Sexuality and the Sacred

Sexuality and the Sacred

Sources for Theological Reflection

Edited by

**JAMES B. NELSON and
SANDRA P. LONGFELLOW**

Westminster/John Knox Press
Louisville, Kentucky

Book design by Publishers' WorkGroup
Cover design by Drew Stevens
Cover illustration: Gustav Klimt's The Kiss. *Courtesy of Superstock.*

First edition

Published by Westminster/John Knox Press
Louisville, Kentucky

This book is printed on acid-free paper that meets the American National Standards Institute Z39.48 standard.

PRINTED IN THE UNITED STATES OF AMERICA

9 8 7 6 5 4 3 2 1

Library of Congress Cataloging-in-Publication Data

Sexuality and the sacred : sources for theological reflection / edited by James B. Nelson
and Sandra P. Longfellow. — 1st ed.
     p.   cm.
  Includes bibliographical references.
  ISBN 0-664-25529-9 (alk. paper)
  1. Sex—Religious aspects—Christianity. I. Nelson, James B. II. Longfellow,
Sandra P.
BT708.S4797 1993
233'.5—dc20   93-39390

For
Maren Longfellow
Christopher Longfellow
Mary Nelson
and Stephen and Denise Marcoux Nelson

Contents

Contributors   xi

Introduction   xiii

Part 1: *Methods and Sources*

Introduction   3

1. Notes on Historical Grounding: Beyond Sexual Essentialism
   CARTER HEYWARD   9

2. Sexuality and Christian Ethics: How to Proceed
   LISA SOWLE CAHILL   19

3. New Testament Sexual Ethics and Today's World
   L. WILLIAM COUNTRYMAN   28

4. Sexual Ethics
   MARGARET A. FARLEY   54

Part 2: *Sexuality and Spirituality*

Introduction   71

5. Uses of the Erotic: The Erotic as Power
   AUDRE LORDE   75

6. Wonder, Eroticism, and Enigma
   PAUL RICOEUR   80

7. Sleeping like Spoons: A Question of Embodiment
   JOHN GILES MILHAVEN   85

8. The Sexuality of Jesus and the Human Vocation
   JOAN H. TIMMERMAN   91

9. While Love Is Unfashionable: Ethical Implications of Black
   Spirituality and Sexuality
   TOINETTE M. EUGENE   105

Part 3: *Gender and Orientation*

Introduction   115

Gender Relations

10. The Christian Mind and the Challenge of Gender Relations
    MARY STEWART VAN LEEUWEN   120

Women's Experience

11. Pain and Pleasure: Avoiding the Confusions of Christian Tradition
    in Feminist Theory
    BEVERLY WILDUNG HARRISON and CARTER HEYWARD   131

12. The Moral Significance of Female Orgasm: Toward Sexual Ethics
    That Celebrates Women's Sexuality
    MARY D. PELLAUER   149

13. Lovingly Lesbian: Toward a Feminist Theology of Friendship
    MARY E. HUNT   169

Men's Experience

14. Explaining Men
    PHILIP CULBERTSON   183

15. Embracing Masculinity
    JAMES B. NELSON   195

16. Men's Studies, Feminist Theology, and Gay Male Sexuality
    J. MICHAEL CLARK   216

Part 4: *Ethical Issues in Sexuality*

Introduction   231

Rethinking Sexual Ethics

17. Common Decency: A New Christian Sexual Ethics
    MARVIN M. ELLISON   236

18. Sexuality and Social Policy
    BEVERLY WILDUNG HARRISON   242

Singleness, Marriage, and Celibacy

19. Appropriate Vulnerability
    KAREN LEBACQZ   256

20. Sex before Marriage
    MONICA FURLONG   262

21. Sex within Marriage
    JACK DOMINIAN   264

22. Celibate Passion
    JANIE GUSTAFSON   277

Sexuality and Disability

23. Persons with Disabilities
    OFFICE OF THE GENERAL ASSEMBLY, PRESBYTERIAN
    CHURCH (U.S.A.)   282

Sexuality and Aging

24. The Change of Life
    PENELOPE WASHBOURN   288

25. Older Adults
    OFFICE OF THE GENERAL ASSEMBLY, PRESBYTERIAN
    CHURCH (U.S.A.)   297

HIV/AIDS

26. AIDS, Shame, and Suffering
    GRACE JANTZEN   305

27. AIDS, High-Risk Behaviors, and Moral Judgments
    EARL E. SHELP   314

Sexual Violence and Pornography

28. Violence against Women: The Way Things Are Is Not
    the Way They Have to Be
    MARIE M. FORTUNE   326

29. Refusing to Be "Good Soldiers": An Agenda for Men
    MARVIN M. ELLISON   335

30. Pornography: An Agenda for the Churches
    MARY D. PELLAUER   345

Part 5: *Sexual Orientation: A Test Case for the Church*

Introduction   357

31. Homosexuality and Religious Life: A Historical Approach
    JOHN BOSWELL   361

32. Sources for Body Theology: Homosexuality as a Test Case
    JAMES B. NELSON   374

33. Homophobia, Heterosexism, and Pastoral Practice
    ROSEMARY RADFORD RUETHER   387

34. Church at the Margins
    DAN SPENCER   397

Acknowledgments   403

Contributors

JOHN BOSWELL is the A. Whitney Griswold Professor of History at Yale University, New Haven, Connecticut.

LISA SOWLE CAHILL is professor of theology at Boston College, Chestnut Hill, Massachusetts.

J. MICHAEL CLARK teaches at both Georgia State University and Emory University, Atlanta, Georgia. He acknowledges the contribution of Bob McNeir to the development of his article.

L. WILLIAM COUNTRYMAN is professor of New Testament at Church Divinity School of the Pacific, Berkeley, California.

PHILIP CULBERTSON is professor of pastoral theology at the University of the South, Sewanee, Tennessee.

JACK DOMINIAN is senior consultant psychiatrist at the Central Middlesex Hospital, London.

MARVIN M. ELLISON is professor of Christian social ethics at Bangor Theological Seminary, Bangor and Portland, Maine.

TOINETTE M. EUGENE is associate professor of Christian social ethics at Garrett-Evangelical Theological Seminary, Evanston, Illinois.

MARGARET A. FARLEY is professor of Christian ethics at Yale Divinity School, New Haven, Connecticut.

MARIE M. FORTUNE is founder and director of the Center for Prevention of Sexual and Domestic Violence, Seattle, Washington.

MONICA FURLONG is a theologian, journalist, scriptwriter, and BBC producer for religious broadcasts, who lives in London.

JANIE GUSTAFSON is a writer, composer, and artist, and a member of the Sisters of St. Joseph of Carondelet in Venice, California.

BEVERLY WILDUNG HARRISON is the Carolyn Beaird Professor of Christian Ethics at Union Theological Seminary, New York, New York.

CARTER HEYWARD is professor of theology at Episcopal Divinity School, Cambridge, Massachusetts.

MARY E. HUNT is Cofounder and Codirector of the Women's Alliance for Theology, Ethics, and Ritual (WATER), Silver Springs, Maryland.

GRACE JANTZEN is lecturer in philosophy of religion at King's College, London, and an editor of *Theology*.

KAREN LEBACQZ is professor of Christian ethics at Pacific School of Religion, Berkeley, California.

AUDRE LORDE was an African-American poet, essayist, and activist who lived in New York City and St. Croix, Virgin Islands. She died in 1992.

J. GILES MILHAVEN is professor of religious studies at Brown University, Providence, Rhode Island.

JAMES B. NELSON is professor of Christian ethics at United Theological Seminary of the Twin Cities, New Brighton, Minnesota.

MARY D. PELLAUER was, at the time this essay was written, coordinator for research and study at the Commission for Women of the Evangelical Lutheran Church in America, Chicago, Illinois. She is currently a freelance theological writer.

PAUL RICOEUR is the John Nuveen Professor Emeritus in the Divinity School and professor emeritus of philosophy at the University of Chicago.

ROSEMARY RADFORD RUETHER is Georgia Harkness Professor of Applied Theology at Garrett Evangelical Theological School, Evanston, Illinois.

EARL E. SHELP is executive director and senior research fellow at the Foundation for Interfaith Research and Ministry, Houston, Texas.

DAN SPENCER is instructor of religion at Drake University, Des Moines, Iowa.

JOAN H. TIMMERMAN is professor of theology at the College of St. Catherine, St. Paul, Minnesota.

MARY STEWART VAN LEEUWEN is professor of interdisciplinary studies at Calvin College, Grand Rapids, Michigan.

PENELOPE WASHBOURN was assistant professor of religion and coordinator of the women's studies program at the University of Manitoba in Canada when she wrote this essay.

Introduction

"The famous gesture of Adam covering his genitals with a fig leaf is, according to Augustine, not due to the simple fact that Adam was ashamed of their presence, but to the fact that his sexual organs were moving by themselves without his consent. Sex in erection is the image of man revolted against God. . . . His uncontrolled sex is exactly the same as what he himself has been toward God—a rebel."[1] In these words the French historian Michel Foucault captures much of the accepted Christian legacy about sexuality, particularly as that tradition has reflected the male experience: sexuality equals genital sex, and genital sex is intrinsically uncontrollable and antithetical to authentic spirituality. Augustine's distortion of Adam's sexuality finds its parallel in Tertullian's caricature of Eve, who, as female, was more fleshly and carnal than her male counterpart, and hence she was the particular locus of sin. Tertullian's accusation leveled against any woman is this: "She would carry herself around like Eve, mourning and penitent, that she might more fully expiate by each garment of penitence that which she acquired from Eve—the degradation of the first sin and the hatefulness of human perdition. . . . You know not that you are also an Eve?"[2]

The essays in this volume depict a different view. While varying interpretations are presented, while different accents and even disagreements will be found among them, there is a broad consensus that Augustine's and Tertullian's perceptions will no longer do. A revision of much Christian understanding of sexuality is necessary, and it is in process. The selections that follow reflect that process.

Thus, we have made no attempt to represent the whole range of Christian thinking about sexuality. Rather, we have tried to furnish contemporary theological sources that, contrary to much in our legacy, reflect two basic convictions. First, sexuality is a far more comprehensive matter, broader, richer, and more fundamental to our human existence than simply genital sex. And second, our sexuality is intended by God to be neither incidental to nor detrimental to our spirituality, but rather a fully integrated and basic dimension of that spirituality.

What, then, are the central meanings of human sexuality? That exploration is the task of this volume. We have approached the selection of articles with several basic assumptions, some of which are about *the nature of sexuality itself.* While sexuality may well include our desires for experiencing and sharing genital pleasure, it is far more than this. More fundamentally and inclusively, it is who we are as bodyselves—selves who experience the ambiguities of both "having" and "being" bodies. Sexuality embraces our ways of being in the world as persons embodied with biological femaleness or maleness and with internalized understandings of what these genders mean. Sexuality includes our erotic orientations—our attractions to the other sex, to the same sex, or to both. Sexuality includes the range of feelings, interpretations, and behaviors through which we express our capacities for sensuous relationships with ourselves, with others, and with the world. While sexuality is always rooted in our bodily realities, it is much larger than these, always involving our minds, our feelings, our wills, our memories, indeed our self-understandings and powers as embodied persons.

Theologically, we believe that human sexuality, while including God's gift of the procreative capacity, is most fundamentally the divine invitation to find our destinies not in loneliness but in deep connection. To the degree that it is free from the distortions of unjust and abusive power relations, we experience our sexuality as the basic eros of our humanness that urges, invites, and lures us out of our loneliness into intimate communication and communion with God and the world. It is instructive to remember that the word "sexuality" itself comes from the Latin *sexus,* probably akin to the Latin *secare,* meaning to cut or divide—suggesting incompleteness seeking wholeness and connection that reaches through and beyond our differences and divisions. Sexuality, in sum, is the physiological and emotional grounding of our capacities to love.

Thus it is impossible for the authors of the following articles to speak of sexuality without speaking, at the same time, of *spirituality.*[3] While various understandings of spirituality will be discussed in the introduction to Part 2, at this point we can simply define the term as signifying the response of our whole beings to what we perceive as the sacred in our midst. And, precisely because it is the response of our whole beings, our sexuality is inevitably involved.

Almost all writers in this volume speak out of a Christian spirituality wherein the sacred power is God as known through the community of Jesus Christ. Readers will detect that these writers commonly are making *incarnationalist* assumptions. That is, they assume that God's very being still becomes flesh and dwells among us full of grace and truth. And in becoming flesh God is revealed through the sexual dimensions of our lives.

Making this assumption, the writers engage in *sexual theology.* Throughout most of Christian history the vast majority of theologians who wrote about sexuality tried to approach the subject from one direction only: they began with affirmations and assertions of the faith (from the scriptures, from doctrines, from churchly teachings, and so on) and then applied those to human sexuality. Now, theologians such as those included here are assuming that the other direction of inquiry is important as well: What does our sexual experience reveal about God? about the ways we understand the gospel? about the ways we read scripture and tradition and attempt to live out the faith?

This means a discovery of *the church as a sexual community,* another theme common to these authors. If through most of Christian history the church has understood sexuality either as incidental to or detrimental to its life, a new understanding has emerged—largely spurred by feminist theologians and by gay and lesbian theologians. Those oppressed or discounted because of their sexuality have long known that the church has always been, among other things, a sexual community. It has incorporated a host of sexual understandings—for good and for ill—into its language and images, into its worship and leadership patterns, into its assumptions about power and morality, and into its definitions of membership. The church has been doing this, often quite unconsciously, while at the same time believing that it could write and teach about sexuality from a standpoint of faith quite unaffected by sexual assumptions. Now many of us believe differently. Recognizing that at the same time the church is a community of faith, worship, and service it is also a sexual community opens the door to new consciousness of sexual oppressions and new possibilities for life-giving transformations.

One additional understanding generally pervades the articles in this book: however deeply personal it is to each of us, *sexuality is invariably social and public* in its implications. The feminist insight that "the personal is political" marks the insights of the authors included here. When they speak of "intimacy," for example, they exhibit a common understanding that our sexuality invites us to intimacy not only with the beloved person but also with all creation. It is intimacy marked by right relationships, mutual power, and justice in our social structures.

The literature on human sexuality is vast. Even though we have limited the volume to contemporary theological treatments, the selection process was difficult. We have chosen those pieces we think particularly helpful for the reader who wishes to grasp the major issues in current theological and ethical thinking about the transformation of the sexual tradition. For reasons of space we have, with permission, edited some of the articles.

A word about the book's omissions: We are aware of three such areas. One is denominational studies. While most denominations in the United States and Britain have produced sexuality studies in recent years, any attempt to represent them adequately or to compare them to one another would require excessive space.[4] However, two brief topical excerpts from one of the more inclusive studies, that of the Presbyterian Church (U.S.A.), will provide a feel for this material.

A second area is that of certain sexual subjects we deem beyond the scope of this volume, particularly abortion, contraception, sterilization, and reproductive technologies. Again, space limitations make it impossible to do justice to the range and complexity of interpretations of these issues. Moreover, bioethical anthologies on these subjects are readily available elsewhere.

Finally, though we had wished to include certain important subjects congenial to our selection pattern, we were disappointed in the dearth of adequate theological treatments of them. These include issues as diverse as childhood sexuality, bisexuality, and certain sexual variations (for example, transsexualism and transvestism).

Brief comments on the organization of this volume are in order. "Part 1: Methods and Sources" speaks to two issues. The first is "From whence come the meanings of our human sexuality?" Here we visit the current debate between "essentialists" (who argue that certain meanings are intrinsic to our created sexuality) and "social constructionists" (who argue that sexual meanings are created through processes of social interaction). The second issue involves the appropriate sources for theological reflection on sexuality.

"Part 2: Sexuality and Spirituality" engages some basic philosophical and theological issues concerning the relation of these two dimensions of our lives. While the dualistic strain in the Christian tradition has divorced them, the authors included here hunger for a reunion in which the rediscovery of the spirituality of eros is central.

"Part 3: Gender and Orientation" focuses on "the ethics of agency"—Who are the actors in the sexual drama? Men and women differ in both their physical bodies and their patterns of gender role socialization. And, while lesbians and gay men share a common social oppression, there are also significant differences in their experiences because of gender. Nevertheless, the contributions in this section make it clear that the commonalities we all share in our divinely created sexuality are more fundamental than our differences.

"Part 4: Ethical Issues in Sexuality" does not introduce ethical issues for the first time in this book. Such issues are clearly present throughout the previous sections. Here, however, is a focus on how we might reflect critically on the morality of specific ways of being and acting. Christian ethical reflections on celibacy, marriage, singleness, disability, aging, HIV/AIDS, sexual violence, and pornography illustrate the broader question: What makes certain sexual ways of being or certain sexual acts good, right, and responsible?

"Part 5: Sexual Orientation: A Test Case for the Church" shifts to a particular case study for ethical focus. The authors here show varying ways of using theological sources, perceptions of moral agency, and critical reflection on moral action as they deal with the most divisive and yet potentially most liberating issue for today's churches.

Without any exaggeration, we can safely say that the past twenty-five years are without parallel in the long history of the church in terms of the amount of critical focus on sexuality issues. Never before has the church witnessed so many articles and books, so many denominational reports, so many debates, so many divisions, so much ferment about changing the church's sexual attitudes or preventing unwanted change, so much hope and so much fear about things sexual. We live in an exciting and perplexing time regarding Christian perceptions of sexuality. We wish the reader a good journey in wrestling with the meanings of God's good gift.

The encouragement to edit this volume originally came from Davis Perkins, Director of Westminster/John Knox Press, and Judith Longman, Publisher of A.R. Mowbray & Co., Cassell Publishing Company. We are grateful that they gently and persistently nudged us toward a project that we also believed was needed to enrich the current theological discussion of sexuality. As our work progressed, Stephanie Egnotovich, Managing Editor of Westminster/John Knox, has given valuable guidance in innumerable ways, and we thank her.

Believing it would enhance the usefulness of this volume to include selections deemed important by others in the field, we canvassed a number of members of the Society of Christian Ethics who teach courses in sexuality, ethics, and theology. Their names are too numerous to list, but we acknowledge with pleasure the enormous helpfulness of their generous suggestions and course syllabi. Further, the staff of The Institute for the Study of Christianity and Sexuality in London gave valuable counsel. We hope that the resulting volume reflects the wisdom of this "cloud of witnesses" that surrounds us.

The locale for our work on this project has been a community that is deeply part of our lives, United Theological Seminary of the Twin Cities. It is a seminary that has long believed in the vital importance of these issues of sexual theology for the churches, and we have been encouraged by the supportive atmosphere and by conversations with faculty and students throughout our work. In addition, we want to thank several persons who in very particular ways have provided tangible support: Benjamin Griffin, President; Wilson Yates, Dean; Sue Ebbers, Librarian; Dale Dobias, Technical Services Librarian; and ViAnn Keller, Administrative Secretary.

We believe sexuality, most broadly and richly interpreted, is the divinely given energy for connection. We have experienced connections with all these people in working on this volume, and we celebrate them.

James B. Nelson
Sandra P. Longfellow

NOTES

1. Michel Foucault, quoted by James W. Bernauer in *The Final Foucault* (Cambridge, Mass: M.I.T. Press, 1988), 51.

2. Tertullian, *The Apparel of Women*, quoted in Margaret R. Miles, *Carnal Knowing: Female Nakedness and Religious Meaning in the West* (Boston: Beacon Press, 1989), 85.

3. For more extended discussions of spirituality, sexual theology, and the church as sexual community, see James B. Nelson, *The Intimate Connection: Male Sexuality and Masculine Spirituality* (Philadelphia: Westminster Press, 1988), chap. 6.

4. Readers particularly interested in church position statements may wish to consult the most thorough interpretation of ecumenical sexuality documents thus far: Robin Smith, *Living in Covenant with God and One Another: A Guide to the Study of Sexuality and Human Relations, Using Statements from Member Churches of the World Council of Churches* (Geneva: World Council of Churches, 1990).

PART 1

Methods and Sources

Carter Heyward
Lisa Sowle Cahill
L. William Countryman
Margaret A. Farley

Introduction
to Part 1

What does our human sexuality mean? That is the larger question addressed throughout this volume. In this section we focus on two background questions. The first is this: From whence come those meanings? Are they intrinsic to our sexuality? just there? implanted by our Creator? On the other hand, do we create those meanings through our interaction with others? Or, in some sense are both of these things true? The second question is this: Regardless of the source of those sexual meanings, what are the important and appropriate sources for Christians to use in discerning them?

Turning to the first question, the two theories currently vying with each other are social constructionism and essentialism. *Social constructionism* emphasizes our active roles as human agents deeply influenced by our social relations in structuring or "constructing" our sexual meanings and values. While our capacities to feel and to act sexually are, of course, rooted in the sexual and bodily realities that are given to us, the meanings of those feelings and expressions vary greatly over time and among different cultures. For example, whereas persons in most cultures consider a kiss on the lips to be a positively charged sexual gesture, some Inuits find such kisses repulsive, and not the least bit erotic. In another example, traditional native Americans avoid making eye contact during conversation, a practice that may seem evasive to European Americans. The Indians, however, regard sustained eye contact as rude and invasive. Thus, the social constructionists say, we socially attach symbolic meanings to our bodily and sexual expressions, meanings that are not intrinsically coded into people.

In contrast, the *essentialists*, or empiricists, emphasize the objectively definable reality of sexual and bodily meanings. The body, they claim, has its intrinsic and given meanings, quite apart from whatever we happen to believe about it. Though sexuality may well be acted out differently in various times and places,

3

there is something universal and constant about its core reality. For example, the official Roman Catholic understanding of natural law states that sexual expression has an intrinsically procreative meaning. Hence, all sexual expressions (such as contraceptive sex, oral sex, anal sex, and masturbation) that deliberately frustrate the procreative possibility are unnatural—against the given, essential nature of our human sexuality.

Carter Heyward's essay makes a strong case for social constructionism. She maintains that "our sexual relations, indeed our sexual feelings, have been shaped by historical forces—the same contingencies, tensions, politics, movements, and social concerns that have shaped our cultures, value systems, and daily lives."[1] She argues that a historical reading of sexuality is an interpretation of power—whether that is power over other persons or mutually empowering relationships. If we accept the radical relationality and historicity of who we are as persons, we will not succumb to the belief that our sexuality is fixed or unchanging. Such a social and historical perspective, she believes, frames our sexual ethics around issues of what we *do* rather than what we *are*.

Lisa Sowle Cahill frames the question with a more essentialist emphasis. The problem, she says, is that in the unity of our personhood we experience our sexuality as a duality—both physical and spiritual. Sex is physical, urgent, and pervasive. It is also an avenue for the deep expression of emotion and spirituality among persons. Our sexuality cannot be reduced simply to its procreative potential or its physical pleasure, for it is also a constituent of those relationships that are most distinctively human. Thus, "It is possible to define at least approximately, some *'essential'* or *'ideal'* *meaning* of sexuality, despite actual historical distortions or adaptations of it in the human sexual reality, and despite the limits of the human mind in seeking to discover it."[2] Cahill joins those philosophers and theologians who wish "to affirm *the essential character* of sex in relation to human being, the meaning of sex as expression of interpersonal relation as well as procreation, and the equal dignity of man and woman."[3]

One way of grasping the difference between these two writers is to ask, What are they fundamentally worried about? Heyward is concerned that essentialism is often used to oppress persons (for example, lesbians and gay men) whose sexuality does not conform to certain notions of a given and unvarying truth of sexuality (for example, procreation). Cahill, on the other hand, is more concerned that without claiming something essentially given about sexuality we fall into an utter relativism about its meanings, a relativism incompatible with Christian faith.

Both authors, we believe, have some truth in their positions. We have chosen to represent both social constructionists and essentialists throughout this volume, though with some accent on the former. But the positions need not be seen as polar opposites. We emphasize constructionism because we believe our sexuality is, indeed, subject to a vast range of socially constructed meanings, and those meanings are often related to social power. Hence, we believe that the major focus for our theological and ethical questions should be on the *meanings* of our ways of being sexual, not upon the physical contours of specific *acts*. Further, if sexual meanings are socially constructed, they can also be reconstructed in ways that are more just, more whole, more life-giving. By the same token (and here is the truth of an essentialist emphasis), sexual meanings are not entirely relative. There *is* something "given" in our sexuality—not intrinsically embedded in certain specific acts, but intended by God for our sexual *relationships*—that our relationships be those marked by justice, wholeness, and life-giving love.

Turning to the second major question, we ask, With what sources might we work as we do our sexual theology? Cahill points to four complementary sources for Christians to use in sorting out the problematic qualities of sex. They are (1) the Bible (the foundational texts of the community), (2) tradition (the historic teachings, practices, and understandings of the church), (3) philosophical accounts of essential humanity (normative accounts of what human beings truly ought to be), and (4) descriptive accounts of what actually is the case regarding our sexuality. All four of these, she maintains, are indispensable and, indeed, mutually correcting. Even though it is never a simple matter, a faithful and judicious balancing of these sources is what we need. A slightly different way of naming these four ("the Wesleyan quadrilateral") will be illustrated in James B. Nelson's article on homosexuality in part 5.

The importance of these mutually complementary and mutually correcting sources has been recognized in various parts of the Christian community, even though some Christians emphasize one more than the others. Many Protestants have attempted to turn almost exclusively to the Bible as their authority. L. William Countryman demonstrates the futility of this approach but also argues that the scriptures are powerfully relevant.

Countryman argues that the Bible's *specific* sexual norms are largely alien and irrelevant to us today, for the significant texts dealing with sexual morality were framed by purity and property systems that we have, with good reason, abandoned. Ancient purity laws with a particular focus on bodily boundaries dealt with those actions deemed clean or dirty, pure or impure. Our biblical forebears' main concern in these laws was not the ethical quality of the sexual acts as such, but what certain bodily acts symbolized regarding the boundaries of the chosen, holy people. When in the course of time the gospel message cast into doubt the principle of the purity system, the New Testament writers still appealed to another principle—property. The patriarchal household, with its male ownership of women and children, was kept as the building block of the sexual property system. Thus, adultery, fornication, and incest were defined as violations of sexual ownership and family lineage.

While those ancient systems of purity and property are no longer appropriate for us, Countryman argues that there is great scriptural relevance for sexual theology and ethics. The Bible is important precisely because it is alien to our historical-cultural situation and therefore relativizes it. The scriptures relativize our sexual norms to make fresh room for the gospel of God's grace. Further, the

Bible shows how the grace of God broke into the self-sufficiency of another culture, and hence how it can shatter our own self-sufficiency as well. Country-man then proposes a set of basic principles along with some "derived guidelines" to illustrate how the scripture can subject our own sexual patterns and institu-tions to the gospel. His essay thus argues for the critical importance of scripture in doing sexual theology, without claiming that scripture alone is sufficient.

Margaret Farley addresses tradition, the second major source named by Cahill. Farley's overview shows how "the teachings within the Christian tradition regarding human sexuality are complex, subject to multiple outside influences, and expressive of change and development through succeeding generations of Christians."[4] Careful attention to tradition serves several pur-poses in doing sexual theology. Perhaps most obvious is that it helps us grasp why and how we have come to our present positions (and to our present confusions) about sexuality.

An important illustration of this is Farley's summary of the Gnostic and Stoic influences. Both Gnosticism and Stoicism were profoundly dualistic in their understandings of human nature. Both sharply separated spirit from body, with the spirit believed to be good and eternal while the body was seen as mortal, suspect, and the particular locus of evil. Gnosticism, however, led to two different extremes—the complete rejection of sex and the embrace of sexual licentiousness. It was in the Stoic justification of sexual intercourse for the sole purpose of procreation that early Christians found the answer to the Gnostics. That justification allowed them to affirm procreation as the central rationale for sex and still to maintain the spiritual superiority of virginity. With this, as Farley observes, "the direction of Christian sexual ethics was set for centuries to come."[5] Though such Stoic reasoning may seem archaic and foreign to modern Christians, few of us have been untouched by religious suspicions regarding sexuality per se, and by negative evaluations of those sexual acts that are inherently nonprocreative, such as oral sex, masturbation, and homosexual intercourse. Tradition, indeed, helps us understand why we are as we are.

This same illustration, however, suggests a second contribution of tradition. Late Hellenistic dualism as expressed in both Gnosticism and Stoicism did not originate in Jewish or Christian sources. Yet it profoundly influenced all subsequent Christian understandings of sexuality. Thus, grasping something of the tradition helps us comprehend the ways in which sexual theology is never "pure," but always finds its shaping in relation to the cultural contexts in which Christians live. Moreover, understanding of our religious heritage assists us to recognize ways in which the tradition itself is susceptible not only to modifica-tions but also to fundamental shifts regarding human sexuality. Farley points out how the shift away from the centrality of the procreative norm began in the fifteenth century, when certain theologians began to justify the good of sexual pleasure itself for the well-being of persons. A century later, in the Protestant Reformation, John Calvin affirmed that "the *greatest* good of marriage and sex is the mutual society that is formed between husband and wife."[6] Hence, tradition is neither monolithic nor unchanging.

The branch of the church that has most strongly emphasized the continuity of tradition is currently the site of considerable ferment in sexual theology. Many leading Roman Catholic theologians now defend pluralism on numerous sexuality issues and the importance of distinguishing between what is central to the faith and what is peripheral. Charles Curran, for example, writes, "In my view, dissent from the authoritative, noninfallible hierarchical teaching of the Roman Catholic Church is an effort to support, not destroy, the credibility of the teaching office. The theological community can play the critical role of the loyal opposition, thus in the long run enhancing the church's teaching role. . . . The primary teacher in the church remains the Holy Spirit—and no one has a monopoly on the Holy Spirit."[7]

In addition to scripture and tradition, reason and experience are the remaining sources to which sexual theology turns. We have not included specific articles on these latter two, for they are amply illustrated in many of the selections throughout the remainder of the book. Reason, as Cahill notes, includes philosophical accounts of what human beings truly ought to be. We suggest that some elements of Cahill's fourth source, "descriptive accounts of what actually is the case regarding our sexuality," might also be included in our understanding of reason. It is, after all, the disciplined exercise of reason as found in the various sciences concerned with human sexuality (such as biology, medicine, anthropology, psychology, and sociology) that attempts to describe "what actually is the case." That these elements of reason—insights about sexuality from the sciences—are present in most of the selections and interacting with scripture and tradition will be apparent.

The fourth source is experience. Some would include the sexual work of psychologists, sociologists, and anthropologists under this rubric, inasmuch as they attempt to describe the ranges of human sexual experience. Others would say that since these sciences are attempts to give objective and rational interpretation to sexuality, they are rightly understood as exercises of reason. The categorization, however, is not important. Our awareness of and use of the multiple sources of insight are the critical elements.

But there is one other area of experience crucial for sexual theology, an area only indirectly addressed by the behavioral sciences. It is our personal and communal experience as sexual beings. Ever since the rise of theological liberalism in the early nineteenth century, much of the church has recognized human experience as a valid and important source of Christian theology. In the latter part of the twentieth century various forms of liberation theology have boldly named experience as central to the theological task. In selections throughout this volume we shall see writers drawing heavily on their own sexual experiences as sources of theological insight—in dialogue with scripture, tradition, and reason. Often that experience is some form of sexual oppression. Or it is the experience of sexual intimacy. At other times it is sexual experience particular to female or to male bodies. Or it is sexual experience in physical disability or in aging. In all cases, the writers claim that a viable sexual theology cannot omit this realm of God's revelation.

Although we have used a number of labels and categories in this introduction, reality is not all that neat. Our interpretations of sexual meanings need to be informed by the positions of and the debates between social constructionists and essentialists. We also think it important to name and be conscious of the several major sources of insight and arenas of revelation in doing sexual theology. But these labels should not imply neat boxes into which dimensions of sexual theology can be sorted. The labels are simply tools—no more, no less—for better understanding what we are trying to do when we think theologically about the perplexing, mysterious, sometimes painful, hopefully wonderful reality of being sexual in God's creation.

NOTES

1. Carter Heyward, *Touching Our Strength: The Erotic as Power and the Love of God* (San Francisco: Harper & Row, 1989), 38.

2. Lisa Sowle Cahill, *Between the Sexes: Foundations for a Christian Ethics of Sexuality* (Philadelphia: Fortress Press; New York: Paulist Press, 1985), 10. Emphasis added.

3. Ibid. Emphasis added.

4. Margaret A. Farley, "Sexual Ethics," *Encyclopedia of Bioethics*, vol. 4 (New York: Free Press, 1978), 1578.

5. Ibid, 1579.

6. Ibid., 1581. Emphasis added.

7. Charles E. Curran, "Roman Catholic Sexual Ethics: A Dissenting View," in *Sexual Ethics and the Church: A Christian Century Symposium* (Chicago: The Christian Century Foundation, 1989), 54–55.

1

Notes on Historical Grounding: Beyond Sexual Essentialism

CARTER HEYWARD

Our history is inseparably part of our nature, our social structures are inseparably part of our biology.

JOAN L. GRISCOM[1]

From my "Holiness" Christian background, complete with sexual taboos, I discovered and hid in puberty the pleasure of masturbation, a delicious bathtime/bedtime thrill. Fantasies and pictures of Marilyn Monroe were hidden too, and I was constantly convicting myself of the sinfulness of my nightly obsession.

I began dating after I left my parsonage home for college. I thrilled at the first touch of a woman's thigh. I fell in love repeatedly and ached for intimacy. But at my religious college, my few serial loves considered sexual exploring ("feeling them up") to be prurient—and spiritual exploring was unheard of. I was rejected by a woman (to whom I had proposed marriage) because of my "weird" ideas—like seeing nothing wrong with sex as long as she didn't get pregnant.

After a stint in the factory, as a graduate student in philosophy at a midwestern university, I blossomed. I saw movies, drank beer, smoked pot, and fell in love twice again. I discovered sexual intimacy with each of these women, and they marveled at the wonder with which I touched their bodies. Yet, despite my devotion, each left me.

For the next seven years, I explored a number of liaisons, sharing sexual intimacy in most but finding no lasting spiritual connection. Beginning to practice Buddhist prayer, I enlarged my agenda from only desires for sexual intimacy to attention to the others' depths of concern. . . .

Sexual relationships became fewer. In 1982, after six years of Buddhist fellowship, I was expelled by my fellow Buddhists for theological questioning, and I became socially isolated.

> Grant,
> theological student

Our sexual relations, indeed our sexual feelings, have been shaped by historical forces—the same contingencies, tensions, politics, movements, and social concerns that have shaped our cultures, value systems, and daily lives.

In *The Handmaid's Tale*, Canadian Margaret Atwood portrays with chilling, imaginative insight the centrality of sexual control in the new christian fundamentalist nation of Gilead, formerly the United States: White women are forced to breed and are forbidden to have sex except with the Commanders, the white men who own them. Gaymen and lesbians are summarily executed. Black people are ghettoized in Detroit. These are the very forces about which social anthropologist Gayle Rubin speaks: "The right has been spectacularly successful in tapping [the] pools of erotophobia in its accession to state power."[2]

Good social history is written not just from the perspective of "the winners." It teaches us about the connections between the control of women's bodies for procreation; the suppression of homosexuality; the economic system and conditions of a particular place and time; the virulence of such forces as racism and anti-Semitism; and the exercise of social control by institutional custodians of such normative "virtues" as spiritual growth, mental health, and physical well-being.

It would be small solace for us to imagine that we are nearing the end of a period of blatant political reaction against sexual and gender justice in the United States. Even if this were superficially the case, the radicality of the injustice in our power relations goes deeper than any one political party or heyday of the religious right. The problems in our sexual and gender relations are historical, they are critical, and they connect us all.

A historical reading of sexuality is a reading about power in relation, specifically about how people historically have or have not embodied our capacities for mutually empowering relationships. The study of sexuality is also an exploration of how the exercise of power-over (power-as-control by kings, customs, corporations, gods, and so forth) has shaped our capacities and incapacities to act mutually.[3]

We use and abuse power in relationships. We also are used and abused in relationships. Our capacity to act as cocreative subjects in the dynamics of mutually empowering relations is affected, and determined in some cases, by how we have been objectified and acted upon in our significant relationships. An example of the connection between how we are treated and how we treat others and ourselves is the large extent to which abusive adults have been battered and abused as children.

The late French structuralist Michel Foucault (and, with him, radical British social historian Jeffrey Weeks and feminist liberation theologians in the United

States such as Sharon Welch and Beverly Harrison) insisted that no experience of power, sexual or other, is intrinsic to a person or to a relationship, but rather that our experiences of power-in-relation are socially constructed. Sexuality is socially constructed. . . .

For example, few people in Euroamerican culture are strangers to feelings of sadomasochism in our social relations, including our sexual relationships, regardless of how we may act. Ours is a society fastened in dynamics of control and subjugation. None can escape the psychosexual or spiritual fallout of such a system.[4]

In an appreciative but unapologetic critique of such sexologists as Havelock Ellis, Jeffrey Weeks charges, "Possibly the most potent of their legacies is what is now generally known as 'sexual essentialism.' " Weeks is referring to "ways of thinking which reduce a phenomenon to a presupposed essence—the 'specific being,' 'what a thing is,' 'nature, character, substance, absolute being'—which seeks to explain *complex* forms by means of an identifying inner force or truth."[5]

A historical reading of sexuality will move us beyond sexual essentialism as explanation of anything, including either homosexuality or heterosexuality. If we accept a relational, historical matrix as our origin, the womb of who we are becoming, we will not fall into believing that either our identities or our relational possibilities are fixed and unchanging. This is because relationality—the basis of historical agency—presupposes relativity: All of us, and all of everything, is relative to everything else—changing, becoming, living, and dying in relation.

There can be nothing static in a personal identity or relationship formed in such a matrix. There is no such thing as a homosexual or a heterosexual if by this we mean to denote a fixed essence, an essential identity.[6] There are rather homosexual and heterosexual people—people who *act* homosexually or heterosexually.

Relationality relativizes our essence. We are only who we are becoming in relation to one another. Self-knowledge is steeped in awareness of movement and change.

Because history involves change and movement, understanding our sexualities involves knowing in what ways our sexualities are changing and in being open to changing understandings of our sexualities as we continue to learn about our bodyselves. Not only are we not living in the nineteenth century, we are not living in the 1950s or 1960s in terms of how we may experience nutrition, sexual activity, pregnancy, disease, and other bodyself phenomena. Understanding our sexualities historically involves understanding ourselves as people whose sexualities are in flux.

A historical rather than an essentialist perspective on sexuality involves framing our sexual ethics around issues of what we *do* rather than of what we *are*: What we do as hetero/homosexual persons—how we act in relation to lovers and friends—is the stuff of sexual ethics, rather than whether it is right or wrong to *be* heterosexual or homosexual.

A historical reading of sexuality may make living as lesbians and gaymen more difficult, because we cannot plead for acceptance on the basis of being something we can't help and therefore of needing special sets of rights and understanding because we are homosexuals who didn't choose to be who we are. When we are clear with ourselves and others that our sexual identities are not "essential" but rather are being shaped by many factors, including our own "permission," the difficulties we may incur politically will be offset by our own shared sense of the relational power born among us as we call each other forth and help shape each other's identities.

We no longer have to wage our campaigns for "rights" on the basis of being homosexuals who can't help it because it's just the way we are. Rather, whether we are heterosexual or homosexual, we expect our society to offer basic conditions of human worth and self-respect to *all* people, regardless of sexual preference.

A historical reading of our sexualities that is rooted in our assumption of responsibility for what we do demands responsible engagement from others. It is easy enough for many christian liberals to "love" gaymen, lesbians, divorced women and men, single parents, people with AIDS. It is harder, but more honest and of deeper social value, for us to engage one another's lives in a spirit of mutual respect and discovery. And what better definition of love?

A historical perspective on sexuality is important also because such a view enables us to envision and perhaps experience our own possibilities as sexual persons beyond the constraints of any particular failure in historical imagination—whether the failure be religious, psychological, economic, or cultural.

Dorothee Soelle writes of *phantasie,* a creative mix of intuition and imagination that enables us to participate in shaping the future even as we are grounded in the present.[7] Our *phantasie* helps us experience and understand sexuality as an open, changing, relational dynamic. Our sexual future is not set or predetermined. We are involved in shaping our own dreams.

A historical reading of sexuality moves us beyond sexual essentialism toward understanding ourselves radically as persons-in-relation. We move through *phantasie* toward questions that we would miss altogether unless we were thinking historically, such as Jeffrey Weeks's question about when heterosexual behavior became an ideology—when it began to develop into "compulsive heterosexuality" or "heterosexism." No one knows the answer to this question; but it is interesting and it could become a locus of historical inquiry further into connections between sex, women, and political control.[8]

The christian church plays the central formative role in limiting and thwarting our sexual *phantasie,* or sexual imagination. Most historians, sexologists, and others who are interested in how sexual practices and attitudes have developed historically seem to agree that in the realm of sexual attitudes, Western history and christian history are so closely linked as to be in effect indistinguishable.[9] That is to say, the christian church has been the chief architect of an attitude toward sexuality during the last seventeen-hundred years of European and

Euroamerican history—an obsessive, proscriptive attitude, in contrast to how large numbers of people, christians and others, have actually lived our lives as sexual persons.

The church's antisexual preoccupation dates from early in the church's history. The Council of Elvira (Spain), at which for the first time an explicitly antisexual code was made law for western christians, was held in 309 C.E. This was on the eve of the Constantinian settlement, in which the church formally made its peace with the state and in so doing lost a major element of its identity: its role as a body of resistance to oppressive power relations.

Historical theologian Samuel Laeuchli writes of the Council of Elvira:

> In the turmoil of a decaying empire the Christian Church attempted to find its communal identity; in the crisis that had come about at the twilight of antiquity, the Christian elite [bishops and presbyters] sought to carve out a clerical image. Both of these struggles rose to the surface whenever the synod of Elvira dealt with matters of sexuality. By establishing sexual codes the synod meant to define the particular character of Christian life; by setting sexual taboos, the synod meant to create the image of an ascetic clerical leadership. . . . [These texts] were of far reaching import for the history of Christianity. Few ancient texts provide such evidences and opportunity to examine the purpose behind the Christian elite's antisexual drive as do these canons.[10]

Laeuchli goes on to suggest five reasons why the church's elite became preoccupied with sexual control of the clergy and, to a lesser extent, the laity. First, the need to carve out a new identity for christians as the old identity (of contending against the state) faded into oblivion. Second, the determination on the part of the clergy to establish themselves as powerful in a new sociopolitical context in which christian laity would be looking to Roman leadership as locus of power. Third, the overwhelming emotional and physical demands of becoming part of the Roman world in its expansive, urbane environment. Fourth, the disquieting urbanization of christians who, as increasing numbers became city dwellers, lost their tribal and rural ties. And finally, the breaking apart of religious mythology, both pagan and christian, as the claims of each relativized the other. Laeuchli writes,

> It is no coincidence that the second-century movement which so desperately tried to recover the mythological canopy, namely Gnosticism, picked Genesis 3, the idea of a fall, as the starting point for its remythologication in which sexual copulation belongs to heaven, as an abstract cosmic event beyond human reach. Nor is it a coincidence that the philosophical parallel to Gnosticism, middle Platonism . . . , declared body and matter as evil. When man began to lose his secure place in the mythic-cosmic structure which he had hewn for himself, he was thrown into crisis. Perhaps he lost his place because he became urban, and thus conscious of man's universal predicament. No matter what caused this crisis, the bishops and presbyters of Elvira, as the leaders of an exclusive religion, offered an alternative which reckoned with the sexual dilemma of their age.[11]

Ideas, or philosophical possibilities, are seeded in social realities—political, economic, and so on. In periods of social unrest, theologians historically have idealized the human condition by spiritualizing it. At Elvira, this spiritualization took the shape of calling men (it was addressed to males by males) to rise spiritually above their sexual bodies.

Laeuchli's primary thesis is that the church's ordained leadership tightened the sexual reins of the church during a period of confusion and chaos. It was the only control they had. Moreover,

> the decisions of Elvira show . . . a crisis in male identity. In the image of manhood which these canons presuppose, the woman as a sexual being was excluded. Where such sexual dualism was predicated, man no longer defined himself in relation to woman . . . or expressed the conflict creatively; instead, he defined himself in separation from the woman.[12]

Laeuchli notes that the christian church still operates on the basis of this same antisexual dualism, which is, in effect, an antifemale dualism.[13] From the second century on, the church had portrayed sex as something pertaining to women and as evil, "the devil's gateway."[14] This attitude, for the first time, is canonized at the dawn of the era in which the church's social, political, and economic power is inaugurated.

The Elvira synod illustrates that a historical perspective on sexuality in western societies involves understanding the antisexual and antifemale (as well as anti-Semitic) character of christian teachings as a means of maintaining control in what was experienced as a chaotic social milieu, much like our own historical period.[15]

Understanding sexuality historically involves making connections between the social control of sexuality and the social control of women. Not only in christian history but moreover in western history (in which social control has been dominated by the church), the connection between women and sex has been so close as to be synonymous.

"The place of women in this chaotic world" is one of toil and trouble, scapegoating and violence, hatred and trivialization, poverty and despair.[16] Economically, under global structures of late capitalism, women are kept in poverty.[17] It is the way profit is maximized. Womens' bodies are kept in the service of heterosexist patriarchy—as wives, whores, fantasy objects, and as a vast, deep pool of cheap labor.

We cannot comprehend the meaning of sexuality from a historical perspective without viewing its place in the context of power relations between genders. In particular, we must understand sexism, the oppression of women in which men are expected to play their manly roles—on top of women, enforcing the rules by which patriarchal, androcentric society is naturally and rightly ordered.

Behind the hostile slogan that "what a lesbian needs is a good fuck" is the less individualistic and more honest threat that what the society needs, in order to be well ordered, is for men to make women "enjoy" being dominated, held down, and screwed.

A historical reading of sexuality will teach us that sexual performance is often less a matter of enjoyment or pleasure—especially for women—than of necessity. Weeks writes of the modern movement for sexual liberation in the United States and Europe:

> The sexual liberation of women was developing in a dual context: of male definitions of sexual need and pleasure, and of capitalist organisation of the labour market and of consumption (including consumption of sex in all of its many, frequently pornographic varieties). The junction of the two—(male definitions of sexual need and capitalist organization of labor) came through the material reality of family life. The economic position of most women—lower pay, fewer job opportunities—still ensures that marriage is seen as a gateway to financial as well as social security and position. And increasingly during this century, sex or at least sexual allure, has emerged as a guarantee for attaining status and security. We pay homage to an ideology of voluntarism in relation to marriage; the reality is often of an iron determinism, especially for women: economic, cultural, moral *and sexual*.[18]

For many women much of the time and some women all of the time, sex is not fun, it is not pleasurable, and yet it is what we are here to do—provide it for men. A historical understanding of sexuality demands that this reality be recognized.

Although Western societies historically have been patriarchal and, on the whole, erotophobic, at no historical period have the links between sexual, gender, and economic control been more pernicious than today. Advanced capitalism literally feeds off of men's control of women's bodyselves, including the production of pornography, prostitution, rape, and other forms of sexual exploitation. Sex pays; and, in a culture of power-over social relations, coercive sex—involving pain and humiliation—pays best.

As a window into viewing our power in relation, a historical understanding of sexuality might help us begin to envision sex as erotic—the "life force" of the later Freud.[19] In his early writings, Freud linked sex and death. He never got fully away from this, but he did begin to move away from his own theory. Building on the later Freud, Herbert Marcuse speaks of the "eroticization of the entire personality."[20] In so doing, he prefigures Audre Lorde's articulation of the erotic as the source of our creativity, the wellspring of our joy, the energy of our poems, music, lovemaking, dancing, meditation, friendships, and meaningful work.[21]

History, including the stories of our own lives and those of our forebears in relation, can teach us something about the erotic as creative power. The testimonies are there. Theologically, we are speaking of our power in right relation; from a christian perspective, the power of God.

Understanding sexuality historically might enable us also to experience sexual pleasure as good, morally right, without need of justification. Viewed through the traditional christian lens, this perception is scandalous—that our sensual, sexual pleasure is good, in and of itself, not merely as means to a good end.

In doing sexual ethics, we can refuse to play a defensive role. We do not need to justify pleasure. Let us rather have to justify pain—try to understand in what ways pain and suffering may be unavoidable, and sometimes necessary, in our lives. If we are to live with our feet on the ground, in touch with reality, we must help one another accept the fact that we who are christian are heirs to a body-despising, woman-fearing, sexually repressive religious tradition. If we are to continue as members of the church, we must challenge and transform it at the root. What is required is more than simply a "reformation." I am speaking of revolutionary transformation. Nothing less will do.[22]

Beverly Harrison, Dorothee Soelle, Margaret Huff, Janet Surrey, and other feminist liberation theologians and relational psychologists do not accept the concept of a personal "self" or "identity" apart from the relational matrix in which it is shaped. Theologically and ethically, our questions must include what it means for any of us to know her sexual "identity" in the relational praxis of transformation.

Language and change are a difficult fit. Words seem static, not fluid, which is why adjectives and transitive verbs tend to serve us better than nouns and intransitive verbs. And yet we must speak words as best we can. At no time has the urgency been more acute than today for us to share honest words about our bodyselves.

Our silence will not protect us.[23] Our best protection is to speak the truths of our lives insofar as we can, with one another's presence and help, and cultivate carefully together those truths we cannot yet speak, truths that may be still very unformed and young. We are shaping history with our words. Either we speak as best we can or our power in relation will slip away like a thief in the night.

NOTES

1. Joan L. Griscom, "On Healing the Nature/History Split," in *Women's Consciousness/Women's Conscience*, edited by Barbara H. Andolsen, Christine E. Gudorf, Mary D. Pellauer (San Francisco: Harper & Row, 1985), 97.

2. Quoted in Jeffrey Weeks, *Sexuality and Its Discontents: Meanings, Myths and Modern Sexualities* (London: Routledge & Kegan Paul, 1985), 44.

In his *History of Sexuality*, Michel Foucault asks how power has become a factor in sexuality. His understanding of the sexual relation is one in which relations of power are immanent to it. Sexuality is one of the "specific domains formed by relations of power." Rather than acting out of a mutually empowering relation, Foucault accepts that "disequilibriums" are embedded in the sexual relation. Further, a competitive, aim-oriented power relation gives power to some ("men, adults, parents, doctors") and denies it to others ("women, adolescents, children, patients"). Michel Foucault, *History of Sexuality*, vol. 1 (New York: Vintage, 1978), 94–95, 99.

3. The body is a site for historical moulding and transformation because sex, far from being resistant to social ordering, seems peculiarly susceptible to it. We know that sex is a vehicle for the expression of a variety of social experiences: of morality, duty, work, habit, tension release, friendship, romance, love, protection, pleasure, utility, power, and sexual difference. Its very plasticity is the source of its historical significance. Sexual behavior would transparently not be possible without physiological sources, but physiology does

not supply motives, passion, object choice, or identity. These come from "somewhere else," the domains of social relations and psychic conflict. If this is correct, the body can no longer be seen as a biological given which emits its own meaning. It must be understood instead as an ensemble of potentialities which are given meaning only in society. Weeks, *Sexuality and Its Discontents,* 122–23. See also Mario Mieli, *Homosexuality and Liberation: Elements of a Gay Critique,* trans. David Fernbach (London: Gay Men's Press, 1980).

4. Weeks, *Sexuality and Its Discontents,* 8.

5. Ibid.

6. Ibid. Jeffrey Weeks challenges the idea of a "pre-given essence of sexuality." Weeks understands sexuality to be open, fluid, and flowing, influenced by changing elements in the culture. Sexuality is moved and shaped by a variety of circumstances. A "fixed identity," one that is static and eternal, inhibits this "flow of different forces and influences." Weeks, *Sexuality and Its Discontents,* 121–22. See also Mieli, *Homosexuality and Liberation;* and Beverly Wildung Harrison, "Misogyny and Homophobia: The Unexplored Connections," in *Making the Connections: Essays in Feminist Social Ethics,* ed. Carol S. Robb (Boston: Beacon Press, 1985).

7. Dorothee Soelle writes, "In German, *phantasie* has a potentially far more positive value than the word "fantasy" has in English. Its meaning includes the dimensions of imagination, inspiration, inventiveness, flexibility, freedom and creativity." Dorothee Soelle, *Beyond Mere Obedience: Reflections on a Christian Ethic for the Future,* trans. Lawrence W. Denef (Minneapolis: Augsburg Publishing House, 1970), 10.

8. Further resources that discuss sex, women, and political control are Harrison, "Sexuality and Social Policy," in *Making the Connections,* 83–114; Weeks, "The 'Sexual Revolution' Revisited," in *Sexuality and Its Discontents,* 15–32; and Sheila Briggs, "Sexual Justice and the Righteousness of God," in *Sex and God: Some Varieties of Women's Experience,* ed. Linda Hurcombe (New York: Routledge & Kegan Paul, 1987), 251–77.

9. In the early christian church, sexual dualism intensified to the point that sexuality was hyper-regulated and made permissible only through pure and exclusive love. Samuel Laeuchli writes that it was a conflict won over by "a tipping of the scale so against sexuality that sexuality becomes synonymous with evil. The sexual act becomes abhorrent and people either flee into deserts or write books on the perfection of virginity." Samuel Laeuchli, *Power and Sexuality: The Emergence of Canon Law at the Synod of Elvira* (Philadelphia: Temple University Press, 1972), 103.

Elaine Pagels discusses the struggle within the church in the first three centuries for control over people. Pagels notes that sexuality is one distinct area of people's lives that the church can regulate, thus regulating their theology and social lives. See Elaine Pagels, *The Gnostic Gospels* (New York: Vintage Books, 1981).

10. Laeuchli, *Power and Sexuality,* 88.

11. Ibid., 112–13.

12. Ibid., 104.

13. Laeuchli notes that the church is still not willing to open the explosive, yet crucial, issue of sexuality (114). The Council of Elvira's refusal to confront the issue of sexuality perpetuates its hierarchical, ecclesiastical authority when dealing with contemporary matters of the modern world. The church's refusal to face its antisexual stance keeps it from confronting relational and interactive issues around sexuality. Laeuchli, *Power and Sexuality,* 122–23.

14. Tertullian, quoted in Mary Daly, *The Church and the Second Sex* (New York: Harper & Row, 1968), 45.

15. Examples of canons that expose the antifemale, antisexual, and anti-Semitic characteristic of teachings include the following: Number 72: "If a widow has intercourse

with a man and later marries him, she shall be reconciled to communion after a period of five years, having completed the required penance; if she marries another man, having left the first, she shall not be given communion even at the end." Number 78: "If one of the faithful who is married commits adultery with a Jewish or pagan woman, he shall be cut off, but if someone else exposes him, he can share Sunday communion after five years, having completed the required penance." Laeuchli, *Power and Sexuality*, 134–35.

16. Haunani-Kay Trask, *Eros and Power: The Promise of Feminist Theory* (Philadelphia: University of Pennsylvania Press, 1986), 56.

17. For more on women and poverty, see Caroline Allison, "It's like Holding the Key to Your Own Jail," in *Women in Namibia* (Geneva: World Council of Churches, 1986); Beverly Bryan, Stella Dadzie, and Suzanne Soate, *The Heart of the Race: Black Women's Lives in Britain* (London: Virago, 1985); Victoria Byerly, *Hard Times Cotton Mill Girls: Personal Histories of Womanhood and Poverty in the South* (Ithaca, N.Y.: ILR Press, 1986); Zilla R. Eisenstein, *Feminism and Sexual Equality: Crisis in Liberal America* (New York: Monthly Review Press, 1984), particularly 114–38; Harrison, *Making the Connections;* Karin Stallord, et al., *Poverty in the American Dream: Women and Children First* (Boston: South End Press, 1983); Soon-Hwa Sun, "Women, Work and Theology in Korea," *Journal of Feminist Studies in Religion* 3, no. 2 (fall 1987): 125–35; Rosa Dominga Trapasso, "The Feminization of Poverty," *Latinamerica Press* (May 31, 1984): 5.

18. Weeks, *Sexuality and Its Discontents*, 26–27.

19. In his later writings, Sigmund Freud began to see the "sexual instincts" as the "true life-instincts." He began to understand the sexual instincts as an energy that "preserved life itself." This was a major affirmation not only of the life-instinct in human nature, but the life-affirming instinct of sexuality. Sigmund Freud, *Beyond the Pleasure Principle: The Pioneer Study of the Death Instinct in Man*, trans. James Strachey (New York: Bantam Books, 1959), 74–75, 79.

This was a major shift for Freud, who had earlier considered the sexual instinct to be a death-instinct. The distinction in his theory came about as Freud began to hypothesize on the "ego-instincts," pressured for death, and the "sexual instincts pressured . . . toward a prolongation of life." Ibid., 78.

20. Herbert Marcuse, *Eros and Civilization: A Philosophical Inquiry into Freud* (Boston: Beacon Press, 1955), 201.

21. See Audre Lorde, "Uses of the Erotic: The Erotic as Power," in *Sister Outsider: Essays and Speeches* (Trumansburg, N.Y.: Crossing Press, 1984), 53–59.

22. Mary Daly and Sarah Bentley Doely were two of the first women to recognize that it was not merely changing male god language or ordaining women into the priesthood that was needed for human liberation. They understood that these issues were symptoms exposing the need for vast structural changes within the church. See Mary Daly, *The Church and the Second Sex;* and Sarah Bentley Doely, *Women's Liberation and the Church* (New York: Association Press, 1970).

Radical Christian feminists are continuing to explore and expand on the ideas put forth in the above-mentioned texts. See, e.g., Elisabeth Schüssler Fiorenza, *In Memory of Her* (New York: Crossroad-Seabury Press, 1983); Rosemary Radford Ruether, *Sexism and God-Talk: Toward a Feminist Theology* (Boston: Beacon Press, 1983); and Harrison, *Making the Connections*.

23. Lorde, "The Transformation of Silence into Language," *Sister Outsider*, 41.

2

Sexuality and Christian Ethics: How to Proceed

LISA SOWLE CAHILL

Both sexual ethics and ethical methodology clearly are problems, which is what makes their discussion not only interesting but urgent. One of the many reasons sex is of interest for every adult human being is that all people at least some of the time are unsure how to understand their sexuality and how to behave sexually in ways that are morally praiseworthy rather than reprehensible. Moreover, ethicists want to talk theoretically and normatively about sexuality and sex in ways that are not only praiseworthy but coherent. This ambition too is problematic, peculiarly so for the Christian ethicist. He or she has to take into account factors and perspectives that seem to lead in opposed directions. These include common wisdom; what the empirical studies, which presently command so much attention, reveal about human sexual experience and gender identity; the ways Christian authors and churches traditionally have educated the faithful to perceive male and female relations, sexuality, and sex; what the Bible says or indicates about these subjects; and even central philosophical presentations of them. Perhaps the salient obligation of the moral analyst, given this state of affairs, is to muster the nerve to proceed at all.

Despite its pitfalls, the task of analysis may not be avoided. For humans, "sexuality" is "morality." It is part of our expressing, for good or ill, relationship to the material world, to other life forms, to the self, and to other persons, including God. As our point of departure we will pay attention to the experiential phenomena of sex and sexuality, for they bring home in a most pressing and universal manner the necessity of systematic reflection on the moral life.

SEXUAL EXPERIENCE

Sex is now no more a simple matter than it ever has been, however much in the name of "sexual liberation" we claim to have demystified it. Twentieth-century Americans are no more or less obsessed with sex than our predecessors; it is only that our obsessions take different forms. Sex, despite its prosaic side, was to our grandparents' generation a hidden idol, enshrined in an aura of mystery, fascination, and danger; we glorify, pursue, and parade it to the point of banality. Sex has been connected with elemental and divine powers in certain historical periods and cultures; but our protestations that it is "natural" do not conceal our own fear and even contempt of it. Why is it that sex among human beings is always so puzzling? Why are humans not able, like other animals, to come together by instinctual motives of self- and species preservation, to couple briefly, to conceive, and thereafter to part or affiliate (without problems), motivated again by instinct to do what is necessary to raise the young that result?

It seems to be precisely the animal-like compulsion of sexual yearning that most bewilders and beleaguers the human moral agent, philosopher, and theologian. Augustine of Hippo referred to "the shameful motion of the organs of generation"[1] and went so far as to suggest that in the Garden of Eden sexual intercourse between Adam and Eve would have taken place without any sexual desire at all. Apparently, it seemed to Augustine that the replacement of disorderly passion by a sheer act of the rational will would have been more in keeping with human dignity.[2] While this theory may be extreme, it does represent an influential Christian author's perception of the ambivalence of human sexual experience.[3] Humans have tended to conclude from reflection on the matter that sexual impulses either are in an essential sense anti-human because they cannot be conformed to some ideal of pure rationality and freedom, of absolute self-control; or, on the other side, are so quintessentially, immediately, and irresistibly natural that it is as futile to deny, suppress, or sublimate them as it would be the contractions of the heart muscle. Human beings have a preference for thinking in extremes; it makes matters far more simple. But simplicity in human affairs is more often than not illusory. Sexuality is no exception. Some accounts of human sexuality and its genital expressions construe them as counter-human because they are among those experiences in which humans feel least in control of themselves and most under the influence of instincts and physical responses. To the minds of some of the fathers of the Christian tradition, sexual desire is to be resisted lest it bring humanity to the level of the animals. Such interpretations miss the obvious point that "animality" is not a pejorative term and that, indeed, it is one aptly applied to the species Homo sapiens.[4] But accounts of sex that explain it as a simple, universal, and irresistibly attractive drive ignore the fact that humans are animals of a special sort. Their ability to reflect self-consciously and empathetically on their own and others' needs and interests, to discriminate cognitively and affectively among them in terms of immediate and long-range outcomes, and to act so as to rearrange priorities and redirect impulses in the interests of communities and of other persons is not unparalleled in the animal world, but it is nowhere matched.

We have, then, a certain duality in sexual experience. It is physical, urgent, and pervasive. It is also an avenue of affective and spiritual relations among persons, for good or ill. Yet the human person is not a duality. At least Western philosophical and religious traditions have learned to resist dualistic interpretations of the person, even if they have not overcome them. To cut the person into separate pieces of soul and body, psyche and physique, freedom and determinancy, is again too simple. We shall note that the Genesis creation accounts attest that the human being is one, a unity, which has two aspects but not two discrete components.

It is this duality of experience in unity of being that grounds the problem of human sexuality. Sex in humans is not understood completely if it is explained only as a physiologic species-survival mechanism, or a technique of physical enjoyment. It is also an instrument, or indeed a constituent, of the sorts of interpersonal relations that are most distinctively human. Since humans are as capable of evil, wickedness, selfishness, and manipulation in these relationships as they are of good, rectitude, self-sacrifice, and generosity, sex is a problem. And sinfulness in sex, as in other realms of human existence, often springs from just the fact that humans are slothful and cowardly and shortsighted, and thus refuse to take on the project of reconciling the troublesome human reality of what Reinhold Niebuhr called freedom and finitude, or spirit and nature.[5] The ever-mobile, dialectical relation between these poles is what makes the human situation so precarious and causes our anxiety. It is because we cannot resolve this anxiety, and refuse to endure it, that we attempt to evade it. In so doing, according to Niebuhr, we sin by denial of what it is to be human.

I fear that this beginning has had about it an air of moroseness which, I hope, does not represent adequately the sexual experiences of most people, even of most Christians. But I see it as the necessary backdrop for the project of ascertaining what the Christian religious tradition demands of humans in their sexual being and relationships and acts. It is this ambiguous, problematic quality of sex that has instigated much of the worrying and writing about it that has gone on in Christianity. No doubt, in a profound way sexuality will remain an enigma. It would be naive, ahistorical, and self-aggrandizing to think that we might achieve an unassailable or even unique formulation of the problem of sexuality and its ethical resolution. But we may come to understand it more adequately, if never completely, by recollecting and critically renewing what some of our predecessors have had to say of our common experience.

THE SOURCES OF CHRISTIAN ETHICS

But what are the wellsprings of this process? The interrelation and priority of the sources of Christian ethics is the major methodological theme of [Cahill's book]. This concern is another version of the "reason and revelation" question. How ought the Christian ethicist to include, interpret, and weigh religious and secular sources of moral insight? Not infrequently, Christian authors writing about sexual ethics so stress a chosen point of departure that the contributions of other sources are neglected or virtually excluded. Whether one begins with, for instance, received "natural law" teaching, certain biblical prohibitions, or scientific studies of sexual psychology and behavior, a fully "Christian" process of reflection will permit interpretation and qualification of that initial source by other complementary ones.[6] My thesis, whose lack of originality may be its strength, is that there are four complementary reference points for Christian ethics:[7] the foundational texts or "scriptures" of the faith community—the Bible; the community's "tradition" of faith, theology, and practice; philosophical accounts of essential or ideal humanity ("normative" accounts of the human[8]); and descriptions of what actually is and has been the case in human lives and societies ("descriptive" accounts of the human). While Scripture is the reference point most obviously associated with Christian theological ethics, empirical sciences recently have received most emphasis as sources of insight into human sexuality, sexual behavior, marriage, parenthood, and gender roles. Both Bible and empirical studies present particular problems for the ethicist, for they entail special, internal canons of interpretation, with which the theological ethicist may not have sophisticated familiarity. Yet both sources are indispensable for contemporary Christian ethics. Sometimes Christian theologians have rejected the adequacy for a Christian moral perspective of nonreligious definitions of the normatively human ("human nature"), but Christian ethics is never uninfluenced by secular philosophical anthropologies, even those against which it defines itself. Because it is the fundamental content for explicitly theological ethical reflection, the Christian tradition forms the "hermeneutical circle" within which Christian theology defines itself and interprets its other sources. The most distinctive source of Christian ethics, the Bible, is the product of the most primitive stage in the life history of the community founded in Christ. In a sense, the Bible is not only the basis of the Christian religious tradition, but is actually a representation of the first phases within that tradition. Although "tradition" is sometimes taken to mean dogmatic or moral propositions transmitted from the past, it is better understood as the "story" of a people, "handed on" or "transmitted" for reappropriation in each generation. It includes but is not limited to formulations of dogma and ethics derived from the faith life of the community. Specific criteria for what counts as "tradition" might include antiquity, widespread usage, consensus of the faithful, and authoritative definition. Tradition is the historical identity and self-understanding of the religious community, which is formed by the Scriptures, and which continues to inform its present and future.[9]

I contend that fidelity to these four mutually correcting sources, and success in judiciously balancing them, is a standard by which we can measure the adequacy of various positions in the tradition, including our own. Thomas Aquinas, for example, gives priority to the philosophical element in ethics. He interprets the relation of man and woman, marriage, and procreation on the basis of his understanding of what it would mean to be fully and authentically human, that is, to live in accord with the nature that God bestows in the creation. His philosophical anthropology, however, is informed in a radical way not only by that of Aristotle but also by the perspective of medieval Christianity. Although Thomas accomplishes much in terms of a reasonable account of human existence, he neglects a primary source to which Martin Luther redirects our attention: the Bible. With his radical insistence that ethics be ordered by Scripture, and *sola Scriptura,* Luther revitalizes the nature of Christian ethics as the delineation of the practical consequences of faith and life in Christ. In filling out the details and ramifications of the biblical witness for sexuality and marriage, however, Luther relies a great deal on common experience and common sense. Even the inspired Word of God in Scripture is not a sheer "datum" but an occasion of hearing and understanding the spirit of the Lord present in community.

In contemporary theology, the realization is increasing that it is no easy matter to determine how these four resources of Bible, tradition, and descriptive and normative accounts of the human should be balanced. This is especially so, given the facts that no one source is understood apart from the complementary contributions of the others; and that their perspectives on some moral issues may in the end diverge. . . . For example, the Bible seems to provide clearly negative evaluations of homosexual behavior. Empirical and quantitative studies, however, offer evidence that homosexuality is a result of nature or environment, not choice, that it occurs cross-culturally, and that even an overt homosexual lifestyle of itself precludes neither psychological and social health, nor the exercise of central virtues traditionally associated with Christ-like living. [It is also important] to examine the interface of biblical and empirical studies when we take up the problem of male and female sex differences and gender roles. On either of these questions, homosexuality or gender roles, the ethicist's commitment to his or her task is complicated by the awareness that even the collection of so-called "objective empirical data" is made possible by categories of organization which are not without interpretative elements. By what "scientific" standard, for example, is one's sexual orientation defined as "homosexual" or "heterosexual"; or is a person of either orientation described as "socially well-adjusted"? Or, what are the presuppositions that determine the patterns of family organization that the anthropologist chooses to study? On what premises does he or she draw lines of causation between adult female and male roles in a given society, and that society's patterns of child rearing, or religious symbols, or economic and political systems? What we look for and eventually see in what "is" cannot but be influenced, if not determined, by what we think "ought to be." The ethicist who uses or rejects empirical studies naively will pay with loss of credibility, not only to the broader culture or to the "academy" but also to those in the church who perceive that Christian existence is a form of human experience.[10]

The interpretative problem with which I am most concerned is that of a critical hermeneutic of the Christian Scriptures which is cognizant both of historical-critical research on the biblical texts and their communities of authorship and of the authoritative character of the Scriptures for the ongoing life of the community of faith. . . .

TOWARD A CHRISTIAN ETHICS
OF SEXUALITY

The most important biblical contribution to a Christian ethics of sexual activity and of relationship between the sexes is the placement of morality within the life of the faith community. Morality is not an interest for its own sake, but for the sake of understanding how the people of God will live and act toward one another and toward others if they are faithful. In the Hebrew Bible, or Christian Old Testament, the covenant with Yahweh leads to certain religious and moral forms of existence which are an expression of covenant fidelity. In the New Testament, faith and conversion in Jesus Christ establish membership in the Spirit-filled community. The Christian bears the "fruits of the Spirit," or certain qualities of character that dispose one to act in certain ways. Sexuality receives some attention as a concrete mode of action, but certainly far less than we are inclined to give it.

In examining the biblical witness for sexual morality, we will focus on patterns of male-female relationship and sexual relations that can be referred broadly to canonical material, rather than on the specific content of isolated texts.

Both Old and New Testament resources support a view of sexuality as part of the goodness of humanity's creation, but as also subject to the corruption of sin. Humanity is essentially male and female. Man and woman are created for a physical, procreative, psychological, and social partnership, which presupposes sexual differentiation but not hierarchy. Human sexual acts fulfill cooperation and express community, but are in themselves never the focus of biblical discussions. Morality for both the Hebrew and Christian communities is one aspect of cohesive living in obedience and fidelity. While I would judge that the biblical literature points toward heterosexual, monogamous, lifelong, and pro-creative marriage as the normative or ideal institutionalization of sexual activity, I would not say that the biblical texts represent preoccupation with, or indeed much interest in, the justification or exclusion of other sexual expressions. It will be necessary to turn to additional resources of Christian ethics both to confirm the general scriptural views of male and female, of human sexuality, and of sexual acts; and to consider in what ways the scriptural norm can be realized or adapted in variable concrete situations. As the New Testament divorce texts show us, the process of adaptation begins already within the canon.

Christian authors do better or worse in developing a theology of human sexuality in proportion to their ability to consider, relate, and balance these sources. When the influence of one or more is ignored or minimized, the position becomes less secure. We have indicated already that Thomas Aquinas respects a philosophical perspective on human sexuality, but is not very critical of his cultural milieu and largely neglects the Bible. Luther uses the Bible to criticize received tradition, but finds it necessary to interpret the Bible in the light of concrete experience.

We too will need to complement our reading of the Bible and to respond to the mores of our own culture by attending to all the reference points of Christian ethics. Of the Christian tradition it will be asked what the community of faith consistently has affirmed about human sexuality. A response might suggest the goodness of sexuality as God's creation, male and female differentiation and union, the importance of procreation as a purpose of sexual acts, marriage and family as the institutionalization of procreation, and the social partnership of male and female. The tradition, however, also yields elements that today are regarded as less than normative: the dubious moral nature of all sex, the subordination of women, and intended procreation as the only complete justification of sexual acts. The ambiguity of the tradition, as well as of the Bible, presses us to the question of *criteria* for the elimination or appropriation of biblical and traditional meanings of sexuality and sexual activity. The standard of an adequate Christian theology and ethics of sexuality is precisely the dialectical and complementary relationship of Bible, tradition, and normative and descriptive accounts of human existence.

Since moral philosophy and philosophical anthropologies have many incarnations, it is difficult to isolate a single normative view of the human as central. . . . The classical, medieval, and modern world views entail different presuppositions about whether what is "natural" to humans can be known in any clear and final way, and about whether human "nature" may indeed change. But philosophical accounts of sexual ethics commonly presuppose that it is possible to define at least approximately some "essential" or "ideal" meaning of sexuality, despite actual historical distortions or adaptations of it in the human sexual reality, and despite the limits of the human mind seeking to discover it. Sometimes, of course, such definitions are used in the service of a religious tradition or culture and its view of sexuality, and thus transmit some of the same "values" that were defined above as inadequate components of the Christian tradition. However, most moral philosophers today, as well as some classical ones, at least to a degree, may be understood to affirm the essential character of sex in relation to human being, the meaning of sex as expression of interpersonal relation as well as procreation, and the equal dignity of man and woman.

Descriptive accounts of what the human situation actually is like give us a "window" onto the normative. In our century, the empirical sciences have become preeminent sources of such factual information. Another form of describing the human situation is the "personal story," which is then generalized, implicitly or explicitly, to persons in situations similar to that of the author of the account. Empirical or other descriptive resources serve as correctives to biblical, traditional, and normative accounts that simply do not correspond to the realities of human experience.

Although . . . attention to several sources will be profitable for Christian ethics, especially a Christian ethics of sexuality, I must acknowledge . . . that my proposals, both methodological and substantive, will be provisional. For one, the quadruple enumeration of Christian ethics' sources certainly will be subject to restatement or refinement. For another, assessment of their contributions can be carried out most successfully by those who have in regard to them more specialized expertise than I. By no means have I discussed Bible, tradition, philosophy, and descriptions of actual experience comprehensively. I have chosen instead to focus on certain aspects of each, with the aim of demonstrating the interconnection of our understanding of any one with that of all the others. My purpose in writing will have been accomplished if others are induced to undertake more proficiently the task, which I have set for myself, of construing Christian ethics as a dynamic yet ordered form of fidelity to the central Christian symbols of beneficent Creator, righteous Judge, gracious Redeemer, and transforming Spirit. These symbols require us to attend to our own experience, to view critically all our ideas and actions, and to take the experience of God in community as the beginning point of reconciliation of body and spirit, self and others, and humanity and God.

NOTES

1. Augustine, *City of God* XIV.19, 21.

2. Ibid., XIV.23–24.

3. Although the "irresistibility" of sexual drives indeed has been a major component in Christian reflection on sexual ethics, I wonder if it is not more an element of the male experience of sex than of the female. It was precisely the involuntary movements of the male sexual organ that Augustine seemed to find so shameful and even frightening. (See David F. Kelly, "Sexuality and Concupiscence in Augustine," in *The Annual of the Society of Christian Ethics: 1983,* ed. Larry L. Rasmussen [Southern Methodist University: Society of Christian Ethics, 1983].) A complementary (not opposite) female perspective on the experience of sexuality was offered by Karen Lebacqz, who was a member of a panel that responded to my Earl Lectures at the Pacific School of Religion (February 1983). Lebacqz offered that our sexuality is an avenue of *vulnerability,* because through it we both need and are open to other persons. Lebacqz did not suggest that vulnerability is a characteristic of the woman's sexuality only, nor is the experience of an urgent physical drive only the man's. However, the male and female experiences of sexuality (which certainly differ physically and may differ psychologically and emotionally) may enable men and women to be more sensitive to its various aspects. The philosopher Sara Ruddick also comments that in the most complete sexual exchanges "vulnerability is increased for *both* sexes by the active desiring of the partners" ("Better Sex," in *Philosophy and Sex,* ed. Robert Baker and Frederick Elliston [Buffalo: Prometheus Books, 1975], 97).

4. Mary Midgley, *Beast and Man* (Ithaca, N.Y.: Cornell University Press, 1978).

5. Reinhold Niebuhr, *The Nature and Destiny of Man,* vol. 1 (New York: Charles Scribner's Sons, 1964), chap. 7.

6. For a critical discussion of the use of sources in recent Christian ethics of sexuality, see my "Sexual Issues in Christian Theological Ethics: A Review of Recent Studies," *Religious Studies Review* 4/1 (1978):1–14.

7. Several who heard the Earl Lectures pointed out the resemblance of my method to the Methodist "quadrilateral" test, inspired by John Wesley. Although this test is formulated somewhat differently, I take its similarity to confirm my conviction that the

sources I name are no novelty, but substantive for Christian theology and ethics. Another discussion of the method of Christian ethics, which resembles mine in appealing to several sources but which is much more exhaustive, is provided by Robert J. Daly, *Christian Biblical Ethics: From Biblical Revelation to Contemporary Christian Praxis* (New York: Paulist Press, 1984). See especially Part 1, chap. 3, "The Bible and Ethics," The book began in a task force of the Catholic Biblical Association, and incorporates chapters by members of that group, woven by Daly into a lengthy study. Daly and others raise many of the hermeneutical questions that I do, come to a consensus that Christian ethics is both a science and an art, and address issues of practice such as nonviolence, marriage, divorce, and politics.

8. "The normatively human" is a phrase borrowed from James M. Gustafson ("Genetic Engineering and a Normative View of the Human," in *Ethical Issues in Biology and Medicine,* ed. Preston N. Williams [Cambridge: Schenkman, 1972], 46–58). It indicates what is to be valued and promoted in human existence, or what is fulfilling for humanity, but is free of the connotation of the classical term "human nature" that essential human being is an ahistorical and clearly knowable entity.

9. See James Hennesey, S.J., "Grasping the Tradition: Reflections of a Church Historian," *Theological Studies* 45/1 (1984):153–63.

10. In chap. 1 of *The Analogical Imagination: Christian Theology and the Culture of Pluralism* (New York: Crossroad, 1981), David Tracy speaks of the three "publics" of theology: society, academy, and church (3–46).

3

New Testament Sexual Ethics and Today's World

L. WILLIAM COUNTRYMAN

A close reading of the New Testament . . . shows how alien its sexual ethics are to the world of today. They are framed in terms of purity and property systems that no longer prevail among us. Although we have grown accustomed to reading the Bible as if it pertained directly to our own experience, such a reading ignores much that is important in the texts themselves and is, for the most part, incapable of dealing with them literally—that is, in terms of their simplest, least adapted sense. The reader may therefore be tempted to conclude that the sexual ethics of the New Testament are now irrelevant, even for Christians, and that we must begin from the beginning to construct some kind of sexual ethic suitable to our own era. I believe this conclusion would be mistaken.

As I have argued elsewhere, one of the primary contributions which Scripture makes to the work of the Spirit in the life of the Christian community is that it stands outside our present and therefore prevents us from treating our contemporary world as an inevitability. The antiquity of the biblical writings means that they give Christians other models of social life to stand alongside those we know directly. These models come from the past and are therefore in some sense irretrievable. Every culture, including that of the first-century Mediterranean world, is a whole and not recoverable in isolated pieces; even when isolated pieces survive or are consciously revived, they will no longer mean the same thing in their new contexts. The first-century Mediterranean world—or its sexual ethics or any other single aspect of its culture—is not, then, of the substance of the gospel. To suggest that it is would be to place the gospel forever beyond our reach. The spiritual function of the Bible's antiquity is rather to relativize the present, to rule out in advance the notion that things can be only as they are. We cannot return to the past, and we do not know what shape the future will take. What we can do is seek, with the help of the past, to understand the present in its own terms and proclaim the gospel in ways pertinent to it.[1]

In sexual matters, as elsewhere, this is the goal of Christian theology. The dominance of dogmatic or systematic theology in Western Christianity since the Scholastic period has created the unfortunate illusion that the gospel is a system of ideas which can be fully comprehended by any person of adequate intelligence quite apart from any necessity of personal transformation. Nothing could be further from the teaching of Jesus, as presented in the New Testament Gospels. This teaching is unsystematic in form; but, what is more important, it is devoted to the transformation (*metanoia,* conversion) of the hearer rather than to the creation of a theological system. In the earlier eras of Christianity, the "theologian" was preeminently one whose encounter with God shaped the person with such power that he or she could speak of God with the authority of grace.

Such speech was more often "occasional" than systematic; that is to say, it responded to occasions of immediate concern, seeking to explicate them in terms of grace and making no pretense to a complete or exhaustive knowledge of God. Thus, Paul wrote to the Corinthians in order to speak to conflicts and problems raised in the life of their congregation, not to explicate the whole of his gospel. Dogmatic theology has sometimes pretended to a complete and perfect knowledge of things sacred, and it has suggested such pretensions to the unreflective even when it has known better than to take them seriously itself. The idea that an ordinary human being could, through a form of intellectual endeavor, be fully in command of the mysteries of the gospel or that anyone could progress toward knowledge of God faster than one was in fact being transformed by that knowledge is fundamentally alien to early Christianity.

Theology, in the older, presytematic sense, assumes that we live in our own moment, our own historical and cultural context. We meet, in that context, God's grace as definitively made known through the ministry, death, and resurrection of Jesus. We experience grace as transforming our life; and we proclaim the power of grace as we have known it. This is not to say that all theology must always take the form of personal testimony. In most cases, this would prove boring—for the very good reason that one person's experience becomes relevant to another only insofar as the one can show the other how they belong to the same world and share the reality or possibility of intimately comparable experience. What this means, rather, is that all theology must be true to the speaker's living, not spun out as the logical consequence of an objectivized intellectual system, but cohering with an experience of grace in the world we actively share. If this theology is to be, moreover, Christian theology, then it must meet the further criterion of continuity with the experience of grace expressed in the New Testament.

This brings us to the other side of the New Testament's relevance today. If Scripture is important partly because it is alien to and therefore relativizes our own historical-cultural situation, it is even more important in that it can show, by reference to the way the grace of God broke into the self-sufficiency of another culture, how it breaks into our own as well. The New Testament writers did not try to construct a new sexual ethic from the ground up. They took over the existing cultural patterns and refocused them, pushing some elements from the center to the periphery, altering the balance of powers allotted to various members of society, and, most important, relativizing the familiar life of this world by subordinating it to the reign of God. The result was that Christians could, in many ways, continue to conform to familiar cultural mores while, at the same time, understanding these familiar institutions in ways which undermined their absolute claims.

This suggests a pattern worth applying to the present situation. Ideally, it would invite us to comprehend the nature of sexual institutions in our own time and culture, and then to subject them to the same kind of critique on behalf of the gospel of God's grace. This will prove difficult. The difficulties arise both from the side of the modern world and from that of the gospel. Our world has been (and perhaps still is) passing through an era of great changes, making it difficult for us to know what in fact our social structure provides in the way of sexual institutions. The world of the first century was probably more fixed and settled in this regard. At the same time, the demands of the gospel of grace are being constantly renewed and fitted to new situations by the Spirit who animates the church. There is no simple list of them that can be lifted out of Scripture or the church's past experience and reflection and applied without further ado to the present.

This is not a task for one theologian, but for the church. It will require insights from many perspectives, both on the modern world and on the Bible, brought together in what I suspect will be a long conversation. I am not so foolish as to propose, in one chapter, to resolve all the relevant questions or even to raise them. I hope rather to show that the major emphases of the New Testament, if applied with appropriate sensitivity to our cultural and historical distance from the first-century Mediterranean world, will yield the outlines of a sexual ethic that is both intelligible and practicable in our world and also coherent with the gospel of grace.

[*At this point the author urges readers to interpret the following discussion in light of the preceding chapters in his book. We believe that this material is intelligible in its own right, but we would strongly commend the rest of Countryman's book to all readers.—Ed.*]

In the following pages, I shall first put forward a series of principles drawn from the preceding study. I call these principles "generative" because I believe that, when applied, they will give rise to explicit ethical guidelines, such as I have sketched in the latter part of this chapter. These, in turn, I present not as invariable rules, but as a kind of alarm system whose violation signals a very high probability (amounting in some cases to a practical certainty) that the principles behind them are being violated. Throughout the present chapter, I am writing as a Christian for Christians. In the present confused state of our culture, I presume that any coherent statement of a sexual ethic will hold some interest for a larger public, but I do not propose what follows as a universally applicable ethic, for it is directly dependent on the message of the gospel.

GENERATIVE PRINCIPLES

The preceding historical study of the New Testament [not here reproduced] has provided a basis for defining six principles that must enter into the formation of any Christian sexual ethic today. Most of them are drawn directly from the New Testament; one of them (the third) speaks rather of the distance of the first-century world from our own time. These are not "first principles," for they are themselves dependent on more fundamental assertions about God, God's grace, and humanity under God's grace. The oneness of God, which implies a oneness of this created world and of humanity in it; the absolute priority of God's action over our own, both in creation and in subsequent acts of grace; the sinfulness of humanity, which becomes most destructive in the form of claims to righteousness; God's presence in flesh through the incarnation; the call to *metanoia* (repentance, conversion, transformation) and the demands made on us in this world by our citizenship in the age to come; the equality of all human beings under grace and the priority of love over all other virtues—all these are prior to the principles enunciated here. The links which lead from the ones to the others can, in fact, be made explicit, but this is not the place to do so. At present, it is enough to have shown that these generative principles are those which the New Testament itself lays down for dealing with the questions of sexual ethics or which the change of cultures compels us to take into account.

1. *Membership in the Christian community is in no way limited by purity codes.* Individual Christians may continue to observe the purity code of their culture, but they may not demand that other Christians do so. If one wishes to assert that any given proscription is a part of Christian sexual ethics, one must justify that claim by showing that the act in question infringes some principle other than purity. Any claim that a given sexual act is wrong in and of itself will be found ultimately to represent either a lack of ethical analysis or a hidden purity claim.

2. *Christians must respect the sexual property of others and practice detachment from their own.* There are two points to be made here. The first is that the New Testament interests itself in property not so much in order to defend me against my neighbor as to defend my neighbor against me. Paul, for example, wrote to the Corinthians that it would be preferable for them to suffer injustice and deprivation at one another's hands rather than take their cases to the public courts where they would themselves probably be seeking to commit injustice (1 Cor. 6:7–8). The second is that property also had value, for the New Testament writers, as an extension of the self; in this respect, the essential question was not "How shall I maintain what is mine?" but "How shall I dispose it in obedience to the reign of God?" The self is not something to be preserved

and enhanced at all costs, but rather a means by which we become compatible with and enter the world to come.

3. *Where, in late antiquity, sexual property belonged to the family through the agency of the male householder, in our own era it belongs to the individual.* The difference between the ancient and modern worlds in this respect is one of focus. The ancient householder could say "mine"; the modern individual is usually still implicated, to some degree, in the restrictions and pressures of a family. "Family" and "individuality" are the poles of a continuum, with life taking place in the area of tension between. Nonetheless, the brief treatment of family-oriented society provided [earlier in Countryman's book] should be enough to show the distance between a world in which the individual is the primary arbiter of his or her sexual acts and one in which these were functions of the life of a family. If the New Testament's critique of sexual property is to be illuminative in our present world, we must take into account that the type of "owner" has changed; and such a change in ownership will always imply a change in the character and understanding of what is owned.

4. *The gospel can discern no inequality between men and women as they stand before God's grace.* The New Testament writers came to accept a good deal of inequality between the sexes in day-to-day life; but this represented an accommodation to existing patterns, not the working out of the gospel principle. Perhaps this principle could never have been worked out very effectively in a family-oriented society, since it implied the destruction of the existing family order. The early Christians, in general, found it achievable only in the context of celibacy. It remained, however, a principle of basic importance.

5. *Marriage creates a union of flesh, normally indissoluble except by death.* This principle brought sexual union into the family in a new way which rivaled the existing family structure; indeed, had not Paul and some later New Testament writers reaffirmed the subordination of women, it would have dissolved the ancient family. In a society which defines the individual as the basic social unit rather than the family, the meaning of "one flesh" must necessarily go through some redefinition if this principle is still to be challenging, intelligible, and useful.

6. *The Christian's sexual life and property are always subordinate to the reign of God.* This is not a rejection of the values of sexual life, but rather a focus on God's calling of each person under particular circumstances, which may demand sacrifice of lesser to greater good. Since Christ "owns" all believers, their lives must cohere with this reality—not by some show of pietism, transforming each aspect of life into a kind of religious show, but by the clear linking of what is more peripheral to what is more central.

To say how these principles give rise to a sexual morality in our own time calls for an exercise of judgment in relating them to the facts of our sexual life. Grace calls us not to leave this world, but to live in it, wherever God calls us to be, as citizens of God's reign. This calls for ethical discernment of the problems and possibilities implicit in our milieu in order to see what God asks us to do in this context.

DERIVED GUIDELINES

Rejection of the Requirements of Physical Purity

When the New Testament rejected the imposition of the purity codes of the Torah on Gentile Christians, it was not in order that a new, distinctively Christian purity code might take their place. Except for hints of such developments in Jude and Revelation, the New Testament did not justify any sexual rule by appeal to physical purity. Indeed, it exhibited a strong concern that purity, as a distinction dividing human societies from one another, should give way before a massive awareness of the grace of God, extended impartially to all human beings. The creation of its own purity code has been one of several ways in which the church has at times allowed itself to become a barrier to the gospel of God's grace. A Christian sexual ethic that remains true to its New Testament roots will have to discard its insistence on physical purity.

The great difficulty of this demand is that it excises what has become, at least for many Americans, the very heart of Christian sexual morality. It therefore places the churches under a great test—essentially the same test as that which confronted the pious among the Jewish people during Jesus' own ministry and the circumcision party within the earliest Christian church at the time of Paul's Gentile mission. Will the churches hang onto their own self-defined purity and so hold themselves aloof from those excluded by it, or will they proclaim the grace of God which plays no favorites? Will they make their existing purity codes conditions of salvation, or will they acknowledge that they have no right to limit what God gives?

To be specific, the gospel allows no rule against the following, in and of themselves: masturbation, nonvaginal heterosexual intercourse, bestiality,[2] polygamy, homosexual acts, or erotic art and literature. The Christian is free to be repelled by any or all of these and may continue to practice her or his own purity code in relation to them. What we are not free to do is impose our codes on others. Like all sexual acts, these may be genuinely wrong where they also involve an offense against the property of another, denial of the equality of women and men, or an idolatrous substitution of sex for the reign of God as the goal of human existence.

Christians have increasingly accepted that masturbation or even nonvaginal heterosexual intercourse, in and of themselves, are not wrong. Bestiality, where it is the casual recourse of the young or of people isolated over long periods of time from other humans, should occasion little concern. It is probably too isolated a phenomenon to justify strong feelings. More difficulty may attach to the other issues in the list. They therefore call for a somewhat more detailed discussion.

Polygamy is more likely to be a serious issue in the Third World than in the modern West. Nowhere, however, does the Bible make monogamy a clear and explicit standard for all Christian marriage. Our usage in this matter must derive from the Greco-Roman milieu in which the church spent its formative early centuries. This does not mean that the modern church should seek to reinstitute polygamy where there is no cultural demand for it; but it does mean that, in cultures which have hitherto been polygamous, monogamy as such should not be made a condition of grace. The church, however, should concern itself with the question of the equality of women and men, particularly with regard to the way marital patterns affect the status of women. Monogamy offers no guarantee of equality; but the relative benefits of monogamy and polygamy in this respect should be the principal point at issue wherever the church must make such decisions.

Homosexual orientation has been increasingly recognized in our time as a given of human sexuality. While most people feel some sexual attraction to members of both the same and the opposite sex and, in the majority of these, attraction to the opposite sex dominates, there is a sizeable minority for whom sexual attraction to persons of the same sex is a decisive shaping factor of their sexual lives. It appears that this orientation is normally inalterable and that there is no strong internal reason for the homosexual person to wish to alter it. To deny an entire class of human beings the right peaceably and without harming others to pursue the kind of sexuality that corresponds to their nature is a perversion of the gospel. Like the insistence of some on the circumcising of gentile converts, it makes the keeping of purity rules a condition of grace. It is sometimes suggested that homosexual persons be told to become celibate. While celibacy is a venerable Christian tradition and may even, as Paul suggested, be called for under certain circumstances, it is also a *charisma* (gift) and can never be demanded of those to whom such a gift has not been given. Paul indicated that the presence of this gift is known by the ability of the celibate person to deal with ungratified sexual desires without being dominated by them. For those without this gift, Paul considered the satisfaction of their desires, so long as it was within the boundaries of the property ethic, entirely appropriate. Any insistence on celibacy for homosexuals as such is, accordingly, contrary to the New Testament witness.

Erotic literature and art (commonly called "pornography")[3] form a wide-spread and diverse phenomenon which may at times be contrary to Christian ethics, particularly when they set up idolatrous ethical standards which treat the self and its sexual gratification as the final goal of all existence or when they present as acceptable the degradation of adults (usually women, in our society) or abuse of children. Explicit verbal and pictorial representations of sexual acts are not forbidden by the gospel—apart from such considerations which may render one or another particular item ethically obnoxious. By the traditional standards of Western Christianity, however, whatever is sexually explicit is impure. Although we tend to think of the issue of pornography as limited to newsstands, so-called "adult" bookstores, and theaters, actually it permeates our whole society, as attested, for example, by our lack of an ordinary vocabulary in English (as distinct from a medical or an obscene one) for the discussion of sexuality. Anxiety about the erotic is, most importantly, the thing which prevents the clear and open sexual education of our young. We are currently reaping the consequences of this purity rule in the form of widespread pregnancies among teenagers who are neither capable of nor very interested in the rearing of children. And we shall be very lucky indeed if we do not promote the rapid spread of AIDS by our unwillingness to speak explicitly to children in the educational process. The pleasure attached to explicit sexual portrayals, in words or pictures, should be accepted as the powerful ally of any effort to teach the responsible use of so beautiful a thing. We cannot, however, expect to forbid sexually explicit representations in most respects and still make good use of them in one narrowly permitted area, namely, education. Children will not usually trust claims on which they have no independent controls whatever.

The New Testament, of course, does not demand that those Christians whose consciences are committed to some purity law give up the practice of it. No one should be required to take an interest in erotica or to indulge in sexual practices which, however permissible, seem to that person a violation of conscience. For that person, they would indeed be wrong actions. Conscience, of course, is not fixed in its final form, and one must expect that it will mature along with our comprehension of other aspects of God, the world, and the gospel. It remains true, however, that every Christian is responsible to his or her own present understanding. Those whose confidence in grace is great enough to free them from purity codes (the "strong," as Paul called them) may not force their position on others; but neither may those who observe such codes (the "weak") refuse the strong the right to follow their consciences. Since neither group has any right to deprive others of what properly belongs to them, it follows that the weak should not attempt to prevent open sexual education, outlaw erotic art and literature, or keep homosexual persons out of the church and ministry. The strong, on the other hand, must not make their standard of conduct a prerequisite of grace any more than the purity rules are. Paul urged the strong to avoid occasions of public offense to the weak. This is good, so long as the weak also commit themselves to a clear recognition that the strong have a part in the church; it would be betrayal of the gospel, however, if the needs of the weak were made an excuse for the reinstitution of purity law as a condition of grace.

There has been a tendency, over the past century or so, to reinstitute purity law under the guise of mental health, by claiming that deviations from it are a kind of sickness. Our society, having made a religion of medicine and a priesthood of physicians, is tempted to invoke the word "sickness" as a mere synonym of "impurity" without imparting any definite meaning to it. This sham was long used to threaten children who masturbated with such dire consequences as insanity; but the most obvious and shameful use of it has been against homosexuals, who have been labeled as sick merely because they differed from the majority. Even though intelligent and truly comparable studies have now shown that there was never any foundation for such claims, there are those who, on dogmatic grounds (nothing else being available), still make them.

The identification of sickness and impurity has become even more apparent in the irrational anxieties focused recently on people with AIDS. These anxieties have induced many to seek a radical separation from carriers and potential carriers of the virus, even though competent authorities have repeatedly assured the public that the virus is communicated only in quite specific ways. The irrationality and intensity of such responses testify to the enormous power that the purity ethic can still have for us. It is not death which is the primary source of these fears, for the advocate of quarantines may well be willing to take much greater risks, day by day, in driving metropolitan freeways. The great fear is of contracting a disease as "dirty" to many in the modern world as leprosy was in antiquity.

Those who wish to rescue our society's purity rules by designating everyone who deviates from them as "sick" are merely renaming purity; they are not telling us anything new or illuminating. In many cases, they have even been uttering falsehoods; and, in the process, they have harmed many generations of the young who were forced to fear that masturbation or homosexual attractions were signs of insanity.

Respect for the Property of Others

Where statutory law concerns itself with property mainly in order to conserve what already belongs to me from seizure by another, the great Jewish religious teachers of antiquity were concerned primarily to protect my neighbor from me. This was not unique to the Christian tradition, but is found also in the Mishnah's well-known definition of the four types of human beings: the "type of Sodom," who says, "What is mine is mine and what is yours is yours"; the evil person, who says, "What is yours is mine, and what is mine is mine"; the ignorant person who says, "What is mine is yours, and what is yours is mine"; and the saintly person, who says, "What is mine is yours and what is yours is yours."[4] [The author has examined in an earlier part of the book] the way adultery or incest infringed on the property of others in the ancient family system. These were so intimately involved, however, in that family system that we shall have to reevaluate their meaning, below, in the context of the shift to the individual as the basic social unit.

Under the present heading, I should like to do something simpler, but equally important—suggest what property meant, in a positive vein, for the New Testament writers and relate this to what I believe to be its most significant violation in our era. For the New Testament, property represents a certain personal realm in which one can act in obedience to the reign of God; it is, as in the etymology of our English term, all that pertains or "is proper to" each person. As such, it is something which may be trusted in and hoarded to the soul's detriment, or something to be given in alms or even surrendered entirely, if the claims of discipleship require it. It generates claims and counterclaims; but it is better to suffer loss than to take one's brother or sister to court. In every case, including sexual property, one must administer and care for one's property with a view to sanctification, that is, one's transformation into a citizen of the reign of God. Property, in other words, is the wherewithal of being human in this age—which can also become, by grace, the wherewithal of becoming a fit citizen of the age to come.

The wherewithal of being human must include, at the very minimum, sustenance, space, the means to grow, the community of other humans, and some freedom of choice. Theft of sustenance or space is the most obvious kind of violation of property; yet, violations of that trust which is the foundation of human community or of the freedom of choice are at least as grave. If in antiquity, given the existing concept of family, adultery was the characteristic violation of sexual property, in our own age, it has become rape.[5] When committed by a stranger, it violates the victim's freedom of choice; when committed by a family member or presumed friend, it violates the bonds of human community as well. The metaphorical space which surrounds each of us and which we characterize as "mine" is of the essence of our being human. It offers some protection for the freedom to develop and become what God is calling us to be, which is the principal goal of being human. When it is opened voluntarily to another, it is also a means of community. But when it is broken into by violence, the very possibility of being human is at least momentarily being denied to us. As there is nothing more precious to us than our humanness, there is no sexual sin more serious than rape.

Rape, as property violation, includes not only the use of physical violence to gain sexual access to another, but also the use of social, emotional, and psychological violence. This takes the form of sexual harassment in workplaces, of sexual impositions by trusted authorities upon their clients, and of manipulative pressures in intimate relationships. Our contemporary culture, with its constant glorification of sex, largely for commercial ends, creates a climate in which this sort of violence flourishes. It offers leverage for the unscrupulous to press inexperienced or unwilling persons into acts which they have not freely chosen. Even within marriage or other established sexual relationships, both physical violence and these other forms of rape are by no means unknown.

An ethic consistent with the gospel will condemn not only individual acts of rape, but also those in which whole groups attack other groups to deny them the property necessary to their humanness. Assaults on women or homosexual people, whether as individual attacks or as political and legal campaigns to deny them equality as citizens and human beings, are the most obvious cases in point. This kind of communal violence may also be based on differences other than sexual, especially on racial, ethnic, and economic ones. Even here, however, sexual elements are often entangled in the violence. For example, in the United States, white men have often justified their violence against black men by accusing them of having sexual designs on white women, while reserving to themselves the right to make sometimes violent use of black women. What is more, violence may be done to others' freedom not only through direct assault, but also through patronizing the less powerful, making them dependencies and therefore properties of the more powerful. Both kinds of violence have been characteristic of the relations of men with women and of rich with poor in our culture.

All these kinds of violence have sunk their roots deep in our culture, and it is difficult to imagine their complete eradication. The Christian, however has an obligation to name them and struggle against them inwardly, in personal relationships, and in the larger society. In this respect, it is disturbing that some Christian denominations seem to have taken the side of violence themselves. Their condemnations of homosexual people, for example, are accompanied, at the very best, by only the mildest of rebukes to those who persecute them; some denominations, such as the Roman Catholic and Southern Baptist, even encourage denial of their legal rights. Some who call themselves "Evangelical," "Charismatic," or "Pentecostal" also oppose equal freedom for women and call for complete subservience even on the part of battered women. Until this changes, it is unlikely that our society will begin to treat rape of all kinds with the revulsion that it deserves, for to some extent such violence will always appear to be at least a quasi-legitimate reaffirmation of the dominance of men over women, of heterosexuals over homosexuals, and, indeed, of the powerful generally over the weak.

Sexual Property as Individual Property

When the owner of property changes, the nature of the property changes also. To take a nonsexual example, a piece of farmland that is underlain by coal deposits suitable for surface mining will appear to be various things to various possible owners. If the owner of the coal is a mining company which may not own the surface of the land but has the right to remove it in order to gain access to the coal, the farmland itself will appear to be incidental to the property that matters. In many cases, such a company is not part of the local community and has no bond to either the human or the natural ecosystem in which the farmland participates, but exists only to make a certain profit through the mining of coal. The coal is therefore purely a capital investment, and the company will make decisions about it in the extremely narrow context of profit and loss—unless, of course, the larger community of state or nation forces a greater measure of social responsibility on the company. At the other extreme, if a resident farmer owns both the farmland and the coal under it, the coal is only one aspect of the larger whole to which she relates. It has an economic value, but the owner will balance that value against her self-understanding as farmer rather than miner, against her identity as part of the local community where she lives and farms, against any sense of spiritual connection she may have to the land, and so forth. These do not predetermine her choice whether to mine the coal or not; but they do create a certain distinctive context for the making of that choice. If, to create a third case, the owner is an absentee landlord with at most a remote family connection to the land, both the arable surface and the underlying coal may still be of interest. Yet, with the withdrawal of the landlord from the local human and natural community, the property comes to be identified mainly with its economic value. Such an owner is likely to make decisions based primarily on economic considerations but is not likely to be quite so narrowly focused as a coal company.

Many readers will recognize the above as a sketch of varieties of ownership in parts of the Appalachian region in the United States. The point is that, even if the property remains, physically, the same object, its relationship to various owners can constitute it as, in effect, several different objects. The same is true of sexual property. In the ancient world, where it pertained primarily to the family and secondarily to the male householder as representative of the family, it meant one thing; in the modern world, where it can pertain only to the individual, it means another. It will be useful to say here a few words about the nature of this transition. The individualization of modern American society is a social fact, an aspect of the environment in which we make ethical decisions, not an ethical principle itself. As such, it is neither good nor bad. It represents some losses as against earlier, family-structured eras and also some gains. If the human being now lacks the kind of inevitable links with a social continuum that the earlier society afforded, that loss must be balanced against the fact that individualization has gone hand in hand with—and is probably the condition for—what progress this century has made toward genuine equality of races, nationalities, and the sexes. The ability of modern people to choose for themselves with regard to education, work, living place, life-partner, religion, or politics became conceivable only as the family ceased to be the basic unit of society and was replaced by the individual.

Individuality can become an ethical principle in two ways. Philosophically speaking, it may become so by a recognition that my individuality is intelligible only as an expression of the principle which renders every other human being an individual, too. This principle was already being expressed in late antiquity in the Golden Rule; respect for my individuality implies respect for that of others. As such, it enters into Christian ethics, but it is by no means the crowning element in them. It could not, for example, have generated the sacrifice of Jesus on the cross or the witness of the martyrs, which require the further principles of love, faith, and hope for their understanding. On the other hand, individuality can also become an ethical principle in the form of individualism—an idolatry of the self, which treats the self as its own source and end. Such individualism has been a pervasive ethical influence in the modern West, enshrined in certain forms of capitalist ideology as the image of the "self-made" person—that is, the person who has chosen to forget the role others played in his fashioning and rise and who regards with interest only those people and things that contribute to his own aggrandizement. This individualism, like any other idolatry, is utterly inconsistent with the gospel.

The gospel does, to be sure, call for serious attention to be given to the self. Jesus held up the unjust steward, who threw caution, morality, and household loyalty to the winds in order to ensure his own future, as a model for the Christian (Luke 16:1–13). From the preaching of John the Baptist onward, belonging to the family of Abraham by physical descent no longer counts for anything in the economy of salvation (Matt. 3:9). Yet, the gospel's rejection of the idolatry of family, the social unit of the first century, implies an equally stern rejection of the idolatry of the individual in our own time. The connection between the two was clearly visible at the time of transition between them, the Industrial Revolution, when William Blake declared that the family was simply a grand excuse for selfishness.[6] This was so in several ways. Insofar as the individual is, in a family-structured society, simply an expression of the family, any claim one makes on behalf of one's family is a claim on behalf of one's self. At the same time, the diffusion of the self in the family that is thus achieved will seem to relieve one of the burden of selfishness. As society became more individualized, however, Blake's insight became more literally true; the lesser members of the family (wife, children, slaves, servants) came to be no longer expressions of the family to which they belonged, but extensions of the male individual who owned them. This modern kind of "family" has little to do with the family of late antiquity, is even more repugnant to the gospel than the ancient family, and is probably inherently unstable in its own right.

In the ancient world, the man, on behalf of his natal family, owned one or more women, either as spouses or as concubines or as slaves. The man received sexual satisfaction; the family received as goods the labor of the women involved and, in the case of the spouse, the promise of legitimate heirs. (In very rich households, of course, the number of subordinate women indicated the prominence of the family as well.) The Greco-Roman world limited a man to one wife at a time, and Western Christianity restricted this still further by rejecting the right of divorce. Even then, however, what the man still chiefly sought in marriage was a combination of sexual satisfaction, household labor, and legitimate heirs. Only the first of these was specific to him; the rest benefited the family.

What goods, by contrast, does the modern individual seek in entering upon a sexual relationship? The goods the ancients sought have not, of course, ceased to be of importance. Apart from the most individual of them (sexual satisfaction), however, they will seldom appear as the primary reasons for marriage or other sexual relationships in the mainstream of modern American society. Why do most of us marry, and how do we choose our partners? We seek things that can benefit an individual. The thrill of romantic love is, of course, enormously important; and we typically hope that this will form the basis for a lasting intimacy, in which our spouse will provide friendship, encouragement, counsel, solace, and a new sense of family to supplement and eventually replace the natal family. These are, of course, interior goods—goods which cannot be given without a genuine delight in and commitment to the other; and in this respect they stand in sharp contrast to the primary goods sought in antiquity. To be sure, there are external goods involved in modern marriage as well: the expectation of security, financial support, and perhaps the desire for children. Yet, we are inclined to look askance at those who marry for money, and child-bearing and rearing have become a vast and still largely unacknowledged problem for our society. For us, the heart of sexual property in marriage and in other lasting sexual liaisons lies in the interior goods.

When the nature of what is owned changes, the nature of theft necessarily changes as well. From the perspective of the Appalachian farmer, the destruction of the farm in order to mine the coal underneath it is a kind of theft; from the perspective of the mining company, refusal to allow the removal of this "overburden" would be a kind of theft. In antiquity, theft, as applied to sexual property, was easily defined, since sexual goods themselves were external and therefore easily defined. Adultery meant a man's taking the womb and family resources which belonged to another man and using them for the nourishment of his own seed. We continue, for the most part, in our society to regard adultery as wrong, but we are forced to find a quite different reason for so regarding it. We usually say that it is wrong because it is a betrayal of trust—that is, theft of an interior good. Insofar as this is in fact the case in a given situation, it gives a good account of adultery in our modern context; but it does not go far enough.

Trust is not only interior good essential to marriage or to its equivalents, and the outsider is not the only possible thief. Since, in ancient marriage, the man owned the woman, it was not possible for the man to steal from his wife. If he committed adultery he was stealing from another man. Jesus, however, by redefining adultery, altered this internal balance and made both spouses capable of taking from one another. That is still more true under present circumstances, for partners can easily withhold from each other those interior goods which they have contracted, explicitly or implicitly, to provide; and there is in fact no way to gain them from an unwilling partner. An ancient wife need have no deep affection for her husband in order to bear his children and do her part in the running of the household. Neither partner, in the modern world, can fulfill his or her obligations in such an external, "objective" manner.

The form of adultery most characteristic, then, of our own society, is not adultery with another person, but the purely self-regarding adultery which demands of the partner the full range of goods associated with sexual property but gives few or none of them in return. This is not to discard the older understanding of adultery, in which one person takes from another what belongs to a third party; this is certainly not dead. It is rather to stress the prevalence of adultery in the form of profiteering, the use of a sexual relationship for one's own physical, economic, emotional, or psychological satisfaction with minimal regard for that of the partner. In comparison, the technical act of adultery by sexual intercourse with a third person is a relatively trivial matter.

Our transition from a familial to an individual society has been particularly difficult in the matter of children and lies at the root of many modern troubles, ranging from abortion to unwanted infants to child abuse to educational uncertainties and beyond. Not that these are of a single or simple origin! The increase of child abuse, for example, is probably partly a matter of fact and partly a matter of changed perceptions, for kinds of corporal punishment which were normal parental prerogatives a few generations ago now appear to be abusive. In the familial society, after all, children were the property of the family, part of its assets, and the family's self-interest would dictate that it discipline them without harming them in a way that would damage its own investment. In the individual society, however, children have become an obligation rather than an investment.

This has brought with it the permission for—and even the necessity of—conscious decision making about the conception of children. Agricultural societies, before the advent of modern medicine, might afford the luxury of producing as many children as they could; now, more urbanized societies with lowered birthrates and greater longevity must make deliberate decisions, with the cooperation of those of childbearing age. Since both Jesus and Paul seem to have encouraged celibacy, one cannot imagine that the conceiving of children is any sort of intrinsic Christian virtue. Since it is now also the incurring of a substantial burden which can be born successfully only out of love, no one should undertake it without due consideration. In most areas of the modern world, the use of birth control should be the norm and the conception of children should represent a deliberate and considered departure from it. (A significant exception must certainly be made for those human groups that are threatened with disappearance or with diminution to numbers too small to maintain their cultural traditions.) No existing method of birth control is inherently unacceptable, though certain ways of imposing them may certainly be.

Some particular discussion of abortion is called for. The Bible contains nothing helpful on the subject. Other early Christian literature, too, has surprisingly little, given that abortion was not uncommon in the Greco-Roman world. One must distinguish two separate issues: abortion as therapeutic for the physical, mental, or emotional health of the pregnant woman; and abortion as a means of birth control. While the ancient family ethic may have regarded the legitimate offspring as of greater importance than the mother in some cases, there can be no basis in the New Testament itself for such a judgment. To the contrary, in making the wife equal to her husband, Jesus implied that she was no longer merely an instrument of his natal family in their quest for heirs. This implies that her health is at least as important as that of an uncertain offspring.

The question of abortion as a method of birth control is more difficult. Human societies—and different voices within our own society—disagree about when the fetus should be considered a separate human being. The Greeks and Romans, who allowed exposure of the newborn if unwanted by its family, recognized this as occurring some time after birth; others have placed it at conception (a process little understood at the time of the New Testament writers), at quickening, or at the earliest moment when a premature infant might survive outside the womb. The child who has actually passed through the birth channel seems qualitatively different from one still in the womb; even the Greeks and Romans tended to expose unwanted newborns to be collected by anyone who might want them rather than killing them outright. Still, there is no compelling logic to tell us how to choose among the other three options. The principal consideration must be that the choice in relation to childbearing should always be, if at all possible a choice *for,* not a choice *against.* No one should be obligated to bear children and, given the present threat to the world from its human population, no one should do so unless moved thereto as a specific calling and gift. Christians should not, then, place themselves in the position of having to decide repeatedly not to bear this particular fetus, but rather in the position of deciding when they are called to conceive a child.

Now as in other eras, parents conceive children for a variety of reasons, perhaps including innate biological urges as well as social pressures, sentiment, the desire for some kind of genetic immortality, a sense of social responsibility, pure carelessness, and the rest—perhaps a longer list than any one person can imagine. Yet, once born, the child is, in our age, a quite different matter from what he or she was in the first century. The ancient family had to have legitimate heirs in order to maintain its own existence. But what is the child to a society of individuals? If they are individualists, in the idolatrous sense, the child is, of course, nothing at all except an extension of the parents and insurance against their being left unattended in senility. The individual society, however, is not necessarily committed to individualism of this kind, any more than a familial society is doomed to be torn apart by the grander selfishness of its families. In each, the worst case is a possibility, but not the only possibility. Ultimately, the individual society militates against individualistic megalomania on the part of parents, for the children will learn from the society itself that they, too, are expected to become individuals and will refuse to cooperate with parents who sought to use them purely for their own ends. They may, in turn, adopt the same self-defeating individualism, of course, unless something more rational and loving is offered in its place.

What sort of rational and loving alternative can one suggest? That children should be understood as individuals in preparation. They are, in other words, ultimately their own property, not that of their parents; while the parents have the role not of owners but of educators, those who prepare the child to become the best of herself or himself. The model parent will be one who seeks to discern the child's unique qualities, both good and bad, and help the child form the self-discipline to make the best of his or her resources. This is not a kind of "permissive" project, for the child is not yet a realized individual ready to be in full command; it is, rather, a loving and persistent demand that children become responsible for themselves, their choices, their relationships and community, their work, their world. Parents who understand that the child is not obligated to them to be exactly what they want will be better parents. Children who understand that they cannot evade their responsibilities either by habitually obeying or by habitually reacting against their parents are more likely to become stable, creative, and faithful adults.

Parenting is thus a gift to the child of the child's self; it is the passing on of gifts which the parents received from their own parents and from all the others who contributed to their being who they are. It is more like the work of the educator than any other model—not the educator as a communicator of a single specialized kind of information, but the educator as one who cooperates with the pupil as a kind of critic and guide in the shaping of the educated person. This must of necessity be a somewhat disinterested task. The parent who wants only an athlete for a child will be an incompetent parent to a painter. The parent who wants a substitute for adult companionship from the child, making the child a quasi spouse, will confuse the child into thinking that adulthood is a kind of mannerism and so make true adulthood, which is an inner certainty, the more difficult to identify or to achieve. Above all, the parent or other senior family member who uses the trust which that position bestows in order to make the child his or her lover thereby makes demands on the child totally inconsistent with the disinterested love of one who seeks only the other's good.

While in the familial society of antiquity it was the violation of the patriarch's status which characterized incest, in our own, individual, society it is the violation of the child's individuality. The inequality between adult and child (and, to a lesser degree, between older and younger child) means that, in a sexual relationship, the needs of the child will be subordinated to the needs of the adult. What the child loses in the process is, above all, the preparatory space and time when responsible adults encourage and assist children to know themselves before assuming full adult obligations. This, in turn, renders the child's growth into real adulthood extremely difficult, creating an alienation not only from the available adult models, but from the child's very self. Adulthood comes to seem a rejection of the past instead of something that grows out of the experience of childhood.

In addition, incest also carries with it, in our culture, a strong purity taboo, often used by the perpetrator of incest to frighten the child into silence. While Christians do not make this the basis for their own objection to incest, we must recognize that some part of the harm done to the child in such cases arises not from the sexual act itself, but from the revulsion with which the society at large greets it—a revulsion which almost inevitably spills over onto the child and encourages the child in self-loathing. Christians have a responsibility to reduce their own inner involvement in this kind of purity response, so that they can deal more constructively with individuals who have experienced incest and also can, one hopes, better instruct society at large. The hiding away of this topic or its discussion only in hushed tones and ambiguous language can only work harm, not good.

Sexual abuse of children, in the context of modern society, is a kind of generalized incest. For the child, every older person is to some extent a parent. The child's growth into individual adulthood is promoted if the child has a variety of adult models and so does not identify adulthood with the characteristics of a single person. If, on the other hand, the child encounters adults as people whose only interest is to take advantage of the child for their own satisfaction, the model of adulthood that emerges is disastrous. Most abusers of children, it is said, are adult heterosexual males, frequently friends or relatives of the child's family. In their case, the disadvantage the young girl experiences may be compounded by an unexpressed wish on the man's part that all women would remain children. In any case, all such abuse contains in it the implied desire that the sexual object not grow up. Thus, it is akin to incest in the harm it does to children.

Sexually, the child must be considered his or her own property. As the child grows old enough to begin wanting to make active exploration of sexuality, the parent or other adult guide will contribute most effectively by teaching the child frankly about the realities of sex, including its dangers, and by holding the child to the necessity of making clear and responsible decisions. A stonewalling technique of refusing to discuss the issue or of presenting all discussion in the form of prohibitions denies the child's developing responsibility and status as an adult-in-becoming. As a result, it encourages either repression and much future sexual misery on the part of the quieter, more obedient child or rebellious irresponsibility on the part of the more energetic and active one. Most children will probably do well to pass through a period of experimentation, though they should not be pushed into it against their wills. They should be shown how to do this as safely as possible. Certainly, no child—and probably few teenagers— is prepared to enter upon a true marriage of equal adults such as the gospel calls for.

Even among young adults, the first choice of a sexual partner is not likely to be the best, and their initial picture of themselves in a serious sexual relation- ship is not likely to be fully formed. If marriage is treated in the individual so- ciety simply as license to have sex, we can be quite sure that many will choose marriage partners for the most inadequate of reasons and with poor judgment. If the decision is not merely one about first sexual experience but about life partners, it will be easier for people to make it in a realistic way. Christian thinkers as diverse as Margaret Mead and Archbishop Fisher suggested some decades ago that the church should not rush to make the unions of the young permanent; but we have yet to honor the importance of their suggestions by giving them due discussion.

Finally, with regard to sexual property, it is necessary to speak in our era about the value of physical health as the property of each individual and about one's obligation not to deprive another of it. Although Leviticus probably refers to gonorrhea, the author seems not to have understood that it was a communicable disease. In our own century, we have passed from a time when sexually transmitted diseases were a major threat to life and health to a time when antibiotics could combat most of them and back to a time when, first with herpes and then with AIDS, they have once again moved beyond our ability to cure. Knowingly to endanger another person with such a disease is clearly a transgres- sion of that person's property, in the sense in which I am here using the term, and is prohibited by the New Testament's sexual ethic.

Equality of Women and Men

Both Jesus and Paul laid it down as a principle that women and men are basically equal in marriage. Although Paul, in the circumstances of his own times, did not find it necessary or appropriate to carry that principle into practice in all areas of married life, the church today, with the shift from familial to individual society, no longer has any reason to delay in this process. Indeed, society has led the way in this matter, and it is entirely consistent with New Testament practice for the church to accept the emerging marital customs of the modern West as the basis for its own usage. This is not to suggest that the situation has stabilized, however, or that the acceptance of equality will be easy, either for men or for women.

What is called for is something more than the revision of household rules and the alternation of household roles. It involves new understandings of manliness and womanliness that can come about only with some pain and anxiety as well as some sense of liberation and joy. If the husband gives up the image of himself as sole ruler of the household, waited on by wife and children, his whim the family's law, he must also give up its spiritual equivalent—the image of himself as the family's unique sacrificial sustainer, isolated in his moral strength and grandeur. If the wife gives up being the servant of all, with no life of her own except in responding to the needs of others, she must also give up the spiritual vision of herself as the one who gives all for others' good. Men cannot give up their responsibilities as sole wage earner and still claim the benefits of that position by demanding an uneven distribution of labor and services; women cannot claim equality and still reserve the right to be dependent if equality does not yield what they want. None of this will be easy, but the survival of marriage in our society surely depends on it.

Spouses in heterosexual marriages will have much to learn in this process from partners in stable, long-term homosexual relationships. They have long experienced the difficulties of maintaining enduring relationships in a society which is even less supportive of them than of heterosexual couples; and they have had to do it without socially prescribed divisions of roles and labor. If there are useful models to be had, they will probably be found among them. On a deeper level, the reunderstanding of womanliness and manliness in our changed circumstances will make headway only if the conversation leading toward it includes both heterosexuals and homosexuals. One interesting feature of recent times is the importance of serious, nonsexual friendships between men and women where the man involved is homosexual; perhaps the absence of a sexual factor facilitates this. If heterosexual men were more open to friendships with women, they might find, for the same reason, that they formed them most readily and deeply with lesbian women. While heterosexual men and women begin with the greater attraction toward each other, it does not always lead to real personal knowledge or respect. In a time when the old definitions are no longer serviceable, we shall need the variety of perspective that male and female, homosexual and heterosexual, can offer on one another in order to reach new models of the properties of either sex.

Marriage as Union of Flesh

When the author of Genesis 2 described marriage as making man and woman "one flesh," he was describing their bond as equivalent in power and importance to that of the natal family. Jesus used the phrase as the foundation of his prohibition of divorce. Paul, however, applied it to every act of sexual intercourse, without thereby suggesting that every such act formed an indissoluble union. The image thus raises a number of questions for us to deal with: When is a marriage a marriage? What can the phrase "one flesh" mean in a nonfamilial society? To what extent is the institution of marriage, as transformed by our very different context, still to be understood as indissoluble? What is the role of the church in relation to marriages? To what degree is nonmarital or casual sex permitted or forbidden?

These are difficult questions, but reference to the property aspects of marriage as discussed above may help illuminate them. To begin with, the nature of the property desired in modern marriage, being largely interior and therefore more complex and more difficult to convey successfully, implies that marriage is in itself more difficult to consummate. In the familial world, the first act of sexual intercourse, with its accompanying proof of the bride's virginity, was sufficient, since it showed that the new wife was indeed the property which the husband's family had intended to acquire. Jesus, at least according to Matthew, acknowledged that some marriages were not real marriages, and I have suggested that he was probably referring to those where the bride was found not to be a virgin.

Is there any sensible way to apply a measure of this kind to contemporary marriages, where the purity of the family line is no longer the primary desideratum? The virginity of either spouse is no longer a primary issue, for the goods sought in connection with marriage in an individual society are goods which can best be offered only by a mature person and such a person will more often than not have acquired some sexual experience. What is still more difficult, the goods are not simply brought to the marriage, but must be developed within it in the form of the relationship between the spouses. Thus, it is very difficult to specify a date, even in the most successful of marriages, when it became clear that the property transactions involved were indeed in good order. Certainly, it could not be known at once. Once the initial romantic enthusiasm wears thin, it may become apparent that one or both spouses is unable or unwilling to give anything of importance to the other. Clearly, one should not and seldom would enter upon marriage knowing that to be the case; but the transition from romance to the business of marital living will always be a somewhat risky undertaking, if only because the romantic face is but one aspect of the other person and sometimes a misleading one at that.

Paul did not count every act of sexual intercourse as constituting an indissoluble bond of marriage. We should not do so, either. This means that not every external marriage in our own experience constitutes a real marriage in the more interior sense demanded in our society. We must therefore be prepared to consider the possibility that what some divorces—perhaps a large percentage of them—do is not to end an existing marriage but to announce that, despite whatever efforts were made and ceremonies performed, no marriage has in fact taken place. This insistence on the property involved in constituting a marriage may appear crass to some readers. Yet is is precisely analogous to what was assumed by the biblical writers, and I venture to argue that it is a far more realistic approach to the ethical issues. To characterize Christian marriage, as some would do, as an idealistic commitment to eternal loyalty without any regard for what one receives in return is ultimately destructive of the whole situation. It encourages abused spouses, female and male alike, to remain with those who profit from them in various ways and give nothing in return. In the process, not only does the abused person suffer to no end, but the abusive spouse is seldom effectively confronted with any realization of what he or she is doing. A sound marriage is not, of course, a dispassionate business arrangement, but it ought to be based on perception of mutual benefit arising from mutual devotion and affection.

One part of our present difficulty arises from the church's custom of blessing marriages. Marriage, in the milieu of the New Testament, was typically the celebration of a secular contract. Since, under the ancient circumstances, the property aspects of the marriage were readily and efficiently verifiable, there was no appreciable delay in ascertaining that the contract had been fulfilled. Only in the Middle Ages, it seems, did the church begin to take a part in solemnizing the occasion; but it was an intelligible step, since all the necessities of the case could be verified. At present, however, when the great majority of church people are married with church ceremonies, the rites give an impression of definiteness to the marriage which cannot in fact be verified at once and perhaps not for many years to come.

At the present time, the church would perhaps be better advised not to solemnize marriages at the inception of the relationship itself, but to wait a period of some years before adding its blessing. When it does so, it may as easily bless homosexual as heterosexual unions, for the new definition of the goods making up sexual property, which has already come informally to prevail in our society, makes no distinction between the two. Two persons of the same sex cannot engender children and could not therefore have contracted a full-fledged marriage in the familial milieu of the New Testament itself; they are, however, fully capable of giving one another the interior goods demanded by marriage in our time. Even after the blessing of a union, the failure of a marriage and consequent divorce probably cannot be ruled out altogether. The church should, however, discourage it. It can rightly ask its members not to proceed to divorce without having done all that they could do to compromise their differences, and it can also insist on the exercise of a high degree of responsibility in the contracting of a further marriage. For an unblessed union, that is, one that has not progressed to the point of mutual stability that would justify the church's blessing it, the church might reserve judgment.

Since the solution I have suggested blurs the distinction between marriage and nonmarital sexual liaisons—a blurring demanded by the actual nature of marriage in our times—we must also ask whether all sexual activities of however casual a nature and however little personal involvement are to be permitted. Jesus did not speak to the matter, but Paul clearly would have said no. Sexuality, as an essential aspect of the self, cannot be treated as if it were either trivial or peripheral. Every sexual act does constitute some kind of bond with the partner, and that bond must, at the very least, be free of falsehood and violence toward the partner and in some way be compatible with the Christian person's relationship with Christ. Paul reproved men in Corinth who visited prostitutes though they had open to them the options of either celibacy or marriage. He did not, however, have occasion to address the situation of the person for whom neither option existed—the sailor, to create an example, who did not have the gift of celibacy but whose exceedingly mobile occupation also did not permit permanent cohabitation with a wife.

We might also add, in our own age, the examples of the homosexual person, for whom no marital forms are provided in our society, the young person of either sexual orientation for whom marriage would be premature but who does not have the gift of celibacy, the single person of whatever age who has not met the appropriate person to contract marriage with, or the widowed person for whom a new legal marriage would create financial stringency or unnecessary confusions about inheritance. At one extreme, one cannot defend the promiscuous person who desires only personal gratification at whatever expense to others. At the other, two widowed persons who wish to contract a faithful and giving relationship without benefit of legal marriage seem to create a problem of words more than of things. Between these extremes, there lies a large area of difficult individual decisions. People will have to wend their way through such decisions, however, for the gift of celibacy is not given to all and the property demands of modern marriage are such that one cannot, even if one wishes, enter upon it lightly.

Some nonmarital liaisons may in fact prove to be preparatory to marriage in the stricter sense. Others may serve to meet legitimate needs in the absence of genuine alternatives. Still others may be abusive and exploitative. Only the last are to be condemned. Prostitution appears to belong most often in the last of these three categories, though perhaps at times it may belong in the second. I think, for example, of abnormal conditions where there is a vast disproportion of the members of one sex; in such cases, those who have no other access to sexual gratification are not to be condemned for resorting to prostitutes, though I am not willing to encourage them in it. The person who prefers prostitutes, however, to a sexual relationship which would make greater demands on him or her must be asked whether this is not an avoidance of deeper relationships in general and therefore also an effort to treat one's sexuality as peripheral or irrelevant to one's humanity.

The same question must be put to the prostitute, provided that one is such of one's own will. In antiquity many prostitutes were slaves and had no freedom of choice as to the use to which they would be put. Jesus' abolition of purity requirements gave these people renewed access to God which must not be taken away from any legitimate successors they may have. In our own day, this would include at least those street children whose only alternatives are return to an intolerable home situation or starvation. If those prostitutes, however, who are such by choice—whether because they make a good living or because of attachment to another person who is abusing them—should wish to be fully active participants in the church, the church would legitimately urge them to accept some other occupation and, if need be, assist them to do so, so that they may honor themselves as sexual beings under the reign of God.

Sex and the Reign of God

Although we have said a great deal thus far about what the New Testament sexual ethic forbids and not much about what it advocates, that is largely a function of the style in which the Bible speaks about sexual matters. This study has worked throughout with specifically moral texts—that is, texts which define acceptable and, more often, unacceptable behavior. Some might feel it preferable to begin with texts speaking to the nature of sexuality rather than defining its limits. There are several difficulties with that approach, however. One is that such texts are few and far between in Scripture. The Bible takes sex more or less for granted and does not explicitly lay out a theological or philosophical understanding of it. The few pertinent verses in Genesis 1 and 2, for example, are brief and allusive in their language, which leaves them open to a variety of speculative interpretations. In order to form a well-founded understanding of a viewpoint alien to our own, we have had to find and study a corpus of materials sufficiently rich that we can test our speculations and see where they do or do not account for all the details. This quality, which is lacking in the theological materials on sex, is abundantly present in the moral ones.

The resulting negative bias, however, is misleading insofar as it suggests that the New Testament writers were negative toward sexuality as such. The results of the present study confirm that that was by no means the case. We have seen that Jesus, for example, attacked the institutions of the family rather than sexuality itself and that Paul specifically acknowledged the satisfaction of sexual desire as a valid reason for marriage. In order to locate the New Testament's positive ethic of sexuality, however, one must refocus from the boundary lines marked out by negative pronouncements to the area that they enclose and give shape to. The New Testament's positive account of sex is that it is an integral part of the human person, particularly as joining us to one another, and therefore has a right to be included in the spiritual transformation which follows upon our hearing of the gospel.

The gospel, as it permeates every aspect of life, will and must permeate sexuality as well. If Christian teaching appears to flinch from sex as something dirty or suspect, it is falsely Christian. This does not mean that sexuality, for the Christian, is to be saturated in a kind of pietism, that the bedroom should become a chapel, or that sex should be submerged in prayer. It means rather that sexuality, like every other important aspect of human life, should be clearly related to the center and goal of that life, the reign of God. The life of the world to come, characterized by a joyful reverence and love, is already the standard by which our growth in faith and hope is measured in this life. Sex, therefore, is to be received with delight and thankfulness. It is a gift of God in creation which also reflects for us the joy of God's self-giving in grace and the perfect openness of true human life in the age to come.

If the reign of God is central, to be sure, other things can no longer make that claim. Sex, in other words, is *not* central—nor is knowledge, wisdom, money, power, success, security, one's job or family or marriage, even oneself. None of these things is wrong, in and of itself. They become wrong only at the moment when they become ultimate goals for us. As long as we can name something which is, for us, a condition of God's reign—as long as we find that we must say, "I am ready for God's reign only if it includes this or excludes that"—then we are still placing idols at the center and goal of life alongside God. Yet, insofar as we are ready to hand back whatever God asks of us, then it becomes, to that degree, innocent for us.

Sex is one of the rich blessings of creation, to be received with delight and thanksgiving. At the point when one's actions no longer express that truth, they become wrong. If I grab something for myself that belongs rightfully to another, whether through direct violence or through manipulation or any other means, I acknowledge what I have grabbed as a good, but I no longer confess it as a part of the whole richness of creation—a richness which includes all goods, including myself and the neighbor whom I have robbed as well. If I make satisfaction of sexual desire the overarching goal of my life, I have put the part in place of the whole and thereby lost perspective on its real value. These considerations are what make libertinism wrong, for they condemn any pursuit of sexual pleasure which is based on megalomania and idolatry. What is less commonly observed is that they also make prudery, legalism, and addiction to respectability wrong. For just as sex is not the final goal of the creation, neither is works-righteousness, the fulfillment of the law, or the sense of comfort that comes from having fulfilled the expectations of my neighbors. The world begins in God's free act of creation and concludes in God's free act of grace—or rather in the rejoicing to which it gives rise. Prudery, narrowness, self-confident respectability will be no preparation for the life of the age of rejoicing. It is not surprising that Jesus alienated those who practiced such "virtues."

This is not to suggest that the path to the age to come is all one of ease and pleasure. Its difficulties, however, are not self-induced. We do not have to make the Christian life difficult with the constant recitation and amplification of rules, for there are real challenges, arising both from our own selfish idolatry and also from our times. As Paul stressed the need for a certain kind of preparedness in the face of what he believed would be an imminent eschaton, we, too, must undertake to be prepared in terms of the needs of our own time. As marriage and family could not be a final goal for the first-century Christian, sexuality and self cannot be today. The Christian will find it very difficult to live in an intimate relation with one who does not understand or accept the kind of demands which God's calling makes. While it is not impossible to live in such a relationship with a nonbeliever, the partner must at least be one who respects commitments that may seem unworldly and which do not place self or sexual partner first. The Christian must also retain a certain freedom to respond to God's call loyally in critical times. While we cannot make any confident predictions about the timing of the eschaton, we live in times when great demands are being made of us in relation to justice, peace, and the survival of the world. If relations of dependency prevent us from responding to those demands, we shall have something to answer for.

Finally, the gospel, the news of God's grace in Jesus and the inbreaking of God's reign, has not yet finished transforming us—and will not this side of the grave. If we look at the great exemplars of its work, in the New Testament and afterward, from Jesus to Martin Luther King, Jr., we shall find that it does not normally act to make us more respectable—to produce conventional, predictable husbands and wives, devoted to nothing more than one another's happiness. For that matter, Jesus himself excepted, the gospel does not even work to produce perfect people. The gospel works rather to express the power of God's love, which rejects our rejections and breaches our best defenses and draws us out of our fortifications toward a goal that we can as yet barely imagine. The measure of a sexuality that accords with the New Testament is simply this: the degree to which it rejoices in the whole creation, in what is given to others as well as to each of us, while enabling us always to leave the final word to God, who is the Beginning and End of all things.

NOTES

1. L. William Countryman, *Biblical Authority or Biblical Tyranny? Scripture and the Christian Pilgrimage* (Philadelphia: Fortress Press, 1982), 77–93.

2. I use this term in its common sense of intercourse with an animal, not the technical psychological sense in which it designates a distinctive complex of attractions and behaviors.

3. Some reserve the term "pornography" specifically for those erotic materials involving degradation of women. These, I think, are contrary to Christian sexual ethics, but not because of their erotic element.

4. *Aboth* 5.14. Need one observe that this is yet another piece of evidence to show that the ancients did not typically identify the sin of Sodom as homosexual intercourse?

5. The difference between the cultures in this respect is vividly apparent in Philo, who argued that the law of Moses specified no punishment for the forcible violation of a

widow or divorced woman because that was, in effect, only half the crime that adultery was (*Special Laws* 3.64). So, too, in ancient Athens, rape was considered a less grave offense than seduction (Pomeroy, *Goddesses,* 86–87).

6. At least, I believe it was Blake. The statement stuck in my mind more than twenty years ago, but I have not been able to locate it again.

4

Sexual Ethics

MARGARET A. FARLEY

Like other issues in bioethics, questions of sexuality have entailed questions of the body's relation to the whole person, moral standards for rational intervention in physical processes, and norms for the overall health of the individual and society. More specifically, ethical evaluations of sexual behavior have at times included claims that some sexual behavior is sick (as, for example, when homosexuality has been considered an illness) and claims that some sexual behavior leads to sickness (as, for example, when masturbation has been thought to have medical consequences). Bioethical questions regarding contraception, sterilization, abortion, venereal disease, sex therapy and sex research, and genetics are directly concerned with sexuality. Not surprisingly, health professionals both in the past and in the present have frequently found themselves called upon as counselors with regard to sexual matters.

To the extent that ethical reflections on sexuality can provide a helpful context for issues in bioethics, an overview of sexual ethics is called for. The present state of sexual ethics cannot be assessed without understanding something of its historical antecedents and their more immediate contributions to contemporary theory and practice. It is also necessary to understand in some degree the sources of the widespread contemporary challenge to traditional sexual ethics. This article will limit its concern to Western traditions of sexual ethics (the most systematic of which have been religious). It will begin with a historical overview, consider next those factors which have rendered traditional norms problematic, and finally focus on central issues that now engage ethical reflection on the sexual life of human persons.

THE JEWISH TRADITION

Earliest Hebrew moral codes were simple and without systematic theological underpinnings. Like other ancient Near Eastern legislation, they prescribed marriage laws and prohibited adultery, rape, and certain forms of prostitution, incest, and nakedness. In contrast to neighboring Eastern civilizations, Hebrew belief in a god who is beyond sexuality led to a kind of desacralization of sex. Human sexuality was sacred only insofar as marriage and fertility were part of the plan of a creator God. Such a view of sexuality, however, set the stage for a positive valuation that endured despite later tendencies toward negative asceticism.

Marriage and Procreation

The injunction to marry is central to the Jewish tradition of sexual morality. Marriage is a religious duty, affirmed by all the codes of Jewish law.[1] Two elements in Judaism's concept of marriage account for many other important laws regarding sexuality. The first is the perception of the command to procreate, at the heart of the command to marry. The second is the patriarchal model upon which the Jewish notion of marriage is institutionally based. These two elements help explain prohibitions against adultery and regulations regarding divorce, prostitution, polygamous marriage, and concubinage. Thus, for example, biblical law considered adultery primarily a violation of a husband's property rights. With minor modifications this was true also of talmudic and post-talmudic law. Further, polygamy and concubinage were accepted for a long time as a solution to a childless marriage. Prostitution was forbidden as idolatrous, but no legislation ever applied to the use of female slaves. Early in the tradition, custom recognized an almost unlimited right on the part of the husband to divorce his wife. Later the rabbis introduced various restrictions but did not abolish the right. The obvious double standard for men and for women which marked much of this legislation did not hinder, and in some cases helped, the fulfillment of the law of procreation. It was, moreover, in accord with the subordinate status of women in relation to men. These laws do not by themselves, however, give an adequate picture of traditional Jewish sexual morality.

Sex and the Marital Relationship

In fact, monogamous, lifelong marriage always stood as the ideal context for sexuality. As the centuries passed, that ideal came to be emphasized more and more. It took precedence even over the command to procreate. Gradually polygamy or divorce and remarriage were less and less accepted as remedies for childless marriages. Concern for the value of the marital relationship in itself finally overruled both as options. In the talmudic period monogamy became the custom as well as the ideal, and polygamy later disappeared entirely in Europe. The rabbis came to teach that neither unilateral nor mutually agreed-upon divorce was required or even always justified as a solution to barrenness in a wife.

developed, moreover, the moral tide ran against concubinage, and prostitution was more and more proscribed as a matter of conscience if not of law.[2]

A conflict between the marital relationship and the command to procreate, then, could be resolved in favor of the relationship. The fabric of the relationship has always been of great concern in the Jewish tradition. While the core of the legal imperative to marry is the command to procreate, marriage has also always been considered a duty because it conduces to the holiness of the partners. Holiness here refers more to the opportunity for channeling sexual desire than to companionship and mutual fulfillment, but the latter are clearly included in the purposes of marriage and are an expected concomitant result. Now it is the element of holiness in the Jewish concept of marriage that has proved decisive in determining questions of fertility control. Contraception is allowed for the sake of preserving the existing marriage relationship when a new pregnancy would be harmful either to the wife or to the welfare of existing children.[3] It is morally preferable to abstinence because it is the husband's duty to promote the happiness and holiness of his wife through uniting with her in sexual union.

Unnatural Sex Acts

Judaism traditionally has shown a concern for the "improper emission of seed." Included in this concern are proscriptions of masturbation and homosexual acts. Both are considered unnatural, beneath the dignity of humanly meaningful sexual intercourse, and indicative of uncontrolled and hence morally evil sexual desire.[4] The source of these prohibitions seems to be more clearly the historical connection between such acts and the idolatrous practices of neighboring peoples than the contradiction between sexual acts and the command to procreate. Indeed, the minimum criterion for "proper emission of seed" is the mutual pleasure of husband and wife, not the procreative intent of their act of intercourse.[5]

Contemporary efforts to articulate a Jewish position on questions of sexual morality involve efforts to draw forth as yet unexplicated directions within the tradition and to correct perceived deficiencies in the tradition. Thus, for example, in a tradition where marriage has been the ideal context for sexual activity, contemporary questions of premarital sex are nonetheless not yet settled.[6] And contemporary concern to equalize the relation between women and men encounters the factor of male dominance, which has characterized sexual relationship from the beginning of Jewish history.

ANCIENT GREECE AND ROME

General Attitudes

Attitudes toward sexual behavior differed significantly between the ancient Greeks and Romans. In comparison with Rome, the Greeks seem to have had a balanced, humane, refined culture in which sexuality was accepted as an integral part of life. Sensuality and reason were harmonized in a kind of idealized virtue of the whole person. Rome, too, accepted sex as a natural part of life, but the refinement of Greek culture was missing.

Marriage for both Greeks and Romans was monogamous. In ancient Greece, however, no sexual ethic confined sex to marriage. Human nature was generally assumed to be bisexual, and polyerotic needs especially of the male were easily accepted. Hence, there was what some have referred to as sexual polygamy within marital monogamy. Monogamous marriage in Rome, on the other hand, was the foundation of social life. In fact, the institutionalization of marriage, through the development of marriage laws, was thought to be of central importance in the achievement of Roman civilization.

Both Greece and Rome were male-dominated societies, and a double standard was obvious in regard to sexual morality. Divorce was an easy matter in ancient Greece, but for a long time it was available only to husbands. In Rome, while there was apparently no divorce at all for a period of five hundred years, later a husband could divorce his wife for adultery and a variety of other sometimes trivial reasons. Both Greek and Roman brides but not bridegrooms were expected to be virgins. The only women in Greece who were given some equal status with men were a special class of prostitutes, the *hetairae*. Wives had no public life at all, though they were given the power to manage the home. In the Roman household, on the contrary, the husband had an entirely free hand. Indeed, perhaps nowhere else did the ideal of *patria potestas* reach such complete fulfillment. Outside the home, husbands could also consort freely with slaves or prostitutes. Adultery was not proscribed so long as it was not with another man's wife. Fidelity was required of wives, however, primarily in order to secure the inheritance of property by legitimate children. Though by the first century A.D. women in Rome achieved some economic and political freedom, they could never assume the sexual freedom traditionally granted to men.

Homosexuality was accepted in both Greek and Roman culture. Indeed, the Greeks incorporated societal attitudes toward relationships between men into their most highly developed philosophies of interpersonal relations. Both Plato and Aristotle assumed that the ideal of human friendship was possible only between men. In Plato's *Symposium*, the unequal relationship between a man and a woman could never give rise to the mutual pursuit of higher than sensual goods. Aristotle, in his *Nicomachean Ethics*, could only list the friendship between husband and wife among the lesser forms of friendship that exist between those who are not equal.

Greek and Roman Philosophical Appraisals of Sex

The ethical theory of Greek and Roman philosophers was clearly influenced by the cultural mores of their time. The reciprocal impact of the theory upon the mores is less clear than its later influence upon Jewish and Christian thought.

Overall it must be said that Greek and Roman philosophy contributed to subsequent distrust of sexual desire and negative evaluation of sexual pleasure. The Pythagoreans in the sixth century B.C. advocated purity of the body for the sake of culture of the soul. The force of their position was felt in the later thinking of Socrates and Plato. Though Plato moved from the general hostility to pleasure, which marks the *Gorgias,* to a careful distinction between lower and higher pleasures in, for example, the *Republic, Phaedo, Symposium,* and *Philebus,* sexual pleasure continued to be deprecated as one of the lower pleasures. Above all Plato wanted to unleash, not to restrain, the power of eros, which could move the human spirit to union with the greatest good. If bodily pleasures could be taken up into that pursuit, there was no objection to them. But Plato thought, finally, that the pleasure connected with sexual intercourse diminished quantitatively the power of eros for higher things.

Aristotle, like Plato, distinguished between lower and higher pleasures, placing the pleasures of touch at the bottom of the scale. He was sufficiently more this-worldly than Plato to caution moderation rather than transcendence, however. He never conceived of the possibility of equality or mutuality in relationships between men and women (and opposed Plato's design for this in the *Republic* and *Laws*). The highest forms of friendship and love, and of happiness in the contemplation of the life of one's friend, had no room for the incorporation of sexual activity and even less room than Plato for the possible nurturing power of erotic love.

Of all Greek philosophies, Stoicism had the greatest impact on Roman philosophy and on the early formation of Christian thought. Philosophers such as Seneca, Musonius Rufus, Epictetus, and Marcus Aurelius taught a strong doctrine of the power of the human will to regulate emotion and of the desirability of such regulation for the sake of inner peace. Sexual desire, like the passions of fear and anger, was in itself irrational, disturbing, liable to excess. It needed to be moderated if not eliminated. It could never be indulged for its own sake, but only if it served some rational purpose. The goal of procreation provided that purpose. Hence, even in marriage, sexual intercourse was morally justified only when it was engaged in for the sake of procreation.

The Greco-Roman legacy to Western sexual ethics contained, somewhat ironically, little of the freedom and imagination of sex life in ancient Greece. The dominant themes picked up by later traditions were suspicion and control, elimination, or severe restriction. This may have been largely due to the failure of both the Greeks and the Romans to integrate sexuality into their best insights into human relationships. Whether such an integration was in principle a possibility remained an unanswered question in the centuries that followed.

CHRISTIAN TRADITIONS

Like other religious and cultural traditions, the teachings within the Christian tradition regarding human sexuality are complex, subject to multiple outside influences, and expressive of change and development through succeeding generations of Christians. Christianity does not begin with a systematic code of sexual ethics. The teachings of Jesus and his followers, as recorded in the New Testament, provide a central focus for the moral life of Christians in the command to love God and neighbor. Beyond that, the New Testament offers grounds for a sexual ethic that (1) values marriage and procreation on the one hand and celibacy on the other; (2) gives as much importance or more to internal attitudes and thoughts as to external actions; and (3) affirms a sacred symbolic meaning for sexual intercourse yet both subordinates it as a value to other human values and finds in it a possibility for evil.

Stoic and Gnostic Influences
on Christian Understandings of Sex

Christianity emerged in the late Hellenistic Age when even Judaism with its strong positive valuation of marriage and procreation was influenced by the dualistic anthropologies of Stoic philosophy and Gnostic religions. New Testament writers as well as the Fathers of the church found a special appeal in Stoic doctrines of the mind's control of body and of reason's effecting detachment from all forms of passionate desire. Stoicism, though this-worldly in itself, blended well with the early Christian expectation of the end of the world. More important, it offered a way of rational response to Gnostic devaluation of marriage and procreation.

Gnosticism was a series of religious movements that deeply affected formulations of Christian sexual ethics for the first three centuries.[7] Combining elements of Eastern mysticism, Greek philosophy, and Christian belief, the Gnostics claimed a special "knowledge" of divine revelation. Among other things, they taught that marriage is evil or at least useless, primarily because the procreation of children is a vehicle for forces of evil. That led to two extreme positions in Gnosticism—one that opposed all sexual intercourse and hence prescribed celibacy, and one advocating every possible experience of sexual intercourse so long as it was not procreative.

What Christian moral teaching sought in order to combat both Gnostic rejection of sexual intercourse and Gnostic licentiousness was a doctrine that incorporated an affirmation of sex as good (because part of creation) but set serious limits to sexual activity (and hence provided an order for sexual emotion). The Stoic doctrine of justification of sexual intercourse by reason of its relation to procreation served both of those needs. The connection made between sexual intercourse and procreation was not the same as the Jewish affirmation of the importance of fecundity, though it was in harmony with it. Christian teaching could thus both affirm procreation as the central rationale for sexual union and advocate virginity as a praiseworthy option for Christians who could choose it.

With the adoption of the Stoic norm for sexual intercourse, the direction of Christian sexual ethics was set for centuries to come. A sexual ethic that concerned itself primarily with affirming the good of procreation and thereby the good of otherwise evil sexual tendencies was, moreover, reinforced by the continued appearance of antagonists who played the same role the Gnostics had played. No sooner had Gnosticism begun to wane than, in the fourth century, Manichaeanism emerged. And it was largely in response to Manichaeanism that Augustine formulated his sexual ethic—an ethic which continued and went beyond the Stoic elements already incorporated by Clement of Alexandria, Origen, Ambrose, and Jerome.

The Sexual Ethics of St. Augustine
and Its Legacy

Augustine argued against the Manichaeans in favor of the goodness of marriage and procreation (*On the Good of Marriage*), though he shared with them a negative view of sexual desire as in itself a tendency to evil. Because evil was for him, however, a privation of right order (and not an autonomous principle), it was possible to reorder sexual desire according to reason, to integrate its meaning into a right and whole love of God and neighbor. That was done only when sexual intercourse had the purpose of procreation. Intercourse without a procreative purpose was, according to Augustine, sinful (though not necessarily lethally so). Marriage, on the other hand, had a threefold purpose: not only the good of children, but also the goods of fidelity between spouses (as opposed to adultery) and the indissolubility of their union (as opposed to divorce). Augustine wrote appreciatively of the possibility of love and companionship between persons in marriage, but he did not integrate a positive role for sexual intercourse.

In his writings against the Pelagians (*Marriage and Concupiscence*) Augustine tried to clarify the place of sexual desire in a theology of original sin. Although for Augustine original sin was a sin of the spirit (the sin of prideful disobedience), its effects were most acutely seen in the chaos experienced when sexual desire wars against reasoned choice of higher goods. Moreover, the loss of integrity in affectivity (the effect of original sin) is, according to Augustine, passed on from one generation to another through the mode of procreation wherein sexual intercourse always interferes with self-possessed reason and will. Augustine's formulation of a sexual ethic held sway in Christian moral teaching until the sixteenth century. There were a few Christian writers (for example, John Chrysostom) who raised up the Pauline purpose for marriage—that is, as a remedy for incontinence. Such a position hardly served to foster a more optimistic view of the value of sex, but it did offer a possibility for moral goodness in sexual intercourse without a direct relation to procreation. From the sixth to the eleventh century, the weight of Augustine's negative evaluation of sexuality became even more burdensome. Following the premise that sexual intercourse can be justified only by its relation to procreative purpose, the Penitentials (manuals providing lists of sins and their prescribed penances) detailed prohibitions of adultery, fornication, oral and anal sex, contraception, and even certain positions for sexual intercourse according as they were departures from the procreative norm.

The rise of the courtly love tradition and new forms of mystical ideologies in the twelfth century presented a new challenge to the procreation ethic. Once again the meaning of sexuality in relation to marriage and procreation was questioned, and Christian moral theory reacted by renewing its commitment to Augustine's sexual ethic. In theology, Peter Lombard's *Sentences* led the way in renewing the connection between concupiscence and original sin, so that sexual intercourse within marriage demanded once again a procreative justification. In church discipline, this was the period of Gratian's great collection of canon law, and canonical regulations were shaped with the rigorism dictated by a sexual ethics that held all sexual activity to be evil unless it could be excused under the rationale of a procreative purpose.

While the tradition became more and more emphatic in one direction, nonetheless other directions were being opened. A few voices (for example, Abelard and John Damascene) continued to argue that concupiscence does not make sexual pleasure evil in itself, and that sexual intercourse in marriage can be justified by the intention to avoid fornication. The courtly love tradition, while it served to rigidify the opposition, nonetheless also introduced a powerful new element in its assertion that sexuality can be a mediation of interpersonal love.[8]

The Teaching of Aquinas

Thomas Aquinas came on the scene in the thirteenth century at a time when rigorism prevailed in Christian teaching and church discipline. His massive and innovative synthesis in Christian theology did not offer much that was new in the area of sexual ethics. Yet there was a clarity regarding all that was brought forward from the tradition that made Aquinas's own participation important for the generations that succeeded him. Christian moral teaching as he understood it included a disclaimer regarding the intrinsic evil of sexual desire. Moral evil is always and only tied up with evil moral choice and not with spontaneous bodily tendencies or desires. Yet there is in fallen human nature, as the result of original sin, a loss of order in natural human tendencies. All emotions are good insofar as they are ordered according to reason; they become evil when they are freely affirmed in opposition to reason's norm.

Aquinas offered two grounds for the procreative norm of reason, which the tradition had so far affirmed. One was the Augustinian argument that sexual pleasure always, in the fallen human person, hinders the best working of the mind. It must, then, be brought into some accord with reason by having an overriding value as its goal. No less an end than procreation can serve to justify it.[9] But secondly, reason does not merely provide a good purpose for sexual pleasure. It discovers that purpose through the very facts of the biological function of sexual organs.[10] Hence, the norm of reason in sexual behavior is not only the conscious intention of procreation but the accurate and unimpeded physical process whereby procreation is possible. So important is this process that whether or not procreation is in fact possible (that is, whether or not actual conception can take place—as it could not in the case of the sterile), it is sufficient that the process of intercourse be complete and there be no intention to avoid procreation. If *per accidens* generation cannot follow, nonetheless the intercourse is in its *essence* justifiable.

It was the procreative norm for sexual intercourse that provided specific moral rules to govern, either directly or indirectly, a variety of sexual activities and relationships. In addition to a general proscription of anything that produces sexual pleasure for its own sake (not justified by the purpose of procreation), Aquinas argued from the assumption that sexual intercourse would be procreative to considerations of the morality of instances of intercourse from the standpoint of the progeny that might result. Thus, for example, he argued against fornication and adultery on the grounds that they injure a child born of the union by not providing a responsible context for its rearing. He argued against divorce because the children of a marriage need a stable home in order to grow into the fullness of life. He considered sexual acts that could not meet the requirements of the biological norm for heterosexual intercourse immoral because there was no way in which they could be procreative. And he opposed contraception not only because it was in intention nonprocreative but because it constituted an injury against an unborn child and/or the human species.[11]

Aquinas's treatment of marriage contained only hints of possible new insights regarding the relation of sexual intercourse to marital love. He worked out a theory of love as a passion that had room in it for an assertion that sexual union can be an aid to interpersonal love,[12] and he had the bare beginnings of a theory of marriage that opened it to the possibility of maximum friendship.[13] Indeed, some Thomistic scholars assert that a closer analysis of Aquinas's texts shows that he broke with Augustine's theory of procreative sex and fully justified marital intercourse as an expression of the good of fidelity. In so doing he rejected only *anti*procreative marital intercourse.[14]

Fifteenth-Century Justifications of Nonprocreative Sex

Though what had cystallized in the Middle Ages canonically and theologically would continue to influence Christian moral teaching into the indefinite future, the fifteenth century marked the beginning of significant change. Finding some grounds for opposing the prevailing Augustinian sexual ethic in both Albert the Great and in the general (if not the specifically sexual) ethics of Thomas Aquinas, writers such as Denis the Carthusian began to speak of the possible integration of spiritual love and sexual pleasure. Martin LeMaistre, teaching at the University of Paris, argued that sexual intercourse in marriage is justified for its own sake; that is, sexual pleasure can be sought precisely as sexual pleasure, as the opposite of the pain experienced in the lack of sexual pleasure. When it is enjoyed thus it contributes to the general well-being of the persons involved. The influence of LeMaistre and others was not such as to reverse the Augustinian tradition, but it weakened it. The effects of the new theories of human sexuality were felt in the important controversies of the sixteenth-century Reformation and Counter Reformation within Christianity.

Reformation Teaching on Sex

Questions of sexual behavior played a significant role in the Protestant Reformation. The issue of clerical celibacy, for example, was raised not just as a matter of church discipline but as a question intimately tied into doctrinal controversies over nature and grace, original sin, sacramental theology, and ecclesiology. Martin Luther and John Calvin were both, paradoxically, deeply influenced by the Augustinian tradition regarding original sin and its conse-quences for human sexuality. Yet both developed a position on marriage that was complementary to, if not in opposition with, the procreative ethic. Like Augustine and the Christian tradition that followed him, they affirmed marriage and human sexuality as part of the divine plan for creation, and therefore good. But they shared Augustine's pessimistic view of fallen nature in which human sexual desire is no longer ordered as it should be within the complex structure of the human personality. The cure for disordered desire that Luther offered, however, was not the one put forth by Augustine. For Luther, the remedy was marriage; for Augustine, it was celibacy. And so the issue was joined over a key element in Christian teaching regarding sexuality. Luther, of course, was not the first to advocate marriage as a remedy for unruly sexual desire. But he took on the whole of the Christian tradition in a way that no one else had, challenging theory and practice, offering not just an alternative justification for marriage but a view of the human person that demanded marriage for almost all Christians (*The Estate of Marriage*). Sexual pleasure itself, then, in one sense needed no justification. The desire for it was simply a fact of life. It remained, like all the givens in creation, a good so long as it was channeled through marriage into the meaningful whole of life (which included above all, for Luther, the good of offspring). What there was in it that was a distraction from the "knowledge and worship of God," and hence sinful, had to be simply forgiven, as did the inevitable sinful elements in all dimensions of human life (*A Sermon on the Estate of Marriage*).

Calvin, too, saw marriage as a corrective to otherwise disordered desires. But Calvin went beyond that in affirming that the greatest good of marriage and sex is the mutual society that is formed between husband and wife (*Commentary on Genesis*). Calvin thought that sexual desire is more subject to control than did Luther, though whatever fault remains in it is "covered over" by marriage.[15] He worried that marriage, while it is the remedy for incontinence, could nonetheless be itself a provocation to "uncontrolled and dissolute lust."

The converse of both Luther's and Calvin's teaching regarding marriage was their opposition to premarital and extramarital sex less out of a concern for irresponsible procreation than out of a belief that sexuality not restrained by the marriage bond was wholly disordered. So concerned was Luther to provide some institutionally tempering form to sexual desire that he preferred a second marriage to adultery (yet so inevitable did he consider the need for sexual activity that he allowed adultery for either a husband or wife whose spouse was impotent or frigid). Both Luther and Calvin were opposed to divorce, though its possibility was admitted in a situation of adultery or impotence. Overall, every sexual moral norm was influenced by the belief that any sex outside the forgiving context of marriage was sinful. Hence, Calvin unquestioningly opposed homosexuality and bestiality along with adultery and fornication (though he followed the scholastics in considering the first two a violation of nature).

Post-Reformation Developments

In the four centuries following the Reformation, development occurred, of course, in Christian attitudes and theory regarding sexuality. Yet the fundamental directions of both Roman Catholic and Protestant thought changed surprisingly little before the twentieth century. Even now, basic norms and patterns of justification for norms affirmed by Augustine and Aquinas, Luther and Calvin, remain intact for many Christians despite the radical challenges put to them in recent years. The fundamental struggle in each of the Christian traditions through the centuries has been to modulate an essentially negative approach to sexuality into a positive one, to move from the need to justify sexual intercourse even in marriage by reason of either procreation or the avoidance of fornication to an affirmation of its potential for expressing and effecting interpersonal love. The difficulties in such a transition are more evident in the efforts of the churches to articulate a new position than in the writings of individual theologians.

In Roman Catholicism

During and after the Reformation, new developments in the Roman Catholic tradition alternated with the reassertion of the Augustinian ethic. Though the Council of Trent became the first ecumenical council to treat the role of love in marriage, it also reaffirmed the primacy of the procreative ethic and reemphasized the superiority of celibacy. The move away from the procreative ethic by sixteenth-, seventeenth-, and eighteenth-century Roman Catholic theologians proved to be primarily a move to lean like Luther and Calvin in the direction of justifying marriage for the sake of continence. In the seventeenth century Jansenism reacted against a lowering of sexual standards and brought back the Augustinian connection between sex, concupiscence, and original sin. The nineteenth century stagnated in a manualist tradition that never moved beyond Alphonsus Liguouri's eighteenth-century attempt to integrate the Pauline purpose of marriage with the purpose of intercourse. Then came the twentieth century with the rise of Roman Catholic theological interest in personalism and the move on the part of the Protestant churches to accept birth control.

It was the issue of contraception that served once again to focus Roman Catholic teaching firmly on the procreative ethic. In 1930 Pius XI responded to the Anglican approval of contraception by reaffirming in his encyclical letter,

Casti Connubii, the full rationale for the procreative ethic.[16] At the same time, he gave approval for the use of the rhythm method for restricting procreation, an approval that Pius XII reiterated in an address to midwives in 1951.[17] Theologians such as Bernard Häring, Josef Fuchs, John Ford, and Gerald Kelly began to move cautiously in the direction of allowing sexual intercourse in marriage without a procreative intent and for the purpose of fostering marital union.

The change in Roman Catholic moral theology from the 1950s to the 1970s was dramatic. The wedge introduced between procreation and sexual intercourse by the acceptance of the rhythm method joined with new understandings of the totality of the human person to support a radically new concern for sexuality as an expression and cause of married love. The effects of this theological reflection were striking in the Vatican II teaching on marriage. Here it was affirmed that the love essential to marriage is uniquely expressed and perfected in the act of sexual intercourse (Second Vatican Council).[18] Although the Council still held that marriage is by its very nature ordered to the procreation of children, it made no distinction between the primary and secondary ends of marriage. Nonprocreative marital intercourse thus was accepted by the Catholic community. This was recognized by Paul VI in his encyclical *Humanae Vitae* in 1968, although at the same time he insisted that contraception is immoral. The debate continues between those who reject contraception and those who believe that acceptance of nonprocreative purposes for marital intercourse entails acceptance of contraception. For some, a distinction between *non*procreative and *anti*procreative behavior mediates the dispute.

In Protestantism

In the meantime, twentieth-century theological reflection on sexual behavior has developed as dramatically in the Protestant communities as in the Roman Catholic. After the Reformation, Protestant sexual ethics continued to affirm heterosexual marriage as the only acceptable context for sexual activity. Lutheran pietism and Calvinistic Puritanism continued to justify sex in marriage only as a corrective to disordered sexual desire or as a means to procreation of children.[19] Except for the differences regarding celibacy and divorce, sexual norms in Protestantism looked much the same as those in the Roman Catholic tradition. Nineteenth-century Protestantism was little influenced by the unconventional sexual attitudes of Romanticism (with the exception of perhaps Schleiermacher), and it shared the cultural pressures of Victorianism. But in the twentieth century Protestant thinking was deeply affected by historical studies that revealed the early roots of Christian sexual norms,[20] biblical research that questioned direct recourse to explicit bibilical sexual norms,[21] and new philosophical anthropologies and psychoanalytic theories.

It is difficult, of course, to trace one clear line of development in twentieth-century Protestant sexual ethics, or even as clear a dialectic as may be found in Roman Catholicism. The fact that Protestantism in general was less dependent from the beginning on the procreative ethic may have led it almost unanimously to a much easier acceptance of, for example, contraception. The Anglican Lambeth Conference in 1930 marked the beginning of new official positions on the part of major Protestant churches in this regard. Protestant theologians from Bonhoeffer to Barth, Brunner to Reinhold Niebuhr, Thielicke to Ellul, have concurred with this change.

The fact that Protestant sexual ethics has more frequently been based on a biblical rather than a natural law ethic may account for its earlier (than Roman Catholic) willingness to favor the civil rights of homosexuals. This would not account as easily for the fact that a number of Protestant churches and theologians have suggested a new position on the morality of homosexuality as well. In 1963 a group of Quakers published a formal essay in which a general sexual ethic of mutual consent did not rule out homosexual relationships as a Christian option.[22] The Lutheran theologian Helmut Thielicke[23] and the Anglican Derrick S. Bailey have both advocated a new openness to the needs of the homosexual at least for the pastoral concern of the churches. On the other hand, Karl Barth called for "protest, warning, and conversion," because homosexuality violates the command of God,[24] and the Lutheran Church, Missouri Synod, condemned homosexuality in 1973 as "intrinsically sinful."

Overall, Protestant sexual ethics is moving to integrate an understanding of the human person, male and female, into a theology of marriage that no longer deprecates sexual desire and sexual pleasure as primarily occasions of moral danger. For the most part, the ideal context for sexual intercourse is still seen to be heterosexual marriage. Yet questions of premarital sex, homosexuality, masturbation, and new questions of artificial insemination, genetic control, and in vitro fertilization are being raised by Protestant theologians in Protestant communities.

NOTES

1. David Feldman, *Marital Relations, Birth Control and Abortion in Jewish Law* (New York: Schocken Books, 1974), 27.

2. Eugene B. Borowitz, *Choosing a Sex Ethic: A Jewish Inquiry,* Hillel Library Series (New York: Schocken Books, 1969), 47.

3. Feldman, *Marital Relations,* 42–53.

4. Louis M. Epstein, *Sex Laws and Customs in Judaism* (New York: Block Publishing Co., 1948; reprint, Ktav Publishing House, 1967), 134–47.

5. Feldman, *Marital Relations,* 104.

6. Borowitz, *Choosing a Sex Ethic,* 50.

7. John T. Noonan, Jr., *Contraception: A History of Its Treatment by the Catholic Theologians and Canonists* (Cambridge, Mass.: Harvard University Press, Belknap Press, 1965), 78–136.

8. Denis De Rougement, *Love in the Western World,* trans. Montgomery Belgion, rev. ed. (Garden City, N.Y.: Doubleday/Anchor Books, 1957), 65.

9. Thomas Aquinas, *Summa Theologiae* I–II, 34 1 ad 1.

10. Ibid., II–II, 154, 11; Aquinas, *Summa Contra Gentiles* III, 122, 4 and 5.

11. Josef Fuchs, *Die Sexualethik des heiligen Thomas von Aquin* (Cologne: J.P. Bachem, 1949), 181.

12. Aquinas, *Summa Theologiae* II–II, 26, 11.

13. Aquinas, *Summa Contra Gentiles* III, 123.

14. Fabian Parmisano, "Love and Marriage in the Middle Ages," *New Blackfriars* 50 (1969): 599–608, 649–60; Germain G. Grisez, "Marriage Reflections Based on St. Thomas and Vatican Council II," *Catholic Mind* (June 1966): 4–19.

15. John Calvin, *Institutes of the Christian Religion* 2, 8, 44.

16. Pius XI, "Casti Connubii," *Acta Apostolica Sedis* 22 (1930): 539–92, trans. as "On Christian Marriage," *Catholic Mind* 29 (1931): 21–64.

17. Pius XII, "His Holiness Pope Pius XII's Discourse to Members of the Congress of the Italian Association of Catholic Midwives, Castle Gandolfo, Monday, 29th October, 1951," *Catholic Documents: Containing Recent Pronouncements and Decisions of His Holiness Pope Pius XII,* no. 6, 1952, 1–16.

18. Second Vatican Council, "Pastoral Constitution on the Church in the Modern World," *The Sixteen Documents of Vatican II and the Instruction on the Liturgy* (Boston: St. Paul Editions, 1962), 511–625, esp. chap. 1, sec. 49, pp. 563–64, *Gaudium et Spes.*

19. William Graham Cole, *Sex in Christianity and Psychoanalysis* (New York: Oxford University Press, 1955), 162.

20. Derrick Sherwin Bailey, *Sexual Relation in Christian Thought* (New York: Harper & Brothers, 1959); London ed. titled *The Man-Woman Relation in Christian Thought.*

21. Heinrich Baltensweiler, "Current Developments in the Theology of Marriage in the Reformed Churches," *The Future of Marriage as Institution,* ed. Franz Bockle; Concilium: Theology in the Age of Renewal, vol. 55 (New York: Herder & Herder, 1970), 144–51.

22. Alastair Heron, *Toward a Quaker View of Sex: An Essay by a Group of Friends* (London: Friends Home Service Committee, 1963, 2d rev. ed. 1964).

23. Helmut Thielicke, *The Ethics of Sex* (New York: Harper & Row, 1964), 269–92; Derrick Sherwin Bailey, *Homosexuality and the Western Christian Tradition* (New York: Longmans, Green & Co., 1955). Reprint, Shoe String Press, 1975.

24. Karl Barth, *Church Dogmatics,* ed. by G. W. Bromiley and T. F. Torrance, vol. 3 pt. 4: "The Doctrine of the Word of God" (Edinburgh: T. & T. Clark, 1961), 166.

PART 2

Sexuality and Spirituality

Audre Lorde
Paul Ricoeur
John Giles Milhaven
Joan H. Timmerman
Toinette M. Eugene

Introduction
to Part 2

The term "spirituality" is popular these days, for reasons both welcome and questionable. For some it is a good New Age word meaning almost anything a person wants it to mean. For others it suggests a religious quest without the constraints, pieties, and baggage of organized religion and religious community. While we are interested neither in faddishness nor in religious life disconnected from community and tradition, we believe that the use of "spirituality" in its broad and inclusive sense is helpful. By it we mean the ways and patterns by which persons relate to that which is ultimately real and worthful to them. With this term we signify the response of the whole person—mind and body, feelings and relationships—to the presence of whatever is held to be sacred, of ultimate worth. In this broad sense, spirituality need not be articulated in theological terms, nor need it be explicitly theistic. All human beings have some kind of spirituality, for it is impossible to live without identifying and finding ways of relating to that which is of central worth and importance to us.

The question now is, What do spirituality and sexuality have to do with each other? To pronounce both of these words in the same breath still sounds like an oxymoron to many people—they seem to cancel each other out. Indeed, that reaction is understandable, for the dualistic inheritance of the classical world deeply affected Christianity and shaped the understanding of spirituality into body-denying directions. Spirit was viewed as essentially different from and superior to the suspect sexual body. Hence, the cultivation of spirituality meant the control, discipline, and repression of the body. Christian spirituality was seen as a life controlled by disciplines of meditation and prayer whereby one could rise beyond the flesh to higher communion with the divine.

Some years ago the distinguished French philosopher Paul Ricoeur (in a different essay from that included in this section) noted that there seem to be three major stages in the understanding of sexuality and religion in the West.[1] The first stage, at the dawn of human history, saw no real separation. Sexuality was incorporated into the whole view of the cosmos through religious ritual and myth. But with the second period (the rise of the major world religions) came the great divorce. Increasingly, the sacred was seen as transcendent, while a demythologized sexuality was limited to a small part of earthly life: procreation within institutionalized marriage. When sexuality threatened to break from these constraints, its power was feared and suppressed. Ricoeur noted, however, that in a now-emerging third period there is the strong desire to reunite sexuality with the experience of the sacred. We realize, with insights from the second period, that sexual expression can be distorted and oppressive; hence it does need discipline and ordering. But with the assistance of modern depth psychology we now understand more of the ways that sexuality enters into the deepest dynamics of our humanity. Thus, with those of the first period we now have both a sense of sexuality's inevitability in our central commitments, and also a glimpse of its spiritual power when integrated into the core of our lives.

We believe that our society is edging its way into this third period. With more awareness of sexuality's destructive capacities, we also see a dawning recognition that sexuality is significantly involved not only in our individual quests for meaning and wholeness, but also in the broad social issues of our time (see Part 5). This section will address particularly the issues of sexuality and personal wholeness, though there will also be ample suggestions of its connection to the wider social issues.

We begin with Audre Lorde's widely quoted essay "Uses of the Erotic," which continues to give voice to the intuitive knowledge—"our deepest and non-rational knowledge"—of many feminist thinkers both in the Christian church and in the wider community. Lorde, who was an African-American lesbian feminist poet and essayist, has been an articulate spokesperson for a significant movement to reclaim the goodness and power of the erotic. While she does not articulate a specifically Christian or even theistic position, she clearly speaks of spirituality when she names eros as the source of sacred power. While the erotic has been often misnamed by people and confused with the pornographic, it is truly the creative energy and life force within us. The erotic is that which allows us deep connection with others, giving joy, creative energy, and the capacity for feeling; that which empowers persons to change the world; that which is the deep yes within the self.

In order to appreciate the power that Lorde's reclaiming of the erotic has had for Christian theologians such as Carter Heyward (see Parts 1 and 3) and Marvin Ellison (see Part 4), we think it helpful for a moment to look at some more traditional understandings. The erotic dimensions of love have been held suspect by much of the Christian tradition. In 1932 Anders Nygren, a Swedish theologian, wrote a vastly influential book, *Agape and Eros*. In it he sharply contrasted agapaic love, which he defined as God's self-giving love epitomized in Jesus' cross, with eros, which he defined as selfish and carnal love that seeks only its own fulfillment. The two loves, for Nygren, are diametrically opposed to each other, and the task of the Christian life is to eliminate eros and embrace agape. Although Nygren did not create the antipathy to eros, he expressed it with a power that has influenced much of Western theology ever since.

In contrast to Nygren, to whom eros is clearly bad, and Lorde, to whom eros is unquestionably good, Paul Ricoeur finds it ambiguous. When eros is "a restless desire for pleasure" dissociated from lasting interpersonal intimacy, it is false eroticism, and sexuality falls into insignificance. Yet, Ricoeur defends the erotic as basic to the enigma of sexuality. Eros is nontechnical and immediate. Not a duty, it is impatient with rules. And when eros is mated with tenderness and fidelity, authentic happiness and spiritual fulfillment follow.

Whereas both Lorde's and Ricoeur's essays make strong affirmations about eros, neither attempts a phenomenological description of how the experience looks and feels. In attending to a concrete bodily experience, John Giles Milhaven does just that. Note how clearly he claims experience as an important arena for revelation in sexual theology (see our introduction to Part 1), observing that when theologians and philosophers praise the goodness of the body, they still largely treat the body as instrumental—as that which promotes personal relationship. But what, he asks, of bodily eros? Why do we desire it for itself and not just as a means to something else? Then he puts delightful words to the intense pleasure of falling asleep with his wife as their bodies cradle spoonlike together. Milhaven, a Christian ethicist, does not deal with spirituality or with God by name. Nor does he speak of genital sex. Yet clearly he is reflecting on what to him is a sexual and erotic experience of intense pleasure and spiritual value.

With Joan Timmerman's piece we move into explicitly Christian reflection. "Jesus Christ is the point at which God and sexuality must be discussed together or forever remain separate."[2] If we are to claim the intrinsic relation between the sexual and the spiritual, we must reassess the issue of Jesus' own sexuality. Confusions and silence about his sexual humanity, she argues, reflect confusions about our own. Though the historical quest for data concerning how Jesus expressed his sexuality will bear no fruit, at least it seems probable that the notion of a sexless Christ was the product of later devotional sources and not a genuine bibilical testimony. Whatever Jesus' particular *lifestyle* as a sexual being may have been, his importance for us is not found in imitating how he lived (regarding which we have no historical certainty anyway). Rather, he is a model of *vocation*, the call to full humanity. Because we are constituted as both sexual and spiritual, our vocation is to develop toward full and integrated wholeness. Such vocation, intended for us all, will be marked by a variety of sexual lifestyles. And our choices about the latter are to embody growth in those ways of sexual expressiveness that nurture intimacy and ecstasy, love and justice, peace and joy—in other words, those expressions that keep us open to God's healing and saving presence.

African-American theologian Toinette M. Eugene acknowledges that the black church has neglected the holistic integration of sexuality into life. Identifying ways that racism and the sexual dualisms have diminished black love, she argues that present distrust between black women and black men is a profound spiritual problem. Neither a spirituality unrelated to black bodily existence nor a focus fixated at genital expressions of black love will do. Nevertheless, "It may be historically demonstrated that in times past whenever black women and men consciously and consistently dared to express black love through an integration of their spirituality and sexuality, they became a source for liberating social transformation in both the black community and in the white world around them."[3]

In the five authors in Part 2, then, we see different ways of expressing the sexuality-spirituality connection. On one fundamental thing they agree: a meaningful integration of these dimensions of selfhood is essential to the wholeness of life. Just how such integration might occur, how complete it can be, and what is might look like all find varying expressions. Now the reader is invited into the task of exploring that connection.

NOTES

1. See Paul Ricoeur, *The Symbolism of Evil,* trans., Emerson Buchanan (New York: Harper & Row, 1967).

2. Joan H. Timmerman, *Sexuality and Spiritual Growth* (New York: Crossroad, 1992), 30.

3. Toinette M. Eugene, "While Love Is Unfashionable: Ethical Implications of Black Spirituality and Sexuality," in Barbara Hilkert Andolsen, et al. (eds.), *Women's Consciousness, Women's Conscience* (San Francisco: Harper & Row, Publishers, 1987), 126.

5

Uses of the Erotic: The Erotic as Power

AUDRE LORDE

There are many kinds of power, used and unused, acknowledged or otherwise. The erotic is a resource within each of us that lies in a deeply female and spiritual plane, firmly rooted in the power of our unexpressed or unrecognized feeling. In order to perpetuate itself, every oppression must corrupt or distort those various sources of power within the culture of the oppressed that can provide energy for change. For women, this has meant a suppression of the erotic as a considered source of power and information within our lives.

We have been taught to suspect this resource, vilified, abused, and devalued within western society. On one hand the superficially erotic has been encouraged as a sign of female inferiority—on the other hand women have been made to suffer and to feel both contemptible and suspect by virtue of its existence.

It is a short step from there to the false belief that only by the suppression of the erotic within our lives and consciousness can women be truly strong. But that strength is illusory, for it is fashioned within the context of male models of power.

As women, we have come to distrust that power which rises from our deepest and non-rational knowledge. We have been warned against it all our lives by the male world, which values this depth of feeling enough to keep women around in order to exercise it in the service of men, but which fears this same depth too much to examine the possibilities of it within themselves. So women are maintained at a distant/inferior position to be psychically milked, much the same way ants maintain colonies of aphids to provide a life-giving substance for their masters.

But the erotic offers a well of replenishing and provocative force to the woman who does not fear its revelation, nor succumb to the belief that sensation is enough.

The erotic has often been misnamed by men and used against women. It has been made into the confused, the trivial, the psychotic, the plasticized sensation. For this reason, we have often turned away from the exploration and consideration of the erotic as a source of power and information, confusing it with its opposite, the pornographic. But pornography is a direct denial of the power of the erotic, for it represents the suppression of true feeling. Pornography emphasizes sensation without feeling.

The erotic is a measure between the beginnings of our sense of self, and the chaos of our strongest feelings. It is an internal sense of satisfaction to which, once we have experienced it, we know we can aspire. For once having experienced the fullness of this depth of feeling and recognizing its power, in honor and self-respect we can require no less of ourselves. . . .

This internal requirement toward excellence which we learn from the erotic must not be misconstrued as demanding the impossible from ourselves nor from others. Such a demand incapacitates everyone in the process, for the erotic is not a question only of what we do. It is a question of how acutely and fully we can feel in the doing. For once we know the extent to which we are capable of feeling that sense of satisfaction and fullness and completion, we can then observe which of our various life endeavours bring us closest to that fullness.

The aim of each thing which we do is to make our lives and the lives of our children more possible and more rich. Within the celebration of the erotic in all our endeavours, my work becomes a conscious decision—a longed-for bed which I enter gratefully and from which I rise up empowered.

Of course, women so empowered are dangerous. So we are taught to separate the erotic demand from most vital areas of our lives other than sex. And the lack of concern for the erotic root and satisfactions of our work is felt in our disaffection from so much of what we do. For instance, how often do we truly love our work?

The principal horror of any system which defines the good in terms of profit rather than in terms of human need, or which defines human need to the exclusion of the psychic and emotional components of that need—the principal horror of such a system is that it robs our work of its erotic value, its erotic power and life appeal and fulfillment. Such a system reduces work to a travesty of necessities, a duty by which we earn bread or oblivion for ourselves and those we love. But this is tantamount to blinding a painter and then telling her to improve her work, and to enjoy the act of painting. It is not only next to impossible, it is also profoundly cruel.

As women, we need to examine the ways in which our world can be truly different. I am speaking here of the necessity for reassessing the very quality of all the aspects of our lives and of our work.

The very word "erotic" comes from the Greek word *eros*, the personification of love in all its aspects—born of Chaos, and personifying creative power and harmony. When I speak of the erotic, then, I speak of it as an assertion of the life-force of women; of that creative energy empowered, the knowledge and use of which we are now reclaiming in our language, our history, our dancing, our loving, our work, our lives.

There are frequent attempts to equate pornography and eroticism, two diametrically opposed uses of the sexual. Because of these attempts, it has become fashionable to separate the spiritual (psychic and emotional) away from the political, to see them as contadictory or antithetical. "What do you mean, a poetic revolutionary, a meditating gun-runner?" In the same way, we have attempted to separate the spiritual and the erotic, reducing the spiritual thereby to a world of flattened affect—a world of the ascetic who aspires to feel nothing. But nothing is farther from the truth. For the ascetic position is one of the highest fear, the gravest immobility. The severe abstinence of the ascetic becomes the ruling obsession. And it is one, not of self-discipline, but of self-abnegation.

The dichotomy between the spiritual and the political is also false, resulting from an incomplete attention to our erotic knowledge. For the bridge which connects them is formed by the erotic—the sensual—those physical, emotional, and psychic expressions of what is deepest and strongest and richest within each of us, being shared: the passions of love, in its deepest meanings.

The considered phrase, "It feels right to me," acknowledges the strength of the erotic into a true knowledge, for what that means and feels is the first and most powerful guiding light towards any understanding. And understanding is a handmaiden which can only wait upon, or clarify, that knowledge, deeply born. The erotic is the nurturer or nursemaid of all our deepest knowledge.

The erotic functions for me in several ways, and the first is in the power which comes from sharing deeply any pursuit with another person. The sharing of joy, whether physical, emotional, psychic or intellectual, forms a bridge between the sharers which can be the basis for understanding much of what is not shared between them, and lessens the threat of their difference.

Another important way in which the erotic connection functions is the open and fearless underlining of my capacity for joy. In the way my body stretches to music and opens into response, hearkening to its deepest rhythms, so every level upon which I sense also opens to the erotically satisfying experience, whether it is dancing, building a bookcase, writing a poem, examining an idea.

That self-connection shared is a measure of the joy which I know myself to be capable of feeling, a reminder of my capacity for feeling. And that deep and irreplaceable knowledge of my capacity for joy comes to demand from all of my life that it be lived within the knowledge that such satisfaction is possible, and does not have to be called marriage, nor god, nor an afterlife.

This is one reason why the erotic is so feared, and so often relegated to the bedroom alone, when it is recognized at all. For once we begin to feel deeply all the aspects of our lives, we begin to demand from ourselves and from our lives' pursuits that they feel in accordance with that joy which we know ourselves to be capable of. Our erotic knowledge empowers us, becomes a lens through which we scrutinize all aspects of our existence, forcing ourselves to evaluate those aspects honestly in terms of their relative meaning within our lives. And this is a grave responsibility, projected from within each of us, not to settle for the convenient, the shoddy, the conventionally expected, nor the merely safe.

During World War II, we bought sealed plastic packets of white, uncolored margarine, with a tiny, intense pellet of yellow coloring perched like a topaz just inside the clear skin of the bag. We would leave the margarine out for a while to soften, and then we would pinch the little pellet to break it inside the bag, releasing the rich yellowness into the soft pale mass of margarine. Then taking it carefully between our fingers, we would knead it gently back and forth, over and over, until the color had spread throughout the whole pound bag of margarine, leaving it thoroughly colored.

I find the erotic such a kernel within myself. When released from its intense and constrained pellet, it flows through and colors my life with a kind of energy that heightens and sensitizes and strengthens all my experience.

We have been raised to fear the yes within ourselves, our deepest cravings. For the demands of our released expectations lead us inevitably into actions which will help bring our lives into accordance with our needs, our knowledge, our desires. And the fear of our deepest cravings keeps them suspect, keeps us docile and loyal and obedient, and leads us to settle for or accept many facets of our oppression as women.

When we live outside ourselves, and by that I mean on external directives only, rather than from our internal knowledge and needs, when we live away from those erotic guides from within our selves, then our lives are limited by external and alien forms, and we conform to the needs of a structure that is not based on human need, let alone an individual's. But when we begin to live from within outward, in touch with the power of the erotic within ourselves, and allowing that power to inform and illuminate our actions upon the world around us, then we begin to be responsible to ourselves in the deepest sense. For as we begin to recognize our deepest feelings, we begin to give up, of necessity, being satisfied with suffering, and self-negation, and with the numbness which so often seems like their only alternative in our society. Our acts against oppression become integral with self, motivated and empowered from within.

In touch with the erotic, I become less willing to accept powerlessness, or those other supplied states of being which are not native to me, such as resignation, despair, self-effacement, depression, self-denial.

And yes, there is a hierarchy. There is a difference between painting a back fence and writing a poem, but only one of quantity. And there is, for me, no difference between writing a good poem and moving into sunlight against the body of a woman I love.

This brings me to the last consideration of the erotic. To share the power of each other's feelings is different from using another's feelings as we would use a Kleenex. And when we look the other way from our experience, erotic or otherwise, we use rather than share the feelings of those others who participate in the experience with us. And use without consent of the used is abuse.

In order to be utilized, our erotic feelings must be recognized. The need for sharing deep feeling is a human need. But within the european-american tradition, this need is satisfied by certain proscribed erotic comings together, and these occasions are almost always characterized by a simultaneous looking away, a pretense of calling them something else, whether a religion, a fit, mob violence, or even playing doctor. And this misnaming of the need and the deed give rise to that distortion which results in pornography and obscenity—the abuse of feeling.

When we look away from the importance of the erotic in the development and sustenance of our power, or when we look away from ourselves as we satisfy our erotic needs in concert with others, we use each other as objects of satisfaction rather than share our joy in the satisfying, rather than make connection with our similarities and our differences. To refuse to be conscious of what we are feeling at any time, however comfortable that might seem, is to deny a large part of the experience, and to allow ourselves to be reduced to the pornographic, the abused, and the absurd.

The erotic cannot be felt secondhand. As a Black Lesbian Feminist, I have a particular feeling, knowledge, and understanding for those sisters with whom I have danced hard, played, or even fought. This deep participation has often been the forerunner for joint concerted actions not possible before.

But this erotic charge is not easily shared by women who continue to operate under an exclusively european-american, male tradition. I know it was not available to me when I was trying to adapt my consciousness to this mode of living and sensation.

Only now, I find more and more woman-identified women brave enough to risk sharing the erotic's electrical charge without having to look away, and without distorting the enormously powerful and creative nature of that exchange. Recognizing the power of the erotic within our lives can give us the energy to pursue genuine change within our world, rather than merely settling for a shift of characters in the same weary drama.

For not only do we touch our most profoundly creative source, but we do that which is female and self-affirming in the face of a racist, patriarchal, and anti-erotic society.

6

Wonder, Eroticism, and Enigma

PAUL RICOEUR

RESTLESSNESS AND EROTICISM
VERSUS TENDERNESS

. . .The term "eroticism" is ambiguous: it can designate, first, one of the components of human sexuality, its instinctual and sensual component. It can also designate the art of loving built upon the cultivation of sexual pleasure. As such it is still an aspect of tenderness, as long as the concern for reciprocity, mutual gratification, of gift, wins out over egoism and the narcissism of enjoyment. But eroticism becomes a restless desire for pleasure when it dissociates itself from the network of tendencies linked by the concern for a lasting, intense, and intimate interpersonal bond, and at this point it becomes a problem. Now we have learned from Freud—principally from *Three Essays on Sexuality*— that sexuality is not simple, and that the integration of its multiple components is an unending task. This disintegration of components, no longer experienced as a failure, but sought after as a technique of the body, makes eroticism the opposite of tenderness. In tenderness, the relationship to the other becomes dominant and can enlist eroticism as the sensual component of sexuality. In eroticism, an egoistic cultivation of pleasure wins out over mutual exchange.

Eroticism, in the limited and derogatory sense of the word, has always existed—indeed, certain of our correspondents, as we shall see, even declare that it is declining in a utilitarian civilization based on work. The cultivation of pleasure is a fundamental possibility of human sexuality, due to the simple fact of not letting itself be reduced to animal reproduction. There is an element of play in it and it becomes play. The cultivation of pleasure is summoned by tenderness and can always turn against it; it is the serpent that tenderness nourishes in its bosom. We must know that this is so and accept it. The demonism of Eros is the dual possibility of eroticism and tenderness. The restraint that the institution has always exercised on tenderness constantly reactivates the centrifugal tendency of eroticism, at the same time that the institution struggles to integrate it within tenderness.

But if eroticism is a possibility and an internal danger of sexuality insofar as it is human, its contemporary modalities appear new, and it is these which we propose to elucidate in what follows. I shall limit myself here to calling attention to three groups of phenomena, which are connected and reciprocal. There is, first, what I shall call the fall into insignificance. The removal of sexual prohibitions has produced a curious effect, which the Freudian generation had not anticipated, the loss of value through facility: sexual experience having become familiar, available, and reduced to a simple biological function becomes rather insignificant. Thus the extreme point in the destruction of the cosmo-vital notion of the sacred also becomes the extreme point of the dehumanization of sex.

Many circumstances have contributed to this first phenomenon: the mixing of sexes in economic life and in studies, woman's gaining of an equality which provides access to a sexual liberty which was formerly the privilege of man—in sum, everything that makes sexual encounter easy, also tends to make its meaning and value drop to zero.

To that is added the fact that vulgarized sexological literature has entered the public domain. Man knows himself better, and at the same time his sexuality becomes public. But in losing its clandestine character, it also loses its intimate character. "We other mammals," said Beguin. . . . There is something irreversible here: as they are diffused, human sciences become in turn a new cultural phenomenon which is part of the total human situation.

Finally, sexuality suffers the repercussion of all those other factors which make for depersonalization and anonymity. The testimony of American psychoanalysts is instructive in this regard. They notice the disappearance of the obsessively inhibited type, characteristic of the Victorian era, and the increase of more subtle symptoms: a destruction of the emotional contract, a powerlessness to love and to hate. Their clients complain more and more of not being able to experience an affective engagement of their entire personality in the sexual act; such people make love without loving.

The fall of sexuality into insignificance is both the cause and effect of this affective failure, as if social anonymity and sexual anonymity helped to activate each other.

A second phenomenon is that at the same time that sexuality becomes insignificant, it becomes more imperative as a response to the disappointments experienced in other sectors of human life. Sexuality, exasperated by its function as compensation and revenge, becomes in a way distraught. What are these disappointments?

First, there is disappointment in work. There are important studies to be made on the relationship of a civilization of work and sexuality. The Freudian school of *ego-analysis* (Hartmann, Erikson, etc.) has amply shown that, by its antilibidinous character, work serves to educate instinct. The personality is built up, the ego gains its autonomy beginning with conflict-free situations (at least, from the instinctual point of view). Along with language and the apprenticeship of life in institutions, work is one of the conflict-free spheres of which Erikson speaks. But the corollary is also important: the experience of modern man is that he is not "happy" in society conceived as an organized struggle against nature. His disappointment is deeper than a simple refusal of the economic-political regime of his work; he is disappointed by the technological world itself. Therefore, he seeks the sense of his life in leisure rather than in work, and eroticism begins to appear as a dimension of leisure. The vulgar form of eroticism is often simply the cheapest available leisure-time activity.

Along with a disappointment in work, there has been a disappointment in politics. We are witnessing a certain failure of the political definition of man. Weary of making history, man aspires to nonhistory. He refuses to be defined by a social role and dreams of being a man outside of all civil definitions. Reports on adolescents today would indicate a basic disinterest in their social-political role. Is this true in all the "advanced" nations, which now seem to be deprived of a vocation in the world? I do not know. In any case, eroticism appears as a formidable revenge, not only of leisure on work, but of private life on public life as a whole.

Lastly, and more profoundly, eroticism expresses a more radical disappointment, the sense of having been cheated by the established "meanings." There is a secret bond between eroticism and absurdity. When nothing makes sense any longer, there remains instantaneous pleasure and its artifices. This characteristic puts us on the track of a third phenomenon, which allows us to see the nature of eroticism better; if restless sexuality is both insignificant and imperative as revenge, it must still be made interesting. Eroticism is then a revenge not only on the insignificance of work, politics, and speech, but on the insignificance of sexuality itself. Hence we find the search for a sexual mythology. This search liberates a fundamental possibility of human sexuality which we have already evoked: that of separating pleasure not only from its function of procreation (which love-tenderness also does), but from tenderness itself. Man is engaged in an exhausting struggle against the psychological poverty of pleasure itself, which is scarcely susceptible of perfection in its biological brutality. So eroticism will construct its mythology in the interval of hedonistic dissociation and within the limits of affective finitude. This explains the almost desperate character of its enterprise: the quantitative eroticism of a life devoted to sexuality, refined eroticism constantly looking for variety, imaginative eroticism of showing while hiding, of refusing while saying yes, and the cerebral eroticism of the voyeur who insinuates himself as a third party into all erotic roles. A sexual mythology has been developed for all of these, and projected into various heroes of sexuality; but from one form to the other we see it slide from promiscuity to desolate solitude. The intense despair of eroticism—which recalls the famous leaky cask of the Greek legend—is that it never compensates for the loss of value and meaning while accumulating substitutes for tenderness.

THE ENIGMA OF SEXUALITY

I should prefer not to end on this pessimistic note, but rather to bring together the two halves of my analysis. In the way both of tenderness and of eroticism, it can be noticed that sexuality remains perhaps basically impermeable to reflection and inaccessible to human mastery. It is perhaps this capacity which prevents it from being contained either in the ethic of tenderness or in the nonethic of eroticism; perhaps it cannot be reabsorbed in either an ethic or a technique, but only symbolically represented by means of whatever mythical element remains in us.

Ultimately, when two beings embrace, they don't know what they are doing, they don't know what they want, they don't know what they are looking for, they don't know what they are finding. What is the meaning of this desire which drives them toward each other? Is it the desire of pleasure? Yes, certainly. But this is a poor response, for at the same time we feel that pleasure does not contain its own meaning, that it is representational. But of what? We have the vivid and yet obscure feeling that sex participates in a network of powers whose cosmic harmonies are forgotten but not abolished; that life is much more than life—that is, much more than the struggle against death, or delaying the time when the debt must be paid; that life is unique, universal, everything in everyone, and that sexual joy makes us participate in this mystery; that man does not become a person, ethically, juridically, unless he also plunges again into the river of Life—such is the truth of romanticism as well as the truth of sexuality. But this vivid feeling is also an obscure feeling, since we well know that this universe in which sexual joy participates has been sunk within us, that sexuality is the flotsam of a submerged Atlantis. Hence its enigma. This dislocated universe is no longer accessible to simplicity, but to the learned exegesis of ancient myths. It lives again only thanks to hermeneutics—that is to say, an art of interpreting writings which today are mute. And a new hiatus separates the flotsam of meaning which this hermeneutics of language restores to us and that other flotsam of meaning which sexuality discovers without language, organically.

The enigma of sexuality is that it remains irreducible to the trilogy which composes man: language, tool, institution. On the one hand, indeed, it belongs to a prelinguistic existence of man. Even when it makes itself expressive, it is an infra-, para-, superlinguistic expression. It mobilizes language, true, but it crosses it, jostles it, sublimates it, stupefies it, pulverizes it into a murmur, an invocation. Sexuality demediatizes language; it is Eros and not Logos.

Eros, on the other hand, belongs to the pretechnical existence of man. Even when man becomes responsible for it and integrates it to a technique of the body (whether it be the art of sexual adjustment, or more specifically, a preventive technique of procreation), sexuality remains hyperinstrumental; its instruments must be forgotten. Sexuality remains basically foreign to the "intention-tool-thing" relationship. It is a surviving example of noninstrumental immediacy. The body to body relationship—or better, person to flesh to flesh to person—remains basically nontechnical. As soon as attention is drawn to and settles on the technique of adjustment or the technique of sterility, the charm is broken.

Lastly, whatever one may say of its equilibrium in marriage, Eros is not institutional. One offends it by reducing it to a contract, to a conjugal duty. Its natural bond does not allow itself to be analyzed into a duty-debt. Its law, which is no longer law, is the reciprocity of the gift. In that respect it is infrajuridical, parajuridical, superjuridical. Thus by its very essence it must threaten the institution with its demonism—any institution, including marriage. Love, such as our culture has fashioned it, walks between two abysses: restless desire, and a hypocritical wish for constancy—a harsh caricature of fidelity.

Happy and rare is the meeting, in living fidelity, between Eros, impatient with all rules, and the institution which man cannot maintain without sacrifice.

7

Sleeping like Spoons: A Question of Embodiment

JOHN GILES MILHAVEN

THE PHILOSOPHER'S QUESTION

The other evening, I held forth to my friend Fergal, poet, farmer, and family man, on recent erotic poetry by women, such as Audre Lorde, Alice Walker, Adrienne Rich, Susan Griffin, Judy Grahn, Maya Angelou, Erica Jong, and Marge Piercy. Over beer and chips, I expounded my view that writing like this helps a Christian philosopher like me. . . . The poems illustrate what is true of much more than sexual love. . . . Human love of all sorts is bodily. . . . In all sorts of love, the bodily is precious for its own sake. . . . Christian thinkers from the beginning and still today neglect this truth.

They may not seem to neglect it. For decades now, "body" has been "in." What Christian today would not declare that the human body is good? But, said I to Fergal, it is applied chiefly to the esoteric and aesthetic. When I hear praise of the bodily, the speaker or writer usually goes on to give as illustration forms of meditation or diet or exercise or spending time in nature or art appreciation or art creation. What of the ordinary bodiliness of most human lives above the poverty line? I hear little of this. Are there not values here a Christian might tend to neglect and should appreciate more?

True, all Christians discoursing today on sex affirm the goodness of the bodily in making love. But it is, for the most part, an unexamined slogan. None whom I have read identifies what is so good about this bodiliness itself, what makes it peculiarly valuable for its own sake. Even those who denounce a "dualistic" view of sex go on usually to see the sexual value of the bodily, not in itself, but in expressing something else, some deeper or higher value. For them, the bodily is good not for itself but because it expresses the personal.

Why then do lovers—spouses, for instance—happily and wisely will bodily excitement and satisfaction for its own sake, and not just for what it may express and serve? What is there in this turbulent, fleshy need and in this opaque, overwhelming pleasure that God sees is good? Could it be that this bodily tumult not only expresses the personal but is itself precious because it is peculiarly personal?

I cannot find ethicists who inquire in a coherent, sustained way: What is the bodily in making love? What are the bodily feelings here? Writers call "bodily" the sexual values they affirm, but could not an angel experience what they go on to describe? Pioneering Christian ethicists, such as James Nelson, Karen Lebacqz, and Andre Guindon, have begun a phenomenology of the bodily in sex, but they have only begun.

My point—I gestured vigorously to the patient Fergal—is not sex. But by neglecting the bodily in sex and elsewhere, ethicists bypass a great good. They detour around commonplace, vulgar, precious human eros. Praising it vaguely, they look away from its peculiar nature and value. From Griffin, Rich, Lorde, Dorothy Dinnerstein, and Haunani-Kay Trask, I have started to learn how consistently our civilization pushes our eros out of our sight. Our loss is disastrous.

As these writers illustrate in poetry and explicate in prose, the eros that makes good sex is the same eros that makes all good love in human life. Good sexual lovemaking simply exemplifies it vividly. Sex is only one helpful paradigm for eros. These writers are right, I cried, and with the great mystical theologian of Christian East and West, Dionysius the Areopagite, I "dare to affirm" that God is eros. All movements of creatures to unite with each other and, harmoniously, each in its own way, to rise toward God are nothing but their sharing of divine eros. The sacrificial, giving love, the Christian agape, is just another side of eros.

Our eros, therefore, is usually not sexual. But good sex suggests how the rest of our eros is also thoroughly bodily, and its bodiliness is thoroughly personal. In all eros, I submit, the bodily does not merely express the personal. It is personal: intrapersonal and interpersonal.

And I went on to Fergal: this raises the question that I am struggling with: But how? *How* in our experiences of good bodily eros, sexual and otherwise, is the physical personal? I want a general phenomenology of eros, more explicit and systematic than my female teachers offer. The congenial writings of Matthew Fox, Tom Driver, Sam Keen, and Charles Davis fall far short, it seems to me. I am ready to attempt the phenomenology myself, but first, I must listen further to individual, concrete experiences of eros. I need to reread the sexually erotic poems of women. But much more, I need accounts of individual erotic experience that is not sexual. The recent lecture by my teaching assistant, Diana Cates, on the erotic nature of her two home births, instructed me greatly.

I'm looking for something like Suzanne Miller's essay here, said I to Fergal, but not sexual. I held out to Fergal my copy of *Pleasures: Women Write Erotica*,[1] with a marker at Miller's "Awakening." If you think of anything, let me know.

Fergal nodded, took the book, changed the subject, and a week later passed me the following:

FERGAL'S REPLY

In the essay you gave me, Miller reports that a "familiar yet ever unexpected gesture" of her husband, sleeping in bed with her, continues to move her. "Elliot's hand comes to immediate and reassuring rest upon the small of my back, as it unfailingly does when he lies next to me as I stir into awakening." Suzanne Miller, before going on to describe her experience of this gesture and its aftermath, remarks that she and Elliot "don't sleep like spoons."

That made me stop. Julie, my wife, and I sleep like spoons. Not every night, nor the whole night when we do. Not in the hot weather. But in the cool and cold weather most of the time. We do it automatically, taking it for granted, hardly deciding. Our minds are on sleep and this is the way we sleep.

A spy, peering at us, would be amused at our danse militaire. When during the night one wakes and turns, so does the other, both hitching then to maximal touching. If we were both facing the wall, we both now face the window, still snugly fitting into each other. Sometimes one leads. Sometimes the other. It must look comic since I'm a scarecrow and Julie is short and plump.

I try, in what follows, to describe just what I feel in spoon-sleeping, though I have always presumed Julie feels the same. She has read what follows and says it's pretty much her experience, "if I understand what you're saying." But when I say what "we both feel," it's only what *I* feel we feel. You can talk to Julie if you want.

My experience of spoon-sleeping lasts a matter of seconds. I go to sleep immediately when we close together. I curl around Julie (or vice versa), feel her warm, silk heaviness with mine, and yield to sleep, scarcely knowing I do. I am amazed, when I start to describe this brief bit of routine, how many things I feel.

Some of what I feel, I would call "erotic." Betty Miller, in *On the Side of the Angels*, identifies the moment when Claudia, after long resistance to the advances of a man she hardly knows and neither likes nor respects, is overcome by feeling for him. They are sitting by a stream. He embraces her. She stiffens in resistance. He considers her, bends over her, kisses her. "The resistance went out of her, momentarily he had her full weight on his arm." That is something like I feel when I curl up with Julie. The resistance goes out of me. The bed has my full weight on it. The nothingness of sleep has my full weight on it. All of me falls. Nothing holds back.

Why do I call it erotic? It is not sexual, at least not in a genital sense. It seems to be love of sleep rather than love of Julie. Or love of self? It is a blissful giving way by bodily self to itself. A sweetness of complete relaxing, of luxurious letting go of muscles, skins, nerves, and all. An effortless, sensuous shedding of all concerns, worries, even thoughts. I am the kind of man who can't eat, drink, make love, play, or anything without simultaneously thinking about it. But as I slope down with Julie to sleep, thoughts float off. I don't think. I enjoy. I enjoy myself.

It's hard to describe since it lasts only seconds and I scarcely notice it happening. The bliss is not just in the losing of tension, concerns, thoughts, etc. Voluptuous fullness takes over me. I am filled by the pleasure of swelling desire and the pleasure of desire collapsing into satisfaction. Gluttonous, needy, triumphant desire of the enveloping darkness.

It makes no sense when I think about it. How does unconsciousness appear so desirable to me that I dive into it with abandon? I know of course that my biological nature forces sleep on me so my body can rest and replenish its forces. But I am not conscious of this as Julie and I curl together. I just blissfully need and want to fall blissfully asleep. And do. There is no sense to it. Nor should there be, that I can think of.

I relish even more the deliciousness of it when we wake during the night. "What time it is?" I whisper, who see little without glasses. Some hours left. We turn, staying joined. Sometimes I fall back asleep instantly. Other times I hold a moment. Weighed down with sleep, I anticipate the joy of giving in totally. I savor the moment, and then plunge with lusty, incredulous will. It is unbelievable that it is all right for me to yield totally to his languor. Sometimes—you may find this hard to believe—I murmur, "God is good!"

Falling asleep is not the most intense pleasure I experience in my life, but it is relatively rare inasmuch as it is complete pleasure. I mean: pure pleasure. I have pleasure and nothing else. Nothing else on my mind. No subsequent letdown or restlessness. A perfection of pleasure.

Occasionally I am alone when I fall asleep this way. It happened last Friday in the upper field as I rested after lunch. I stretched out and in a moment was riding down from the sun shining through my eyelids, down into the black abyss. I could have read my Hopkins, which I had in my sack. I could have walked in the woods as I often do. They're gorgeous this time of year. I chose sleep and my sinking was voluptuous.

You talk about "values." Those are big values in my life: poetry reading, woods walking, and falling asleep. They are important to me. Which of the three is more important? Better? Of higher value? Greater? I don't know. I can't rank them. I can't even compare them. They're very different. They each make my life more worthwhile. I live in a garden and I'm showing you three of the flowers.

As usual, you will ask, "Why?" Why is this banal, run-of-the-mill falling to sleep so precious to you? I answer, as usual, "I don't know." Well, perhaps I know a bit of what I feel. As I slide into oblivion, I seem to rejoin a hidden part of myself. I enter into a strain of my life that is inaccessible to me most of the time. I come upon and hug an old friend. I greet me as I meet me, for that fleeting instant. As I fade out, I feel larger in life. I feel more whole, more one.

Falling asleep with myself, I call an erotic experience! How much more erotic is falling asleep with Julie! This is a plain fact of experience. But, as I try to anticipate your philosophical questions, it becomes mysterious. For my going to sleep glued to Julie is obviously centered on myself.

Through my head flow unchecked thoughts, arising from my day just past. I have no idea what thoughts go through Julie's head. I think mainly of my going to sleep, and only peripherally, if at all, of Julie's. As thoughts vanish and I slip gladly into the quicksand, Julie is out of my mind.

And yet. And yet. Friday's nap by the field was exceptional. Rarely do I fall to sleep so easily and voluptuously without Julie. Not always as spoons. We, too, know that touch of the hand Suzanne and Elliot know. But if Julie's not there, it takes me close to an hour to fall asleep, as it did before I married and in the first years of marriage.

Only lying in touch with Julie can I count on getting swiftly that kinesthetic sense of security in sliding down. The heavy, sweet sleep I seep into is my sleep, not hers, but it is rarely so quickly overpowering as on feeling Julie and forgetting her. What takes over me that I drift so surely, so languorously, so complacently into that invisible vortex? What brings about this quick fading of all fears? This crass confidence in free fall?

I don't understand how it comes about. Julie and I are fearful persons. She is not—not when we go to sleep anyway—a protective parent for me. Nor I for her. But when we curl together at the end of the long day, the air becomes too thick for fears to penetrate. Our feeling each other is not only sensual pleasure, but sensual trust. Wrapped together in our bodily trust we slide into the abyss. Nothing bad can happen right now, we fondly feel.

Whence our complacency? Obvious: from our knowing we're together, going to sleep. Nothing dramatic. Routine we don't pay attention to. We're tired together. We go together to sleep. I don't think it's true to say: we sleep together. We each sleep our private sleep. But it is true: We go together to sleep. And often during the night we come together out of sleep and go back in together.

Spoon-sleeping in not an I-Thou relation. I do not "encounter" Julie—that favorite verb of yours. Julie and I go together to encounter sleep. During the night, we may wake and bob up, luxuriously relishing each other, and then bob down again with common will and desire. It is a we-relation. Is it irrelevant that in body we do not face each other, but ride on each other's back?

I don't think of Julie as I go off to sleep. She's not in my mind. But she's in my legs, torso, and arms. Not in my head. Without thinking of it, I know her there going to sleep like me. I know her knowing me the same way. This must be why that trust rises swiftly and fills us. We're together though our minds are elsewhere. We know each other letting go, giving in to sleep. We . . . we . . . we . . . I don't know. That is all I can think of for now. I'm getting to the heart of it but I'm tired out. Writing for philosophers is exhausting.

You said you want in your writing and teaching to make clear the valuable things of human lives. Well, sleeping like spoons with Julie is one of mine. When

I drive out on a morning in my tractor, I feel rich. Part of that feeling is the dimming memory of last night's sleep.

The memory is only one of many riches, "values" if you will. I am a rich man. If, by some permanent ailment of one of us, Julie and I had to sleep in separate beds for the rest of our lives, I'd sure miss it. But I'd still be rich. Just to point to some of the larger coffers: I have countless other ways of being with her, countless ways of being with our kids, countless ways of being with our land, friends, a nice pregnant daughter-in-law, health, house, weather, some material security. I could go on.

It remains true that sleeping like spoons with Julie is a jewel I have and softly hold. This banal, undramatic, scarcely attended to, monotonously recurring moment of my life is one I feel happiest about and proudest of when I think of it. No. I feel happy and proud of it all the time, whether I think of it or not. Why? I leave it to you philosophers to answer. Sip and savor my vin ordinaire with your conceptual spoons.

NOTE

1. Lonnie Barbach, ed., *Pleasures: Women Write Erotica* (New York: Harper & Row, 1984).

8

The Sexuality of Jesus and the Human Vocation

JOAN H. TIMMERMAN

The perfecting of human love has always been recognized as a goal of religion. It is markedly so when a religion, such as Christianity, affirms the vocation to love as the primary way of identifying with the creative, redemptive, and transformative activity of the divine. Theologies of Jesus as the Christ and the Christ as God would be expected to emphasize love as the path of imitation of Christ. What is surprising is that the love modeled by the archetypal figure of Christ should emphasize the commitments of parent and neighbor to the practical exclusion of conjugal, erotic love. Of course such preferences can be explained historically. My point here is that to appeal to the life of the historical Jesus to ground such a preference is mistaken.

The humanity of Jesus, like femininity and masculinity, is constructed by us as a cultural symbol. Those things which reflect the aspirations of our own ways of being human are included; those things which incorporate the confusions and conflicts we wish to reject are left out. This need not, indeed could not, be a reflective, intentional process, but nonetheless there is evidence that the affirmation "Jesus Christ is truly human" has shifting content. Its content depends on the adequacy of the anthropological assumptions that underlie its doctrinal formulation. Edward Schillebeeckx has written that our problem with developing an adequate Christology is not that we do not know enough about God, but that we do not know enough about what it means to be human.

When the classical descriptions of Jesus' manhood were formulated, it was in line with the conventional dualistic model, biased in favor of the concept of rationality in Greek thought. It was unthinkable to include in normative humanity those things associated with women, connectedness, vulnerability, immersion in nature. Today a hundred-and-eighty-degree turn has been made: any formulation about the human which fails to take into account the experience of women is simply wrong: it represents not the normatively human but the male; it is vitiated because it is the partial pretending to be the universal. There is, of course, also the problem of anachronism, for each age attempts to read its own preferred values into the image of the God-man.[1] So Jesus has been cast as one of the desert hermits, as a royal ruler of the imperial kingdom, as a bishop shepherding the flock, as a divine physician healing plague-stricken victims, as a reformer cleansing old institutional forms, as the divine teacher of conventional morality, as the liberator, urging people to claim their intrinsic dignity, and of course as the supreme celibate who, free of all concupiscence, was never even tempted to intercourse with women. All of this is of course appropriate to a mythic, paradigmatic figure. Only when formulated as if it were to be taken as revelation of the full and literal God-willed way of being human, and, as such, becomes the object of faith, only then does it become oppressive. The mythic becomes pernicious when it is understood and applied literally. That many take the belief statements of the past with regard to Jesus' sexuality as literally true and absolutely founded was demonstrated dramatically, if ridiculously, when the film *The Last Temptation of Christ* was released. The presence of a sequence of scenes wherein Jesus loved and married a woman who bore his children and lived the life of a householder was widely regarded as obscene and blasphemous, even though the scenes were presented as the content of a hallucination.

The doctrine of faith, the formulated content of revelation, is that Christ is fully human and fully divine. The belief statements, written or unwritten, regarding what kind of sexual fulfillment full humanity entailed in Jesus, or in us, are subject to change. They are formulated according to historical and cultural insights and limitations, and to pretend otherwise is to mistake the words of men for the Word of God. Anyone sensitive to his own life knows that the experiences of loneliness, doubt, powerlessness, and fear have a different character when they are filtered through adult sexual awareness. To exclude on principle both this pleasure and this pain from Jesus' human life seems an impoverishment indeed. The greater impoverishment of course is ours. The precise function of the Holy Spirit, given by the risen Jesus to the community he left, was to lead that community continuously into deeper and fuller knowledge of Christ. The Spirit has only just begun to speak to the churches about the sexuality of Jesus. Why? Because just as our appreciation of his humanity is dependent on our insight into our own, so is our acceptance of his sexuality conditional upon our esteem for our own. The incarnation, in a real sense, is not complete until the community of people discovers God disclosed in their own humanity; just so, an element of Christology is lacking until we can allow ourselves to formulate images of Jesus entering as deeply into the passion of his sexuality as we have done regarding the passion of his suffering.

There have, it seems, been moments of such insight in the history of ideas. Leo Steinberg, an art historian, has defended the thesis that much Renaissance painting and sculpture, both Italian and Northern, had its inspiration in the theological thesis that Jesus assumed a humanity "complete in all its parts."[2] The reference to "all its parts" was a way of acknowledging explicitly Jesus' sexual anatomy and thereby the unquestionable completeness of his humanity. Paintings of the infant as well as the dead and risen Christ displayed or emphasized the genitalia of Christ for the purpose of exhibiting what might otherwise by denied. The total nudity of the child in many of the paintings had become so conventional that for most of the last four hundred years the point was missed: in each of more than two hundred depictions the focal point of the paintings' composition is an *ostentatio genitalium*, that is, a stylized gesture in which the mother points to the infant's genitals, the grandmother fondles them, or the adult Christ himself points to or holds them in the midst of his death agony. Besides the pointing and touching, there is unmistakable evidence of erection in the infant, the dying man and the risen God-man. Amazing to reviewers of Steinberg's book are neither the theological motivation nor the performance of the art depicting the sexual awareness and potency of Jesus. Rather what is perplexing is that the post-Renaissance religious community failed to have seen and understood the artists' intention in all these works of art. As the iconography of the East worked out in nonverbal form a theology of the divinity of Christ, so the Renaissance artists used bodily detail to flesh out a theology of his humanity. Why has it been so undeveloped in words? Denial seems the only explanation, and fear that the official Christology that from the sixteenth century had fallen into Docetist patterns should be protected from change. Further, a social system that considered the clandestine as the proper arena for sex could not easily support its explicit use as the warrant of wholeness. The Renaissance artist, frank about the sexual and unambivalent about its beauty, could celebrate the sexuality of Jesus. When the humanity of the God-man was out of theological fashion, how settle the doubt better than by calling attention to the Christ's physicality? The epiphany of the divinity may have been in the blinding light of the mountain of transfiguration, but the epiphany of Jesus' real humanity continues in the warm comfort of the genitals, ordinary like anyone else's.

A later age did not ask about the nude body: Is this true, good, or beautiful? but Is this seemly? It's the later age not the earlier that should have to justify itself. Up until the time of Rubens the erotic was entirely acceptable as the content of church art. From the nineteenth century on, the erotic has been judged unseemly for the house of God. This can, I think, be read as a statement by default about the superficiality of contemporary belief in the reality of the incarnation. The later age also asked anxiously, "Weren't they too preoccupied with sexuality?" demeaning the artists of the past by painting diapers on the cherubs and infants. It has been unable to apply one of the psychological insights of our time: shame, not acknowledgement, produces unhealthy preoccupation.

If the formula "Jesus is like us in all things save sin" is in fact understood popularly to mean he is like us in all things except sex, then the problem for a theology of sexuality and spiritual growth is at least clear. It is already commonplace to acknowledge that the Gospels do not address the issues of Jesus' personal lifestyle. Some would interpret this to mean that Jesus was not extraordinary in his sexual expression, and would even conclude that the absence of direct statements about his celibacy would point to the probability that he was indeed married for at least part of his life. The same position could claim further evidence by omission by pointing to the fact that Paul, when he was justifying his own celibate status, did not call upon the example of Jesus, which would have been significantly more persuasive than the arguments Paul finally hit upon (1 Cor. 7:7—"I say this by way of concession [to those who wanted to disregard the teaching about conjugal rights between husband and wife and the need for mutual consideration], not of command. I wish that all were as I myself am. But each has his own special gift from God, one of one kind and one of another").[3] An obvious reason Paul would not call upon Jesus' celibacy to authorize his own and justify an admittedly dangerous lifestyle (v. 2) could be that the tradition of Jesus' celibacy derives from later devotional rather than biblical or theological sources authoritative in the early communities. Clement of Alexandria argued that the ascetics had exaggerated and misunderstood Paul's teaching, and said that although Jesus never married, he did not intend for his human followers, in this respect at least, to follow his example: "the reason that Jesus did not marry was that, in the first place, he was already engaged, so to speak, to the church; and, in the second place, he was not an ordinary man."[4] It is evident that Clement is accepting the assumptions of his day and trying to make them coherent with contemporary needs; he is certainly not questioning the assumptions regarding marriage and asceticism. Believing Paul to be the author of both the early epistles, for example, Romans and Corinthians, and the later Pastorals, for example, Timothy and Titus, he claims, as the church does generally in its exegesis, that Paul endorsed both marriage and celibacy, teaching "self-control and continence," but nowhere excluding "self-controlled marriage." Clement rejects the view held by Tatian and others that the sin of Adam and Eve was sexual intercourse. Sexual intercourse he declares to be from nature, by which he clearly meant from God. To assume Jesus was never "tempted" sexually, and that that loaded term means he never experienced desire or arousal is simply absurd. He is not only responsive to sensuous goods, including wine, but he is actually shown in the Gospels as tempted to other sins. To use the word *temptation* with regard to natural movements of sexual response to stimuli is to assume that it, the response and the stimulus, was a result of the Fall, not part of the original goodness of created man. It would be instructive about our attitudes to use the word *tempted* to describe normal desire for food. That simple linguistic exercise would show how extended, through rigorism and asceticism, had become the range of the illicit in comparison with the licit in sexual options for the good Christian, not to mention the good Christ. Of course the conventional views of Augustine and Thomas would not have allowed Jesus either erection or masturbation.[5] Symeon the New Theologian (d. 1022) assigns distinct functions to the members of the body of Christ conceived as a figure of the church. Among these members the "thighs" stand for "those who bear within themselves the generative power of the divine ideas of mystical theology and who give birth to the Spirit of salvation on earth."[6]

The tradition that Jesus adopted celibacy, at least after his baptism and reception of the Holy Spirit, has been read by some as indicating the influence of Essenism on Christian practice. Scholars also point out the obvious, that to argue from omission is weak. On both sides, those who assume Jesus' celibacy and those who argue for a more conventional lifestyle for his time, all that can be gathered is supposition, not fact. Any historical search for the sexuality of Jesus is doomed to failure. But the issue is not really Jesus' sexuality; that does not need proof. What is needed is a new awareness in his followers. More than textual witnesses, a credible theological way of relating the sexual with the holy is needed. That is why I would hope to highlight the fact that the humanity of Jesus, as we have it, is a symbol, and a symbol that is incomplete to the point of uselessness for human life without its fully developed sexuality.[7] A student wrote out the following question, as if to speak it aloud would be unacceptable:

> If sexuality is sacred and essential to a wholly integrated human experience; if sexuality may be considered an expression of God's grace and love; and if Christ was indeed fully human, is it not appropriate to consider that perhaps Christ did not abstain from sexual activity?

After all, Jesus Christ is the point at which God and sexuality must be discussed together or forever remain separate.

VOCATION AND LIFESTYLE

The source of much of the urgency as well as the confusion on the issue of Jesus' sexuality is confusion between the notions of vocation and lifestyle. So long as the term "vocation" is used exclusively for the celibate lifestyle, a not-so-subtle demeaning of sexual activity is commonplace. By analogy, marriage, and less frequently, the chosen single life have been referred to as vocations. But that analogous use of terminology has neither cleared the confusion nor increased the sense in people of valued options. Marriage was considered in medieval times as an *officium,* an order, in the church. Vowed celibacy too is an order, that is, an institution, an endorsed and public lifestyle. These exist for the sake of the community to realize some aspect for the growth of that community. Spouses are not called to marriage, but within marriage they are called to completion of life, to union with God in co-creating, co-redeeming, and co-sanctifying activity. Priests and religious are not, precisely speaking, called to the "Evangelical" life in the sense of "Gospel living" but to the evangelical life in the sense of a life of supererogation, that is, one which commits itself to more than is required. It is within the particular definition of the lifestyle of the evangelical counsels that vowed persons are presumed to be able to find the life with God to which they feel called. The call to completion is vocation; the daily arrangements are lifestyle. Vocation is the larger category, shared by all.

Jesus is paradigm of the call to fuller humanity envisioned by Christians. Jesus then is a model of vocation, not lifestyle.

The imitation of Christ, as spiritual writers have always affirmed (even though parenthetically), is compatible with every station in life and reserved to none. Adhering to the holy one, continuing to strive to be what we are called to be, "belonging to the Lord," that is what matters above all details of daily arrangements. But Jesus is not and should not be used as a literal model to be imitated in lifestyle. His "way" is to be followed, his task of taking on mankind's cause as his own is to be accepted. To live in the same way as Jesus lived means to discover for ourselves today a way of being that corresponds effectively to what Jesus' mode of existence was in his own times. He lived his life as a man for others. He loved and served, not only those it was socially acceptable to love but also the outcasts and pariahs of his society.

A lifestyle is chosen, but only within the limitations of the larger call that the person hears. They are not unconnected, for obligatory ways of living grow out of vocation. Concrete factors, unique to the person in her place and time, affect the evolution, or sometimes the invention of an appropriate lifestyle. A student reflected on the experience of life as a call.

> Vocation is an overarching, heartfelt sense of call which inspires persons to participate in and contribute to the world. For example, an individual may respond to the call to love within the context of married or single life. Individuals may find that their experiences of love are most profound, most vital outside the norm of heterosexual relations and inside the realm of homosexual, bisexual, or even celibate living.

The division of the religious community into an elite which withdrew from the world in order to be free from the constraints of sexuality and the masses which remained embedded in the profane world of everyday society was one particularly brilliant historical solution to remaining on the horns of the dilemma (how relate sex to sanctity). The laity reproduced itself within the restrictions of church-supervised monogamy. The elite withdrew into celibacy and monasticism, recruiting members through "vocations" rather than through sexual interaction. Sexual activity, in theory at least, was the province of the laity. To order the irrational and destructive manifestations of sexual desire was one of the most important tasks of human social organization. But extreme forms of asceticism, some rejected as heretical, developed and continue to recur. Ironically the very increase in rigidity and numbers of rules could be read as a sign that the asexual life never successfully took hold as a viable ideal. The purification rituals of the Old Law, circumcision and food taboos, returned as taboos regarding sexual practices. But the priority of sexual control over sexual development was effectively established. The more appropriate priority, I argue here, is not that of restraint over indulgence but that of vocation over lifestyle. "First choose your path, then choose your partner," is one way the order of importance has been expressed. The fundamental option is vocation; the series of choices by which that option is lived out is lifestyle.

In terms of sexuality, the person's vocation is to develop toward full and integrated wholeness, the fruit of which is freedom, out of which one is able to have possession of oneself in order to give oneself fully to shared life. In his *Familiaris Consortio,* John Paul II wrote: "Creating the human race in his own image and continually keeping it in being, God inscribed in the humanity of man and woman the vocation, and thus the capacity and responsibility, of love and communion. Love is therefore the fundamental and innate vocation of every human being" (par. 11). We are constituted as sexual and spiritual, and in the particular mode of being human each is condition for the other. The norm and expectation, therefore the vocation of a human being, must be seen as toward sexual expressiveness. The form and frequency of the activity, the lifestyle, stands under the same sort of givens and guidelines that limit and enable all other human development within an interpersonal context. It will be virtuous insofar as it expresses and causes love and justice, peace and growth, joy and beauty, life that is centered and productive. The perception that abstinence from coitus defines the norm for Christian love, and that those who cannot accept omission as a norm are allowed sexual activity only for procreation, has lost its following. This is not to say that such limits, at certain times, for certain people, within certain situations are not appropriate. But that the normative human life is to be without sexual expression, development, or fulfillment is a failed concept.

Completion is the work of grace, and grace is capable of functioning within any natural structures. There must be a structure, but what form this structure will take depends on what best does the opening, the surprising, the healing at a given time. Can anyone dictate in the abstract what is the best structure for a couple in love during wartime? for refugees separated for decades from legal spouses? for lesbian women? for an incest survivor who is a single parent with a deep suspicion of men?

Consequent upon progress in the vocation to grow sexually, one does have choices between good and evil. They are choices of how and in what pattern of human relationships a person's development toward wholeness, in this real situation in which he finds himself, can best proceed. Where the individual person experiences greater coinherence with the Spirit, there lifestyle choices would be discerned as better, but better in degree not in kind, and better for the individual not for humankind. The optimum relationship for men and women in any cultural epoch must be that which best keeps them open to God's healing and saving entry into their lives. For most women, for most of history, the choice, assumed to be inevitable, between a serious spiritual and sexual life, meant acquiescence to their reproductive destiny and the internalization of the false notion that they belonged more to the flesh than the spirit, more to the husband who needed their services than to the holy God whose image they embodied. Now the revolution is entering its second, long overdue phase, when women, with a sense of the sacredness of their sexuality, claim rightful place in the sphere of Spirit.

The traditional teaching on law and grace is in keeping with the order of this dynamic. It is not the renunciatory lifestyle that produces grace, but the response to grace that takes forms sometimes of detachment and sometimes of attachment. In the history of spirituality, perhaps because it was largely written or censored by men, perhaps because of the exegetical tradition, letting go, detachment, has been interpreted to have greater intrinsic value. But the movements of the Spirit toward embodiment, engagement, of taking hold are the fruit equally of grace. Neither embracing nor renouncing sexual pleasure is in itself a state to be preferred. Both are necessary phases in the dynamic of a responsive individual or institution.

A young lesbian woman, speaking to a group about the dilemma in which she lived, being Catholic in a committed lesbian relationship, cut through it all with the clarity of her evaluation: "I tried religious life at one time, but I had to leave. My experience of God comes much more strongly through human love." When lifestyle and vocation are in step, confidence glows; life is luminous.

Discernment

Discernment, a skill intensified as a gift, is important for people trying to make good faith choices regarding lifestyle. Whatever its content, a lifestyle conducive to spiritual growth will be characterized by a number of qualities, including progress toward personal freedom, increased capacity for intimacy, and an environment in which ecstasy is possible.

Progress toward personal freedom might be recognized, not so much by autonomy as by interdependence. Its opposite is addictive behavior, sometimes described in psychological terms as compulsion or obsession. The scriptural reference might be Paul's declaration against excessive dependence on the Law: "For God has called us to peace. . . . Only, let every one lead the life which the Lord has assigned to him, and in which God has called him" (1 Cor. 7:15, 17). This is the effective spiritual criterion that has led many a woman to reject a previous lifestyle, for example, a patriarchal marriage in which roles of domination and submission were lived out, for an autonomous lifestyle.

> The single most important life experience concerning my sexuality was when I admitted to myself how unhappy I was sexually and made the decision to work through my fears and rage in hopes of finding a sexuality of my own. This was a huge decision for my life. I separated from the man I had desperately committed myself to when I was fourteen, I lost friends that couldn't understand what I was doing and I enraged my family for not going along with what has been expected. . . . Happily, I am learning what feels healthy and right for me sexually, I have choices.

Whatever its difficulties, including loss of financial support and spousal companionship, divorce has been perceived by some as a move that is necessary for the salvation of their personhood, their "souls." A significant number of men have also invoked this criterion to leave the celibate lifestyle required by the Roman Catholic priesthood to carry out what they recognized to be larger vocations as human beings. Leaps of faith and steps in spiritual progress are made daily by men and women who change jobs, professions, habits ingrained over long periods of time, because they recognize in them a bondage that prevents integration and full self-possession. There is some evidence that, in our time, the preoccupation with sex that takes people away from their vocation to wholeness is more the result of false guilt, poor self-understanding and self-acceptance, artificial stimulation through media images and general lack of balance in the ordering of life than it is of intentional bodily expression of excess sexual passion. The use of sex is a relative value; the lack of use of sex is a relative value. Neither is to have power over the person. Both are powers of the person. These are lifestyle choices within the absolute (though ambiguous) mandate of the vocation to human becoming. Yet in the performance of the sexual choices of daily life, I reveal more than this or that particular and relative thing about my lifestyle. In choices, such as who and how to touch, where and with whom to be intimate, when and why to refuse the gift of presence, I create connections with the Absolute. More than my way of being teacher, lover, aunt is at stake. What is actually composed day by day is myself as a person in entirety, a vocation. At the same time as I know pleasure in a friend, there is ecstasy in the Spirit; my being there for my students is a performance also of my "belonging to Christ"; and while having fun with nieces and nephews, I know what it is to play in the sight of the Lord of the universe. My vocation is a robe woven by way of my lifestyle; I am not called out of my lifestyle into a vocation.

In a Christian theology of the discernment of a call there are a number of elements. The person always has some sort of inner experience of call. Practically speaking this might be no more than an internalized sense of one's religious or spiritual identity. For Christian theology, it is an inner experience decisively begun in the externally visible event of baptism, explicitly affirmed as having taken hold in confirmation, and continually deepened and integrated into daily life through frequent liturgical celebration of the eucharist. For once-born personalities, to use the intriguing concept formulated by William James,[8] there may be no single dramatic moment associated with the experience of inner call, but it is known nonetheless to be real when reclaimed reflectively. For twice-born personalities, the call, as well as the experiences of infidelity and reconciliation to it, may be quite dramatic. Stories of conversion are stories of vocation recognized. When those stories can be told, a milestone has been reached in the spiritual life.

In addition to the inner experience of call, a theology of discernment requires objective evidence that the person has the ability to meet its practical demands. A "call" can be tracked as a continuous line between the divine energy and this particular individual, but the fulfillment of the call requires human credibility. Joan of Arc was able to complete what she perceived to be asked of her by God's voices also because she had considerable military genius and was able to gain credibility with the troops she was called to lead. We are called within our personal situation to a human way of being. Whoever wants to affirm the accuracy of their inner sense of call, must look to what is given in their intelligence, character, circumstances, opportunities, as verified by someone outside themselves. I can be absolutely sure I am not called to parenthood in a physical sense if I am physically incapable of conceiving or carrying a fetus to term. Not my natural limitations but my tendency to settle for less than I can achieve when enhanced by the Spirit are transcended in the notion of vocation. The Spirit drives out fear, self-hatred, small-mindedness, narcissim. I may not always know at the outset what is attainable from what is beyond me, but that only serves to reemphasize the point: only that can be required of me for which I have the necessary qualities and conditions.

A third point in the theology of vocation insists that the specification of the call be affirmed by others in the community. Some kind of credentialing, formal or informal, through ritual or by the literal undergoing of transformation through illness or trauma is likely always to be associated with the discernment of vocation. Here emerges one of the crucial points in human development. The peculiar inequities of vision and power have produced situations in which only some within the human community are presumed capable of a spiritual life. The greatest sin against our own sexuality and that of others has been the blindness which has prevented us in general and the lack of love which has prevented us in particular from affirming in each other the call to love God by becoming as fully loving sexual human beings as possible. The inexplicability of it all is demonstrated through a number of institutional power issues.

For no apparent good reason, many Catholics are left for years "outside the church" because of a second marriage after divorce, which the official community did not recognize, in fact which it condemned as living in sin. For easily apparent poor reasons, marginalized groups have been rejected even from the act of worship because their sexual orientation or practice was considered deviant, among them gay men and lesbian women, divorced and remarried persons, those who support women's responsible ownership of their own reproductive capacity, especially if they are politically active for a pro-choice position. If persons, Christian or otherwise, do not live their sexual lives as vocation, it is at least partly due to the lack of this third requirement: they have not been called by the community to do so; moreover, in some instances they have been actively prevented from so doing.

Intimacy

A second criterion by which any lifestyle could be measured as compatible with vocation is intimacy. The capacity for intimacy, which I will define as the experience of being wholly and deeply touched by others, is a mark of maturity and a fruit of the Spirit. It involves an awareness of one's own depths, along with the recognition that feelings are not in themselves suspect. Feelings are always good, always to be accepted as normal. Acceptance of feelings enables a person to be intimate with herself in moments of solitude. Otherwise, she tends to become anonymous to herself, to have no inner life.

I have been monogamous all my life, but have achieved intimacy only when I was willing to risk sharing my emotions and only when the man I was with was willing to accept me and also willing to share himself. . . . I don't believe that most people open themselves up to each other the first time they meet. The experience didn't happen to me until a time when I was comfortable enough with myself to be myself and to share that person with someone else. When I learned to accept and love the person I am, I could be that person with someone else without fear of rejection. I could go into a relationship saying in effect, this is who I am. If you like who I am that's fine; and if you don't, that's fine, too. In former relationships my partner and I didn't seem to be able to allow each other the time to explore and discover ourselves. There's a certain amount of self-awareness that can only be learned over a period of time, I believe. Some people are able to learn and grow together and some aren't.

Those who deny their bodies and their feelings, thinking that the real self is the mental subject, are never wholly available. Some part, the vital, spontaneous part, is always under constraint. Touch is always feared. An aspect of mystery, interpersonal mystery, is forever closed to them because it is revealed through reciprocal attention to our male and female bodies. This absence from one's own emotional self has been called repression. As a habitual state of being, it has consequences not just for self-intimacy but for shared intimacy.[9] Repressed persons must avoid personal situations, for such situations always hold the possibility of a tender moment, and tenderness leads to danger. They anxiously scan the social horizon to insure that no one violates their sacred space. They are intolerant of the intimacies of others even as they revel in seeking them out for condemnation. They glare at sexual expressions but do not permit themselves to see anything that expresses human sexuality positively. They are alienated and hostile to play and self-expression. Insisting on governing all relationships, they fall into considering "illicit" those which they themselves have not permitted. How absurd this can become was illustrated recently by the director of a Center for Fitness and Wholistic Living who questioned a group for going on an "unauthorized" hike. Repressed persons are especially dangerous in positions of authority. For many cultures, the capacity for intimacy is a mark of mature leadership. It might well become a key indicator for readiness for religious or political candidates for leadership at this time in the technologically developed cultures when know-how is less rare than relatedness. No one skill or structure, including a monogamous relationship, is able to guarantee intimacy. It is developed more than chosen, and its presence in a person's relationships is more a sign of the stage of development of the persons involved than a function of a particular framework.

Ecstasy

As important as intimacy to test the rightness of a lifestyle, so is the availability of moments of ecstasy. Excitement, adventure, being beside oneself with feeling are not luxuries but are the essential integrators of human life. Ecstasy is the experience of the temporary dissolution of boundaries. The moment, and it is always momentary, is one in which some otherwise distant reality is glimpsed as here and now, one with oneself. The "unitive glimpse" is capable of completely reorganizing a life, a fact to which the accomplishments of many a mystic point. More often, we hear about the accomplishments but are unaware of the ecstatic moments at their source, until allowed through an autobiography or journal to gain insight into a process that is always creative and revolutionary. But the ecstatic moment recreates the personality as well as introducing new insights, inventions, and lives into the universe. When the boundaries re-form, it is never with quite the same configuration as before. Scientists concerned to understand the chemistry and motivation of human drug use tell us that it is not only human beings who experience, indeed create situations in which they can experience, an altered state of consciousness. There is no mammal who does not try by some means, physical or chemical, to alter its state of consciousness. Small animals twirl around in circles or mimic attack and escape patterns, presumably to stimulate release of varying levels of drive chemistry. The command center in the human brain, known as the hypothalamus, releases varying levels of epinephrine (once called adrenalin); dopamine, a very powerful pleasure substance; endorphins, recently discovered reward substances; and serotonin, a substance associated with sleep or rest. These natural biochemicals can be mimicked by the use of alcohol, heroin, opiates, and various depressants or stimulants. Research has shown that it is probable that the hypothalamus is suggestible and programmable. This only confirms empirically what religious liturgies have always understood intuitively and incorporated into worship. Current research suggests that chemical dependency and eating disorders are the result of a drive process gone awry. This happens when a substance (alcohol, drugs, food) begins to mimic natural reward, and reward reshapes the drive. During the process of romantic love, the substance phenylethylamine has been discovered in human beings. Sex is rewarded by dopamine, norepinephrine, and endorphins which produce powerful pleasure rewards after sex. In a similar way, but with a different intensity, serotonin and other biochemical elements may reward rest, also called sexual "afterglow." These behaviors are reinforced by the command center and are necessary for the continuation of life and the human species.[10] Therefore it is suggested by some researchers that so-called sexual addictions, like chemical addiction or eating disorders, is a drive process in disarray. Individuals who abstain from one mood altering substance which might in fact mimic the natural biochemicals the body produces may seek a similar mood-altered state produced biochemically through sex. In such a theory it is not the substance (sex, food, alcohol) addicted individuals are dependent upon, but they are dependent physically and psychologically on the mood-altered state provided by the biochemicals released in the human body during the sex act. Further research may ultimately provide additional answers to managing the body's ability to provide altered states of consciousness. For this consideration of sexuality and spirituality, it is already clear that here is something that is clearly symbolic of the unity of body and mind. Persons' freedom with regard to ecstatic experience in relation to their overall well-being is a spiritual concern. Compulsions destroy lives. With accurate information, with growth toward the ability to make and live with choices, and with the support of an involved community, individuals can ultimately be empowered to choose to cease behaviors that may be causing harm in their lives. But never should the specter of abuse and addiction in particular lives overshadow the promise of ecstasy in a union based on the joy of free and mutual love. When genital feelings are properly cultivated, tenderness, lived out as respectful affection, can be the transforming and exhilarating result. For adults, genital feelings are a primary source of ecstatic experiences. Intellectual, aesthetic, and religious intimations of union are also part of a full human life. Any lifestyle that is so constituted as to prevent peak experiences, one that fits so poorly that in it an individual has no room to know the excitement of newness, leaves little room for spiritual growth.

NOTES

1. On the ways in which different generations and cultures have appropriated Jesus for their own times: Jaroslav Pelikan, *Jesus Through the Centuries: His Place in the History of Culture* (New Haven: Yale University Press, 1985).

2. Leo Steinberg, *The Sexuality of Christ in Renaissance Art and in Modern Oblivion* (New York: Pantheon Books, 1983).

3. On 1 Corinthians 7 as interpretation of what matters above all: See Josef Fuchs, *Christian Morality: The Word Becomes Flesh,* trans. Brian McNeil (Washington, D.C.: Georgetown University Press, 1987), 84–101. Fuchs shows Paul as answering those in Corinth who believed the Christians should change their normal lifestyle: ". . . each should live the life which the Lord has assigned to him, and in which God has called him. This is my rule in all the churches" (v. 17), and Fuchs comments: "One who believes that, as a Christian, he must alter his lifestyle, has not yet grasped that it is belonging to Christ that matters, and that in comparison to this any particular lifestyle is simply not important" (p. 84). Verse 7, especially the phrase *per indulgentiam* or *per veniam*, was interpreted by St. Augustine not as concession, but as forgiveness, and implied for him that where forgiveness is required sin must exist. It follows that when married people come together in order to escape the danger of fornication, rather than because of procreation—which was for Augustine the only aim of marital union—there necessarily exists (at least venial) sin. This understanding of St. Augustine, based on questionable exegesis, determined the Christian teaching on marriage for many centuries. It gave relatively few married people the chance to belong wholly to the Lord (p. 87).

4. For Clement's discussion: *Stromata 3,* 49, in *Alexandrian Christianity,* vol. 2, 40–92, in The Library of Christian Classics, trans. J. Oulton and H. Chadwick (Philadelphia: Westminster Press, 1954).

5. Augustine, *The City of God Against the Pagans,* Book XIV, XXIII in Loeb Classical Library, IV, trans. Philip Levine (Cambridge, Mass.: Harvard University Press, 1966), 379–85; Thomas Aquinas, *Summa Theologica 3,* q. 14, a. 4; q. 15, a. 2, in *Summa Theologica,* vol. 2 (New York: Benziger, 1947), 2104, 2106.

6. Symeon the New Theologian: *Ethical Treatises* 1, 6; in Wainwright, Geoffrey, "Types of Spirituality." In *The Study of Spirituality,* ed. Cheslyn Jones, Geoffrey Wainwright, and Edward Yarnold, S. J. (New York: Oxford University Press, 1986), 241.

7. I am aware that this assertion contradicts the position elaborated by Michel Foucault, who wrote: "We are often reminded of the countless procedures which

Christianity once employed to make us detest the body; but let us ponder all the ruses that were employed for centuries to make us love sex, to make the knowledge of it desirable and everything said about it precious. . . . These devices are what ought to make us wonder today. Moreover, we need to consider the possibility that one day, perhaps, in a different economy of bodies and pleasures, people will no longer quite understand how the ruses of sexuality . . . were able to subject us to that austere monarchy of sex" (*History of Sexuality,* vol. 1, 159). He finds not "liberation" but enslavement in the explicitation of sexual symbols. Perhaps in another situation I would agree. For the present, the absence of sexual referents in religious symbols is indeed one of the factors that account for women undervaluing their own being. (See Foucault, Michel. *The History of Sexuality. Vol. 1, An Introduction.* (New York: Random House, 1978).)

8. Once-born and twice-born personality types are described in *The Varieties of Religious Experience,* ed. Martin E. Marty (New York: Penguin Books, 1982), 80, 139–44, 239 n. 2. People of the former personality type are those for whom adjustments to life have been straightforward and whose lives have been more or less a peaceful flow from the moment of their births. The twice-borns, on the other hand, have not had an easy time of it. Their lives are marked by a continual struggle to attain some sense of order. Unlike the once-borns, they cannot take things for granted. According to James, these personalities have different world views. For a once-born personality, the sense of self, as a guide to conduct and attitude, derives from a feeling of being at home and in harmony with one's environment. For a twice-born, the sense of self derives from a feeling of profound separateness. A sense of belonging becomes practically significant when individuals see themselves as perpetuating and strengthening existing institutions. They are in harmony with ideals of duty and responsibility. The sense of self flows easily to and from the outer world. Those who seek out or initiate change tend to be twice-born personalities, people who feel separate from their environment, including other people. They may work in organizations, but never belong to them. Their sense of who they are does not depend upon memberships, work roles, or other social indicators of identity. They search out ways to profoundly alter human relationships.

9. Thomas Tyrell, *Urgent Longing: Reflections on the Experience of Infatuation, Human Intimacy, and Contemplative Love* (Whitinsville, Mass.: Affirmation Books, 1980), 52.

10. On the biochemistry of pleasure: Ron Rosenbaum, "The Chemistry of Love," *Esquire* 101/6 (June 1984) 100–111.

9

While Love Is Unfashionable: Ethical Implications of Black Spirituality and Sexuality

TOINETTE M. EUGENE

Black spirituality and black sexuality, properly understood as aspects of the holistic life-style of Afro-American women and men, are a closer fit than hand and glove. Nonetheless, taken together these issues also represent two of the most serious ethical challenges that the contemporary black church must address.

We must acknowledge at the outset a widespread and well-known experience within the black community. Michelle Wallace, among others, agrees that experience of distrust has driven a wedge between black women and black men:

> For perhaps the last fifty years there has been a growing distrust, even hatred between black men and black women. It has been nursed along, not only by racism on the part of whites, but by an almost deliberate ignorance on the part of blacks about the sexual politics of their experience in this country.[1]

This basic distrust between black women and black men accounts for the inability of the black community to mobilize as it once could and did. The religious aspect of *black sexuality,* by which I mean the basic dimension of our self-understanding and way of being in the world as black male and female persons, has been distorted into a form of black sexism. Because of this basic distrust, the beauty of black sexuality, which also includes our sex-role understandings, our affectional orientations, physiological arousal and genital activity, and our capacity for sensuousness, has become debilitated. The power of black sexuality to contribute to our liberating mission to change our oppressive condition has been weakened. This basic distrust disables and distracts us as we strive to bring about the reign of God, which is a theological, as well as a political reality, for black women and black men.[2]

Theologian Jacquelyn Grant adds another significant aspect of the nexus between black spirituality and black sexuality: the effects of sexism on the kerygmatic and proclamatory mission of the black church. She insists:

> If the liberation of women is not proclaimed, the church's proclamation cannot be about divine liberation. If the church does not share in the liberation struggle of Black women, its liberation struggle is not authentic. If women are oppressed, the church cannot possibly be "a visible manifestation that the gospel is a reality"—for the gospel cannot be real in that context. One can see contradictions between the church's language or proclamation of liberation and its action by looking both at the status of Black women in the church as laity and Black women in the ordained ministry of the church.[3]

The holistic expression of black spirituality is a central part of what is at stake in liberating relationships between black women and men in the church and society.

Spirituality is no longer identified simply with asceticism, mysticism, the practice of virtue, and methods of prayer. Spirituality, i.e., the human capacity to be self-transcending, relational, and freely committed, encompasses all of life, including our human sexuality.

Specifically, Christian spirituality involves the actualization of this human transcendence through the experience of God, in Jesus the Christ, through the gift of the Spirit. Because God, Jesus, and the Spirit are experienced through body-community-history, a black Christian spirituality includes every dimension of black life. We must begin to re-employ the power of black spirituality as a personal and collective response of black women and black men to the gracious presence of the God who lives and loves within us, calling us to liberating relationships with one another and with all people on Earth.

RACISM AND SEXISM AS CRITICAL FACTORS AFFECTING THE BLACK QUEST FOR MUTUALITY

Racism and sexism, operative in our midst, are the two primary negative factors which affect black male/female relationships. Any ethical reflection on the issue of sexism in relation to racism requires a coming to terms with the suffering and oppression which have marked past pathological relationships between black women and black men. Honest reflection on the issue of sexism in relation to racism may also highlight positive aspects of the challenge and conversion available to black and believing women and men who want to deal with their own spirituality and sexuality as a means of coming to terms with a new life in God.

Jacquelyn Grant explains the effects of sexual dualism on the self-image of black people. "Racism and sexism are interrelated," she says, "just as all forms of oppression are interrelated."[4] Racism and sexism have provided a theological problem within the Christian community composed of both black women and men who theoretically are *equally* concerned about the presence of freedom and justice for all. "Sexism, however, has a reality and significance of its own because it represents that peculiar form of oppression suffered by Black women at the hands of Black men. It is important to examine this reality of sexism as it operated in both the Black Community and the Black Church."[5]

A careful diagnosis of the sickness and the sin of sexism within the black church calls forth a challenge to ministers and laity alike. The failure of the black church and of black theology itself to proclaim explicitly the liberation of black women indicates, according to this assessment, that neither theology nor the church can claim to be agents of divine liberation or of the God whom the evangelist describes as the Author and Exemplar of black love. If black theology, like the black church, has no word for black women, then its conception of liberation is inauthentic and dysfunctional.

There are two basic forms which such sexism takes in black male/female relationships: sexist and spiritualistic splits or divisions within reality.

Sexist dualism refers to the systematic subordination of women in church and society, within interpersonal relationships between males and females, as well as within linguistic patterns and thought formulations by which women are dominated.[6] Hence the term "patriarchal dualism" may be also appropriate, or more simply, the contemporary designation of "sexism" may be used. *Spiritualistic dualism* has its roots in the body-spirit dichotomy abounding in white western philosophy and culture introduced at the beginning of the Christian era. Hence, the term "Hellenistic dualism" may also be appropriate. It must be noted in offering these descriptive distinctions about sexual and spiritual dualisms that African philosophy and culture was and still is significantly different from these white western conceptualizations.[7] It is this African worldview which has given rise to the holistic potentiality residing in authentic expressions of Afro-American spirituality and sexuality today.

Sexist dualism has pathologically scarred not only the white community from which it originated but has also had its negative effect within the black religious community.[8] Sexist dualism, which has been organized along racial lines, refers to "schizophrenic" male attitudes toward women in general who are imaged as either the virgin or the whore—the polemical Mary or Eve archetype represented by the female gender. The prevailing model of beauty in the white, male-dominated American society has been the "long-haired blond" with all that accompanies this mystique. Because of this worldview, black women have had an additional problem with this pseudo-ideal as they encounter black men who have appropriated this norm as their own.

Sexist as well as racist dualisms have elevated the image of the white woman in accordance with the requirements of a white worldview into becoming the respected symbol of femininity and purity, while the black woman must represent an animality which can be ruthlessly exploited for both sex and labor. Similarly the sexist dualism present within pseudo-biblical teaching argues that *woman* is responsible for the fall of "*man*kind," and is, consequently, the source of sexual evil. This dualistic doctrine has had its doubly detrimental effect in the experience of many black women.[9]

The self-image and self-respect of many black women is dealt a double blow by both black religion and black society. Thus, black women are made to believe or at least accept on the surface that they are evil, ugly, insignificant, and the underlying source of trouble, especially when the sense of intimacy begins to break down in black love relationships.

This dualistic doctrine has nurtured a kind of compensatory black male chauvinism (as evidenced in typical black church patterns and black nationalism movements) in order to restore the "manliness" of the one who had traditionally been humiliated by being deprived (according to a white patriarchal model) of being the primary protector for his family. In such manner, sexist dualism has been a central limitation in the development of a black love which at its zenith is the most authentic expression we have of the unity of black spirituality and sexuality.

A disembodied spirituality has also been a central limitation in the development of black love. Spiritualistic dualism has been a central factor in persistent efforts to portray faithful black love as an unfashionable and hopelessly anachronistic way of establishing black liberation and black material success and achievement. Eldridge Cleaver obviously recognized the racism and sexism in this spiritualistic form of dualism. Cleaver readily identified bodily scapegoating as an aspect of the sickness within racist/sexist relationships: "Only when the white man comes to respect his own body, to accept it as part of himself will he be able to accept the black man's mind and treat him as something other than the living symbol of what he has rejected in himself."[10] Bodily scapegoating implies a discomfort with our own bodies which leads us to discredit any human body-person which differs too much in appearance and similarity from our own. This scapegoating is particularly evident in racist, white-black relationships. But it is equally obvious in the revealing and discrediting attitudes of some men, white and black, about the assumed menstrual "uncleanliness" of women, or the intrinsic "repulsiveness" of the pregnant female form.

Because blackness has long been understood as a symbol for filth as well as evil, a spiritualistic dualism prevalent in the worldview of many white persons has allowed them the racist option of projecting onto black persons any dirty or disgusting bodily feelings which they may harbor within themselves. Because of the fertility potential symbolized by the female menstrual and pregnancy cycles, a spiritualistic and sexist dualism has also been created and sustained by white and black males which has allowed them to act out their own latent anxieties and hostilities by sexually depreciating the value and worth of the black female person.

As long as we feel insecure as human beings about our bodies, we will very likely be anxious or hostile about other body-persons obviously racially or sexually different from our own embodied selves. Thus, the most dehumanizing spoken expressions of hostility or overt violence within racist and/or sexist experiences are often linked with depreciating the body or body functions of someone else. Worse yet, though, the greatest dehumanization or violence that actually can occur in racist and/or sexist situations happens when persons of the rejected racial- or gender-specific group begin to internalize the judgments made by others and become convinced of their own personal inferiority. Obviously, the most affected and thus dehumanized victims of this experience are black women.

Racism and sexism diminish the ability of black women and men to establish relationships of mutuality, integrity, and trust. Racism and sexism undermine the black communities in which we live, pray, and work out our salvation in the sight of God and one another. However, in coming to terms with racism and sexism as oppressions affecting us all, the black church does have access to the black community in ways that many other institutions do not. The black church has a greater potential to achieve both liberation and reconciliation by attending carefully to the relationships which have been weakened between black males and females.

Because the black church has access, and is often indeed the presiding and official agent in the process of sexual socialization, it has a potentially unlimited opportunity to restore the ancient covenant of Scripture and tradition which upholds the beauty of black love in its most profound meaning. Wherever black love is discouraged or disparaged as an unfashionable or unattainable expression between black women and black men, the black church has an unparalleled option to model these gospel values of love and unconditional acceptance. By offering from its storehouse an authentic understanding of black spirituality and sexuality, the black church becomes paradigmatic of the reign of God materializing and entering into our midst.

I have referred to spirituality as a commitment and life style, as the growth and response of the human personality to the beauty and benevolence of a liberating God. For black Christians in particular, the praxis of spirituality is a conscious response to the call for discipleship by Jesus. It is intimately related to the moral and ethical conviction which moves us from the private, prayerful posture of bowed head and bent knee to the public, prophetic position of proclaiming before oppressor and oppressed alike: "Thus saith the Lord of Justice. . . ."

For black Christian women and men, the importance of the spiritual life cannot be overplayed. It is what unites those of African ancestry in the possession of a distinctive *ethos*. For black Christians, our African heritage allows us to comprehend spirituality as a *Lebenswelt*—as a life-experience—as well as a worldview. Our African heritage allows us to share in a collective mindset that recognizes yet does not rigidly separate the sacred from the secular, or insist on negative, polemic (i.e., Hellenistic) distinctions about the relative merits of the ideal and actual, the body and the spirit, or the profane and the pristine.[11]

Dualisms, sexist or spiritualistic, have no place within the seamless garment of authentic black religious experience. It is this integrative understanding implicit and inherent in the Afro-American religious *Lebenswelt* that allows spirituality and sexuality to be considered together and as aspects of a holistic religious experience for black women and men in the church and society. Whatever one decides in the historical debate surrounding the actual degree of African retentions in the New World, it is certain that the black church in America has thrived on the dynamic qualities of an African spirituality. History has evidenced a faith affirmation among black religionists that indicates "both the individual and community have a continuous involvement with the spirit world in the practical affairs of daily life."[12]

A striking description of African Christian spirituality provides in summary format a black perspective:

[African Christian] spirituality is a dynamic and outgoing concept. . . . There is nothing cerebral or esoteric about spirituality; it is the core of the Christian experience, the encounter with God in real life and action. Spirituality is the same thing as continuous or experiential prayer—prayer as a living communion with God who is experienced as being personally present in the relationships of humanity. It is the mode of living, the essential disposition of the believer, and it imparts a new dimension to the believer's life. In other words, it is not only a new way of looking at human life, but a new way of living it. It is unnecessary, perhaps, to draw any sharp dividing line between theology and spirituality. Theology should be spiritual theology . . . it should not be merely speculative, but should encourage active commitment.[13]

Because of this overarching emphasis in black spirituality on human persons, relationships, and values, the black church is in a prime position to invite and reestablish in creative ways a dialogue between black women and black men. Because the black church is seen to be the driving force of the movement toward the recovery of a meaningful value system for the black community, it has tremendous potential for fostering constructive, instructive, and reconciling discussion on issues of mutuality, sexuality and spirituality for black women and men. It is obvious that the foundational theory and the theology are all in place to accomplish this dialogue, yet the praxis is still limited or lacking if we are at all honest in our reflection upon our lived experience. The recovery of a meaningful value system enriching the relationships between black women and men still remains underdeveloped, or at best only moderately achieved.

The tendency to opt for a spirituality which is unrelated to our black bodily existence or the temptation to become too heavily fixated at the level of the physical, material, or genital expressions of black love keeps us off balance and unintegrated in religiously real ways. Thus, relationships between black women and men in the black church and community still struggle to reveal that *imago Dei* of which Scripture speaks:

Then God said, "Let us make man in our image, after *our likeness*" . . . so God created . . . Male *and* female . . . (Gen. 1:26f [emphases added]).

For as many of you as were baptised into Christ have put on Christ. There is neither slave nor free, there is neither male or female; for you are all one in Christ Jesus. (Gal. 3:27f.)

It is impossible to adequately establish any Christian perspective on human sexuality without first returning to and affirming the value that God has forever made human flesh and "body-persons" the privileged place of the divine encounter with us. Perhaps, as we are able to deepen our understanding of black spirituality as an embodied, incarnational, holistic and earthy reality and gift given to us by the God who became enfleshed to dwell with us as a "body-person," we may become better at the praxis which this implies.

If God has so trusted and honored the human body by taking on a human form and accepting human sexuality as a way of entering into relationship with all humanity, how much more must we strive to imitate the model of spirituality and sexuality offered to us by the Word-Made-Flesh. God freely chose to become a body-person as we are. I am persuaded to think that many of us are simply too afraid to take ourselves that seriously and act "freely mature with the fullness of Christ himself" (Eph. 4:13).

In the process of exploring theologically how this ontological blackness points to the *imago Dei* in black humanity we are immediately referred back to the context of the feminist challenge. To theologically explore ontological blackness requires us to engage in open and nondefensive dialogue with others about creative use of sexually inclusive *language* for God as well as sexually inclusive *images* which serve to symbolize God. Although we may take great pride and satisfaction in the language and image of the phrase "God is Black," there is still a black feminist question which is appropriately raised for our consideration: "Have we simply shifted from imaging and thinking of God in white male terminology into conceiving and speaking of God as a black male figure?"

James Evans offers a straightforward reply to this concern in his article on "Black Theology and Black Feminism."

> If blackness is an ontological symbol [pointing out the *imago Dei* in humanity] then it means more than physical blackness and also more than maleness. . . . Blackness must mean the racism and liberation from it experienced by black men. It must also mean the racism/sexism and the liberation from them experienced by black women. If blackness as an ontological symbol refers to authentic humanity, then it cannot become simply a "living testament" to failure in white male/female relationships, but must point to new relationships.[14]

This consideration of new relationships between black women and black men and with a God whom we choose to image as black and as androgynous within our contemplation and conversation necessarily urges us onward in the ethical task of reintegrating and restoring the fullness of meaning to black spirituality and sexuality. The search for ways of expressing and experiencing an inclusive vision of God calls us to the task of offering and receiving black love which joins and sustains our spiritual and sexual lives in appropriate ways.

Through a deepening trust and mutuality in our relationships with God, self, and others, the expressions of black love which may seem so unfashionable or unsophisticated to the world may serve to bond black women and men even more closely together in our worst periods of trial and tribulation as well as in our best moments of joy and achievement.

NOTES

1. Michelle Wallace, *Black Macho and The Myth of Superwoman* (New York: Dial Press, 1979), 13.

2. See J. Deotis Roberts, *A Black Political Theology* (Philadelphia: Westminster Press, 1974), for further explanation of the reign of God as both a theological and political reality.

3. Jacquelyn Grant, "Black Theology and the Black Woman," in *Black Theology: A Documentary History, 1966–1979,* ed. Gayraud Wilmore and James H. Cone (Maryknoll, N.Y.: Orbis Books, 1979), 423.

4. Grant, "Black Theology and the Black Woman," 422.

5. Ibid.

6. James B. Nelson has made extensive use of the concepts of "sexist and spiritualistic dualism" in *Embodiment: An Approach to Sexuality and Christian Theology* (New York: Pilgrim Press, 1976). See especially chap. 3. I have attempted to turn his categories into explicit reflection on black sexual experience.

7. See John Mbiti, *The Prayers of African Religion* (Maryknoll, N.Y.: Orbis Books, 1975) and *Concepts of God in Africa* (London: SPCK, 1970) for further connections made on the nexus between black spirituality and an integral worldview.

8. See Rosemary Radford Ruether, *New Women, New Earth: Sexist Ideologies and Human Liberation* (New York: Seabury Press, 1975), chap. 5.

9. Grant, "Black Theology and the Black Woman," 422.

10. Eldridge Cleaver, as quoted by Robert Bellah in *The Broken Covenant: American Civil Religion in Time of Trial* (New York: Seabury Press, 1975), 105.

11. See John Mbiti, *African Religion and Philosophy* (Garden City, N.Y.: Anchor Press, 1969), for additional emphasis on the integration of African lifestyles and value systems: epistemology and axiology.

12. Gayraud Wilmore, *Black Religion and Black Racialism* (Garden City, N.Y.: Anchor Press, 1973), 197.

13. Aylward Shorter, ed., *African Christian Spirituality* (Maryknoll, N.Y.: Orbis Books, 1978), 47.

14. James H. Evans, Jr., "Black Theology and Black Feminism," *The Journal of Religious Thought* 38 (spring-summer 1982): 52.

PART 3

Gender and Orientation

Gender Relations
Mary Stewart Van Leeuwen

Women's Experience
Beverly Wildung Harrison and Carter Heyward
Mary D. Pellauer
Mary E. Hunt

Men's Experience
Philip Culbertson
James B. Nelson
J. Michael Clark

Introduction
to Part 3

The sexual issues now dividing religious communities the most are clearly those related to gender and to sexual orientation. In Part 3 we do not aim to present all sides of the current debates. Rather, we have chosen representative voices who speak for the transformation of sexual oppressions. Even among such voices, however, the theological spectrum is wide.

We open with an introductory article by a scholar who identifies with evangelical Protestantism. Mary Stewart Van Leeuwen reasons dialectically—from scripture to gender and from gender experience to the Bible. Consistent with her evangelical theological stance, she maintains that scripture must be central, taking priority over human experience. Nevertheless, she approaches the Bible well versed in current theories and interpretations of sexuality from the behavioral sciences that supplement her interpretation of scripture.

Van Leeuwen believes that gender equality is the clear mandate of the Bible. Yet, the gender fallenness depicted in Genesis 2 and 3 still affects men and women, and in different ways: "The male propensity to abuse dominion seems compulsively matched by the female propensity towards the securing of relationships, even unhealthy ones, no matter what the cost."[1] We now live between the times, in the era of "the already, but not yet." Our gender relations are still profoundly distorted. Thus, Van Leeuwen argues, "middle-class men often become ulcerous workaholics and middle-class women often suffer from depression." Nevertheless, this author's Calvinistic theology holds a strong view of God's grace, offering the possibility of transformation.

Next we move to three authors who reflect specifically on women's experiences. All are strongly feminist, and the essays include both heterosexual and lesbian experience. Beverly Harrison and Carter Heyward argue, as did Audre Lorde, that eros is the source of creative personal power and is essential to women's well-being, while distorted sexuality expresses conquest and surrender rather than mutually empowering relationships. Their focus is on "the subtle connection between relational dynamics of domination and submission and erotic experiences of pain and pleasure."[2]

Whereas erotic pleasure is a significant source of moral good, Harrison and Heyward maintain that in our culture sexual desire has been shaped around the dynamic of dominance and submission, conquest and surrender. When sexuality is distorted in this way, we perceive that true pleasure is available chiefly through pain and through the deprivation of sexual pleasure. But this spiritualizing of deprivation and suffering leads us astray, for then we see suffering and pain as an intrinsic moral or religious value. Solidified in Christian atonement theories, this anti-body glorification of suffering has become an essential note of the Christian pilgrimage, affecting both men and women, but especially women. Although the Christian tradition has also eroticized male-male relations of dominance and subordination, the heart of the problem is women's socially conditioned and reinforced masochism—the psychosocial result of the patriarchal aim to have women accept, even enjoy, their pain and powerlessness in relation to men. The authors' hope lies in a mutually empowering eroticism, a sexual dynamic of mutual pleasure "that grows from the soil of nonalienated relationship as a profound source of an experience of transcendence."[3] They envision good sex as the experience of one's own empowerment while the lover's well-being simultaneously is enhanced.

Mary Pellauer's article clearly shows how one can explore sexual experience and find it a medium of revelation. Her focus is a woman's experience of orgasm. She recognizes the difficulty of such reflection: orgasms are brief, they are difficult to remember in detail, for each woman they are different at different times, and who knows if they are alike for women generally? Nevertheless, Pellauer finds six important elements in her own experience of orgasm: being here-and-now, varieties of vibrant sensations, an ecstasy that melts one into existence and embodies one fully, the experience of gracious vulnerability, the experience of the partner's and one's own power, and the immense varieties of orgasmic experience.

Pellauer acknowledges that describing and interpreting female orgasms is difficult. In patriarchal interpretations of sexuality, men are able to take pleasure for granted while women cannot. Also, both sexes still lack the power of language to communicate about body experience. Further, Pellauer wonders to what extent she, as a long-married heterosexual, can represent other women's experiences. Nevertheless, without making the orgasmic experience central to sexuality, she wants to claim it as an experience of grace for herself and, hopefully, for others. As grace it is a gift both from her partner and from her own body, a gift that can help her experience more of life as significant.

Mary Hunt identifies her reflections on women's sexuality as those of a lesbian feminist who has been taught in patriarchy that a woman should not love either other women or herself. Now, however, with the sexual revolution, the women's movement, and the lesbian/gay movement lesbians can find a new voice. Hunt claims that lesbian reality often is different from gay reality. Being lesbian means "women loving women without fixating on the presence or absence of genital activity to define it."[4] Hunt stands with many lesbian feminist writers, such as Adrienne Rich, in this understanding of lesbianism in its deepest, most radical sense.[5] Whereas some would use the threat of lesbianism to divide women from one another, such a nonpatriarchal definition of lesbianism shows it to be paradigmatic of all types of friendships in a culture often hostile to people who relate to one another in uncorrupted ways.

Hunt claims that something new is struggling to be born in women's friendships, a major contribution to our culture that no other source, including the churches, is making: "a self-conscious effort to improve the quality of love."[6] Woman-woman love at its best is committed to authentic mutuality, is community-seeking, is honest about sexual dynamics, is flexible, and is other-directed— qualities needed in all human love relationships. Hunt ends her essay by showing how woman-woman friendships can provide particular theological lenses through which to explore freshly major Christian theological claims about God, humanity, and the world. Note how clearly Hunt moves from sexual experience to theological revisioning.

As we turn to men's experience, a comment about "the men's movement" is in order. Clearly, it has been derivative from the women's movement. Its organizational structures are diverse and its ideological spectrum wide. Its most conservative (often reactionary) manifestations are the "men's rights" groups. These men are tired of being blamed by feminist women for the world's ills. They are angered and threatened by job competition from women and by their treatment in court during separations and divorces. Their ideology is geared toward reclaiming traditional gender roles and reclaiming those male rights they feel are being threatened.

A second ideology in the men's movement has received more publicity. It is from the "mythopoetic" or "masculinist" groups who see the core problem as the loss of an archetypal masculinity that men once possessed but no longer do. Through myth, poetry, archetypes, fairy tales, and initiation rituals deemed important to masculinity, they seek bonding with other men and reconnection with their fathers and other elder male mentors. While clearly less anti-woman and anti-gay than the first group, this ideology nevertheless does not perceive the depth of the misogynist and homophobic dimensions of current cultural constructions of masculinity.

Our selection of articles is more representative of a third approach, the "men's liberationist" viewpoint, one that takes seriously the wounds and hungers of individual men but also takes with equal seriousness the feminist critiques of patriarchy, the importance of gay inclusiveness, and the public nature of gender issues.

In the first men's essay, Philip Culbertson hopes for a transformed society in which "men can articulate their identities in support of and in relation to the new ways of living that have rightly developed out of the women's movement."[7] If this transformation is to occur, however, men will need to deal more creatively with four basic male experiences that are both formative and problematic, experiences so significant that most men spend the rest of their lives in some kind of response to them. They are: "(1) prenatal development from female to male; (2) inability to accommodate determined by anatomy; (3) the learned value of success; and (4) separation/individuation from the mother."[8] When these experiences are not dealt with well, the results are often an excessive genital focus, a premium on rugged self-sacrificing independence, an anxious quest for professional success and status, and a heterosexual identity based on a pathological homophobia. Culbertson's approach draws on insights from both social constructionists and essentialists. While eschewing biological determinism, he wants to take biological realities seriously. Males and females *are* different, he claims, and those differences do give rise to different experiences.

The excerpt from James B. Nelson emphasizes the spiritual significance of male genital experience. Nelson is aware of walking a fine line with this focus. On the one hand, this approach seems to contribute to an already overly genitalized male image of sexuality. On the other hand, however, ignoring the problematic male genital experience leaves the body without healing integration. Thus, Nelson decides to move *through* the genital focus, not around it. He does so by showing that, while the experience and symbolism of the phallus (the erect penis) is important, it is insufficient for masculine spirituality. Equally important is the flaccid, unaroused penis, which has been seriously neglected as a masculinity symbol and experience. Taking the undervalued soft penis seriously leads, Nelson believes, into the development of an underdeveloped part of masculine spirituality, the "Via Negativa." It is the way of emptying, of darkness, of sinking, the way that knows the grace of simply *being* rather than doing. Reclaiming the masculinity of genital softness also invites the revaluation of power and size. All of this leads Nelson to reconsider androgyny and Christology. Once again, notice the ways in which reflections about sexual experience can be placed into dialogue with scripture and tradition.

In the final essay in this section, J. Michael Clark foresees a second wave of gay liberation—liberation from genitally focused promiscuity into genuinely intimate relationships. He discovers that genuinely fulfilling sexual pleasure requires an intimacy involving the investment of the whole self into the relationship. When viewed from the vantage point of intimacy, he argues, one's whole interpretation of sexuality is opened to reconceptualization. Then one's sexuality becomes not merely a series of genital events, but rather a deep connection to the erotic energy that heals life, allows persons to be vulnerable and playful, and yet seeks ongoing mutuality. Sexuality, Clark maintains, is not finally about our genitals. It is about a mode of relationality that yields intimacy and communion. From this assumption the writer moves into the complex question of the meanings of monogamy and fidelity in gay relationships.

In Part 3 we see that women and men do differ from each other both in bodily realities and in patterns of gender role socialization. Further, while lesbians and gay men have much in common because of their social oppression, there is no unified or single "homosexual experience." Lesbians and gay men also differ from each other in significant ways, ways that are clearly related to their genders. Nevertheless, it is clear to the writers in Part 3 that, regardless of dissimilarities in gender and orientation, we are all bound together as sexual human beings whose commonality is far greater than our differences. A common thread runs through these seven articles. It is the conviction, variously stated, that our human sexuality has fundamentally to do with connection, with communion, and with life-giving intimacy.

NOTES

1. Mary Stewart Van Leeuwen, "The Christian Mind and the Challenge of Gender Relations," *The Reformed Journal*, vol. 37 (September 1987): 22.

2. Beverly Harrison and Carter Heyward, "Pain and Pleasure: Avoiding the Confusions of Christian Tradition in Feminist Theory," in *Christianity, Patriarchy and Abuse*, ed. Joanne Carlson Brown and Carole R. Bohn (New York: Pilgrim Press, 1989), 150.

3. Ibid., 166.

4. Mary E. Hunt, "Lovingly Lesbian: Toward a Feminist Theology of Friendship," in *A Challenge to Love: Gay and Lesbian Catholics in the Church*, ed. Robert Nugent (New York: Crossroad, 1983), 139.

5. Poet and essayist Adrienne Rich defines lesbian feminism as "that love for ourselves and other women, that commitment to the freedom of all of us, which transcends the category of 'sexual preference' . . . to become a politics of *asking women's questions*," in *On Lies, Secrets, and Silence: Selected Prose 1966–1978* (New York: W. W. Norton & Co., 1979), 17.

6. Hunt, "Lovingly Lesbian," p. 148.

7. Philip Culbertson, *New Adam: The Future of Male Spirituality* (Minneapolis: Fortress Press, 1992), 12.

8. Ibid.

10

The Christian Mind and the Challenge of Gender Relations

MARY STEWART VAN LEEUWEN

The particular challenge I have chosen to address—the challenge of gender relations—may at first glance seem a very odd choice for a college graduation-week address.* Universities and colleges, after all, are traditionally concerned with the discovery, appreciation, and transmission of *universal* truths—those stable underlying principles of reality which transcend the concrete details of history, culture, and individual behavior. There are, of course, colleges and universities in our increasingly secularized society that seem to have given up on the communal quest for universals, substituting instead a kind of learned ignorance which leads its holders to scoff at the very suggestion that there might be stable general principles by which the universe operates.

But to the extent that colleges and universities retain this vision of seeking after universal truths, they are continuing a tradition which goes right back to the academies of ancient Greece, but which also, in the case of the Christian college, rests in the confidence that the Word of the Lord endures forever—that this revealed Word can speak to us truly at all times, in all places, regardless of individual and cultural differences. And in such a vision of higher education, it is sometimes argued, the very category of gender has little, if any, place. According to this vision, you are here at Wheaton (are you not?) to explore and appreciate those things which are universally human. Consequently, to focus on the particularities of gender may seem decidedly parochial and unscholarly, particularly to students (of *both* sexes) who have performed with as much academic competence as I'm told all of you have done.

---

*This article was originally delivered as a Wheaton College Honor Society address in May 1987.—ED.

However, I am here as a *Christian* scholar this morning to argue otherwise. I am here to argue, on the very basis of biblical revelation, that your Christian liberal arts education is going to be incomplete if you do not respect, ponder, and struggle with both the idea and the concrete realities of gender—whether or not this subject is acknowledged in the structure of the formal college curriculum. And I base my argument not on any claim to a privileged understanding of Scripture in all its detail (for I know that many Christian traditions are represented here today, and we are each tempted to think of our tradition's handling of Scripture as the only really adequate one!). I want to appeal rather to the essentials of the "biblical drama"—to that cosmic, overarching story of creation, fall, redemption, and future hope which in broad outline forms what C. S. Lewis called "mere Christianity," and about whose basic significance for both individual *and* corporate human history I think we can all agree. I want to say something about the significance of the first three acts of the biblical drama (creation, fall, and redemption) for relations between you as men and women—academically gifted men and women specifically—and to suggest some applications along the way which I hope will be of help to your present task as students and your future task as probable leaders in church and society.

I begin with creation, not just because it is the first act in the biblical drama, but because creation theology is the very basis for the existence of the Christian liberal arts college. If we did not think we could learn of God from the book of nature as well as the book of Scripture; if we did not affirm that the broad image of God resides in *all* persons (not just confessing Christians), and that as a result we can respect truth from whatever quarter it emerges; if we did not take seriously our mandate from Genesis 1 and 2 to fill the earth and subdue it, to till the earth and keep it; if we did not believe that we are to exercise responsible dominion as "kings and queens in Narnia" (to borrow another phrase from C. S. Lewis)—then there would be no point in *having* a Christian liberal arts college. We would assume instead that it would be both dangerous and unnecessary to study anything over and above the Scriptures.

But your very presence here today is a testimony against such a mentality. As students, faculty, and supporters of a Christian liberal arts college, you have affirmed, explicitly or implicitly, that you expect to study Scripture here—yes, indeed—but more than this, to look at *all of creation* through the *lens* of scriptural truths: to use the Word of God as a lamp to light every path, but not to declare any path, or any aspect of God's creation, off-limits. If this is the case, then the topic of gender relations is anything but irrelevant or secondary; to the extent that gender is part of the creation order, we have a divine mandate to respect it, to study it, and (where it is fallen) to bring the healing power of redemptive truth and action to bear on it.

Well then, what does the creation account tell us about gender relations that we need to know as Christian liberal arts scholars? First of all, it suggests that we need to make a distinction that is seldom acknowledged nowadays. Contemporary social science theory does make a distinction between biological sex on the one hand and socialized gender roles on the other—a distinction, that is, between what is thought to be "naturally" male or female and what is merely the product of culturally based learning and therefore more changeable. Moreover, knowing that almost all talk of innate "differences" between men and women becomes talk of "deficits" in women, there is a strong reluctance among most social scientists to concede anything at all to biology in this matter. It is assumed, in other words, that some combination of biology (a very little bit) and learning (a great deal) accounts for all that we need to know about males and females.

But the Bible is neither a biology nor a social science text in the usual meaning of that term. It tells us not about natural or social history so much as about "metahistory"; that is, it deals with universal truths about God, human beings, and their interaction throughout time which profoundly affects all aspects of life, but which cannot be reduced to either nature or nurture, important as these both are and insistent as social scientists may be that they are the whole story. So the distinction between natural and social accounts of gender on the one hand and the supernatural, biblical account on the other is the first thing we need to recover.

Over the past two decades or so, biblical scholars and theologians with a high regard for the authority of Scripture have more thoroughly studied the question of men and women in the Bible than perhaps at any other time since the biblical canon was closed. It is a topic whose time has come. And it is surprising how much agreement these scholars display, despite great diversity in ecclesiastical background, in their understanding of the Genesis creation accounts. For example, I cannot think of a single evangelical scholar well-trained in Hebrew exegesis who does not affirm that God called both sexes, without favor, to exercise accountable dominion over the creation. Nor can I find any who argue that Eve's being a "helper fit" for Adam in any way argues for her secondary status. All of them realize that the Hebrew word for "helper," as used in Genesis 2, refers overwhelmingly in the Old Testament to God himself—to the God who, for example, has been our "help" in ages past. Finally, I know of no serious scholar who argues that Adam's calling Eve "woman, because she was taken out of man" (Gen. 2:23) in any way gives him dominion over her. They are well aware that the standard Hebrew formula by which one "*calls* [a child, an animal, a place, etc.] *by name*" and therefore claims it as part of one's estate is, significantly, not used by Adam with regard to his wife until the end of Genesis 3, *after* the fall has occurred and God has announced its consequences.

So it seems that men and women were meant from the beginning to be "joint heirs" of creation, just as they are joint heirs of salvation in the third act of the biblical drama. And, again, your very presence here today testifies that you share that belief. For if we really believed that women were by creational status less accountable to God than men for the exercise of their talents, or that those talents were at all times and in all places to be put only at men's disposal, then surely we would have to say that Wheaton, Calvin, and other Christian liberal arts colleges, by virtue of having the same set of liberal arts and disciplinary requirements for both sexes, are being dangerously unbiblical.

But we do not say that. In fact, by keeping our liberal arts requirements both diverse and uniform, we are even ignoring the consistent, empirical finding that men, on the average, have a slight edge over women in certain mathematical skills, while women, on the average, have a slight edge over men in certain language skills. It is not that our college administrators are unaware of these differences, nor even of the fact that these differences may in part be biologically determined. But they have chosen to ignore them precisely because they affirm, implicitly if not explicitly, that exercising accountable dominion over creation is the task of *both* sexes and that to do justice to such a task at this point in our culture, all students need a certain minimal level of linguistic and mathematical sophistication.

All of this may seem so terribly obvious and simple as not to bear mentioning at all. And, indeed, the perplexities of life in general and of gender relations in particular *would* be rendered simple if we were still only in the first act—the creational act—of the biblical drama. But we are not. The fall has intervened, and despite the resurrection of Christ and the outpouring of the Holy Spirit, through which we have the promise of "all things made new," our re-creation is not complete, nor will it be until Christ returns to establish total lordship over all principalities and powers. In the meantime, we live in the metahistorical era of "the already, but not yet," or, as Oscar Cullmann put it, in an era rather like the time between D-Day and V-Day during World War II, when the decisive turning point of the war had been reached, but a great deal of painful "mopping up," with not a few casualties, had still to be done.

Nor do I have to remind you (I hope) that the fall is no respecter of intelligence—and here again we make a distinction that is too often lost in contemporary social-science theorizing. There are theorists of moral development (Lawrence Kohlberg, for example) who come dangerously close to asserting that the most intelligent people (as we in the Western world reckon intelligence) will also be the most moral people—that virtue is, at root, a function of cognitive sophistication. But the Bible is ruthlessly democratic in its response to such a suggestion: not only are we all equally fallen, but there is no function *within* any of us—be it cognition, emotion, perception, or (you've guessed it!) gender—which is not in some way, much of the time, distorted by the ravages of the fall. As a matter of fact, God apparently felt that the distortions wrought upon gender relations by the fall were so serious that they needed special mention before Adam and Eve were evicted from the garden. "Life will certainly not be a rose garden for the two of you after this," he warned them. "Not only will the earth fight back as you try to wrest a living from it, but that sense of complementarity and mutual dependence the two of you used to feel as man and woman—that too will be badly distorted by your joint disobedience."

Now I want to be very careful what I say here. The last impression I want to give is that the fall has turned gender relations completely sour, negative, or evil. For one thing, that would be a very un-Calvinist conclusion, because the Calvinist idea of total depravity (contrary to its popular understanding) never meant that human beings could never do anything right again. On the contrary, Calvinism retains a very strong creation theology and a very strong view of God's common grace, working through his broad image in all persons. Both of these doctrines (as I suggested earlier) argue for a positive appreciation of creation and the confidence that human beings can, at least some of the time and if appropriately motivated, separate truth from falsehood in their intellectual, social, and other endeavors. But while the doctrine of total depravity does not mean that our human functions are totally tainted, it does mean that *none* of those functions is spared the distorting influence of the fall. All of them, without exception, are in some way affected. What this means is that we have to be alert to the possibility—indeed, the inevitability—of sin in all areas of life. We may try to rationalize it or to whitewash it, but in the end we are always forced to concede that sin is more deeply at work in us than we realized.

Throughout the history of humankind, it seems that gender relations have been particularly susceptible to this kind of rationalized distortion. Worse still, so has the scriptural exegesis which is supposed to dictate the shape of those relations. A particularly glaring example has been the justification of male dominance by an appeal to the second half of Genesis 3, as if this represented a creational norm to be preserved, rather than a consequence of the fall to be mourned and resisted.

Now at this point I can imagine some of you beginning to shift in your seats. "Here it comes," you may be thinking, "the predictable feminist commercial. She's about to tell us that male sexism is the original sin, and women are the new creation. Time to tune out!" Well, as a matter of fact I'm not going to do any such thing. Indeed, it would be altogether inconsistent of me to suggest anything of the sort, since I have just finished affirming that the fall has affected *all* functions in *all* people, with no exceptions. It is quite true that there has been an appalling tradition of misogyny throughout the history of biblical exegesis. It stretches back to Chrysostom, who proclaimed that "Woman taught once, and ruined all!" and to Augustine, who concluded that God gave Eve to Adam purely to help reproduce the species, but that for every other kind of activity, another man would fit the bill much better; and it continues to this day in various theologies of womanhood, although in subtler forms. But there is no virtue in simply substituting female for male chauvinism; moreover, I am willing to bet that if women, rather than men, had been the dominant sex throughout history, they would have been just as condescending, and just as prone to eisegesis, in their theology of manhood.

What I want rather to suggest is that the fall, although it has affected both men and women equally, may have affected men and women in somewhat different ways. Let me confess as a psychologist that I have nursed an ongoing compulsion, dating back almost fifteen years, to understand as fully as possible the meaning and implications of Genesis 3:16. That is the verse in which God, announcing the consequences of the fall, tells Eve that despite the suffering that will accompany the birth of children to her marriage, "your desire shall be for your husband, and he shall rule over you." Now, the first thing you find out when you try to exegete this mysterious verse is that the Hebrew word translated as "desire" occurs only three times in the Old Testament—and this, of course, makes the business of understanding its intent somewhat difficult. So I am grateful to one of Wheaton's own biblical scholars, Gilbert Bilezikian, for the extensive work he has done on this verse in his book *Beyond Sex Roles*. In that volume, he compares the uses and contexts of this word "desire" and makes a convincing case that the verse really is talking about an unreciprocated longing for intimacy:

> [The woman's] desire will be for her husband, so as to perpetuate the intimacy that had characterized their relationship in paradise lost. But her nostalgia for the relation of love and mutuality that existed between them before the fall, when they both desired each other, will not be reciprocated by her husband. Instead of meeting her desire . . . He will rule over her. . . . [In short], the woman wants a mate, and she gets a master; she wants a lover and she gets a lord; she wants a husband and she gets a hierarch.[1]

Now let us again clarify what is *not* being said here. It is not the case that the positive, mutual interdependence intended between men and women at creation has totally disappeared (although given the current rate of divorce in America, I am sometimes tempted towards pessimism in this regard). Nor is it the case that being a "master," a "lord," or a "hierarch" is totally against the creation order. The human abuse of power is possible only because, in the first instance, human beings were created in God's image and given the freedom to exercise accountable dominion over the creation. But what I take God to be saying in Genesis 3:16 is that as a result of the fall there will be a propensity in man to let dominion run wild—to impose it in cavalier and illegitimate ways not only upon the earth and upon other men (remember Cain's murder of Abel, the first act of warfare), but also upon the person who is "bone of [his] bones and flesh of [his] flesh—the helper corresponding to [his very] self." And so throughout Scripture we have what Old Testament scholar Phyllis Trible has called "texts of terror," in which the cruel objectification of women by men is reported in unsparing detail: the sordid deeds of David to secure Bathsheba; the royal rape of Tamar by her brother Amnon; the fatal gang-rape of the Levite's concubine; the sacrifice of Jephthah's daughter for the sake of a rash vow made by her father, to mention only some. These are not pretty tales; and frankly, if I believed for a moment that they were in any way intended by God to be normative, I simply would not be a Christian. Again, this is not to say that all men at all times behave this way towards all women: creation, common grace, and redemption have made certain that this will not be the case. But I think it does mean that there is something akin to a congenital flaw in men, going right back to Genesis 3:16 and reducible neither to biology nor to socialization, which makes it all too easy for them to assume the right to dominate women.

Now, again, I can see you squirming in your seats and starting to glance towards the nearest exit. "There she goes; she's doing it after all, even though she promised she wouldn't. She's saying that men are constantly being heavy-handed with women, while the women always respond with self-sacrificing patience and turn the other cheek to the point of death." Is this not, in effect, saying that sexism on the part of males *is* the original sin and that women are the new creation, exhibiting the fruits of the Spirit long before Paul identified them as the marks of a redeemed Christian? Well, no; because, you see, we have not yet finished exegeting the implications of Genesis 3:16. For this is a verse that I suspect is really being quite even-handed in its prediction of sinfulness in *both* sexes. Let me now try to explain why.

I reminded you earlier that accountable dominion is part of the image of God in both sexes; I also reminded you, in so many words, that men and women were intended from the beginning to be mutually interdependent. Trinitarian theology tells us that right from the beginning God was a unified plurality of persons; that is presumably why he said "Let *us* make humankind in our own image," an image which includes, as well as accountable dominion, an inherent sociability. Thus Christians, unlike the philosopher Thomas Hobbes, can never say that people are inevitable individualists who grudgingly enter into a social contract with others merely to advance their own private interests. On the contrary, we are so unshakably created for community that we cannot even become full persons unless we grow up in nurturing contact with others. And so, just as there is something creationally legitimate about the man's desire for dominion (even though it is misused against women) there is also something creationally right about the woman's desire for complete union with a man and (as a result, and despite the attendant pain) for the creation and maintenance of a family.

But because of the fall, Genesis 3:16 seems to imply, this desire on the part of women for community is also distorted by sin. Because, you see, there are two opposite ways we can abuse our God-given exercise of accountable dominion. The first (the man's sin) is to try to exercise dominion without regard to the Creator's original intentions for male-female relationships. But the second—the peculiarly *female* sin—is *to use the preservation of those relationships as an excuse not to exercise accountable dominion in the first place.* In other words, the *woman's* congenital flaw in light of Genesis 3:16 is the propensity to evade personal responsibility. Now this is very seductive temptation indeed, for it so very easily masquerades as virtue. After all, haven't we acknowledged that self-sacrificing servanthood and the desire to maintain peace and interpersonal unity are essential fruits of the Spirit? Well, yes and no, depending on the context. If women insist on peace at any price—if they settle for an abnormal quietism as a way of avoiding the risk and potential isolation that may come from opposing evil—then they are *not* exhibiting the fruit of the Spirit; they are sinning just as surely as the man who rides roughshod over relationships in order to assert his individual freedom.

I have already suggested that King David, in his determination to have Bathsheba, is a paradigm of male abuse of power which must needs be repented of. But recently a perceptive young seminarian pointed out to me that the Bible may also contain a paradigm of the female evasion of responsibility, which needs just as much to be renounced—and this is seen in the person of Queen Esther. Esther, after all, was the darling of King Ahasuerus' harem. She seemed quite happy to keep her Jewish identity a secret, and even when her uncle Mordecai asked her to intercede with Ahasuerus to rescue the Jews from Haman's genocidal plot, she answered, in effect, that she would rather not take the risk. But then comes Mordecai's rebuke, as telling as the prophet Nathan's judgment of David:

> "Think not that in the king's palace you will escape any more than all the other Jews. For if you keep silence at such a time as this, relief and deliverance will rise for the Jews from another quarter, but you and your father's house will perish. And who knows whether you have not come to the kingdom for such a time as this?" (Esther 4:13–14)

Esther, like David, is turned around by this prophetic rebuke, and after asking the Jews to fast and pray for her (thus manifesting the *right* sort of communal solidarity), she finally says, "I will go to the king, although it is against the law; and if I perish, I perish." The rest, as we know, is metahistory: the Jews are again spared to continue as God's carriers of the Messianic promise, in part because a young queen overcame the negative legacy of Genesis 3:16.

I have said that I am not merely trying to be militantly feminist in the points I am making. But in trying to understand women's tendency to avoid responsibility, I do in fact owe a rather large debt to a number of contemporary feminist psychologists. For despite the progressive removal of *external* barriers to women's achievement, these psychologists have noted with much distress and puzzlement that women still seem to have enormous *internal* barriers to overcome. The titles of books that have been written on this subject are telling: *Women Who Love Too Much; Why Do I Think I am Nothing Without a Man?; Sweet Suffering: Woman as Victim;* and perhaps most striking of all, *Men Who Hate Women and the Women Who Love Them.* Now the writers of these books share with other social scientists the error of trying to reduce this problem of overdependence on males primarily to the way women have been socialized throughout history. They do not realize (or refuse to admit) that there is an inescapably religious dimension involved even prior to socialization. But be that as it may, they have done a remarkable job of documenting the empirical effects of what is noted in Genesis 3:16 on the lives of their women clients. And it is distressing to me, as a Christian psychologist, that so little work has been done on this from a confessionally Christian perspective.

But there are exceptions, and one of them is a book written by a feisty

Wheaton graduate named Kari Malcolm. In *Women at the Crossroads,* she speaks of the profound shock she experienced when she came to college in 1946 and found almost all her fellow women students essentially marking time until a husband appeared on the horizon. Raised a Norwegian by missionary parents in China, she had survived three years as a teenager in a Japanese concentration camp during World War II. Malcolm sees that camp experience as the crossroads of her particular life—where she learned that nothing could separate her from the love of God, and that Christ must be her first love. To her, it was tragic when one of her most vibrant friends decided against medical school and the mission field when a man came into her life:

> It seemed as if the child within her—the dreams and aspirations of many years—had died. . . . I could not see why marriage and medical school had to be an either/or proposition. But for many women marriage was such a top priority that careers, as well as love for Jesus, had to be relegated to second place. [Others] stuck to their career goals, setting aside both human *and* spiritual relationships. Love for Christ took a back seat to secular ambitions. Nevertheless, I did find women . . . who put Jesus first in their lives, [preparing] to serve Christ through their careers, either at home or abroad, without wavering from their purpose each time their hearts felt a flutter. For many of them marriage was postponed until they met husbands with similar goals and aspirations, so that as joint-heirs with Jesus Christ they could accomplish God's will for their lives. By waiting, these women chose marriage *and* mission instead of marriage *or* mission.[2]

Malcolm is well aware of the psychological and sociological forces that contribute to women's desire to evade risk and responsibility by attaching themselves to other people. But as a biblically literate Christian, she realizes this is not the whole story. Underneath these mechanisms lies the fear of losing security, family, and even one's femininity—a fear that can be cast out only by the redemptive love of Jesus Christ. And, writes Malcolm, "the woman who responds to God's love with all her heart and soul will walk tall and straight as a daughter of the King."[3] Because, of course, that is what Christ came to do: to reverse the effects of the fall in both men and women and in their relations with each other. One of the tragic things about our fallenness, as expressed in Genesis 3:16, is that it seems to be so horribly complementary in its effects on the sexes: the male propensity to abuse dominion seems compulsively matched by the female propensity towards the securing of relationships, even unhealthy ones, no matter what the cost.

Moreover, it is significant that one of the things Malcolm documents in her book is the almost total disappearance of arguments about gender roles during times of spiritual revival. When the Spirit of God is poured out, it seems, Genesis 3:16 fades into oblivion as men and women alike respond to the call to action *and* the call to communal self-sacrifice. When Christians first became involved in the abolitionist movement, for example, one of their number, Theodore Weld, observed how women came to realize that they were holding back from the fight against slavery by invoking the excuse of feminine propriety: "The very week I was converted," he wrote to two fellow abolitionists, "and the first time I ever spoke in a religious meeting, I urged females both to pray and speak if they felt deeply enough to do it, and not to be restrained from it by the fact that they were females. . . . The result was that seven female Christians confessed their sin in being restrained by their sex, and prayed publicly in succession in that very meeting."[4]

Malcolm rightly contrasts this revival-based equality of the sexes with the present-day, picky insistence many Christians have for figuring out every last jot and tittle of a "correct" view of headship and submission. "We have a world to win for Christ," she writes. "The ship is sinking, we are standing on the shore arguing about who should go to the rescue—men or women."[5] When we do so, regardless of the apparent sincerity of our motives, we are largely retreating from the current act of the biblical drama—the act of redemption—in which God has placed us, preferring instead to respond to the regressive pull of the fall on gender relations. And, as I have tried very hard to point out, both women and men must assume some blame for allowing this. If Malcolm is correct that one of the hallmarks of revival is the blossoming of a true priesthood of all believers, with no regard for gender, then how many of us, male or female, can claim to have been revived?

But to those Christians, both male and female, young and old, who have found that radical first love of which Malcolm wrote, Jesus Christ brings redemption to the area of gender relations, as to all other areas of life. To the woman who reduces all of womanhood to the nurturing of relationships and cries out to him, "Blessed is the womb that bore you, and the breasts that nursed you," Christ replies, "No; blessed rather are those who hear the word of God and keep it" (Luke 11:27–28). Conversely, to the male disciples who have been taught by their rabbis to believe that the primary function of women is to be man's sexual partner and that the automatic result of public contact between men and women can only be lust (thus justifying horrendous restrictions on women's movements and activities), Christ asserts in Matthew 5 that male lust—one of many ways of objectifying women—not only can, but must be controlled. In the perceptive words of Mary J. Evans (a biblical scholar at London Bible College),

> Jesus . . . completely dismisses [the disciples'] suggestion that lust is inevitable. He does not [like the rabbis] warn his followers against looking at a woman, but against doing so with lust. Women are to be recognized as subjects in their own right, as fellow human beings, and not just the objects of men's desire. Once it is recognized that women are people who can be related to in other ways than that of sexual desire, and once it is acknowledged that lust is not only sin, but deliberate sin, an act of the will as is adultery, then there is no longer any necessity to avoid social contact. Therefore Jesus accepts women into the group of disciples because he expects his disciples to control their desires.[6]

I have affirmed throughout that both dominion and sociability are essential aspects of the image of God in all persons. I have also argued, especially in light of Genesis 3:16, that the fall has tended to distort the first of these more in men, and the second more in women. Moreover, young people of today live with the heritage of the 19th-century industrial revolution, which further tore apart the organic unity of family life, taking men away from their household-based work to the waged labor of urban factories, and leaving women at home as socio-emotional specialists, stripped of the essential economic roles they shared in the pre-industrial economy. Only now are Christians beginning to realize that assigning the invisible labor of domesticity entirely to women, and the burden of breadwinning entirely to men, is not necessarily biblical at all.

So the young men and women being honored here today have their work cut out for them. Life at a Christian college nowadays is often unrealistic in terms of gender relations. The course requirements, and most professors, are scrupulously even-handed in their treatment of both sexes; nor do women have to worry (I trust) about being sexually harassed, as they often are in more secular settings. But the real test of their having overcome the legacy of Genesis 3:16 has yet to come. I have been known to say to my own students that the real test of their commitment to healed gender relations will come not after graduation, nor even upon marriage, but when they start to have children. Because then, of all times, it is seductively easy to decide that men were "really" designed for dominion and women were "really" designed for the maintenance of relationships. In the process, we often turn fathers into absentee landlords who barely know their children—a denial of their creational call to intimacy; at the same time, we isolate mothers in nuclear-family households, denying them the exercise of the cultural mandate that is just as much a part of *their* creational call. And then we wonder why middle-class men often become ulcerous workaholics and middle-class women often suffer from depression.

It is an ironic tragedy that the church of Jesus Christ, called to be light and salt to a decaying world, and to role-model redeemed relationships in all areas of life, so often merely follows the distorted drumbeat of the world around it. But it is never too late to repent and recover our heritage of redemption, for as the popular saying has it, our God is a God of the second chance. He is also the God of the Holy Spirit, whose power and wisdom he never withholds from those who truly want it. There are myriad contemporary challenges crying out for attention from gifted young people today—but to my mind, the challenge of gender relations is one of the most urgent. So let us all wake up, and be about the work of the Creator.

NOTES

1. Gilbert Bilezikian, *Beyond Sex Roles* (Grand Rapids: Baker Book House, 1985), 55, 229.
2. Kari T. Malcolm, *Women at the Crossroads: A Path Beyond Feminism and Traditionalism* (Downers Grove, Ill.: Inter-Varsity Press, 1982), 26–27.
3. Ibid., 33.
4. Quoted in ibid., 122.
5. Ibid., 132.
6. Mary J. Evans, *Woman in the Bible* (Downers Grove, Ill.: Inter-Varsity Press, 1984), 44–45.

11

Pain and Pleasure: Avoiding the Confusions of Christian Tradition in Feminist Theory

BEVERLY WILDUNG HARRISON
CARTER HEYWARD

As political repression accelerates in the United States, feminists must sharpen their critiques of the cultural, social, religious, and economic roots of women's oppression. It is imperative, moreover, that in this reactionary climate feminist theorists admit the complexity of the reconstructive perspectives they are attempting to forge. Theories that oversimplify the constructive feminist agenda or challenge the troubling dualisms of patriarchal culture in an overly reactive way merely feed the divisiveness among women that political repression seeks to sow.

Contemporary feminist politics and theory, liberal and radical, converge in the face of pervasive violence against women and mounting efforts to foreclose the already limited options that women have regarding reproductive choice and health care. But in discussions about pornography, or about what constitutes an optimal conception of women's eroticism, consensus among feminists gives way to acrimony, and our politics tend to become a battleground of conflicting normative theories and strategies.[1] In matters of sex, more than in any other political arena, feminists are inclined simply to superimpose their individual preferences or senses of morality upon others. In this way, the feminist insistence that "the personal is political" (and, conversely, that the political always yields personal, concrete meaning) ironically receives skewed, negative confirmation rather than constructive expression. That the personal is political is a social fact, and our personal preferences and sensibilities always are steeped in a more complex social dialectic. These personal preferences acquire moral meaning in relation to the well-being of a larger social-cultural order. As it is, among contemporary feminists, wherever eros, sex, and sexuality are envisioned differently, conflicting personal agendas jockey competitively to become the "right" answer to the public question of which strategies and policies actually contribute to the liberation of women.

While we agree with Mariana Valverde that "the debate on sexuality has not been one of the success stories of the women's movement,"[2] we also acknowledge the oft-repeated claim that, from a historical point of view, the greatest breakthrough of contemporary feminist theory is precisely this securing of the cultural and intellectual space to forge a genuine female "discourse on sexuality."[3] Conflict over sexuality should not obscure this gain. The burgeoning feminist literature on sexuality, including discussions of pornography and sadomasochistic practice among women, has brought sex out of the closet into the realm of public discourse and has sharpened reflection among feminists on their values. On all sides of these contemporary debates, feminists agree that relational dynamics of domination and submission, images and acts that ritualize violence, make widespread contributions to the sexual pleasure of men—and women—in our society.[4] In other words, it is beyond dispute that many women find sexual pleasure in patterns of erotic domination and submission, whether these images lurk largely in the realm of women's sexual fantasies or are acted out in women's sex lives.

We are grateful for the work of the many secular feminists who have been unwilling to let specific questions of eros and sex go unexplored, a failing, as we see it, of many religious feminists. This essay is an attempt by two religious feminists to integrate and expand insights from this discussion of women's eroticism and genital pleasure. We share with many secular feminists a conviction that feminist theory must incorporate a profound positive evaluation of the vitality of the erotic in women's lives. We understand eros to be body-centered energy channeled through longing and desire. With Audre Lorde we affirm eroticism as essential to our well-being and believe it to be the source of creative personal power and, as such, essential to creativity.[5] In our work, we have attempted to show how eros also is central to an adequate feminist theory not only of politics but of religious and moral experience.[6] We also share the suspicion, now widely voiced in feminist literature, that resistance to pervasive pornographic manipulation is tempting some feminists to embrace a subtle prudery or a new antisexual moralism.[7] That women now must seek sexual fulfillment in a context where "pleasure and danger"[8] are intertwined seems to us obvious. The threat of violence and the objectification of women's bodies create genuine barriers to women's realization of the erotic, but the way forward is not to adopt prematurely a feminist theory of women's sexuality that portrays women's sexual needs simplistically, as if our desires were homogeneous or untouched by the disordered power dynamics of patriarchal eroticism.

Feminist theorists whose insights contribute most to the emerging discourse on sexuality are those who have been most attentive to the sociohistorical shifts in patterns of eroticism, recognizing that forms of sexual expression and erotic desire, while rooted in physio-psychic potential, are shaped by complex cultural dynamics—recognizing, that is, that sexuality and eroticism have a history. This history of sexuality is embedded in social structures of patterned power relations such as institutionalized heterosexism, racism, and cultural imperialism.[9] To explore how senses of personal power and eroticism have been linked historically in heterosexist patriarchy is to begin also to see that the self-other relation which elicits strong erotic desire frequently is one of domination and submission. As such, sex is often experienced as a dynamic of conquest and surrender rather than as power in mutual relation.[10]

In such "eroticization of domination," sexual desire is linked with either self-oblivion or self-assertion. It would be ahistorical and naive to imagine that *anyone's* eroticism in this culture could be untouched by this dynamic.[11] Feminists such as Valverde and Linda Gordon insist that the "eroticization of equality" must be understood as a historical project of feminism. They acknowledge, however, that this project is necessarily long term,[12] so securely fastened in our society, and our psyches, is the felt need for a sexual mediation of relational power to confirm our superiority or subjection in relation to others, whether for a moment or a lifetime.

To probe the linkage of erotic desire and inequality so characteristic of patriarchal culture we need to focus on the subtle connection between relational dynamics of domination and submission and erotic experiences of pain and pleasure. We realize that this connection—between experiences of relational power or powerlessness and of sexual pleasure enhanced by pain—might be approached critically from a number of directions (e.g., natural or social science; art, literature, or film; comparative studies of religion or culture), as well as with different focuses (e.g., gender relations, sexual customs, ascetic traditions). As feminist ethicists and theologians who are Christian, we approach this issue with a critical interest in the role of Christianity in developing and sustaining a social (not only sexual) relation—a sadomasochistic relation—in which pleasure is available chiefly through pain. We are committed, moreover, to participation in the reconstruction of theological and moral theory which is both socially responsible, contributing to the creation of justice for all, and deeply affirmative of erotic pleasure as a source of moral good.

We will now examine some Christian theological roots of the equation of pain with pleasure and also suggest ways in which the legacy of liberal individualism, the dominant ideological underpinning of Western society, tempts feminists to reformulate the dilemmas of female eroticism in a way that perpetuates rather than challenges this theologically legitimated confusion. We shall conclude with images showing how erotic relationships might contribute to fully socialized, self- and-other-empowering relations.

PAIN AS PLEASURE:
CHRISTIAN FOUNDATIONS

Christian orthodoxy (culminating for the Western church in Augustine) eschewed the notion of a radical dualism in which Creator and Creation exist in a posture of *unmitigated* opposition. Orthodox Christian dualism, by comparison to more radically dualistic religious systems eventually deemed heretical, has been more experientially complex, more dialectical in the relation between cosmologically "higher" and "lower" realities.[13]

Still, the primary architect of the identification of pain with pleasure in Western culture has been the Christian church with its basically dualistic anthropology. On the basis of Neoplatonic cosmology, early church fathers explained their religious experience as essentially that of breaking tension between such oppositional realities as spirit and flesh, male and female, light and dark, good and evil.[14] The role of religion in general, Christian religion in particular, was thus to mitigate the opposition by enabling the two forces to "co-operate" rather than to compete for the headship of society as well as the human soul. Such opposites as spirit and flesh, male and female, could be cooperative only insofar as the higher was in control of the lower—and as the lower accepted its place as a weaker reality, both naturally and morally subordinate in relation to the higher. Whether by will or force, the resolution of tension between potentially competitive cosmic forces was to become a test of Christian faith: a faithful Christian woman, for example, would accept her role gladly as man's helper and a faithful Christian man would accept his role cheerfully as head of the household. Patristic theological discourse bears written testimony to social relations of domination and subjugation in which "the fathers" of the family (both civil and ecclesial households)[15] believed that they should be in charge of women, children, slaves, and all other creatures—and in control, moreover, of their own "lower" selves: flesh, body, passions, and eroticism.

Because in this system good Christian men—and through men's authority, women as well—must deny the enjoyment of flesh, females, darkness, evil, and the sensuality associated with these negativities, early Christian anthropology required that *pain*—the *deprivation of sensual pleasure*—be accepted as an important element in attaining the joy of salvation. We cannot trace here the long process by which this dualistic asceticism in which the exercise of faith involved attempts to transcend the sensual pleasures of human being—hunger for food, warmth, and touch—became in time not only acceptable as a dimension of Christian spirituality, but moreover normative for it: to be Christian was to accept or even to seek pain.

This establishment of antisensual pain as a foundation of Christian faith is a complex story informed by diverse historical processes. For example, the extended sociopolitical repression, torture, and martyrdom that some Christians endured and that threatened others in the Roman Empire in the middle of the third and during the early fourth centuries contributed to the spiritualizing of deprivation and suffering. But it is one thing to accept suffering for the sake of a moral or religious good when confronting unjust power, and another to perceive suffering as itself an intrinsic moral or religious value, the point to which much institutional Christianity came after the collapse of the Roman Imperium.

The earlier anti-material, anti-body, anti-woman dualisms of Neoplatonic patriarchal Christianity laid the groundwork for this romanticization of suffering but the full flowering of masochism in the Christian ethic can be best measured by the increase, over time, of a sex-phobic and sex-preoccupied focus within the Christian ethic.[16] Historian Samuel Laeuchli has traced one strand of the story of this move from a Christian spiritual discipline focused at least in part on resistance to the Roman state to one morbidly preoccupied with the control of human sexuality.[17] Laeuchli acknowledges that this development had deep roots in early dualistic patristic theory about spirit and flesh and in the developing church's transparent fear of women.[18] Not insignificantly for feminist theory, Laeuchli also connects this impulse to sexual control and the rapid development of centralized ecclesiastical hierarchy within Western Christianity. We can only speculate as to how such dynamics of pain and pleasure took hold of Christian experience such that the suffering associated with sensual self-denial became *essential* to Christian spiritual and moral life, and thereby a source of spiritual satisfaction. Without pain, pleasure was immoral; whereas by pain, with pain, and through pain, pleasure became a happy consequence of the Christian pilgrimage.

This spiritual paradigm of Christian pain as virtue and as pleasure was also developed theologically: The Christian drama of salvation has been staged historically as a transaction between an almighty God and a powerless humanity. As the lower relational entity, humanity has been cast as a "fallen" partner, able to be "saved" or "redeemed" into right relation only insofar as human beings know ourselves to be unworthy of anything but punishment from God. Into our unworthy lives comes Jesus, the Christ, to bear our sins and to submit, on our behalf, to the Father God's Will. Thus, standing in for us (as only the elder obedient Son is worthy to do in this patriarchal schema), Jesus is humiliated and killed, becoming thereby a perfect sacrifice to the Father. As the classical portrait of the punitive character of this divine-human transaction, Anselm of Canterbury's doctrine of the atonement (1093–1109) probably represents the sado-masochism of Christian teaching at its most transparent.

But there is a subtler sadomasochistic hue to Christianity, an effect also of the litany of dualistic oppositions such as those between earth and heaven, flesh and spirit, and present and future. The patriarchal Christian story is basically one of a fierce war between good and evil forces in the cosmos, from the farthest outreaches of the universe to the individual's soul. In this praxis of opposition, Christians have believed that, in fact, God—the supreme force for good— already has won the war. This faith has reflected the Christian experience on two different levels of meaning in their lives: God's victory is on a spiritual level whereas the numerous incessant battles which constitute the war are material as well. Christians have believed that the spiritual power of the resurrection has overcome human history and thus the pain of the cross, so real in "this world" has been vanquished by the power of God in the "other world" above or beyond us. We may catch glimpses even now of the spiritual world through faith that embodied life as we know it is not all there is.

But for most people on the earth embodied *pain* is much of all there is—the pain of poverty, oppression, alienation, loss and, from a liberation perspective, the pain incurred in struggling against injustice and oppression. In Christian theology, eternal joy may have the upper hand and the spiritual victory, but daily pain and sorrow play the more visceral, sensual roles in shaping the lives of most women, men, and children on earth. This split sensibility between what is experienced and what is yearned for provides, for many Christians, a foundation for their faith. This faith in turn functions as a state of mind, a cosmology, and as a way of interpreting daily events and historical movement.

In this dualistic praxis that is not peculiar to Christianity, yet which takes a distinctive shape in Christian theology, *pain* in the present and *hope* for the future together form a bridge between earth and heaven, human and divine life, estrangement and unity, conflict and resolution. Pain and hope thereby constitute the link for most Christians between such immediate sensual experiences as hunger and loneliness and such "delayed gratification" as food and intimacy. This tension, existential and political, personal and historical, provides an eschatological back-drop against which sadomasochism is acted out as the most typically "Christian" of all social relations: We learn to experience the deprivation of pleasure—the pain of being hurt, hungry, or rejected; of feeling weak, stupid, bad in the immediate present—as a moment filled with intense anticipation of pleasure that is yet to come. In short, Christians learn theologically to equate the anticipation of pleasure with pleasure itself. This disembodied sensibility, in which *pleasure is fundamentally a state of mind,* is steeped in the eschatological promise that the realm of the divine—a spiritual arena of unity, joy and ecstasy—is, for Christians, here but not quite here; now but not quite yet.

The covert popularity among Christians of pain-filled sexual (and other social) relations can be explained in part by this politic of pain and hope that is so basic to classical Christian practice and theory and that is as forceful and erotic a politic in the lives of women as of men. This difficult social relation is rooted most deeply, we submit, in the pain of alienation generated historically by political and religious structures of domination and control. Such structures as male gender superiority and white racial supremacy have shaped to an extent the relational dynamics and erotic feelings of all members of all institutions and societies that are themselves established on these foundations of domination and control. Thus do *all* Christians, as well as many others, bear scars of sadomaso-chistic relations.

Beyond a common experience as dreamers of an eschatological relief and pleasure, Christian men and women have a very different political and sexual history, a point that, thanks to feminist religious scholarship, is finally widely acknowledged today.[19] The differences between them are nowhere more appar-ent than in the ways in which Christian sadomasochism is actually embodied by the sons of the Father, on the one hand, and his daughters on the other.

Consider the sons: Unless reconstructed along the lines of a feminist liberation hermeneutic, or of a radical womanism, Christianity—even in its most liberal dress—remains quintessentially a religion about men controlling men's bodies, men's women, men's children, and men's other property. This fundamental male-male relation is imaged as that between father and son. The father is willful and benevolent, loving and just, one who desires—but does not always receive—obedience from his sons, in which case the sons can be punished justly. (Apologists for the sexism of Christianity are apt to insist that the "sons" include the "daughters." To the extent that the daughters fall for such patriarchal "inclusion," we can read ourselves into this drama of disobedience and discipline.)

The explicit sadomasochistic dynamics of classical Christianity do not often receive voice in "modern" Christian theologies. Even so, they live on in the sexual fantasies of many Christian men and are frequently expressed in closeted homosexual eroticism so much denied and so widely practiced among Christian males. This is especially true among those men drawn to traditional Catholic liturgical spirituality—perhaps because this spirituality offers such dramatic opportunity to dress up, role play, and act out a very sensual relation between men. In a much more literal way than at the altar, the "meat-rack" is often the arena for enacting the justice of the father who must whip his sons, humiliate them, and require them to beg for his mercy. The sons' pain is merely in proportion to what they deserve for the sin of their disobedience which, in the dualistic praxis we have described above, *includes their experiences of sexual passion*. The sadistic father will feel pleasure in disciplining his sons "for their own good." Masochistic sons will enjoy the discipline because it will set them into right relation with their father, whose love they seek.

But did not Jesus suffer and die in their stead? Why is there this violence between father and son if the ransom for the wages of sin has been exacted already? Perhaps it is the guilt of the younger sons in relation to the innocent Jesus? Or their catholic desire for participation? Or simply their need for hands-on experience? Most of these sons believe that with Jesus they too must be beaten and broken in order to satisfy their almighty father. Becoming Christlike—good sons, submissive to the father's will—is accomplished repeatedly and ritualistically through a pain which the sons experience as the love of God and as such a source of deep satisfaction and pleasure. In this erotic fantasy, the father is turned on by his absolute power over another.

A theology of scourged buttocks and torn anuses, and the accompanying violence, can nevertheless be understood as a yearning, a reaction, of Christian men *against* the dualistic character of the divine-human relation in which no son except Jesus has immediate access to the Father; nor for that matter does the Father have intimate relations with his human sons. The sadomasochistic sexual relation between Christian "fathers" and "sons" might be comprehended as a father-son transaction in which is expressed their mutual desire for immediate and intimate relation.[20]

To be sure, not all Christian men are driven to enact this sadomasochistic imaging of divine-human relations. But we believe that Christianity has intensely eroticized male-male transactions of subordination and dominance, obedience and defiance. In the face of this we interpret much male fear of sexuality as a defense against these desires and interpret the lure of celibacy within Christianity as a fragile defense against them.

Since the Protestant Reformation, which reestablished "compulsory heterosexuality," male sexual transactions with women have frequently been interpreted as "duty"—a "burden" to be assumed by spiritual and intellectual superiors toward inferiors. We perceive the continuing split in male eroticism, in which sex and intimacy are rarely associated, as historically conditioned by these dynamics of gender inequality. Men who are "turned on" to women are rarely turned on by strong, self-reliant women or women who make demands for full integrated relationship. The objectification of women as "sex objects" is sustained primarily by the split in men's lives—between sex and intimacy, friendship and eroticism, man and man, and man's sense of "spirit" and his own body. "Woman" has become historically a convenient scapegoat for men's lack of sexual and spiritual integration.[21]

Consider now the daughters of God. However harshly men may be dealt with by God in the sadomasochistic imagination, the raison d'être behind the discipline they receive is to make them worthy to share in the father's inheritance, his power and dominion over his kingdom. Patriarchal daughters by contrast are not heirs at all but rather are their brothers' helpers on the way toward men's appropriation of the power of God. As the sons are redeemed by their obedience to God, so too are the daughters redeemed by their obedience to the sons.

Patriarchal heterosexism is founded less upon deep male heterosexual desire than upon men's use of women's bodies as a means of public social control. In this situation, women have no body rights, no moral claim to our bodies as self-possessed. In Christianity, woman is equated with flesh, body, but Christian women have no integrity of embodied selfhood; no authoritative voice in determining where we put our bodies/ourselves, with whom we share our bodies/ourselves, where we put our embodied energies, time, and talents. *Women in Christianity are meant to live for others.* The inability of so many women even to imagine that they should be well-treated in a relationship with a man or that they deserve physical and emotional pleasure is conditioned by the demand that we have our being for others.

Women's bodies, sensual and hungry, are on the one hand needy impediments to the sacrifices expected of us. On the other hand, our bodies are all we have, all we are, and as such are our best and only hope. If Christian women are to be liberated, it will be through the aegis of our sensual, hungry, needy bodyselves, which we learn are dangerous, dirty, and bad—and, at the same time, the source of our power. Such body alienation is then reinforced by the pervasive threat of rape, sexual harassment, and other widespread forms of bodily exploitation. Thus do we learn to live in radical ambivalence toward our bodies/ourselves. The very womanly flesh we learn to despise is the source of our redemption—from material and spiritual bondage, from self-loathing and from our contempt for women in general. As feminists attempt to show, the possibility of women's liberation is seeded in women's self-respect, a revolutionary act because it embodies a challenge to fundamental assumptions about womanhood which have been espoused both by the church and by Western societies for two milleniums.

While feminists speak often with passion and good reason about women's self-respect, being woman-identified, taking women seriously, we should not underestimate the force—and devastating effects—of misogyny in patriarchal heterosexist Christianity and in those cultures shaped largely by it. It is far easier to embrace feminist ideology in our public work than to live radically in a strong love for our bodies/ourselves, or with love and advocacy for our sisters.

While we acknowledge the sexual sadomasochism acted out among Christian women as well as men, we believe that sexual sadomasochism is, as we have suggested, a sexual politic of male-male relations—even when the participants include females. All women in patriarchy are, to a degree, male-identified. To that extent, we are likely to enjoy sadomasochistic relations, sexual and other.[22] The shape of sadomasochism among women, however, is probably less genitally sexual than among men. More often, female sadomasochism is more generally sensual, more a matter of women's body-integrity.[23] For this reason a more clearly female embodiment of sadomasochism originates not in our desire to control others but in an ambivalence toward our bodies. This is reflected in bodily obsessions such as fear of aging, fixation on cosmetic beauty, and eating disorders which have grown to epidemic proportions in our time and culture.[24]

Eating disorders provide an especially poignant illustration of sadomasochism among women because they embody, literally and vividly, the confusion of pain and pleasure. Whether an eating disorder takes the form of anorexia nervosa (self-starvation), bulimia (gorging oneself with food and then purging oneself of it), or compulsive overeating, its source is pain—social, political, and emotional pain—and its consequences are a short-lived pleasure which becomes pain and which continues the cycle of self-destructive behavior. The eating disorder signals a woman's resistance to the role imposed upon her body/herself by her religion or culture.[25] It represents, moreover, a woman's ambivalence toward her body/herself. An anorexic woman, for example, wants to be thin since thinness is a virtue, and a pleasure, in men's eyes (and, thereby, her own). She is willing to starve herself, literally to death if need be, to become thin enough to enjoy herself. Another woman, who is bulimic, takes pleasure in eating—and wants to be thin. She experiences tension between pleasing herself with food and pleasing men (and, thereby, herself) with a trim figure. This tension generates a pattern of compulsive eating finally more painful than pleasurable, to be followed by compulsive elimination of the food. For the bulimic the pleasure of eating has become painful, and the pain of induced vomiting becomes a relief and a pleasure. Rather than make public challenge to institutions that teach misogyny, or embody this protest in her work and relationships (perhaps more common today), the woman internalizes the misogyny and punishes herself for daring to dream of her own liberation. From a psychoanalytic perspective, the daughter has internalized the father and, as such, acts sadistically toward herself—and toward her mother. The heart of the problem, the woman's masochism, far from being "natural," is the psychosocial result of the patriarchal aim to help women accept, even enjoy, our powerlessness in relation to men and the pain we necessarily will incur if we attempt to alter this relation.

The dynamics of Christian heterosexist sadomasochism, sketched only in bold relief here, are no longer *explicitly* emphasized in the theologies of liberal Christianity, that is, in those Christian communities that do not contend against the modern scientific world view. Here Christian asceticism has given way to a qualified embrace of the value of the created world. The blatant antisensuality bias of the highest forms of patristic and medieval spirituality has been replaced by the more dialectical dualism characteristic of the early church. Liberal Christians affirm embodied sensuality when it is expressed in heterosexual monogamous marriage, perceiving that interpersonal intimacy and love redeem sex; they have transmitted eros to a spiritual plane.[26] Christian women, in particular, learn an erotic patterning in which eros is affirmed if and when it is expressed in "love" relations with men. The modern female disposition to "fall madly in love," to be "swept away" in order to justify sexual desire, surely has its roots in this liberal shift.[27]

In our view, the Christian theological liberal response to the need for a more adequate theory of eros is unsatisfactory. Some theological liberalism, for instance, rejects sadomasochistic imagery of divine mediation by qualifying or repudiating the Anselmnian doctrine of atonement.[28] While stressing the ethical character of divine and human interaction, this theological posture nonetheless maintains a bias toward the spiritual, thereby perpetuating a subtle devaluation of both material and female existence.[29] Here the doctrine of the inferiority of women is replaced by a complementarity doctrine in which women (good women, those who express their sexuality in lifelong committed heterosexual relations) are in fact more spiritual, less carnal, than men. This teaching, which continues to tempt Christian feminism and postchristian theory to adopt a dualistic doctrine of female erotic supremacy in which women are more spiritual than men, serves to reduce the pressure for a theological reconstruction of the terms of divine-human interaction predicated by Christian patriarchal imagination. It also frequently leads Christian or formerly Christian feminist theorists to evade the full religious and ethical impact of the secular feminist struggle to place women's sexuality at the heart of a feminist liberation theory.

FEMINIST RESPONSE TO
PATRIARCHAL CHRISTIAN MASOCHISM

Even so, most postchristian and Christian liberation feminists have positioned themselves in opposition to the basic masochistic assumptions about women's spirituality generated by orthodox patriarchal Christianity. Insofar as religious feminists acknowledge embodied pleasure as fundamentally life-enhancing, we join many secular feminist theorists and, with them, affirm a post-Enlightenment, modern stance against the antisexual obsession of Christian metaphysics. In our view, a dramatic recovery of a world-affirming, sex-affirming perspective could not have occurred without the rupture that post-Enlightenment modernity created between dominant Christian ecclesiastical culture and a secular, world- and human-experience-centered way of interpreting the world. Though many interpreters have recognized that the basic cultural shift stemming from the Enlightenment led to a recovery of this-worldly interest, few have observed the fact that the shift characteristic of this transition is one in which concrete, worldly pleasure is positively embraced. In some post-Enlightenment theory it is even predicated as "the highest good."[30] One need not endorse a full-scale hedonistic psychology or the monistic value theory that it entails in order to acknowledge the critical character of this shift for human well-being.

The long struggle required to recover a respectful appreciation of the centrality of pleasure to human fulfillment and the essential role of eros and sex in human well-being would never have occurred if the political and theological control exercised by patriarchal Christianity had not been displaced. Yet we submit that it is one thing to break the ecclesiastical monopoly on the definition of the relation of spiritual pleasure and physical pain, and another to disentangle, at the level of personal erotic experience, a clear difference between what hurts and what gives pleasure. Physiologically, the line between pain and pleasure is at times a fine one. It is not surprising that human beings learn a psychological preference for an eroticism that is tinged, if not with pain, with tension that is close to pain. We suspect, however, that the widespread cultural entanglement of violence and sex reflects a blurred distinction between pain and pleasure in many people's experience, and moreover that few people experience tension-free relationships as erotic.

It is the clear intent of most feminist theorists to affirm pleasure and the importance of seeking its enhancement as a path to deeper personal power. Were the modern post-Enlightenment embrace of the erotic its only legacy, feminist reconstruction could proceed with an agenda of affirming women's eroticism without contradiction. But Enlightenment tradition, with its gradual affirmation of embodiment, nevertheless maintained a strong continuity with Christian patriarchal interpretation of the meaning of *personal power in relationship*. In fact, modern liberal theory, with its uncritical commitment to capitalism, exacerbated the patriarchal imaging of self-other relations as nonmutual. The individualism of the Enlightenment became, increasingly, a conception of social relations in which power-in-relation, if not antagonistic, is at least competitive such that either self *or* other must prevail. In this schema, personal power and personal fulfillment are envisaged as the realization of "autonomy," understood as "self-possession" or as *freedom from dependency*.[31]

The basic philosophical and political tenets of so-called free societies are suffused with such assumptions. Feminists too have been schooled by life as well as books in a highly individualized and possessive understanding of personal power: an ability to generate action, a capacity to effect. Our power, we see clearly, includes our feelings which can serve to catapult us into commitment or action. We must not forget that in the West (especially in the United States), our senses of personal power (including our feelings), our sexualities (how we use this power), and our eroticism (our specifically *sexual* feelings) *always* are mediated to a degree by these deities of individualism and possession. A feminist reconstruction of sexual theory must acknowledge that the continuing confusion between pain and pleasure that besets patriarchal Christianity cannot be disentangled without also challenging the bias that personal pleasure consists primarily in the realization of independence. Both patriarchal Christianity's hierarchical social relations, characterized by domination and submission (however benignly exercised), *and* a feminist commitment to a woman's self-possession (rather than her being possessed by others) continue to reflect a dualistic apprehension of embodied power and thus an erotic split.

The effect of the split between top and bottom and between male and female (patriarchal distinctions), and between belonging to oneself and belonging to others (a liberal dichotomy sustained in much feminism) is to associate the erotic with ongoing tension. Patriarchy has conditioned us to feel, as erotic, the tension between top and bottom, male and female, self and other. While most feminists have rejected flatly the hierarchical- and gender-based dualisms, individual feminists often remain captive to the need for relational tension.[32] Even some of the most subtle feminist theory has not yet adequately repudiated the association of eroticism with the split between self and other that is endemic to the patriarchal view of reality. In other words, if we are likely to be "turned on" in patriarchal praxis by being on top or on bottom, giver or receiver, in traditional male or female roles, we may still, in feminist praxis, be "turned on" by a sense of being *either* self-possessed *or* belonging to another. In the context of this dualistic eroticism, *for a woman to feel that she belongs both to herself and to another is rare.* To do so involves breaking the tension generated by the split between oneself and others. To those shaped by the power relations of patriarchal culture (all of us), the loss of such tension is experienced unavoidably as the diminishment or elimination of erotic power. Few are able to find their way, in this dualistic praxis, to full eroticization in mutuality.[33]

This may suggest why so many people (feminists and others) find it hard to sustain high levels of sexual excitement in the context of friendship.[34] It suggests also that the erotic split is the ground upon which we learn to feel as pleasurable or sexually stimulating that which in fact is the source of much pain to us: our alienation from one another, as people who have difficulty *feeling* power by *sharing* it. To put it another way, it is rare in this culture to experience power when shared as *genuine power* because we are inured to perceiving as powerful anything that does not have a zero-sum quantity, that does not appear "over against" us or someone else. As we have already insisted, the identification of eros with the tension created by power disparity cannot be transcended until we repudiate the legacies of patriarchal social relations at root, rejecting the way patriarchy images self-other relationship. . . .

PLEASURE AND TRANSCENDENCE

Transcendence, the wellspring of religious intuition and spiritual resourcefulness, is the power to cross over from self to other.[35] It is the act of making connections to one another, to the rest of creation, and, from a monotheistic religious perspective, to the source of our creative power in relation. Transcendence is also the resource of the desire to overcome structures of alienation such as heterosexism, sexism, racism, and class exploitation that impede even our best efforts to love our neighbors or ourselves very well. If sex is experienced as enhancing a shared sense of power, it is an avenue to transcendence, to deepening our relations with the world.

If self-other dynamics are fated to bear the mark of tension between self- and other-possession, then good sex can be at best an occasional, even accidental, striking of delicate balance. But experiences of good sex, however rare, precisely *lack* this quality of balance. The pleasure of sex is in its capacity to enhance sensuality; the full-body orgasm feels good because it increases a sense of well-being, of integrated bodily integrity. The pleasure in making love comes from experiencing one's own sensuous empowerment while being present to that of one's lover. Good sex involves a simultaneous enhancement of one's own and one's lover's well-being. Good sex does not involve simply one partner giving and the other receiving, one empowering and the other being empowered. The causes and effects of good sex are more complex, more dialectical, more interesting, and more difficult to categorize on the basis of separate roles or functions.

Insofar as sex is merely a balancing act, a matter of reducing tension, it is an alienated act which, while it may embody a desire to transcend alienated power in relation, can do no more than momentarily resolve it. Experienced simply as an exchange of power or as a means of resolving emotional and physical friction in our relational lives, sex cannot move us beyond the zero-sum experience of personal power in which one person's gain is another's loss. As long as this remains our primary experience of sexual activity or desire, we are likely to be titillated by fantasies of being taken, ravished, or raped by those who hold power over us. Conversely, and less frequently among women in the dominant culture in the United States, our erotic images may be fueled by a desire to take, ravish, or rape those whom we wish to have power over or experience as powerless. We have tried to show that this sexual dynamic is a disturbing, often violent, embodiment of a broader social relation, and that this social relation lays bare the core of sadomasochism: *the embodied, sensual appropriation of absolute power, or abject powerlessness, in relation to others.* Our dominant culture and theological systems continue to legitimate this zero-sum power arrangement in which giving or enduring pain signifies good sex or good behavior. Whether we personally view this situation through moralistic, deterministic, hedonistic, or playful lenses, none of us as individuals, or as sex partners, can simply rise above the sadomasochism that deforms our common life.

We can re-vision, however, our life together in such a way that we participate in sparking a sexual *phantasie* the presses beyond sadomasochism. We borrow Dorothee Soelle's term to denote a reality that is more than simply "fantasy." *Phantasie* is generated by the collective power of human beings actively to "imagine" a present-future and, in so doing, to begin to create it among ourselves.[36] In our sexual *phantasie*, sex is fueled by the realization of ourselves as subjects of our own lives and as partners in the realization of common pleasures. In this sexual relating, which is political and spiritual as well, we realize our power as we are touched, delighted, and moved by others and experience them as subjects of their own lives rather than of ours. We discover that our pleasure is not largely in exchanging power or reducing tension but rather in realizing together the power that we have in relation to one another. Indeed, as [Jessica] Benjamin would suggest, erotic pleasure may always be enhanced to some degree by the tension between self and other. But our sexual *phantasie* is that the strongest and most durable pleasure has little to do with tension reduction between people who possess unequal quantities of power. It is rather a matter of relational celebration between people who realize sensually—in our bodies— that genuine personal power belongs to either only insofar as it belongs to both and who know deeply that sharing common goods, such as pleasure and self-esteem, generates more rather than less power and pleasure for all.

NOTES

1. Carol Vance, ed., *Pleasure and Danger: Exploring Female Sexuality* (Boston: Routledge & Kegan Paul, 1984); Ellen Willis, "Feminism, Moralism and Pornography," in *Powers of Desire: The Politics of Sexuality,* ed. Ann Snitow, Christine Stansell, and Sharon Thompson (New York: Monthly Review Press, 1983), 460–68; Varda Burstyn, ed., *Women against Censorship* (Toronto: Douglas & McIntyre, 1984); Robin Linden, Darlene Pagano, et al., *Against Sadomasochism* (Oakland: Frog in the Well Press, 1982); Laura Lederer, ed., *Take Back the Night: Women on Pornography* (New York: William Morrow & Co., 1986); Andrea Dworkin, *Pornography: Men Possessing Women* (New York: A Perigee Book, 1979); *Coming to Power,* 2d ed., Samois Collective, a lesbian feminist S/M organization (Boston: Alyson Publications, 1982); "Sex Issue," *Heresies* 12, 3, no. 4 (1981); Haunani-Kay Trask, *Eros and Power: The Promise of Feminist Theory* (Philadelphia: University of Pennsylvania Press, 1986).

2. Mariana Valverde, *Sex, Power and Pleasure* (Toronto: Women's Press, 1985), 14.

3. Ibid., 9–46. See also Linda Gordon, *Woman's Body: Woman's Right. A Social History of Birth Control in America* (New York: Viking-Penguin, 1976); Adrienne Rich, *On Lies, Secrets and Silence: Selected Prose 1966–1978* (New York: W. W. Norton, 1979), 185–94, 199–202. For reviews of the development of literature on women's sexuality in the United States, see Introduction, in Snitow et al., eds., *Powers of Desire.*

4. Vance, ed., *Pleasure and Danger;* Linden et al., *Against Sadomasochism;* Samois

Collective, *Coming to Power;* Snitow et al., eds., *Powers of Desire;* Valverde, *Sex, Power and Pleasure;* "Sex Issue," *Heresies.*

5. Audre Lorde, "Uses of the Erotic: The Erotic as Power," in *Sister Outsider* (Trumansburg, N.Y.: Crossing Press, 1984), 53–59.

6. Carter Heyward, *Our Passion for Justice: Images of Power, Sexuality and Liberation* (New York: Pilgrim Press, 1984); Beverly W. Harrison, *Making the Connections: Essays in Feminist Social Ethics,* ed. Carol Robb (Boston: Beacon Press, 1985), 3–21, 81–173; idem, "Human Sexuality and Mutuality," in *Christian Feminism: Visions of Humanity,* ed. Judith J. Weidman (New York: Harper & Row, 1984), 141–57.

7. See the following essays in Vance, ed., *Pleasure and Danger:* Vance, "Towards a Politics of Sexuality," 1–27; Linda Gordon and Ellen Carol Dubois, "Seeking Ecstasy on the Battlefield: Danger and Pleasure in Nineteenth-century Thought," 31–49; and Alice Echols, "The Taming of the Id: Feminist Sexual Politics, 1968–1983," 50–72. See also Willis, "Feminism, Moralism, and Pornography" in Snitow et al., eds. *Powers of Desire,* 460–68.

8. From Vance, ed., *Pleasure and Danger.*

9. See Cherrie Moraga and Gloria Anzaldua, eds., *This Bridge Called My Back: Writings by Radical Women of Color* (Watertown, Mass.: Persephone Press, 1981); Cherrie Moraga, *Loving in the War Years* (Boston: South End Press, 1983); Rennie Simpson, "The Afro-American Female: The Historical Context of the Construction of Sexual Identity," in Snitow et al., eds., *Powers of Desire,* 229–35; Jacquelyn Dowd Hall, "The Mind That Burns in Each Body: Women, Rape, and Racial Violence," in Snitow et al., eds., *Powers of Desire,* 328–50; Barbara Omalade, "Hearts of Darkness," in Snitow et al., eds., *Powers of Desire,* 350–67; Bonnie Thornton Dill, "On the Hem of Life: Race, Class and the Prospects for Sisterhood," in *Class, Race and Sex: The Dynamics of Control,* ed. Amy Swerdlow and Hanna Lessinger (Boston: G. K. Hall, 1983), 173–88; Paula Giddings, *When and Where I Enter: The Impact of Black Women on Race and Sex in America* (New York: William Morrow, 1984), 84–94, 299–357; Bell Hooks, *Feminist Theory: From Margin to Center* (Boston: South End Press, 1984); Adrienne Rich, "Compulsory Heterosexuality and Lesbian Existence," in Snitow et al., eds., *Powers of Desire,* 177–205; and Joanna Ryan, "Psychoanalysis and Women Loving Women," in Sue Cartledge and Joanna Ryan, *Sex and Love: New Thoughts on Old Contradictions* (London: Women's Press, 1985), 196–209. See works by Linda Gordon, Mariana Valverde, and Carol Vance already cited; and Ellen Ross and Rayna Rapp, "Sex and Society: A Research Note from Social History and Anthropology," in Vance, ed., *Pleasure and Danger.* See also Rosalind Pollack Petchesky, *Abortion and Woman's Choice: The State, Sexuality, and Reproductive Freedom* (New York: Longmans, Green & Co., 1984); Beverly Wildung Harrison, *Our Right to Choose: Toward a New Ethic of Abortion* (Boston: Beacon Press, 1983); Rayna Rapp and Ellen Ross, "The Twenties' Backlash: Compulsory Heterosexuality, the Consumer Family, and the Waning of Feminism," in Swerdlow and Lessinger, eds., *Class, Race and Sex,* 93–107.

A few male writers provide extremely helpful historical-structural reinterpretation of the history of eroticism and confirm dynamics discussed here. E.g., Marco Mieli, *Homosexuality and Liberation: Elements of a Gay Critique* (London: Gay Men's Press, 1977). Mieli interprets male homosexual desire as universal and male heterosexual attraction to women as "split off," a form of hostility. He argues that so-called "heterosexual male sexuality" is always suffused with homosexuality. A British historian whose works are also important is Jeffrey Weeks, *Coming Out: Homosexual Politics in Britain from the 19th Century to the Present* (London: Quartet, 1977); idem, *Sex, Politics and Society: The Regulation of Sexuality Since 1800* (London: Longmans, Green & Co., 1981); and idem, *Sexuality and Its Discontents: Meanings, Myths and Modern Sexuality* (London: Routledge & Kegan Paul, 1985).

10. On mutual relation, see Carter Heyward, *The Redemption of God: A Theology of Mutual Relation* (Lanham, Md.: University Press of America, 1982); and idem, *Our Passion For Justice*, 83–93, 116–31. See also Harrison, "Human Sexuality and Mutuality," in Weidman, ed., *Christian Feminism*, 141–57.

11. Popular studies of women's sexual fantasies make clear that fantasies of seduction and domination are widespread and that even the repression of such sexual imagery may be understood as a response to domination.

12. Gordon, *Woman's Body: Woman's Right;* Valverde, *Sex, Power and Pleasure.*

13. Margaret Miles has argued for this dialectical viewpoint in her study of Augustinian theology; see her *Fullness of Life: Historical Foundations for a New Asceticism* (Philadelphia: Westminister Press, 1981).

14. J. N. D. Kelley, *Early Christian Doctrine*, 2d ed. (New York: Harper & Brothers, 1960), 15–17, 127–37, 163–88, 459–79. Once the Neoplatonic dualism is presupposed, the dichotomy worked its way into Christian christological discussions. This discussion can be traced in Richard A. Norris, *The Christological Controversy* (Philadelphia: Fortress Press, 1980).

15. Elisabeth Schüssler Fiorenza has carefully reconstructed the repatriarchalizing process that occurred in early Christianity through the household codes; see her *In Memory of Her: A Feminist Theological Reconstruction of Christian Origins* (New York: Crossroad, 1983), esp. chap. 7.

16. John Boswell, *Christianity, Social Tolerance and Homosexuality: Gay People in Western Europe from the Beginning of the Christian Era to the Fourteenth Century* (Chicago: University of Chicago Press, 1980); and Bernadette J. Brooten, "Paul's View on the Nature of Women and Female Homoeroticism," in *Immaculate and Powerful* ed. Clarissa Atkinson, Constance H. Buchanan, and Margaret A. Miles (Boston: Beacon Press, 1985), 61–87.

17. Samuel Laeuchli, *Power and Sexuality: The Emergence of Canon Law at The Synod of Elvira* (Philadelphia: Temple University Press, 1972), 56–113; Anne L. Barstow, *Married Priests and the Reforming Papacy: The Eleventh Century Debates* (Lewiston, N.Y.: Edwin Mellen Press, 1982); and Harrison, *Our Right to Choose*, 119–53.

18. Laeuchli, *Power and Sexuality*, 57–72, 102–13.

19. A few examples of this massive feminist research are: Rosemary Radford Ruether, *New Woman/New Earth: Sexist Ideologies and Human Liberation* (New York: Seabury Press, 1975); Schüssler Fiorenza, *In Memory of Her;* and idem, *Bread Not Stone: The Challenge of Feminist Biblical Interpretation* (Boston: Beacon Press, 1984); Phyllis Trible, *Texts of Terror: Literary-Feminist Readings of Biblical Narratives* (Philadelphia: Fortress Press, 1984); Rosemary Radford Ruether and Eleanor McLaughlin, eds., *Women of Spirit: Female Leadership in the Jewish and Christian Traditions* (New York: Simon & Schuster, 1979); Atkinson, Buchanan, and Miles, eds., *Immaculate and Powerful;* and Elizabeth A. Clark, *Jerome, Chrysostom, and Friends: Essays and Translations* (Lewiston, N.Y.: Edwin Mellen Press, 1979).

20. The theological significance of immediate relation is illumined in Heyward, *Redemption of God*, 2–9, and chap. 2. Heyward's discussion of "mutual relation" is indebted to the work of Jewish theologian Martin Buber. This work is also critical for understanding feminist theological claims that the effect of Christian dualism was to *denigrate* the human.

21. The tendency of men to separate "sex" and "intimacy" is widely acknowledged in the literature on sexuality. What is less frequently acknowledged is that this split reflects the social reality of sexist society: that men are to "desire" women sexually but are encouraged to locate equality in friendship—with men like themselves. Integration of sexual desire and intimate friendship remains a difficult task for men. We believe that Miele's analysis, *Homosexuality and Liberation*, explains not only why homoeroticism

suffuses male sexuality but why so much male eroticism toward women depends upon women conforming to male tastes regarding proper femininity.

22. Samois Collective, *Coming to Power*. We note, in women's defense of sadomasochism, the characteristic claim that it is a way to come into one's power. Our uneasiness with this defense rests not in the fact that ritualized sadomasochism is too sexual but that its proponents tend to equate coming to power with personal *autonomy*. As we will argue below, such an equation incorporates a conception of power and relationship that extends the traditions of patriarchal social theory.

23. The importance of the Boston Women's Health Collective, *The New Our Bodies, Ourselves* (New York: Simon & Schuster, 1984) rests precisely in its stress on *teaching* bodily integrity to women. As such, it deserves the accolade "the bible" of the women's movement.

24. Susie Orbach, *Fat Is a Feminist Issue* (New York: Berkley Publisher, 1982); and idem, *Hunger Strike: The Anorexic's Struggle for Survival as a Metaphor for Our Age* (New York: W. W. Norton, 1986). See also Kim Chernin, *The Obsession: Reflections on the Tyranny of Slenderness* (New York: Harper & Row, 1982); and idem, *The Hungry Self: Women, Eating and Identity* (New York: Harper & Row, 1985).

25. The role of Christianity in anorexia is illumined in Leadoff M. Bell, *Holy Anorexia* (Chicago: University of Chicago Press, 1985). Orbach has illumined this thesis of female protest in her works.

26. Christian sexual ethics cannot fully transcend this spiritualizing tendency until or unless that ethic officially ceases to privilege lifelong marital sexuality as "the" proper normative form of sexuality. For a philosophical analysis of this problem see Dorothea Krook, *Three Traditions of Moral Thought* (Cambridge: Cambridge University Press, 1959), 333–47. A Christian ethic cannot celebrate sexuality as per se good because sex is only good when it functions to support other values—procreation, or, in liberal theology, "unitative" or "communicative" values. Even the most progressive Christian reinterpretations of sexuality tend to extend this spiritualizing tendency. When, for example, sexuality is affirmed because of its unitative and integrative functions, it is assumed that what sexual longing involved is the desire for *merging with another*. See Anthony Kosnick et al., *Human Sexuality: New Directions in American Catholic Thought* (New York: Paulist Press, 1977), 48–52. Charles Davis, a progressive who purports to affirm bodily sexuality in an unqualified way, nevertheless insists, "One yearns for the other as for a lost part of oneself, with a longing to merge oneself and one's life with the other into a single person and a single life," *Body as Spirit: The Nature of Religious Feeling* (New York: Seabury Press, 1976), 134. A Protestant example of the tendency to spiritualize love and evade sexuality is Frederick Sontag, *Love Beyond Pain: Mysticism Within Christianity* (New York: Paulist Press, 1977), 59ff.

27. It is interesting that there is a spate of recent bestsellers dealing with women's difficulties with heterosexual love and/or sexual relations. See Carol Cassell, *Swept Away: Why Women Confuse Love and Sex . . . And How They Can Have Both* (New York: Bantam Books, 1983); Robin Norwood, *Women Who Love Too Much* (New York: Pocket Books, 1986); Connell Cowan and Melvyn Kinder, *Smart Women: Foolish Choices* (New York: Crown Publisher, 1985); Christine Dowling, *The Cinderella Complex: Women's Hidden Fear of Independence* (New York: Summit Books, 1981). While several of these books are indeed helpful to women in disentangling their lives from destructive relationships with men, the latter two blame the victim and discourage women's relational expectations. What is more important to acknowledge is the *destructiveness of male socialization* that encourages fear of dependency. We also need a more rigorous critical perspective on female socialization in relation to the institution of compulsory heterosexuality than these works provide. See, e.g., Michelle Barrett and Mary MacIntosh, *The Anti-Social Family* (London: Verso Press, 1982).

28. Daniel Day Williams, *What Modern Day Theologians Are Saying*, rev. ed. (New York: Harper & Brothers, 1959), 135–37.

29. Harrison, *Our Right to Choose*, 67–90.

30. The classic formulation of pleasure as the central, and except for immunity from pain, the only, good is Jeremy Bentham's hedonistic utilitarianism. See Jeremy Bentham and John Stuart Mill, *The Utilitarians* (Garden City, N.Y.: Doubleday & Co., 1961), 100–125.

31. For an excellent analysis of the way male socialization conditions preoccupation with self-possession, see John R. Wikse, *About Possession: The Self as Private Property* (University Park, Pa.: Pennsylvania State University Press, 1977).

32. This is probably the real source of the "difficulties" women have with sexual and intimacy relations discussed in the recent popular literature cited in n. 27. What troubles us is a tendency in feminist theory to encourage female independence, predicated upon a male model, rather than mutual relation as the simultaneous realization of self-possession and other-dependence.

33. The recognition that the experience of eroticized mutuality is so rare is one of the many insights that commends Mariana Valverde's analysis; see *Sex, Power and Pleasure*.

34. This theme of the eroticization of friendship is helpfully explored by Mary Hunt in *Fierce Tenderness: Toward a Feminist Theology of Friendship* (New York: Harper & Row, 1986).

35. Heyward, *Our Passion For Justice*, 243–47.

36. Dorothee Soelle, *Beyond Mere Obedience* (Minneapolis: Augsburg Press, 1970), 62–67.

12

The Moral Significance of Female Orgasm: Toward Sexual Ethics That Celebrates Women's Sexuality

MARY D. PELLAUER

*For a feminist like me, there are many lovely puzzles in sexual ethics in the western tradition. None, however, is so basic as the curious notions of women's sexuality. To correct these misbegotten notions, it is not enough just to criticize the errors. We must create more adequate accounts of female sexuality. As one small step in that project, in this essay I will explore one aspect of women's sexual experience—orgasm.

I do so for a set of interconnected reasons. For the last fifteen years I have been deeply involved in the movement against physical and sexual abuse. The feminist movement has asserted that sexual violence is not sex, and we have worked to make this new distinction persuasive. To get further with this project, we need to pay at least as much attention to our joys and delights as to our pains and disappointments. Otherwise we limit our own thriving.[1]

While orgasm is not a sufficient condition for good sex, it may be among the

*This essay springs from my joy in the company of Beverly Wildung Harrison as a colleague in ethics. When I was a graduate student in this field in the late sixties and early seventies, there were so few women in ethics that I nearly memorized her early articles. My pleasure in her as a colleague deepened in the six years I taught at Union Theological Seminary in New York. In those years I occasionally taught two courses with her and others: Ministry in Feminist Perspective and Feminist Ethics (so far as I know the first course with that title). I cannot count the ways I am indebted to her even when I am disagreeing.

Many conversations with other women have contributed to this essay. Special thanks over the years to Christine Gudorf, Sarah Bentley, and the members of the Mudflower Collective; more recently to Sherry Harbaugh, Janet Larson, Karen Bloomquist, Patricia Jung, Adele Resmer, Anita Hill, Daryl Koehn, John Ballew, Elizabeth Bettenhausen, DeAne Lagerquist, Susan Thistlethwaite, Margie Mayman-Park and Anne Gilson, who all read drafts of this essay.

149

necessary ones. Thus the text below will describe some experiences of female orgasm, prospecting for *concepts* appropriate for this moral terrain.[2] I will suggest from this account a few themes to which we could usefully pay more attention. I invite my colleagues in feminist ethics to work this area further.

This invitation is not pro forma. I need help. I find this topic confusing—sometimes literally beyond words, sometimes just not fitting well with other ethical language. This may be due to my lack of skill or to problems inherent in this topic, or both. I have no qualms about admitting I need help; this area has been systematically overlooked and distorted in the previous centuries of sexual ethics. Female orgasm is problematic from the start. Before we look specifically at my account, we need to glance at some of the problems.

WHAT HAPPENS WHEN WE THINK ABOUT FEMALE ORGASM?

We find out it's not easy. Female orgasm is problematic in a surprising number of ways. These difficulties group themselves into three large sets: First, we cannot take the experience for granted. This is extremely odd, and the more we think about it, the odder it becomes. The issues about whether women experience orgasm soon coalesce into a second area, intellectual or conceptual problems. Third, some features of the experience itself make it difficult to communicate.

The Experiential Problems

Even sexually active women cannot take orgasms for granted. Faking orgasms is a topic we now find portrayed in popular movies like *When Harry Met Sally* or discussed in magazines on the supermarket stand.[3] Even in these decades after Masters and Johnson and the whole sex therapy industry spawned by their work, sexologists find many women unsure what orgasm really is.

Anorgasmia among women appears to be common in our society, though perhaps less common than it once was. Its exact extent, now or earlier, is not clear.[4] The best contemporary evidence about the extent women experience orgasms comes from the 1990 *Kinsey Institute New Report on Sex:*

> Approximately 10% of all women have never had an orgasm by any means (this is called total anorgasmia). Between 50 and 75% of women who have orgasms by other types of stimulation do not have orgasms when the only form of stimulation is penile thrusting during intercourse.[5]

"Orgasmic dysfunction" is now *defined* as the inability to reach orgasm while masturbating. This definition conceals an enormous range of problems in sexually active relationships.

Note that these 1990 Kinsey Institute figures are stated as blunt facts, unqualified by social group, culture, or historical period.[6] Indeed, for total anorgasmia, figures in the 10% range have been constant through the last two decades. For earlier in the century the classic Kinsey reports are indispensable. It is rarely noticed that to the "0–6" continuum of heterosexual—homosexual orientation, the Kinsey team added another category—type X. Type X appeared for the first time in *Sexual Behavior in the Human Female,* for this category was composed almost entirely of women. Individuals were rated X if they did "not respond erotically" to anybody, neither the other nor the same sex. From the description, I cannot tell whether the individuals of type X were anorgasmic or asexual altogether. The Kinsey team categorized 9% of the sample as anorgasmic, but also named 2% as asexual.[7]

Before Kinsey, numbers like these did not exist. Prescriptive literature of the Victorian period took female disinterest in sexuality for granted. Sexual anesthesia was expected. (The cleverness of Kinsey's strategy was to assume that women had orgasms, asking only how often and with whom.) We now know that this ideology was not so all-encompassing as historians once thought. Prior to the Victorian period, information is murkier yet, but sexual anesthesia was not assumed.[8]

Partial anorgasmia, or occasional sex-without-orgasm, is harder to count. Figures about the proportion of women's sexual experiences that include orgasm are not very precise. The 1990 Kinsey Institute *Report* tells us:

> About 23% of women have experienced their first orgasm by age 15 and 90% by age 35. These figures include orgasm from masturbation, a partner's manual and/or oral stimulation of the genitals, nocturnal dreams, fantasy, and other sources—not just intercourse.[9]

The diversity of women's experiences of sex in these dry numbers is fascinating. More importantly, it is fundamental to any discussion of female sexuality. Women cannot take orgasms for granted. Men apparently do so, at least for most of the lifespan. Female orgasm does not come "naturally." We have to *learn* it. While this may also be true of male orgasm, it is emphatically the case for women. What is learned may be learned askew, idiosyncratically, or may be biased by hidden assumptions. Many layers of interpretation swathe experiences of orgasm like veils or shawls—thus pressuring us toward the second layer of problems.

Interpretive Problems

Several issues arise. Some, easier to name than to overcome, arise from social pressure: What will people think? When I told several women I was writing about orgasm, the range of responses was intriguing. "So many women are so far from there—they can't talk about sexuality at all, not even the simplest and most basic parts," said one. (This is true.) Others were tired of the pressure to have orgasms or the immense relationship issues. A third group hinted that perhaps I thought I was better than other women. Still others were simply silent. A small group said, "Neat, I'll look forward to finding out what you have to say." Some ethicists may dismiss social pressure as negligible; I cannot. It created internal inhibitions and self-doubts about this work, a tidal pull through which I had to wade in order to persevere, not always clear why I was doing so.

Responses like these raised a myriad of questions about what orgasm means to women. What differences are important between women who find this topic energizing and those who find it wearisome? Between those willing to talk and those who are silent? Does having orgasms confer moral status? Can sex-without-orgasm still be good sex? Is orgasm a male-dominated standard for evaluating sex?

Whether we experience orgasm may be related to the conflict of interpretations. Earlier in this century, women who did not have vaginal orgasms were called frigid. By now almost everyone knows about the errors of the Freudian school, with its misbegotten notions of the women who had not made a successful transfer of sexual energies from the clitoris (childish) to the vagina (mature). Though the Kinsey team was critical of this understanding and emphatic about the need for more empirical data, it was the work of Masters and Johnson in their laboratories, and the many women who volunteered there, that corrected basic errors of this interpretation.[10]

Most recently, the discovery of sexual violence has shifted interpretations once again. Today we are much more likely to learn that abusive experiences, especially in childhood, are the prime reasons that otherwise healthy women have sexually dysfunctional experiences.[11] (And this is what we call them: "dysfunctions.") The studied disinterest in sexual violence that prevailed in the first two-thirds of the century has been overwhelmed by the detailed exploration of several kinds of sexual abuses.

However, it remains the case that women who have not been directly victimized by sexual abuses may still not experience orgasm. We also need, by and large, accurate information about female sexuality, personal sexual knowledge of the kind gained by masturbation, and if in a relationship, a partner informed (informable?) and willing to respond to the woman's specific needs. This is a complex combination of conditions.[12]

What it means to us, what differences between us are crucial—these issues encroach on others that are akin. An account is a created artifact, a second-order phenomenon. To recognize that sexuality is always already interpreted—even in the driest of scientific or medical tomes—is indispensable.[13] To create an "account" means to describe in words, and written words at that.[14] Writing not only inscribes this description, fixing and distancing it, but it shapes these words by genre.

Until very recently, written accounts of sexuality were dominated by a few genres—medical/scientific and confessional/pornographic, in particular.[15] These genres may inflect women's accounts into line not only with sexist expectations but also with newly formed feminist expectations that may be short-sighted or too small. Much as I might wish for a new genre to realize the newness of accounting for female sexuality, I have no such exalted end here. Some commentators suggest that first-person descriptions of experience by ordinary women are a new genre, and I will employ this method here as the starting point for ethical reflection, together with comments on the problems of giving such an account.[16] Whether in the long run this practice will yield new methods in ethics, I cannot say.

Phenomenological Problems

Knots and snarls of other kinds also appear in the topic. If I persist despite the previous layers of problems (no small effort) and scrutinize my experiences, four specific features of orgasm as experienced also make an account problematic.

To begin with, orgasms are brief, even ephemeral; they are bursts of intense pleasure that may be overwhelming. Even if one has several, each is fairly short.[17] The fleeting nature of the experience makes it hard to capture; "overwhelming" is tricky both to live through and to describe.

Second, to describe an orgasm ordinarily means to remember it. This requires special skills or insight—memory, for instance, or a gift for words. Trying to describe one while it is occurring is odd (though one might try this, for instance, to heighten the pleasure of one's partner), but I usually find that words disappear or they reduce to expressive noises. When I try to remember an orgasm, it proves tricky to recall a specific one. They run together in my mind.

Even so, third, they are not all alike. Some are intense bursts, some are more diffuse. (So much so, in fact, that I can now wonder if the first problem is stated properly.) Some are better than others, and I am not sure if this is always a case of "more" (more pleasurable) or if there are qualitative differences. They group together in families, or perhaps arrange themselves on a continuum. Furthermore, while there are things I can do to ensure that I experience an orgasm, I am not in control of the kind of orgasm I experience on any given occasion. If I notice that I am forgetting the more diffuse ones, I cannot plan to have one in order to explore its details.

Fourth, how do I know that the experiences of other women are like mine? Women do not often talk about orgasms. Indeed, they are so very personal that we may suspect that we are not experiencing the same thing. "Did the earth move?" asks a character in a Hemingway novel. Well, maybe not. Should it? I have felt shaken, almost shivered apart, but I have never felt the earth move. If another women says it is like a hiccup (another image I cannot relate to) are we different in some fundamental way? Are there correlations between these chasms or nuances of experiences and other factors, such as social class, culture, race or ethnic background, sexual orientation, religion? We don't know exactly.

That there may be such correlations leads me to name at least the clear limits, right at the start, of this sample of one. I am predominantly heterosexual, a "1" on the Kinsey scale.[18] I have a doctoral degree. I am white by "race," though beige and pink in fact. Today I have a lot of money by our culture's standards, though I remember what it was like to be poor. Both class and education correlate with specific strands of sexual experience in our society, though perhaps more so for men than for women. And in Kinsey's sample and some other studies since, for women (but not for men), we must add religion.[19] I am Lutheran by denominational heritage and ongoing choice, though denomination is too crude a measure for the real differences among women. It is important that I heard in confirmation (1958–60) that God created human sexuality and declared it to be "very good," a cause for celebration, though subject to sin. (I was later surprised to find that all Lutherans did not learn this in confirmation, indeed, that very few did.) That is a lot of limits.[20]

These limits may be insurmountable hazards. Alerted to them, however, we can guard against universalizing any particular instance without serious checking with the varieties of women's experiences. I acknowledge these limits; indeed, I embrace them. They are the roots of my standpoint in the world. If we do not tell the truth as it appears to us from our many standpoints, we have no hope either of broadening our range of vision or of finding any similarities between us. My experience is not enough, to be sure, but it is enough to begin.

My account will be conspicuously heterosexual. It is safer in this homophobic and heterosexist society for a heterosexual account to take public form. It is also relatively safe for me to describe my sexual experiences because I am in a long and stable marriage. If I were a lesbian, and/or if I were single, it could be extremely dangerous to do what I will do here. If I were African American, Asian, Native American, Hispanic, or Jewish, I would risk setting off racism. This is tragic. It is straightforwardly unjust. It strikes at the heart of our ability to assess the moral significance of female orgasm. It means that the best discussions of these issues may never occur in public. Male ethicists may never hear them. I may not either. (Safety is not morally neutral.)

Some readers may be thinking: With such an array of problems, why bother? I too might grow weary just at this point, but I don't. Problems can also be sources of curiosity and creativity, provided we linger with them, mull over them. I experience a curious exhilaration about these problematic layers, each one multiple: Why are there so many? It would be enough to have one set. (It certainly would be enough to have the problems of whether we are experiencing orgasm.)

The presence of three distinguishable layers of problems leads me to speculate that female orgasm is *overdetermined as problematic*. I begin to suspect that female orgasm is very important indeed. What stirs in our orgasms, that there should be so many obstacles around them? And this lures me on: the prospect of pleasure, rejoicing, delight. Whether absent or present, what does pleasure mean? Is it essential or accidental? Is it ethically significant, even foundational? To get at those issues, we must look closely at the experience.

STALKING THE BIG O

At the risk of being overprecise, I find six important elements in my experiences of orgasm. I do not claim them as normative, but as suggestive, provocative, intriguing. They are worth lingering over.

1. *Being Here-and-Now.* There are no recipes for love-making to orgasm (except this one). It is not capable of being routinized. What gave me a

delicious tingle yesterday may be ho-hum blah today, and vice versa. Yesterday's slow and languorous time may be today's urgency and snap changes, or vice versa. Yesterday's silly mood may be today's solemnity or earnestness. Every time I must enter fully and freshly into just what is here-and-now, the precise sensations that occur in the blending of our bodies.

And this is difficult. Any number of distractions can endanger full awareness—muscle cramps, odd mental associations, ill health, differences in timing. (We can also add pain, unpleasantness, aversion to certain behaviors, numbing out, flashbacks.) Cracker crumbs in the sheets, for instance, left there by a child reading, can become boulders when all the nerve endings are firing. At other times, oddly the focused human spirit can shut out everything but the luminous glow of the other's skin/self, magnetically pulling me away from the rest of the universe so completely that nothing else can get in, not even those same cracker crumbs. Which will be the case on any specific occasion, is impossible to foretell.

Concentrating, focusing—these are "mental" abilities that are as much a part of sex as any purely physical abilities. Being fully present, where is the language for this? Meditation is the closest analogue I know; this comparison is surprisingly apt, for both are disciplines of being here-and-now, of letting go. This is to be receptive in a way that is not the opposite of sometimes insisting or demanding. Forcing or faking are the enemies of this state.

2. *Varieties of Sensations.* So, what is it like? I descend into our skins, attention riding the places where we touch, following the curve of this back under my fingertips and palms, following the electric trail of these hands on my planes, the sweated prairies of our torsos pressed into each other, the moisture of the inside velvet of this mouth joining with mine, the blessed smells of sweat rising as incense, the rises of flesh where little hairs entice me to run and play like a child in the woods. We mingle and mesh. Hands are electric. The passage of palms and fingertips over my skin leaves lightning trails of incandescence behind to mark where they move. In early states it is all surface.

At some point this glowing heat intensifies, shifting inward and downward inside me. But what these feelings gain in intensity, they lose in clarity. The middle is often confusing. I often do not know exactly what I want or need at this time. This stage does not supply me or my partner with clear guidance about how to satisfy these deep undercurrents. Sometimes I flail around. But in the farther reaches of this phase, I would do anything to make this last forever. (I think this is what the sexologists call the "plateau phase.") There is something greedy and isolated in this experience, especially in the last moments. I am both completely focused on my partner's touches and yet somehow the other almost disappears, leaving me riding this flesh.[21]

There is a directionality here. I seek to go further, riding the edges of the eruption to tip into the volcano. To stop here is frustrating, incomplete; it leaves me with a sense that it is not over, that there is more. Yet it is not automatic that I will go over the edge to this something else.

If I am lucky, I do go over the edge. Tremors center in my pelvis, vibrating me like a violin string. As I am shaken from the hips outward, my bones turn to lava, languorous liquid fire, heated jelly in the pelvis and thighs, magma coursing molten down.

Sometimes it is not this strong or vibrant. If I try to replicate yesterday's experience, I am frustrated. If I expect magma to course down my legs, a spasm of calm surprises me, like a cool ripple in a pond, more a release from tension than shaking in a vast hand.[22] All I can do is to remain open to the flaring guidance I receive from the impulses and feelings as they arise, little beaconlights summoning me forward.

Though there is pleasure in plenty here, pleasure alone does not do justice to this experience. Pleasure has been present all along the way. There is more. But this language suggests that the difference between orgasm and what precedes it is only quantitative. This is mistaken. It is also a difference in quality. To elucidate this change in quality, I add another element.

3. *Ecstasy*. At the moment/eternity of orgasm itself, I melt into existence and it melts into me. I am most fully embodied in this explosion of nerves and also broken open into the cosmos. I am rent open; I am cleaved/joined not only to my partner, but to everything, everything-as-my-beloved (or vice versa), who has also become me.[23] The puny walls of my tiny separate personhood either drop so that I-you-he-she-we-they-it are one *or* they build up so thoroughly that all/me is one.[24] Either way of stating it calls out for its opposite: paradoxland.

An alternate reading of this quasi-mystical dimension: My partner's skin is an icon of the universe. I am enraptured, captivated, mesmerized, by the planes of this back, arms, navel plain, thighs, the globes of this rearend blending gracious curves into thighs and back, and by my own as well. I fall/slide into them, and they turn into the universe. When I am in this state, reverently and greedily cherishing these gracious plains of flesh, whole-self-as-caress, I want to cherish every plane in the world with this same tenderness—the wood of the bedside table, the walls of the room, the grass of the yard outside, the iron bars of the back fence, the gnarled bark of trees, all call out to me to caress them in this same tender mood, not to intrude upon them my sexuality, but to cherish them as I cherish our skin-self.

Orgasm is sui generis. It is paradoxical. Ecstasy is what is at stake here.[25] *Ek-stasis*, standing outside the self, is the closest word for this state. At the same time, it is the most definite incarnation I know outside of childbirth, for in it I am most completely bound to the stimulation of my body. Thus, immanence and transcendence meet here, another paradox. The experience is peculiar/wondrous in other ways as well. To everyday consciousness, the dissolving of ego's boundaries, nonseparateness, may always look like nonexistence. It scares me. It also makes me thrive. Now I know the full range of my capacities and my ownmost being. It is a limit-experience.[26]

4. *Vulnerability.* As our relationship deepened and improved, as we learned together about female orgasm, I became heartshatteringly threatened by the *goodness* of this experience, this ecstatic union with my beloved. Some of that was intrinsic to the paradoxes above, but not all. It slowly became apparent that my partner eagerly and persistently sought *my* pleasure. My ecstasy excited and touched him; he was eager for my orgasm. This was daunting, especially if I grew impatient. On the occasions when I felt that I would never get it off, and that it was time to quit, he would not.

That my pleasure was important to him, this was hard to accept, to let in. That he would refuse his own release till I had mine, that he was willing to persist in trying to bring my release/ecstasy, that he reveled in it: This shook me very deeply. It was so very unexpected. My surprise about this says more about me than it does about him. I did not expect to be loved. I did not expect him to have the capacity to put me before himself. I expected only to be secondary.[27]

There is an ambiguity here. Some partners and some circumstances might make his stance oppressive. Some may consider the pursuit of orgasm to be a distortion of sexuality, another instance of male goals and male will overriding female choices. I can only report that I did not and do not experience it this way. I experience it as grace, an instance of his vulnerability-to-me reaching out to meet my vulnerability-to-him.[28]

5. *Power.* Perhaps it could easily become domination, because there is power in this transaction. Indeed, sometimes I balk at this ecstatic explosion precisely because of the power. Sex with him is a living icon of the power in his body, making me tingle along every nerve at his touch, making me rouse urgently toward him. That is because I love him and he turns me on. There is a dialectic here of his power meeting mine, that is, he has this power because I respond to him and this response is mine. But I only "know" that, in a kind of distanced way. I do not experience it, I have to reason it out. When his hands glide along my skin, I experience it as the power of his hands and not the power of my response. He may experience it as the power of my response, but I do not. And possibly I cannot, because what is "really" happening here is the power of the connectedness between us. The tingle is neither in his hands nor in my skin, but only at the interface between them. Separated, there is no tingle, no power. Our nonrelational language makes it difficult to say this and sometimes difficult to perceive it. (And "interface" is not a very sexy word.)

But, as we touch, mingle, play together in our bed, I experience these connections occurring as *his power*, the more so the closer I approach to orgasm. Therefore, I experience an orgasm and all the impelling feelings before it as his power over me. This frightens me. I must open myself up to his power over me in order to receive this ecstasy, and this is not easy. It depends upon trust that is built up in many elements of our relationship—the mutuality growing, the confidence in reliability, the sense that this person will not hurt me on purpose, our abilities to forgive each other.

6. *Nothing Above Can Be Taken for Granted.* All of this is complicated by the fact that I do not experience this tingling/burning/melting every time we touch, nor even continuously during our lovemaking. Indeed, most of our touch is warm, nurturing, nonsexual touch. Only sometimes do these sparks flare.

Part of the difficulty of making love is right there. Either of us can be mistaken about whether the other is turned on by something we are doing. It requires communicating about which is which, and what we want. I have to say what I want. I am not always good at that; sometimes I am a coward, yes, but sometimes I literally do not know. Sometimes the effort of concentration does not seem worth it. And on those occasions, not always, but often, no orgasm.

On the other hand, sex-without-orgasm is not nothing. Besides the pleasure inhering in every stage before orgasm, there is also warmth, comfort, intimacy, the experience of belonging in an embrace. I would not trade these non-orgasmic goods of sexuality even for ecstasy.

FLIRTING WITH THE EDGES
OF SEXUAL ETHICS

So, what does it mean? There is too much here for one essay to tidy up all the loose ends, and I affirm that.[29] I intend to conclude this essay only in the minimal sense of ending it. I find it hard to draw conclusions in the sense of coming to rest in a particular insight. (This may be inevitable since I have stressed the boundarylessness of orgasm.) I have been tempted to start several new essays at this point. I suspect this is because concentrating on female sexuality is potentially system-generating, that is, it points us toward a different way of life as well as a different way of thought, or several.

This leads into a first set of concluding comments. *We need a multiplicity in feminist sexual ethics that can at least match the multiplicity of women's sexual experiences.* Ethical reflection on female orgasm could go in many different directions, and these differences enrich rather than threaten our work. I invite my colleagues to give more attention to several clustered themes.

The power issues are familiar. Though feminist ethics has done more to illuminate mutuality than any other kind of ethics, we have hardly exhausted the topic. Considering trust, vulnerability, and openness may be key for moving the discussion another notch.[30]

Some readers may wish to raise issues about the sacred. Some empirical studies since the Kinsey reports stress that religion continues to make a difference in whether women experience orgasm. If this is so, it raises a host of intriguing questions. Further, if I am right that ecstasy is a limit-experience, then religious issues are inherent in orgasm. Whether, and if so how, specifically Christian ethics or theology may be related to female orgasm is an open question.

Historical and social topics, touched briefly in the section on anorgasmia, are worth pursuing. The historical character of sexuality is strongly resisted in our culture. That we are malleable in our most intimate places, our muscles and cells, leads me to paradox again. (This might explain body-mind dualism without falling into it.) We could also use some serious interpretation of the fact that sexuality is learned (rather than "natural") and what difference this makes to ethics.

Warmth, comfort, touch, intimacy, the nonorgasmic goods of sexuality, could all bear much more reflection. How we might talk about a sense of belonging that could be distinguished from patriarchal ownership (belonging with versus belonging to) could be crucial. Obviously I have laid aside desire, imagination/fantasy, and masturbation-to-orgasm—all extremely important topics for female sexuality.

Though my darling is an important background presence here, I have bracketed all questions about the sexual experiences of men. Having women comment about male sexuality would at least be a refreshing change from the prior centuries. I believe that we can do this empathetically and insightfully, because otherwise what would be the point?

If I had many more pages, I would reflect on the changing boundaries about sexual matters in our society and the need to dance between the polarities of uniting and differentiating. I would want to work out the ways that experiences of good sex ground the movement against sexual abuses, since hostility and domination do not mix with any of the six elements of orgasm.

Issues about writing may also be important. How do I communicate the bursting delight, the delicious melting-into-existence of good sex? The language of so much academic prose is dreary, boring, and distanced. These qualities contradict the experience. I do not mean only that we need more passion in sexual ethics, but we need the whole range of emotional expressiveness. Besides being passionate and intense, good sex can also be fun, humorous, and lighthearted. I'd like to encourage my colleagues to try out various tones of voice—rushing breathlessness, lyrical modes, perplexity, tenderness, frustration. It would be good if we thought more seriously about genre as well as about concealing and revealing in nonfiction. Issues about writing are in part issues about language. So we need to open space for a second set of comments.

What Ethical Language Fits?

When I consider the language of ethics and my experiences of orgasm, I am confused. Little of it seems relevant to the specific character of ecstatic union. Even if we begin with simple, basic ethical terms, something goes awry.

Consider "should." It is instructive to notice what happens if we ask: "Should women have orgasms?" or more precisely, "Should women have orgasms when we have sex?" In several ways this question is odd. Consider, for instance, its parallel, "Should men have orgasms?" or "Should men have orgasms when they have sex?" In almost all cases (before advanced age or specific dysfunctions such as retarded ejaculation), if a man is having sex, he is having an orgasm.[31] Most men cannot imagine having sex regularly, let alone for years, without orgasms.

Just as peculiar is what happens when we try to answer the question. The consequences of saying *either* no or yes are odd. Though at first glance, I want to say, "yes of course," this does not accomplish much in the way of healing. Indeed, it may be actively harmful for anorgasmic women. "Should" can deepen women's problems rather than transform them.[32] On the other hand, saying no commits us to enshrining women in deprivation: clearly unacceptable.

These same problems arise for other varieties of ethical language: orgasm is not a duty or an obligation. (This line of thinking may be what creates faking.) I have problems asserting that it is a right, though the consequences of arguing that it is not a right are unacceptable. It is not a virtue; it neither produces virtue nor proceeds from virtue. (On the other hand, female orgasm is emphatically not a vice.) It is not a privilege or a luxury. It is a good, and a very high-level good at that, but a peculiar one. It is not an achievement, however much I have worked hard.

The language that feels closest for me may raise other feminists' hackles—the theological language of gift or grace, the surprisingly unmerited, gratuitous gift. The heterosexuality of my account creates some of these problems. It may suggest that our orgasms are at men's disposal; out of the abundant generosity of their hearts, they provide them for us. Such thoughts of course do extreme damage to the mutuality of the experiences I have with my beloved. We both had to learn; we both had to work hard; nonetheless, there is a gratuitousness to the fact that orgasms resulted. It was more like good fortune, luck, chance, or accident. Chance and luck have disappeared from ethics altogether, let alone sexual ethics. I invite my colleagues in ethics to meditate on the dangers and possibilities of chance for women's sexuality.[33]

In one sense, whether orgasm is a gift from a partner is beside the point. Orgasm is a gift I receive *from my own body.* My very flesh has this capacity to burst me open to existence, to melt me down into a state in which my connections to the rest of the universe are not only felt, but felt as extremely pleasurable, as joyous.[34] But to this foundational celebration of female embodiment and the fragile chanciness of good relationship, I must add the vagaries of culture: available accurate information, both physiological and experiential; the new trust and courage of many women willing to explore and report on our sexuality as we live it; the writers, publishers, and feminist booksellers who make knowledge accessible (at a price); the rape crisis centers, women's shelters, therapists, and other healing agents who make personal/social change possible (sometimes at no price, sometimes at very high prices).

It is peculiar that so few ethical discussions of sexuality take up female orgasm, let alone its problematic character or its importance to flourishing. Much more emphasis and lingering philosophical care has been spent on desire.[35] This may be one of the distinguishing marks of patriarchy in sexual ethics: Men are able to take pleasure for granted in sex. Or perhaps they translate pleasure into desire (as in "she wants it" or "I want it"). The progress from desire to pleasure to ecstasy is precisely what women cannot take for granted in our society.

The Western tradition has been quick to talk about the need for spirit or mind to rule the body with its imperious passions. We have been less apt to talk at length about the gifts body gives to the spirit. Perhaps they have been taken for granted by the men who have always known *ek-stasis* and its releases, with or without that of their partners in bed. Perhaps they have always been able to explore these pleasures more freely than women.

We do not have a language fully empowered and inflected with women's sexual experiences. The time has more than come to talk publicly about the body as women experience it, to see what new concepts would await us there, and to incorporate—that is, take into all our bodies, those of groups as well as of individuals—the insights we need in order to be gentler on ourselves, each other, people far away, and also on the very planet's skin. Body does have gifts to give. and what helps us to experience more of life as cherishable, this can only be a help to our choices in daily life.

What we linger over tells us what is important to us. Indeed, I suggest that *lingering* is part of the ethical language we need. Along with lingering, I have found myself using other terms that are not usually on the tip of the ethicist's tongue: Inviting. Safety. Diversity. Healing.[36] Let's linger a while more on the constructive possibilities of female orgasm.

The Moral Significance of Ecstasy

This experience makes me wonder many things: Why do we think we are really "separate" from each other anyway? Do men experience orgasm as melting union? If women could take orgasms for granted, what exactly would be the consequences? Or, should men take orgasms less for granted? Do they need to have less sex so that they can value it more deeply?[37]

The mystical character of my description may be what is most striking. What does it mean? Is it normative? And what does "normative" mean in this context? (1) Does it mean that it is a source of values and norms, standards by which I evaluate the rest of life? (2) Does it mean that all women "should" experience orgasm as I do? That the norms and values I find here extend beyond my skin out into the universe? I am reluctant to conclude that it is normative in this second sense, for several reasons.

First, I am mystically inclined in general. This may be true of many women, but not all. Like social location, personal idiosyncracies like this may tempt us into universalizing what cannot bear this moral weight.[38]

Second, some women explicitly resist giving orgasm any "meaning," let alone the expansive sense of ecstatic union in my account. "Sex is just—sex," they say, sometimes with a shrug. Or "an orgasm is an orgasm is an orgasm."[39]

Third, the most important moral questions here are precisely about these differences. How do we deal with persons whose experience is different from our own? Do we shut them out or shut them up? I invite my colleagues with different experiences of orgasm to describe what it is like for them, to dissent, to add nuances, or to start over in a different place. (Like safety, invitation is not morally neutral, especially in sexual matters.) That we listen respectfully and attentively for the differences is very important.

There may be still other reasons to resist assigning too much ethical weight to ecstatic union. Everyday consciousness in our society, even my feminist consciousness, resists living with the paradoxes of ecstasy. *Paradoxes are hard to live with.* They feel in the first instance like contradictions. To tell a paradox apart from a contradiction is not easy. Therefore to dwell on them is potentially crazy-making. (And too many nuances risks losing the ability to communicate with the woman on the street.) In the second instance (that is, after thinking about it), some of the paradoxes result from the limits of language. We just can't say it right, the words make it sound like a muddle. Falling silent, as many women do, may be an appropriate response when language does not provide concepts that *fit* experience. (There is no way around the problems of language. We must go through them.)

Several other serious puzzles arise when we linger over female orgasm. If women experience more sexual pleasure, do we become more demanding outside of bed as well (and vice versa)? Does good sex make us more capable of valuing excellence in other realms of life? Is making love a means of grace? Is it insightful to speak of our sexual pleasure as "the advent of non-sense that multiplies sense," granted to women "provided it isn't discussed"?[40] Can all these be right at once? How does this immanent/transcendent joy relate to others?

A good sexual experience is a source of worth and value to the participant(s). To touch and be touched in ways that produce sweet delights affirms, magnifies, intensifies, and redoubles the deep value of our existence. Ecstasy spills over onto the world outside the bed, not accidentally but intrinsically. It awakens rejoicing, but more: wonder and reverence, the poignant astonishment that we are here, that we live, that anything at all is here, that life can enfold such bursting joy. What if more of life were like this? In my experience, female orgasm is so rich, so abundant in meaning that it is supersaturated with it. It is superabundant, a treasure trove. Women wondering, women marvelling: Is this different from Socrates' besotted *thaumazein*? Or from the reverence and awe that are its counterpart in Israel and the Christian theological tradition? Or for that matter, from the laughter of Aphrodite?

After reading a version of this essay, my darling said, "Too much *schlag*," thinking of viennese pastries mounded with whipped cream. And as with any diet overdosing on one rich element, this very superabundance signals that we can overdo it. Though this cannot be an ethics of scarcity, nonetheless we must be able to look at scarcity and surplus together, to hold one in each hand, so to speak. Ethics differentiates. To forget anorgasmia while we are talking about the significance of orgasm is to falsify women's sexuality.

I am reluctant to conclude more about female orgasm until we are more sure about how to encompass graciously the diversity of women's sexual experiences. The fact that women cannot take orgasm for granted while having sex is among the most important aspects of this topic. Most certainly this points us toward the strange and distorted twists of sexuality under patriarchal conditions. But more than that, it may offer unlooked for grounds of hope in reconstructing sexual ethics on a new basis. Questioning what is taken for granted by previous models is typical of paradigm shifts.[41] Not being able to take ecstasy for granted opens a space for inquiry, an expanded vision. Women's experiences of sex-without-orgasm may therefore be as crucial as orgasm for a developed feminist sexual ethics. Both provide loci for examining a whole range of intertwined and complex goods in sexuality that have not been explored.

We need to follow the trails of our joy with the same persistent adventurousness with which we have explored the pains of sexual abuses. We need to explore this terrain in a mood that can acknowledge the disappointments without letting go of delight—balancing them, so to speak, one in each hand. (This may return us to the language of rights.) Ethics is certainly fueled by the insistent No to wrongs and injustices. But we need equally lavish insistence on the Yeses, the visions and joys that lure us toward them.

Celebrating women's sexuality is key to good sexual ethics, feminist or not. Such a celebration requires a many-meaninged, many-valued, many-voiced complexity that can rejoice in the fact that we are many and not one. Appreciating that sexuality is multivocal and multivalent is not usual in sexual ethics. We are right now in a transition state. We need many more voices raised to describe, to speculate, to linger over the meaning of our delights.

NOTES

1. Audre Lorde's classic essay, "Uses of the Erotic: The Erotic as Power," in *Sister Outsider: Essays and Speeches* (Trumansburg, N.Y.: Crossing Press, 1984), 53–59 touched off some of this discussion more than a decade ago. Carter Heyward's *Touching Our Strength: The Erotic as Power and the Love of God* (San Francisco: HarperSan Francisco, 1989) mines this vein for feminist theology.

2. Just as I did in "Moral Callousness and Moral Sensitivity: Violence against Women," in *Women's Consciousness, Women's Conscience: A Reader in Feminist Ethics,* ed. Barbara Andolsen, Christine Gudorf and Mary Pellauer (Minneapolis: Winston Press, 1985).

3. See for instance, Susan Jacoby, "When Women Lie about Sex," *New Woman,* December 1991, 32–34, or Lesley Dormen, "Honey, You're a Great Lover . . . *Not!*" *Ladies' Home Journal,* July 1992, 70–75. Faking orgasms is a moral issue unique to women and may be uniquely illuminating for the moral structures of women's experience under western patriarchy.

4. To do justice to anorgasmia requires a whole essay in itself; though I preter to call it sex-without-orgasm. I believe we need to look at three different groups of experiences of sex-without-orgasm: aversive sexual experiences (consenting encounters that include serious turn-offs), pre-orgasmic experiences, and experiences in which the woman, for whatever reasons, chooses not to have an orgasm.

5. June M. Reinisch with Ruth Beasley, *The Kinsey Institute New Report on Sex: What You Must Know to be Sexually Literate* (New York: St. Martin's Press, 1990), 203.

6. The *Kinsey Institute New Report on Sex* has no references for race or ethnic groups anywhere in the text, nor any comments on this silence. The original Kinsey team in the 1940s was explicit about excluding two groups of women: 915 white females who had served prison sentences, and the 934 members of the "non-white sample." See Alfred C. Kinsey, Wardell B. Pomeroy, Clyde E. Martin, and Paul H. Gebhard, *Sexual Behavior in the Human Female* (Philadelphia: W. B. Saunders and Co. 1953), 22. Shere Hite's questionnaire did not ask its respondents any questions about race and was sent to groups with overwhelmingly white audiences. See *The Hite Report: A Nationwide Study of Female Sexuality* (New York: Dell, 1976), 39, 23–24. Masters and Johnson employed an all-white sample from the upper middle class. See William H. Masters and Virginia E. Johnson, *Human Sexual Response* (New York: Bantam, 1966), chap. 2, "The Research Population," 9–23. For a good analysis of these and other flaws in sexology, see Janice Irvine, *Disorders of Desire: Sex and Gender in Modern American Sexology* (Philadelphia: Temple University Press, 1990).

7. For data on anorgasmia from the early 1970s, see Helen Kaplan, *The New Sex Therapy* (New York: Brunner/Mazel, 1974) or Lonnie Barbach, *For Yourself: The Fulfillment of Female Sexuality* (Garden City, N.Y.: Doubleday, 1975). For the basic description of Type X, see Kinsey, et al., *Sexual Behavior in the Human Female,* 472; for the percentages, see pp. 513, 512, where some were described as also not erotically responding to masturbation, sexual fantasies, or dreams. On the other hand, they also said "it is doubtful whether there is ever a complete lack of [orgasmic] capacity" (373). "Inhibitions" were cited as the primary reason for not reaching orgasm (see pp. 374, 329).

8. See Nancy Cott, "Passionlessness: An Interpretation of Victorian Sexual Ideology, 1790–1850," in *A Heritage of Her Own: Toward A New Social History of American Women,* ed. Nancy Cott and Elizabeth Pleck (New York: Simon and Schuster, 1979); and James Mahood and Kristine Wanburg, eds., *Clelia D. Mosher: The Mosher Survey* (New York: Ayer Company Publishers, 1980). For pre-Victorian medical manuals that discussed women's orgasms, as well as the changes in the mid-1800s, see John S. Haller, Jr., and Robin M. Haller, *The Physician and Sexuality in Victorian America* (Champaign: University of Illinois Press, 1974). A good survey of sexuality in U.S. history is John D'Emilio and Estelle B. Freedman, *Intimate Matters: A History of Sexuality in America* (New York: Harper & Row, 1988). A recent work on the earlier centuries is Thomas Laqueur, *Making Sex: Body and Gender from the Greeks to Freud* (Cambridge: Harvard University Press, 1990).

9. Reinisch, 85. Those last three words were a veiled critique of the original Kinsey team's preoccupation with orgasm during coitus. As Kinsey said, "There has, of course, been widespread interest in discovering what proportion of the coitus of the average female does lead to orgasm, and in discovering some of the factors which account for such *success or failure in coitus*" (374, emphasis mine). After lengthy cautions about the many variables that make it difficult "to calculate what percentage of the copulations in any particular sample lead to orgasm," *Sexual Behavior in the Human Female* said that "the average (median) female in the sample had reached orgasm in something between 70 and 77 percent of her marital coitus" (375) and in about 40% of the unmarried coitus (330). The highly visible charts in the chapter on marital coitus differentiated only between

women who "never" experienced orgasm and those who did "plus or minus always." This makes me wonder about spurious precision. If it is true that half to three-quarters of women in the United States cannot experience orgasm from intercourse alone, then these numbers are highly questionable. Other methods were called "pre-coital petting techniques" by the Kinsey team.

10. The *big* qualifier in *Human Sexual Response* was that women reach orgasm "with effective stimulation" (see p. 4 and following).

11. See the review of the evidence in the appendices in Wendy Maltz and Beverly Holman, *Incest and Sexuality: A Guide to Understanding and Healing* (Lexington: Lexington Books, 1987).

12. While the proportion of U.S. women who masturbate has grown over the last fifty years, it still does not reach the same level as among men. "Among the thousands of people interviewed by Kinsey during the 1940s and 1950s, 94 percent of males and 40 percent of females reported having masturbated to orgasm. More recent studies report that about the same percentage of males masturbate but that the percentage of females has increased to around 70 percent (or more, depending on the study)," says Reinisch, 95.

13. Irvine, *Disorders of Desire,* is the most comprehensive commentary on the politics of interpretation among sexologists. See also Carol Vance, "Gender Systems, Ideology and Sex Research," in *Powers of Desire: The Politics of Sexuality,* ed. Ann Snitow, Christine Stansell, and Sharon Thompson (New York: Monthly Review Press, 1983), 371–84.

14. Not that writing is the primary element in sexuality; far from it. Nor is writing the primary mode of doing ethics, sexual or otherwise. Problems arise when we identify writing as a privileged entree into female sexuality, as French feminist Helene Cixous entices women to do: "To write. An act which will only 'realize' the decensored relation of woman to her sexuality, to her womanly being, giving her access to her native strength; it will give her back her goods, her pleasures, her organs, her immense bodily territories which have been kept under seal." Or again, "And why don't you write! Write! Writing is for you, you are for you; your body is yours, take it." This lovely French intellectualism is not a good guide to sexuality. Cixous does not exhort women to build houses, quilt, or any other kind of physical activity (not even exercise) to gain access to our sexuality. These comments can be found in "The Laugh of the Medusa," in *New French Feminisms,* ed. Elaine Marks and Isabelle de Courtivron (Amherst: University of Massachusetts Press), 250, 246.

15. Mariana Valverde, *Sex, Power and Pleasure* (Philadelphia: New Society Publishers, 1987) draws attention to the hazards of these two genres for feminist reflections. Thus she omits the novel, therapeutic/instructional manuals, and theological or ethical work. Still, Valverde's work has much to recommend it, including a chapter on "pleasure and ethics." I agree that a feminist ethics aims not to provide rules or recipes but "to provide women with the intellectual skills to reason about their particular situation, paying close attention to the interconnections between the sexual and non-sexual aspects of our lives" (185), though what women lack is not skills but *concepts.*

16. Barbara Ehrenreich, Elizabeth Hess, and Gloria Jacobs, *Re-Making Love: The Feminization of Sex* (New York: Doubleday, 1986), 78–81.

17. "A few seconds," says *Human Sexual Response,* 6. Even the longer experience Masters and Johnson called "status orgasmus" lasted only 20 to 60 seconds (131).

18. The 0–6 scale has been frequently criticized, but it remains useful. It has been complicated by using several overlapping scales rather than one. See Eli Coleman, "Assessment of Sexual Orientation," *Journal of Homosexuality* 14, no. 1 (1987): 9–24.

19. For the lack of correlations between women's experiences of orgasm and factors of education or class, see 520–21, 529, of *Sexual Behavior in the Human Female.* In contrast, they found religion "definitely and consistently" affected women's orgasms.

They differentiated religion by large groups (Protestant, Catholic, Jew) and within these by intensity (religiously devout, moderately devout, and inactive). For married women, they concluded: "In nearly every age group, and in nearly all the samples that we have from Protestant, Catholic and Jewish females, smaller percentages of the more devout and larger percentages of the inactive groups had responded to orgasm after marriage. Similarly, the median frequencies of orgasm for those who were responding at all were, in most instances, lower for those who were devout and higher for those who were religiously inactive" (529). For single women, see 515–16 and 521–22.

20. These pale, however, by comparison with the fact that I grew up in an abusive home. My mother was a battered woman, and I was incestuously abused by my father. The incest I experienced colors much of my adult experiences of sexuality. It gave me concepts before I was ready for them—shame, secrecy, aversion, flinching, flashbacks. I am forced to place these ideas next to more usual ones: attraction, pleasure, joy. I spent more than a decade healing from these wounds. (The literature on healing after sexual abuses has grown large. For a good guide to "how" in a case like mine, see Ellen Bass and Laura Davis, *The Courage to Heal: A Guide for Women Survivors of Child Sexual Abuse* [New York: HarperCollins, 1988]).

21. Extreme bodily states may all have this isolating quality. Serious pain, for instance, is also difficult to communicate. See Elaine Scary, *The Body in Pain: The Making and Unmaking of the World* (New York: Oxford University Press, 1985).

22. For other descriptions of women's orgasms, especially their varieties, see: Sheila Kitzinger, *Woman's Experience of Sex: The Facts and Feelings of Female Sexuality at Every Stage of Life* (New York: Penguin Books, 1983); Shere Hite, *The Hite Report*. Though fiction is outside my boundaries here, see also: Louise Thornton, Jan Sturtevant, and Amber Coverdale Sumrall, eds., *Touching Fire: Erotic Writings by Women* (New York: Carroll and Graf, 1989); Michelle Slung, ed., *Slow Hand: Women Writing Erotica* (New York: HarperCollins, 1992); Margaret Reynolds, ed., *Erotica: Women's Writings from Sappho to Margaret Atwood* (New York: Fawcett, 1990).

23. This melting union is where I would begin a critique of Masters and Johnson, churlish as this may seem when we owe so much knowledge of female orgasm to them. Their descriptions of orgasm are limited to sensations; any sense of unity with the partner disappears, as do any other wider feelings (such as love). This may have been because so much of their work was based on masturbation, or because of other assumptions. For an analysis of a "materialism" Masters and Johnson shared with Kinsey, see Paul Robinson, *The Modernization of Sex: Havelock Ellis, Alfred Kinsey, William Masters and Virginia Johnson* (New York: Harper & Row, 1976, 1989). Robinson suggests that Kinsey made "a decision to evaluate sexual experience strictly in terms of orgasms, and orgasms themselves strictly in terms of numbers. This meant he took no statistical note of how orgasms differed from one another in intensity or in the emotional values associated with them . . . he distrusted those who imputed that the physical reality of sex was somehow trivial when compared to its psychology. 'Such thinking,' he wrote, 'easily becomes mystical' " (57). Obviously, I have become mystical.

24. This language of union may lead readers to assume that I am describing intercourse, a literal uniting of bodies by putting the penis inside the vagina. I have been careful not to describe how ecstasy is reached, not only because I am not writing an instructional manual, but also in order to leave this question open. If the empirical studies cited in the first section are to be trusted, most women (including me) do not experience orgasm as a result of intercourse alone.

25. Ecstasy language appears more often these days. See for instance, Margot Anand, *The Art of Sexual Ecstasy: The Path of Sacred Sexuality for Western Lovers* (Los Angeles: Jeremy P. Tarcher, 1989), though she contrasts ecstasy with "ordinary genital orgasm" (p. 3); or Linda Murray, "Sexual Ecstasy," *New Woman*, April 1992, 57–59. (The

headers for this essay say that "there is an erotic pleasure greater than orgasm" and that women can go "beyond ecstasy.")

26. I have formulated "limit-experience" by analogy to "limit-question." Steven Toulmin, *The Place of Reason in Ethics* (Chicago: University of Chicago Press, 1987).

27. Readers may be jarred by the sudden appearance of male pronouns here. Perhaps an experiential account cannot avoid some references to the gender of one's partner, and my partner is male. But homophobia/heterosexism is not to be swept aside by this bare assertion, which evades the moral onus of the charge. In fact, I have written elements 1–3 *deliberately* in inclusive language because I believe these three dimensions are the *same* regardless of the gender of a woman's partner. Elements 4 and 5, on the other hand, are written differently because gender is essential to differences of vulnerability and power in our society.

To illuminate these differences, I invite the reader to try a thought-experiment. Change the pronouns in this account to explore what difference they make: "My ecstasy excited and touched her; she was eager for my orgasm . . . on the occasions when I felt I would never get it off, and that it was time to quit, she would not. That my pleasure was important to her, this was hard to accept, to let in. That she would refuse her own release until I had mine, that she was willing to persist in trying to bring my release/ecstasy, that she reveled in it: This shook me very deeply. It was so very unexpected. My surprise about this says more about me than it does about her. I did not expect to be loved. I did not expect her to have the capacity to put me before herself. I expected only to be secondary." For me, there are significant differences between these lines and those in the body of the text. They shift in moral status for two reasons: (1) They change in genre from nonfiction to fiction. This is a technical issue about writing, and whether it is large or small depends on the relationship of truth-telling to genre. (For instance, how does fiction tell the truth?) (2) His maleness was the fundamental reason that I expected to be secondary in our sexual relationship. This is a large social issue that has nothing to do with expertise or technical questions. Since this is not an essay about homophobia, I invite readers to explore for themselves whether changing the pronouns changes the moral structure of the argument, both here and in element 5, and to reflect on why.

28. I have learned from Karen Lebacqz to highlight vulnerability in thinking about sexuality. See "Appropriate Vulnerability: A Sexual Ethic for Singles" in *After the Revolution: Sexual Ethics and the Church* (Chicago: The Christian Century, 1989).

29. As I have said in another context, tidiness is not useful for feminist reflection, at least not right now. See Mary Pellauer and Susan Thistlethwaite, "A Conversation on Healing and Grace," in *Lift Every Voice: Christian Theology from the Underside,* ed. Mary Potter-Engel and Susan Thistlethwaite (San Francisco: HarperCollins, 1990).

30. Jessica Benjamin, *The Bonds of Love: Psychoanalysis, Feminism and the Problem of Domination* (New York: Pantheon, 1988) suggests the primal necessity of recognition for both mutuality and female desire.

31. English has amazingly strong street language to disapprove of a woman who arouses a man but does not satisfy him. We have *no* comparable language for the reverse.

32. This is why many sex therapists avoid or even attack ethical language. For example, Barbach says "this confusion between sexuality and morality has been another source of conflict for many women" (*For Yourself,* 20, but see similar comments on 6, 8, 9, 16, 21, 88, 92).

33. Martha Nussbaum, *The Fragility of Goodness: Luck and Ethics in Greek Tragedy and Philosophy* (New York: Cambridge University Press, 1986) may open a space for thinking about fortune and ethics.

34. In another sense, of course, I do receive this gift from my partner, and I cannot separate this fact from the rest of our relationship. That my beloved lingers over my pleasure until it culminates in ecstasy tells me vividly that I am his beloved, that I am truly

valued by him as I value him. This ecstatic union overflows into the rest of our relationship, as we circle around the well of abundance in the center of our love, dipping in and out of it.

35. For instance, Roger Scruton's *Sexual Desire: A Moral Philosophy of the Erotic* (New York: Free Press, 1986) contains only passing references to orgasm, though he is not alone in that.

36. There may be many others as well. In addition to references elsewhere, other useful published sources include: Sarah Lucia Hoagland, *Lesbian Ethics: Toward New Value* (Palo Alto, Calif.: Institute of Lesbian Studies, 1988); Katie G. Cannon, *Black Womanist Ethics* (Atlanta: Scholars Press, 1988); Beverly Wildung Harrison, *Making the Connections: Essays in Feminist Social Ethics,* ed. Carol S. Robb (Boston: Beacon Press, 1985); Eve Browning Cole and Susan Coultrap-McQuin, eds., *Explorations in Feminist Ethics: Theory and Practice* (Bloomington: Indiana University Press, 1992); Claudia Card, ed., *Feminist Ethics* (Lawrence: University of Kansas Press, 1991); Susan E. Davies and Eleanor H. Haney, eds., *Redefining Sexual Ethics: A Sourcebook of Essays, Stories and Poems* (Cleveland: Pilgrim Press, 1991).

37. Kinsey, and many sexologists after him, seem to think "more is better." We may have many reasons to question this.

38. Even all mystical experiences are not the same. I have them in many other areas of life besides orgasm, in nature or in worship, but most vividly in public transportation, historical sites, and large crowds. I am not primarily a sexual mystic, nor a nature mystic, but a social mystic. These differences, once again, are important. (I learned these distinctions from a presentation by Naomi Goldenberg at the AAR more than a decade ago.)

39. Betty Dodson, *Sex for One: The Joy of Selfloving* (New York: Crown, 1987), 87. This point is partly to oppose any notion that the way a woman reaches orgasm makes any moral (or other) difference. Ehrenreich, Hess, and Jacobs go further: "Sex should have no ultimate meaning other than pleasure, and no great mystery except how to achieve it," and it is obnoxious to have "every pleasure and sensation burdened with 'meaning' " (*Re-Making Love,* 194–95, 205). On the other hand, they note that "the consumer culture offers the ultimately meaningless version of sexual revolution" (205). (I agree.) The Kinsey team defined orgasm as "an explosive discharge of muscular tension at the peak of sexual response," akin to a sneeze; they were ascerbic about claims that it was more (*Sexual Behavior in the Human Female,* 627 ff.).

40. For others' reflections on these questions, see respectively: Dorothy Dinnerstein, *The Mermaid and the Minotaur: Sexual Arrangements and Human Malaise* (New York: Harper & Row, 1976), esp. 73–75; Audre Lorde, "Uses of the Erotic: the Erotic as Power"; Rebecca Parker, "Making Love as a Means of Grace: Women's Reflections," *Open Hands* 3, no. 3, (Winter 1988): 8–12 (thanks to Anita Hill for drawing my attention to this essay); Julia Kristeva, "Oscillation between Power and Denial: An Interview with Xaviere Gauthier," in *New French Feminisms,* 165–66.

41. Thomas Kuhn, *The Structure of Scientific Revolutions* (Chicago: University of Chicago Press, 1970).

13

Lovingly Lesbian: Toward a Feminist Theology of Friendship

MARY E. HUNT

What is lesbian feminism? Where did it come from and why won't it go away? Why use the word *lesbian*? Can't women just be friends? Why isn't there a new word for it? These are the kind of first-level questions which need to be answered in order to move on to creative analysis.

The theopolitical reality of lesbian feminism is that it can only be understood in a particular social context. That context is both patriarchal and heterosexist. By patriarchal, I mean that the entire social fabric is so imbued with the normativity of male experience that female experience is excluded. This means that schools, churches, businesses, governments, etc., are arranged according to male principles of competition, aggression, and production to the extent that so-called female characteristics of cooperation, agreeability, and process are negated. Patriarchy expresses itself in sexism in the culture, and has been responded to in some initial ways by what is known as feminism. Feminism is the insight into the historical and contemporary oppression of women, and at the same time a movement dedicated to strategies for overcoming it. Major work has been done on sexism from a theological perspective by Sheila Collins, Mary Daly, Rosemary Ruether, and others, and from a theoretical angle by Charlotte Bunch, Susan Griffin, Adrienne Rich, and company. More recently however, we have come to understand that this same patriarchal context is heterosexist as well.

The insight into heterosexism is just beginning to be explored logically by a generation of scholars who have benefited from the work which has been done on sexism. Heterosexism means that normative value is given to heterosexual experience to the extent that legal and acceptable expression of homosexual experience is excluded. As in patriarchy, there is no claim that heterosexual experience as such (like maleness as such) is bad. Rather, its normativity to the exclusion of homosexuality (just as the exclusion of women) makes it oppressive. When all social relationships and social institutions are arranged according to heterosexist principles, i.e., male-female dating and marriages, child rearing in heterosexual families, and the presumption that all are heterosexual until proven otherwise, it is nearly impossible for healthy, good, and natural homosexual relationships to flourish. That they do is some proof of grace.

Women whose experiences do not conform to this model realize early on that the context in which definitions are born is patriarchal and heterosexist. They realize that all women are defined not only according to their gender but according to their sexual relationships with men as well. The litany is something like the following: married women sleep with men, divorced and widowed women used to, separated women might again, single women would like to, lesbian women do not, and nuns, well, they are not even supposed to talk about it. Thus the "normal" (Webster's) definition for a lesbian in this context is "a female homosexual," the word itself coming from "the reputed homosexual band associated with Sappho of Lesbos." Here it is clear that even a lesbian in heterosexist patriarchy is defined in male terms, that is, as homosexual who does not happen to be male. Even the word chosen for such women is defined in terms of male fantasies about Sappho's friends.

So it goes, but the confusions are even helpful for understanding what a lesbian is not. A lesbian is not defined by her sexual partner any more than she is defined by those with whom she does not sleep. This is to fall into the patriarchal trap of defining women according to sexuality, which only serves to divide us. What we need is to be united in order that our strength will free all of us. A lesbian is an outlaw in patriarchy. But she is the herald of the good news that patriarchy is in its decline. A lesbian is a woman who in the face of heterosexist patriarchal messages not to love women—the others, the outsiders, the de-spised—indeed not to love herself as woman, in fact does both. She loves other women as friends, that radical relationship of laying down one's life that has always been valued in Christianity. And by loving other women she comes to that authentic self-love which is, in the words of novelist Doris Grumbach, "It was the very opposite of narcissism—it was metamorphosis."[1] To be a lesbian is to take relationships with women radically seriously, opening oneself to befriend and be befriended, so that by loving, something new may be born. When all women are free to have this experience, then, and only then, can we say that any women are free.

This renewed definition of lesbian comes from a particular social context. Three social movements paved its way. They are: the so-called sexual revolution, the women's movement and the lesbian/gay movement. I will treat each one briefly so that we may see the backdrop for this new definition. Agreeing with these movements is not important, but being aware of them as forming part of our history in the evolution of a postpatriarchal, postheterosexist culture, is.

First is the sexual revolution, perhaps the most dubious of all three. This was the much heralded and mercifully short-lived revolt against puritanical ways in the sixties. It was made popular through such slogans as "Free Love," "Abortion on Demand," "Make Love Not War," etc. The very expressions themselves give away the patriarchal nature of this movement. For men it meant license for sex wherever and whenever with whomever, taking away from women the "nice girls don't" excuse. For women it meant the need for more birth control, more abortions, and ultimately less freedom to really choose. Heterosexual activity in and of itself was seen as revolutionary, for still inexplicable reasons. But if anything positive did come out of this rather virulent period it was the fact that people finally began to talk more freely about sexuality. This was no small matter when we reflect that even to the present day, discussion of sexuality is taboo in some circles, including most of theology.

The second and far more significant social movement to have an impact on the definition of lesbian was the women's movement. This movement recognized the class nature of women's oppression in the historical and contemporary scenes. At the same time it began to use women's experience as the starting point for developing strategies to overcome oppression of all types. In consciousness-raising groups women not only mentioned sexuality but took it as a major focus, seeing it as the mirror which reflected all of women's treatment in the society. The woman who was oppressed in bed, who was raped or beaten, whose husband or lover did not use birth control, the woman who was called frigid, the postmenopausal woman, all of these are various facets of the same woman, namely, the oppressed woman in patriarchy.

Lesbians were told to keep their voices down during the early years of the women's movement. Betty Friedan and others (who later, happily, repented publicly) referred to lesbians as the "lavender menace," and made it clear that lesbians could cost all women their rights if lesbians insisted upon theirs. So, dutifully the dykes closed their mouths, remained invisible, and worked on birth control, abortion rights, child care, etc., for what amounted to straight women's liberation. It was only with the lesbian/straight split in the women's movement (1970–71) that feminists began to understand the politics of lesbianism. As Charlotte Bunch indicated, "lesbian feminist politics is a political critique of the institution and ideology of heterosexuality as a primary cornerstone of male supremacy."[2] Until this cornerstone is removed, the structures of patriarchy will stand firm.

The point is not that every woman act in a particular way, but that every woman be freed from the constraints that patriarchal heterosexism places upon her. Then and only then can women make real choices about relationships with particular people, not excluding a whole class of people (women) from the beginning. This same dynamic of instant exclusion of whole classes of people is operative in racism, in classism, in discrimination toward the differently able, those from Third World countries, etc. It is this dynamic that lesbian feminists seek to change in its many manifestations.

The third major social movement which set the stage for present thinking about lesbianism is the lesbian/gay movement itself. When gays first fought back against police at the Stonewall bar on New York's Christopher Street in 1969, they opened a new era for homosexuals. No longer were same-sex relationships simply the stuff of back rooms and Mafia-run bars. Homosexuals were persons with dignity and (eventually) legal rights equal to all others. The movement was primarily male in that the leadership, focus, and values were basically derived from male experience. But women, even women who were not feminists, could see their rights as well. And everyone was finally able to see the lives and contributions of lesbians and gay men throughout history, who could now be celebrated by the gay community.

Feminists quickly became aware that being part of the gay community was important but no panacea. *Gay* had become another false generic like *man*, referring to both male and female homosexuals. This symbolized the values of the movement as well, which were focused on making male homosexual expression valid, and little else. Feminists could not stop our analysis with the sexual, but always understood our sexuality within the complex constellation of racism, classism, sexism, etc. The "natural alliance" between lesbian feminists and gay men was not so natural after all. This is not to say that there are not some obvious and important links, but it is to say that very different emphases have been made from the two perspectives.

Gay males, for example, have emphasized their sexual lives as the locus of their liberation. But since *gay* is not a generic word we can conclude that the lesbian emphasis is quite different and not to be homogenized. Lesbian feminists have not defined ourselves according to sexuality, although that has been important. Rather, we have defined ourselves according to certain relational commitments to other women, or what I am calling female friendship. The nature of our relationships with regard to the specifically sexual aspect is quite simply no one else's business. This is not to say that lesbian feminists are in the closet about our sexuality, nor that we advocate continuing the hidden relational lives of our foresisters with the women they loved. Far from it. Rather, the goal from a lesbian feminist perspective is that persons eventually be allowed to love whom they will without current heterosexist gender restraints.

To achieve such a goal, we are reclaiming the word *lesbian* for what it has always meant, namely, women loving women without fixating on the presence or absence of genital activity to define it. What we are talking about is the basic feminist truism that the personal is political. This is important to distinguish from the private, which has never been claimed to be political. Concretely, that I take my relationships with women seriously is an important personal choice in patriarchy which has clear political implications. But that my friend and/or sexual partner is Susie and not Debby is private, therefore not political, though it is of course both public information in a certain way and something which we choose to share among our families and friends. This distinction is important because it allows lesbian feminists to have private lives like everyone else. We can live without having our sexuality politicized beyond what relationships can handle. At the same time, we can make claims about the political nature of loving women within a patriarchal, heterosexist culture without those claims being tied to one or another relationship. In short, sexuality is not privatized, but neither are specific relationships publicized, at least not beyond the usual small circle of friends who know, support, and critique any human relationships.

This analysis must be seen in the light of contemporary women's studies and what we might call lesbian feminist theory. Adrienne Rich has suggested that the cost of heterosexism has been so high as to erase the lives and loves of many lesbians from history.[3] The threat of lesbianism has served to divide women, alienating them and making them fearful of one another. The ultimate epithet for any woman, regardless of her sexual preference, is *lesbian*. To diffuse this, Rich has suggested the notion of the lesbian continuum, placing all women somewhere on the continuum. This would include married women who take their relationships with women friends seriously on the one hand, and women who live together in primary affective relationships on the other, and everyone in between.

Rich's analysis suggests that when all women can embrace and celebrate the lesbian in them the distinctions between "who is" and "who is not" will finally fall away. It has been suggested that perhaps letting all women onto the continuum might degrade or de-emphasize the value and dignity of those relationships which are on the latter end of the spectrum, those which would traditionally be defined as lesbian anyway. However, it is clear that such a wholesale identification of women as lesbians is not about to happen, though for those few who do so identify there will undoubtedly be a warm welcome. The idea, rather, is that all women take seriously their friendships with women, and the only word which we have to indicate this revolutionary reality is *lesbian*. Thus, it is at our peril that we back off of the word. To do so is to deny the powerful women's reality which has gone before us and probably to short-circuit what is ahead. I feel for women who say that they agree with the concept— frightening as it is for many of them to think of the implications of taking relationships with women seriously—but only wish we could employ another word, please. As yet there is no word, so I simply remind them that there was a time not so long ago when the word *woman* had distinctly sexual overtones. All females were described as "girls" and "ladies." How quickly language and concepts change together. The point is that no one knows all of the implications of integrating sexuality into women's friendships. But we do know that the important thing is not that they necessarily do it, but that they do it lovingly and responsibly.

This is why we insist on reclaiming the word *lesbian*, wrenching it from its patriarchal context, à la Mary Daly, and giving it a content worthy of the lives of some great women friends throughout history. Inviting all women to share its richness, it is important that *lesbian* not be forced to carry the symbolic freight of sexuality for all women. Instead, we can insist on our self-identification as friends in a culture which tells all of us to keep our distance from one another. Thus *lesbian* takes on a new meaning. It becomes paradigmatic of all types of friendships in a culture which provides precious few structures for women and men, men and men, women and women to relate to each other as friends without the corruption of such unions with partial, distorted notions of heterosexism.

Throughout the country and in fact in many places in the world a women's community is emerging. This community is made up of women who understand and value the necessity of women's friendships for our collective survival. Here, female friendships can flourish in places and spaces where they go unquestioned in themselves and are subsequently evaluated according to the persons involved. Music, art, poetry, drama, dance, etc., can be shared in the women's community without the annoyance of male objectifiers or the more subtle drain of liberal male hangers-on. The community is dynamic and shows its resourcefulness by great mobility and simple comfort. It is, however, almost completely white and middle class, something which limits its value, although women of color are beginning to make their voices heard as well in contributions which promise new life for all of us.[4] The women's community, however, is a tiny fraction of a percentage of the general culture where women's lives and friendships are trivialized unto death.

However, lesbian feminism and the women's community are having a significant impact in the culture if reports in popular news magazines can be taken seriously. For example, it seems that lesbians on campus are more visible than ever before, and that their visibility is both political as well as personal. They are not simply part of the larger male gay movement. They evidence instead a clear awareness of how relationships with women offer them more depth and possibilities for growth. There are even reports of some straight women wondering about themselves, whether they are whole persons or if indeed there is something wrong with them. While I have some sympathy for their confusion, I encourage their line of thinking. It points to what lesbian feminists are saying, namely, that loving other women, thus being free to love oneself, is good for every woman's health. This is nearly impossible under patriarchal, heterosexist influences.

Just as quickly as this insight into what we call woman identification out of lesbian feminism comes to consciousness, Hollywood and Madison Avenue are right there to counteract it. We can expect a spate of films of the *Personal Best* caliber which will capitalize on and trivialize women's friendships. These films play on male fears and fantasies about what the world would really be like if women loved women. Of course the results are predictably shallow, neurotic, one-dimensional, stereotypic, sexually focused relationships. These simply do not ring true about most lesbian feminist friendships, where it is not an instant attraction due to a compatibly toned body, but an attraction born of friendship with a sister in the struggle, and perhaps a sister in the snuggle too! These are the life-giving friendships which grace women even in a patriarchal, heterosexist culture, and which give some hope and role models for the next generation.

Lesbian feminist friendships are known to us through a variety of sources. I look at my own experience and smile to think how blessed I have been with a very particular friendship, but also with a constellation of friendships which participate to one degree or another in the richness which is lesbian feminism. I look at my friends' experiences and the quality of relationships we share. It is astonishing how in the midst of our culture any women's friendships can flourish. But they do and we cultivate them like out-of-season flowers because we know all of the forces which mitigate against them.

We have other sources on women's friendships now. Finally the literature is coming to the fore. We have the formidable collection *Surpassing the Love of Men*, which details literary loves over the past centuries,[5] and few have missed the adventures of Molly Bolt, who made *Rubyfruit Jungle* the first feminist best seller.[6] This was a far cry from *The Well of Loneliness*, which convinced a whole generation that love between women had to be role-defined and tragic.[7] We learn about women's friendships from women's music, that growing group of compositions for, by, and about women. Meg Christian's "Ode to a Gym Teacher," sometimes referred to as the lesbian national anthem, provides a satirical look at the desperate search for role models prior to feminism. There are also the tender, powerful love songs of Holly Near and Chris Williamson, as well as the bawdy tunes of Teresa Trull, all celebrating the fact that women do love women. And there are the haunting melodies of Sweet Honey in the Rock, assuring us that "Every woman who ever loved a woman you ought to stand up and call her name."[8]

All of these give us clues to women's friendships, clues earlier generations simply did not have. The clues are as varied as the friendships. But there are some general lines of agreement. Women are not to be possessed but to be shared. Friendship means support through the difficulties. Making love with a woman can be a delightful experience. Many women have loved women. These kinds of cultural affirmations allow women to see that their experiences are not unique, that the most natural feelings in the world have been distorted by patriarchy. This does not mean that solving the riddles of patriarchy will result in hassle-free relationships. But it does mean that the challenge of loving well is tough enough without having a whole layer of cultural negativity to make it even tougher.

These sources show that something new is struggling to be born in women's friendships. Perhaps it is that the cynicism and exploitation which mask love in straight society are finally being overcome. The mockery which has been made of love in patriarchy, the pain and prerequisites which prevent people from embracing one another in a deep, life-giving way are being put to rest. This is a major contribution to Christian culture, one which can model for relationships of all kinds the way into the future. No other contemporary source, neither the churches nor the gay male movement, nor even the straight women's movement, is making such a self-conscious effort to improve the quality of love.

Classical male qualities of friendship include such characteristics as care, responsibility, respect, and knowledge, according to such writers as Eric Fromm, etc. But for lesbian feminists it seems that some other characteristics come to the fore. The first of these is *mutuality,* that quality of a mature friendship when giving and taking are possible between equals, when one can truly complement the other not from role expectations but because of gifts. It is a rare, if existent, heterosexual relationship which is truly mutual. This is because in a heterosexist, patriarchal world women and men cannot be equal. This is the nature of patriarchy. Thus a friendship which is characterized by mutuality is possible only when a man and a woman live in contradiction with the prevailing culture. Living in this state of contradiction, conscious of all of its pressures, is usually more than most such friendships can take. However, friendships between women, on the other hand, can have this quality by their very nature. There can be an honest assessment of the strengths and liabilities of each one, and some sharing accordingly to each one's ability and each one's needs can be actualized. Then roles can be tossed aside and new possibilities emerge. Hence it is friendships between women which model mutuality for everyone.

A second characteristic of a woman-woman friendship is *community.* It seems that there is some urge in women to broaden, nurture and enlarge a friendship so that it will always exist in a network of relationships. This urge toward community is exactly the opposite of what happens in a male-female relationship in patriarchy when the urge to possess, to close off, and to protect seem to overpower even the most communally oriented of couples. Conversely, in women's friendship there seems to be a desire not to close off relationships but to join them with other similar friendships and create a kind of community. This may simply be a survival mechanism, a response to the fact that in patriarchy friendships between women are dangerous and need all of the support they can muster. But I like to think of it as a programmatic commitment on the part of women to give friendship a communal dimension. It seems also to guarantee a much healthier life-style, where neurotic minuets will be minimized and where groups in which ups and downs, holidays and tragedies may be shared will be the norm.

We are only beginning to structure friendships in this communal way. As noted above, it will be some time before those already in communities will be able to come out about the friendships which exist among them. But I submit that when both of these processes get under way, when communities are built intentionally on friendships and when communities make explicit their friendships, then the richness and power of women's friendships to transform the culture will really be felt. This kind of community building based on friendship will be the stuff of the ecclesia of women to which theologians refer when talking about the impact of feminism on the churches.[9] I support this move and only hope that the lessons of friendship and community building which will result from it can be broadened to include all members of the ecclesia.

A third aspect of women's friendships is a direct dealing with sexuality and the consequences of doing so, namely, *honesty.* This is perhaps the single greatest contribution of lesbians to all women, in that lesbians have urged upon all women an honest and forthright dealing with sexual dynamics which exist between them. It seems that up until very recently women functioned toward one another as if out of a completely heterosexist mind-set. Sexual dynamics were something one had to confront with men, always and everywhere, but friendships with women were cultivated without such complications. I have even heard straight women say that they do not confront sexuality with women because their experience with men is that when sex is no longer a part of the relationship the relationship itself is gone. They claim they do not want to risk this with their women friends, whose friendships are too important to them. The implications for their relationships with men are frightening. However, we have learned more recently that all mature, adult relationships have some kind of sexual component. We have found that it is better to face and deal with such dynamics than to let them stand in the way of quality relating.

This is not easy, given our socialization. But the rewards are many. What lesbian feminists have learned is that acknowledging and facing honestly the fact that in some friendships, for reasons which remain altogether mysterious, there may exist between two women sexual energy which calls for resolution. If the friendship is to flourish, this resolution is imperative. Otherwise, there is great risk of thwarting an otherwise good friendship.

Dealing directly with sexuality in any situation is simply a question of honesty. Failure to do so means introducing distrust into the relationship, distrust which will usually manifest itself in other aspects as well as the sexual one. What it means to be lesbian in a nonpatriarchal, nonheterosexist age is to take the risk which comes with acknowledging sexual energy and resolving it. The experience of many women is that not every friendship leads to the expression of sexuality. This is a myth created by the media to sell everything from liquor to paper towels. But it is equally women's experience that some kind of attraction often needs to be named, simply named. But in those cases where sexual dynamics do come into play there will often need to be some exploration between friends, which more often than not will result in a mutual decision that sexual expression will not enhance and might detract from the friendship. This is simply because we find that sexuality involves so much time and energy and emotion, participates on so many symbolic levels which for women are usually well integrated into the entire personality fabric (unlike men, who seem to have greater ease at distancing their sex life from the rest of their personalities), that we do not have the resources for too many such relationships in a lifetime, and rarely for more than one at a time.

In those few and cherished friendships in which the integration of sexuality is desired by both friends there is a symbolic signaling of a deepening of friendship and commitment. This is never a decision taken lightly. But it is one which involves the friends in each other's lives in ways that demand responsibility, ongoingness, nurture, etc. We are only beginning to see how such relationships, when encouraged and celebrated by families and friends, will transform the relational life of the church.

Of course, the fact that women do not have to worry about birth control in their sexual explorations is no small incentive for greater honesty with women. Imagine if this same depth of honesty could be realized between women and men. Imagine the improved quality of friendships and even marriages which might result if the dynamics of dishonesty, which are so often set up at the sexual level and played out at every other level in relationships, were not in play.

Another characteristic of women's friendship is their *nonexclusivity*. Of course we can all think immediately of exclusive, clingy relationships between women which make the most possessive male-female relationships seem positively open. But contemporary lesbian feminist friendships simply are not that way. On the mixed side these were the result of male property orientation toward women, and on the female-female side a kind of shutting out of the world from that one little peaceful relational spot which women had found. Now we are creating a women's community in the broader culture so as to create the space that women's friendships need. The formation of solid bonds between and among women over generations and national boundaries is another attempt at creating womanspace adequate to the expansive nature of growing friendships. Thus friendships can be open and inviting, letting in the light of other friendships and sharing the goodness without fear of loss or trivialization. This invites women not to relational or sexual promiscuity but to the creation of friendships in a communal context which will in the long run mean added strength and richness for each one. The implications of this model for the entire church remain to be spelled out, but it seems clear that opening the space for women will only lead to greater openness for women and men, as well as for men with men.

Another characteristic of female friendship is *flexibility*. Flexibility means the freedom to express oneself and grow with others in a variety of ways. It means letting go of the old role models which lesbians and gay men picked up from the only (heterosexual) model which existed. It means having to come up with new categories through which to explain and nurture friendships, because the ones we have are simply inadequate. Are Susie and Cathy lovers? Well, Susie and Cathy are friends. Why do you need to know more, so that you can discriminate? This is the kind of response which comes when the categories are no longer adequate.

We are learning to be flexible about our loving. We are learning that we do not necessarily have to live in the twos of the nuclear family. We are learning that we can have intense, romantic friends but still live in the wider community or in fact even alone if that seems best. We are learning to develop the communities and networks of communities which multiply our options and spread out the energy of friendship where it is so badly needed.

Finally, female friendships are remarkable in their *other-directedness*, the extent to which they point beyond themselves to something larger, something more beautiful, something more inclusive, some might even say something divine. This is something which male-female relationships in a patriarchal, heterosexist culture strive to attain but never reach. The reasons for this are historical in that female friendships have been forced outward, forced to understand and relate to the culture in order to survive. On the other hand the usual heterosexual relationship, which all too often is not even a friendship underneath it all, is focused in on itself, trying to reach some norm which patriarchy has established as the most effective way of stifling growth. Hence it is women's friendships which hold the key to transcendence, because they must transcend what *is* in order to be at all. This is a burden for women, but one which promises to make all things new if only women can survive long enough.

I have suggested that women's friendships are mutual, community seeking, honest about sexuality, nonexclusive, flexible, and other-directed. These qualities, it seems to me, have tremendous potential not simply for relationships among women, though that potential has yet to be explored, but for the whole church. It is these characteristics which will transform our culture and create the preconditions for the possibility of the reign of God. I am not arguing that all women's friendships participate in these qualities as yet. That is wishful thinking. Rather, by naming them I hope to make it so, or at least bring to consciousness what might be possible in women's lives so that our contribution to the whole church can be forthcoming.

A theology adequate to this kind of friendship model is much more promising than the theology of sexuality which some of us have hinted at in the past. It is more adequate because it acknowledges that it is not sexuality per se but friendship which determines what the quality of life can be. In patriarchy it is certainly the sexuality dimension which makes the difference. But after patriarchy it is the entire relationship which makes the difference.

New constructive theologies are recognized as such by their saying something new about the fundamental theological categories God, humanity, and the world. This is done in a systematic way when some new insight, experience, or concept is used to illumine these basics. Friendship, it seems to me, is in its postpatriarchal, postheterosexist potential an insight, experience, and concept able to carry us to new heights in theology. Although I will save a full exploration of this possibility for a later essay when we have had more time to live into the idea, I offer now a few hints toward such a theology. To do so I will make certain Christian presuppositions which can be summarized by the normativity of love and justice as the essence of revelation. And of course since this constructive theology attempts to be systematic, the three concepts, God, humanity, and world, are each interdependent. They will be explored according to the six characteristics proposed for female friendships in hope that the specific new content about friendship can be brought to bear.

We begin by exploring who God is, what language and characteristics we can use for meaningful talk about God. The model of friendship, while not in and of itself adequate to exhaust the reality of God, is surprisingly helpful. No longer are we left with Father, Lord, Ruler, and King, nor even with Spirit and Mother Hen, which are often trotted out to balance the gender. But now we have the androgynous, unfettered notion of God as friend to add to the list.

Two of the characteristics gleaned from female friendships which are useful for understanding God as friend are mutuality and the urge toward community. Mutuality is suggested by process theologians who are concerned with how God is affected by humankind, and obviously vice versa. Mutuality is that quality of the otherness of God which is really God's oneness with us. To characterize otherness as mutuality is to say that God can only be understood in human terms, but that the very understanding is affected by our belief in God. In short, mutuality means that our relationship with God, like all friendships, is freely chosen on both sides (unlike family or government images like Father and Lord, in which the relationships are not necessarily intentional and gratuitous). More needs to be explored, of course, but it is clear that God as friend opens up a new paradigm for our understanding.

A second characteristic of female friendships, the urge toward community, is an essential aspect of the Christian God. The idea of the reign of God, the omega point, the gathering of all that is into a harmonious community, these are all Christian ways of talking about the God-human cooperation which will result in salvation. Jesus is the force in Christianity, the friend whose relationship with us is manifested by our being part of the Christian community. This membership is evidenced by the work of love and justice. This is not the pietistic "what a friend we have in Jesus." Rather it is the experience of being part of a historical group of friends. Jesus' friendships, especially the example of his particular friendship with the beloved disciple (John 13:23, 21:7, etc.) as well as with his immediate community of women and men, are a model for contemporary Christian life. This is the community which derives its identity from the laying down of life for friends. Again, much remains to be explored, but we can conclude that the missionary urge which springs from Christianity is in fact to go and make friends in all nations.

Likewise the theological concept of humanity can be understood anew using friendship as the defining model. We have been developing what humanity will look like in postpatriarchal, postheterosexist age, and we have looked at characteristics of female friendships. Focusing on two more of these, honesty and nonexclusivity, gives us a way to see the friendship model operating on the macro as well as the micro level.

The honesty which begins with direct dealing on sexuality questions in a relationship is the same habit of honesty which is needed for a renewed human family. It is the honesty which invites people to see our common heritage rather than stressing the accidental differences like age, race, nationality, sexual preference, physical handicap, etc. It is in the most optimistic of moments this honesty which could lead nations to face the nuclear threat and act like friends for once. It is a dream of course, but why not when options are limited?

Nonexclusivity as a characteristic of female friendship is helpful for imagining a renewed humanity. This could mean an end to preserving national boundaries at all costs while at the same time inviting international cooperation. Nothing would be seen as exclusively mine. Rather, things and people and ideas would be seen as here for the sharing not for the taking; they would be seen realistically as part of what is given to be enjoyed and given back. Nothing and no one would be seen as object or property, only as participating in a kind of cosmic subjectivity which encompasses all of creation. Needless to say, we are some distance from such values. But they give us goals against which to measure our collective progress as well as something toward which to aspire. This is, after all, the task of theology: to develop ethics and strategies to bring us closer to our goals.

Finally, the third theological basic, world, can be reunderstood in the light of a friendship model. World is a great abstraction, almost too great for meaningful discussion. But understood in terms of the earth and all nonhuman life, it is easy to see how flexibility and other-direction, characteristics of female friendships, are helpful lenses through which to examine it.

Flexibility means the freedom to develop a new relationship to the earth. In a nuclear age it means scaling down our grandiose notion of humanity and letting it come into line with the more modest role that was meant for us in creation. Likewise it means changing our attitudes toward the earth, understanding that our very future is tied up with our practices of ecology.

Other-directedness too helps us to see how the world is really oriented not for our pleasure but for our collective future. The pleasure of a few cannot be allowed to determine the future of everyone, or what will surely be no future at all at the rate we are going. This need for balance is critical over against the contemporary nuclear myopia, and it may be this insistence on balance which saves us from ourselves. To whom or to what we ought to be directed is not clear. But what is clear is that an orientation beyond what we know is the hallmark of faith, faith in a friendly future.

This treatment of lesbian feminist friendships . . . and the beginnings of a theological sketch are an attempt to clarify some basic concepts, most of which have been previously misunderstood. Clarification is but a first step toward embracing the new, risking the friendship itself. It is that risk which will open the way for an enrichment of the God-human-world friendship in which we are all invited to participate.

NOTES

1. Doris Grumbach, *Chamber Music* (New York: Fawcett, 1979), 203.

2. Charlotte Bunch, *Lesbianism and the Women's Movement,* ed. Nancy Myron and Charlotte Bunch (Baltimore: Diana Press, 1975), 10.

3. Adrienne Rich, "Compulsory Heterosexuality and Lesbian Existence," *Signs: Journal of Women in Culture and Society 5,* no. 4 (Summer 1980): 631–60.

4. The best example of this emerging contribution is a collection entitled *This Bridge Called My Back: Writings by Radical Women of Color,* ed. Cherrie Moraga and Gloria Anzaldua (Watertown, Mass.: Persephone Press, 1981).

5. Lillian Faderman, *Surpassing the Love of Men: Love Between Women from the Renaissance to the Present* (New York: William Morrow & Co., 1981).

6. Rita Mae Brown, *Rubyfruit Jungle* (Plainfield, Vt.: Daughters, 1973).

7. Radclyffe Hall, *The Well of Loneliness* (New York: Simon & Schuster, 1974). Original publication: Covici-Friede edition, 1928.

8. Lyrics from the popular song "Every Woman" by Bernice Johnson Reagon, recorded by Sweet Honey in the Rock on their album *B'lieve I'll Run On . . . See What the End's Gonna Be*, Redwood Records, Ukiah, California, 1978.

9. Elisabeth Schüssler Fiorenza, "Gather Together in My Name . . . Toward a Christian Feminist Spirituality," in *Women Moving Church*, ed. Diann Neu and Maria Riley (Washington, D.C.: Center of Concern, 1982), 11; reprinted as the epilogue to Elisabeth Schüssler Fiorenza's *In Memory of Her: A Feminist Theological Reconstruction of Early Christian Origins* (New York: Crossroad, 1983).

14

Explaining Men

PHILIP CULBERTSON

Who are men? The question is as old as classical literature and as fresh as the feminist critique. But in our time, as the women in our lives demand equality and justice, as our relationships in the workplace change in bewildering ways, as we struggle to restore the intimacy that we have expected from our relationships with women but lost, and as our assumed positions of privilege crumble, the question has taken on a new urgency for men and for men-sensitive women. Who are men? What drives us? What feeds us emotionally? How can we fill anew the emptiness in our lives? What is the future of our uniquely masculine spirituality? Where can we turn for clarity, for vision, and for a self-understanding that does not embarrass us in the presence of our wives and intimate women friends?

Within the past ten years, we have begun to witness the growth, though nascent, of something called the men's movement, sometimes referred to in academic jargon as "post-feminist men's studies." Post-feminist men's studies is a bit of a misnomer; men cannot themselves be feminist; they can know a lot *about* women, but they can never know how it feels *to be* a woman. Lots of men are not post-feminist, and in many regions, the term "post-feminist" hardly seems to register at all. The field also appears to be threatening to some women, who incorrectly assume that the men's movement represents a trend by men to retrench in the previous despicable traditionalism. I remember the first time I told a feminist friend in a small Southern town that I was giving a speech at a conference on men's studies. She cried in anger and frustration while accusing me of abandoning her in a struggle in which she already had so little support.

As an observer and student of the men's movement, that is not how I understand what is going on. Rather, I see a significant number of men who wish to take the women's movement seriously and have learned much from that movement about human identity in principle, people in general, and men's and women's differences in particular. Men who are attempting to mold the men's movement are not withdrawing their support and encouragement from women's efforts to say who they are and what they need; rather, they are attempting to apply the lessons men learned from the women's movement to men's own sense of identity in a world that has changed quickly. We hope thereby that in a transformed society, men can articulate their identities in support of and in relation to the new ways of living that have rightly developed out of the women's movement.

Some of the observations currently proceeding out of the literature of the men's movement can be organized around four experiences that happen to men so early that men have no control over them. Most men spend the rest of their lives responding to these four experiences: (1) prenatal development from female to male; (2) inability to accommodate determined by anatomy; (3) the learned value of success; and (4) separation/individuation from the mother. Men do not have to be victimized by these early events; instead they can raise their own sensitivities so that they are not entrapped by the dark sides of the male cultural heritage. These four experiences are unique to men—they do not happen in the same way to women. We can understand in these events equal potential for tragedy or creativity.

FROM FEMALE TO MALE

The first early experience of men is the biological change from being female into being male. At conception all fetuses are, in nature and in structure, female; it is only six to seven weeks later, when the production of testosterone kicks in due to the presence of the Y chromosome, that some fetuses switch from female to male. Apparently then, it can be said that femaleness is the basic blueprint for animals (and humans), and maleness is simply an overlay. It might also be said that being male is a sort of altered state (some feminists might claim that it is a birth defect), a final state that differs 180 degrees from a man's conceptual beginnings. It can only be concluded that the account of creation in Genesis 2 is backwards: Eve produces Adam, rather than the other way around. Men seem somehow to be male as a kind of afterthought of nature. Such a conclusion is clearly controversial, as is indeed the entire field of psycho-biological determinism, but the work of medical researchers such as Dr. James Michaelson of Harvard and Dr. Estelle Ramey of Georgetown University opens up the possibility that there may be some genetically conditioned drive that inspires men to spend part of their lives trying to overcome that original mutation by trying to convince women that men are the superior of the two sexes.

This kind of postnatal overcompensation takes many forms: the attempts by some men to convince women that they are genitally deficient; the concomitant exaggerated pride that some men take in their own penises or the opposite anxiety that their penises are somehow "too small"; or other men's attempts to convince women that they are dumber or weaker or less capable than men, maybe even less qualified to be ordained, and that these deficiencies are part of the natural order. At least we can say that if there is some sort of psycho-biological predeterminism, it seems not to become dangerous until it is strongly reinforced by the cultural conditioning and sex-role stereotyping that virtually all men and women in our society suffer.

The issue of biological determinism is a dangerous one. As women have correctly pointed out, the argument that biology is destiny—that is, we can only become the product of our individual genetic heritage—creates potential support for theories of genetic superiority and inferiority and ultimately the potential conclusion that women are biologically inferior to men and can thus never really be men's equals. Recognizing these dangers, however, it still must be said that men and women *are* biologically different one from the other. Men have larger brains, but women have larger fibers in the corpus callosum, connecting the right and left hemispheres. Men's brains decrease more in size as they age, and men recover less quickly from strokes that damage the brain. Recent studies by the Kinsey Institute suggest that the male and female brains are different structurally, and probably chemically, and this in turn means that male and female behaviors are going to be different—overlapping but different. Because more hormonal variables are involved in the maturation of the male brain (males are exposed to greater levels of testosterone in their brains) it is possible that boys' higher rates of developmental oddities (left-handedness, nearsightedness, predisposition to allergies, migraines, dyslexia, stuttering, and even abnormal sexual syndromes, all of which are more common in men than in women) may result from the greater potential for error in their neuro-endocrinological development.

Most of our life performance exhibits proof that both culture and education provide opportunities in which we learn to overcome the biogenetic differences between men and women. Yet too much emphasis on social constructionism as the predictable correction to biological determinism also opens up false expecta-tions that individual genetic differences can be eventually overcome by cultural and educational leveling. While the differences between any two men may be much greater than the differences between a given man and woman, it is still true that each of us is a combination of all three factors working on each other: genetic heritage, education and life experience, and cultural particularism. These three factors seem to be able to combine in a remarkable variety of ways, each perceived as a valid expression of masculinity. As David Gilmore observes: "Manliness is a symbolic script, a cultural construct, endlessly variable, and not always necessary." Biology is destiny *and* culture is destiny.

As men grow, they learn, according to Anthony Astrachan, that as men they have four kinds of power: (1) the power to name; (2) the power to mobilize destructive aggression; (3) the power to organize societal, economic, and political life; and (4) the power to direct others' uses of skills. Men learn that all these forms of power can be used to keep women in a position of inferiority, if men so choose and women cooperate. Men learn to use the power of naming against women by controlling language, by teaching women their place in the world through the words which people use to communicate. Men learn to use the power to mobilize destructive aggression against women by abusing them physically, sexually, and emotionally (over 90 per cent of women in the Hite Report [*Women and Love,* 1987] report being emotionally and psychologically harassed by the men they love) and by defining human worth in terms of the ability to be strong enough to go to war. Men learn to use the power to organize societal, economic, and political life against women by excluding them or by refusing to share with them the knowledge necessary to enter these arenas as equals. And men learn to use the power to direct others' use of skills against women by directing women to continue to play secondary roles that will keep men in the limelight and in power. Of course most of these forms of power are traditionally handed to men by society or learned from men such as our own fathers, but men succumb to the temptation to use them, perhaps, because men are still struggling with a competition which originates in the womb.

NONACCOMMODATION AND LONELINESS

A second experience that happens long before men have any control over their own destiny is that they are born with anatomical differences that seem to predetermine a course of male loneliness. Anatomically women are born with the capacity to accommodate; they can accommodate vaginally, and they can accommodate in utero (a single form of womanpower against which men have traditionally used all their other forms of power), but anatomically males seem to be able to accommodate no one. This early "accident" appears also to have consequential long-term ramifications. In relationships men seem much slower to accommodate than women. Some men have extraordinary resentments over a woman's ability to nurture inside her a child. Men do not nurture inside, but they do tend to bottle up inside. And men, who are anatomically not accommodating, seem most strongly to express this fact by going through life without friends. Virtually every study done on men and friendships reveals that men rarely have close friendships during their adult lives, except sometimes with their wives, though even that seems to be the exception. Judith Viorst tells of a man who described his relationship with his three best friends: "There are some things I wouldn't tell them. For example, I wouldn't tell them about my work because we have always been highly competitive. I certainly wouldn't tell them about my feelings of any uncertainties with life or various things I do. And I wouldn't talk about any problems I have with my wife or in fact anything about my marriage and sex life. But other than that I would tell them anything." After a brief pause, he laughed and said: "That doesn't leave a hell of a lot, does it?"

Men learn to talk about things that men consider to be safe. Studies of male conversation patterns reveal that men limit their conversations with each other to five safe areas: their professional success; sexual conversation, usually dirty, about women; political issues; sports; and equipment such as guns, sound systems, and computers. Men learn early, even from the cradle, not to talk about feelings or fears or weaknesses with women, and particularly not with men. Studies show that female babies are picked up more often when they cry than male babies. Parents unconsciously try to teach their male babies that a man's crying will produce no results. The research of Lawrence Kohlberg and Carol Gilligan suggests that boys see problems as something to be solved like a math equation, and girls put problems into a larger, more complex, ongoing context. In the same manner, masculine theology sets up differences and oppositions, while feminist theology emphasizes connections. Men learn to be independent and self-sufficient, and men learn to be rugged loners. Writer Herb Goldberg says: "We become anesthetized and robotized because we have been heavily socialized to repress and deny almost the total range of emotional and human needs in order that nothing interfere with our 'masculine' style of goal-directed, task-oriented, self-assertive behavior." Yet of course we cannot suppress our capacity for feelings generally without suppressing our capacity for sexual feeling. To be alive includes being sexually alive, and in suppressing one source of vitality, we suppress another.

It is no wonder, given these beginnings, that Goldberg could also observe: "Asking a man to feel is like taunting a crippled person to run." Men pay a price for being so unaccommodating and so anesthetized. Sometimes they binge or go crazy by hitting women or getting drunk or having a destructive affair; sometimes they get resentful that they are not understood by the women who say they love them; sometimes they develop psychopathological diseases common to the repression of feelings, like bowel problems or headaches or ulcers. Fatal diseases more likely in women between forty-five and sixty-four are asthma and high blood pressure. Fatal diseases more likely in men of the same age are emphysema, atherosclerosis, ischemic heart disease, cerebro-vascular disease, liver disease, other selected heart diseases, and stomach or duodenal ulcers. Sometimes men despair of the loneliness they feel and so force themselves even farther away from relationships; and sometimes they numb the pain of being so self-sufficient through alcohol or drugs or compulsive and consuming work. And they justify all these twisted reactions by saying, "A man's gotta do what a man's gotta do."

THE LESSON OF SUCCESS

A third experience that happens to men very early in their lives is that they learn the value of success. In the poignant lines of her poem "Doing it differently," Marge Piercy writes: "remember that every son had a mother/ whose beloved son he was,/and every woman had a mother/whose beloved son she wasn't." A boy learns to earn the gleam in his mother's eye by doing well, and so begins the lifelong male pattern of behavior that says men gain the attention of women by being successful, and so men know who they are by being successful. The workplace becomes the arena where many men express their idea of what masculinity is supposed to look like. Such men express it competitively with other men, but in spite of this competition with other men, they continue to exclude women, because at least men know what the rules of the game are.

Men learn to measure their worth by whether they have fulfilled their vocational or professional hopes and dreams and whether they have been good enough at it that society (we might also say the church) awards them a degree of status. And men carefully guard their work arena from any interference, for it is only in their work arena that they are at all clear about who they are and whether they are worth anything. Men strive for what Daniel Levinson calls "becoming one's own man," which means pursuing a professional dream, setting goals, and then driving to achieve them, all of which take an enormous amount of self-investment and energy. Men learn that they find happiness by performing and that they find women by performing. This performance includes repressing their feelings of being exploited by society.

Men must face that they are compromising themselves; whatever they are doing to succeed and thereby to be reassured that they are masculine is simultaneously turning them into something that they don't like and don't want to be. Men work hard to repress their feelings of being exploited, because their exploitation deems them weak and powerless. But since men can't be weak and powerless (because then they would be women), they must continue to convince themselves that they are strong and powerful even when they're not. They must become careful not to talk to other men too much about their jobs, so that other men won't find out that these men are powerless. For many men, the lesson of success leads them to commit themselves to their families. For most men, working too hard is the primary way they try to be effective parents.

SEPARATION FROM THE MOTHER

A fourth male experience, which begins around age three, is the anxious process of separating from the most powerful woman in their lives, their mother. Male children develop what Samuel Osherson calls a symbiosis anxiety, that is, a fear of over-identification with women. Not only must men separate from their powerful mothers—they face two additional complications. First, they are surrounded by women: they have women babysitters, most people who work in places where they go with their mothers are women, and almost all primary and elementary school teachers are women. Boys spend the first ten years or so of their lives surrounded by women, and they must work hard to remain separate from them and to avoid over-identification with them.

The second complication arises when boys try to turn away from mother and other women to father or some other man with whom they can identify. For many boys there is no father to turn to. Father is at work, or if he is at home, he is emotionally and/or physically unavailable. The lesson boys learn is that to be masculine means to be rejecting, incompetent, or absent. In most cases this is a tragic misunderstanding of the father's intentions, but it is nonetheless the lesson that most boy children deduce out of their limited experience. As infants and children, we love our fathers, but when they are absent, we must interiorize and then bury our homoerotic longings for them. The most common future outlet is friendship with other men; if we don't form these, we will always mourn the lost homoerotic relationships with our fathers in a twisted way.

As today's fathers realize how much they were hurt, they are attempting to express their affection more openly, although they have not yet determined to restructure their professional lives. In the *New York Times,* 18 February 1990, Anna Quindlen observed, ". . . fathers today do seem more emotional with their children, more nurturing, more open. Many say, 'My father never told me he loved me,' and so they tell their own children they love them all the time. When they're home."

Men learn to fear all things that smack of women or of femininity, and in the absence of a male role model, they learn to walk around alone in pain. But here the lessons are perhaps the strangest lessons of all, for here male sexuality becomes tragically warped. Men learn to desire women sexually, and yet they fear being absorbed by them or over-identifying with them. They yearn for fathers yet learn to keep their distance from physical contact with men, because that is feminine, and men must reject feminine activities for fear of becoming feminine. We err by setting up an artificial opposition between masculinity and femininity. At times it sounds almost as though femininity were something contagious; for example, homosexual elementary school teachers are said to be "contagious," a threat to true masculinity.

Men learn to desire women and yet readily admit that they do not understand them. Even Freud admitted he was "psychologically unable to solve the riddle of femininity." Men learn to desire women and yet fear them. As Warren Farrell writes: "Look at the praying mantis or the black widow spider. The male and female are making sex. The male gets so involved he cannot undo himself. The female satisfies herself, then bites off the head of the male. The male is so locked into the sexual act that he cannot prevent himself from being consumed. The ultimate in vulnerability." This is many men's experience with women. Many married men will admit to an occasional overwhelming fear when coming home at the end of the work day. They are suddenly afraid to enter the house, to hear the sounds of the family in the kitchen, and feel like they are about to be swallowed up. So men stay at work, or they walk in the door with an isolation barrier already surrounding them to protect them from their own families.

Yet at the same time that men fear the women from whom they have struggled so hard to separate themselves, they are sexually drawn to them, even against their wills. Perhaps this desire is something else: perhaps men realize that in a man's world without friends, the one hope men have of friendship is a wife. Or perhaps men want to live out the deeply repressed feminine side of themselves by marrying and allowing their wives to express the husband's own feminine side from a safer distance.

Men do marry, sometimes again and again. Yet they also fear commitment. Commitment for many women means achieving their primary fantasy of a home and a family and security; for many men it means giving up their primary fantasy of success and independence and widely available sex. Sometimes men also realize that they are being used by the women they marry. Men have worked hard to earn their success, whatever it may be, but there are women who will seize the opportunity to have that success in an instant just by marrying it and who will keep it long after the men die young. That is what Warren Farrell calls "women's flashdance to power and status."

Not only do men learn an odd way of relating to women, they also learn an odd way of relating to men. Men yearn to find the father who was never there, and yet they fear intimacy with men, for that intimacy implies that the men themselves are feminine. We teach men in our society a most crippling form of homophobia. If fathers have been physically affectionate with their sons at an early age, they stop holding and kissing their sons somewhere about the age of five, although they continue holding and kissing their daughters until they reach puberty. Men learn that physical touch is sexually loaded, and so men learn to fear touching a man or being touched by one. Often our fear causes us to skip a critical stage in male ego individuation. The skip is potentially disastrous when we have already lost all opportunity for traditional adolescent rites of passage.

Joyce McDougall observes that adolescent homosexuality is a natural extension of our personality, as we create the perfect friend in another person of our same sex. In order to sort out the "you" and the "not you," a young man must pass through a phase when other young men are his love objects for they are the perfectly projected creations of himself. Narcissistic idealization is a defense mechanism by which we develop a sense of self. The idealization is then normally devalued once the individual self is identified and developed. From there, we may deal with our growing fear of homosexuality by constructing an artificially black-and-white world, ignoring the Kinsey scale of human sexual orientation and the fact that most real homosexuality (the term was not coined until a hundred years ago) is constitutional, rather than volitional. As a constitutional condition, even Freud, in a 1935 letter, recognized that "homosexuality is assuredly no advantage, but it is nothing to be ashamed of, no vice, no degradation, it cannot be classified as an illness. . . ."

Men become so fearful of homosexuality that they cut off a large portion of their innate human potential for both growth and intimacy, for by cutting themselves off from other men, they cut themselves off from forty-nine percent of the human race. The women's movement is light-years ahead of the men's movement on this score, for women long ago learned how much other women can give them in terms of healing and supportive physical touch. Men have learned instead the "correct" ways to be physically intimate with another man: hit him, like football players slap each other's bottoms, or hug another man from the chest up, all the while pounding his back (notice the way males pass the peace to each other during worship). Men learn that men do not care for men, so men go through life not caring for other men. Men also go through life not caring for themselves as men or for their bodies, and so they die eight to ten years earlier than women.

Men learn that what men do instead of being intimate is mutilate each other, in war, in the business world, or even on the football line, while women stand on the side and cheer them on. Masculinity exists primarily in the eye of the beholder, but we cultivate a bevy of beholders in order to reassure ourselves. Men get so used to competing with each other that they do not know how to nurture each other. Or they mistake male-bonding and the tenuous loyalty that goes with it for intimacy. Or they get so involved with what Letty Pogrebin calls "men's life-long pissing contest" that they never learn how to tell other men anything that really matters, or even to tell other men the truth. For example, research studies indicate that men who feel strongest about men appearing masculine are the most likely to drop out of therapy. They will not even tell themselves the truth. The ways that men learn to relate to women in our American society are tragic. But the ways men learn to relate to other men are equally tragic.

Sociologist Don Sabo writes of his own high school athletic career:

> Today, I no longer perceive myself as an individual ripped off by athletic injury. Rather I see myself as just one more man among many men who got swallowed up by a social system predicated on male domination. Patriarchy has two structural aspects. First it is a hierarchical system in which men dominate women in crude and debased, slick and subtle ways. . . . But it is also a system of intermale dominance, in which a minority of men dominates the masses of men. . . . Patriarchy's mythos of heroism and its morality of power-worship implant visions of ecstasy and masculine excellence in the minds of the boys who ultimately will defend its inequities and ridicule its victims. . . . Male competition for prestige and status in sport and elsewhere leads to identification with the relatively few males who control resources and are able to bestow rewards and inflict punishment.

It is men themselves who made "non-male" behavior by males a punishable crime.

From these four lessons, men have been handed a heritage that attempts to define what it means to be masculine. From the first early occurrence, beginning female and turning into male, men learn to define themselves as the ones with the penises, even to the point of developing the opposite of penis envy, that is, penis pride. (On another level, of course, it can be claimed that the erect penis does not belong exclusively to men, for it is the symbol around which both men and women often organize their sexual fantasies.) From the early lesson of being built not to accommodate, men learn to define themselves as strong, independent, and self-sufficient, regardless of the cost. From the early lesson of being a beloved son, men learn to define themselves on the basis of success and achievement. And from the early lesson of turning away from mother, men learn to define themselves on the basis of a controlled sexual prowess with women and a phobic distancing from men. The four marks, then, of the traditional American male are: penis pride, rugged self-sacrificing independence, professional success and status, and a mixture of sexual activity with women and a frequently pathological homophobia.

DEVELOPING A NEW
MASCULINE AGENDA

This would seem to be an accurate description of what might be called the male condition. I don't think, however, that the male condition is all bad; in fact, I know a lot of happy men, myself included. But even the happy men that I know would like things to be different, not because women tell us that things need to be different, but because deep down inside our human selves, men know that we need not be imprisoned for our whole lives by these four early experiences.

I also know a lot of men who right now are responding to the women's movement with a mixture of rage and confusion. Although I can also empathize with the bitter frustration of women who time after time have men turn away from listening to them, it seems that confrontive criticism often heard from the women's movement is about the worst way to effect change in anyone. The criticism at times comes from unexpected quarters. Freeman Dyson tells the follow humorous story, with a bitter edge:

> I cannot regard humanity as a final goal of God's creation. Humanity looks to me like a magnificent beginning but not the last word. Small children often have a better grasp of these questions than grown-ups. It happened to me that I adopted a stepdaughter. I moved into her family when she was five years old. Before that, she had been living alone with her mother. Soon after I moved in, she saw me for the first time naked. "Did God really make you like that?" she asked with some astonishment. "Couldn't he have made you better?"

Instead of expending their energies being angry or confused by the women's movement, a better approach would be for men to get their own acts together and to set for themselves a threefold agenda: (1) supporting those requests from the women's movement that they know will enhance the rich heterogeneity of humankind and affirm women as having been created in God's image; (2) plotting concrete ways to change how men's traditional sex-stereotyping heritage imprisons them; and (3) affirming the many experiences and characteristics of being male that are good and creative and constructive.

I like much about being male. I like work, even the extremely stressful parts. I, like virtually every human being, like power, although I try to be cautious about its misuse. I like my body the way it is, and I like taking care of it through regular exercise and diet. But there are some things I would change, three in particular: (1) I wish men were better about feeling and expressing those feelings. I believe we can learn this, not through criticism but through coaxing and encouragement by women who still have the patience to help. (2) I wish men would radically change the way they parent so that when little boys and little girls individuate from their mothers, there really is a father to turn to. (3) I wish men would learn new ways to relate to other men physically, through tenderness instead of pounding on each other, and most importantly, through emotional intimacy, divorced from crippling homophobia. I think we can learn to feel, parent, and relate to other men differently, and I think that the best way to learn is through men helping other men, perhaps in support groups similar to those modeled for us by the women's movement. Katharine Hepburn is reported to have said: "Sometimes I wonder if men and women really suit each other. Perhaps they should live next door and just visit now and then." As we sort out who we are, there may be more truth to this than humor.

But even support groups seem hard for us. Letty Pogrebin tells the story of a group of divorced and divorcing men who got together to form a men's support group. In a typically masculine way they met, set measurable tasks and goals, accomplished the tasks and goals, and then seeing no further reason to be together, disbanded. We won't have men's support groups as long as we approach them from a business model. But whether through support groups or some other way, men can begin to change most effectively by opening up with other men, by sharing in trust and without competition their hopes and dreams and feelings, their failures and weaknesses and fears. We can start with men rather than with women, for men understand men in the same way that women understand women; the levels of potential trust are already there and don't have to be built from scratch.

Too many women either do not understand what we are trying to do or reject it. Todd Erkel uses a memorable image: "The new man, if he has arrived, is being received like an errant package from UPS. Women want to know: Is *this* what they ordered?" If we rely too heavily on women's permission or approval, the package may be refused, returned, without ever being opened to see what is actually inside.

In spite of what the most radical branches of the women's movement are saying, I continue to believe that it is a very good thing to be male. Having said that, I would like to learn how to be male in such a way that my son Jacob and my daughter Katie can grow into a world that is more honest, more peaceful, more sensitive, and more open to the fullest development of both men's and women's potential. That sounds to me like the liberating good news of the gospel of God's generous love.

SOURCES CITED

Astrachan, Anthony. *How Men Feel: Their Response to Women's Demands for Equality and Power*. Garden City: Doubleday, 1986.

Dyson, Freeman. *Infinite in All Directions*. New York: Harper & Row, 1988.

Farrell, Warren. *Why Men Are the Way They Are*. New York: McGraw-Hill, 1986.

Freud, Sigmund. *The Standard Edition of the Complete Psychological Works of Sigmund Freud*. Translated by James Strachey. 23 vols. and supp. London: Hogarth, 1963. See especially "Analysis Terminable and Interminable" in Vol. 23.

Gilmore, David. *Manhood in the Making*. New Haven: Yale University Press, 1990.

Goldberg, Herb. *The Hazards of Being Male: Surviving the Myth of Masculine Privilege*. New York: New American Library, 1976.

————. *The Inner Male: Overcoming Roadblocks to Intimacy.* New York: New American Library, 1987.

Levinson, Daniel J., with Charlotte N. Darrow, Edward B. Klein, Maria H. Levinson, and Braston McKee. *The Seasons of a Man's Life.* New York: Ballantine, 1978.

Osherson, Samuel. *Finding Our Fathers: The Unfinished Business of Manhood.* New York: Free Press, 1986.

Piercy, Marge. *To Be of Use.* Garden City, N.Y.: Doubleday, 1973.

Pogrebin, Letty Cottin. *Among Friends: Who We Like, Why We Like Them, and What We Do with Them.* New York: McGraw-Hill, 1987.

Sabo, Don. "Pigskin, Patriarchy and Pain." In Abbott, Franklin, ed. *New Men, New Minds: Breaking Male Tradition.* Freedom, Calif.: Crossing, 1987.

Viorst, Judith. *Necessary Losses: The Love, Illusions, Dependencies and Impossible Expectations That All of Us Have to Give Up in Order to Grow.* New York: Simon and Schuster, 1986.

15

Embracing Masculinity

JAMES B. NELSON

What are the spiritual meanings of the male genitals? The question seldom has been asked, particularly in Christian conversation and literature. There are predictable and important questions about the appropriateness of even considering the issue. Before we go further, we must attend to them.

First, some will simply find the question distasteful. Anti-body feelings nurtured by centuries of sexual dualism are strong indeed. And the genitals are the supreme test. Discomfort over seriously considering the body to be of spiritual significance becomes repulsion when the focus is the genitals. The reaction is predictable, but deeply regrettable. God has created us good in all our parts, and an incarnationalist faith bids us celebrate *all* of the body as vehicle of divine presence and meaning.

Can the sexual feelings, functions, and meanings of our genitals be important modes of revelation? Admittedly, the thought has been far from commonplace in Christian theology. Yet a broader view is needed. The distinguished historian of religion Mircea Eliade saw our human sexual experience as an "autonomous mode of cognition." It is, he believed, a fundamental way of knowing reality immediately and directly. Eliade went so far as to declare that sexuality's "primary and perhaps supreme valency is the cosmological function. . . . Except in the modern world, sexuality has everywhere and always been a hierophany, and the sexual act an integral action and therefore also a means of knowledge."[1] Sexuality thus is a pathway into the mystery of the cosmos. As a hierophany it is a manifestation of the sacred, revealing to us what is beyond our conscious rational apprehension. True, this is a bold claim that goes against the accepted view. Centuries of dualism have taught us that the body (especially in its sexual dimensions) reveals nothing of the spirit. But a holistic spirituality demands that we make this bold claim.

Even if this is granted, however, some will object that such a focus for the masculinity question will simply invite back all the distortions of genitalized masculinity. I am sympathetic with this concern. Such distortions are prevalent in men's experience, and they are serious. Let us name them once more. There is the genitalization of sexual feeling, the Pinocchio-like experience of life in the one organ while the rest of the body feels lifeless and deprived of eros. The consequences are manifold. . . . There is the one-sided phallic interpretation of reality, which overvalues the linear, the vertical, and the hard while undervaluing the cyclical, the horizontal, and the soft. Again, the results in men's one-sided shaping of their world are enormous. Also, there are the ways in which the penis becomes associated with violent and detached meanings, as its slang names amply suggest—cock, prick, tool, rod, and even a gun with its bullets. Such meanings do not readily suggest the genitals as graciously integrated into the body of love. And there are body-affirming feminists, men as well as women, who will resist the thought of *any* kind of male genital affirmation precisely because they are so keenly aware of the wounds caused by phallic violence. Attention of any kind given to the penis might suggest just another thinly disguised form of masculinist oppression. These suspicions, sadly enough, are understandable.

Where are we left? One option seems to be the firm discipline of the genitals. If my penis seems to have a mind of its own, I must deprive it of that freedom. I will be its master and keep it from running amok. The trouble with servants and slaves, however, is that they seldom know their place. They are treated as machines, whose only purpose is to perform the functions determined by their masters. But either as slave or as machine, that part of me will be dead. I will have deprived it of its right to live *except* as slave or machine. This puts me right back into the dualism of control: the higher over the lower, master over servant. The spirit or mind with its higher capacities for thought and virtue must control the body, especially the penis, with its physical appetites.

Even though many Christians seem to hold a different theological theory about the body in all of its parts—good because made by God, and a temple of the Holy Spirit—a simple test proposed by H. A. Williams suggests another reality.[2] Suppose that in church on Sunday morning this lesson from Paul is read: "I appeal to you therefore, . . . by the mercies of God, to present your bodies as a living sacrifice, holy and acceptable to God, which is your spiritual worship" (Rom. 12:1). What prospects come into our imaginations as response to this exhortation? Does it conjure up images of physical pleasure and ecstasy? "Not at all," says Williams. "The prospect conjured up is the dreary duty of controlling the body, or if the body is recalcitrant of forcing it, negatively, not to do this, that, or the other, and positively to energize itself in the performance of this or the other kind of good works. But whether understood negatively or positively the exhortation is taken automatically as a call to the joyless task of disciplining the body and oppressing it by imposing upon it an alien will, treating it in short as a dead object to be pushed around."[3] If that is true of our actual functioning attitudes toward the body as a whole (regardless of the theological notions we might have in our heads), how much truer it probably is of our genitals.

However, the master-slave discipline of the genitals will not work. They are finally treated not as a vital part of us but as something denied the right to live except as slave machines. Nor will it work to ignore our genitals or consign them to hell as beyond redemption. It will not work because that which is consigned to hell just will not lie down. While Williams is speaking of bodies in general, his words are just as true of our genitals in particular: "Being in hell, the place of the undead, they are always somehow planning and threatening their revenge, and they may in the end catapult us into nuclear catastrophe. . . . The body deprived of *eros* inevitably becomes the champion of *thanatos*. Better to die completely than to fester in hell."[4] Indeed, hell is the place of the dead who will not accept their death.

The alternative, however, is not to give our genitals the freedom of their demands. That was the solution for some people in the "sexual revolution" of recent decades: if in the past we have oppressed our bodies and genitals, let us now give the slaves their freedom. But subjecting our genitals to oppression has made them subject to compulsions, and compulsions do not satisfy. They give only fleeting, momentary relief. Compulsions of genital instinct just replace compulsions of the head, but there still is no fulfillment. We still remain divided. Only the balance of power has changed. What we need is truly the resurrection of the body in all its parts. We do not need the crazy behavior of the slave let loose for the evening.

Still, we cannot insist on utter clarity or purity in our experience. Williams's words are wise: "For in experience compulsion and resurrection are often mixed up together. Indeed the experience of resurrection often grows from what was originally an experience of compulsion. If we are perfectionists or purists here we shall find ourselves cut off from all experience of love."[5] Sometimes illusion is the midwife of reality, and paralysis from the fear of illusion may mean that reality will forever escape us.

In recent years a number of feminist women have fruitfully explored the spiritual meanings of their own female body experiences—the nature of their breasts and genitals, their experiences of menstruation and birthing. We men traditionally have identified women with their biology and neglected our own. It is time that we inquire about ourselves.

PHALLUS

In his suggestive book *Phallos: Sacred Image of the Masculine,* Eugene Monick explores the psychic and religious dimensions of the male experience of his phallus, his erect penis.[6] Every male, he asserts, directly knows the meanings of erection: strength, hardness, determination, sinew, straightforwardness, penetration. Because erection is not fully under a man's conscious control, because the penis seems to decide on its own when, where, and with whom it wants erection and action, the phallus seems to be an appropriate metaphor for the masculine unconscious.

From time immemorial it has fascinated men. Numerous ancient expressions of phallic art and worship are well known, from the common representations on ancient Greek pottery, to the huge erection of the Cerne giant (carved in the first century B.C. by the Celts into a chalk hill in Dorset, England), to the modern-day Hindu cult of Shiva, where the phallus is an image of divinity.[7] Beyond such outward evidences of religious veneration, men of every time and place have known a religious quality to their phallic experience. To adapt Rudolf Otto's words, it is the *mysterium tremendum*. Such encounters with the numinous produces responses of fascination, awe, energy, and a sense of the "wholly other."[8] Through the phallus, men sense a resurrection, the capacity of the male member to return to life again and again after depletion. An erection makes a boy feel like a man and makes a man feel alive. It brings the assurance and substantiation of masculine strength.

Yet, as with other experiences of the holy, males feel ambivalent about the phallus. Erections must be hidden from general view. They are an embarrassment when they occur publicly. Men joke about erections with each other but cannot speak seriously. The secret is exposed only with another person in intimacy or when a male permits himself to experience his potency alone. If the mystery is exposed publicly, somehow the sacred has been profaned.

Furthermore, there is a double-sidedness to the phallic experience. One dimension is the *earthy* phallus.[9] This is the erection perceived as sweaty, hairy, throbbing, wet, animal sexuality. In some measure it is Bly's Iron John maleness. Men who have rejected this may be nice and gentle, but they seem to lack life-giving energy. Their keys remain hidden under the queen's pillow—indeed, with the cooperation of the king, for the powers of social order always distrust the earthy phallus. And there is reason for distrust, because there can be an ugly, brutal side to the earthy phallus that uses others for gratification when this part of a man's sexuality does not find balance with other sides. Yet without the positive presence of earthy energy a man is bland. There is gentleness without strength, peacefulness without vitality, tranquility without vibrancy.

Men also experience the *solar* phallus.[10] Solar (from the sun) means enlightenment. A man's erect penis represents to him all that stands tall. It is proud. The solar experience of erection puts a man in touch with the excitement of strenuous achievement. It is the Jacob's ladder and the mountain climb, which rise above the earthy and the earthly. It is the satisfaction of straining to go farther intellectually, physically, and socially. Solar phallus is transcendence. It is the church steeples and skyscrapers that men are inclined to build. Solar phallus represents what most men would like to have noted in their obituaries. In Carl Jung's thinking, solar phallus is the very substance of masculinity. It is, he believed, *logos*, which transforms thought into word, just as eros (which he called feminine) transforms feeling into relatedness. I believe Jung misled us with his bifurcations of masculine and feminine principles, unfortunately grounding them in common gender stereotypes. Nevertheless, logos is an important part of the male experience both represented and invited by the solar phallus.

As with the earthy phallus, there is a shadow side to the experience of the solar phallus, too. It is the patriarchal oppression of those who do not "measure up." It is proving one's worth through institutional accomplishments. It is the illusion of strength and power that comes from position. It is the use of technical knowledge to dominate. It is political power which defends its ideological purity at virtually any price and then prides itself on standing tall in the saddle. It is addiction to the notion that bigger is better. The distortions of solar phallus are legion. Yet without its integrated positive energy, a man lacks direction and movement. Without the urge to extend himself, he is content with the mediocre. Without the experience of the wholly other, life loses its self-transcendence.

Thus far I have agreed in broad outline with Monick's significant analysis: the importance of both the earthy and the solar phallus, their integration, and the dangers of their shadow sides. Here, however, Monick stops. He believes that phallus, the erect penis, is *the* sacred image of the masculine. That seems to be enough. But it is not. Left there, I fear we are left with priapism.

In Roman mythology Priapus, son of Dionysus and Aphrodite, was the god of fertility. His usual representations were marked both by grotesque ugliness and an enormous erection. In human sexual disorders, priapism is the painful clinical condition of an erection that will not go down. Priapus and priapism are symbolic of the idolatry of the half-truth. Phallus, the erection, indeed is a vital part of the male's experience of his sexual organs. Hence, it is usually a vital part of his spirituality. But it is only part. Were it the whole thing, his sexuality and his spirituality would be painful and bizarre, both to himself and to others. That this in fact is too frequently the case is difficult to deny. Our phallic experience gives vital energy, both earthy and solar. But we also need the affirmative experience of the *penis*.

PENIS

In our daily lives, almost all men are genitally soft by far the greater share of the time. Genitally speaking, penis rather than phallus is our awareness, insofar as we are aware at all. (For economy in words, I will use "penis" for the organ in its flaccid, unaroused state.) We are genitally limp most of our waking moments, and while erections come frequently during sleep we are seldom aware of them.

Psychically, the experiences of phallus and of penis seem very different. An erection during waking hours claims my attention. Frequently I choose not to act upon its aroused urgency, and sometimes in embarrassment I hide its evidence. But its claims on my psychic awareness have an undeniable phallic imperiousness. The penis is different. Most of the time I am unaware of it. It is just there, part of me, functioning in my occasional need to urinate, but most often invisible from my conscious awareness, much as an internal organ. But when I am conscious of it in dressing or undressing, I am aware of its difference from phallus. Penis is considerably smaller. It is wrinkled. There is even something comical about the contrast (as a man's wife or lover occasionally might tell him). It has a relaxed humility. In its external existence it seems vulnerable, and with the testicles it needs jockstrap protection during the body's vigorous athletics.

In spite of the quantitative dominance of penis time, men tend to undervalue penis and overvalue phallus. Part of that, indeed, simply stems from conscious awareness. When the phallus is present, it demands our attention. The penis does not. Part of the difference, however, is a matter of intentional valuation. We have been taught and have learned to value phallic meanings in patriarchy: bigger is better (in bodily height, in paychecks, in the size of one's corporation or farm); hardness is superior to softness (in one's muscles, in one's facts, in one's foreign policy positions); upness is better than downness (in one's career path, in one's computer, in one's approach to life's problems). In "a man's world," small, soft, and down pale beside big, hard, and up.

Penis is undervalued, also, because we so commonly identify male energy and true masculinity with the vitality of young manhood. Infant males and little boys have frequent erections, but true phallus—the heroic sword raised on high—is the property of young manhood. As age comes upon a man, hardness changes and modifies. It is less apparent, less urgent, less the signature of his body. Phallus bears intimations of life and vigor, while penis bears intimations of mortality. Fearing mortality, men tend to reject the qualities of penis and project them upon women who are then seen to be small, soft, and vulnerable, qualities inferior to the phallic standard. Wrinkles, so typical of penis, are not permitted in women if they are to retain their womanly attraction.[11]

But the undervaluing of penis and the overvaluing of phallus take their toll. The price is paid by all who suffer because of patriarchy, for this spiritual body dynamic, while hardly the sole cause of such oppression, surely contributes to it. But oppressors themselves are also oppressed in the process. So what is the price paid by men? One cost we must look at is the deprivation of a significant kind of masculine spiritual energy and power.

The history of western spirituality reveals two traditional paths to the presence of God: the Via Positiva and the Via Negativa, the positive way and the negative way.[12] The former is a way of affirmation, of thanksgiving, of ecstasy. It is the way of light, the way of being filled by the sacred fullness and rising to the divine height. The Via Negativa is a way of emptying and being emptied. It is the way of darkness. It is sinking into nothingness and into the sacred depths. In spirituality, each way needs the other for balance and completion. The overdevelopment of one to the detriment of the other brings distortion. I believe that in the male experience the Via Positiva has profound associations with the phallus, while the Via Negativa correspondingly is connected to the penis. And in most men it is the latter which remains underrecognized, underclaimed, underaffirmed.

Consider some aspects of the Via Negativa as expressed by a great Christian mystic who knew this way, Meister Eckhart (1260–1327). It is quiet, not active: "Nothing in all creation is so like God as stillness." It is the darkness more than the light: "The ground of the soul is dark." It appears to be less rather than more: "God is not found in the soul by adding anything but by a process of subtraction." It is a deep sinking and a letting go: "We are to sink eternally from letting go to letting go into God." It is the abandoning of focus and attention: "One should love God mindlessly, without mind or mental activities or images or representations." It is the paradox of nothingness embracing something: "God is a being beyond being and a nothingness beyond being. . . . God is nothingness. And yet God is something."[13]

All such modes of the Via Negativa are a man's experiences of his penis, not his phallus. Think of sinking and emptying. The penis is empty of the engorging blood that brings hard excitement to the phallus. Its flaccidity is a letting go of all urgency. It has nowhere to go. It just is. It just hangs and sinks between the legs.

Sinking, emptying, is a way of spirituality.[14] It means trusting God that we do not need to *do,* that our *being* is enough. It means yielding to our tears that keep coming and coming once they begin. It means trusting ourselves to the darkness of sleep, so like the darkness of death. It means abandoning our own achievements and resting in the depths of meaning we do not create. Men often resist these things. But sinking and emptying are as necessary to the spirit's rhythms as they are to the genitals'. Without periods of genital rest, a man lacks phallic capacity. Without times of retreat to the desert, there is no energy for greening.

Or consider darkness, another theme of the Negativa. It seems related to the cosmic womb of our origins, and it has its own energy. Rainer Maria Rilke writes, "You darkness, that I come from/I love you more than all the fires that fence in the world . . . and it is possible a great energy is moving near me/I have faith in nights."[15] But most men are less at home in the darkness than in the light. We are heirs of the Enlightenment, a male-oriented rational movement that sought to shed light on everything. Our psyches seem to link darkness with death, and fear of death is characteristic of the patriarchal society. Starhawk, speaking of the holiness of darkness, maintains that the dark is "all that we are afraid of, all that we don't want to see—fear, anger, sex, grief, death, the unknown."[16]

The penis, in contrast to the phallus, is a creature of the dark. It is resting. Asleep. Usually we are unaware of its presence. But we are conscious of the presence of phallus, just as we are aware of the presence of light. Taught to prize light and fear the dark, we have also been taught to prize the phallic virtues and to fear the meanings of penis. Its quiescence seems symbolic of death, its limpness the reminder of male-dreaded impotence, and fears of death and impotence are the cause of much destruction. But without the darkness there is no growth, no mystery, no receptivity, no deep creativity. Without the gentle dark, light becomes harsh.

MASCULINE ENERGY:
BEYOND ANDROGYNY

For a variety of reasons, men have come to believe that phallus is the emblem of masculinity, the signature of true maleness. But this is only partly true, and partial truths taken as the whole truth become both demonic and self-destructive. A man's penis is as genuinely his reality as is his phallus, and just as important to his male humanity. Spiritually, the Via Negativa is as vital to him as the Via Positiva. It may also be the case that men's overvaluation of phallus, and the undervaluation of penis, is one important reason for our confusions about gender identities and the notion of androgyny.

The concept of androgyny has been commonplace for some years.[17] Most simply put, it denotes the integration within a single person of traits traditionally identified by gender stereotypes as masculine and as feminine. Thus, androgynous people characterize themselves both as strongly self-reliant, assertive, and independent, and as strongly understanding, affectionate, and compassionate. Androgyny is an appealing alternative to the oppressiveness of gender role stereotypes. It goes beyond the false dualism of the belief that there are certain inherent personality traits of the male and of the female. It moves us beyond oppressive gender expectations into the possibility of a more genuinely human liberation for each and for all.

The concept seems appealing theologically. Nicolas Berdiaev, the Russian philosopher-theologian, pressed the idea in 1914, long before its currency in social psychology. There is, he declared, a fundamental androgyny of the human being created in the image of God, an androgyny that the gender roles of the world have not destroyed. "In fact, 'in the beginning' it is neither man nor woman who bears the divine similitude. In the beginning it is only the androgyne . . . who bears it. The differentiation of the sexes is a consequence of the fall of Adam." Now, estranged from our essence, we have a compelling desire to recover our lost unity through recovery of the lost principle. "It is by means of this femininity that the male-human can once again be integrated to the androgynous source of his nature, just as it is through this masculine principle that the female-human can be . . . integrated to her lost androgynous source. . . . Ultimately it is in God that the lover meets with the beloved, because it is in God that personality is rooted. And the personality in God, in its original state, is androgynous."[18]

Berdiaev was ahead of his time. Most later male theologians of this century have not seriously raised the androgynous theme but rather have emphasized the need of gender complementarity. Karl Barth is typical.[19] He believes that our humanity, created in the image of God, is "fellow-humanity." We are incomplete by ourselves. Men and women come into their fullness only in intimate relation to persons of the opposite sex. Barth's position rests on the assumption that by nature the personalities and qualities of the two sexes are essentially different and that each needs the other for completion. There is no androgyny.

Barth draws a clear conclusion from this concerning homosexuality: it is perversion and idolatry. One who seeks same-sex union is narcissistically seeking the self. It is a quest for self-satisfaction and self-sufficiency, but such aims can never be realized because the two sexes are fundamentally necessary for each other. While I find Barth's emphasis on the *social* nature of our true humanity commendable, his notion of gender complementarity is deeply flawed. It rests on the uncritical use of gender stereotypes, and it particularly oppresses gays and lesbians, all who are female (because those stereotypes do), and all who are single (among the latter, Jesus included). The notion of gender complementarity is a giant step backward from androgyny.

Androgyny is an ancient theme, prevalent in classical mythology. In Christian thought it was present far earlier than Berdiaev. Yet I believe his was the first clear statement of the essential androgyny of *both* sexes. Earlier versions, blatantly patriarchal, found only the male androgynous. Woman was made necessary as a differentiated sexual being only because man had lost his state of perfection and needed her feminine principle for his human completion. She, however, remained half human.

Nevertheless, androgyny as a theological concept, even in Berdiaev's promising way, runs into some of the same problems as are present in current social psychology. One problem is both definitional and practical. Does the concept mean that both "feminine" and "masculine" characteristics somehow essentially (by nature or by God's design) exist together in every individual, and thus they should be developed and expressed? This seems to be the most common understanding. In the psychological literature sometimes it is labeled "monoandrogynism," to distinguish it from variations of the theme. But this can be oppressive in its own way. Now each person has two sets of gender traits to learn and incorporate instead of one. Now everyone is expected to acquire thoroughly both "instrumental/agentic" ("masculine") and "expressive/nurturant" ("feminine") characteristics in equal amounts, a standard that would seem to double the pressure that people traditionally have felt.

Even more basically, another problem is that androgyny is based on the assumption that there are, indeed, two distinct and primordial sets of personality characteristics—one "masculine," the other "feminine." Even if we assume that each sex is capable of developing both sets of traits, the definition itself perpetuates the very problem it had hoped to overcome. It still locates one constellation of qualities essentially and dominantly in men and the other constellation essentially and dominantly in women. Jung's psychological thought exemplifies this, as do those who draw upon him, for example, in speaking of the male's need to develop "his latent feminine side." In fact, there is a built-in obsolescence to this concept. For if each sex stopped adhering only to its primary characteristics, and if the two gender stereotypes subsequently became less distinct from each other, androgyny in the current sense would lose its meaning.

One way out of the conceptual difficulty is simply to envision the complete transcendence of gender-role traits (sometimes called the "polyandrogynous" possibility). Here, personality traits are seen as having no connection at all with biological sex. Each individual is viewed as different from every other individual, for each has unique interests and capacities. In many ways this vision is promising. It frees individuals to be who they uniquely are. However, there remains a problem. The notion of gender-role transcendence, while it honors uniqueness, does not hold up any vision of inclusiveness or relative balance in personal qualities. A given individual could still be as one-sided as ever, even though the rigid linkage between certain traits and one's biological sex had been severed.

Nevertheless, an important question still remains. Is there anything *distinctive* to the experience of one's own biological sex that grounds us in the development of a more whole personality, a personhood richer than its specific gender stereotype? More particularly, is there anything in the male body experience that enables him to transcend the traditional cultural images of masculinity?

If that *is* the case, it is difficult to see why the call to more inclusive personhood would be fundamentally oppressive. If as a man I were called upon to acquire feminine qualities *in addition to my natural masculinity*, that would be one thing. I might be capable of doing that, but it would feel much like learning a second language as an adult, adding another linguistic capability to my native tongue. Even if through years of study and practice I become somewhat proficient, my second language would always be that—a second language, added on, requiring additional effort. My strong inclination would always be to see the world primarily through the images of the language of my birth. On the other hand, were I "naturally bilingual"—born into a bilingual family and society, schooled in the images of both from my earliest days—the inclusiveness of languages would not feel like a burden. It would feel natural.

My illustration admittedly suffers, because languages are thoroughly social inventions and learnings. Our bodies are not. While they have many social, learned meanings attached to them, they also have a biological givenness. My point, however, is this: We have been given "bilingual bodies." Even if one language has been developed more than the other, the second language is not foreign to us. It is not something we need to add on. It is just as originally part of us as the language with which, by accident of circumstances, we have become most familiar.

It is time to move beyond the usual meanings of androgyny. The vision for men is not to develop "feminine" energies (or for women to develop "masculine" energies). Rather, the vision for men is the fullest development of our *masculine* energies. But the issue is *fullness*. We are not talking only of phallic qualities. Penis is vulnerable, soft, receptive. Penis represents and invites the spirituality of the Via Negativa. But a penis is not "feminine"—it is as authentically masculine as is phallus. It bears qualities rooted in the fullness of the male's sexual experience, in the fullness of his body affirmation. So we who are men are simply invited to develop the masculine more richly. To speak this way is not to play word games. Linguistic sleight-of-hand tricks are abstractions. Incarnational reflection does not thrive on abstractions, but tries to represent bodily realities honestly.

Finally, it is important to recognize that each dimension of the male genital experience involves the other. Each of us experiences only one body, though in our experience there is the conjunction of apparent opposites. Paradoxically, the opposites are only apparently so. Each is implied by and contained within the other. Penis is always potentially phallus. The soft receptivity of penis implies relationality. But phallus is aroused as the genital aspects of relationship are anticipated or fantasized. So, also, the hard energy of phallus literally bears the signs of gentleness. The lover is amazed at the velvety texture and softness of the head of the man's rock-hard erection. Men know the vulnerability of their testicles and shield them from harm even during arousal and lovemaking. Indeed, male vulnerability is most present exactly at the spot where colloquial language locates male courage: "He has balls."[20]

Such is the marvelous conjunction of apparent opposites in the male's sexual body, a wholeness inviting him to richness of personhood. It is at the same time the bodily experienced invitation to richness of spirituality through the apparent opposites of Via Positiva and Via Negativa. Such is the golden ball of legend, representing connectedness and radiant energy.

POWER AND SIZE

One of the central issues in spirituality is *power*.[21] It is evident whenever personal beings are present to each other. Men's lives—and the lives of all those affected by patriarchy—have been dominated by one particular perception of power. It is *unilateral* power. It is also called zero-sum power, or the power of a closed energy system, inasmuch as it carries with it the assumption that there is only a limited quantity of power available, so that the more one person gets the less is available to the other. Unilateral power is nonmutual and nonrelational. Its purpose is to produce the largest possible effect on another, while being least affected by the other. Its ideal is control.

"In this view," writes Bernard Loomer, "our size or stature is measured by the strength of our unilateral power. Our sense of self-value is correlative to our place on the scale of inequality."[22] But the sense of self one has in this understanding is nonrelational, self-contained. It is the traditional masculine ideal of the Lone Ranger. The aim is to move toward maximum self-sufficiency. Dependency on others is weakness. But this kind of power, in reducing mutuality, produces estrangement among people. We are deadened to our interdependence and to the mystery of each other. This is unmodified phallic power.

Christianity has often embraced this view of power in its views of God. At such times it has seen God as omniscient, omnipotent, and controlling the world by divine fiat. This theology was built upon the same sexual dualism that split spirit from body. Spirit was seen as eternal, complete, and changeless, while body was temporal, incomplete, and changeable. God had unilateral power. "He" was perfect in his completeness and unaffected by those "below."

At the same time Christian theology embraced this unilateral understanding of power as applied to God, it had problems. The gospel message was quite clear that among people this was "worldly" power. Because such power was one-way and controlling, it seemed to be the antithesis of love. When Jesus renounced the power of the world, it was this kind of power he forsook. Thus, in Christianity a view of love as similarly one-way arose. It was the traditional interpretation of agape—a one-way divine love, a concern for the other with no concern for oneself. It was this kind of love that Christians were told to emulate. A one-sided love became the compensation for a one-sided power. One extreme was designed to offset a contrary extreme. The loss of eros and the goodness of the erotic, the confusion of selfishness with self-love—such were the prices exacted by unilateral power and unilateral love.

There is, however, another understanding of power. "This is the ability both to produce and to undergo an effect. It is the capacity both to influence others and to be influenced by others."[23] This is *relational* power. It is generative power, the power of an open energy system. Instead of a fixed, limited amount, the assumption is that shared power can generate more power. People are enhanced by this kind of power, mystery is affirmed, interdependence is celebrated. This, however, is not the power represented by the penis, but by the whole of the genitals and the whole of the body.

These distinctions concerning power bear on the problem of androgyny. Traditional androgyny begins with a combinationist assumption. It takes a fixed notion of the masculine (the active agent), a fixed notion of the feminine (the receiving, nurturing one) and tries to combine them in one person. However, in regard to power, both understandings of gender roles are deficient. The "feminine" principle has been under attack because it suggests a neurotic dependence on others and lack of sufficient autonomy. The "masculine" has been under attack because it suggests the urge to dominate others without being at the same time influenced by them. The point is that both are faulty. Adding one to another to achieve a balance is not the solution. Rather, the solution is understanding that both are definitions marred by fear and insecurity. The "feminine" fears self-dependence, while the "masculine" fears interdependence. Such fear is born of insecurity. It is the absence of authentic power.

Just as wholeness for either a man or a woman is not some combination of the masculine and the feminine, so also authentic relational power is not a neat combination of the active and the receptive. Relational power understands that the capacity to absorb the influence of another without losing the self's own center is as truly a quality of power as is the strength of exerting influence on another.

Loomer calls this kind of strength "size," the capacity to become large enough to make room for another within the self without losing the self's own integrity or freedom. "The world of the individual who can be influenced by another without losing his or her identity or freedom is larger than the world of the individual who fears being influenced. . . . The stature of the individual who can let another exist in his or her own creative freedom is larger than the size of the individual who insists that others must conform to his own purposes and understandings."[24]

Sexual experience always involves power. The experience of phallus without penis is unilateral power. The colloquial male ideal of the phallus is "two feet long, made of steel, and lasts all night." Phallus can handle multiple orgasms (or partners) without being reduced to flaccidity. The phallic perception of woman is as the receptacle for phallic power and emission. The ideal: affect without being affected.

In contrast, the man who affirms his whole sexuality knows that both phallus and penis are one. They are different but interdependent qualities of one male reality. Each at the same time is the other. In spite of the myth of phallic unaffectedness, men know that they are not made of steel, nor do they last all night. Phallus not only delivers effect but is also very much affected. In intercourse it is changed, transformed into penis. "Transformed" is a good word. Sometimes we use the language of death and resurrection about the male genital experience, but it is time to reassess that imagery. It can be highly misleading, even destructive. Yet I fear that the image is fairly common in the male psyche. It suggests that phallus is alive and then, when spent, dies. Penis, then, is the death from which phallus is raised once again. But this interpretation implies a very unilateral understanding of power. Only the phallus has power, the penis does not. Further, the suggestion is that, at least in the heterosexual experience, the woman is somehow associated with "reducing" the phallus to flaccidity. Thus once again we make, even if unconsciously, the connection between woman and passivity. Now the woman somehow is responsible for the man's passivity, his loss of power and agency. But with the language of death and resurrection the psychic connections become more vicious. Now the phallus dies, and the connection is established between the woman and death. And death is assumed to be the enemy.

But when the phallus becomes penis it does not die. There is simply a change to another form of its life. When the phallus becomes penis it does not lose its power, except when that power is understood unilaterally. Rather, the penis has a different kind of power. It is now the man's genital sexuality expressing its capacity to absorb change. What was once hard and imperious is now soft and gentle. In both dimensions the man is experiencing his masculine power, and both are aspects of relational power. True power is mutuality, making claims and absorbing influence. It is different from the "mutuality" of external relatedness, which trades in force, compromise, and accommodation. It understands the paradox that the greatest influence often consists in being influenced, in enabling another to make the largest impact on oneself.

When a man so understands his sexuality he better understands true power, and when he understands power he better understands his sexuality. The same is true of size, for size and power are intimately related. However, "the wisdom of the world" about male genital size measures quality precisely in terms of quantity. Bigger is better. The masculinist fantasy says not only "made of steel" but also "two feet long." It does not matter that sexologists and sexual therapists tell us that the actual size of the male organ is quite irrelevant to effective sexual functioning and the quality of lovemaking—irrelevant except for one thing: too large an organ causes problems. Still, myth and fantasy persist. Pubescent boys still measure themselves and each other. The record holders are honored in the neighborhood gang. And, as noted earlier, Freud continues to be debunked in his contention that penis envy is a persistent phenomenon of the woman's unconscious; rather, it persists in the surreptitious, glancing comparisons made in the men's locker room.

In contrast to such worldly wisdom about size as quantitative, consider Loomer's description:

> By *size* I mean the stature of a person's soul, the range and depth of his [or her] love, his [or her] capacity for relationships. I mean the volume of life you can take into your being and still maintain your integrity and individuality, the intensity and variety of outlook you can entertain in the unity of your being without feeling defensive or insecure. I mean the strength of your spirit to encourage others to become freer in the development of their diversity and uniqueness. I mean the power to sustain more complex and enriching tensions. I mean the magnanimity of concern to provide conditions that enable others to increase in stature.[25]

When a man understands this meaning of size, his genital sexuality is less anxiously, more graciously celebrated. And when that is true, he also better understands the true meaning of size as criterion of genuine power.

If the themes of death and resurrection can be misleading when applied to penis and phallus, surely they have valid and profound meanings for our sexual and bodily lives more generally. The resurrection of the body in our experience means that mind and body no longer make war on each other, each trying to control or dominate the other. Now I can feel that I *am* my body, and that does not in any way contradict the fact that I am my mind or spirit. Death separates. Resurrection and life reunite. To be raised to life is to discover that I am one person. Body and mind are no longer felt to be distinct.

We usually have such an experience now and then. Most likely it is temporary, soon forgotten, for we have lived much of our lives with dualistic self-understandings and dualistic perceptions of reality at large. So body and mind fall apart again, each competing with the other for the prize of being me. Death sets in once more. But resurrections occur, and in those moments I know myself to be one. When that happens, the experience of oneness with myself brings with it the strong sense of connectedness with the rest of the world. I feel connected to—more than separated from—the people, creatures, and things among whom I live. They have their own identities, yet they also become part of me and I of them. My resurrection is the world's resurrection as I know that world.[26] The same applies to a man's genital perception. Resurrection occurs when penis and phallus are one, neither competing for the honor of being the man. When that happens there is true power—and authentic size.

JESUS AS SEXUAL MAN
AND MAN OF POWER

Jesus as the Christ has been desexualized by most Christian piety throughout the ages. Sexual dualism has kept its sturdy grip, and incarnation, the real presence of God in human flesh, has been a scandal too great for most of the church to believe. A spiritualized God, acting in proper taste, simply would not do that sort of thing. Docetism, the belief that, in Jesus, God was not really humanly enfleshed but only appeared to be, was early declared a heresy by the church, but it still is very much alive. And about the most effective way of denying Jesus' full humanity has been to deny (outright or by embarrassed silence) his sexuality. Some of the early Christian Gnostics (who abhorred the flesh) represent the extreme. They could not even bring themselves to believe that Jesus needed to eat; he took food with his followers from time to time so not to alarm them. The thought of Jesus engaged in digestion, defecation, and urination would have appalled them. To the present-day Gnostics of whatever stripe, of course, the thought of Jesus' sexual arousal, erection, and orgasm is at best exceedingly poor taste and at worst blasphemous.

Just as popular piety has been aghast at the thought, theologians for the most part have simply avoided the issue of Jesus' sexuality other than to affirm his celibacy. Only rarely have they faced the question directly. William Phipps, one of the rare ones, has come to the conclusion that Jesus was probably married at one time.[27] Phipps finds no biblical evidence for Jesus' virginity, but rather finds a picture of Jesus as fully immersed in a sexuality-affirming Jewish culture, a culture which in fact rejected celibacy in both theory and practice. Jesus, who was hardly pictured as an ascetic by the Gospels, probably married sometime during those years about which we have no information (between ages twelve and thirty). Before his public ministry began, something—we do not know what—happened to his wife. The idea of a celibate savior, Phipps concludes, is not the product of the apostolic age but rather grew out of Christianity's later contact with the dualism of Hellenistic Greece.

I believe the case for Jesus' marriage is highly debatable. Had it happened, surely there would have been some apostolic mention of it. But whether or not Jesus married is not really the crux of the issue. His sexuality is, and investigations like that of Phipps help us to take the issue with greater seriousness. The question is not an esoteric one. If we who call ourselves Christian are unsure of the full humanity of him whom we call Truly Human, we shall be unsure of what full humanity means for us. If our image of authentic personhood in Jesus denigrates sexuality, we will do the same within ourselves.

Actually, some of the "secular theologians" have most effectively pressed the question of Jesus' sexuality. Nikos Kazantzakis and D. H. Lawrence have done so in literature. A particularly interesting inquiry is provided by a distinguished art historian, Leo Steinberg, in *The Sexuality of Christ in Renaissance Art and in Modern Oblivion*.[28] Steinberg observes that for a millennium of Christian history Jesus' sexuality was disregarded by theology and art, which focused virtually all attention on his divinity. Then came the Renaissance and the rediscovery of the glories of humanity.

Now devout Christian painters from Flanders to Florence removed the drapery from the figure of Jesus and purposely exposed his genitals. "In many hundreds of pious religious works, from before 1400 to past the mid-16th century, the ostensive unveiling of the Child's sex, or the touching, protecting or presentation of it, is the main action. . . . And the emphasis recurs in images of the dead Christ, or of the mystical Man of Sorrows. . . . All of which has been tactfully overlooked for half a millennium."[29] In the great cathedrals hung paintings of the Holy Family in which Mary herself deliberately spreads the infant's thighs so that the pious might gaze at his genitals in wonder. In other paintings the Magi are depicted gazing intently at Jesus' uncovered loins as if expecting revelation. In still others Jesus' genitals are being touched and fondled by his mother, by St. Anne, and by himself. So also in the paintings of the passion and crucifixion, the adult Jesus is depicted as thoroughly sexual. In some, his hand cups his genitals in death. In others the loincloth of the suffering Christ is protruding with an unmistakable erection.

Steinberg gives several interpretations of this Renaissance art. For one thing, it proved to the believer that Jesus' chastity was real and valid. Sexual abstinence without potency is an empty lesson. Abstinence is meaningful only if it is in combination with a vigorous sexuality. "Virginity, after all, constitutes a victory over concupiscence only where susceptibility to its power is at least possible."[30] Further, the shamelessness of exposing the infant Jesus' genitals for the admiration of others points back to our original innocence and points forward to our redemption from sin and shame, as the incarnation promises. His open adult sexuality depicted in the passion art promises our redemption. "Delivered from sin and shame, the freedom of Christ's sexual member bespeaks that aboriginal innocence which in Adam was lost. We may say that Michelangelo's naked Christs—on the cross, dead, or risen—are, like the naked Christ Child, not shameful, but literally and profoundly 'shame-less' "[31] And, most fundamentally, the focus on the bodily sexuality of Jesus demonstrated the thoroughness, the completeness of the incarnation, God's choice to embody divinity in humanity. "Therefore, to profess that God once embodied [God]self in a human nature is to confess that the eternal, there and then, became mortal and sexual. Thus understood, the evidence of Christ's sexual member serves as the pledge of God's humanation."[32]

We have long known how deeply the Renaissance was committed to the goodness and beauty of the human body. Now we know how radically incarnational its theology was, at least as depicted through the world of art. A half millennium has elapsed since those Renaissance artists made their bold statements about the Christ's sexuality, and most people have chosen not to notice the obvious in their art. Such is the "modern oblivion" about the issue. We continue in that oblivion to our profound deprivation.

Nevertheless, the affirmation of Jesus' sexuality raises difficult problems of another sort, precisely because he was male. The maleness of that one believed to be Christ has been used in countless ways as an instrument of patriarchal oppression. It has been used to "prove" the maleness of God, to outlaw women from ministry, to keep men in control. I agree fully with the protest against this oppressive theological misuse of Jesus' maleness, and I stand with those feminist women and men who despair over the church's tortured slowness in being redeemed on this matter. The central issue at stake is not Jesus' maleness but his *humanity*, to which his full human sexuality is crucial testimony. Indeed, Jesus' life, teachings, and the circumstances of his death all were remarkable protests against patriarchy.[33]

My concern at this point, however, is a different one: How can Jesus help men deal creatively with their own male sexuality? I believe that the ways are manifold, and what I have tried to suggest in this chapter are only a few of them. He stands as teacher, embodiment, and releaser of relational power—a judgment on our phallic unilateral power, but also an invitation to a full-bodied life-giving mutuality. His sexuality was present in his power, and his power was present in his healing sexuality.

Jesus stands as central symbol of the sexuality-spirituality dialectic. Renaissance artists saw in him the full and unified genitality of both phallus and penis, and portrayed him (to repeat Steinberg's words) "profoundly shame-less." Correspondingly, he strikingly embodied and taught the spirituality of both the Via Positiva and the Via Negativa, as is evident from the gospel accounts. He stands for us as symbol of our sexual-spiritual hope and possibility.

For human beings Jesus stands as clue to our authentic humanity in ways that far transcend the categories of sex and gender. In a less patriarchal age and culture than his, the person recognized as the paradigmatic Christ figure might well have been female. Yet Jesus was a first-century Jew, and he was male. This does not mean that through him maleness was certified as normative humanity. It does mean, however, that we who also happen to be male can find clues in him toward a richer and more authentic masculinity for ourselves. As a male I see this in the symbolism of Jesus' genital sexuality and the phallus-penis dialectic portrayed by Renaissance artists. I see in Jesus a compelling picture of male sexual wholeness, of creative masculinity, and of the redemption of manhood from both oppressiveness and superficiality. Yet countless women who are Christian also find in Jesus the intimate connection between their own female sexuality and spirituality. I suspect this is the case because Jesus embodies a sexual-spiritual reality that moves beyond our current understandings of androgyny.

I have argued that the notion of androgyny typically operates with a "combinationist" assumption. It begins with a fixed notion of masculine traits and a fixed notion of feminine traits. Then it moves to the contention that these fundamentally different qualities can and should be combined in any one individual regardless of biological sex. We have seen several problems with this concept. One of the major ones is the claim that we are called upon to develop a side of our personalities different from the one that seems rooted in our own particular bodies. The combinationist problem (in whatever form it occurs) is always grounded in an underlying dualism. Regarding androgyny, the dualism lies in the belief that the two sets of gender qualities are *essentially* different from each other, the assumption that authentic masculinity and authentic femininity are mutual opposites. From this assumption it follows that, in developing "the feminine" in himself, a man will add a different "something" on to that which is essentially himself. For example, he must acquire vulnerability and receptivity, qualities supposedly not natural to one with a male organ, to one equipped biologically to penetrate rather than to receive. I have suggested that men have encouraged this gender dualism through a one-sided definition of the masculine, a definition that magnifies the meanings of the phallus and neglects the reality of the penis.

Now the connection to be named is that between Christology and these gender issues. Like our struggle in recent decades to understand gender issues through the concept of androgyny, the Christological concepts that have dominated the centuries of Christian thought and piety have also been combinationist and dualistic. They have largely maintained that divinity and humanity are two essentially opposite realities somehow brought into perfect combination in one unique person. And when that occurred in Jesus it was a miracle which happened once, was sufficient for all time, and was not to be repeated.

But at least two major problems resulted from these prevailing Christologies. First, divinity dominated humanity to the point that Jesus' humanity became an illusion. Countless Christians believed that Jesus Christ was actually God disguised as a human being. It was the Superman/Clark Kent image. Jesus was the celestial visitor from outer space who lived for a time on earth disguised as one of us, did feats of superhuman power, and then returned to his glorious home in the skies.[34] The second problem stemmed from the first. The ordinary believer found it difficult to understand and internalize such a meaning. Since this Christ event was defined by the church as unique, by definition it was also out of the range of daily human experience. It was utterly removed from the humanity people knew to be their own. Hence, the Christic miracle became a formula, to be accepted by faith and mediated by churchly sacraments for the believer's salvation.

Both of these Christological problems have significant connections to the gender issues before us. The divinity that seemed to dominate and squeeze out Jesus' humanity was largely a phallic definition of the divine. It was an understanding of God's power that was heavily unilateral and one-directional. It was a zero-sum perception that magnified divine power at the expense of human power. Suspicious of the relational mutuality of a human Jesus and a divine God, tradition perceived both power and love as one-way streets. So also the masculine side of the androgyny formula has been equally phallic and one-sided. Just as divine and human were seen as opposites, likewise the masculine qualities and the feminine.

The Christological formula became abstract and confusing because it was removed from ordinary human experience. The same has been true with the androgyny formula. When a man is called to develop "his feminine side" but at the same time has been taught that this feminine side is foreign to his own male bodily experience—defined as phallus—a man finds himself striving to develop qualities that seem strange to his own biological sexuality. Some sort of miracle seems necessary if the two opposites are to be combined.

But what if the realities—both Christological and sexual—are significantly different from these accepted formulas? What if the connections are essentially more intimate than we have supposed? How might that look?

I believe that Jesus did not understand himself to be ontologically different from other human beings. Nor did he intend to monopolize the Christic reality (the intimate communion of divine and human). His self-understanding and his mission were precisely the opposite. He did not aim to control and hoard the Christic possibility, but rather to release and share it among and with everyone. His uniqueness lay not in having two natures, one divine and one human, miraculously combined. Rather, he possessed the same human nature we all have, but remarkably and fully open in mutuality with God's loving power. We might recall that even John's Gospel, which contains an exalted view of Jesus as the Christ, maintains that all who believe in him (all who are open to his message of the presence of God) are given the power to become the sons and daughters of God.[35] The authentically human and the presence of the truly divine are, indeed, closer than we had imagined. When we embrace God we embrace that which is not foreign to our own human essence but that which makes us more truly human.

The same principle holds for our sexuality. Women are tracing for themselves the meanings of the richly conjunctive sexual-spiritual reality in Christ. No man can do that for women, nor should he try. We who are male have plenty to do for ourselves in this regard. But now the connections seem to be clearer than before.

Jesus remains the paradigmatic Christ-bearer of Christian faith and life. He embodied the divine-human communion with a fullness that awes, compels, judges, challenges, comforts, and attracts us. He is also the Christ-*barer,* the one who lays bare and open that Christic possibility for us all.

And now it seems clearer that this Christic possibility is intimately connected with our sexual wholeness. What is it to be a man? To be fully masculine is one of the two ways given to humanity of being fully human. To be fully masculine does not mean embracing something of gender foreignness, strange to our own male bodily experience. Rather, it means embracing the fullness of the revelation that comes through our male bodies. There is good phallic energy in us which we can claim and celebrate. It is the earthy phallus: deep, moist, and sensuous, primitive and powerful. The phallic energy in us is also solar: penetrating, thrusting, achieving, and with the desire for self-transcendence. Equally important *and equally male*, there is good penile energy in us. It is soft, vulnerable, and receptive. It is a peaceful power. It knows that size is not merely quantitative; more truly, it is that strength of mutuality which can be enriched by other life without losing its own center.

The orgasmic sexual experience brings its own revelation. The hard and explosive phallic achievement becomes in an instant the soft, vulnerable tears of the penis. Both are fully male. Both are deeply grounded in a man's bodily reality. Both dimensions of life are fully present when a man is most human. And to be fully human is to know the Christ—not as supernatural invader but as that reality truest to our own natures, and as that reality which intimately connects us with everyone and everything else.

NOTES

1. Mircea Eliade, *Images and Symbols* (New York: Sheed & Ward, 1969), 9. Cf. Eugene Monick, *Phallos: Sacred Image of the Masculine* (Toronto: Inner City Books, 1987), 34.

2. H. A. Williams, *True Resurrection* (New York: Harper & Row, 1972).

3. Ibid., 32–33.

4. Ibid., 33.

5. Ibid., 39.

6. Monick, *Phallos.* I acknowledge my particular indebtedness to his insights in the following paragraphs.

7. Mark Strage, *The Durable Fig Leaf* (New York: William Morrow & Co., 1980), chaps. 1 and 5; also Monick, chap. 2.

8. Rudolf Otto, *The Idea of the Holy,* trans. John W. Harvey (London: Oxford University Press, 1923). Cf. Monick, 26.

9. Monick calls this the "clithonic phallos"; see 94–96.

10. See Monick, 48–49.

11. I am indebted to the Rev. Kenneth W. Taylor for these projection insights and also for pressing me to reflect more about the affirmation of genital softness.

12. See Matthew Fox, *Western Spirituality: Historical Roots, Ecumenical Routes* (Notre Dame, Ind.: Fides/Claretian, 1979); also Fox's *Original Blessing* (Sante Fe, New Mexico: Bear & Co., 1983).

13. Quotations from Eckhart are taken from Fox, *Original Blessing,* 132–133, 137, and 139.

14. See Robert A. Raines's beautiful meditation on sinking, in *A Faithing Oak: Meditations from the Mountain* (New York: Crossroad, 1982), 9–10.

15. Rainer Maria Rilke, *Selected Poems of Rainer Maria Rilke,* trans. Robert Bly (New York: Harper & Row, 1981), 21.

16. Starhawk, *Dreaming the Dark: Magic, Sex, and Politics* (Boston: Beacon Press, 1982), xiv.

17. See my fuller discussion of androgyny in *Embodiment* (Minneapolis: Augsburg Publishing House, 1978), 98–101. While I still endorse much of that discussion, I am now inclined to move beyond the concept. A useful summary of the social-psychological

literature on androgyny is found in *Gender Stereotypes: Traditions and Alternatives,* by Susan A. Basow, 2d ed. (Monterey, Calif.: Brooks/Cole Publishing Co., 1986), chaps. 1 and 13.

18. Nicolas Berdiaev's thought on androgyny is found mainly in his work *The Meaning of Creativeness* (1914). I am quoting the summary by Philip Sherrard in *Christianity and Eros* (London: SPCK, 1976), 61–62.

19. See Karl Barth, *Church Dogmatics,* vol. III, pt. 4. (Edinburgh: T. & T. Clark, 1961), esp. 166.

20. Monick, 50.

21. In these reflections on power I have been particularly influenced by Bernard Loomer, "Two Kinds of Power," *Criterion,* vol. 15, no. 1 (Winter 1976).

22. Ibid., 14.

23. Ibid., 19.

24. Ibid., 21.

25. Bernard Loomer, "S-I-Z-E," *Criterion,* vol. 13, no. 3 (Spring 1974): 21.

26. See Williams, *True Resurrection,* 33.

27. William Phipps, *Was Jesus Married?* (New York: Harper & Row, 1970).

28. Leo Steinberg, *The Sexuality of Christ in Renaissance Art and in Modern Oblivion* (New York: Pantheon Books, 1983).

29. Ibid., 1.

30. Ibid., 17.

31. Ibid., 23.

32. Ibid., 13.

33. Patricia Wilson-Kastner's *Faith, Feminism, and the Christ* (Philadelphia: Fortress Press, 1983) is a helpful treatment of this issue.

34. The Superman image is from Tom Harpur, *For Christ's Sake* (Boston: Beacon Press, 1987), 32.

35. See ibid., 118–19.

16

Men's Studies, Feminist Theology, and Gay Male Sexuality

J. MICHAEL CLARK

Among the ways to break the vicious cycle(s) of our socialization [as gay men] is to relearn relational values—essentially to reprogram ourselves for entering into, nurturing, and sustaining relationships. To do so, we will have to confront those fears hidden from our view by the veil of heteropatriarchal machismo. Foremost among these fears remains our culturally maintained fear of intimacy, of vulnerability and openness to another. As men we may well fear that true intimacy will drain away our fragile egos, like Samson's strength to Delilah's deceit. The very core of our being may fear annihilation as the price both of intimacy and of any mutuality wherein we are not in control. [Carter] Heyward has wisely addressed this fear:

> Unless we know fear, we cannot know the courage it takes to step with another into places of sadness, anger, or confusion to discover therein something important we have not known before about ourselves, about others, about the world.
> . . . [Therefore] compassion [our embodied and humble knowledge that our lives are connected and that no one of us is more or less valuable as a person] is in standing with one another through the hard places.[1]

Our fear can then become not merely an obstacle but a doorway instead, a doorway to self-transformation and self-healing; a doorway into the realization that our selves—our selfhood—will not dissipate in relationship; a doorway into mutuality and hence into intimacy and right relation. Acknowledging our fears will finally make intimacy and community possible.

Unfortunately for many men, gay or nongay, sexual interactions only evoke our fears, when instead they should open us to such liberating possibilities for intimacy. In our extremely sex-negative culture, our nakedness in sexuality, both literally and psychologically, provides an extremely powerful encounter with our fears of intimacy and loss of self. Before the onslaught of AIDS, the gay male subculture in particular, far from liberating itself from this vicious dilemma posed by masculine socialization, instead institutionalized patterns of behavior that prevented both healthy confrontation with these fears and any possibility of intimacy. "Glory holes," which revealed not persons but only penises, utterly blocked relational intimacy; darkened, music-filled bathhouses and orgy rooms likewise presented only vague bodily forms in fog and steam, while they precluded intimate communication and reduced the human participants again to merely genital machines; even the seemingly more personal one-night stands with bargoing "tricks" were generally begun under the veil of dim lights, loud music, and alcoholic haze, consummated often enough without so much as an exchange of names, and, after orgasm, cleaned up and cleaned out of one's life as quickly as possible, lest the post-coital awkwardness give way—god/ess forbid— to any undesired intimacy.

If such "sexual freedom" is the only goal of "liberation," then we have been tragically led to an abyss by the Pied Pipers of Patriarchy, bracketing us into the sexual netherworld of the night. Such indulgence in putative pleasure is instead an accumulative gathering unto ourselves of nothingness, of emptiness. As we grow weary of these rituals and emerge from the long night of drugs, alcohol, and disembodied genitals to find ourselves growing older (and wiser?) and alone—and now after a decade of AIDS to also find ourselves surrounded by the fallen bodies of our comrades, those vast numbers of sexual acquaintances whom we never risked making our friends—we are stunned and shocked by this revealing dawn(ing) upon our awareness. The second wave of our liberation will depend upon the survivors, not only those who survive AIDS but also those who are able to free themselves from the heterobracketed gaysexual underworld. The survivors must now wisely show us other ways to be sexual and to be sexual within the context of genuine intimate relation. Avoiding intimacy by means of a sexually driven promiscuity is the real threat to our selfhood—and to our lives—as gay men.

Again, James Nelson helps us see that mutually intimate sexual relationship does not destroy our fragile selves, but instead heals us and gives us back anew, each to each, in the exchange with our beloveds:

> Authentic sexual communion with a beloved human partner . . . is unity, though not unification. Each self respects the other's identity [and ego autonomy or deepest selfhood] and, in the ecstasy of mutual giving and receiving, creative differences remain.
> . . . Relational power understands that the capacity to absorb the influence of another without losing the self's own center is as truly a quality of power as is the strength of exerting influence on another.[2]

Mercifully, a lesson for us to learn in finally confronting our fear(s) of intimacy is that we can "make room for another within the self without losing the self's own integrity or freedom."[3]

EXCHANGING PERFORMANCE
FOR INTIMACY

As we rethink the issues of intimacy and mutual relationship in regard to our sexuality and our sexual behavior, we may also have to reconsider our understanding of sexual pleasure and our socialized male need to be in control. Again, the gay male sexual subculture has vividly exemplified Nelson's concern that our western work ethic, in collusion with our heteropatriarchally enculturated masculine performance anxiety, means "at best we work hard at playing."[4] We compel ourselves always to be erect, to be ready. Moreover, whether as "tops" or as "bottoms," we remain in control, even manipulating our minds and our bodies with drugs and alcohol if necessary to be perfectly tuned sexual machines. We discover, however, that accumulating sexual pleasure as if it were the product of our genital machinery actually deprives us of pleasure; promiscuously avoiding intimacy and controlling our sexual encounters to insulate our innermost selves leaves us wearied, empty, and alone. We have got the idea of sexual pleasure all wrong somehow. Surprisingly for us, genuine sexual pleasure requires neither performance, nor insularity, nor control, but intimacy instead:

> Playfulness means the devaluation of control. Play involves the capacity to trust and to surrender to the moment.
> . . . To experience the heights of sexual pleasure, I must let loose of my need to control. . . . Losing the self means finding the self. Sexual pleasure nurtures the reunion of the self with the self.[5]

Experience has proven that "playtimes" that are rigidly controlled by the partners and "playspaces" that are constructed to forestall threatening intimacy (and the spontaneous freedom from controls by which intimacy breaks in) rarely deliver any sexual pleasure that outlasts the accumulation of the moment of performance. The spontaneity and vulnerability of intimate, mutual playfulness-in-relationship, however, can nurture friendship, transform sex into lovemaking, and yield a healthy self-love for both partners. In fact, intimacy thrives "when control needs are relaxed, when deep desire for connection is admitted. That is an invitation to the holy."[6] Not performance-anxious, specific genital acts, *but rather* vulnerable, spontaneous, sometimes clumsy and even silly erotic interactions give us the deep and lasting pleasure we really need. Our playful pleasuring unmasks our vulnerability, admits our neediness, and enables us (both gay and nongay men) to quit performing and striving. We, too, need to be loved and to play with one another in making love:

> There is relief in admitting neediness. . . . There is a strange, paradoxical strength in claiming my eros, my incompleteness, my yearning, my thirsting, my desire, my trembling for friends.
> . . . The Cosmic Lover is also emotional, desirous Eros.[7]

And yet, such intimate and mutual pleasuring does not come easily for us, as men or as gay men. Despite our inherited Judeao-Christian suspicion of pleasure and our culture's "persistent fear that the bald affirmation of sexual pleasure will invite self-indulgence and destroy true spirituality and communion," in fact "genuine bodily pleasure is important to wholeness and communion."[8] If the gay male sexual netherworld has not only promiscuously given flesh to our sex-negative culture's worst fears, but has also reduced its participants to pleasure*less*, genital performers who can never achieve an integrated sexual wholeness, then we must quickly (re)learn that genuine, mutual "bodily pleasure has the capacity to contribute significantly to human wholeness, and consistent deprivation of genuine bodily pleasure is predictably an invitation to violence"— if not in physical actuality, at least to our own wounded psyches.[9] *Genuinely fulfilling pleasure requires intimacy;* wholeness requires playfulness and mutual pleasure-in-relation, not the severing of ourselves from our sexuality, which we have allowed our heteropatriarchal society to institutionalize for us. We deserve something far better than the genital reductionism and alienated self/sex lives we have accepted as "liberation" for two decades and more:

> Sexual pleasure . . . is more than just good feelings [or the promiscuous accumulation of genital experiences of "good feelings"]. It is the union of bodily, emotional, mental, and spiritual feelings [a wholeness and fulfillment in relation] in ways that we humans experience markedly positive sensations about the self. In sexual pleasure . . . the body-self feels profoundly unified, taken out of itself into another, yet intensely itself. There comes a self-abandonment. The ego surrenders some of its control.[10]

Recently, Judith Plaskow has also addressed our sexuality in a prophetically similar fashion. The goal of our liberation as gay people must not be merely a "blanket permission" for us to act out our sexuality genitally; rather, the goal of our liberation as gaysexual persons must be something more fundamental, more whole. A truly liberated sexuality is one that affirms the wholeness of our being as persons-in-relation:

> The sharing of sexuality with another is something that should happen only by mutual consent, a consent that is not a blanket permission, but that is continually renewed in the actual rhythms of particular relationships.
> . . . Our sexuality is fundamentally about moving out beyond ourselves. The connecting, communicative nature of sexuality is not something we can experience or look for only in sexual encounters narrowly defined [as genital and/or anonymous], but in all real relationships in our lives.[11]

Such utter self-affirmation accrues only without control, even though we find relinquishing control (i.e., vulnerability) frightening and difficult. We see sexuality as merely genital because we cannot handle a more thoroughgoing eros which permeates our lives, breaks down our control, and demands intimacy and relationship to create interpersonal wholeness. We have been taught, in short, that "eros is dangerous for a male."[12]

Reconceptualizing our sexuality, not as genital activities we accumulate separately from our ever-developing sense of self, but rather as the erotic energy that heals our lives, enables us to be vulnerable and playful, and seeks intimate friendship-in-mutual-relation, may altogether yet prove our salvation. For heteropatriarchally socialized gay men in particular, finally allowing the erotic to permeate our lives and to inform our relationships, while displacing the putative value of genital sexual acts, may enable us to achieve a vastly different and more fulfilling (wholistic) liberation than anything with which we have contented ourselves since Stonewall.

For gay men struggling with control and power and intimacy issues, for gay men struggling with self-identity in a homophobic ethos, and for gay men struggling with our ambivalent attraction/repulsion toward orgasms while at the same time promiscuously seeking sexual acts and hurriedly dismissing our sexual partners—for gay men finally laying down the burden of sexual performance and achievement can only come as a great relief. Giving up our facades and our pretensions of ego-inviolability and genital prowess to admit that we need one another intimately and dearly can only free us. Free us from the long night of sexual reductionism. Free us to heal ourselves and our relationships. This is surely what breaking the bonds of heteropatriarchal masculine socialization must mean, what genuine liberation might taste like. Assertively claiming our freedom and claiming the power of eros permeating our body-selves, our lives, and our relationships—with intimacy, vulnerability, and playfulness—can enable us to reconceptualize, to reinvent, our sexuality in ways that shatter our self-punishing pasts with radical visions for the future, visions we must weave in the present.

The Whole Gay Man:
Reconstruction and Liberation

The process of re-envisioning our sexuality begins with the adamant reaffirmation that our sexuality permeates all of who we are as persons and as gay men: our sexuality should *in no case* be reduced to "merely genital functions." The erotic, or more concretely in our experience, our sexuality, becomes a meaningless, genitally-reduced notion *unless* we understand the erotic as part and parcel of our urges toward mutuality and human(e)ness. To be human is to be in relationship—with ourselves, with other persons, with the earth and the cosmos, and with god/ess. Our fundamental need for connectedness, love, and self-affirming acceptance—our erotic and sexual drive toward connectedness with all things—undergirds our quest for mutuality and, through the realization of that quest, for the establishment of justice in *all* relationships, not just our sexually expressed ones. The lovemaking and justice-making (the right-relationship-making) that I begin at home with my spouse should permeate and inform all my relationships and value concerns. *That* is god/ess-with-us! *That* is our numinously informed power that nurtures our nurturing each other (and our nurturing god/ess into fullest being as well) and that also empowers us to befriend sisters and brothers, earth and cosmos.

Carter Heyward's recent work reiterates and supports this vision: she writes that the erotic is "our embodied yearning for mutuality" and our "participation in the universe"; in fact, "real love-making is not simply genital manipulation[!]

. . . Love-making is a form of justice making."[13] She also helps clarify this relationship between love-making and justice-making:

> In a mutual relationship both (or all) people are empowered to experience one another as intrinsically valuable, irreplaceable earthcreatures, sources of joy and love and respect in relation to one another. To experience ourselves genuinely as friends: This is justice. It is the shape of God in our life together and in our lives as particular selves-in-relation.[14]

If we have not distanced ourselves from the activities of our genitals, but have instead fully and wholistically realized the healing and shaping power of the erotic—of our sexuality—as something that permeates every aspect of our lives, and that specifically permeates, shapes, and even creates our drive toward and our energies for sustaining our most intimate relationship(s), how can we *not* experience the energy carried over, carried out of, our committed sexual relationships in such a fashion that it influences all our value-laden interactions with the world? One cannot make-love and make-hate simultaneously.

In other words, unless we are willing to live in conflict with ourselves, fruitlessly attempting to act in diametrically opposing ways at the same time, the care and tenderness of our specific relationships *must* inform all our values, all our ways of relating to and seeking justice within the world. In fact, the very power of even our most intimate and orgasmic moments simultaneously frees us from ourselves, gives us back renewed to ourselves, and spills over as that energy by which we join in the liberation of all the earth:

> Our sexualities are our embodied yearning to express a relational mutuality. . . .
> Sexual orgasm can be literally a highpoint, a climax in our capacity to know, ecstatically for a moment, the coming together of self and other [and, momentarily, the transcendence or dissolution of this very self/other dichotomy by oneness. . . . Our sexuality also includes] a pervasive awareness, even in moments of erotic ecstasy, that the basis of our connection is . . . the friendship [which] brings us into this excitement and releases us into the rest of our lives. . . .
> The erotic is the sacred/godly basis of our capacity to participate in mutually empowering relationships.[15]

James Nelson anticipates both Heyward's and my own radical assertion that sexuality is not so much about where and how we put our genitals, but is rather something that permeates our lives and that both urges us toward and sustains our relationships—even those that are *not* genitally consummated relationships. As the power of relation, our sexuality enables—nay, compels—liberational, justice-seeking activity in the world. In his earlier text, for example, Nelson insists,

> Sexuality always involves much more than what we do with our genitals. More fundamentally, it is who we are as body-selves who experience the emotional, cognitive, physical, and spiritual need for intimate communion, both creaturely and divine. . . .
> The movement toward a more healed, wholistic spirituality and the movement toward a more healed, wholistic sexuality . . . are inseparable elements [in the same pilgrimage toward] full personhood.[16]

Not only are our spirituality and our sexuality one, but this oneness also ideally shapes our deepest valuing and acting in the world; indeed, Nelson concludes that "compassion . . . is intimately related to our sexuality."[17] Clearly, for Nelson, our capacity for compassion and our capacity for justice-making are one and the same; compassion in action, *which is* justice-seeking and -making, is borne in and from our erotically/sexually informed drive toward right-relation. Again anticipating Heyward, Nelson insists that our sexuality—our eroticism—is inseparably connected with our drive toward relationship and communion with another; such right-relationship undergirds community and all our communal efforts toward justice and liberation:

> Through our bodies we learn that the fundamental reality with which we deal is not simply living beings as such, nor objects as such, but rather it is relationships. . . .
> The fundamental purpose of communication is communion. And communion is the essential meaning of our sexuality. . . .
> But [our bodies] are not only means to relationship. [They] are divine revelations of the interrelatedness of all with all. Though our minds are still saturated with . . . dualism . . . our bodies themselves are revelations of the inclusive community [of pluriformity-in-one].[18]

In his subsequent book, Nelson reiterates and reemphasizes these same values for us, again underscoring their importance for all sexual theology, gay or nongay. Sexuality is *not* solely about our genitals, but is rather about that relationality that yields intimacy and communion. Our eros is that power which urges us into relationship and which, through relationship, compels us into compassionate justice-seeking through collective and communal action, well beyond the limited confines of orgasm: "Above all, sexuality is the desire for intimacy and communion, both emotionally and physically. It is the physiological and psychological grounding of our capacity to love."[19] As we men, gay and nongay alike, strive to overcome our heteropatriarchal masculine socialization and the duality and alienation with which that socialization has burdened us and, instead, create wholistic visions of what it means to be sexual in our lives—to live out of the erotic energy that permeates our lives—even then will we join with the companion energy and presence of god/ess with us:

> Increasing sexual wholeness is part of our redemption intended by God. Sexual sanctification can mean growth in bodily self-acceptance, in the capacity for sensuousness, in the capacity for play, in the diffusion of the erotic throughout the body rather than in its genitalization, and in the recovery of lost dimensions of our sexuality.[20]

As we thus create our visions, inspired by god/ess and informed by our healed relationships with one another, we will find ourselves also recreating our values and reappraising our sexual ethics if you will. Here, too, we have wise friends to guide us.

LIBERATING SEXUAL ETHICS

Our process of re-envisioning our sexuality necessarily entails what may be considered ethical discussion. To insist upon integrating our sexuality into the wholeness of our being, rather than accepting or endorsing any genital reductionism of our eros, for example, is clearly a value-laden position. Implicit as well in our insistence upon the connection between our sexuality and our justice-making in the world is the high valuation of our responsibility toward others. Our concern with responsibility, then, opens us to more traditionally "ethical" considerations of our sexuality. Says Nelson, for example, "Growth and integration are promoted by self-liberating, other-enriching, honest, faithful, *socially responsible,* life-serving, and joyous self expression."[21] "Socially responsible" may even be the key phrase for us here: acting out our sexuality does not occur in a vacuum, but rather within relational contexts. With the exception of solitary masturbation, all sexual *behavior* requires other persons, and our engagement with other persons entails *responsibility* rather than the genital reductionism and dehumanization or objectification more often reinforced by promiscuity. Consequently, according to Nelson, we need to first ask ourselves a number of questions about our sexual *actions:* "As beings who seek meaning, we need to ask about . . . occasions of [sexual] intercourse: What is their value? Are they life-denying or life-giving? Do they thwart or fulfill our deepest needs . . .? What is their ultimate meaning?"[22]

Importantly, however, these questions do not lead Nelson into a narrowly traditional position; indeed, he realizes that neither denigration and denial (sexual discipline) nor promiscuity is the answer. Instead, we need an alternative ethical perspective on sexual behavior:

> Disciplin[ing] the genitals will not work. . . . Nor will it work to ignore our genitals or consign them to hell as beyond redemption.
>   The alternative, however, is not to give our genitals the freedom of their demands. . . . Oppression has made them subject to compulsions, and compulsions do not satisfy. They give only fleeting, momentary relief.[23]

While our traditional notions of sexual sin have focused upon genital acts, Nelson's consistent concern is to free us from such a genital focus, whether vis-à-vis traditional "sexual ethics" or vis-à-vis the opposite—our rebelliously promiscuous actions that are just as narrowly genitally focused. Both extremes are equally mistaken: "Sexual sin is the dualistic alienation by which the body becomes an object, either to be constrained out of fear . . . or to be treated as a pleasure machine."[24] A (re)conceptualization of "sexual sin" that avoids the dichotomizations of heteropatriarchy will recognize that what is really sinful is not any specific sexual act but rather our enculturated alienation from our bodies; our reductionism, which views sex as purely instrumental; and our fear of intimacy, which disenables us from a more wholistic understanding of our sexuality-in-mutual-relation.

Nelson's focus is in fact not upon acts but upon accountability and, in summarizing his view, he ardently avoids heteropatriarchal dualism(s) and the double standard(s) those have so often entailed. Although what he offers for our consideration may cut against the grain of much of the gay-sexual underworld, it is not homophobically intended *by any means*. The prophetic edge in his remarks may rather enable us to see that the sexual netherworld is not our only, nor our best, possibility for sexual wholeness:

> . . . The appropriate ethical question is this: What sexual behavior will serve and enhance, rather than inhibit and damage, the fuller realization of divinely intended humanity? The answer . . . is sexual behavior in accordance with love . . . commitment, trust, tenderness, respect for the other, and the desire for responsible communion. It means resisting cruelty, utterly impersonal sex, obsession with sexual gratification, and actions that display unwillingness to take responsibility for their personal and social consequences. *This kind of ethic is equally appropriate to both heterosexual and homosexual.* . . .
>
> What can be said to everyone regardless of [sexual] orientation is this: genital expression will find its *greatest* fulfillment in a relationship of ongoing commitment and communion. That other sexual experiences can have elements of genuine good in them, even when they do not realize the fullest meanings of personal intimacy, remains an open possibility.[25]

Importantly for us, Nelson does not emphatically endorse heteromonogamy. He does emphasize an understanding of sexual accountability that needs no double standard; both gay and nongay are called to sexual accountability in all our relationships, genital and otherwise. This same emphasis on the "relational context of accountability" finds voice more recently in Heyward's work. She says, for example, "Sexual touching is right only when we are faithful to the commitments we have made. In this context . . . sex . . . is sacred. It is sacramental, an 'outward, visible sign' of the power and love of God."[26] Again, however, neither Nelson, nor Heyward, nor even my own recent work in this area suggests that sexual ethics can be simplistically conflated into monogamy.[27] Although we may well choose monogamy as the most meaningful expression of our sexuality, the value(s) undergirding that decision are far more important. And, like my own work as well, Heyward insists on the underlying value of friendship as the best paradigm for constructing our sexual behavior.[28] She encourages us to "act sexually only in mutual relationships" wherein our eroticism and our sexuality can evoke "that which is most fully human in each of us"; consequently, any "violations of our bodily integrity are forms of sexual abuse."[29]

Valuing friendship and sexual wholism also entails recognizing the sacredness of sensuality, erotic power, and healthy, unalienated sexuality, as well as respecting the integrity of our own bodies and the bodies of others. It opposes violations of our bodily integrity such as the "commoditization of sex," whether in sex for profit (e.g., in prostitution or in pornography) or in the trivialization and accumulation of "merely genital experiences."[30] In fact, our paradigm of sexual friendship can help us to revalue some limitations for our sexual behavior.

Sexual liberation does not mean "anything goes"; developing certain limits based on the concept of social or relational accountability can make our sexuality more meaningful and sacramental for us. Says Heyward, "Without a boundaried sense of ourselves [without limits], we are likely to experience sexual energy as [self-devouring] or as an addictive commodity."[31]

But, then, does *not* a "boundaried sense of ourselves" come down to a restrictive monogamy imitative of heterosexual society? Neither Heyward nor Nelson would make that assertion. Both writers leave open the possibility that a whole and healthy sexuality-in-relation may be sustainable outside strictly monogamous relationships. In my own previous effort to do gaysexual ethics, I, too, have insisted that monogamy is not carved in stone; rather, there are simply a number of questions we must first ask ourselves if we are going to be *non*monogamous. In fact, we must admit that, while there is no *a priori* value consigned to either monogamy or nonmonogamy, a decision to frame our sexual behavior within the context of a monogamous relationship is purely *pragmatic,* not divinely given. Conversely, a decision to be nonmonogamous can turn out to be a *very* difficult choice to sustain successfully. Neither nonmonogamous coupling nor uncoupled sexual variety is in any sense morally wrong *a priori;* no prohibition of these options is carved in stone by a divine or any other authority. These options do, however, require a great deal of energy and compassionate sensitivity to ensure fairness—justice—to *all* involved persons, as well as to ensure that no affected relationship or individual is ever devalued or dehumanized. In other words, not only are we confronted with the difficulty of maintaining the special, even sacramental, aspects of our primary sexual and emotional relationships in balance with our outside sexual encounters; now we must also ponder how *not* to make those encounters alienating and objectifying, on the one hand, and how *not* to exclude our partners or threaten our primary relationships if those encounters do develop humanizing sexual friendships, on the other hand.[32]

Clearly, choosing between monogamy and nonmonogamy for a pattern or model for our relationships is not an easy task. Monogamy avoids many of the problems of nonmonogamy, from the tension caused by jealously, envy, and competition, to the trivialization and objectification of our sexuality, and it embodies some very admirable values. The reality among gay men in particular, however, has more often been that strictly monogamous relationships, however satisfying, are often short-lived.[33] Nonmonogamy, by contrast, is at least as difficult if not more difficult to practice successfully. Attempting to sustain a long-term, nonmonogamous primary relationship requires that we always be willing to deal with tension, to work on our feelings of jealousy and envy, and to sort out those issues from issues of self-esteem. It requires constantly battling homophobic messages from our culture, which threaten our self-acceptance and our self-esteem, and living utterly vulnerable before, and trusting of, the loyalty and compassion of our spouses and the soundness of our relationships. Finally, it means seeking that ideal balance that transcends both a patriarchal possessiveness of our primary partners and a patriarchal objectification, trivialization, or dehumanization of our outside partners, while simultaneously *not* allowing our outside sexual friendships to become a threat to our primary sexual friend and lover. Whether, or to what extent, such an ideal balancing act is possible, for the wholeness of *all* concerned parties, clearly remains an open question.[34]

What is ultimately far more important than the issue of monogamy or nonmonogamy is the value of *fidelity,* and none of our wise friends is willing to conflate the concepts of monogamy and fidelity. All too often, monogamy may not include fidelity in its broadest sense, and only empty relationships remain in such instances. At the same time, fidelity includes far more than simple monogamy. It entails much that is not particularly sexual, such as honoring and not abusing the feelings of the partners in a relationship. It includes not only listening well, but also speaking honestly, from our depths—to be vulnerable rather than to hide what we feel. It means "we must be real with one another, really present."[35] Ultimately, for Heyward, fidelity and friendship go hand in hand as the values by which we might best construct our relationships.[36]

As I have indicated elsewhere, our committed relationships assume an ontological reality that is far more than just the two individuals involved; that reality itself requires our care and nurturing. Moreover, I have also argued that the time, energy, and trust already invested together in a relationship constitute the best guarantor of that relationship's long-term durability.[37] Similarly, Heyward's understanding of fidelity embraces the full range of this caring and investment of ourselves and our relational energies. We must be faithful to our values within our relationships; we must cherish openness and honesty and trust one another deeply; we must be committed not only to our individual growth as persons but also to our growth-in-relationship—to the growth of our relationship itself; hence, we must be willing to struggle together, to forgive and to heal one another, and to move together into the future; we must indeed be "at home" with one another, sharing all the multidimensionality of our relationship as the sure foundation, the one "place" where we know most rightly and fundamentally that we belong, and that we belong together.[38]

Once again, we find that Nelson has anticipated this insistence that fidelity and infidelity are not merely notions about genital acts. Like Heyward, he enables us to see that there are underlying values we must consider:

> Infidelity does not have a simple biological [genital] meaning. Rather, it means the rupture of the bonds of faithfulness, trust, honesty, and commitment. . . . Fidelity is understood as enduring commitment to the partner's well-being and growth, a commitment to the primacy of this convenant over any other relationship. . . . [Granted, while] there are undoubted risks in expanding the boundaries of physical intimacy [nonmonogamy], . . . there are also risks to a couple's relationship when it becomes marked by possessiveness or emotional dependence.[39]

Taken together, Nelson's and Heyward's work may prompt us to find some middle ground, to discern and create a monogamy which is not heteropatri-archally possessive and emotionally dependent, but which is instead a commitment to focusing on intimacy, to nurturing the individual partners *and* the relationship, and to growing together. Such guidelines "respect the necessity of personal choice, and . . . include . . . understanding[s] of forgiveness and the possibility of new beginnings."[40]

While some people may indeed be able to sustain multiple sacramental and whole sexual friendships simultaneously, all too often these efforts break down. Our internal, psychological need for a deeper, long-term intimacy shifts the delicate balance somewhere (or, gay men in particular may use each other as sexual objects, and the so-called friendships created thereby remain shallow). In either case, fidelity breaks down and someone gets hurt emotionally. Given our human limitations—our need for our jobs and for other non-sexual and non-work-related endeavors, our needs for emotional healing and for relational security, our needs for time together to deepen and to nurture relationship—it is very hard to sustain more than one authentic and genuinely faithful sexual involvement over time. Monogamy then becomes not simply a restriction upon genital behavior, but rather a pragmatic and mutually chosen means for nurturing the most healthy and wholistic sexuality-in-relation for two people committed to a common process of growth and liberation together. With this broadened understanding of friendship and fidelity, elucidated here as values underlying our pragmatic choice of monogamy, we may then find in Heyward's own liberational insights a co-companion for our journeys as sexual beings-in-relation:

> We may decide to be sexually active in relation to only one person . . . because we believe that this is our best means of taking care of the relationship with a person we have come to love in a primary and special way.
>
> The decision to be monogamous . . . may be an honest way of embodying and sustaining fidelity to the relationship. . . .
>
> [It] may be our least emotionally confusing way of building and sustaining trust in a particular relationship as the locus of what is, for us, an extraordinary, uncommon experience of erotic power as the love of God.[41]

NOTES

1. Carter Heyward, *Touching Our Strength: The Erotic as Power and the Love of God* (San Francisco: Harper & Row, 1989), 140, 141–42.

2. James B. Nelson, *Between Two Gardens: Reflections on Sexuality and Religious Experience* (New York: Pilgrim Press, 1983), 11; and Nelson, *The Intimate Connection: Male Sexuality, Masculine Spirituality* (Philadelphia: Westminster Press, 1988), 102.

3. Nelson, *The Intimate Connection,* 102.

4. Ibid., 57.

5. Ibid., 57, 59.

6. Ibid., 56.

7. Ibid., 57.

8. Nelson, *Between Two Gardens,* 37.

9. Ibid.

10. Ibid.

11. Ibid., 145–46.
12. Ibid., 55.
13. Heyward, *Touching Our Strength*, 3, 24.
14. Ibid., 23.
15. Ibid., 33, 187.
16. Nelson, *Between Two Gardens*, 6, 9.
17. Ibid., 13.
18. Ibid., 22, 34, 35.
19. Nelson, *The Intimate Connection*, 26.
20. Ibid., 121.
21. Ibid., 125, emphasis added.
22. Ibid., 127.
23. Ibid., 91.
24. Ibid., 118.
25. Nelson, *Between Two Gardens*, 124, emphasis added.
26. Heyward, *Touching Our Strength*, 149.
27. J. Michael Clark, *A Defiant Celebration: Theological Ethics and Gay Sexuality* (Garland, Tex.: Tangelwüld,1990), 35–54.
28. Ibid., 65–69ff.
29. Heyward, *Touching Our Strength*, 129.
30. Ibid., 128, n. 2.
31. Ibid., 110.
32. Clark, *A Defiant Celebration*, 52–53.
33. L. A. Kurdek and J. P. Schmitt, "Relationship Quality of Gay Men in Closed or Open Relationships," in *Gay Relationships*, ed. J. P. DeCecco (New York: Harrington Park, 1988), 217–34.
34. Clark, *A Defiant Celebration*, 53.
35. Heyward, *Touching Our Strength*, 131.
36. Ibid., 129, 130, 132–33.
37. Clark, *A Defiant Celebration*, 60.
38. Heyward, *Touching Our Strength*, 129–33.
39. Nelson, *Between Two Gardens*, 125.
40. Ibid.
41. Heyward, *Touching Our Strength*, 136.

PART 4

Ethical Issues in Sexuality

Rethinking Sexual Ethics
Marvin M. Ellison
Beverly Wildung Harrison

Singleness, Marriage, and Celibacy
Karen Lebacqz
Monica Furlong
Jack Dominian
Janie Gustafson

Sexuality and Disability
Office of the General Assembly,
    Presbyterian Church (U.S.A.)

Sexuality and Aging
Penelope Washbourn
Office of the General Assembly,
    Presbyterian Church (U.S.A.)

HIV/AIDS
Grace Jantzen
Earl E. Shelp

Sexual Violence and Pornography
Marie M. Fortune
Marvin M. Ellison
Mary D. Pellauer

Introduction
to Part 4

The title we have given to Part 4 might be somewhat misleading, for the first three parts of this reader have also dealt with ethical aspects of sexuality. In this part, however, we focus specifically on critical reflections on the morality of action. These essays address the question, How might we evaluate the varied expressions of our sexuality?

The first two essays sketch the ways that some Christian ethicists are rethinking the basic issues in sexual ethics. Marvin Ellison and Beverly Harrison both present constructive frameworks for how we might evaluate any particular sexual expression. Ellison's focus is on relationships (with clear implications for social structures), while Harrison's focus is on social structures (with clear implications for relationships).

Ellison proposes "an ethics of common decency." Its normative center is neither sexual orientation nor marital status, but rather justice. "Our problem is not homosexuality or nonmarital sex but conformity to the unjust norm of compulsory heterosexuality and gender inequality."[1] Justice, for Ellison, calls for equality and mutuality; it means the moral obligation to promote one another's common decency and also the obligation to honor our own needs for intimacy and affection. He believes this means a clear movement away from ethics focused on specific contexts such as marriage, or specific kinds of acts such as heterosexual intercourse, to ethics grounded in the qualities of relationships. Ellison celebrates any sexual relation that deepens human intimacy, genuine pleasure, love, responsibility, and justice. Anticipating the charge that in such ethics anything goes, Ellison says that this approach rules out from the start any act or relationship in which persons are abused, violated, and exploited. Such ethics strengthens one's maturity and self-respect. It is a more demanding ethics, for personal wholeness and relational justice are at stake in every act and relationship.

What Ellison has alluded to—the connection between interpersonal love and social change in sexual ethics—Beverly Harrison makes central in her essay.[2] With Ellison, she proposes a relational justice sexual ethic, one that holistically affirms the erotic goodness of sexual embodiment, the respect for bodily integrity, noncoercion, and profound mutual respect. But, Harrison argues, it is not enough to see what ought to be. We must understand the impediments as well. Our culture's almost obsessive search for sexual pleasure and personal intimacy marks a society of depersonalizing work and dehumanizing institutional patterns. In such a society the antidote of genital sexuality is too weak to bear the overloaded expectations we place on it. We have been obsessed with genital sex, and minimal state interference with persons' sexual acts is advisable. The true injustice consists of morally inappropriate power relations and the intentional degradation of persons—the refusal to recognize bodily integrity as sacred.

The liberal churches have been largely ineffective in empowering basic social transformation because they have embraced civil rights without an adequate vision of social justice, Harrison contends. They have failed to see clearly that those most sexually vulnerable and abused are the economically marginalized. If the churches wish to change patterns of sexual injustice, they must attack the economic injustices that underlie them. What our society needs to understand now, in the midst of our "animalistic affirmation and prim denial of sexuality," as she characterizes it, is that our capacity for caring "is grounded in and through our bodies or not at all."[3]

From these outlines of sexual ethics we turn to some specific applications. The writers of the next four essays in this section look at the meanings of sexuality for persons who are single, married, or celibate. The sexuality of single persons has long made the churches nervous. Karen Lebacqz observes in her essay that neither the legalistic approach of earlier Christian morality nor the compulsory permissiveness of contemporary culture makes a satisfactory sexual ethic for singles. In recent years, some in the church have accepted certain nonmarital sexual expressions provided they are within the context of deep couple commitment. But these revisions do not fully accept sexuality outside marriage. In her sexual ethics Lebacqz proposes a norm of "appropriate vulnerability." Not only for singles, this is a useful norm for all—but it is particularly important for singles precisely because they have no protective structures, such as monogamous marriage, to surround sexual expression. Lebacqz suggests that sexuality is to be valued as a particular form of vulnerability; eros and passion are antidotes to the sin of wanting control or power over another. She concludes that this is an ethic in transition, awaiting more adequate expression until we have a theology of vulnerability.

Monica Furlong acknowledges that the traditional Christian norm of absolute premarital chastity had value in recognizing that sexual desire can be destructive. This norm, however, also expressed ambivalence about women, who were still viewed as property to be handed over "intact" from father to husband. (The

English language still has no word that comes, as it were, between "promiscuous" and "chaste.") Yet, Furlong affirms, given the conviction that sex can be healing, joyful, and revelatory of God—sometimes outside marriage as well as within it—we need to struggle for a positive ethic for single persons.

Jack Dominian, a psychiatrist-theologian, takes a more traditional view of sexual ethics in his essay, urging that sexual intercourse is not appropriate apart from the established and maintained marital relationship. He believes that we need both intimacy *and* exclusivity to thrive. Turning to the question of the good of sex within marriage, he suggests that the Roman Catholic Church, to which he belongs, has been preoccupied with the procreative aspect of sexuality. What is needed now is a coherent teaching concerning the nonprocreative value of sexual intercourse. The author warmly describes a series of values that can arise in marital intercourse—personal and sexual affirmation, reconciliation, hope, and thanksgiving. Dominian regrets that Catholic ecclesiastical pronouncements on sex and marriage, written largely by celibates, show so little of the inner meaning of the sexual relationship.

The title of Janie Gustafson's book *Celibate Passion,* from which we excerpt a chapter, joins the words "celibate" and "passion" in a way we think particularly apt. Gustafson wants to redefine those two words, and she wants to hold them together. She argues against the traditional definition of passion as mortally sinful, "concupiscence, lust, libido,"[4] and equally opposes the passionless descriptions of celibacy as a negative and empty state. "It is a sober, somber, bloodless virtue which represses or denies my basic sexuality."[5] Celibate passion is born of eros, the passion for relationship, and erotic passion is crucial for any of us who want a mature, healthy relationship with God, as well as the ability to embrace our full humanness. Without denigrating the possibilities of genital sex, Gustafson makes a strong case for noncoital eros as a profoundly sensual and erotic spirituality.

Persons with disabilities are too frequently desexualized in our society. There are a number of reasons for this: simple ignorance of the sexual needs and capacities of those with functional limitations; our narrow emphasis on penis-in-vagina sex as the only "valid" sexual expression; and our cultural obsession with perfect bodies and the resulting, often unconscious, desire to punish others who remind us of our common susceptibility to injury, disease, and death. The chapter we include here is from *Presbyterians and Human Sexuality,* the controversial study presented to the Presbyterian General Assembly in 1991. It explores what persons with varying disabilities need and deserve from the church.

Next, two essays look at ethical and moral issues involved in sexuality and aging. They offer, as well, good examples of our social construction of sexual meanings: we find our sexuality to be a curse or a gift (to state the extremes) depending on what meanings we and others attach to it. In the first piece on aging, Penelope Washbourn reflects on menopause, a sexual rite of passage that is both a natural part of women's lives and also, often, an acute spiritual crisis.

Her essay, originally published in 1977, was one of the earliest efforts to interpret menopause theologically, and to our minds it remains sound and useful. For women, the end of biological fertility is a time to come to terms with their procreative history, to grieve their losses. It is also a time, Washbourn writes, for women to reassess their worth as persons, to rediscover their ultimate value in relation to all of life—a spiritual crisis that offers, as the Chinese character for "crisis" suggests, both danger and opportunity. The graceful possibilities menopause offers women are new self-understanding, new interpretations of the meanings of their lifelong sexuality, and movement from the old life into a new life of rekindled eros, what anthropologist Margaret Mead once called "post-menopausal zest."

The second essay is taken from the Presbyterian report mentioned earlier. It describes our ageist society, wherein older persons are seen as unwelcome reminders of human fragility, transience, and inevitable loss; our fears lead us to marginalize them. Our collective denial or trivialization of the sexual capacities and needs of older adults is, sadly, a dramatically effective way of punishing the aged. In response, the authors of the Presbyterian report propose an ethic of wholeness and justice for the aging, an ethic that is essential for persons of every age.

Perhaps nowhere is the social construction of body meanings more evident today than in the response to HIV/AIDS. We include two essays that call eloquently for the Christian response of compassion and pastoral concern for persons with HIV/AIDS and their caregivers. In our time no disease has been more punitively moralized in its interpretation. The essay by Grace Jantzen vividly shows the enormous extent to which punishing interpretations have increased the shame and suffering of persons affected by the disease. Jantzen deals insightfully with misguided theodicies and with the dynamics of sexual shame. In his essay that follows, Earl Shelp explores Christian moralities relating to the current pandemic. He argues that the command to love, to exercise human agape, unequivocally mandates that Christians offer compassionate ministry to all those who suffer, and particularly to persons living with HIV/AIDS. To do less is to violate the primary moral obligation of Christian faith.

The final three essays in Part 4 deal with Christian responses to sexual violence and pornography. Marie Fortune is a founding mother of the movement to end violence against women. In her essay she argues passionately and convincingly that our culture links love with violence, distorts the truth of violence against women, and resists naming this violence a sin. What is to be our response? We are to direct our hearts to the victims of violence, stand with them, and speak.

Marvin Ellison's essay offers a welcome male reflection on men's violence—its forms, it sources, and its devastating costs for women, children, and men alike. He presents an exploratory agenda of the work men need to do "in order to reclaim the power to change our lives in more humanizing directions,"[6] and to eliminate violence from men's lives. He proposes that men explore together "(1) studying our lives as men, especially our sexualities, and reclaiming the centrality

of bodily connectedness; (2) breaking our silence about the abuse of male power
. . .; and (3) accounting for the 'faith within us' to sustain the struggle for a far
different world."[7]

Mary Pellauer's essay on pornography, concluding this section, offers a strong
feminist treatment of the issues pornography poses. Those issues include the
inequities of power, the degradation of persons, and underlying economic
injustices. At the same time, Pellauer urges us to celebrate a healthy eroticism.

The essays in Part 4 are varied in emphasis, nuance, and focus. Yet they share
a common thread. Each challenges a traditional act-centered sexual ethics, which
has been graphically described as "the right organ in the right orifice with the
right person." We believe that each of these essays is a thoughtful contribution
to the reformation of Christian sexual ethics. The extent to which each of them
is Christianly faithful, responsible, and life-giving must be pondered by the
reader.

NOTES

1. Marvin M. Ellison, "Common Decency: A New Christian Sexual Ethics," *Christianity and Crisis*, vol. 50, no. 16 (Nov. 12, 1990): 354.

2. Beverly Wildung Harrison, *Making the Connections* (Boston: Beacon Press, 1985).
For reasons of space we have edited out the sections of Harrison's essay in which she
details the varied forms of oppression and injustice that currently surround women, men,
lesbians and gay men, and family structures. In the edited version we are most concerned
to see Harrison's social justice framework for sexual ethics.

3. Ibid., 114.

4. Janie Gustafson, *Celibate Passion* (San Francisco: Harper & Row, 1978), 74.

5. Ibid., 73.

6. Marvin M. Ellison, "Refusing to Be 'Good Soldiers': An Agenda for Men," in
Redefining Sexual Ethics, ed. Susan E. Davies and Eleanor H. Haney (Cleveland: Pilgrim
Press, 1991), 189.

7. Ibid., 190.

17

Common Decency: A New Christian Sexual Ethics

MARVIN M. ELLISON

It should come as no surprise that the church has lost its credibility where sex is concerned. It is also clear by now that if the church is going to regain any credibility, it has to take two immediate steps. It needs to acknowledge that a significant gap exists between official church teaching on sex and most people's lives, and it needs to clarify its theological and ethical mandate, especially where sexuality is concerned.

Even if these steps are taken, new pronouncements will amount to little if the church does not also become serious about developing an alternative sexual ethics—one that takes account of the changes of the last twenty-five years and gives concrete guidance for thinking about sex in everyday life.

Many of the most significant [theological writings] over the last few years have critiqued traditional teaching on sex and set forth a context and framework for a new sexual ethic. That crucial work now needs to be augmented by a willingness to talk about what the new context implies for "real life." This article takes first steps in that direction by presenting in capsule form a new context for sexual ethics and then going on to propose an ethic of common decency.

THE CONTEXT FOR SEXUAL ETHICS

Not heterosexuality, not marriage, but responsibility should become morally normative for a contemporary Christian sexual ethics. The church's traditional ethic—well represented by the phrase "celibacy in singleness, fidelity in marriage"—is woefully inadequate. It denies the rich diversity of sexual experiences and relationships that bear moral substance, and it establishes uncritically the exclusive claim of heterosexual marriage to moral propriety and sexual maturity. It focuses on the form rather than the substance of sexual relations—asking about who does what with whom under what circumstances, instead of asking about the quality of honesty, care, and respect in sexual relationships.

The church's lack of moral leadership on sex has in fact infantilized people, disempowering them to make responsible sexual choices. By defining a whole range of sexual experiences as sinful, the church has promoted guilt rather than sexual maturity; it has not helped people learn how to accept what they need, give and receive sexual pleasure freely, and direct their lives in order to enhance their own and others' joy and self-respect. If the church is going to be helpful here, it has to be willing to undertake a major shift in its ethical sensibilities.

Loyalty to the God "of grace and glory" is the basis of the church's theological and ethical mandate to seek justice passionately, including sexual justice. In accepting this mandate, the church agrees to become a gracious place—a place of hospitality and safety, a kind of "unoccupied territory" where persons can experience and delight in loving and being loved.

If it is going to become a gracious place, the church must honor the goodness of sex and diversity of sexual experience; it must also transform its deep fear of sex and the body and, at the same time, admit its preoccupation, bordering on fixation, with both.

Christians have had big problems gaining a balanced perspective on sex. Doing so might enable us to "come out" and mature *as sexual persons*, to own that erotic power is intrinsic to our humanness, that it often (but *not* always) deeply enriches our connectedness to self, others, and God, and that in and of itself it is the source neither of our salvation nor of our damnation.

Accepting its mandate, the church also agrees to stand boldly with those afflicted by sexual injustice and oppression and to advocate their cause as its own.

Christians' integrity as a people of faith depends on our standing with and demonstrating genuine solidarity with those who suffer sexual oppression and injustice—whether they be gay men and lesbians, or sexually abused children and women. Only from real-life solidarity will we come to appreciate how much our lives are diminished by gender and sexual injustice, as well as by racism and economic injustice. If the church is going to help people critically assess their cultural context and the social forces that shape and misshape human sexuality, personally and corporately, it is also going to have to listen and learn, especially from those calling for a fundamental reconstruction of sexuality and sexual ethics.

All societies organize erotic life. Human sexuality is never simply a matter of "what comes naturally"; it is culturally encoded, given a distinctive shape that reflects certain values and social preoccupations.

Our own culture is patriarchal—built on gender inequality and the legitimacy of men's control over women, children, and men of lesser power. The gender of the person with whom we have sex is the standard used to determine whether persons are normal or abnormal. Beyond that, permission is granted only for sex between a man and a woman within the institution of a male-dominant marriage. More reluctantly, permission is given to sexually active couples on their way to marriage. At the same time, men are encouraged to gain sexual access to any woman, especially any woman not "possessed" or controlled by another man.

Under patriarchy, men are socialized to exercise power over others and to feel uncomfortable when they do not. Staying in control means controlling feelings and remaining "manly," detached and "rational." Women are socialized to accept dependency, emotionality, and powerlessness. Always operating within such differentials (never transcending them), patriarchal sex depends on a dynamic of conquest and surrender, of winning control over or of being placed under someone else's control. "Opposites attract." Inequality is sexy.

We learn, in other words, to accept sexism as natural *in our bodies,* as well as in our psyches, to believe that male gender superiority feels good and is beneficial to men and women alike. Patriarchal sex makes gender injustice appear pleasurable.

Heterosexism complicates matters even more. It reinforces sexism by pressuring people to play their "proper" sex-stereotyped gender roles and to feel pain, fear, and guilt if they do not. It enforces sexism by oppressing, if not punishing, sexual nonconformists. Heterosexism and homophobia operate to maintain gender injustice in our churches and throughout this society.

The moral challenge before the church, therefore, is this: It must choose between perpetuating a patriarchal ethic of sexual control and gender oppression or pledging its commitment to an ethic of gender justice, of mutuality between women and men, and of respect for sexual diversity. Naming the sexual problem accurately is a fundamental theological and ethical task. The sexual problem the church must critique and challenge lies not in people, but rather in prevailing social, cultural, and ecclesial arrangements which stigmatize and devalue self-respecting persons who deviate from the sexist and heterosexist norm. Unless we acknowledge this distortion of human equality and intimacy by sexism and heterosexism, we will remain captive to a patriarchal culture's values and loyalties.

Therefore, we must not shy away from the following declaration: *Our problem is not homosexuality or nonmarital sex but conformity to the unjust norm of compulsory heterosexuality and gender inequality. This unjust norm must be altered, not those who question it.* What is shaking the very foundations of church and society is the open call to struggle for a nonsexist moral order in the family and throughout our public institutions, including the church.

AN ETHIC OF COMMON DECENCY

Articulating a normative vision of sexual justice, applied inclusively regardless of gender, sexual orientation, and marital status, has implications, most of them controversial. The church can't avoid dealing with them as it begins to articulate an ethic of sexual empowerment. Such an ethic might best be termed an *ethic of common decency*. It would look something like this:

Not marriage, not heterosexuality (not homosexuality, for that matter), but *justice in sexual relationships* is morally normative for Christians. Justice includes the moral obligation to promote one another's common decency and to honor our need for intimacy and affection. Our sexuality is who—and how—we experience this quite remarkable emotional, cognitive, physical, and spiritual yearning for communion with others, with the natural world, and with God. Sexual desire and passion ennoble our lives.

Only by unabashedly reclaiming sex as intrinsic to Christian spirituality can we begin to recapture a more earthy, sensuous, and concrete awareness that we are created and destined to be lovers. We are invited to relish receiving and giving sexual pleasure. Affirmation and care are expressed with vitality and integrity whenever we honor our capacity to touch and be touched with tenderness and respect for our common dignity. Literally "staying in touch"—with our senses, with one another, with whatever moves us in delight, horror, or curiosity—is an open-ended sexual and spiritual project, full of surprises and challenges.

From a justice perspective, it is entirely fitting not to grant special status or moral privilege to heterosexual marriage, but rather to celebrate *all* sexual relations of moral substance whenever they deepen human intimacy and love. Marriage retains value and meaning not because it serves as a "license for sex" or a declaration of ownership and possession, but because it offers *one possible* framework of accountability and a relatively stable, secure place in which to form durable bonds of devotion, affection, and intimacy. Marriages should also be expected to strengthen persons to deepen ties of affection and friendship beyond, as well as within, the primary relation, rather than fostering control and dependency.

Some marriages may make room for additional sexual partners while others will thrive only by maintaining genital sexual exclusivity. Although justice requires relational fidelity—honoring and responding fairly to the demands of a relationship—the precise requirements for maintaining faithfulness cannot be predetermined in any formal fashion. Rather, the concrete "terms of endearment" can be detected and refined only as a particular relationship develops. For this reason, the most likely violation of the covenant bond will not be "outside" sex per se or collateral friendships, but the refusal to act in good faith, to remain mutually accountable, and to renegotiate the relations as needs and desires change.

Obviously, what I call "just" marriages require a high degree of moral responsibility and mutual commitment—not to mention a willingness to face the truth. Equally obviously, the right to participate in and receive community support for an enduring, formalized sexual partnership should be available to same-sex couples as well as to heterosexuals. For both alike, the question remains: When is a marriage properly "consummated," and how does one know that?

In this day and age, sexual activity alone does not mark the establishment of a marriage or authentic sexual friendship, nor should it. If sex does not "make" a marriage, however, neither does a church ceremony nor legalizing action by the state. As William Countryman has suggested *(Dirt, Greed, and Sex: Sexual Ethics in the New Testament and Their Implications for Today)*, since the church does not constitute marriages but only offers its blessing, we need to clarify appropriate ethical criteria for knowing when a marriage has taken place.

Marriages "happen" only as persons committed wholeheartedly to empowering each other as genuine equals experience "mutual benefit arising from mutual devotion and affection." For this reason, as Countryman wisely notes, at least some divorces may signal less an "end to a marriage" than the public announcement that "no harm be done." More importantly, it will serve to *strengthen people's well-being and self-respect.* Good sex is good because it not only touches our senses powerfully, but also enhances our self-worth and our desire to connect more justly with others. Sex is not something one "does" to another person or "has happen" to oneself. Rather, sexual intimacy is a mutual process of feeling with and connecting as whole persons. In having sex with someone, we don't "lose" ourselves as much as we relocate ourselves in the in-betweenness of self and other, as we receive and give affection, energy, and passion.

Such respect and pleasure can teach us how wrong it is to regard any and all self-interest as somehow morally tainted. As lovers and friends, we can be rightly interested in our *mutual* enjoyment and well-being. Being interested in others does not detract from but complements our self-interest, and vice versa. What harms or diminishes another can never be good for me. Positively stated, whatever enhances your well-being deepens the quality of my life as well. In a culture that has confused love with controlling others (or with giving over power to another), the church should educate each of us to know that we can connect with others only to the extent that we also stay genuinely present to ourselves, aware of our needs and feelings, and mindful of our obligation to honor ourselves, as well as the other person.

Finally, an ethic of common decency will *raise, not lower our moral expectations.* It will teach us how to demand of ourselves (and of others) what we deserve: to be whole persons to each other and to be deeply, respectfully loved.

GOOD EROTICISM

A gracious, liberating church will teach us to claim our right to a pleasurable and good eroticism. It *may* also impassion us to invest ourselves in creating a more just and equitable church and world. Desire for pleasure can authentically include a desire for community and for a more ethical world. Contrary to many voices inside and outside the church, sex and desire are not necessarily dangerous, selfish, or self-indulgent. Rather, erotic power can be an indispensable spiritual resource for engaging joyfully in creating justice.

And Christian spirituality *without* erotic passion is lifeless and cold. It is also boring. More tellingly, the pervasive fear of sex and of strong passion, so rampant in our churches, is deeply implicated in the difficulty many religious people have in sustaining their passion for social justice.

Sooner or later, the church must face the conflict between a patriarchal and a liberating paradigm of Christian spirituality and sexuality. Passionately challenging sexism and heterosexism is the necessary avenue to reclaiming an erotically powerful, nonexploitative sexuality. And because justice lies at the heart of any Christian spirituality worth having, we may stumble on a pathway to spiritual renewal as well.

18

Sexuality and
Social Policy

BEVERLY WILDUNG HARRISON

In our present society, and far too frequently in our churches as well, persons of very different theological and political persuasions—conservatives, liberals, and radicals—coconspire to keep in place assumptions about human sexuality, ethics, and social policy that block a much-needed rethinking of how our human capacity for intimacy and love and our aspirations for a just social order coinhere. Taken at face value, this claim may seem incredible. Surely, the conservative who longs for clear and precise normative rules about the rights and wrongs of sexual acts on the one hand and who wishes to keep religion out of social policy or politics on the other appears to have little in common with theological liberals or radicals. After all, the latter usually put concern for the justice of social institutions squarely at the center of their religious commitment and are quite likely to take the position that the ethics of sexuality is merely a personal issue and a matter of relative indifference compared with the "grave" issues of social justice. The fact is, however, that both positions accept a set of assumptions about our human personhood that badly need to be challenged. For both, the personal and the political are sealed off from each other, and the dynamics that make for social and personal well-being are not deeply interconnected. The conventional wisdom that sustains this split is precisely what needs to be challenged, I believe, if we are to rise to a major responsibility in our time: rethinking our understanding of human sexuality to appropriate a sexual ethics deep enough to clarify the relation between our capacity for interpersonal love and our ability to struggle effectually for social justice in our common life.

Without a better grasp of the intimate connection between personal and social well-being, our sexual ethic will simply reinforce a growing trend toward privatism and the churches' withdrawal from social engagement. But equally problematic would be any renewed concern for social justice that is devoid of awareness of how our social passivity is rooted in the dynamics of our interpersonal, primary relationships. The churches are always tempted to avoid altogether the volatile questions of human sexuality, abandoning people in the confused struggle to find more adequate paths to personal fulfillment and human intimacy. What we Christians evade is the connection between our silence on sexuality and our general conventionality toward social relations. Even our presumed "social action" often suffers from lack of creativity and imagination.

That we need a new understanding of the dialectic between love and justice is obvious from the way that both conservative and liberal ideologies within Christianity lead to obvious contradictions in the actions and strategies of their respective proponents. For their part, many Christian social activist liberals are perplexed at a growing political apathy in the churches and seem unable to find ways to mobilize social conscience except through the methods of rhetorical moralizing, which were the very means deplored as overindividualistic in the past. At the same time, conservatives who have long cried out for clear-cut standards of right and wrong in personal sexual ethics and who always have insisted that a rigid line be drawn between religion and ethics on the one hand and politics and economics on the other find themselves mobilizing politically to change the direction of social policy to prevent further changes that they deem immoral. So religiopolitical movements against the defeated Equal Rights Amendment and against legal abortion and the civil rights of homosexuals flourish. That many who support these efforts are violating their own deeply held convictions against government interference with or regulation of individual liberty only underscores the inability of established social theory to encompass our lived-world reality.

The complexity of the relation between sexuality and social order becomes clear when we observe how little impact such largely successful political mobilization has on our culture's preoccupation with human sexuality. Legislators can gain support by turning back permissive social policies, but our fascination with genital sexuality and explicit sexual themes seems to increase. We even see the emergence of groups, such as the Total Woman Movement, that combine a celebration of heterosexual genital sexual liberation in marriage with a militant reassertion of traditional notions about "woman's place" in home, family, and society. Evidently, the pleasures of genital-sexual eroticism are here to stay, whatever the outcome of social movements aimed at justice for women. This trend is further confirmed by the response of several television networks to complaints about gratuitous physical violence during prime-time programming. In a number of cases, detective shows and adventure stories have given way to situation comedies that feature a new and presumably "daring" explicitness about sexuality. Since the television media often know more about our collective tastes and attitudes than we ourselves do, the substitution of the titillations of explicit sex for the presumed excitation of physical violence suggests that we are a long way from any shift back toward more traditional sexual reticences.

The fact is that explicit sexuality is very big business in this nation, and our fascination with the technologies of sex, with sexual therapies, and with the paraphernalia of sexual experimentation is flourishing. Those who cry out for a tightening of sexual standards notwithstanding, "sexual liberation," in its tawdry, commercial guise, will not abate until the profit wanes. The anomaly of our situation can be measured by the way in which sexuality is becoming part of the performance- and achievement-oriented ethic characteristic of a business society. We appear so preoccupied by sexual performance that some commentators wonder whether capacity for sexual pleasure may not be giving way to ennui and boredom. If greater sexual genital expression were, in itself, a panacea for what ails us, we would expect clear evidence that a sense of personal well-being was on the rise in our society. In fact, there is no indication that we are experiencing a reduction in loneliness, isolation, competitiveness, or alienation from community.

In the face of all this, the trivialization of sexuality by those whose concerns are presumably focused on the "more substantive" questions of social justice is understandable. Such people consider preoccupation with sexual concerns and sexual pleasure to be a cause of our social malaise. There has been much loose talk about a "new narcissism," turning to self-preoccupation that presumably threatens our capacity to take the reality of other persons seriously. The problem with much of this sort of social diagnosis is that it does not probe deeply enough to lead to a reintegrated sense of how interpersonal well-being interacts with the wider social realities that shape our experience. The analysis of our presumed narcissism too often confuses "cause" with social "symptom."[1] The almost desperate search for physical pleasure and personal intimacy that pervasively characterizes our culture is much more a symptom of the lack of humanly fulfilling opportunities in work and frustration at depersonalized, bureaucratic institutional patterns that suffuse our life than a cause of our social ills. And the tragedy is that the simple pleasures of sex, while real, are not a sufficiently powerful antidote to the wounds to self-respect we endure elsewhere. Genital sexuality, narrowly conceived, is simply too weak a reed to bear the overloaded expectations that people in our society are encouraged to place on it. What is most needed is an approach to sexuality that aims to be holistic, that sets what we know of ourselves as sexual persons in the broadest possible context of our lives within our existing social order.

SOURCES, PRINCIPLES, AND PRIORITIES FOR A MORE ADEQUATE ETHICS OF SEXUALITY

The time is ripe for a reappraisal of our understanding of sexuality, ethics, and social policy, in spite of the controversy such reappraisal engenders. There are two salient and appropriate pressures for a reevaluation in contemporary society, and both provide resources for recovering a deeper, holistic understanding of the nature of our sexuality. The first of these pressures derives from the emergence of basic paradigm shifts in social scientific conceptions of the nature of gender difference and "normal" sexuality. What we are discovering today is how little we really have ever understood about ourselves as sexual persons. The new paradigms of psychosocial development make clear that the meaning of our sexuality involves the integration of many levels of biological and social determinants. More and more, we are coming to realize the full range of possible healthy sexual development that characterizes human life. New knowledge per se does not yield new ethical awareness, but the emerging paradigms are themselves more open to humane value questions.[2] These newer scientific perspectives afford us opportunity to appropriate a more adequate sense of human diversity in sexual development and expression. They correlate well with the best insights of our religious and moral tradition about the interrelationship of human freedom and moral responsibility.

However, Christians have as yet been reluctant to embrace an ethic of maturity where sexuality is concerned. In many dimensions of our life as human agents, Christian ethicists have insisted, explicitly, that we must both accept our power as agents and learn to express that power responsibly, without recourse to unexceptional rules. In relation to our actions as sexual beings, however, there remains a lingering fear of affirming any genuine capacity of moral agents to live responsibly apart from largely prohibitive and constricting action guides.[3]

The second pressure and resource for reappraisal of sexual ethics come from the fruit of women's efforts to achieve full social recognition as persons. In our time, it is the women's movement and, more recently, the gay and lesbian liberation movements that have called into question many of the traditional views formerly held to be "scientific." At the deepest level, the insights of contemporary feminism lead to reappropriation of the meaning of our sexuality, which runs counter to the narrow "sexual liberation" fixation on genital sexuality.

What women have discovered, signaled in the phrase "we are our bodies, ourselves," is that in the absence of freedom to understand, control, and direct our own sexuality, our power as self-regulating moral agents does not develop. Numerous feminists have formulated telling critiques of traditional erotic patterns, insisting, for example, that our modern romantic ideals of love between the sexes involve the celebration of dehumanizing seduction and conquest on the male side and feminine passivity and denial of pleasure on the other.[4] A clear break with male myths regarding female sexuality has enabled women to recognize to what extent such myths have been generated to keep women obeisant to the social function of procreation. The religious dictum that the only moral expression of sexuality is that which is at least open to the possibility of procreation has been a source of many women's inability to achieve a self-defining role in relation to their bodies. Many women have denied their own needs for bodily pleasuring as the cost of being "good" women. Conversely, when women have been sexually active or self-initiating, society has defined

them as "whores" or "deviants." In the positive reappropriation and appreciation of ourselves as embodied persons, women are regaining the capacity to
celebrate our sexuality as inherent in our own embodiedness. But the experience
of genuine embodiedness also leads to rejection of the view that sexual pleasure
is limited to genital contact or that women's sexuality is passive, mediated
exclusively through active relationships with men. The feminist insight is that
sexuality is mutual pleasuring in the context of genuine openness and intimacy.
That such communication is of "ultimate value" only when it is shaped by
procreative potential or procreative intent—the Christian teaching, at least as it
applies to women—is simply lingering male supremacist doctrine that reinforces
male control of women's self-definition.

The social criticism generated by feminism also has led to a fresh analysis of
the way in which sex role patterns in the family operate destructively in relation
to women's self-esteem. These sex role expectations have subtly conditioned us,
men and women alike, to accept inequities of power and differing capacities for
self-direction between men and women in the broader society.[5] It is one thing,
however, for groups of women—and, increasingly, for sensitive men—to begin
to diagnose the destructive aspects of sex role socialization as they affect the lives
of individuals and the broader community; it is another to begin to reverse these
powerfully ingrained patterns of traditional gender socialization in society.

The women's movement and the gay and lesbian movements are resources
and pressures for change, but they do not provide a simple blueprint that enables
us to prioritize issues relating to sexuality and social policy. Insofar as these
movements are limited by theory or practice to the reality of white experience or
fail to address the dynamics of class, identified priorities will be inadequate. In
addition, public knowledge of feminism and gay and lesbian liberation movements is filtered through and conditioned by the mass media that aim to
minimize offense to some presumed "general public" and therefore also aim to
mute serious systemic criticism. This means that it is mostly the priorities for
social policy change that resonate with already existing "public opinion" that are
called to our attention. The full implications of a serious feminist social policy are
rarely understood in public debate.

The corrective for uncritical acceptance of media-interpreted priorities of
these social movements, however, is deeper listening and involvement and a
greater effort to respect the principles underlying the specific priorities of all
social justice movements. For example, in the women's movement, the principle
of bodily self-determination underlies the emphasis on the need for accessible
contraception and the availability of legal abortion. The same principle, applied
in the context of the existing race and class dynamics of this society, requires
equal attention to the abhorrent social practice of developing contraceptive
devices through medical experimentation on poor and nonwhite women and the
too frequent practice of forced sterilization, especially of poor and nonwhite
women.[6] Yet the media focus only on the former issues, leaving concern for the
latter, widespread in the women's movement, undiscussed as a serious social evil.

The fundamental social attitude toward women—that our competence as moral agents vis-à-vis our bodies and reproductive capacities is not trustworthy—inevitably results in divergent patterns of social control across race and class lines. Many middle-strata white women experience social deprivation only when they insist on self-determination that flies in the face of traditional female roles. They may count on family and community support and personal affirmation if they choose childbearing and function as "good" mothers and homemakers. Only when they resist conformity to these conventional roles does their environment grow hostile or suspicious of them as women. Poor and working-class women, by contrast, suffer more acute deprivation; they have neither easy access to prevention of pregnancy nor support for their exercise of women's "traditional" role. Racism and poverty function as coercive pressures against even traditional fulfillment through procreation.

The point is that the social policy priorities of groups aiming at liberation from the various forms of sexual oppression are adequately liberating only insofar as these priorities are defined by how they touch the lives of persons on both sides of the institutionalized and interstructured patterns of race and class oppression. Andrea Dworkin has put this point forcefully:

> The analysis of sexism . . . articulates clearly what the oppression of women is, how it functions, how it is rooted in psyche and culture. But that analysis is useless unless it is tied to a political consciousness and commitment which will totally redefine community. One cannot be free, never, not ever, in an unfree world, and in the course of redefining family, church, power relations, all the institutions which inhibit and order our lives, there is no way to hold onto privilege and comfort. To attempt to do so is destructive, criminal, and intolerable. . . .
>
> The analysis [of sexism] applies to the life situations of all women, but all women are not necessarily in a state of primary emergency as women. What I mean by this is simple. As a Jew in Nazi Germany, I would be oppressed as a woman, but hunted, slaughtered as a Jew. As a Native American, I would be oppressed as a squaw, but hunted, slaughtered, as a Native American. *The first identity, the one which brings with it as a part of its definition death, is the identity of primary emergency.* This is an important recognition because it relieves us of a serious confusion. The fact, for instance, that many Black women [by no means all] experience primary emergency as Blacks in no way lessens the responsibility of the Black community to assimilate this and other analyses of sexism and to apply it in their own revolutionary work. [Emphasis mine][7]

This same insight must be extended to gay and lesbian analyses and sensibilities. The social priorities of gay men do not always adequately incorporate the needs and sensibilities of lesbians or of black people or the poor. In the churches and in the wider gay movement, white gay men are often those who specify the agenda for change in relation to heterosexism. Setting adequate priorities for just social policy in relation to human sexuality will occur only if we learn to ask, How do the matters that are central to my liberation touch the lives of those who are doubly or triply oppressed? We must learn to shape our formulation of sexual justice with this question and these persons in view. No sexual ethic will be adequate unless it incorporates a full appreciation of the interstructuring of social oppression. For example, economic justice as access to and genuine participation in the production, distribution, and determination of the use of a society's wealth is also a condition of genuine sexual freedom. All distortions of power in society reveal themselves in the inequity of power dynamics in interpersonal life. An adequate normative sexual ethic will be predicated on awareness that where people (men, women, *and* children) are socially powerless, they are vulnerable to irresponsible and inappropriate—that is, nonvoluntary and/or nonmutual— sexual transactions. The goal of a holistic and integrated sexual ethic is to affirm sexual activity that enhances human dignity, that entails self- and other-regarding respect and genuine communication. Such an ethic must challenge actions that degrade, disempower, and reduce oneself's and others' esteem or that aim at control, objectification, or manipulation of another.

The basic theological and moral principles implicit in the feminist and gay liberation movements—the affirmation of the goodness of sexuality as embodiment, the respect for bodily integrity, and the appropriateness of self-direction and noncoercion in expressing sexuality—are constitutive of everyone's human dignity. They are foundational to all claims for human well-being, as fundamental to the eradication of racism and ethnic oppression as to women's and gay men's historic emancipation. As such, they are criteria for a sexual ethic that genuinely affirms personal freedom, community, and responsibility.

DIFFICULTIES OF CONSTRUCTIVE SOCIAL CHANGE IN RELATION TO HUMAN SEXUALITY

Another awareness that must inform our efforts to translate social policy priorities into strategy is a recognition of the difficulty of finding effective loci for social change in this society. Genuine implementation of change in relation to our well-being as sexual persons is difficult to achieve. Liberal social reform efforts tend to focus strategies for change primarily through government, aiming chiefly at legal reform and government administrative change. Neither legal nor administrative reform can be neglected in efforts to implement new policies with respect to gender and sexual justice. But it is important to be clear about the role, and also the limits, of law and procedural reform. Liberals frequently misunderstand the role that law plays in strategies for change. In our society, fundamental legal change (including constitutional change, as, for example, the Equal Rights Amendment) or the achievements of administrative fairness are always as much a response to already partially realized conditions for justice as they are initiators of such change. The initiation of conditions for social justice always begins with social movements. Legislation is important because without it or without administrative fairness, the relevant conditions for sustaining justice will never approximate "normalcy" in the wider society. Reversion to repressive policies is always easier if the requisite legitimations in law and administrative procedure have not been realized.

Nevertheless, it is critical to be aware of the actual dialectic between such legal change and wider social change. Genuine change is always the result of hard-won struggle from below. Some groups and some institutions must begin to shape a liberating praxis within the society before there is sufficient pressure to actualize humane conditions as a legal norm. Theological liberalism has misunderstood this fact, which is why liberal church activism for justice has been so inept. Tragically, liberal Christians who aver that the church should avoid controversy until issues are respectable and who refuse liaisons with social movements and activist social policy groups are those who ensure that Christianity will never play an active role in shaping policy development within our society. To "get involved" only when consensus about positive legal change has developed means that such Christians are never influential in the process of change. Social movements are the means whereby any positive change emerges, and the politics of mainstream theological liberals are never engaged enough to interact with such movements.

In sum, double focus on change at the cultural and legal levels offers the best hope for transforming the split between what is presumed to be political or public and what is held to be merely personal or private, a split that reinforces and legitimates our widespread moral schizophrenia and keeps sexual oppression in place. The potential for "radicalizing" people's broader awareness of the importance of social justice by integrating their sensibilities to sexual justice lies precisely here. It is worth emphasizing again that the conventionality of our religion is maintained by our fear of honestly and openly facing issues of human sexuality. If exclusive reliance on the power of government to initiate change is one fallacy of much liberal social strategy, the tendency to overestimate the capacity of formal education to transform personal values is another. "Public" education (and, by default, most "private" education as well) is in a weak position to challenge the dominant or established understandings of human sexuality that are transmitted powerfully in our society. "Sex education" in our schools can at most challenge the miasma of misinformation, fear, and prejudice with respect to human sexuality. Furthermore, what actually goes on in the name of "sex education" has some way to go to reach even this minimum standard of effectiveness and moral adequacy. The truth is that our so-called public schools are often rendered educationally ineffectual because of fear of conflict. With respect to sexuality, as at so many other points, this fear often results in an educational strategy that postures a reductionistically "scientific" approach. Sexuality is dealt with from a physiological stance in which human reproductive biology is taught abstractly, in an environment where discussions of values are avoided to evade conflict.[8] The result is a bland conventionality that is more devastatingly effective in reinforcing the status quo than a more explicitly reactionary stance would be.

A strong case can be made that on this issue, at least, the liberal churches (regretfully, by default) have a genuine opportunity to serve the social good by a humane educational approach to human sexuality. Yet because of sexism, that is, the disvaluation of women, and fear of sexuality, the churches are not better equipped than other institutions for this task. Liberal churches, in particular, need a critical perspective on their own past social praxis in relation to public policy. Most of the public utterance of liberal churches vis-à-vis social policy questions has taken the form of voicing support for "the rights of individuals" against state intrusion on those rights. Even the most liberal of our churches have gone only so far as to ground support for sexual liberation in statements that affirm individual civil liberties. Some liberal churches have urged the state to avoid heavy-handed enforcement of sexual morality; they have affirmed women's individual freedom of conscience in seeking access to legal abortion; they have accepted the appropriateness of civil liberties for gay people. Such a posture and such policy positions have been legitimated with reference to a theology that is not substantively social. The bottom line for the liberal churches has been to oppose policies in relation to sexuality that deny status and dignity to the individual within the "public" sphere. These policy positions have helped to reduce pressure from other, more reactionary quarters for more oppressive public policies, but they lack moral vision. We need to recognize that a more adequately social theology would provide a substantive positive political rationale that would go beyond this individualistic bottom line. As it is, liberal Protestant churches have a public policy stance that suggests that it is acceptable for us to be "political" only if and when individual rights have been demonstrably violated. Whether or not the social system itself is just appears, from this perspective, to be a matter of indifference.

The very fact that we resort to such individualistic justifications—supporting individuals' civil rights rather than embracing positive and substantive moral principles rooted in an adequate vision of social justice—bespeaks the disorder of the churches' theological approach to sexual ethics. Because this is so, such defensive, "individual rights" policy stances are ineffectual. They appear to the wider society as hypocritical because they are predicated on a moral double standard that all the world reads (and reads properly) as Christian double-talk. Gay people, we claim, deserve "civil rights," but they do not receive full human affirmation and respect in the churches. Women should have the "civil right" to elect legal abortion, but abortion continues to be viewed as, at best, morally dubious, an evil necessity. The churches have not affirmed people's sexual well-being as basic to their personal dignity. The state is not charged to *support* citizens' sexual well-being but simply to desist from meddling. Because the churches do not embrace theologically the positive, nonfunctional good of human sexuality or affirm the positive principles related to sexual well-being as substantively moral, our "liberal" stance is dismissed as mere accommodation to modern culture. Because we do not accept the mandate to active solidarity with those who are the victims of sexual oppression, our social policy positions appear equivocal. We deny our own best understanding of the inherently theosocial nature of persons and community, and speak instead as individualists whose message to society is that it must adopt a moderate tolerance of human sexual expression, a moderate tolerance that we, within the churches, are not even willing to exemplify in our own community.

There is a long roster of social policy concerns that come into view when we actually embrace a positive, holistic understanding of sexuality. In addition to the policy issues I address here, this roster should include the question of how children and the sexual well-being of the differently abled can be protected and how sexual manipulation of inmates of "total institutions" can be prevented. Here I have limited my discussion to analyzing the way in which an adequate view of human sexuality requires us to take an inclusive view of women's lives and to identify some of the needed social policy concerns affecting men, gay men and lesbians, and families.

As I have already made clear, any identified social policy issue has an economic aspect. Among other things, this means that the matters I address here gain their urgency as social policy questions from the fact that they hold no "priority" in the regular, day-to-day workings of our present political economy. Serious social vulnerability in this society rests on economic marginality; hence, children and older people, all women and gay males, as well as nonskilled males (mostly, though not exclusively, nonwhite) are vulnerable as groups, which also makes them especially susceptible to sexual exploitation, violence, or forms of "benign neglect." Since the capacity to produce income and to accumulate wealth (not to be equated with wages) is *the* measure of personal worth in this society, anyone who does not participate in money-making will also be a priori a victim vulnerable to sexual oppression or to being treated as a nonperson sexually. The elderly or physically handicapped, for example, are frequently characterized as "beyond sexuality" for just this reason. . . .

In keeping with the principles identified earlier, we need always to ask how these policy matters affect persons differently, how the dynamics of class and white supremacy intersect with the social dynamics of human sexuality and gender difference.

CONCLUSION

Many of the thorniest questions of social policy in relation to sexuality will continue to pose dilemmas for morally concerned persons whatever happens in the future. Even if we succeed in deepening our awareness of the connections between personal intimacy patterns and the sociopolitical and economic forces that mold our lives, the constructive shaping of our personal-social relationships is a challenge that does not admit easy solutions. How societies should function, through government, to influence individual behavior is always a difficult question. How and in which ways sexual behavior should be shaped is, perhaps, the hardest question of all.

Efforts to regulate sexual conduct between consenting adults are notoriously difficult and, as I have observed, are fraught with potential for the abuse of state power. Enforcement of laws regulating sexual conduct are more the exception than the rule. The temptation of government authorities to use techniques of police entrapment to catch "sexual offenders" seems inexorable, and the tendency toward corrupt use of public authority in enforcement is strong. This state of affairs is probably inevitable because sexuality involves intimate spaces— where we sleep, dress, and retire for privacy. Given our dominant value patterns, such enforcement will always catch the poor, relatively powerless, socially marginated offenders, while more privileged lawbreakers go free. Conversely, sexual entrapment can always be used against those whose political views are unpopular. Nothing can reduce the tension between those provisional rights to privacy that we all need and initiatives to use law to encourage a positive moral climate regarding sexual conduct because monitoring sexual conduct requires intrusive observation. As a result, our presumptive stance should be that restrictive law needs to be used sparingly where sexuality is involved. In the face of this fact, all of us should exercise caution in looking to government for simple redress of grievances because others' sexual conduct offends our personal moral sensibilities. In spite of considerable social pressure on the churches to demand legal action to curtail "dubious" sexual behavior, we need to exercise critical sensibility and a healthy dose of skepticism as to what such laws actually accomplish.

How a society may best live with this tension between the diverse personal sensibilities of adults and the need for a degree of public order will always be subject to debate. I have already made it clear that we would be well served by considerably "desexualizing" our criminal codes. Morally evil behaviors that are frequently classified as sex offenses—molestation or exploitation of young children, rape, publicly intrusive pandering of sexually explicit or obscene material, and the offensive hawking of sexual devices, including solicitation for prostitution—are wrong, in different degrees, not because they involve genitally explicit activity but because they express morally inappropriate power relations between people—physical and psychic assault or obvious insensitivity to the dignity of another person's rights and capacity for self-direction. The most heinous of these so-called sex crimes are not more "especially wrong" than other acts of violence, unjustified coercion, or manipulation, though in a sex-phobic society "sex crimes" are experienced as especially "dirty" or polluting. These acts are wrong because they involve the harassment or the abuse and degradation of persons who are relatively powerless to resist. Such acts *intend* humiliation or control. Genital or sexual intrusion is perceived as the best way to express contempt or to establish power over another person. Legal changes that desexualize criminal law while strengthening legal sanctions against any bodily harassment or assault toward children or nonconsenting adults might go a long way toward helping us disentangle our fears of sexuality from our fears of being humiliated by other persons through contemptuous physical abuse aimed at the most vulnerable areas of our bodies. No unjustified violence toward another's body, against that person's will, should ever be construed as a sign of positive erotic capacity or mature action. Rather, such actions are usually rooted in fear of closeness and mutuality. They express a need for control and a disordered incapacity for relationship over an appropriate capacity for interdependence. Victims of so-called sex crimes often are more stigmatized than the perpetrators of the crimes because such offenses stereotype victims as sexually "impure." It is time to recognize that those who are recipients of violent "sexual" acts are *not* sexually polluted; they have been victimized by ugly acts of human retribution, evil because of the contempt for persons they express rather than the genital contact they involve.

If acts of coercion and violence involving genitals are "desexualized" and understood as crimes of assault and bodily intrusion, it may be possible to see more clearly why minimal regulation of sexual conduct between consenting adults by the state is desirable, even a positive moral good. If there is any "zone of privacy" that requires, seriously, to be sacrosanct and respected, it is a person's right to bodily integrity. Our body-selves, the zone of body-space we possess by virtue of our being embodied persons, deserve explicit protection from arbitrary interference and unjustified coercion. "Consent" at this level is a condition of having a moral relationship. From a moral point of view, embracing "consent" as a criterion is not to deny a norm or to be merely "permissive." In our most intimate, interpersonal relations, consent or self-direction is a critical condition of human well-being. Space in which it can be expressed is a social good. Those who govern with regard for the conditions of a just society do well to respect this reality. Honoring the decisions regarding sexual expression between consenting adults is not a negative moral norm but a positive moral value. We ought to possess the conditions for nonconstrained expression of intimacy.

We must not be romantic about the quality of sexual communication that characterizes our society. We are sex-preoccupied but neither genuinely sensual nor genuinely pleasure-oriented. Because much that passes for sexual liberation is only a blend of alienated technological consciousness with the most puerile notions of what good male-female eroticism involves—notions, alas, often imitated in same-sex eroticism—we have no reason to celebrate the actual "quality" of the presumed new "sexual liberation" overall. Nevertheless, there are hopeful indications that through "our bodies, ourselves," some of us are learning to ground our capacity for personal fulfillment and for genuine mutuality. The affirmation of our capacity for giving and receiving pleasure and for appropriating our self-worth in and through our bodies has also begun to lead to an important demystification of our sexuality. The ancient idea that sexuality itself is an irrational, alien, even evil power, deeply foreign to our personal integrity and outside the range of our self-direction, is giving way to new integrations of psychosexual identity with socially fulfilling action. The fact that some can now celebrate sexuality as an important, albeit not all-controlling, aspect of selfhood, having learned to value it as a deep mode of communication, is a great step forward. Sexuality involves pleasure and erotic intensity, but it also expresses playfulness, tenderness, and a generalized sense of well-being.

Our culture expresses simultaneously an animalistic affirmation and prim denial of sexuality. We do not yet see clearly that our capacity for caring, for expressing and receiving deep feeling, for reaching out to others is grounded in and through our bodies or not at all. Given this insight, the way is now open for us to affirm genuinely what we have long given lip service to in our theologies—that our sexuality is a gift of God. Positive affirmation of our sensuality leads to the understanding that when we abuse our sexuality, it is not because we have been too free or too permissive or too spontaneous. Rather, it is because our capacity for intimacy and sensual communication has been twisted and distorted by manipulative and nonmutual patterns of relationship. If we cannot tolerate mutually respectful and mutually enhancing erotic communication, if we prefer relational patterns of conquest or subservience, sadism or masochism, or if we are stuck in compulsive, inappropriate, and repetitive patterns of action, it is because we have failed to find the positive power of our own being as sexual persons. If this is so, no repudiation of sexuality, as such, will deliver us. Rather, what we need is a deepened and more holistic sense of ourselves that will enable us to grow sexually, to celebrate, and to respect our own sexuality and that of others. Today no Christian ethics of sexuality can straddle the fence or hedge positive affirmations with qualified Victorian bets of modified prudery. Too many have learned to celebrate the wondrous gift of our created being to want to go back on the discovery.

NOTES

1. I have complained of a related confusion elsewhere. See the discussion in particular of Christopher Lasch's work in Beverly Wildung Harrison, *Making the Connections* (Beacon Press, 1985), 293, n. 7.

2. Ibid., 274, nn. 24–27; 284, n. 4; and 293, n. 5. For a telling critique of empiricist social science, see Liam Hudson, *The Cult of the Fact* (New York: Harper & Row, 1972).

3. "Unexceptional action guides" are, in contemporary moral philosophic parlance, rules or principles that do not admit of conditions or exceptions. Most moral philosophers and Christian ethicists believe that we should treat rules and principles as if they create a presumption for or against acts such that we need to marshal serious reasons if they are not to be honored. Nevertheless, Christian sexual ethics continues to be discussed as if unexceptional rules exist. . . . See Gerard Fourez, *Liberation Ethics* (Philadelphia: Temple University Press, 1982), particularly parts 1 and 2. I share Fourez's assumption that such rigid rules reflect taboo structures and that these are maintained often by the ideology of dominant groups to serve their interests. See also John Lewis, *Marxism and the Open Mind* (Trenton, N.J.: Rutgers University Press, 1957), 211–12.

4. References valuable in discussing sex roles are found throughout the notes of this book, *Making the Connections,* especially those for essays 1, 3, and 7. See also Peter Gabriel Filene, *Him/Her Self: Sex Roles in Modern America* (New York: Harcourt Brace Jovanovich, 1974). Also Helen S. Astin, Allison Parelman, and Anne Fischer, *Sex Roles: A Research Bibliography* (Washington, D.C.: Center for Human Services, 1975).

5. Robin Ruth Linden, Darlene R. Pagano, Diana E. H. Russell, and Susan Leigh Star, eds., *Against Sadomasochism: A Radical Feminist Analysis* (East Palo Alto, Calif.: Frog in the Well, 1982); also Pamela Kearon and Barbara Mehrhof, "Rape: An Act of Terror," in *Radical Feminism,* ed. A. Koedt, E. Levine, and A. Rapone (New York:

Quadrangle, 1973); Maria Roy, ed., *Battered Women: A Psychosociological Study of Domestic Violence* (New York: Van Nostrand Reinhold, 1977); and Carol Vance, ed., *Pleasure and Danger: Exploring Female Sexuality* (Boston: Routledge & Kegan Paul, 1985).

6. Bonnie Mass, *Population Target* (Toronto: Toronto Women's Press and Latin American Working Group, n.d.); Dr. Helen Rodriguez, "The Social Politics of Technology," *Women's Rights Law Reporter 7,* no. 5 (1983). Also see Beverly Wildung Harrison, *Our Right to Choose: Toward a New Ethic of Abortion* (Boston: Beacon Press, 1983), 272, n. 20; 273, n. 29.

7. Andrea Dworkin, *Woman Hating* (New York: E. P. Dutton, 1974), 22–24.

8. Mary Breasted, *Oh—Sex Education* (New York: New American Library, 1971).

19
*Appropriate
Vulnerability*

KAREN LEBACQZ

All of us spend our first years single. Most of us spend our last years single. As adults, many of us are single by circumstance or by deliberate choice. Given these simple facts, it is surprising how little attention and how precious little support the churches have given to singleness (except for the monastic tradition, with its very particular demands and charisms). The scriptural witness on singleness is virtually ignored, despite the fact that Jesus never married and Paul preferred singleness. Throughout history, churches have simply assumed that marriage is the norm for Christians.

Single sexuality, when it is discussed at all, falls under the category of "premarital sex." Churches clearly expect that those who are single will get married and that those who have been married and are now single through divorce or widowhood will simply disappear into the closet until they marry again. The slogan recently adopted by the United Methodist Church might stand as a summary of the traditional Christian view of sexuality: "celibacy in singleness, fidelity in marriage."

A new ethic for single sexuality is needed, for the tradition that requires celibacy in singleness is not adequate. This situation does not mean that anything goes or that the church has nothing to offer by way of a positive ethic for single people. The task is to thread our way between two views of sexuality: the "old testament" or "thou shalt not" approach exemplified by much of church tradition, and the "new testament" or "thou shalt" approach evident in much of our current culture.

The "old testament" or legalistic approach to single sexuality is well summed up in a delightful limerick by Joseph Fletcher:

There was a young lady named Wilde
Who kept herself quite undefiled

by thinking of Jesus
and social diseases
And the fear of having a child.[1]

The "thou shalt not" ethic was characterized by fear—fear of pregnancy and venereal disease—and by a series of "don'ts": don't have sex, don't take pleasure in it (at least, not if you are a woman) and don't talk about it. As the limerick suggests, sexual involvement was regarded as "defiling." "Bad girls" and "good girls" were defined according to their willingness to be sexual or not. There was no discussion of the sexuality of divorced or widowed men and women, and gay men and lesbian women simply stayed in the closet.

With the advent of the so-called "sexual revolution" and the birth-control pill, fear of pregnancy was gone. After the "thou shalt not" of Christian tradition, we encountered the "thou shalt" of contemporary culture. Here, "love" was all that counted. Women were "liberated" and virginity was redefined as "bad." Now people talked about sex all the time, with everyone. Far from being defiling, sexual involvement was regarded as mandatory. Sex was supposed to be pleasurable, and "how-to" manuals abounded. Finally, everyone knew how—but had forgotten why. In short, fear was replaced by pressure— pressure to engage in sex, to do it right, to enjoy it, and to let the world know how much and how well you were doing it.

The result is a clash often internalized into a "Catch 22." In the wonderfully perceptive comic strip *Cathy*, Cathy Guisewite captures the confusion of many. As the almost-but-not-quite-liberated Cathy is getting dressed to go out on a date, she reflects: "I'm wearing the 'heirloom lace' of my grandmother's generation . . . with the conscience of my mother's generation . . . coping with the morals of my generation. . . . No matter what I do tonight, I'm going to offend myself."

Neither the legalistic approach of earlier Christian morality nor the permissive approach of contemporary culture provides a satisfactory sexual ethic for singles. And without a good sexual ethic for singles, there cannot be a good sexual ethic for couples either.

Can we construct a positive, Christian sexual ethic for single people? I think so. Let us begin with Christian tradition, which affirms that sex is a gift from God. It is to be used within the boundaries of God's purposes. As part of God's creation, sex is good. Like all of creation, however, it is tainted by the fall, and therefore becomes distorted by human history. It needs redemption. Such redemption is achieved by using sexuality in accordance with God's purpose and through God's grace.

The two redeeming purposes of sexuality have always been understood as procreation and union. With these purposes in mind, Christian tradition maintained that marriage was the proper context for sex, since it was the proper context for raising children and for achieving a true union. Catholics have tended to stress procreation as the primary purpose while Protestants have stressed union, but both agree on the fundamental purposes of sexual expression.

This tradition has had enormous practical implications for singles. The tradition condemns all genital sexual expression outside of marriage on the assumption that it violates the procreative and unitive purposes of sexuality. Nongenital sexual expression is also suspect, because it is thought to lead inexorably to genital expression. Given such a view of sexuality, it is difficult for single people to claim their sexuality or to develop a positive ethic for that sexuality.

Standards within both Catholic and Protestant traditions have recently loosened, but there has been no fundamental challenge to this basic paradigm. Today, some Catholics and most Protestants accept "preceremonial" sex between responsible and committed adults.[2] Both traditions have moved toward affirming union as primary, while still upholding the importance of procreation. The meaning of the two fundamental purposes has been expanded by replacing the term "procreative" with "creative" and the term "unitive" with "integrative."[3] Thus, there is some acceptance of nonmarital sexual expression, provided it is in the context of deep interpersonal commitment.

But however important such revisions may be, they do not really accept sexuality outside marriage. Single sexuality is still difficult to claim. Neither Catholic nor Protestant tradition provides a totally satisfactory explanation of why sexuality should be fully expressed only in marriage or in a "preceremonial" relationship that will eventuate in marriage. Both traditions still uphold marriage as the ideal, but give no satisfactory reasons for that ideal.

I accept part of the *method* that has led to the traditional interpretation, but wish to offer an additional insight into the nature of sexuality that might provide a fuller appreciation of the ethical context in which sexuality is expressed. I agree with the traditional understanding that sex is a gift from God to be used within the confines of God's purposes. However, I would add to the traditional purposes of union and procreation another God-given purpose of sexuality that I believe opens up a different understanding of human sexuality and of a sexual ethic for singles (as well as couples).

Sexuality has to do with vulnerability. Eros, the desire for another, the passion that accompanies the wish for sexual expression, makes one vulnerable. It creates possibilities for great joy but also for great suffering. To desire another, to feel passion, is to be vulnerable, capable of being wounded.

There is evidence in Scripture for this view of sexuality. Consider the Song of Songs (the "holy of holies"), which displays in glowing detail the immense passion and vulnerability of lovers. This is not married or "preceremonial" sexuality, nor are children the justification for the sexual encounter. It is passion pure and simple. And it is graphic sex. The Stoic fear of passion is not biblical. From the Song of Songs we can recover the importance of sexual desire as part of God's creation.

It is equally important to recover the creation stories in Genesis, which are often the grounds for our interpretation of what God intends human sexuality to be. It is from these stories that we take the phrase "be fruitful and multiply" and turn it into a mandate for procreation. It is from these stories that we hear the deep call for union between sexual partners: "This at last is bone of my bones and flesh of my flesh . . . and the two shall become one flesh."

Without denying the importance of these phrases and their traditional interpretation, I would stress another passage—one that has been ignored but is crucial for completing the picture. The very last line in the creation story in Genesis 2 reads: "And the man and his wife were both naked, and they felt no shame" (Gen. 2:25). In ancient Hebrew, "nakedness" was a metaphor for vulnerability, and "feeling no shame" was a metaphor for appropriateness.[4] We can therefore retranslate the passage as follows: "And the man and his wife experienced appropriate vulnerability." As the summation and closure of the creation story, the verse tells us that the net result of sexual encounter—the purpose of the creation of man and woman as sexual beings who unite with one another to form "one flesh"—is that there be appropriate vulnerability.

Vulnerability may be the precondition for both union and procreation: without a willingness to be vulnerable, to be exposed, to be wounded, there can be no union. To be "known," as Scripture so often describes the sexual encounter, is to be vulnerable, exposed, open.

Sexuality is therefore a form of vulnerability and is to be valued as such. Sex, eros, passion are antidotes to the human sin of wanting to be in control or to have power over another. "Appropriate vulnerability" may describe the basic intention for human life—which may be experienced in part through the gift of sexuality.

If this is so, then a new approach to sexual ethics follows. If humans are intended to have appropriate vulnerability, then the desire to have power or control over another is a hardening of the heart against vulnerability. When Adam and Eve chose power, they lost their appropriate vulnerability and were set against each other in their sexuality. Loss of vulnerability is paradigmatic of the fall. Jesus shows us the way to redemption by choosing not power but vulnerability and relationship.

The implications for a sexual ethic are profound. Any exercise of sexuality that violates appropriate vulnerability is wrong. This includes violations of the partner's vulnerability and violations of one's own vulnerability. Rape is wrong not only because it violates the vulnerability of the one raped, but also because the rapist guards his own power and refuses to be vulnerable.

Similarly, seduction is wrong, for the seducer guards her or his own vulnerability and uses sex as a weapon to gain power over another. Any sexual encounter that hurts another, so that she or he either guards against vulnerability in the future or is unduly vulnerable in the future, violates the "appropriate vulnerability" which is part of the true meaning and purpose of our God-given sexuality. Prostitution and promiscuity are also generally wrong. In each there tends to be either a shutting down of eros or a form of masochism in which the vulnerability is not equal and therefore not appropriate. Sex is not "just for fun," for play, for physical release, for showing off or for any of the host of other human expressions that are often attached to sexuality. It is for the appropriate expression of vulnerability, and to the extent that that expression is missing, the sexual expression is not proper.

Nothing in what has been said so far suggests that the only appropriate expressions of vulnerability are in marriage. Premarital and postmarital sexuality might express appropriate vulnerability. Gay and lesbian unions, long condemned by the church because of their failure to be procreative, might also express appropriate vulnerability. At the same time, some sexual expressions within marriage might not be an appropriate expression of vulnerability—for example, spousal rape or unloving sexual encounter. We must beware of the deceptions through which we reduce or deny vulnerability in sexuality—both the "swinging singles" image and notions of sexual "duty" in marriage deny appropriate vulnerability.

But what about singleness specifically? Is there any need for a special sexual ethic for single people? Precisely because sexuality involves vulnerability it needs protective structures. A few years ago, the United Church of Christ proposed a "principle of proportionality" for single sexuality. According to this principle, the level of sexual expression should be commensurate with the level of commitment in the relationship. While I have some problems with this principle, it does have the merit of suggesting that the vulnerability involved in sexual encounter requires protection. The more sexual involvement there is to be, the more there needs to be a context that protects and safeguards that vulnerability. As Stanley Hauerwas puts it, "Genuine love is so capable of destruction that we need a structure to sustain us."[5]

Traditionally, monogamous marriage has been understood to provide that needed context. Whatever the pitfalls and failures of marriage in practice, certainly in theory the commitment of a stable and monogamous marriage provides a supportive context for vulnerable expressions of the self. Marriage at its best ensures that the vulnerability of sexuality is private and that our failures remain protected in a mutually vulnerable and committed relationship.

Singleness carries no such protections. It is an unsafe environment for the expression of vulnerability. No covenant of fidelity ensures that my vulnerability will not lead to my being hurt, foolish, exposed, wounded. In short, in singleness the vulnerability that naturally accompanies sexuality is also coupled with a vulnerability of context. Thus, singleness is a politically more explosive arena for the expression of vulnerability in sex because it lacks the protections of marriage. It heightens vulnerability.

An adequate sexual ethic for singles must therefore attend to what is needed for appropriate vulnerability in sexuality. Attention must be paid to the structural elements in the particular situation that heighten or protect vulnerability. For example, a sexual ethic for singles might take one form for those who are very young and another for those who are older. The protections of age and experience may make it sensible to permit sexual encounter for those who are older and single, while restricting it for the very young. Unequal vulnerability is not appropriate. Therefore, in a culture where men tend to have more power than women and women are more vulnerable to men great care will be needed to provide an adequate context for the expression of sexuality.

We need a theology of vulnerability. Until such a theology is forthcoming we can only struggle toward a proper sexual ethic. Single people will have to explore their own vulnerability to find its appropriate expression in sexuality. Neither the "thou shalt not" of traditional prohibitions nor the "thou shalt" of contemporary culture provides an adequate sexual ethic for singles. "Celibacy in singleness" is not the answer. An appreciation of the link between sexuality and vulnerability is the precondition for an adequate sexual ethic.

NOTES

1. Joseph Fletcher, *Moral Responsibility: Situation Ethics at Work* (Philadelphia: Westminster, Press, 1967), 88.

2. Paul Ramsey argues that this is marriage in the moral sense. See his "On Taking Sexual Responsibility Seriously," in *Social Ethics,* ed. Gibson Winter (New York: Harper & Row, 1968), 45ff.

3. See Catholic Theological Society of America, *Human Sexuality: New Directions in American Catholic Thought* (New York: Paulist Press, 1977), 86.

4. On this topic I am indebted to the work of Stephen Breck Reid of Pacific School of Religion.

5. Stanley Hauerwas, *A Community of Character: Toward a Constructive Christian Social Ethic* (Notre Dame, Ind.: University of Notre Dame Press, 1981), 181.

20

Sex before Marriage

MONICA FURLONG

I think it was John Wilson who pointed out that the English language has no word which comes, as it were, between promiscuous and chaste. If you are not promiscuous then you are chaste, and if you are not chaste you are promiscuous—an odd quirk of language which owes more to the rather wistful Christian sexual ideal than to the reality of life as most of us observe it around us.

For, even if we take the line that many Christians do that marriage is a form of chastity (a little oddly, I always think—my dictionary defines chaste as "virgin" and "abstaining from intercourse"), it can scarcely be accurate to describe as promiscuous, i.e., indiscriminate, someone who has three or four deeply-loved partners in the course of a lifetime, whether married to them or not.

This gap in our language, and therefore in our thinking, is being brought home to us in an acute form by our young people, and more particularly by the student generation—that is, those who have to wait longest for marriage. When I was that age only the most daring young people, at least in my circle, slept openly together; a girl was told that she must "keep herself for marriage" and that her husband "wouldn't respect her" if she was no longer a virgin—a fairly powerful disincentive.

It was partly to do with religion (I remember a clergyman telling me when I was about twenty that the choice before me was either marriage or life-long chastity, which made me feel I must get a husband at all costs), but also to do with social convention. Thus my parents, who had no particular religion, would have been just as horrified as the clergyman if I had broken the convention.

The world has changed a great deal in the intervening twenty years, and in nothing has it changed faster than in the refusal of young people to accept the taboo on premarital sex. I have a number of young student friends; and, as soon as they know me well enough, they begin to tell me of the boy or girl they live with and boys and girls their friends live with. You couldn't call it promiscuity and you couldn't call it chastity—more a recognition that it is pleasant and natural to make love within an ongoing relationship, but that poverty and extreme youth are not a basis for a life-long union.

It is not easy for traditional Christians to know what to make of these semi-permanent liaisons, so firmly have we believed that the only positive alternatives open to a Christian believer were those which I was offered in youth. Yet I see in many of these young people a real devotion to their partner, and a real healing of the wounds and self-doubts of adolescence that probably could take place in no other way. I also see that these partners are not necessarily the ones who will be right for them at twenty-five, still less at forty-five.

Such liaisons carry a lot of joy and pain, and joy and pain lead to growth. Looking at them, I cannot feel that my own inhibited youth, with the ever-present need to "take care," was a better introduction to life and love than theirs. Yes, I do know that some of these liaisons lead to tragedy of one kind and another, but there were tragedies in my youth too—tragedies of extreme inhibition, of couples who married "just for sex," and of "shotgun" marriages.

But what, in the face of these empirical observations, can I say of the long and rigid Christian tradition of absolute premarital chastity? First, that it expressed a real and precious insight that sexual desire can be destructive, that *real* promiscuity encourage a split between love and desire that erodes relationship.

Second, that it expressed an ambivalence about women. On the one hand it protected them from the ravages of male desire at a time when no reliable contraceptives were available to them. On the other hand it viewed them not so much as persons as property to be handed over intact from father to husband (the sub-plot of *Much Ado about Nothing* reveals this in a peculiarly chilling form), with relationship seen only as a lucky incidental.

Third—and from our point of view much the most important, since this is where we have to start thinking and questioning—it ignored the positive value of sexuality, grudgingly allowing it as a practical necessity within marriage for the "procreation" of children but implying that in an ideal world everyone would live like a monk.

It is this latter Muggeridgean view that some of us feel a need to reject both in our own lives and, so far as we can influence them, in the lives of others. That sex can be healing and joyful (sometimes outside marriage as well as in it), that it can lead to personal growth, that it is a way of knowing God, above all that it is *good,* still takes a certain nerve to say in Christian circles; and I have no doubt that I shall undergo the usual penalties for saying it.

But the repressive and sex-hating voices still seem to dominate our discussion of sexual morals, and it seems important that other voices should speak up. For it is, I have come to believe, by knowing the wonderful goodness of sexuality and by valuing it as we value all good things, that we can work best against those who try to make it trivial or impersonal. If we despise the body and its delights, we open the way to the cynical exploiters.

21

Sex within Marriage

JACK DOMINIAN

It has been argued that coitus is not appropriate during the decade of separation from parents, concluding in the early twenties, when a final choice is made of establishing a permanent relationship called marriage, within which children are born and reared and the spouses grow and develop over a possible span of over fifty years of life. Within the context of marriage, that is, in an established relationship, the value of coitus is to be found in its ability to maintain the relationship.

Before examining the capacities of coitus to maintain a bond, a brief reference has to be made to the permanent relationship we call marriage. Marriage and the family are institutions with ubiquitous presence proclaiming something basic about human nature. Sociologists will claim that the family is necessary for the birth and raising of the next generation and the mutual support of the spouses. Psychologists would argue that in fact human beings are programmed to form relationships based on attachment and that marriage is the adult equivalent of the childhood bonds between child and parent.

This is not the place to discuss in detail why marriage and the family are such basic ingredients of humanity, but it is important to note that alternatives have always been suggested. While everyone agrees that couples are needed to have children, it has been postulated that children can be raised by the state, thus eliminating the need for the family. Such alternatives have never found favour and even the kibbutz accepts an increasing involvement of parents in the care of their children.

Thus having and raising a family is one of the basic reasons for marriage; but not the sole reason. The human propensity for attachment means that a close relationship is the norm for optimum realisation of human potential. Once again it would need a whole book to consider in detail why human beings need intimacy and exclusivity to thrive. But here it is sufficient to note that since time immemorial marriage and the family have provided the conditions for the continuity of the race. In the West today the duration of marriage has increased considerably, placing a great strain on the permanency of the relationship. Considerable advances in medicine have made pregnancy reliable and predictable and have meant that women do not have to spend a major part of their life in procreation. An increasing understanding of the dignity of life has shifted emphasis from numbers of children to the quality of their lives and the size of the family has been gradually reduced. In addition the advent of widespread and effective contraception has made conception a deliberate and planned activity, allowing the desired family size to be achieved with the minimum of sexual activity, leaving the major part of sexual intercourse free from procreation. This liberation of coitus from its procreative intent is also realised by Roman Catholics who use the infertile period method. Thus for the whole of Western society, and increasingly for the rest of humanity, a point has been reached when the overwhelming majority of sexual intercourse is knowingly, consciously and deliberately non-procreative. This transformation is a basic challenge to a world that has linked coitus with procreation ever since the dawn of time. For me this is one of the most basic questions of our age. If the main reason for sexual intercourse is not procreation then what is its meaning? Has it got any value other than providing sexual pleasure? One of my greatest concerns is that this question has been largely ignored by society and by Christianity.

The absence of a coherent answer as to the non-procreative value of sexual intercourse has been the single most important reason for the ascendancy of hedonism and the indifference shown to the Christian teaching of chastity. Men and women know intuitively that coitus has other values and have looked in vain to Christianity for a lead. I consider the answer to this question to be fundamental for society and Christianity and, as far as my own Roman Catholic Church is concerned, far more important than whether every sexual act should be open to life, the argument which has preoccupied the Catholic Church for the last twenty years.

In this chapter I offer an outline of the answer to the meaning of coitus beyond its procreative potential. I do not imply that my suggestions are exhaustive but they do point to an inner world of richness reinforcing the widespread conviction that sex offers far more than pleasure and procreation, and recalling far more fundamental reasons for the pursuit of chastity, which for me is the attempt to safeguard all the potential characteristics of sexual intercourse.

ATTACHMENT

Medieval moralists in particular, following a long tradition of comparing human to animal behaviour, saw fertility as the common link. Even within this line of thought the view is fundamentally wrong. The prime purpose of sexuality, so clear in humanity, is to form pairing: the formation and maintenance of attachment which then allows for procreation. Without attachment there would be no marriage, which precedes procreation. So in searching for the fundamental meaning of sexual attraction we find it in the facilitation of human bonds between men and women, and thereafter in their maintenance through sexual intercourse. It can be argued that human bonds are found not only through sexual attraction but through sibship and friendship. That is perfectly true; but looking at the overall human situation one cannot help reaching the conclusion that the fundamental unit of society is the man-woman relationship of marriage and the family, from which spring the wider possibilities of attachment. Sexual attraction and intercourse have as their principal meaning then the unity of the sexes. The search for the fundamental value of coitus has to be directed at its capacity to maintain the man-woman relationship. How does it do this?

BODY LANGUAGE

Sexual intercourse is an intimate encounter of bodies in which the genitalia play a pertinent part but at the same time the act involves whole persons. When persons meet in such intimacy they give messages to each other. Sexual intercourse is a specific act which occurs within the context of a continuous relationship. It is not just a meeting of genitalia but of persons with a past and a future. The whole experience, with its accompanying intense pleasure, becomes a body language in which the sexual components become the means of reaching and addressing each other. The language is rich and the challenge is to decode its messages. What are husbands and wives saying to each other?

FEELINGS

The first point is that a couple make love against a background of feelings about themselves and each other. The first feeling is that of sexual arousal. Here men are more often sexually aroused when they approach their wives than their spouse who often needs tenderness, affection and sexual stimulation to become as ready as their husband. Such mutual arousal needs awareness, discipline and sustained gentle effort to bring each other to a high pitch of sexual readiness for penetration. The husband, who is often more aroused, does not always remember to prepare his wife adequately for intercourse. So an element of selfishness can enter from the very beginning of the act.

The second range of feelings is the state of the spouses who may be relaxed, tense, irritable, tired, in pain or not interested in sex at all. A positive response to the overtures of their spouse may often involve overcoming a whole range of feelings which are opposed to having sex. Here effort, sacrifice and love come into operation as a man or woman shifts from inhibition to sexual assent.

Thirdly the couple have feelings for each other. This is particularly true of the wife, for whom the desirability of sexual intercourse is often placed in the context of the quality of the prevailing relationship, and in particular what has transpired between the spouses during the preceding twenty-four hours. It is self-evident that there is an intimate connection between the feeling atmosphere in the couple's life and the consummation of sex. In this respect there is a gradual reconciliation over time between the different needs of the couple. The husband's approach to sexual intercourse is largely influenced by physical needs and the wife's by her overall feeling state, although there is a good deal of overlap between the two. In due course men have to learn to pay more attention to the wife's feelings and women to their husband's physical needs. This is a reorientation which takes place over time and is one of the several reasons that sexual intercourse naturally belongs to a continuous relationship.

PERSONAL AFFIRMATION

When a married couple agree to have sex, they are assenting to a great deal more than just to unite genitally. They are making themselves totally available, body, mind and feelings and are thus indicating an enormous degree of acceptance of each other. Human beings have a whole range of possibilities with which they indicate approval of each other. People smile, shake hands, agree about things, share, co-operate, give things to each other; but the greatest donation we have to offer is the whole of ourselves and that is precisely what happens at the moment of intercourse. Coitus demands a total surrender of ourselves to another person and has become a symbol of total availability of love to another person. There is nothing more of ourselves left to offer.

People make this extremely generous donation of themselves when they receive a signal which invites them to become the most important person in the life of another human being. When couples make love they signify to one another that they recognise, want and appreciate each other as the most important person in their life. The sensual excitation, intromission and friction leading to the orgasm are powerful physical commitments to give the maximum significance to the personal encounter. Spouses come to the end of intercourse with their whole body involved in a mutual surrender which has spelt out that they are the most significant person in each other's life. Coitus has thus the capacity for a personal affirmation of immense proportions.

It is this affirmation which is diminished in causal intercourse because the couple in these circumstances do not have such meaning for each other. They are often strangers who have no personal significance. Since coitus cannot by itself give them enough meaning, its significance is confined to its orgastic possibilities. This is the inverse of the potential meaning of the act. In reality the physical component becomes the basis for reinforcing the personal meaning of the couple.

That is not to say that such rich involvement is always present in the life of married couples. Clearly husbands and wives are in various stages of awareness of each other. What I am suggesting is that their free consent to intercourse implies a degree of mutuality which is always reinforced.

This advance in personal significance grows as the relationship deepens and then sexual intercourse becomes the means of strengthening the attachment. This personal significance is non-existent in causal relationships, as mentioned before, and develops only as the couple become more important to each other. The richest realisation of the potential for personal affirmation comes about in those circumstances when a couple have the greatest meaning for one another, which is achieved when they have decided to commit themselves fully in marriage. What comes first is the attachment: when the attachment is forged, intercourse sustains and deepens it. Thus in the presence of a loving relationship sexual intercourse becomes a symbol which signifies and achieves the unity of the couple.

RECONCILIATION

This unity of the married couple is constantly open to misunderstanding, conflict, anger and alienation. Couples argue, quarrel, feel hurt and are rejected by one another. The idyllic marriage which has no alienation is a dream that does not exist in reality. Most of the conflict between husband and wife is resolved quickly. Spouses apologise to one another and this is followed by forgiveness and reconciliation.

But sometimes the pain caused by one another is much deeper and is not easily forgiven or forgotten. At these times the couple become estranged. They are angry with each other and the first thing that suffers is their sexual relationship. If sexual intercourse was a mere physical entity it could be indulged in whatever the mood or feelings of the couple; but it is not. It is a meeting between persons with its own language. In these unresolved circumstances the language is of anger, and the desire is to punish rather than to please.

This state of tension can continue for days, weeks or even months when the couple are separated from each other by hostility. Then they decide, despite their estrangement to make love. They may agree to have intercourse out of care, concern or compassion, even if they are still hurt and feel rejected. And then a miracle takes place. After intercourse they are no longer estranged. The act, with its powerful affirmative characteristics, has the capacity to heal the rift between them. Spouses emerge from sexual intercourse affirmed and reunited, so that they are lovers once again. Thus, beyond the capacity for personal affirmation, coitus is capable of bringing about reconciliation.

SEXUAL AFFIRMATION

In the course of sexual intercourse couples caress the sexual parts of their bodies. The husband is aroused by his wife's breasts and other parts of her body and she by his physical contours. This is an exchange of sexual recognition in which the husband appreciates the feminine qualities of his wife and she in turn his male characteristics. In this way couples confirm in each other their sexual identities.

These sexual characteristics carry the credentials of each other's total identity. Their manhood and womanhood stand for their whole self, and so coitus becomes a moment of immense intensity when their personhood is recognised through their sexual features.

The importance of this mutual sexual recognition is expressed in the time, effort and money spent in personal adornment. Male theologians have tended to dismiss this preoccupation as mere vanity, particularly where it concerns women. But this universal concern is far more than vanity. It is one of the most important ways that our identity is formed.

Every time we make love and find each other's bodies stimulating and pleasurable we affirm the sexual significance of each other, and through the sexual dimension our personhood. This affirmation of the whole person becomes increasingly significant as we grow older and we lose our sexual attraction. In remaining faithful to each other we not only continue to give encouragement and meaning to the sexuality of our partner, but we go on reassuring them that we desire and need them as the most important person in our life. This continuity of acceptance contrasts with transient sex when we pick up and drop sexual partners as our fancy takes us. In the process of such rapid change, we offer recognition one moment and rejection the next. It is not surprising that in order to minimise this hurt men and women devalue the whole of sex and strip it of its personal characteristics. As a pure leisure-time activity it no longer matters with whom one has sex, because its meaning of personal and sexual affirmation has been removed.

HOPE

Continuing with the personal meaning of sexual intercourse in marriage, we come next to its characteristic of repetition. The frequency with which intercourse is desired is much more than a response to physiological sexual needs. Human beings are far more than animals and are capable of controlling mere instinctual drives.

Couples who are in love with one another want to make love frequently. Every pleasurable sexual act stimulates the desire for repetition the same night, the next day, the day or week after. Built within coitus is the wish for an extension of the joy experienced. Essential to this characteristic is the presence of hope that our partner will continue to love us and in this way accept us for further acts of intercourse. Thus, coitus plays a vital part in the continuity of our acceptance as a lovable person.

The desire for frequent sexual intercourse is not confined to marriage. It can also be the mark of promiscuity. In the case of the latter there is no expectation that we will continue to be meaningful to the same person over time. Coitus does indeed become a discharge of sexual energy, often coupled with an unrecognised inner despair of remaining continuously important to the same person. Hence the necessity for a variety of persons.

Within marriage this hope of repeated intercourse fades and disappears when we are no longer interested in our partner. There is no more convincing evidence of the personal significance of sex than the gradual disappearance of the desire to have intercourse, when the partner has ceased to have personal meaning. Then hope is replaced by indifference.

THANKSGIVING

When a couple make love they usually experience a peak of sexual joy. Each has become the channel of intense pleasure to the other. The consequences are that in the aftermath there is a desire to express thanksgiving. Such thanksgiving can be done verbally but it is more usual to translate it in the physical dimension of lying in each other's arms and enjoying the presence of the other. It is a time of pleasurable exhaustion in which gratitude is expressed by the complete and alert awareness of the source of such delight.

Against this desire to express gratitude and thanksgiving to someone well known to us, we need to contrast the encounter of strangers, who, having become the means of mutual orgasm, have no other meaning for one another. All the desire to rejoice with the partner is stifled by the distance that divides the participants of casual sex.

MARRIAGE AND THE CHURCH

By describing the characteristics of personal and sexual affirmation, reconciliation, hope and thanksgiving I have described a range of characteristics of intercourse which can only be realised to the full in a relationship which has the continuity, reliability and predictability of marriage and contrasts sharply with the transience, shallowness and inconsistencies of casual sex.

But in describing these qualities of sex I am also trying to show that, to be revealed, this inner world of richness needs marriage. And it is the revelation of the inner meaning of coitus that is singularly absent from ecclesiastical pronouncements written, ultimately in the Roman Catholic tradition, by celibates. This is not a criticism of celibacy; but it is a world far removed from that of marriage, and the insights of celibacy, however rich, rely on intellectual abstractions which have no intimate connection with the reality of married life. It is this feeling that official documents speak about married life from the outside that makes married Catholics concerned as to whether their conjugal experiences can be really grasped. That is not to say that the church is not aware of the link between sexuality and love. It is, as the following passage from *Familiaris consortio* shows:

> Consequently, sexuality, by means of which man and woman give themselves to one another through the acts which are proper and exclusive to spouses, is by no means something purely biological, but concerns the innermost being of the human person as such. It is realised in a truly human way only if it is an integral part

of the love by which a man and a woman commit themselves totally to one another until death. The total physical self-giving would be a lie if it were not the sign and growth of a total personal self-giving, in which the whole person—including the temporal dimension—is present.

The trouble with such a statement, examples of which abound in *Familiaris consortio,* is that the sentiment is right but the language is wrong. What married men and women need is an accurate description of their love, not in theoretical terms of its possibilities, but in a language and a manner which reveals and illuminates their experiences. This has to be a language which uses psychology, which is the nearest efficient tool we have of reaching the contemporary understanding of love.

In criticising the last important document from the Roman Catholic Church on the family, I am not suggesting that other churches have been more success-ful in capturing the essence of sexual intercourse. It is because the matter is so important and so urgent that I am urging a repeated return to this crucial human activity, particularly at a time when there is a need for a new moral initiative.

At the centre of sexual morality today is (as already mentioned) the critical advance from a conceptualisation which is ultimately based on biology to that which captures the mystery of love. Men and women have to be persuaded that intercourse confined to marriage really realises the richest potential of its possibility. That means that we have to unravel its deepest personal significance, which requires us to tap the experiences of married couples and invite them to offer the fruits of their understanding to the whole Christian community. As far as the Roman Catholic Church is concerned this will not be realised by appointing to church institutes concerned with the family only married men and women who are compliant with the authoritarian teaching of the church. While obedience is an excellent quality, it is not the sole arbiter or guarantee of the truth.

CONTRACEPTION

It will have become abundantly clear by now that I dissent from the official teaching of the Roman Catholic Church on contraception. I do this with intense regret and with a total absence of any desire to rebel. I am well aware that some faithful Catholics, who may not be interested in the details of the argument, are extremely bothered to know how the church can possibly be wrong in such a fundamental matter, and are concerned about its credibility in its teaching on faith and morals. This concerns me as much. This is not the place to discuss the details of the church's infallibility. It is sufficient to say that the "clear theological consensus today maintains that in the area of morality the magisterium has never exercised its official teaching authority in an infallible way by means of any solemn definition issued either by a pope or by the college of bishops gathered together in an ecumenical council."[1] The ban on contraceptives belongs to the category of authentic fallible church teachings and that means that responsible dissent is a duty for those Catholics who, in conscience, believe that the church must ultimately develop its teaching further.

That the church does in fact change its pronouncements is clear for anyone to see who has studied its theology of marriage closely. Anyone familiar with this theology will know how extensive, controversial and critical were the discussions in the 1930s, 1940s and 1950s of the definitions of the ends of marriage. In 1944 the Holy Office formulated the following question:

> Can we admit the opinion of some recent writers who either deny that the primary end of marriage is the generation and bringing up of children or else teach that the secondary ends are not essentially subordinate to the primary end, but are in fact equally primary and independent? The answer given to this question is "NO."

Some twenty years later the Second Vatican Council not only abolished the usage of the terms "primary and secondary ends," but had this to say, in direct contradiction to the answer of the Holy Office:

> Hence, while not making the other purposes of matrimony of less account, the true practice of conjugal love, and the whole meaning of the family life which results from it, have this aim: that the couple be ready with stout hearts to cooperate with the love of the Creator and the Saviour, who through them will enlarge and enrich His own family day by day.

In this statement the church places the personal and procreative elements on an equal footing.

I mention all this not to indulge in any special plea which shows the church to be fallible. I rejoice in the capacity of the church to examine the truth, formulate and teach it. I also agonise when that same church finds itself in isolation from the rest of the Christian community and from the overwhelming majority of its own people. Then, far from its teaching being prophetic, it becomes a danger to its task of revealing Christ to the world. It is no secret that one of the most urgent problems facing the church in Europe today is that survey after survey show that the majority of people believe in God but have withdrawn from the institution of the church. This withdrawal is a complex phenomenon but part of the problem is the inability of the church to speak accurately to man's contemporary experience. In sexual matters the church is not trusted. The constant answer to this aloofness is that the church possesses eternal truths which cannot be adapted to the popular whims of the day. This is perfectly true, but in matters of morals its teaching is based on a combination of scripture and natural law, and the veracity of this teaching does not depend on mere repetition, however loud and authoritative, but on the humble and constant search of the meaning of the scriptures and the upholding of natural law. This requires a much greater co-operation between clergy and lay people than has been the habit in recent centuries.

The teaching of the Catholic Church on contraception is based on the conviction mentioned previously, that the sexual act has two meanings, a unitive and a procreative one, which must not be separated. In contraception there is a distortion of the "total" donation of the husband and wife to each other.

To uphold this teaching it has to be shown unequivocally that there is a clear indication that the sexual act has two meanings, the unitive and the procreative, which must never be separated. This teaching is not drawn from the scriptures, as is that of fornication and adultery. I mention this, not to disparage the contribution of natural law to human thinking and the formulation of morality, but to make the point that our understanding of natural law is constantly developing as our knowledge of human nature unfolds. It is essential to moral thinking, based on natural law, that it changes as authentic insights about human nature make changes necessary.

One of the reasons why the teaching on contraception is so important to some Catholics is because of its continuity from the earliest days of Christianity. This is not the place to go into details, but it has to be admitted that the goodness of coitus was seriously questioned in the early centuries of the church, although never repudiated. Against this hostile background procreation became a powerful and justifying element for its existence. Indeed a history of Christianity's attitude to sexual intercourse is intimately linked with the subordination of the personal loving meaning of coitus to the procreative one, which for a long time was its main justification. Thus when the church considers the subject of contraception, there is a long history in favour of the procreative potential and a relatively short and limited understanding of its unitive meaning. Since the married faithful, who are the principal agents of the meaning of coitus, have not played a crucial role in formulating the teaching, it is not surprising that their insights have not seriously contributed to it.

At its crudest, this teaching requires that every act of sexual intercourse should allow the unfettered deposition of semen in the vagina with no interference to the procreative potential of the fusion of sperm and ovum. At this level it is pure biology and must be assessed as such. Such a view is a throwback to the ignorance of sexual physiology when the sperm was considered to be the agent of fertilisation. The discovery of the essential need of the ovum is of recent origin. If we look at God's design we find that women ovulate once a month, the ovum is capable of fertilisation on average for up to twenty-four hours and so the possibility of procreation is confined to an extremely limited period in each month. There is thus overwhelming evidence that the design of nature is not one that lends itself to find a procreative and unitive meaning in each and every sexual act.

A little more sophisticated argument indicates that procreation ultimately has nothing to do with the intricacies of biology, but with the human intention of bringing new life into being and loving it. Life is precious, not because it follows the rules of biology, but because of the richness of love. Furthermore the human propensity to create covers the whole period of fertility of the woman; there is not one iota of evidence which demands blind adherence to physiology in every act of coitus. Couples decide to have children when they are in the best position to look after them and love them. There is no rhyme or reason why they should not control their fertility in the best possible way to facilitate their family formation.

So far I have suggested that there is no evidence of any design in nature that demands that every sexual act should be open to life and no reason why the available fertility should not be controlled. But the protagonists of the teaching would proclaim that I am missing the point. The teaching is based on personal donation. Those who use contraception reduce their "total" self-giving by suppressing the biological dimension. They are saying to each other that they are closed to a powerful dimension of their being. And even if they mutually agree to this, they have no right to do so because they remove a God-given potential.

My answer is that it is nowhere clear, as mentioned above, that the procreative potential has to be interpreted in every sexual act as against the fertility of the whole duration of marriage. The use of the infertile period closes the whole range of fertility of the couple. But the argument goes on that the use of the infertile period does not withhold the procreative potential, it chooses the natural periods of infertility. What it does, however, is far more serious, namely to withhold the persons of the spouses from each other.

Returning to the issue of personal donation of the spouses, the teaching on contraception argues that the frustration of the possible union between sperm and ovum is a vital distortion of the act: but this is a claim that is not recognised by every couple. Spouses know that their married love lies in the integrity of their relationship and this authenticity is to be found in their love. This love is directed first and foremost to the maintenance of their bond, that is, in the unity dimension of their relationship. If any one characteristic is appreciated as essential, it is the availability, in every act of intercourse, of the capacity to reinforce their bond. Men and women experience intercourse as a personal encounter of love in which the human characteristics, not the biological, are the supreme values. What matters to them primarily is the wellbeing of their spouse, not their fertility. Provided they are capable of having children, their mutual fertility is of no consequence to them. Indeed given that they are fertile and have had their children, the continuing presence of fertility is of little value except, after the possible death of one spouse, its use in another relationship.

This order of values between the procreative and the unitive is not appreciated by the teaching, which places them on an essentially equal basis. This is not how couples experience intercourse. For them, what is inherently needed in every act is the unitive potential described in this book as personal and sexual affirmation, reconciliation, hope, trust and thanksgiving. The creative potential has a strictly limited application. Proponents of the teaching insist that the removal of this possibility will have dire personal and psychological consequences and point to the use of contraception before and outside marriage. My reply is that what is being discussed is contraception within marriage. In any case, sexual intercourse before and outside marriage has always been a temptation even before the advent of modern contraception. The other point made is that the non-availability of procreation has some dire psychological consequences. The suggestions for potential damage are numerous and varied but there is no convincing evidence for any. In particular, the one that is offered on behalf of marital breakdown, namely, that those who divorce are more prone to use contraceptives, is a reason that has no serious social or psychological support. It is suggested above all that contraceptive intercourse dehumanises the couple because it removes the procreative potential. This is a theoretical supposition that has no evidence to support it. One has to remind the protagonists of these dangers that contraception has been around for a long time and, if discernible dangers to couples and society clearly existed, there would be irrefutable evidence, as there is in the case of marital breakdown.

In my writings I have suggested that, while I cannot follow the strict teaching on contraception, I can see that some contraceptives deter from the integrity of the sexual act, as for example in the case of the condom.

Finally the point is made that the use of the infertile period is a time of mutual sacrifice which is beneficial to the couple. The answer here is that married couples exercise a great deal of self-control at times of illness and non-availability for a variety of reasons. In my view the richness of coitus is such that there have to be excellent reasons for limiting its use.

For these and many other reasons I cannot in conscience follow this particular teaching, and in this respect, I have urged the church to reconsider it. The simplest way to do that is to ask the hierarchies of the world to test the opinion of their flock. This is one teaching that has been given but not received and, if authentic teaching has any meaning, it must express the life of the community of the faithful. The magisterium without the people of God is incomplete. While its teaching can never be based on popular consent, what it teaches must reflect the truth of the behaviour it describes. This truth cannot be based on theoretical abstracts but must be verified by human experience. In sexual matters it should reflect the wisdom of the married who are in a very much better position to test its accuracy. While I do not subscribe to the view that celibates are not capable of evaluating married truths, I am deeply concerned when the formulation of sexual ethics ignores the persistent and clear voice of the married. Is it likely that the grace of God, the discernment of the Holy Spirit, has deserted in substantial numbers the married whose sacrament makes them the most accurate interpreters of the meaning of sexual love?

One final point. The teaching on contraception, based on natural law, is meant to be clearly self-evident. Men and women abide by the rules. Why has so much of humanity become blind over contraception? Is it likely that, in this instance alone, there is widespread hardness of heart or clouding of the intellect? When so many of its own children and so much of the rest of the world are dissenting, is it surprising that there is such a large-scale ignoring of this teaching and would it not be more appropriate to think afresh? After all, no harm will be done to take the faithful into its confidence and ultimately express a view that reflects the whole Christian community. There is no point in describing the church as a *koinonia* and then to treat is as if it did not exist.

NOTE

1. Vincent J. Genovese, S. J., *In Pursuit of Love: Catholic Morality and Human Sexuality,* Theology and Life Series, vol. 18 (Wilmington, Del.: Michael Glazier, 1987).

22

Celibate Passion

JANIE GUSTAFSON

Sadly enough, both celibacy and passion have been badly misunderstood for centuries. Their meanings have been obscured and tainted by moral nuances, and have been, for the most part, obliterated with antiseptic, inhuman definitions. Although traditional Christian moralists have upheld celibacy as a virtue, they have certainly not presented it as very appealing. I often find their definitions of celibacy negative and empty. This celibacy seems to be merely the unripe virginal state, the incomplete situation of being unmarried and unloved. It is a sober, somber, bloodless virtue which represses or denies my basic sexuality. At the same time, however, attracted as I am to the enriching vitality of passion, I often find myself inhibited by passion's traditional definition of being mortally sinful: concupiscence, lust, libido. This passion is irrational and animal; it somehow pertains to my weaker, "lower" self.

Although I am still trying to understand the place of celibacy and passion in my own life, I know that I value them both highly and I do not think they can be strictly opposed to one another. My celibacy has got to be passionate, and my passion, my desire for union with another, must have its celibate dimensions. Passion, as I experience it, is not something I consider dark or evil. It is a push, a drive from within, an energy which moves me into relationship with others. It is an intense thirst for intimacy, a yearning for real living, which at the same time affirms and accepts me as separate and individual. It is a passion which I hope will integrate all my inner forces into a single, fierce, and all-consuming love for heaven and for earth.

Celibate passion, I believe, is in every way the passion of eros. But eros, too, has been grossly misunderstood by our culture. This is partly due to the influence of Freud, who, in his early writings, identified eros with lust or libido. Quite understandably, whenever we now hear the word *erotic* we think of *erotica,* or

277

pornography. In his later work, which has not yet been popularized, Freud makes a great distinction between the passion of libido and the passion of eros. Lust or libido is the biological drive toward coitus, a mere physical act. Eros, however, is the passion for relationship; it is the desire for goodness as much as for union and communion. Libido seeks release from physiological tension; its end point is the gratification of orgasm and its post-climactic relaxation. Eros, however, cherishes tension and seeks to sustain a homeostatic balance between relating opposites.

The man-woman relationship that is erotic but not coital could be the greatest single witness to society of the inadequacies of mere libido. This, I think, is one of the reasons why men and women who accept their innate celibacy are so desperately needed in today's world. These men and women stand apart from the common stream of humanity and face the reality of solitariness head-on. They can stand alone, in need, accepting that need, and refusing to manipulate God or another person to satisfy it. Their lives and their loves tell us that true freedom implies separation and uniqueness. True intimacy involves, first, a wholeness from within, and second, a sensitivity to the other person, with no infringement upon his or her individuality. The persons who have integrated within themselves the opposing masculine and feminine forces will discover the truth of Erich Fromm's contention that "the ability to be alone is the condition for the ability to love."[1]

A mistake many in today's society make is to substitute the coital man-woman relationship for the person-God relationship. In striving for full human maturity and individuality, some of us have mistaken the lure of libido as the passion of eros. We have erroneously believed that sexual intercourse must be the only and the inevitable conclusion of our various expressions of sexuality. Instead of relating creatively to the other, we have merely entered the impersonal mainstream of Mother Nature's drive for biological preservation of the species.

Indeed, intimacy with God can keep expressions of our intimacy with each other within appropriate limits. However, erotic intimacy is never an easy thing to achieve nor is it ever safe. As St. Teresa says, we must place ourselves unconditionally in the hands of the beloved. We must be completely open to a presence that demands death, that demands total surrender to the transforming fires of love. We must enter into a closeness that demands detachment, so that the beloved may be forever enlivened and freed to "grow maturely into the full stature of Christ" (Eph. 4:13).

Being intimate is the vocation of every person, single or married, lay or cleric. It is the most human behavior possible, and simultaneously, the most divine. At the same time, however, we fear intimacy more than anything else, and rightly so. As Irene de Castillejo points out, with intimacy there is always "the fear of being taken advantage of, and the terror of possible involvement which we had never intended."[2] Intimacy with God or with another person can become too much to bear. It is like a cosmic electricity, a totally free and universal energy that threatens to destroy us.

We desiccate passion whenever we use sex as a means to our own sexual gratification and pleasure. Where sex becomes utilitarian, eros is destroyed. As Rollo May remarks, "By anesthetizing feeling in order to perform better, by employing sex as a tool to prove prowess and identity, by using sensuality to hide sensitivity, we have emasculated sex and left it vapid and empty."[3] Furthermore, we desecrate ourselves and one another by the overuse of technology and technique. All too easily can we become psychologically and spiritually castrated, with feelings of despair and of having been used.

If I were to advocate a heightened awareness of celibate passion while maintaining a utilitarian philosophy, I would have to insist that we meet strict and rigid standards in our interpersonal relationships. No embrace, no kiss, no touch would ever be allowed, because to permit any of them would be considered a consent to the whole act to which these were preludes.[4] Such rigidity is quite different from the love Jesus lives out. His love is fully sensuous and spontaneously tactile. But it centers on whole-personed intimacy and relishes each expression of communication as an end in itself. The effects of such love are stunning. His erotic love for Magdalen irreversibly shocks her from libido. His passion arouses others from their apathy.

Erotic celibate passion involves a leisurely attitude toward another which does not seek to dominate or exploit. It necessitates a contemplative reverence for the beloved and an acceptance of each expression of intimacy for itself, with no thought of inevitable progression. So few of us today have this sense of leisure that this form of love-making may well be confined to a very small number of persons, persons, I am quite sure, who know the meaning of such love from their experience of prayer. In *Nature, Man and Woman*, Alan Watts writes of such love-making:

> Contemplative love, like contemplative meditation, . . . has no specific aim; there is nothing particular that has to be made to happen (e.g. it does not purposely aim at orgasm). . . . In a relationship which has no goal other than itself, nothing is merely preliminary. One finds out what it can mean simply to look at the other person, to touch hands, or listen to the voice. . . . The psychic counterpart of this bodily and sensuous intimacy is a similar openness of attention to each other's thoughts, a form of communion which can be as sexually "charged" as physical contact. This is the feeling that one can express one's thoughts to the other just as they are, since there is not the slightest compulsion to assume a pretended character. This is perhaps the rarest and most difficult aspect of any human relationship. . . . Yet this is quite the most important part of a deep sexual relationship and it is in some way understood even when thoughts are left unsaid. . . . To unveil the flow of thought can therefore be an even greater sexual intimacy than physical nakedness.[5]

Although the troubadours of the Middle Ages were not necessarily contemplatives, they were acquainted with the philosophy of leisure. Thus a practice of courtly erotic love developed quite separately from the tradition of procreative, orgasmic love associated with marriage. No behavior of this courtly love was regarded as "foreplay"; everything was considered in the light of a leisurely, playful expression of intimacy.

Even in the final stage, the behavior of the lover and his lady was, by most standards, curious, if not altogether improbable. For they were very likely to indulge repeatedly in protracted sessions of sex play, unclothed and in bed, without yielding to the imperious drive toward completion. . . . And scores of rhapsodists of *l'amour courtois* scorned the culmination of the sex act as false love while extolling as true love the pure kissing, touching, fondling, and naked contact of the lovers.[6]

Prolonged coital union was indeed present in these relationships, but if historians are correct on this matter, it was *coitus reservatus,* coitus without orgasm.

The purpose of medieval erotic love was not a mere physical feat, but the opening of two persons to an intimate oneness. Orgasm in not the only way, and is not even necessarily *a* way, of achieving this whole-personed communion. Herbert Richardson, in *Nun, Witch, Playmate,* points out that conversation, the honest sharing of one's heart, mind, and spirit, was considered by the courtly lovers as a greater expression of intimacy than coitus. Thus, kissing on the mouth was considered the highest form of physical affection.

Genital union is a way of uniting only bodies but kissing is a way of uniting oneself with that part of the body that is the organ of the soul. Through the mouth, not through the genitals, the true intercourse between a man and woman is created. Hence the act of kissing is the act of honoring and loving the organ through which spiritual communion is sustained.[7]

In his *Treatise on Spiritual Friendship,* the twelfth-century abbot Aelred of Rievaulx writes about three types of kisses: the bodily physical kiss, the kiss of the spirit or of Christ (the union of hearts), and the kiss of the mind (infusion of grace into the soul through God). Courtly love may not have always resulted in heightened spirituality, but it did aim at intimacy and reverence between whole persons.

I am not suggesting that all expressions of courtly erotic behavior are always appropriate and moral in a relationship between any man and any woman. However, I am suggesting that all of our love-making, regardless of who we are or what we are committed to, should be purposeless and leisurely. In an erotic relationship involving singles, vowed religious, or two people not married to each other, abstinence from intercourse can be one expression of such leisurely love. Likewise, in the erotic relationship of married persons who do not desire children, abstinence from orgasm can be a viable alternative to artificial means of contraception. The desire for communion in selfless erotic love cannot be the desire to possess or "own" another. Action which progresses to orgasm, especially in the relationships just mentioned, may abort the limitless creativity which lies in the man-woman relationship.

NOTES

1. Erich Fromm, *The Art of Loving* (New York: Harper & Row, 1962), 112.

2. Irene Claremont de Castillejo, *Knowing Woman: A Feminine Psychology* (New York: Harper & Row, 1973), 21.

3. Rollo May, *Love and Will* (New York: Dell, 1969), 64.

4. An example of this thinking may be found in the following passage: "Even the smallest degree of incomplete venereal pleasure has reference by its very nature to legitimate sexual intercourse and to that alone. . . . It is grievously sinful in the unmarried deliberately to procure or to accept even the smallest degree of true venereal pleasure; secondly, it is equally sinful to think, say, or do anything with intention of arousing even the smallest degree of this pleasure." Henry Davis, *Moral and Pastoral Theology* (London: Sheed & Ward, 1936), vol. 2, 180–82.

5. Alan Watts, *Nature, Man and Woman* (New York: Pantheon Books, 1958), 196–201, and passim.

6. Morton Hunt, *The Natural History of Love* (New York: Alfred A. Knopf, 1959), 55.

7. Herbert W. Richardson, *Nun, Witch, Playmate: The Americanization of Sex* (New York: Harper & Row, 1971), 55.

23

Persons with Disabilities

OFFICE OF THE GENERAL ASSEMBLY, PRESBYTERIAN CHURCH (U.S.A.)

Betty, afflicted with cerebral palsy, had severe body limitations. Though confined to a wheelchair and often unable to hold her head upright, she successfully completed both college and seminary and was ordained. However, until she learned about a medical school's sexual rehabilitation program, no one had ever talked to her about her sexuality. After going through the new program, Betty discovered that she was, indeed, a sexual person capable of intimacy and meaningful physical response. She described her discovery as "a profound spiritual rebirth."

Henry, born with severe disfiguration of his face and one leg, went through adolescence as a loner. Other youth shied away from his strange and frightening appearance. While he had all of the sexual feelings of other adolescents, no adults or peers ever talked to him about these things. In his pastor's office one day, Henry noticed a book on sexuality on a shelf. Too shy and ashamed to ask, yet starved for information, Henry literally broke into the church that night to get the book. It was the beginning of a new awakening for him. His process later led to a series of facial reconstruction surgeries and the beginning of a new life. And, as Henry says, much later he did return the book, with an explanation and a hope that others in similar situations would not need to feel such desperation.

Though a positive affirmation of one's own sexuality is fundamental to everyone's personhood, common social attitudes still seriously desexualize "persons with disabilities" (the general term presently preferred by most persons who have various physical and mental limitations). Upwards of 10 percent of all people and 50 percent of those over 50 years of age currently experience some form of disability, and yet their sexual concerns are seldom taken seriously. Such attitudes of neglect and prejudice are typically based on several things. One is simply ignorance of sexual needs, desires, capacities of persons with functional limitations. Another is our society's obsession with perfect bodies and with the-penis-in-the-vagina as the only valid form of sexual expression. Still another may be fear and the desire to punish. Those with disabilities remind everyone else of their own susceptibility to illness, injury, and mortality. Such reminders can beget the impulse to punish those who arose such anxiety.

The elimination of such oppressive sexual attitudes is imperative because our commitment to God's justice demands it. Sexuality involves the need to give and receive love, both emotionally and physically, a need that is universal. By convincing persons with functional impairments that they are not, cannot be, nor do they deserve to be sexual, society deprives them of many opportunities for warmth, touch, companionship, and love. But the vast majority of those with functional impairments are fully capable of rich sexual feeling and expression. The human mind and body have astonishing capacities to adjust to difficult situations, and sexual expression is no exception. When persons are desexualized through silence or rejection concerning their sexuality, their self-esteem is undercut, their sense of personal power diminished, and they are dehumanized. In such situations, they may experience loneliness, anxiety, anger, depression, and behavior problems. When these things are caused, there is an affront to God's inclusive justice.

Elimination of desexualizing attitudes and practices is also in the interests of the majority who are presently free from serious limitations. We often forget that "the able" are only temporarily so. Sooner or later, everyone will experience significant limitations in physical and/or mental capacities; hence, everyone's humanity is ultimately at stake. All of us need to encounter our common vulnerability to accident and disease. All of us benefit from facing our mortality realistically and faithfully. Our attitudes toward sexuality and disability are crucial in this.

The range of functional limitations is great, and each person with disability has his or her own special needs and possibilities. Nevertheless, we can consider three general kinds of situations: physical disability, mental disability, and serious illness.

1. PERSONS WITH
DISABLING PHYSICAL CONDITIONS
AND MOBILITY IMPAIRMENTS

a. Fred, coping with cerebral palsy all of his life and confined to a wheelchair, had reached his mid-thirties without knowing what was sexually possible for him. He finally located a woman who agreed to help him explore his sexual responses. When the appointed time came, a friend carried Fred up three flights of stairs to her apartment. That evening the woman helped Fred discover that he was capable of arousal and orgasm. Yet, he needed direct genital stimulation that he was incapable of giving himself because of limited hand control. Fred has chosen to remain single and to find his sexual outlet through masturbation, which he can now experience with an electric vibrator. He testifies that this sexual expression is enormously important for his own sense of well-being and for the self-esteem he needs to function in his work.—A personal story.

b. George, a handsome and athletic young man of nineteen, suffered a severe spinal cord injury in a motorcycle accident. After months of initial treatment in the general hospital, he was transferred to a rehabilitation facility where he remained for another year and a half. During that entire period, no one—no doctor, nurse, physical therapist, minister, or family member—ever spoke to George about his sexuality. As a result of the silence, he assumed that his sexual capacity had been permanently destroyed. Throughout those long months that assumption deepened his depression. Later George did find professional sexual rehabilitation therapy. Now happily married, he has a mission to save others with such injuries from the silence and despair that he suffered for almost two years.—A personal story.

Disabling physical conditions and mobility impairments can be relatively stable and nonprogressive—as in brain and spinal cord injuries, amputations, genital injuries, deafness, or blindness. However, such conditions may be progressive—as in cystic fibrosis, heart disease, muscular dystrophy, diabetes, multiple sclerosis, and end stage renal disease.

Any of these disabilities indeed may inhibit certain forms of sexual expression, but none of these conditions by itself makes the person nonsexual or devoid of the desire for emotional and physical intimacy. Nevertheless, persons with such conditions commonly experience sexual difficulties because of social attitudes.

It is true that people with no obvious functional limitations may encounter similar desexualizing attitudes. However, those with established disabilities are far more heavily impacted. They are often treated (sometimes from early childhood) as asexual. Significant persons in their lives, often their parents, simply deny their sexuality, assuming it is "not there." Medical professionals and clergy often treat their sexuality with silence, awkwardness, or incompetence. As a result, many with disabilities continue for years in ignorance without knowing what is sexually possible for them, internalizing negative body images. They may be paternalistically sheltered from others, thus finding few opportunities to form intimate relationships.

In all of this, self-fulfilling prophecies may result: functionally limited persons may start believing that they are in fact asexual or that they actually cannot hope ever to have a fulfilling relationship. Coupled with such attitudinal difficulties, many may frequently experience physical problems that hamper more traditional sexual expressions, including intercourse: paralyzed or uncontrolled limbs, lack of bowel or bladder control, spastic motion, appliances, genital impairments, or general mobility limitations.

What do such persons need and deserve? Just like those who are "temporarily able," they need and deserve adequate and positive sexuality education, including encouragement to form meaningful relationships. In addition, special information about sexual options and possibilities for their particular situations is crucial. Permission and encouragement to experiment with pleasurable and nonexploitive sexual expressions is important. For example, sexual aids such as vibrators can make satisfying masturbation possible for many with limited arm and hand mobility. Additionally, many parts of the body are potentially erogenous, not only those commonly associated with sexual activity. Some spinal cord injured persons and others have learned to experience intense sexual pleasure even though their genital ability has been functionally impaired. Fundamentally, persons with disabling physical conditions simply need and deserve to be treated and respected as sexual human beings by their families, their pastors, their church members, their health-care professionals, and by society.

2. PERSONS WITH LIMITED MENTAL FUNCTIONING

a. Joan is twenty-one, a regular worshiper in her family's Presbyterian congregation, and has Down's syndrome. Because previous clergy in her church discouraged it, Joan had not been baptized. Prevented by her mother from taking communion as an unbaptized person, Joan pressed the question. The current pastor invited Joan to discuss the matter with the session. The session was encouraging, yet puzzled about the baptismal form. It could not be infant baptism, obviously, but could she understand enough to make it believer's baptism? The pastor asked Joan two questions: "Do you think Jesus loves you? Do you love Jesus?" To each she responded with an enthusiastic "Yes!" After Joan's first communion, she reported to her pastor, "I did it! And I know how to love!" In the months that followed, Joan seemed to have a noticeable growth in her ability to relate well to others in the congregation.—A personal story.

b. Marie, age seventy-six, visited her husband of fifty-three years in the nursing home every afternoon. John, long confined to bed by a series of strokes, had severely limited mental responsiveness. The doctor doubted that John was aware of any interaction with his environment. Yet, both the physician and the nursing home staff cooperated with Marie's request that each day at two o'clock John's door would be shut and the couple would have complete privacy until Marie again opened the door. They knew and honored Marie's desire to undress each afternoon, to lie in bed with John, and to hold him close to her body for an hour.—A personal story.

About 3 percent of the U.S. population have IQs below 70, which is the usual definition of mental retardation. Approximately two-thirds of these are mildly limited, live in noninstitutional settings, and frequently are ill-trained and ill-taught for dealing with their sexuality. Some of the sexuality problems mentally-limited people face are similar to those with physical disabilities, while other problems are different. Yet, except for the most severely limited, the same basic human need for relational intimacy exists and with it the possibility of sexual expression.

Persons who are born with limited mental functions often face sexual difficulties simply because they have not been taught basic social skills. They have been treated either as having no sexual capacity or, if having capacity, as obligated not to express it. Thus, they have seldom been taught relationship skills, nor have they been instructed in what kinds of sexual expressions are appropriate in certain contexts. Because of this lack of instruction, many may be unaware of the need for and the methods of contraception. (Sterilization was once thought to be the solution to this problem; however, free and informed consent was usually absent, and subsequently many states forbade such sterilizations.) Their limitations, through no fault of their own, may render them less capable or incapable of adequate parenting should pregnancy occur. Lacking social skills need for self-protection, many will be more vulnerable to sexual exploitation and sexually-transmitted diseases, including AIDS.

What do persons with limited mental functioning need and deserve? First, they need and deserve understanding. Second, adequate education and training for social-sexual activity is crucial, including clear, useable directions and guidance for safe and fulfilling sexual conduct. For heterosexuals this includes training in contraceptive methods, and for everyone it means education in disease prevention, safer sex, and defense against sexual exploitation. A minority of the population may be so profoundly limited that relational intimacy is not realistic. These persons need guidance and support from their care-givers regarding masturbation, together with the privacy that makes such self-pleasuring appropriate and possible. Fundamentally, persons with mental limitations, like everyone else, need basic affirmation as sexual human beings who have the right to sexual expression and, when they are capable, to nonexploitive intimate relationships.

3. PERSONS WHO ARE SERIOUSLY ILL

a. Helen developed vaginal cancer and was treated with surgery and radiation. Her physician urged her to dilate her vagina with regular exercises to preserve her capacity for intercourse with her husband. Helen, however, had been taught from early childhood not to touch herself "down there," and had great difficulty following her doctor's advice until a frank conversation with an understanding pastor relieved her mind.—A personal story.

b. Harold, permanently on a respirator in the hospital, was increasingly uncooperative and difficult as a patient. The nurses and chaplain discovered that, though his wife visited him daily, he and Marge had had no sexual expression since the onset of his serious illness. Despite the severity of his condition, Harold still had sexual feelings and wanted his wife to perform oral sex on him. The chaplain facilitated a discussion with Marge and the medical personnel. Thereafter the staff found ways of ensuring regular privacy for Marge and Harold to express their sexual intimacy. While Harold's physical condition gradually deteriorated, his emotional condition showed marked improvement.—A personal story.

Sometime before we die, the vast majority of us will experience serious and possibly prolonged illness. Such illness—e.g., cancer, strokes, heart, liver, and kidney diseases—usually affects sexual functioning. But, the ill person remains a sexual person until death comes. If there is consciousness, usually there is also the continuing awareness of one's own body image and gender, and of one's desire and need for human touch. Indeed, these desires may actually increase when serious illness brings awareness of the fragility of life.

Like those with other disabling conditions, however, the seriously ill are often treated as if they were asexual—devoid of sexual feelings, desires, and needs. When this happens, problems usually associated with the particular illness are compounded. The person's sense of loss of bodily functions brought on by the disease is now augmented by the sense of sexual loss. Gay and lesbian patients may suffer additionally, since hospitals and care facilities frequently do not honor their partners as legitimate family members.

What do seriously ill persons need and deserve? Encouragement is needed from partners, family, pastors, friends, and medical personnel to communicate about their desires, needs, and possibilities. Often they need assistance to discover what is physically possible and medically safe for their own sexual expression. Permission and encouragement are important for them to experiment with new ways of sexual pleasuring. Appropriate nurturing touch, particularly during long-term hospitalizations, is often highly desirable and warranted. Reassessment of hospital and long-term care facility policies that restrict sexual contact between patients and their partners is long overdue, along with the affirmation of and respect for patient's own chosen partner, whether spouse or lover. In short, like all others with limiting conditions, those who are seriously ill need and deserve fundamental affirmation of their sexuality by the persons, communities, and institutions that touch their lives.

4. CONCLUSION

Persons with disabilities, no less than those who are temporarily able, are graced by God as sexual beings desiring intimacy and wholeness. Often deprived of their own eros and passion by insensitive and ill-informed attitudes of others, they deserve the church's special understanding and support as they seek to reclaim as far as is possible their own bodily integrity, self-direction, and relationships of mutuality and fidelity. Each of the stories told in this chapter is true. Each story represents thousands of others in similar situations—persons who need and who deserve the church's celebration and affirmation of their sexuality.

24

The Change
of Life

PENELOPE WASHBOURN

Mary Wollstonecraft, writing at the end of the eighteenth century, cited an "unnamed gentleman" who wondered what possible use a woman over the age of forty had on this earth.[1] This unkind speculation reflects a real problem: What possible use do I have in my later years? My youthful beauty is gone, my childbearing years are over, and my fertility disappeared with the advent of menopause. The physiological hormonal alterations of the "change of life" often coincide for the unmarried and the married alike with an identity crisis common to the middle years in men and women.[2] The physiological changes of menopause come at a time when the structure of life shifts—children grow up and move away, husbands reevaluate their masculine identity, often searching for affirmations of their worth through changes in career or through sexual escapades. The divorce rate in our society peaks for men and women in their middle years, struggling to find a new identity for the remainder of their lives.

This midlife crisis is preeminently, however, a woman's crisis. A woman's fertility *definitely ends,* whereas a man's gradually tapers off. The hormonal changes that accompany menopause *may* cause varying degrees of unpleasant physiological symptoms—the renowned hot flashes, irregular bleeding, mood changes. Medical journals refer to this phenomenon as "degeneration" of the female body structure.[3] There are changes in skin elasticity; there are changes in the bones and in the vertebrae which can eventually lead to "dowager's" hump and loss of height. Women fear the possibility of breast cancer and hysterectomies. The menopausal period is also a time of psychological danger, for female suicides are at one of their peak levels (the other is in early adulthood, 24–34 years).[4]

In our modern times it is claimed that the use of estrogen therapy can prove helpful to many women in alleviating the so-called degenerative processes and mitigating some of the unpleasant physical symptoms associated with hormonal changes. Is this all there is to it? Are we to assume with the makers of estrogen that better hormone therapy will successfully handle "the change of life"?

> Today, this upheaval in a woman's body can be avoided. The intelligent woman will not unnecessarily accept undue and rapid aging. Her physician will be able to determine when she is on the threshold of her "change of life." And it is within his power to alleviate these symptoms so that the continuance of life becomes more vital, healthier, and happier.
>
> [In response to the issue of depression, the pamphlet advises] "menstrual blues? cheer up. Gather up all those 'somedays'—someday you'll do this, someday you'll try all those wonderful things and start making them come true!"[5]

I believe that this approach to menopause, which is now being questioned as to its long-term effects, does *not* sufficiently recognize the nature of this crisis to enable a woman to come to a new form of self-understanding.

The change of life is a crisis for the married and the unmarried woman that is as significant as the onset of menstruation. It marks the end of one life and the beginning of another. Menopause is not, however, as sudden as the onset of menstruation. Over a three- or four-year period the inevitable process occurs, and one day the menses is gone. Fertility is over.

Primitive women rarely faced this last crisis of sexuality. As actuarial tables show,[6] the average life span of women has lengthened dramatically over the last one hundred years. Better medical care in childbirth, the advent of birth control, and limiting the size of families means that most women do have a life—a whole other third of their lives—*beyond* the childbearing years. In earlier times a woman did not survive beyond her fertility. There was no real role for them outside of childbearing; thus Jesus was particularly concerned about the plight of widows. In light of these circumstances, primitive societies have no "rites of passage" for the woman's loss of her fertility. Women beyond childbearing age were not even regarded as women; they were seen as men.[7] There is no folk wisdom or religious rite to interpret this most significant change in a woman's life. It is a change that *needs* symbolic interpretation, for it, above all others, presents itself initially as a death, an end, a decay, a degeneration.

The need of the modern woman to find a symbolic framework for this fundamental stage of life is acute. She needs a new basis for self-understanding outside her earlier interpretation of her sexuality. The issue facing her is whether she can find new purpose, new identity, new worth, a new self-concept, and a new sense of ultimate meaning as she passes into middle age. The crisis is more than a physiological adjustment to declining hormone levels. A woman must come to terms with herself and the meaning of life on a radical level. Perhaps the reason this crisis is so difficult and has so many aspects is that it foreshadows the end, death itself, the last crisis. The end of a woman's fertile years intimates the decline of the whole body and signifies a gradual approach toward the end of its powers in death. Menopause unmistakably marks the slowing of the whole system before we are ready for it. In midlife we are still strong; we are often healthy, and yet one element of our body's creative powers is now over and forces us to recognize our gradual movement toward death.

For this reason the crisis of menopause affects married and unmarried alike. For the never-married it can represent the loss of an unrealized potentiality—childbearing. The end of my fertility may bring regrets, for my freedom of choice concerning the use of my female procreative powers is now over. Even if I have gladly forsaken bearing children for the other values in earlier years, whatever regrets there may have been are now intensified, and I may question the rightness of past decisions. What would it have been like to bear a child? I face impending old age aware that I will have no one to care for me.

For the never-married or the once-married menopause may also signal the end of hopes for being able to find a life partner. Marriage without the possibility for childbearing, while greeted with joy in the later years, may appear an unlikely possibility for a woman facing menopause. She fears that the end of her fertility is the end of her sexual attractiveness. She fears that the hoped-for union which has eluded her or failed her in earlier years is now finally beyond her grasp. She is alone forever and will never experience her bodily capacities as a mother or find her sexuality fulfilled.

For the married woman who was never able to conceive, menopause repre-sents the end of a dream. Being unable to conceive is a deep sadness for many women. Wanting to conceive and being unable to do so leads to real regret even though children may have been adopted. The process of being able to conceive, of giving birth, is significant, not only because of the child, but because it can symbolize a woman's strength, a valuable element of her psychosomatic personal unity. For her, as for others at menopause, lingering hopes and regrets surface and must be dealt with.

For the married woman who enjoyed her sexuality as the bearer of children, menopause may also be full of regrets. There will never be any more children; her biological role of mother is now over. Menopause is a particularly deep crisis for women who have devoted themselves exclusively to mothering. The children are often grown up and leaving home as the woman wonders who she is now that her role as mother seems to be over. The demands of parenthood are over; the house is quiet, and the woman asks herself, Is there anything left? The end of her role of mother carries no accolades, no promotion, no thanks. The children are often grateful to be gone after the confrontations of the adolescent years. The woman who has found her identity exclusively in mothering faces the crisis of middle life with the least resources. She may find her physiological symptoms part of a larger crisis in which the essential elements of her very life are uprooted. She feels tricked and cheated and that her children are ungrateful. She experiences, not joy that the demands of parenthood are over, but *emptiness*. The promise given to her that she will find herself through motherhood has proven hollow. She is no longer "needed," no longer loved; she feels no productive role in society.

The mythology that suggests that motherhood is the essential role of the woman is most cruel at this point. The years that are filled with doing for others, often to the exclusion of self-interest and self-development, of striving to fulfill the ideal of the good mother, end, not with a sense of fulfillment, but in confusion, and with a lack of preparedness and inner resources to cope with the changes.[8] The paradox of a woman's attempt to live up to the traditional image of the mother or wife who gives her life for her children is that she above all has neglected her personal and spiritual development. For such women, the change of life brings the hardest challenge.

The change of life is indeed *a change* and offers a woman the possibility for a new direction and focus for interpreting her identity in relation to the meaning of life as a whole. If she feels that her life is over now that her sexual attractiveness begins to decline, she will also feel an ever-increasing sense of insecurity about her worth as an individual. Our culture emphasizes youthful female sexual attractiveness as the major criterion of female worth and thereby engenders fear and mistrust in the middle-aged woman. Compulsively reaching for cosmetics, fad diets, and youthful clothes can be a way of dealing with this anxiety. This sort of resolution is only temporary. More energy and time will continually be spent on packaging the exterior to fit the youthful self-image and hiding an ever-deepening inner sense of insecurity.

Another manner of handling the crisis of middle age, more familiar to men than to women yet common to women perhaps more in fantasy than in reality, is to have an affair. To find oneself as a woman again, to solve the crisis in sexual identity by searching for sexual fulfillment in a new love, may indeed feel like a resolution of the crisis. The rejuvenation brought about by feeling loved, not in the firm body of a young woman but in the body of a mature woman bearing the stretch marks of motherhood, can bring new feelings of self-worth. To be loved in *this body* by one who finds you attractive as you *are* and not in the memory of what you *were* can bring a new self-confidence and joy. This resolution, however, does not in fact prove lasting or finally satisfactory for negotiating a new form of self-understanding. Looking to others, whether lovers, substitute children, or a new husband, only as a means to escape the confusion of personal identity will lead to increasing bitterness and demands upon those to whom we reach out. The potential for falling into this form of demonic resolution of this major crisis is strong in our society that emphasizes youthful sexual attractiveness and/or motherhood as the exclusive definitions for female identity.

Our society also places great value on achievement. The woman, like her male counterpart, who has attempted to find herself in a career generally faces a severe midlife crisis. She realizes that she is no longer a "promising young hopeful." She feels undermined by younger women and sees the future as gradually more closed rather than infinitely open. Her creative powers seem to have settled into boredom and frustration.

How then can the contemporary woman find grace rather than destruction in the change of life? To come through the crisis with a new focus on oneself, a new sense of one's female identity, is important, not just for the woman herself, but in terms of her attitude toward others and her effect upon all her significant others.

Possessiveness, lack of trust in others, feelings of insecurity, frustration, and blame can characterize the woman from the middle of her life onward. Her friends and family attempt to withdraw from the emotional burdens she places upon them.

To discover new depths of self-understanding requires first of all a recognition of the nature of the crisis. The physiological symptoms of menopause and any effects that they have on mood may be helped by chemical means. The problem is that the woman finds it difficult to distinguish what part of the depression is caused by changes in her life situation and what part is a result of hormonal imbalance. Separating the physiological from the psychological factors is indeed impossible. As in all other life-crises there *is* a distinct physiological process at work. In some women it has marked effects; in others, almost none. In fact, women who have felt very well during pregnancy may be "estrogen sensitive"[9] and experience more depression postpartum and during menopause. To recognize the nature of the crisis in both its physiological and its emotional forms is essential for a graceful resolution. Hormonal therapy, if proved safe, may indeed ease the physical changes, but the personal issues need to be recognized in all their implications for a new life-pattern.

Something dies at menopause; the fertile female potential is over. For this there needs to be mourning as well as thankfulness. The ability to experience a new body, free from menses, free from the fears of unwanted pregnancy, depends, I believe, on acknowledging and grieving for what is no longer—the end of one stage of life. All the joys and sorrows, hopes and disappointments, connected with the experience of one's sexuality in its procreative function need expression. Acknowledging this sorrow and expressing it without guilt to oneself and to others will eventually enable new hope to emerge. The new self cannot grow until the process of mourning and grief has been completed.

There is new life and new identity beyond the change of life. This crisis, perhaps more crucial than the others since it extends over a period of years, calls us to an awareness that the process of dying may be slow and will encompass the regrets, the guilt, and the painful coming to terms with that which remained unborn, both physically and spiritually. The change of life is a reordering of the personality and of the body. For there to be a new order, the old one must be displaced. As we go through the change of life, we do not know that the new order *will* emerge. We only know that the familiar forms are slowly eroding; the body chemistry is changing. The pattern of life is changing, and the values of the old life are being challenged. This feels like death, and we have no hope that there can be anything new.

The crisis of menopause may indeed involve physiological changes. It is, however, essentially a spiritual crisis. During the change of life I am challenged to come to terms with what I have left behind, with whatever I have done or not done with my female sexuality in its procreative aspect, with whatever I have done or not done in my youth with my early vitality. Midlife is a time for mourning; it is also a time to forgive oneself and others. It is a time for reassessing one's worth as a woman, as a unique individual; it is a time for realigning and rediscovering one's ultimate value in relation to the whole.

The ability to recognize the nature of this crisis, to express the fears, confusion, regrets, and bitterness, will allow the individual woman to come into a new life as the process of mourning for the end of youth gives way to the reemergence of hope. Life comes, for out of the end of the old, something new emerges—perhaps unbidden. Risking, trusting the future, finding hope that new forms of personal self-understanding and worth will emerge are qualities that are given, *discovered*. The new identity, the new strength, the new direction that can emerge for a woman as life changes come not so much from conscious planning but from parts of the self hidden and unexpressed for many years.

The outcome of the change of life can be truly graceful if one avoids desperately hanging on to an old identity and a fixation with a single view of one's female sexuality. The new body may indeed, once achieved, offer a new hope, a new freedom of female sexual expression. Released from the anxiety and fear of pregnancy forever, many women achieve a new freedom, a deeper level of sexual expression and vitality. Sexuality returns to its autonomous nature in its nonprocreative aspect, and a woman can enjoy it in a new way. Freed from menses and her particular pattern of psychosomatic responses to the fluctuation in hormone levels, a postmenopausal woman is offered a new body relieved of any possible discomfort associated with menstruation. Her physical health may be better, and her spirit may be better as the burdens of her procreative sexual being are left behind.

Middle life represents a crisis. The old breaks up so that the new may emerge. The woman must decide whether she will trust the open future or attempt to hold on to the past. Many will break the old patterns of relationships and risk the insecurity of the future, the loneliness, and the self-doubt. Divorce, separation, and new ventures in education and careers are all characteristic of this stage. Risking the future always includes leaving, loneliness, and spiritual reckoning in which the self struggles with the agony of self-doubt. Enrichment will emerge if the risk is made; new strengths will be found, new forms of self-understanding will emerge, and new relationships will be formed.

The change of life offers a woman the possibility of coming to terms with her unique individuality outside of (though inclusive of) the procreative nature of her sexuality. She is now free to come to terms with herself. She need no longer sacrifice herself for the sake of her children or the achievement of her husband. She can give attention to her own values and worth, her own sense of creative center, and her own responsibility to the life that is within her. Freed from obligation, false achievements, making it financially, and living for others, a woman may discover that the change of life offers her the possibility of discovering herself in a new manner.[10]

Perhaps the mythological image of the Virgin Goddess is an appropriate symbol for this stage of a woman's spiritual journey. The Virgin Goddess has risked and suffered, borne children, and loved many. She is a virgin, however, because she finds her sense of spiritual wholeness within herself; she is a woman unto herself. The movement of life that propels us ever forward toward death is nevertheless not identical with physical decline but can be seen as a spiritual journey reaching to deeper levels, as the Jungian psychologists have suggested.[11] The change of life offers a woman a new opportunity to recognize her buried strengths, to realize the wholeness of her identity. New directions, new forms of creativity, new levels of self-understanding can emerge, and a woman finds freedom to *be* herself.

The change of life opens the door for a blossoming of the spirit. It may be a time for more inner activity. The preceding years busy with external activity in the "productive" phase of life, both physically and mentally, can now give way to a time of inner productivity—a psychological and spiritual growth of the total woman.[12] Irene Claremont de Castillejo writes, "If we are wise we shall notice that our concerns change too. As we advance in years the inner demands which have rightfully lain dormant during youth, claim our attention more and more."[13]

The question that must be answered by the individual is, Who am I now that my life begins its descent toward death? What am I worth now that my primary productivity is over? What does my female identity mean as I leave my youthful sexuality behind? The need to find an answer to these questions is acute; the manner in which the crisis of the change of life is handled will determine how the woman experiences herself in the gradual process of aging. If she emerges from the crisis with a new sense of self-trust, with a new belief in her creative role in the universe and in relation to others, and with a new sense of joy about the potential strength in her own maturity as a woman, she will be able to face the final crisis of life, the anticipation of death. Indeed these years postmenopause bring many trials for the woman. In our culture, given the extra longevity of women, it is most likely that she will eventually face burying her husband. During these years illness may impinge on her life; aged parents may need to be nursed and buried. These are the years when the woman will of necessity be more involved with death and the intimation of death. Where will she find strength to face the separations involved—the loss of children from the home, the loss of parents by death, the possibility of widowhood or of reaching the awareness that one will have to negotiate the post-retirement years alone? The ability to discover the strength lies in trusting oneself as an inherently worthy individual woman, letting go of the past, and embracing the future. The trust that there are always new levels of growth for the woman even as the past patterns recede and our relationships are forced to change through separation and death is an ability to trust in the movement of life itself. That is why the crisis of the change of life is spiritual.

Many women are freed by the change of life from past limiting patterns of interpretation of sexual identity. Broken marriages often result. Emerging from the crisis of the change of life enhanced and not diminished is a blessing, not merely for the woman, but for those around her. The destructive solution to the crisis may mean bitterness, regrets over the past, blaming husbands and children, a false sexual self-image in desperately striving for youth, displacing the mothering image on others in manipulation and control, feeling insecure and worthless, losing hope. Without hope there can be no life, no value, no joy.

Irene Claremont de Castillejo describes the individual psyche as a garden that we are responsible for tending to enable it to grow. It is a spiritual responsibility, not only to ourselves, but also for others.

> It is in the latter part of life that people need to turn attention inwards. They need to do so because if their garden is as it should be they can die content, feeling that they have fulfilled their task of becoming the person they were born to be. But it is also an obligation to society. What a man or woman is within affects all those around. The old who are frustrated and resentful because they have omitted to become in life the persons they should have been, cause all in their vicinity to suffer.[14]

The crisis of the change of life can therefore be a process of death and rebirth, a change from the old life into the new. There will be some suffering, and yet from that it is possible for the woman to build a new sense of female identity. The tragedy of this crisis is that the possibility for grace may never come, and many women find themselves facing the process of aging with ever-deepening despair and dread. The discovery of the hidden creative powers within is unfortunately never made, and the woman fails to enrich the lives of those she touches. To find new trust is, however, to be reborn through the change of life and is an experience of joy for the woman and those around her.

NOTES

1. Mary Wollstonecraft, *A Vindication of the Rights of Women* (New York: W. W. Norton, 1967), 36.

2. George and Nena O'Neill, *Shifting Gears* (New York: Avon, 1975). Discusses how to handle the changes that often occur in the middle years as identity is redefined.

3. See Howard J. Tatum, "Current Concepts of Hormonal Treatment of the Menopause," *Proceedings of the Third Asia and Oceania Endocrine Congress, Manila Philippines,* January 2–6, 1967.

4. Ibid., 54.

5. *The Change of Life* (Montreal: Ayerst Laboratories, Division of Ayerst, McKenna and Harison Ltd.), 7, 12.

6. Actuarial tables quoted by Howard Tatum suggest that the average life expectancy for women in 1900 was 38 years. It is now 78 years.

7. Margaret Mead, *Male and Female: A Study of the Sexes in a Changing World* (New York: Dell Publishing Co., 1949), suggests that women after menopause were treated like men in many societies; they were no longer potentially harmful to men (229, 187).

8. Simone de Beauvoir, *The Second Sex,* trans. and ed. H. M. Parshley (New York: Alfred A. Knopf, 1952), comments that though menopause frees a woman from a patriarchally imposed slavery she is immediately put into "retirement" (550).

9. "Menopause and Estrogen Therapy," a roundtable discussion in *Journal of Reproductive Medicine,* 11, no. 6, December 1973: 235.

10. See Clara Thompson's discussion of the psychological aspects of the change of life

in "Middle Age," reprinted in *Women Body & Culture,* ed. Signe Hammer (New York: Harper & Row, 1975), 223–34.

11. C. G. Jung, "The Stages of Life," *Collected Works,* 1975.

12. De Beauvoir, *The Second Sex,* noted the turn to religion common to women in their search for a new life—in illusion and fantasy (546–57).

13. Irene Claremont de Castillejo, *Knowing Woman: A Feminine Psychology* (New York: Harper & Row, 1973), 146.

14. Ibid., 161.

25

Older Adults

OFFICE OF THE GENERAL ASSEMBLY, PRESBYTERIAN CHURCH (U.S.A.)

1. TOO OLD FOR LOVE?

Americans, generally speaking, find little overtly triumphant in the late years of life. Shaped by a culture that prizes youth, vigor, and quantifiable achievement, we tend to view aging as a threatening reality, an unwelcome reminder of fragility, transience, and inevitable loss. Our profound discomfort with, and distrust of, our own embodiment and the difficult changes in ability that aging brings lead us to marginalize older adults, excluding them from centers of economic, political, and social life. Such "ageism" is particularly evident in our tendency to reserve sexual pleasure for the young and to deride the sexuality of the old. . . . At a certain age, we seem to believe persons simply become too old for sexual love.

Our collective denial of the sexual needs and capacities of older adults, while ill-founded, has powerful effects of truth. Put simply, it promotes the sexual incapacity it assumes. We begin by telling ourselves that older adults have somehow ceased to need or desire sexual intimacy. Institutions for the aging are then structured in ways that segregate women and men, affording little or no opportunity for intimate relationships to develop. Medical professionals neglect issues of concern to older adults, such as the effects of commonly prescribed medications on sexual desire and capacity, and shy away from discussing the sexual needs of their older patients. Family members discourage, directly or indirectly, expressions of sexual interest and emotional need in their widowed or divorced parents and grandparents. Such patterns result in a self-fulfilling prophecy for many older persons: "Lacking social permission to express their attraction to another person, afraid of appearing ridiculous or immature if they were to reveal their sexual needs, overwhelmed with confusing guilt feelings about sexual desires, they themselves deny their own sexuality."[1]

The problems stemming from this collective denial of the sexuality of older adults go far beyond the embarrassment and confusion of the individual. This denial has isolating and dehumanizing effects that ultimately undermine the concrete well-being of both individuals and communities. "It makes difficult, and sometimes impossible, correct diagnoses of medical and psychological problems, complicates and distorts interpersonal relations in marriage, disrupts relationships between children and parents thinking of remarriage, perverts the administration of justice to older persons accused of sex offenses, and weakens the whole self-image of the older man or woman."[2] It is, in short, an immense obstacle to social justice. In our struggle to be faithful to God and to secure sexual justice for all, we are called to confront this obstacle head on by giving special attention to the issues and concerns of older adults.

Just who are the "older adults"? The membership of this particular group is not quite as unambiguous as that of "singles" or "teens." Indeed, when we hear the phrase "older adults," our first inclination might be to ask, "Older than whom?" Any numerical figure we may set—such as 60 or 65 years of age—will undoubtedly be somewhat arbitrary. For some individuals, a sense of old age may come early in life as a result of physical and emotional misfortunes. For others, a sense of youthful vigor may continue far beyond any socially imposed definition of old age. We resist, therefore, the temptation to set a numerical figure. Furthermore, we prefer to speak of "older adults" rather than "the old" or "the elderly" precisely because we believe the phrase "older adults" conveys something of the relativity of this designation and lessens the sense of separateness and difference that underlies so many of our negative attitudes toward persons who are no longer young. As William Hulme has observed, "Old is the stigma of an ageist society."[3]

However the population of "older adults" might be defined, one thing is clear: it is getting larger all the time. Because more persons than ever before are living into their 70s and 80s and birth rates are declining, both the number of persons over 65 and its percentage of the total population have grown rapidly in recent years. These numbers will continue to increase significantly for at least the next forty years as the so-called "baby boomers" (persons born in the years 1946–1964) swell the ranks of those 65 and over.[4] Furthermore, the fastest growing age-group in the country is 85 and over. This group now accounts for 38 percent of all persons over 65, and by 2035 it will account for nearly half.

This so-called "graying" of America is even more pronounced in the churches, where trends in society as a whole are accentuated by the fact that large numbers of the generation now 30 to 45 years old have shunned church membership. This means that the percentage of church membership made up by older adults is increasing dramatically. Already in the Presbyterian Church (U.S.A.), for example, the average age is 54, and 29 percent of the total membership is over 65. Given trends in society as a whole, we can expect these numbers to increase over the next several decades.

Because of such trends, the interests and concerns of older adults command ever-increasing attention from church and government officials, employers, physicians, and others. Nevertheless, issues surrounding the sexual needs and capacities of older adults remain woefully neglected. Even the Presbyterian Church (U.S.A.) has been silent on such issues, despite the large number of older adults in its ranks.[5] We must not hesitate to break this silence now, if we are to ensure the concrete well-being of a vast segment of both church and society now and in the coming decades. As John Lindquist warns: "The unmet needs of the elderly are already a problem of monumental proportions. They are nought compared to what will exist in the early decades of the twenty-first century. Ignoring them will not make them go away. The churches and denominations of America must gird themselves today in order to begin the battle which will surely face them tomorrow."[6]

2. BEGINNING THE BATTLE FOR SEXUAL JUSTICE

Be gracious to me, O Lord, for I am in distress;
    my eye wastes away from grief,
    my soul and my body also.
For my life is spent with sorrow,
    and my years with sighing;
my strength fails because of my misery,
    and my bones waste away.
I am the scorn of all my adversaries,
    a horror to my neighbors.
an object of dread to my acquaintances;
    those who see me in the street flee from me.
I have passed out of mind like one who is dead;
I have become like a broken vessel.
                                        —Psalm 31:9–12

In the battle to establish sexual justice for older adults, our most formidable adversary is the intransigence of unexamined assumptions that lead us to deny the sexual needs and capacities of those who are no longer young. One such assumption is that the older person becomes "like a broken vessel" and is no longer physically able to function sexually. This is simply not true. Sexual capacity does decline somewhat with age, but sexual activity can and does continue into the later years of life. One well-known study of 260 men and women over the age of sixty found that "from 40 to 65 percent of the people between the ages of sixty and seventy-one were still having sexual intercourse with some frequency, and of those aged seventy-eight and older upwards of 20 percent still reported sexual activity."[7] Given the social obstacles to this activity, such figures are remarkable.

The causes of sexual inactivity in older adults are many and complex. Most research indicates, however, that physiological factors are not determinative. Except for the onset of seriously debilitating illnesses, the physiological changes that come with age do not significantly diminish sexual capacities for arousal, intercourse, and orgasm in either men or women. For those older adults with a partner, the single greatest determinant of continued sexual activity is the maintenance of sexual activity throughout the middle years of life. Put simply, those who enjoy regular sexual activity earlier in life continue to be sexually active in later years, while those who are inactive continue to be so.

While older adults in general can and do remain sexually active, there are significant differences between men and women in sexual capacity and interest over the life span. After reaching a peak of sexual responsiveness in adolescence, the sexual capacities of men decline in a gradual linear fashion. Testosterone level decreases somewhat, as does ejaculation, and erection requires more time and increased direct stimulation to achieve. Nevertheless, as the research of Masters and Johnson indicates, it is psychological factors, not physiological ones, that tend to determine the level of sexual activity and interest in older men. Of the six main reasons they identify for decreasing levels of sexual activity, five are primarily psychological: "monotony or boredom in sexual relations, preoccupation with career and money, mental and physical fatigue, over-indulgence in food and drink, and performance fears relating to these factors."[8] This last factor seems to be particularly incapacitating in that once a man experiences impotency under any circumstances, he often withdraws from sexual activity altogether in order to avoid risk of repeated failure.

The fact that decreased sexual activity among older men is often psychologically rather than physiologically induced raises important issues regarding sexual justice. It dramatizes the way in which the patriarchal beliefs and structures so widespread in our society dehumanize men as well as women. Put simply, the assumption that men are and must be active, powerful, and "in control"—an assumption internalized by most, if not all, men in our society—presents a serious obstacle to sexual satisfaction and integrity in old age, when weakness and vulnerability can no longer be denied. As a result of the inability to move beyond the equation of impotence with weakness and failure and to affirm the goodness and desirability of other, less genitally-oriented forms of sexual expression, many older men find themselves cut off from life-giving human relationships.

Unlike men, women reach a peak of sexual responsiveness in their mid-30s and tend to maintain this level throughout the rest of their lives, given regular sexual activity. Physiological factors related to endocrine imbalance may produce thinning of the vaginal walls, reduced vaginal lubrication, and painful uterine contractions during orgasm, but the potential for orgasm remains high and in some cases continues to increase well into a woman's later years. Menopause is a potentially liberating experience, and many women experience it as such, enjoying a new found freedom from the worries of pregnancy and childrearing.

Despite the physical and psychological potential for continued sexual satisfaction, however, older women tend to be less active and less interested in sex than older men. There are two main reasons for this discrepancy. First, unlike men, older women have a difficult time finding suitable partners. After age 65 there are four single women for every single man.[9] Inasmuch as older men often seek the company of younger women, many older women harbor little hope of escaping the loneliness and frustration of their situation. Second, like men but to an even greater degree, older women internalize ageist and sexist assumptions that denigrate their sexuality. As Shevy Healey has trenchantly observed, "All the adjectives that are most disrespectful in our society . . . are part of the ageist stereotyping of old women: pathetic, powerless, querulous, complaining, sick, weak, conservative, rigid, helpless, unproductive, wrinkled, asexual, ugly, and on, ad nauseam."[10] Thus, the sexist assumption that "women are only valuable when they are attractive and useful to men" combines with ageist biases to lead many older women to devalue and disregard their sexual identity. Perhaps we should see it as a hopeful sign of the power of grace and of the human spirit that older women remain as sexually vital as they do.

3. RECLAIMING EROS FOR PERSONS OF ALL AGES

What then does it really mean to grow old? For me . . . to be old is to be myself. No matter how patriarchy may classify and categorize me as invisible and powerless, I exist. I am an ongoing person, a sexual being, a person who struggles, for whom there are important issues to explore, new things to learn, challenges to meet, beginnings to make, risks to take, endings to ponder. Even though some of my options are diminished, there are new paths ahead.[11]

We have seen that, despite widespread beliefs to the contrary, older adults do not cease to participate in or desire sexual activity. Our collective denial of this activity, however, does not stem simply from our ignorance of the physiology of aging. Rather, behind our belief that older persons no longer can function sexually is the notion that they no longer should. Here we must take note of the ways in which religious beliefs and practices have contributed to a strong ascetic tradition in the West. This tradition shies away from affirming the goodness of sexuality in itself, linking it almost exclusively to childbearing. Although there has always been some appreciation within Christianity for elements of intimacy and companionship in sexual relations, these generally have been eclipsed by an emphasis on procreation. This emphasis has been shifting in recent years, but the link between sex and childbearing is strong enough in the minds of many older adults to discourage sexual activity beyond their reproductive years. Increasing numbers of persons now live two or three decades beyond those years. Many find themselves partnerless, isolated, unwanted, and insecure. What are the options for such persons? Must they accept old age as a sexually barren wasteland?

Faithfulness to the gracious God who has created us for wholeness requires that we affirm another possibility. This is the possibility of securing sexual justice for older adults, of transforming relationships, of reclaiming God's gift of eros for persons of all ages. As sexual beings, we require and reach out for the physical and spiritual embrace of others. As Christians, we seek to make such embrace possible for all persons by securing right relatedness and the concrete well-being of individuals and communities.

We must be open to a range of possibilities if we are to secure sexual justice for older adults. The traditional norm of "sex only in marriage, celibacy in singleness' is extremely limiting for older adults. Remarriage is a near-impossibility for many persons due not only to the lack of available partners, but also to welfare and social security restrictions that make marriage financially burdensome. Thus we must continue to resist restrictions on welfare and Social Security benefits to older adults regardless of their marital status. In addition, we must eliminate ideas of strict age limits for appropriate partners of older adults and redefine family in a broader, Christian sense. These efforts would reduce the isolation of older adults by providing a greater variety of human contacts from which intimacy might grow including recognition of gay and lesbian relationships among older adults.

Older persons, as well as younger persons, are rethinking human sexuality, including sexual relations outside marriage, as well as same-sex intimacy and friendships. Given the lack of available partners, many older adults also acknowledge that masturbation is a desirable form of sexual expression for them. Masturbation can provide both the physical stimulation and release desirable for good health and the continuity in sexual activity that is so important in maintaining sexual vitality into old age. We must be careful, furthermore, not to limit our understanding of sexual expression to genital activity. "Even when genital activity, for varying reasons, has severely diminished or even ceased in the elderly person, she or he continues to be very much a sexual being."[12] Recognizing this, we may wish to turn our attention to what some experts call "pleasuring"—that is, forms of sexual expression that are not necessarily genitally-oriented. "Pleasuring refers to any form of physical activity or arousal that feels good. It sets no goals or 'musts.' . . . According to the pleasuring principle, tactile and oral contact as well as other forms of stimulation and arousal can be valid and satisfying ends in themselves."[13] Redefining sexual pleasure in a way that emphasizes elements of affection, touch, companionship, and compassion is important for persons of all ages. In this task, we can learn much from the experience of older adults.

Acknowledging and affirming a range of sexual possibilities for older adults challenges not only our ageist biases, but our deepest fears and anxieties about full sexual expression as well. We must not evade this challenge, difficult though it may be. Rather, drawing strength from our faith in a God who calls us to sexual and spiritual wholeness, we must speak openly about the possibilities of sustained sexual activity into old age, and the various forms of pleasuring that are physical and intimate, but not genitally oriented. Only through such open and concrete exploration can we affirm the sexual needs of older adults, encourage their continued sexual expression, and so make possible the sexual integrity of a vast segment of persons both within the church and society as a whole. If we back away from discussing these possibilities in fear or shame, we may deny the genuine needs of older adults and perpetuate the distrust of embodiment that divides individuals and communities, rendering us less than whole.

Finally, a word of caution. We must be careful not to equate happiness in old age with sexual happiness. A superficial reduction of human fulfillment to sexual satisfaction is quite common in our popular culture, and falling prey to it would result in just the kind of "cultural captivity" we seek to avoid. We affirm, by contrast, that happiness at any age stems from the concrete well-being of individuals in community, a situation of right relatedness that is based on inclusivity and mutuality and includes respect for the sexual integrity of all persons. Furthermore, it is not our intention to impose an overly narrow conception of sexual satisfaction on older adults. As Karen Fischer suggests, "It is important to point out that the psychological changes connected with aging do not dramatically affect the capacity for sexual arousal, intercourse, and orgasm, [but] it is a mistake to use these as the major norm for evaluating sexuality in later life. There is a danger that youth will once again be the standard by which the later years are judged. Perhaps it is time to reverse this one-sided standard and allow older people to share important insights which can help all ages better understand the meaning of human sex and sexuality."[14]

Indeed, inasmuch as it is our intention to promote sexual justice by giving voice to those who are presently excluded, we would do well to listen to, and learn from, the experience of older adults.

> Do not ignore the discourse of the aged,
> for they themselves learned from their parents;
> from them you learn how to understand
> and to give an answer when the need arises.
> —Ecclesiasticus 8:9

NOTES

1. James B. Nelson, *Embodiment: An Approach to Sexuality and Christian Theology* (Minneapolis: Augsburg, 1978), 222.

2. Isadore Rubin, "The 'Sexless Older Years'—A Socially Harmful Stereotype," in *Let's Learn About Aging: A Book of Readings,* ed. John R. Barry and C. Ray Wingrove (New York: Schenkman, 1977), 247.

3. William E. Hulme, "Quality Aging," *Journal of Religion and Aging* 1 (winter 1984):55.

4. The number of persons age 65 and over will begin to decline after 2030 as the baby boomers are replaced by the "baby busters" (persons born after 1965). John H. Lindquist, "Prognosis for the Future: Looking at the Past," *Journal of Religion and Aging* 3 (winter 1986):110.

5. Presbyterian Church (U.S.A.), Stewardship and Communication Development Ministry Unit. John P. Marcum, director.

6. Lindquist, "Prognosis for the Future," 114.

7. Nelson, *Embodiment,* 222.

8. Nelson, *Embodiment,* 223.

9. George L. Maddox, ed., *The Encyclopedia of Aging* (New York: Springer, 1987), 606.

10. Shevy Healey, "Growing to Be an Old Woman: Aging and Ageism," in *Women and Aging: An Anthology by Women,* ed. Jo Alexander (Corvallis, Ore.: Calyx Books, 1986), 62.

11. Healey, "Growing to Be an Old Woman," 62.

12. Nelson, *Embodiment,* 224.

13. Maddox, ed., *The Encyclopedia of Aging,* 608.

14. Karen R. Fischer, *Winter Grace: Spirituality for the Later Years* (New York: Paulist Press, 1985), 73.

26

AIDS,
Shame,
and Suffering

GRACE JANTZEN

A man with AIDS wrote,

> At the age of 28 I wake up every morning to face the very real possibility of my own death.
>
> Whenever I am asked by members of the media or by curious healthy people what we talk about in our group I am struck by the intractable gulf that exists between the sick and the well: what we talk about is survival.
>
> Mostly we talk about what it feels like to be treated like lepers who are treated as if they are morally, if not literally, contagious.[1]

People with AIDS and HIV are the lepers of modern society. They are looked upon with horror, revulsion and fear. There is fear about any form of contact, from eating together to sharing a communion cup to offering an embrace or a kiss of peace and welcome. Like the lepers in medieval times, people with AIDS and HIV face not only physical revulsion but also moral disapproval, the attitude that their condition is a punishment for sin or that they have brought it upon themselves through sexual activity or drug use that is feared and condemned by the majority. Their human dignity is undervalued and undermined, not least by the church.

Yet the church has had better examples of how lepers should be treated, and it is worth considering one such example as we try to come to a more Christian response to AIDS. According to his biographers, Francis of Assisi was a fastidious young man. He was horrified by poverty and by all forms of suffering, but nothing raised his revulsion so much as leprosy. If he chanced to see a leper while he was out riding, he would dismount, hold his nose, and send a messenger to give some alms. Then one day, at the beginning of his conversion, he came unexpectedly upon a leper on the road. His first impulse was to recoil: then he remembered his desire for discipleship.

He slipped off his horse and ran to kiss the man. When the leper put out his hand as if to receive some alms, Francis gave him money and a kiss.[2]

This was for Francis a significant turning point in his understanding of Christ. Now that he had identified himself with Christ and with the lepers, in action and not merely in theory, his practical understanding of the incarnation deepened in direct proportion to his active obedience.

From that time on he clothed himself with a spirit of poverty, a sense of humility and a feeling of intimate devotion. Formerly he used to be horrified not only by close dealing with lepers but by their very sight, even from a distance; but now he rendered humble service to the lepers with human concern and devoted kindness . . . because of Christ crucified, who according to the text of the prophet was despised *as a leper*. He visited their houses frequently, generously distributed alms to them, and with great compassion kissed their hands and their mouths.[3]

It is clear that his biographers do not see this connection as accidental. It was as Francis responded to the invitation to follow Christ in his identification with the lepers that his spiritual vision was enlarged: his love for Christ increased in direct relation to his involvement with the outcasts of his society. Nor do his biographers intend us to see this increased understanding and love as a sort of divine reward for heroic behaviour. Rather, it is because Christ really is the one who made himself one with the outcasts that he can be found in solidarity with them. The lepers constituted a concrete opportunity to learn to know and love Christ.[4]

I wish to suggest that as the lepers for St. Francis, so people today with AIDS and HIV offer us the opportunity to rediscover Christ. I am not saying that the church is being offered an opportunity for condescending charity or alms to "victims" while we keep well out of the way and metaphorically hold our noses. I am not even saying only that the AIDS crisis offers the possibility for genuine service, though it certainly does. I am making the much stronger claim that for all the human tragedy of AIDS, like the human tragedy of leprosy, it is also an opportunity to reopen ourselves to people who have the virus, to their love and dignity as well as their suffering and fear, their sexuality and mortality—in short, their humanity—*and our own*. And if the incarnation is about the solidarity of God with humankind, then practical identification with people with AIDS can send us back to reading the New Testament with joyous insight that we didn't have before.

One of the avenues along which we may grow together in a deeper openness to incarnation is by exploring the revulsion and shame associated with AIDS and HIV. Like St. Francis cringing with revulsion from the lepers, our first reaction is often to cringe from those with AIDS. Now, although we need to explore what we do with that revulsion, I would suggest that we should not be too hard on ourselves for having it in the first place. It is an entirely human reaction to recoil from the sight of disease, deformity or pain, or even from the awareness of serious illness where no symptoms are apparent. We are horrified by these things, and we should be. They are horrific. They are not to be romanticized or sentimentalized; and our revulsion to them should not be suppressed, lest we develop calluses around our souls.

Furthermore, encounter with serious disease is a reminder of our own mortality. Again, it would be inhuman not to cringe from death. It may be that we can face it and come to terms with it, but to be unmoved by it is subhuman, not superhuman. When we face our own mortality in the body of another it is right to be appalled, for their sake and our own. The question is not whether we feel fear and revulsion but what we do with it. I have suggested that what we must *not* do is deny those feelings, pretend they are not there, refuse to let the symptoms and suffering of fellow human beings bother us, or repress our fear at their mortality and ours.

Another common way of coping with our feelings of horror is to offer compassion at a distance, as St. Francis did, keeping our own noses carefully covered while sending charity, perhaps very generous charity, by way of a messenger or go-between, but avoiding contact at all costs, lest somehow we be polluted. But what does this accomplish? The recipients of the charity, while perhaps having to accept it out of their necessity, are diminished in their humanity by it, forced to receive condescension, to accept the role of victim. They have to see themselves as people whom no one wishes to touch, people who cause revulsion, people who cannot be received and loved. When one is already suffering and fearful, the burden of such rejection is intolerable. As for us as givers of such charity, we are isolated not only from those who suffer but from our own humanity as well by such refusal to encounter disease and death. We refuse ourselves the opportunity to come to terms with them, and by keeping our distance from those who suffer, distance ourselves also from learning about the dignity and courage, humour and hope available to those who use their illness to discover their meaning and their worth. We deprive ourselves of truth and of love. We deprive ourselves also of God, for God sits with the sufferer against whom we hold our nose.

A further way in which we deal with our feelings of revulsion, especially if we are theologians, is to construct a theory about suffering. Suffering is horrifying: surely a compassionate God must be as horrified as we are? Why then does God continue to permit such suffering, when surely it is within the competence of omnipotence to intervene? These are genuine questions, and it is right that we should ponder deeply the nature of God in the face of suffering. But what can too easily happen is that as we seek for answers to our concerns we turn the whole thing into an intellectual exercise, offering explanation and counter-explanation, theodicy and counter-theodicy, until what may have begun as an effort at understanding human suffering ends as an insulation against it.[5]

Particularly insidious is the sort of theodicy which is so intent on preserving God from all responsibility for suffering that it attributes the responsibility to the sufferer. In some contexts the so-called "free will defence," the theory that all suffering is to be attributed to the free choices of moral agents, reads like a classic exercise in blaming the victim. It is a syndrome only too well known in cases of rape and violence against women: somehow the victim must have asked for it, must be at fault. And it is applied with particular venom to people with HIV and AIDS: they must be deserving of illness because of their sexual practices or drug use or even, in the case of African and Caribbean people with AIDS, because of the race to which they belong. The natural physical revulsion that we feel about suffering and death is turned into a moral revulsion, an imputation to the sufferer of moral failure for which they are being justly punished. By such a strategy it is possible to preserve both our own righteousness and God's, setting ourselves up as with divine authority against the ones "contaminated" through their own fault. . . .

What I wish to do . . . is to draw attention to the connection between fear and blame that is apparent in such a stance. As already noted, we are all afraid of suffering and death; we are also afraid of the unknown and the marginal. Now for many of us sexuality represents something that is deeply unknown and problematical. That is of course not to say that we are not sexually active; but for many of us our sexual impulses and involvements are more complicated than we like to admit. Our society is strongly heterosexist; that is, it sees heterosexuality as the biological and moral norm. In such a society there is an enormous investment in denying, even to ourselves, any homosexual feelings or relationships, and refusing to acknowledge that part of ourselves which is drawn to the same sex. This is true even though it has been widely known for some time that most people are in fact drawn to both sexes to a greater or lesser degree.

Now although AIDS and HIV are by no means restricted to homosexuals, they are popularly so associated in the public mind. This means that when we confront a person with AIDS we are confronted not only by our revulsion at sickness and death but also by our ambivalent sexuality. Many of us find this—especially the combination—deeply threatening. If within ourselves there is repressed discomfort about homosexuality, AIDS is available to become a focus for our fear and uncertainty. As Seymour Kleinberg has said,

> Since the late sixties we have all been living in a society at war, mostly with itself, under dire stress, and the sexual behaviour of gay men has become the radical exponent of tension and disaffection widespread in all adult life. We have come to symbolize every confusion about sexuality in modern history, and thus, we are objects of fascination and abhorrence.[6]

Our societal anxieties emerge as anger against homosexuals, and blame heaped upon those who have AIDS and HIV. The church has much to answer for in this, both in its frequent eagerness to be the ringleader of the stone-throwing brigade, and more fundamentally, in its failure to develop a theology of sexuality. It is deeply ironic that a religion named after one who was incarnate love should have so total a vacuum in its theology of embodied desire, and be so frightened of public discourse about sexuality.

For people who have contracted HIV or AIDS, the effect of all this is invidious, leading all too easily to an internalization of the shame and revulsion which society projects on to them, and eroding their sense of self-worth. Anyone who has a serious illness which may generate painful or difficult-to-manage symptoms is already confronted with bewilderment about her body, fear, physical and mental pain, anger, and often revulsion at the abhorrent symptoms. She may also have to confront not only her own fear and grief but also that of her friends and family as they try to cope with their own reactions, and with a certain level of stigmatization from society. As Dennis Altman has pointed out,

> To be stigmatized because of illness is hardly confined to people with AIDS: anyone suspected of carrying a disease will experience stigma, and it is a stigma that often extends to non-contagious diseases such as cancer and schizophrenia.[7]

But in the case of an illness like cancer, the attitude of society and church is generally sympathetic and supportive: people consider it important to overcome such fear and revulsion as they might feel. Messages of love and encouragement pour in from family, friends and colleagues; at times when morale is low it is possible to ask for support and be confident that such a request will find a sympathetic response. This cannot take away the pain or the fear or even the sense of isolation in the face of possible death, but it does assure the ill person of her worth to those who love her, and of all the care and comfort they can give. It is very common for a person with a life-threatening illness to have periods of anguished questioning: Why me? What have I done to deserve this? But in the case of an illness like cancer it is possible to express such doubt and confusion to a friend or to a visiting minister and to receive assurances that the illness has nothing to do with sin, let alone with God's punishment: that these are natural and normal questions but that they are expressions of understandable rage and bewilderment, not signs that the ill person is particularly sinful or perverse.

People with AIDS and HIV ask these questions too. But because of the fear and suspicion and blame in society and in the church toward drug use and homosexuality it is by no means a foregone conclusion that they will be offered the care and moral support that someone with some other life-threatening illness can count on. If a person with AIDS asks the vicar, "Why me? What have I done to deserve this?" she or he may well get, not comfort, but a list of accusations probably coupled with an invitation to repent. At a time when vulnerability is highest and morale is lowest, self-esteem is further eroded by the opprobrium heaped upon them even by well-meaning individuals, let alone by attitudes of society percolated through the media. A person who is ill and frightened needs a lot of hugs: who will hug a person with AIDS?[8]

Even at the level of medical care major differences can arise. A person with cancer can rest assured of skilled and sympathetic medical attention and does not need to add to her fears and grief about death any worry about whether appropriate funeral arrangements can be made. But for a person with AIDS it is always possible that some of the medical staff will be hostile; and there are still many undertakers who refuse their services. As well as the anxiety which such attitudes generate for the person with AIDS, there is inevitably a strong reinforcement of self-revulsion and shame.

By no means all people with AIDS and HIV are homosexual, but for those who are, such undermining of self-worth strikes at a very vulnerable point. All of us who are lesbian or gay have had the task of coming to terms with our sexuality in an oppressively heterosexist society, and for many of us it has not been easy. If we are Christians it has probably been more painful rather than less, as the church has reinforced the attitude that respectability is to be accorded only to heterosexual marriages or to total celibacy. We have all been aware of how our families and friends and colleagues would prefer us to keep silent: as long as we do not confront them with the fact of our homosexual choices they will pretend that we are "normal" and accord us respectability.

Yet we know too that respectability based on silence and pretence is bought at the expense of our self-esteem. Of course our sexuality is not the only or even necessarily the most important thing about us, any more than skin colour is the only or even the most important thing about blacks; but if this is the focus of denigrating attitudes, whether sexist or racist, then it must be affirmed with pride over and over again, partly to do what we can to change such attitudes, and partly to keep ourselves from colluding with the silence that offers respectability at the price of betrayal of a fundamental aspect of our identity. If this is hard for a person in a heterosexual marriage to understand, they might try to imagine what it would be like for them if they were placed in a situation where they could be accepted and esteemed only if they pretended that their spouse and children did not exist, or that their relationship with them was only casual.

For many of us, the decision to be open about being lesbian or gay has been costly even while also being enormously liberating and joyful. Attitudes of the unacceptability of homosexuality have been so internalized that even though we have begun to find our voice and our dignity and our pride it does not take much to tip us back into feeling vulnerable and insecure, uncertain of our value. Self-questioning and shame are easily induced.[9]

Accordingly, when a homosexual person contracts AIDS or HIV, and is faced with the revulsion and opprobrium of society and the church, how can they help but find in themselves feelings of shame and guilt about their sexuality? How can they *not* feel angry with themselves and their lovers, horrified at what is happening, as if they are to blame and are being punished not only for their acts but for their very being? How can anyone not in their position begin to grasp the level of courage required to face their illness with dignity and without self-loathing?

When we try, however, inadequately, to imagine ourselves in their position we can see how enormously important it is that the church should be able to offer resources of dignity and support, not attitudes of shame. Like St. Francis, the church needs to stop holding its holy nose and take the men and women with AIDS and HIV into its arms and learn from them to see Christ. If the Gospels are about anything, they are about God coming alongside us, not identifying with the self-righteous, but giving dignity and esteem and support to those who were the outcasts of society by eating and drinking with them, touching them, being their friend. One thing that Jesus did not do was to reinforce internalized shame: what he did was to set people free to see their worth in his eyes and in God's.

In a Psalm which the church has regularly taken as descriptive of Christ, one of the qualities calling forth awe is his readiness to be alongside a sufferer:

> For he has not despised or abhorred the affliction of the afflicted;
> and he has not hid his face from him,
> but has heard, when he cried to him.
>
> (Psalm 22:24, RSV)

The Hebrew word translated "abhorred" is *shiqef:* it means "to shrink from, to detest or abominate." It is used of the loathing that someone might have for filth, or for the detestation for idols that was to be engendered in the Israelites.[10] Such abhorrence would have been as familiar to those with leprosy in Jesus' time as it is to people with AIDS today: people would shrink from them, seeing them as filth and probably as wicked, coupling their fear and revulsion with moral rectitude.

We need to hear it plainly: *such an attitude is not God's attitude.* It is not God's attitude even if it is widely held in society. It is not God's attitude even if it is held by many who profess to speak in God's name. In Jesus we are shown that God does not detest or shrink from the affliction of the afflicted, but comes alongside in tenderness and brotherhood.

Such coming alongside is enormously important for the recovery of dignity. As Arnold Isenberg has pointed out, shame can only be healed by replacing it with self-worth. Such healing is to be contrasted with two inadequate efforts to deal with shame. The first of these is "forgetfulness": that is, trying to pretend that the cause of shame is not there by thinking about other things, while still leaving intact the external and internal value judgements on which the feelings of shame feed. The other is "consolation," in which the shame is not forgotten, but substitutes or compensations are suggested as though somehow if there are other good things about the person then the shameful things don't matter. Neither of these really resolves the shame; they only push it away, making it even harder to deal with. The only way in which it can be resolved is not by resorting to either pretence or substitutes, but by confronting the value judgement from which the shame originates.[11]

This is precisely what Jesus did. The society of his time shrank from and abhorred its outcasts, seeing them as sinners punished by God. Jesus counted them his friends, ate meals with them, spent time with them, thus reversing the value judgement that they were not of worth. It is also what St. Francis did. He overcame his revulsion and his condescending charity by embracing the lepers, facing his own initial value judgement with the human reality of the sufferer. It is important to notice that he did not stop feeling revulsion first and then went and embraced the leper. He went and embraced the leper, and the love that he gave and received melted the revulsion away.

And this is what Christians are invited to do in response to people with AIDS and HIV. We need to confront our own value judgements which generate shame and fear with the loving acceptance of Christ. If we open ourselves to love people with AIDS and to receive love from them we will find that we can let go of our projections of shame and revulsion. As we spend time together we can find our attitudes being healed and our being alongside one another opening us to the presence of Christ. We may be challenged to be more in touch with our own sexuality and our mortality by women and men who have much to teach us about both. Who knows, we may even lose some of our self-righteousness!

Yet it would not be true to say that Jesus never expresses shame of anyone. In the Gospel of Mark there is a poignant sequence of events, Jesus performs miracles, multiplies loaves and fishes, heals a blind man. Then he asks his disciples who they say that he is, and Peter answers, "You are the Christ." But when he begins to teach them what that means, how being Christ means being on behalf of those who are seen as sinners and accepting the consequence of the cross and its shame, the disciples cannot handle it at all: Peter begins to rebuke him. The disciples wanted a Christ of power and invulnerability; Jesus offered them a totally different perspective. He taught them (and us) something about what following him means: it means taking up one's cross, doing in our own lives what Jesus did in his, giving our love and if necessary our reputations and our lives in being alongside those who suffer, just as Jesus was alongside them. And as Jesus concluded this teaching, for the only time in the Gospels Jesus speaks of shame: not shame at a sinner or a sufferer or an outcast, but shame at the pretended followers of his who disown the cross and the solidarity with human shame and suffering it represents.

> For whoever is ashamed of me and of my words . . . of them will the Son of man also be ashamed, when he comes in the glory of his Father with the holy angels.
> (Mark 8:38; par. Luke 9:26)

Jesus projects no shame on those who suffer, not even when by the standards of his society they are sinful. But he expresses deep shame of those of us who affirm him as Christ, call ourselves after his name, and yet refuse to follow him in a vocation of being alongside. This, not suffering or the rejection it attracts, is shameful, abhorrent to God, contrary to Jesus, and contrary to our own souls as followers of his. And from the shame of God, who will deliver us?

NOTES

1. Michael Callen quoted in F. and M. Siegal, *AIDS: The Medical Mystery* (New York: Grove Press, 1983), 182–83.

2. Bonaventure, *The Life of St. Francis*, I.5, in Ewart Cousins, ed., *Bonaventure*, Classics of Western Spirituality (London: SPCK, 1978), from Thomas of Celano, *Second Life*, 9.

3. Bonaventure, I.6; Thomas of Celano, I.17 and II.9.

4. See Leonardo Boff, *Saint Francis: A Model for Human Liberation* (London: SCM Press, 1981), 23–28.

5. For an investigation of the insulating effects of theodicy, see Ken Surin, *Theology and the Problem of Evil,* (Oxford: Basil Blackwell Publisher, 1986).

6. Seymour Kleinberg, "Dreadful Night," in *Christopher Street* #76, 1983.

7. Dennis Altman, *AIDS and the New Puritanism* (London: Pluto Press, 1986), 59.

8. See ibid., 25.

9. For further discussion of the relationship between societal attitudes and shame, and its distinction from guilt, see John Rawls, *A Theory of Justice* (Cambridge, Mass.: Harvard University Press, 1971), 442–46.

10. Nahum 3:6; Zech. 9:7; Deut. 7:26.

11. "Natural Pride and Natural Shame," in *Explaining Emotions,* ed. Amélie Rorty (Berkeley, Calif.: University of California Press, 1980), 368.

27

AIDS, High-Risk Behaviors, and Moral Judgments

EARL E. SHELP

Sickness, loss, isolation, dependency, death, and grief are occasions for God's people to offer ministries of care and concern. These ministries are representative and expressive of God's love for humanity. In addition, they are obedient responses to the love command, provided to people regardless of whether or not they are members of a faith community. Implicitly, if not explicitly, such ministries affirm the beliefs that all people are made in the image and likeness of God and, as such, are loved by God and deserving of the love of God's people.

With the appearance of AIDS among certain groups of people, these typical ministries and beliefs have tended to be qualified, conditioned, or restricted because of moral disapproval of behaviors by which the AIDS virus is transmitted. The relevant condemnations are said to apply to the objectionable behaviors and not to the people who engage in them. In reality, however, it is difficult to hate the "sin" but not hate the "sinner." Favorable or unfavorable feelings about a person's conduct always influence estimates of a person's character and relationship with that person. Thus, moral judgments about sex and intravenous drug use, the primary modes by which the AIDS virus is transmitted, have helped to inhibit a compassionate response to people touched by AIDS. This situation is contradictory to the church's ethos, placing the church in an untenable, ambiguous position. When condemnation of behavior replaces love of people as a first priority, opportunities for ministry are neglected and failures in discipleship occur. This situation equally is unfortunate for people touched by AIDS. They are denied the experience of God's love and grace embodied in and mediated through the church. This situation of mutual loss appears based on misunderstandings of Christian morality, pastoral care, and the relationship of each to the other.

CHRISTIAN MORALITIES

There are individuals and groups who hold their particular Christian moral viewpoints to be unexceptionable and normative for believers and non-believers alike. Often these individuals and groups are intolerant of differing moral perspectives, religious or secular. Even though this sort of exclusivist orientation tends to deny the validity of alternate moral understandings, it is an inescapable fact of modern life that the moral order is composed of people who embrace differing respected moral visions. The differences may be between moral traditions (secular and religious) or within moral traditions (philosophical: deontological ethics and utilitarianism; or religious: Christian, Jewish, and Moslem). In addition, there may be conflicts among groups within secular or religious traditions. For example, Roman Catholics may hold certain moral views about an issue that Protestants may not. Further, there may be diverse opinions among Protestants or Roman Catholics about an issue. Thus, the moral order is composed of particular communities which often express distinct differing moral viewpoints. In the words of theologian Ted Peters, the differences that mark contemporary moral reflection "cannot be washed away; they cannot be uprooted or overcome, absorbed or ignored, assimilated or dissipated. They are an indelible characteristic of life."[1] Equally characteristic of life in a moral pluralism is the seemingly endless debates and discussions about issues that are particularly divisive, e.g., abortion and homosexuality.

Christians often participate in these moral controversies, offering their opinions and, like other participants, trying to convince others of the validity of that opinion. These judgments reflect certain understandings of God, God's will for human social intercourse, resources for moral instruction, and the facts of the case or topic at issue. Since these judgments reflect a theocentric orientation, they are confessional in nature and supported by reasoned arguments. They may incorporate many of the moral rules and principles that are accepted by nearly all moral communities and traditions. One distinctive element of a Christian morality, however, is the primacy of human agape or the love command.[2] As a moral principle, human agape requires love of neighbor as a primary, related, and equal component with devotion to God as one condition of Christian discipleship (Matt. 22:37–40).

Human agape or love, in a moral sense, is not a human emotion or sentiment. It is an imperative to which attitudes and conduct are to conform. Luke records Jesus to say that love is not conditioned on expectations of reciprocity or evaluations of a person's worthiness. Christians should love even their enemies, a standard of conduct that transcends customary rules of morality (Luke 6:27, 32–33). Experience teaches that human agape, therefore, is not an easy moral command to obey. It is a command that all who claim Jesus as Lord are to affirm by actively valuing others, even if they are enemies. Jesus expected his followers to embrace a morality that requires a constructive, compassionate, unconditional, and concrete commitment to other persons and their needs.[3] Agape or love summons Christians to exemplary living, marked by a regard for the fullness of life for all.

Christians generally will be comfortable with this general, formal understanding of the love command. Individuals and groups may disagree, however, about what love requires in a particular instance. A common and revealing example of disagreement is the issue of abortion. Without recounting the respective detailed arguments, some people argue that all abortions are contrary to Christian morality, others argue that some, but not all, abortions are permissible according to Christian morality, and a smaller number argues that all abortions are permissible. Presumably all parties to the dispute about the morality of abortion are people of faith, honestly attempting to discern right and wrong, and making a sincere effort to live morally. But given the moral disagreements among them and an inability to settle their dispute empirically, they can attempt to settle the issue by coercion or by persuasion. Yet in most instances, a coercive solution appears incompatible with moralities that are confessional in nature and grounded in theological beliefs.[4] Confessional moralities require a method of discourse that invites assent or wins agreement through convincing arguments. This is true particularly in a moral pluralism where disputes properly are addressed and resolved by cogent arguments. Mutual respect for people of good will and toleration of reasoned and reasonable moral differences are necessary conditions for peaceful coexistence in such an environment.[5]

HIGH-RISK BEHAVIORS AND MORAL JUDGMENT

There are many issues about which individuals and groups disagree morally. If the seemingly endless debate about abortion is an indication, the prospects for consensus regarding other disputed issues do not appear bright.[6] However, a failure to establish a single morality and a single set of moral norms, whether rooted in philosophy or religion, may not be a cause for despair. Rather than viewing moral pluralism as an indication that moral agents and society have gone astray, perhaps the existence of competing moral visions should be seen as a safeguard against self-righteousness and unjust intolerance, as well as a reminder that knowledge of right and wrong, like knowledge of God, is imperfect and in the process of being refined. In addition, whatever discomfort is felt because of moral differences may occasion an honest, sincere, and open exchange of views that leads to greater mutual understanding, if not consensus. Critical reflection and dialogue about the nature of morality, and its many expressions, may lead to a clearer comprehension of the concepts, principles, and values that constitute its core substance. Such a clarification would be valuable, even if there is no agreement about divisive issues. Perhaps the suspicion, distrust, and condemnation that frequently stem from ignorance of another person's rational, though different, opinion will subside and be replaced by mutual respect and tolerance based on a more mature understanding of reasonable differences. Such an attitude and approach seems particularly required of individuals and groups whose moral vision is based on an *invitation* to faith and discipleship.

Certain behaviors linked to transmission of the AIDS virus are subjects of moral debate.[7] Anal intercourse (heterosexual or homosexual), heterosexual intercourse outside of monogamous marriage, oral-genital, oral-anal, and other sexual activities that may provide passage of the AIDS virus from one person to another are variously condoned and condemned by representatives of secular and religious moral communities. The other primary means of transmission (sharing needles by intravenous drugs users and intrauterine infection of a fetus by an infected woman) are subjects of moral concern, not only because of judgments about certain behaviors, but also because of confusion about where to attach responsibility. There is intense disagreement about the morality of these behaviors, and whether moral or legal sanctions should exist to regulate these activities.

The respective moral argument about high risk behaviors and proposals regarding their control cannot be summarized here.[8] Neither would it be appropriate at this point to state my positions about these matters. Such an excursus would distract unnecessarily from the primary concern of this article. The focus here is whether moral judgment or disapproval of behaviors or persons should be a barrier to ministry. Our stance is that it should not. One reason already has been implied in the foregoing discussion of the pluralistic character of the moral order; that is, despite the high confidence that is placed in religious beliefs and the moral judgments derived from them, these beliefs and judgments always should be tentative. By definition, people of faith should remain open to new insights into the nature and will of God, and to new understandings of right and wrong. If God's revelation were complete and if humanity had perceived all of God that there is to understand, then the ministry of the Holy Spirit would not be necessary. In addition, what we are as humans, why we are the way we are, and why we do what we do are being better understood as scientific studies provide a more complete picture of humanity. And lastly, theological and biblical studies are continuously clarifying the meanings and applications of authoritative sources with respect to God, humanity, and the relation of each to the other.

Christians are people of faith. Faith is not knowledge or certainty. What understandings of God and morality Christians hold are incomplete. They do not, at present, constitute all truth. As a confessional people, Christians have responded to the revelation of God in Jesus. The discipleship and moral vision of Christians are grounded in the witness of Jesus. Loving one's enemies, like believing in God, is optional or voluntary. As a moral norm, therefore, human agape is an obligation for Christians, but optional for people who do not confess Jesus as Lord. For Christians, human agape supersedes all other rules of conduct. Therefore, enabling, sustaining, and enriching ministries should be offered in obedience to the love command to all people regardless of a Christian's moral evaluation of the behaviors that contributed to the creation of need.

The devastation brought about by HIV disease presents the church with opportunities for ministry, as well as an opportunity to reflect on its identity and its mission. An examination by the church of whom it represents, what it is, and how it should act, however, ought not to be merely repetitious of received and unexamined teachings or assertions. AIDS is unprecedented, as these theme articles serve to illustrate. Faith statements and moral judgments that seemed valid in an earlier time and responsive to past circumstances may be found wanting with respect to the current AIDS crisis. AIDS presents the church with an opportunity to think critically about what it means to be a servant people serving a servant Lord.[9] The church is forced by AIDS to reconsider what human agape means and requires in the face of a fear-evoking pandemic. The sort of study and reflection envisaged here may be stressful for individuals, congregations, and denominations. The stress, however, may reflect the sort of creative tension out of which deeper, more mature understandings of God and Christian discipleship can emerge.

As a Christian response to AIDS is contemplated, a study of human sexuality including sexual conduct might be undertaken. Since the inauguration of the AIDS interfaith council in Houston, its members have been at pains to establish that their compassionate response to the epidemic must be entirely separate from moral judgments of expressions of human sexuality. Having established this basis for service, however, the fact that HIV disease is primarily a sexually transmitted disease inevitably has drawn attention to the failure of the church to give adequate attention to human sexuality education. What it means to be a sexual being, forms of sexual expression, and the factors that influence sexual self-perceptions and behavior are among the appropriate topics for enquiry. Scientific data regarding these matters can be compared with authoritative or influential religious resources. Both resources should be approached fairly, realizing that they present snap-shots of reality and truth, not necessarily all reality and truth. As with human agape, there are other norms of conduct that Christians may hold but other people may not. A failure of some people to subscribe to certain Christian norms does not necessarily invalidate the norms to which other people subscribe, nor does it mean they are immoral or evil people. This lack of consensus among people of good will merely reflects the morally pluralistic character of modern life. A Christian ideal of conduct is not necessarily a norm that justifiably can be forced on others. When seen in an informed and uncritical light, previously unexamined norms and consequent condemnations might be affirmed, revised, or rejected. If not affirmed, prior declarations regarding sexual "sin" might be modified. A difference is not necessarily a sin or moral wrong. Christians, acknowledging that more is to be understood about God and God's will for humanity, should also be cautious before making categorical and irrevocable judgments of sin and moral wrong.

A similar educational process could be undertaken regarding intravenous drug use. It is appropriate to learn about the culture of drug users and the individual and societal factors that contribute to drug use in general and IV drug use in particular. Alternatives with potential to enrich individual opportunity and quality of life, rather than summary condemnations, may appear more appropriate and forthcoming. Similarly, we may understand intravenous drug users not to bear sole responsibility for their behavior. The societal and ecclesiastical contribution to behaviors with high risk for the transmission of the AIDS virus might be recognized. Thus, a propensity to blame the "victim" of AIDS virus infection might be challenged on factual and moral grounds. Instead of responding to people touched by AIDS with condemnations, the church has no option but to respond with compassion and humility. Such an approach to the crisis is required by the first principle of Christian conduct (human agape). A loving response to people in need does not mean necessarily that moral judgments are incorrect or invalid. It simply means that assertions of moral innocence or guilt are secondary and that supportive ministries are not conditioned on agreement with or conformity to confessional moral norms. In short, moral judgment is not a legitimate justification for neglecting people in need.

PASTORAL MINISTRIES

The needs of people touched by AIDS and the opportunities for ministry generated by the losses caused by the AIDS virus are [another area of consideration]. The ministries . . . are pastoral in the sense that they are sustaining, enabling, and enriching. They are person-oriented activities of engagement and identification. As such, pastoral ministries are incarnational. They are ministries of presence, involvement, and redemption in the midst of travail. They are manifestations of God's concern and participation, implying a belief that God too is vulnerable, that God shares the pain and grief of illness, disability, dependency, and death. These ministries affirm the value of all people to God and to God's people, regardless of identifying characteristics or how they came to be in a situation of need. Christians, by definition, cannot neglect or reject people in need and claim to act as God acts, feel as God feels, or do as God wills. Pastoral ministries, therefore, are tangible demonstrations that God does not abandon a person, people, or world in distress.

Pastoral ministries or care should be freely given and the recipient should be free to accept or reject them.

Christians are obliged to offer pastoral care, unconditioned by a judgment of the person's moral guilt or innocence. A person in need, however, is free to refuse an offer of care. Just as people are free to accept or reject participation in God's saving activity, so people are free to accept or reject God's caring activity mediated through the pastoral ministries of God's people. A person's weakness, vulnerability, and dependency ought not be exploited. Offers of care and support should express genuine concerns for a person's welfare, and should not camouflage an evangelistic, moralistic, or political agenda. If the latter is the case, these otherwise morally laudable and theologically justified ministries become tainted by an interest other than the care, comfort, and enrichment of the person in need. What was undertaken as moral activity, an activity grounded in human agape, deteriorates into a morally questionable activity of exploitation and coercion.

Pastoral ministries or care that primarily focus on the welfare of people in need properly are grounded in a sense of Christian mission and discipleship. They are valid and good in and of themselves. No other agenda or end needs to be served in order to justify the offer or activity of care. If the care is accepted, then both the giver and recipient gain. The caregiver is permitted to do that which is essential to his or her Christian identity. The person in need freely accepts the love, affirmation, and assistance that the provider gives. Though the exchange arises from a situation of inequality, the people involved are respected and relate as equals. Pastoral care, according to this understanding, is a moral activity, characterized by a primary concern for the welfare of a person in need and a respect for that person's freedom to decide what is good for him or her.

This approach suggests that people who offer ministry will do so with an attitude of humility and confidence. So disposed, a caregiver is freed to risk entry into different situations without feeling compelled to ridicule or disparage that which is different. The freedom of the prospective recipient of care requires that he or she be regarded as an equal. His or her moral values and commitments do not have to correspond to those of the pastoral caregiver. They deserve to be acknowledged and accepted because they represent that person's notion of the life worth living. They do not necessarily require assent, however. Given this understanding, the integrity of the provider and recipient of care is respected. The relationship between the parties is on an adult-adult level, rather than an adult-child level (care-giver and care-receiver, respectively).

Where two or more people are brought together out of mutual need and relate on a level of mutual regard, there is a risk that one or all may change as a result of the encounter. In relationships of this description, moral perspectives may be explained, analyzed, and evaluated. This sharing is an implicit invitation to change, as much as the witness of Jesus is an invitation to faith and discipleship. People are free to accept or reject both invitations. The people of God, however, are not free to reject Jesus' command to love others, even if the others are different or considered morally deviant.

The tendency of Christians to concentrate on their differences with others can impede ministry. These differences may be doctrinal, racial, ethnic, economic, educational, cultural, sexual, or moral. Value judgments may be attached to these differences in an effort to justify failures to provide supportive, sustaining, concrete ministries to people in need. However, it is for this reason that differences ought not be considered as a condition for providing or denying ministry to people in need. The parable of the Samaritan provides an excellent object lesson.

Recall that in Luke the parable immediately follows Jesus' summary of the law. After saying that one is to love God and love one's neighbor, Jesus tells the parable in which a man was robbed, injured, and left half-dead along a road. A

Samaritan passerby saw the man, recognized his need for help, and had compassion, attending to his wounds and providing for his care (Luke 10:25–37). It should be emphasized that nothing is known about the injured man other than he was in need.[10] Everything about the victim apparently was irrelevant to Jesus except his need. His race, nationality, sexuality, or cause of distress are not known to the travelers down the road. He simply is a man in need to which the Samaritan responded with acts of care. If this parable instructs Christians about what love means and requires and who is one's neighbor, then neither identifying characteristics nor the causes of a person's need are relevant conditions for ministry. A person's need, and that alone, is sufficient to require of God's people a loving response. All other considerations have no role. From a perspective of Christian discipleship and Christian morality, to be moral and to be a faithful witness to Christ, the needs of others cannot be ignored.

This unconditioned and unqualified call to care for people in need is reiterated in the Sermon on the Mount. Jesus, according to Matthew, cautions his disciples against judging others. The mercy that a believer experiences from God should be generously expressed toward all others without exception.[11] Dietrich Bonhoeffer expressed powerfully the significance of Jesus's teaching regarding the danger of judgment to love: "Christian love sees the fellow-man under the cross and therefore sees with clarity. If when we judged others our real motive was to destroy evil, we should look for evil where it is to be found, and that is in our own hearts. But if we are on the lookout for evil in others, our real motive is obviously to justify ourselves, for we are seeking to escape punishment for our own sins by passing judgment on others, and are assuming by implication that the Word of God applies to ourselves in one way, and to others in another." Bonhoeffer regards such a stance as highly dangerous and misleading because it indicates that we are trying to claim for ourselves a special privilege which we deny to others. It should be clear, he argues, that Christ's disciples have no rights of their own or standards of right and wrong which they can enforce with other people; they have received nothing but Christ's fellowship. As disciples, therefore, we are not to sit in judgment over our fellows because that would wrongly usurp the jurisdiction.[12] Having experienced the reconciling love of God, Christians are to express reconciling love to all others. We are to give freely what we have received. Nothing else is acceptable.

The care provided to people with need on the basis of the need alone not only benefits the person served, but also sets an example for others to follow. It challenges people and communities who subscribe to other, perhaps less demanding, moralities to see the intrinsic worth of a love ethic which incorporates but goes beyond justice. The emphasis in pastoral care, according to the perspective offered here, should be on being a moral agent, obeying the love command, freely and without condition committing oneself to the welfare and well-being of others.

Pastoral care, therefore, is a gift of self and sustenance to others. It is a witness to faith in God. It is an act of obedience. It does not exploit a person's need or vulnerability in order to coerce that person to believe in God or accept the caregiver's notion of Christian morality.

GOD, AIDS, AND PASTORAL CARE

Despite the warnings of Jesus regarding the destructive potential of judgment to love, some Christians claim to know God's mind and attitude toward certain people based on the prosperity or adversity they experience.[13] In the present AIDS epidemic, as in past epidemics, preachers have asserted that a dreaded disease represents a punishment by God upon an offending person or people. For example, Jerry Falwell claims that "AIDS is a lethal judgment of God on the sin of homosexuality and it is also the judgment of God on America for endorsing the vulgar, perverted and reprobate lifestyle. . . . He [God] is . . . bringing judgment against this wicked practice [homosexuality] through AIDS. . . ." According to Falwell, AIDS has its roots in the male homosexual community and it is a "due penalty of their [homosexuals'] error." He acknowledges that a cure or vaccine is not within sight which apparently is cause for grave concern because "the AIDS virus is now coming into the heterosexual community and infecting innocent people."[14]

Falwell's rhetoric was even more histrionic and harsh in a televised sermon titled "How Many Roads to Heaven." After asserting that AIDS is a consequence of a sexual revolution, Fallwell stated that "God almighty brought an end to it, for that permissive crowd is scared to death. They are scared to walk near one of their kind right now. And what we have been unable to do with our preaching, a God who hates sin has stopped it dead in its tracks by saying do it and die. Do it and die."[15] If Falwell's assessment is correct, then all efforts to find a cure, comfort the sick, and console the grieving should cease lest one act contrary to God's will. Such a response, however, would be contrary to the teachings of Jesus discussed above.[16]

Falwell's interpretation of the AIDS crisis is incorrect scientifically and sociologically, and misleading theologically. It is true that AIDS was first described in the United States among homosexual males in 1981. Epidemiological studies have shown since that the AIDS virus originated in central Africa where the disease seems to affect dominantly heterosexual men and women in about equal numbers. The roots of AIDS, therefore, are in Africa, not the United States, and among heterosexual people, not homosexual men. In addition, it simply is not true that gay men are afraid of each other because of AIDS. Organizations committed to the support of people with AIDS and to risk reduction educational programs were founded by gay men. Gay men cared for one another early in the AIDS crisis because of their concern and because most others were afraid. These supportive and educational efforts are continuing.

Finally, Falwell's conclusion that AIDS evidences God's anger over homosexuality is erroneous for several reasons. If the association of a disease with a people is an indication of God's displeasure with that people, then Tay-Sachs disease is

God's punishment upon Jews, sickle cell anemia is God's punishment upon blacks, hemophilia is God's punishment upon men, vaginal and breast cancers are God's punishment upon women, and Legionnaires' disease is God's punishment on members of the American Legion! This sort of association is logically absurd and theologically incorrect. In addition, if Falwell is correct several questions must be answered. Why did God wait so long to express anger over homosexuality? Why are lesbians allowed to escape punishment for their sexual misdeeds? Is God so inept as to permit some homosexual people to escape what they allegedly deserve? If "innocent" people suffer because of God's misdirected wrath, is God morally blameworthy, or could it be that God's aim is bad? These questions may appear humorous or ridiculous, but they represent serious questions about the nature and character of God that Falwell's assertion implicitly depicts. These images of God as vengeful and arbitrary are contradictory to the incarnational theology of Christianity that portrays God as loving humanity and suffering with humanity. The incarnational God of Christianity invites people to fellowship and reconciliation, not condemnation and estrangement. The incarnational God of Christianity shares the suffering of broken humanity. God does not delight in it, and neither should God's people!

The notion that AIDS is God's punishment on any person has no theological merit, as this overly simplified refutation has shown. Since this claim is invalid, it cannot be used to justify failures by God's people to offer compassionate ministries to people touched by AIDS. Whatever moral views a Christian may hold about any feature of a person's life, they do not justify a failure to minister to a person in need. The command to love, even one's enemies, is unequivocal and unexceptionable. It is the centerpiece of Christian ethics, the premier standard by which discipleship is measured. It is a person-centered principle of conduct grounded in the revelation of God in Jesus. Love requires that human needs be met, unconditioned by moral norms according to which judgments of blame, guilt, praise, or innocence are otherwise made. Love requires the mitigation of suffering. It does not sanction any action or attitude that compounds suffering. Where moral judgments impede or deny supportive, compassionate ministries to people in need, Christians fail in their witness and the love command is denied.

CONCLUSIONS

Human agape or love, as a moral principle, requires that a person's need take priority over judgments about any conduct or characteristic of that person. The single most important moral consideration for God's people in the AIDS crisis is how they are going to love their neighbors caught in the suffering that AIDS generates. For purposes of pastoral care, all other moral concerns are secondary and operationally irrelevant. These matters, like other issues of controversy, can be debated within the moral pluralism, but offers of ministry to people with need cannot be conditioned on the resolution of disagreements, doctrinal confession, or conformity to a particular code of conduct. There may be many barriers to ministry in the AIDS crisis, but this brief discussion shows that moral judgments about high-risk behavior ought not be one of them. The opportunities and challenges for ministry that AIDS presents constitute an invitation to God's people to set an example of love for all to follow.

NOTES

1. Ted Peters, "Pluralism as a Theological Problem," *The Christian Century,* vol. 100 (Sept. 28, 1983): 843.

2. For extended analyses of the love command, see Gene Outka, *Agape: An Ethical Analysis* (New Haven, Conn.: Yale University Press, 1972); and Victor Paul Furnish, *The Love Command in the New Testament* (Nashville, Tenn.: Abingdon Press, 1972).

3. Furnish, *The Love Command,* 66.

4. The confessional aspects of Christian moralities are their grounding in certain beliefs about God and those features, like loving enemies, that go beyond widely shared notions of morality. Clearly there are components of Christian moralities that correspond with basic rules of conduct necessary to social life that are nearly universally shared. These basic rules of social order accepted by Christians are not necessarily grounded in confessional propositions, but they may be. These rules of social order are justifiable apart from statements of faith. As such, they can be accepted by almost all segments of the moral order, constituting the procedural rules by which a peaceable society will function. Actual or threatened force or coercion may be associated with these basic rules as a means to promote respect for persons and property, for example.

5. A brief, but more extensive, discussion of decision making in a moral pluralism is found in Earl E. Shelp, *Born to Die?* (New York: Free Press, 1986), 7–25. The issue here is the management of severely impaired newborn infants. However, the analysis and approach are applicable to other issues, including behaviors associated with transmission of the AIDS virus.

6. Cf. Alasdair MacIntyre, *After Virtue* (Notre Dame, Ind.: University of Notre Dame, 1981), 6.

7. Infection by the medically prescribed use of contaminated blood seems to be accepted broadly as an unfortunate outcome, not a morally blameworthy act. Thus, people infected by these means or infants infected *in utero* tend to be seen as morally blameless for their infection.

8. Literature providing insight into the factors that contribute to drug abuse and the difficulty of altering behavior is extensive. These analyses should inform moral judgments and efforts to control this behavior. See, for example, Saul Shiffman and Thomas A. Wills, *Coping and Substance Abuse* (Orlando, Fla.: Academic Press, 1985); Charles W. Lidz and Andrew L. Walker, *Heroin, Deviance, and Morality* (Beverly Hills, Calif.: Sage Publications, 1980); Arie Cohen, "A Psychosocial Typology of Drug Addicts and Implications for Treatment," *International Journal of the Addictions,* 1986, vol. 21: 147–54; George Serban, ed., *Social and Medical Aspects of Drug Abuse* (Jamaica, N.Y.: SP Medical and Scientific Books, 1984): Ann F. Brunswick and Peter Messeri, "Drugs, Lifestyle, and Health: A Longitudinal Study of Urban Black Youth," *American Journal of Public Health,* 1986, vol. 76:52–57; and Michael D. Newcomb and P. M. Bentler, "Substance Use and Ethnicity: Differential Impact of Peer and Adult Models," *Journal of Psychology,* 1986, vol. 120: 83–95.

The moral debate by Christians about homosexuality has been energetic in recent years. A disapproving argument is contained in the Roman Catholic Doctrinal Congregation's Letter to Bishops, "The Pastoral Care of Homosexual Persons," *Origins: NC Documentary Service,* 1986 (Nov. 13), vol. 16:378–82. For positions more accepting of homosexual people, see George Edwards, *Gay/Lesbian Liberation: A Biblical Perspective* (New York: Pilgrim Press, 1984); Robert Nugent, ed., *A Challenge to Love: Gay and Lesbian Catholics in the Church* (New York: Crossroad, 1983); James B. Nelson, *Embodiment: An Approach to Sexuality and Christian Theology* (Minneapolis: Augsburg Publishing House, 1978); John Boswell, *Christianity, Social Tolerance, and Homosexuality* (Chicago: University of Chicago Press, 1980); and Letha Scanzoni and Virginia Ramey Mollenkott, *Is the Homosexual My Neighbor?* (San Francisco: Harper & Row, 1978).

9. Earl E. Shelp and Ronald H. Sunderland, eds., *The Pastor as Servant* (New York: Pilgrim Press, 1986).

10. Jay Jones helped us to appreciate the significance of this feature of the parable.

11. Archibald M. Hunter, *A Pattern for Life* (Philadelphia: Westminster Press, 1965, 86.

12. Dietrich Bonhoeffer, *The Cost of Discipleship* (New York: Macmillan Co., 1959), 206.

13. Charles E. Rosenberg, *The Cholera Years: The United States in 1832, 1849 and 1866* (Chicago: University of Chicago Press, 1962); and Allan M. Brandt, *No Magic Bullet: A Social History of Venereal Disease in the United States Since 1880)* (New York: Oxford University Press, 1985).

14. Jerry Falwell, "AIDS: The Judgment of God," *Liberty Report,* 1987 (April): 5, 7.

15. Jerry Falwell, "How Many Roads to Heaven," Old Time Gospel Hour—760, audiocassette tape.

16. For a more extensive discussion of illness in Christian perspective with special reference to AIDS, see Earl E. Shelp and Ronald H. Sunderland, *AIDS and the Church* (Philadelphia: Westminster Press, 1987), chaps. 3 and 4.

28

Violence against Women: The Way Things Are Is Not the Way They Have to Be

MARIE M. FORTUNE

PART I

Alice Walker begins her book *The Color Purple* thus: "You better not tell nobody but God. It'd kill your mammy." So Celie proceeds to tell God the truth about her life. In her first letter to God, Celie describes the rape by her stepfather. When she cries out in pain, her stepfather chokes her and says "you better shut up and get used to it." She writes, "but I don't never get used to it."[1]

Violence against women is a fact of life in the United States. It is the common thread of women's existence which binds us together across race, age, class, sexual orientation and religious preference. This violence is not random; it is not accidental. It is directed at us by men, strangers or intimates, simply because we are women. Because of our gender, we are perceived to be available victims: powerless, vulnerable, deserving of abuse. Statistically, we are most likely to be assaulted by a family member or acquaintance: hence the most dangerous place for a woman to be is in a relationship.

Nearly 1 out of 2 women has suffered rape or attempted rape,[2] 1 out of 5 wives has been a victim of physical abuse by a husband,[3] 59% of battered women have been raped by the batterer,[4] 1 out of 3 girl children is sexually abused before she is 18 years old.[5] Simply because of our gender, we are viewed as legitimate targets for male aggression and violence. Every woman carries either the fear of violence or the memory of violence in her life.

The violence takes many forms: physical, psychological, sexual. Whether it is the brutalization of [an acquaintance], or the beating of a wife, or the molestation of a 3-year-old girl, or the unwanted hand on your thigh in the subway. Women and girls live with violence everyday.

The corollary to the fact of violence against women is that women are discouraged from reporting or talking about violence done to us. We are taught to accept violence and abuse as normative: for example, when women are assaulted by husbands, boyfriends, or acquaintances, they are unlikely to report the crimes. Only 5% of undergraduate women who experienced forced sex reported it to the police.[6] Other studies of rape victims found less than 10% reporting to the police.[7] There are multiple reasons for women not reporting these crimes to the police, not the least of which is the frequent lack of response or insensitivity of response by police. For example, in St. Petersburg in 1984, in only 1.7% of the "domestic dispute" calls made to police was there an arrest made.[8] Women do not expect to be believed when they report crimes done to them by people they know. In particular, most women of color do not expect the legal system to advocate for them or protect them from further violence. Many of the laws themselves would indicate this: as of 1987, marital rape was still legal in 36 states and only 5 states and the District of Columbia require mandatory arrest in domestic violence cases.[9] The legal system teaches women to accept violence and abuse as just the way things are.

Unfortunately our religious institutions frequently convey the same message. The pastor who responds to a battered woman with perfunctory prayer and counsel to return home and try to bring her husband to Jesus remains all too common. Likewise the church which punishes the very children who come to it for help when they are being abused by a parent: a woman called our office who had discovered her husband sexually abusing their children. She had had him arrested and removed from the home in order to protect the children. She went to her church and asked for support. She was told that she could not teach Sunday School any more and that her children could not attend Sunday School. Nothing was said to the offender.

These two conveyors of powerful social norms in our society, the legal system and religion, by and large still promote acceptance of violence against women as normative. Both women and men have learned to accept this norm.

Having set this context for our discussion, I would like to make [two] observations. These comments come out of my 15 years of working to end violence against women. There are several contemporary realities which reveal much to us about the power of the norm of violence against women.

First, the linking of abuse and love romanticizes violence against women. There is a song ["He Hit Me"], written by Carole King and Gerry Goffin in 1962, which has been rerecorded by a group called the Motels.

This song [in which a woman says it "felt like a kiss" when her man hit her][10] reflects the classic romanticization of violence that both men and women are taught: the pairing of love and violence, legitimated as a means of control. Jealousy is the excuse, violence is the means, control is the outcome. A 14-year-old female member of a church youth group explained to me once that she didn't think her boyfriend really loved her because he had not hit her yet.

Violence against women is not only romanticized; it is offered as entertainment for men in our society. The paired images of explicit sex and explicit violence dominate pornography of both the soft and hard core varieties. The message is that violence is sexy and good sex is violent. In the Philippines, in bars owned by Americans and patronized by U.S. servicemen, the floor show is a boxing match in which Filipinas are required to box each other, getting paid for each bruise or cut that they raise on the other woman. American men pay money to other men to see Third World women beat each other up. The women do this in order to feed their children.

Whose interests are served by romanticizing violence against women, by denying the truth of its pain and suffering, by the promotion of women's acceptance of violence as our lot in life?

My [second] observation has to do with our culture's inability to name violence against women as wrong, or in theological language, a sin. Let me illustrate first with a story from Hebrew Scripture found in Judges 19.

> There was a Levite who had a concubine. She ran away from him because he mistreated her and went back to her family. He pursued her to bring her back to his home. As they were traveling on the return journey, night drew near and they stopped in a village to seek shelter. As was the custom, they waited in the village square for someone to come and take them in. Finally an old man came and seeing them, took them to his home and gave them shelter and a meal.
>
> As they were making their hearts merry, behold, the men of the city, base fellows, beset the house round about, beating on the door; and they said to the old man, the master of the house, "Bring out the man who came into your house, that we may know him." And the man, the master of the house, went out to them and said to them, "No, my brethren, do not act so wickedly; seeing that this man has come into my house, do not do this vile thing. Behold, here are my virgin daughter and his concubine; let me bring them out now. Ravish them and do so with them what seems good to you; but against this man do not do so vile a thing." But the men would not listen to him. So the man seized his concubine, and put her out to them; and they knew her, and abused her all night until the morning. And as the dawn began to break, they let her go. And as the morning appeared, the woman came and fell down at the door of the man's house where her master was, till it was light.
>
> And her master rose up in the morning, and when he opened the doors of the house and went out to go on his way, behold, there was his concubine lying at the door of the house, with her hands on the threshold. He said to her, "Get up, let us be going." But there was no answer. Then he put her upon the ass; and the man rose up and went away to his home. And when he entered his house, he took a knife, and laying hold of his concubine he divided her, limb by limb, into twelve pieces, and sent her throughout all the territory of Israel. And all who saw it said, "Such a thing has never happened or been seen from the day that the people of Israel came up out of the land of Egypt until this day; direct your heart to her, take counsel, and speak."
>
> (Judges 19, RSV, alt.)

How many of you from Jewish or Christian backgrounds have ever heard a sermon preached on this passage? There is another version of this which is probably more familiar to most of you. It is the Sodom and Gomorrah story. I'm sure many more of you have heard that preached on and in the context of condemnation of gays and lesbians.

In fact, as is very clear in Judges 19, this is a story about rape, the attempted rape of the Levite and the actual rape and murder of his concubine. It is a story told in frightening detail of the expendability of both the virgin daughter of the host and of the concubine. And it is not at all clear in the end whether anyone understood that the crime here was the brutal torture and murder of a woman. Rather it appears that the people of that time saw the crime to be the destruction of the Levite's property. In any case, the traditional contemporary usage of both versions of this story has focused erroneously on the immorality of homosexuality and ignored the violence done to this woman.

This is not the only time that the Jewish and Christian faiths have had difficulty naming the sin of violence against women.

A more contemporary example: several years ago I attended a United Methodist conference on pornography. It was an attempt to bring together the wide divergence of opinion within the Methodist Church on this issue.

So we had feminists and reactionaries, scholars and civil libertarians, liberals and conservatives. I was presenting with Ed Donnerstein who is a researcher on pornography. As part of the presentation, Ed showed a 4 minute film clip from the movie *Tool Box Murders,* which is a teen slasher film. The clip began with a nude woman getting into a warm bath, pleasant music playing, a very relaxing scene. As she settles into the bath, she begins to masturbate. The pleasing, relaxing scene now becomes erotic. Then the scene shifts. A strange man comes into the woman's apartment. He is carrying a tool box. He is clearly an intruder. He walks through the apartment looking for the woman. He puts down his tool box and gets out his power nailer. She hears something and interrupts her bath. She gets up to check on the noise as he comes into the bathroom. She runs; he pursues her around the apartment. He finally corners her and proceeds to shoot nails into her, killing her in a scene of graphic, brutal violence. End of clip.

We asked the audience to react to this clip. A man stood and with a trembling voice expressed his outrage at showing a woman masturbating on film. He was appalled that teenagers could see such things. He said nothing about the fact that the woman had been murdered on film and that his sons and daughters were seeing that image juxtaposed with a very erotic image, that his daughters in particular were learning from that film that sexual pleasure for women is dangerous, that we can be killed if we seek to pleasure ourselves.

Why is women's sexuality so offensive but women's victimization is not? Why is the church so quick to name sexuality a sin and so hesitant to name the sin of violence against women?

In light of these observations, the linking of love and violence, the distortion of the truth of violence against women, and the difficulty in naming this truth a sin, what are we to do?

"Direct your heart to her, take counsel, and speak." This is the instruction which follows the telling of the concubine's story. Direct your heart to *the victim.* Consider her experience, her perspective, her powerlessness. Try to comprehend what it must have been like for her. Then speak. Break the silence which surrounds her death.

Not to speak is to be complicit in the terror which continues to shape women's lives. Elie Wiesel reminds us: "Let us remember: what hurts the victim most is not the cruelty of the oppressor, but the silence of the bystander." The silence of the church, the synagogue, the university, the courts, the family has been the predominant response to the truth of women's suffering.

The silence is a lie, a lie we tell ourselves, a lie we tell each other, a lie we let them tell about us, a lie we think protects us from violence. We must not lie anymore about the truth that we know. There are two truths: one is the truth of our experiences of violence; the other is the truth that it doesn't have to be this way.

"Direct your heart to her, take counsel, and speak."

To say that the way things are is not the way they have to be, to assert that violence against women is not a part of the created order, to suggest that women should not live in fear simply because of our gender is nothing less than a statement of faith in this time. There is little in our experience which tells us that women should be able to live free from fear. So we make this assertion on faith alone. As the writer of Hebrews said, "Now faith is the assurance of things hoped for, the conviction of things not seen." And after listing numerous foremothers and forefathers, the writer concludes: "These all died in faith, not having received what was promised, but having seen it and greeted it from afar, and having acknowledged that they were strangers and exiles on the earth." As women we are strangers and exiles to this patriarchal land. It is our job to speak the truth so that our daughters and granddaughters will know that the way things are is not the way they have to be.

PART II

A hundred years ago among the Tlingit people living in what is now southeast Alaska, there was a belief that one should not beat one's wife. If ever a husband deviated from this norm and beat his wife, his clan was required to pay her clan in material goods. The whole community came together for a potlatch to exchange the goods. The whole community knew why they were there. Wife-beating was expensive; wife-beating was shameful. There was very little wife-beating among the Tlingit people a hundred years ago.

The way things are is not the way they have to be. This is a lesson which we sometimes forget in our painful, cynical world views of this present age.

But in fact we face every day the aftermath of violence against women, in the midst of the injustice of rape, battering, child molestation. What do we do with these shattered lives?

"I was 11, at the end of 1982, when he sexually molested me. It was early in 1983 that I finally had the courage to tell my mother. I was very lucky because she believed me and got a restraining order to get my dad out of our house. I think the worst thing was when he pleaded not guilty to the criminal charges when he had already confessed to many people. I had to testify at the trial along with my sister. My mother and a therapist also testified. The jury decided that my father was guilty as charged. We were really glad. The day of his sentencing was unbelievable. My dad's new therapist testified and said that my father had no problem and that my dad said he knew what he did was wrong and that he would never do it again. He also said he didn't deserve any jail time. The judge didn't give him any jail time either. He got three years probation. . . . My dad got away with everything. He doesn't get punished, not only for what he did to me, but for what he did to my half-sister. He has ruined her life. . . . I just hope my dad and all the other molesters in this world get the punishment they deserve, so victims like me get justice."[11]

I'm sure we have all at some point in our own experience or in working with others, felt similar things:

—anger and frustration with the legal system
—anger and frustration when family members want to forgive and forget
—anger and frustration that offenders seem to be allowed to keep offending and victims ultimately are held responsible for the abuse.

In the midst of these feelings, I am convinced that we long for healing, for restoration, for reconciliation. We use words like "justice" or "forgiveness" because we hope that these are mechanisms to accomplish that which we long for.

And yet we long for healing from the very depths of our being—not expecting that everything will be fine or just like it was before, but that it will be made right in some way. That the brokenness which resulted from the acts of abuse will be made whole somehow. This is what we long for—whether we are victim, non-offending parent, friend, helper, or offender. We long to be made whole again.

It is my bias that some experience of *justice* is necessary in order for healing to take place, in order for a victim to become a survivor.

The imperative to do justice is based on three assumptions:

1. Embodiment is a crucial fact of our existence and requires that we take violations of bodily integrity seriously.
2. Relationship between and among persons is a primary value.
3. Persons can and should act in the face of injustice rather than remain passive (moral agency).

When we place three assumptions in the context of two additional working principles gleaned from liberation and feminist theologies, we realize the mandate to do justice. These principles are:

1. We must begin with the lived experience of persons.
2. We must take the side of the powerless and victimized.

This mandate propels us into the chaos of injustice and violation as we seek order, justice, and healing.

So what does this mean to a rape victim? It means that the truth of her rape is important both because it violates her bodily integrity and because it shatters any relationship with her offender in the past or the future. It means that she and we can act in response to her rape. It means that whatever we do begins with her experience and that our job is to take her side and stand by her throughout the process of justice making. The goal of justice making is the restoration of right-relationship, whether between her and her community, her family, or between her and her offender.

Now what is required? What are the particulars of doing justice? What does it look like to try to restore right relation?

1. *Truth-telling:* the silence which surrounds the violence is broken. Truth-telling is not merely a rendering of the facts; it is giving voice to a reality.
2. But truth told must also be truth heard. Hearing the truth means acknowledging the violence that has occurred. This *acknowledgment* needs to be spoken, simply and clearly: "You have been harmed by this person. It was not your fault. This is wrong and should never have happened. We regret that it happened to you." This acknowledgment can come from a friend, a pastor, the legal system, etc. But it needs to come from somewhere.
3. *Compassion* is the willingness to "suffer with" combined with efforts to alleviate the suffering. Rather than trying to minimize, explain away, or avoid the suffering of another, we should be present with them.
4. *Protecting the vulnerable from further abuse* means that we do whatever is necessary to protect the victim and others from further harm. This may mean restraint of an offender prior to and after conviction or it may mean helping a battered woman change her identity and move to another state.
5. *Accountability* is confrontation with the offender, the one responsible for the violence, which hopefully results in confession or acknowledgment by him of his responsibility. Willard Gaylin argues that: ". . . those of us who transgress have a right to *receive* punishment; if we are not punished adequately for our crimes, we are being treated as less than persons. . . . As a tribute and testament to the aggressor's freedom, we must dignify him by making him pay for the evil actions he commits. We show our respect by making him accountable."

6. *Restitution,* making payment for damage done by violence, is a concrete means of renewing right-relation. Not only does material restitution help pay for actual expenses incurred as a result of the victimization, it is highly symbolic. It is a tangible sign of an attempt to restore that which was lost due to an assault.

7. *Vindication* for victims is the substance of justice and mercy. Vindication refers not to vengeance and retaliation but to the exoneration and justification of those harmed. The obsolete definition of vindication is "to set free"; hence to be vindicated is to be set free from the bondage of victimization.

Now how does all of this work in our lives? Let me illustrate with a story about a woman who came to me who had been molested as a child by her uncle. After meeting with me for several weeks, she began to let loose her anger at what he had done to her. And she quickly felt ready to confront him; she wanted to tell him what he had done and what it had cost her over the years and how angry she was at him. But she could not because he was deceased. So where was she to put her anger and her truth-telling? She decided to write to her father, whose brother had molested her. She told him the whole story. She did not know what her father would do with this piece of news. She and he had a fairly good relationship and saw each other once a year. But she was unsure how he would receive this information. Her father came to her immediately after receiving her letter. The first thing he said was, "I'm sorry." He said, "I didn't know that this was happening to you but I knew that something was wrong, that you were having trouble and I didn't ask to find out. In any case, I should have been there for you. I should have protected you; I am your father." When I saw her a week later, she was a different person. The burden of the memory of her childhood victimization had been lifted from her. Her father had listened to her truth without questioning it, he acknowledged it, he was compassionate, and he took responsibility, not for his brother's offense, but for his inability at the time to protect her. He was accountable. He also offered to help with her medical and counseling expenses.

This woman experienced justice in a 10-minute conversation with her father. And having experienced justice, she was able to let go of the powerful, painful memory of what her uncle had done. She was able to forgive.

In forgiving, she did not say that what was done to her was now okay. She did not have to make herself forget what was done to her. But she was able to release herself from its power so it no longer victimized her or diminished her life. She could now go on and live her life. Forgiveness is about letting go . . . for the sake of the victim, not for the sake of the offender.

This is a justice that is life-giving, that enables restoration, that creates the possibility of reconciliation and renewal of right-relation. This is the justice that we must demand from our churches and synagogues, from our legal system, from our families and friends.

Is such justice possible? Yes. Because we make it possible. We make it possible because, like Celie in *The Color Purple*, we never get used to the violence. And because we never let go of the anger we feel when we see, or hear about, or experience violence against women. Such justice is possible because we make it possible. We make it possible because, to paraphrase Andrea Dworkin:

In our hearts, we are mourners for all of those who have not survived.
In our souls, we are warriors for those who are now as we were then.
In our lives, we are both celebrant and proof of women's capacity and will to survive, to become, to act, to change self and society.
And each year, we are stronger, and there are more of us.[12]

NOTES

1. Alice Walker, *The Color Purple* (New York: Washington Square Press, 1982).
2. Dianna Russell, *Sexual Exploitation* (Phoenix: Sage Press, 1984).
3. Dianna Russell, *Rape in Marriage* (New York: Macmillan Publishing Co., 1982).
4. Lenore Walker, *The Battered Woman Syndrome* (New York: Springer, 1984).
5. Russell, *Sexual Exploitation*.
6. Koss, *Journal of Consulting and Clinical Psychology*, March 1987.
7. Russell, *Sexual Exploitation*.
8. *St. Petersburg Times*, May 21, 1984.
9. National Center on Women and Family Law, 1987.
10. Carole King and Gerry Goffin, "He Hit Me," Screen Gems—EMI Music Inc., 1962.
11. *Seattle Times*, Aug. 13, 1984.
12. Andrea Dworkin, "The Bruise That Didn't Heal," *Mother Jones*, July 1978 (altered).

29

Refusing to Be "Good Soldiers": An Agenda for Men

MARVIN M. ELLISON

In the past two decades, male violence has been the focus of intense debate within the feminist movement. Men have rarely participated in that movement, but their absence is not entirely due to antifeminism. As Bell Hooks observes, some women, especially those who have identified all men as the enemy, have perpetuated a traditional (that is, sexist) sex-role division by assigning to women exclusively the task of "cleaning up the mess" and creating a feminist revolution. At the same time, Hooks rightly acknowledges that all men do support—and benefit from—sexist oppression in one way or another, but even so,

> it is crucial that feminist activists not get bogged down in intensifying our awareness of this fact to the extent that we do not stress the more unemphasized point which is that men can lead life-affirming, meaningful lives without exploiting and oppressing women.[1]

Men, as well as women, are socialized passively to accept sexism as the "natural" order of things and to internalize its ideology and norms as fixed and unalterable. While none of us men in Western culture is more "blameworthy" than another for the sexism we have internalized, each of us must assume responsibility for eliminating sexism and ending our complicity in the oppression of ourselves and others.

Becoming responsible as men does not mean leaning on women to do our political and emotional work for us, nor does it mean taking charge of the feminist movement. Rather, we men have our own work to do in order to reclaim the power to change our lives in more humanizing directions, as we become strong advocates for the well-being of women and children and for their increased empowerment to become the "subjects of their lives."

I suggest three areas for us men to explore together in order to strengthen ourselves for constructive participation in the movement to eliminate violence from our lives: (1) studying our lives as men, especially our sexualities, and reclaiming the centrality of bodily connectedness; (2) breaking our silence about the abuse of male power and supporting *and* confronting one another as we do so; and (3) accounting for the "faith within us" to sustain the struggle for a far different world, one without patriarchal privilege and devoid of the violence that sustains male gender superiority.

What follows is exploratory and suggestive of only a partial agenda, that men will need to delineate and refine together. I address these remarks directly to men because it is our work of which I am speaking, but I trust women will participate in the process as well, if only to continue to hold us accountable for our words and our deeds.

One preliminary observation: patriarchy, the social structure built on male gender privilege and the power of men to control women and less powerful, socially marginalized men, is perpetuated by the acceptance and internalization of its ideology of masculinity. Insofar as men identify and comply with patriarchal ideology, we will seek but also most often exaggerate the power that this system grants to us as men. Although men as a group do have more power than women, the majority of men do not exercise significant personal power in Western society or experience secure control over our own lives. Moreover, no matter how much power the system has given to any one of us, this power is useful only in keeping things going according to present rules and dynamics, not in changing things in any fundamental way. When men deviate from, or actively resist, the status quo, power is taken away from us. Often that resistance is met with punishments, including the loss of job, status, social respectability, and life itself. Gay men, as nonconformists to patriarchy, are the prime illustration of those considered traitors to the "male cause."

The power to change comes not from the patriarchal system but from another source—our ability to connect with ourselves and others and then passionately to forge an alternative possibility. The good news, as Tony Eardley identifies it, is that while "the ideology of masculinity is generalized and pervasive, and molds us all," none of us is simply a passive recipient of it, "any more than all women have accepted their own ideological designation."[2] To own up to the discrepancy between the ideological standard for men and our own lived experience makes possible a way to reinforce our need and our responsibility to make choices that are life-enhancing both for ourselves and for others.

STUDYING OUR LIVES,
OUR SEXUALITIES

For us men to study our lives, we need to look carefully at our own experiences and struggles. At the same time, we need to understand how others perceive us and how we and the world we have created are experienced by others, especially by those least powerful and well placed in Western society. Examining our role in that preeminently masculine occupation, war making, is a good place to start.

Training to be a "good soldier" is a process of instilling macho-masculinity, an intensification of the typical male socialization process in which men are trained to be violent, aggressive, controlling, and emotionally detached. Men are socialized to "toughen up" in order to be able to dominate and coerce other people without self-reflection or guilt. Such toughening is necessary so that men will willingly use violence and inflict suffering upon others, as well as tolerate their own pain and risk their own deaths.

Military training involves distancing the self from one's own body, from other people's bodies, and from the emotions. During basic training, a young recruit's insecurity about his own sexuality and manhood is systematically manipulated in order to link sexuality with aggression and domination. Because manhood is a quality to be achieved and, therefore, something that can either be lost or never firmly established, men are threatened with basic insecurity about their own worth in a male system that generates fear, uncertainty, and self-doubt about one's adequacy and ability to "make the grade." To avoid becoming an "unreal man," that is, like a woman or like less powerful men in this culture, men strive desperately to establish their superiority. They prove their fitness to do their duty by assuming control, by violence if necessary, over their own bodies and bodily senses, but also by controlling others and nature itself. As one Vietnam veteran describes his experience in basic training,

> The primary lesson of boot camp, towards which all behavior was shaped, was to seek dominance. . . . All else was non-masculine. . . . Recruits were often stunned by the depths of violence erupting within themselves. Only on these occasions of violent outbursts did the drill instructor cease his endless litany of "you dirty faggots" and "Can't hack it little girls?" After a continuous day of harassment, I bit a man on the face during hand-to-hand combat, gashing his eyebrow and cheek. I had lost control. For the first time the drill instructor didn't physically strike me or call me a faggot. He put his arm around me and said that I was a lot more of a man than he had previously imagined. In front of the assembled platoon [he] gleefully reaffirmed my masculinity.[3]

The ideology of war and the ideology of masculinity are intertwined. Both are based on contempt for women and on a corollary fear of homosexuality. Homosexuality is especially fearful because it represents a deviation from and break with the strongest and most familiar social control on sexuality in Western culture, the patriarchal social pattern of compulsory heterosexuality. Heterosexism insists that both men and women conform to sterotypic gender roles and to dominant-subordinate power dynamics. This elaborate social construction of human sexuality is ideologically built on two assumptions: on gender dualism, that there are fundamental differences and an unalterable inequality between men and women, and on gender hierarchy, that male superiority and control over women is natural and good.

According to this heterosexist code, which the military strenuously reinforces, moral legitimacy is granted only to certain configurations of power and only to certain sexual and social relationships. When men are on top, all is well with the patriarchal world. Men remain members of the club especially by avoiding the realm, the tasks, and the concerns of women, Men who do not play their dominant role, either by choice or by accident, are viewed as failed men. They are perceived as homosexuals, whether accurately or not, and like women, that is, without power and status. Winner or loser, on top or on bottom, are the only outcomes available to the patriarchal imagination.

The modern soldier as a "killing machine" bears a striking resemblance to modern patriarchy's other cultural hero, *homo economicus,* the corporate executive who makes a killing in the market or arranges for plant closings without serious regard for the human and social costs involved. Both roles reflect the abstractionism, or remoteness from reality, that is so characteristic of the masculinist ethos. Taught to fear and repress their feelings, especially feelings of pain and vulnerability, men literally lose connection with themselves and others, so that "the man who kills from a distance and without consciousness of the consequences of his deeds feels no need to answer to anyone or to himself."[4]

Disassociation from the body and from the emotions is at the root of this absence of moral sensitivity to the suffering men inflict on ourselves and on others. Since we are connected to ourselves and to the world only in and through our bodies, when we no longer feel and experience our bodily connectedness, we literally lose touch with reality. As men who batter others give ample testimony, those not able to feel their own pain are more likely to inflict pain on others. In the process, they may in fact not know what they are doing or what is being done in their name, a situation also true in war.

How might we deal with this emotional illiteracy and engage in a process to, literally, "come to our senses"? Glenn Gray offers a provocative suggestion that the appeals of war will dissipate only as men experience a radical inner change and emotional reorientation, a process of gaining genuine closeness and intimacy with ourselves, other people, and the natural order. Physical proximity by itself does not guarantee such intimacy, as battered women can certainly attest. Genuine relationship, or deep connectedness, is possible only as we recover intimacy, the embodied capacity to let go of control and experience mutual delight in one another's company.

Deepening awareness of our need and capacity for intimacy in relation to women is critical but not more so than in relation to other men, both those more powerful and those less powerful than ourselves. As Joseph Pleck has rightly observed, "Ultimately, men cannot go any further in relating to women as equals than they have been able to go in relating to other men as equals."[5] Examining issues of intimacy with other men is especially needed, for homophobia and heterosexism teach us that "real men" must exercise power over other men as well as over women and that closeness to other men signals effeminacy and loss of manhood.

For me, the gift of the profeminist men's movement has been the invitation together with other men to explore friendship and take mutual delight in sharing physical touch and gestures of care and nurture. Because patriarchy assigns women to deal with matters of intimacy and emotional nurture, we men have depended almost exclusively on women friends and female lovers to find the personal support and comfort that now we are slowly discovering we can both give to and receive from other men. In honoring our love for other men, we also come to celebrate our love for our own selves. Only in self-acceptance do we find the source of our personal power to live securely in touch with our own value and the value of others.

Regaining intimacy also requires reclaiming the centrality of erotic power in our lives. Embracing the erotic and the sensuous as a source of our knowledge and empowerment goes against the dominant culture's wisdom that men are associated only with the "higher" things of the mind, of the spirit (not body), and of the will's control over the body and over nonrational spontaneity. It also challenges the patriarchal assumption that the passions are tainted and intrinsically corrupt and corrupting. As Audre Lorde argues,

> We have been raised to fear the yes within ourselves, our deepest cravings. . . . When we live outside ourselves, and by that I mean on external directives only, rather than from our internal knowledge and needs, then . . . we conform to the needs of a structure that is not based on human need, let alone an individual's. But when we begin to live from within ourselves . . . then we begin to be responsible to ourselves in the deepest sense.[6]

Women, first of all, but also gay men are the designated "carriers" of the erotic in Western culture. The best test of men's willingness to take the body seriously is how well gay men are respected and listened to as unique male resources for living passionately and gaining strength, through bodily intimacy, in the struggle to resist the dynamics of masculinist oppression. Because gay men celebrate love for men's bodies and refuse to "disincarnate" their own lives by insisting upon the integrity of body *and* spirit, they embody a wisdom empowering for all men to honor the erotic as creative life-source as well as the well-spring of desire to value our own unique identities in relation to others. As we gain trust in our ability to name ourselves and our needs and to discern what is genuinely life-giving for us, we also learn to respect and appreciate that process in others.

In patriarchy, as in capitalism, all self-directed human needs and desires are denied or strenuously frustrated, except those that have been cultivated to maintain the smooth functioning of the present social order. Enormous pressure is applied to discount one's own feelings and sensibilities as "merely" subjective and idiosyncratic and to accept external guides for what is "truly" desirable and worthy of our respect. That so many men put up with unsatisfying jobs, for example, in exchange for the dubious reward of being considered a "real man" who earns his own keep and can rule the roost when he goes home is but one illustration of how our manly acceptance of "doing our duty" thwarts us from living on the basis of our own deepest desires and needs. When we fear and ignore the erotic, we also give over our trust and power to external authorities to know better than ourselves what is life-giving for us.

Whenever we are cut off from the sensuous wisdom of the body and from the knowledge that our feelings communicate, we lose the much needed capacity to experience our own pain and joy, as well as losing a deeply felt sense of connectedness to all that is around us. When we are deeply in touch with our own desires, vulnerabilities, and passion for life, we will be less inclined to inflict pain on others, but equally important, we will also become less willing to tolerate abuse of ourselves. Recovery of body connectedness and of our capacity to give and receive pleasure, therefore, has direct bearing on the problem of violence in our culture. As James Nelson comments, there is now considerable research that shows "close connections between peacefulness and the experience of body pleasure, and between violence and suppression of body pleasure."[7] Studying our lives and our sexualities in order to increase our ability to experience body pleasure is thus our first work in eliminating violence from our lives.

BREAKING OUR SILENCE ABOUT
MALE VIOLENCE

As men we rarely gather to talk about our lives and discuss how we are implicated in violence. When the subject is addressed, my experience has been similar to Tony Eardley's that we men "are often confused, defensive, self-doubting or self-hating and resentful. A challenge to sexual violence may itself produce a violent reaction."[8]

That silence might be explicable if all men were, indeed, rapists or batterers. The fact that only some are does not explain our general reluctance to address the problem of male violence. Another explanation might be that all men feel the guilt and shame of male violence, but as studies regularly indicate, men who are violent against women and children rarely, if ever, experience remorse or contrition. The fact that women, not men, have traditionally been the service providers, relegated to "bind up the wounds" of those who have been violated and abused by others, may account for some of our distancing from these issues, but I have another hunch about our silence and confusion.

As part of a patriarchal society, we men fear isolation and rejection from the company of men. To acknowledge candidly the reality and depth of the problem of male violence requires courage for any man who dares to risk speaking the truth and to hold himself—*and other men*—accountable. Because any departure from the dominant male role, as well as all direct confrontations about the "limits of masculinity," incurs costs for the individual man, speaking out about male violence is likely to generate fear in us of being repudiated by other men as disloyal and "unmanly." Precisely for this reason, I think Sally Gearhart is right to argue that the danger for most women is not the individual man, who may in fact be deeply sympathetic to feminism and engaged in personal resistance to dominant male gender roles. Rather, the danger is "in the phenomenon of male bonding."[9]

Glenn Gray is helpful on the reality of men closing ranks with one another. He notes that in war, "the most potent quieters of conscience are evidently the presence of others who are doing the same things," as well as the awareness that the soldier is acting under orders from those "superior" to himself who will answer for his own conduct.[10] I would add that a more telling possibility is that individual men who abhor violence keep silence for fear of alienating other men or of being themselves subjected to their ridicule and other men's violence.

Two social psychologists, John Sabini and Maury Silver, have examined various research projects about the formation of moral conscience and the capacity of persons to challenge institutional dynamics of injustice and oppression. They argue that "moral drift" occurs when individuals are afraid to speak publicly about their objections to violation and abuse. In one experiment they reviewed, a model prison was set up and staffed by volunteers, each assigned to a role as prisoner or guard. Although many of the "guards" soon displayed acts of brutality toward their "prisoners," some men showed moral sensitivity and refrained from any violence or abuse. These "good guards," however, never spoke out to reproach any of their comrades for their misconduct, and the brutality rapidly escalated unchecked. As Sabini and Silver conclude, "The failure to establish publicly the wrongness of a particular action gives it an implicit legitimacy." Although the public establishment of a moral consensus among men about the limits of acceptable male behavior may not, by itself, restrain or inhibit certain actions, "at the very least, the *failure to condemn* allows those who ignore simple moral requirements to do so more easily."[11]

We men do violence by our silence, as well as with our fists. Men who batter their partners, for example, believe that most men support them. Therefore, it is particularly important for us to communicate, in visible, outspoken ways, that abuse by men is unacceptable behavior and will not receive our endorsement. Moreover, we must model publicly as well as privately our enthusiastic support for the empowerment of women as agents of their own lives and well-being and accept our responsibility to educate and work with other men to change our own masculinist behavior patterns and attitudes. Only when we men passionately and energetically join in a broad-based social-protest movement to critique and challenge male violence will a strong enough shift occur in the prevailing moral climate, which, at present, too easily minimizes or denies these abuses of male power.

One lesson for us is a warning "not to go it alone" but to connect with other men for mutual support and empowerment. Power for change is found in collective, shared power. The lone warrior, even the most courageous moral crusader, is too easily intimidated and isolated or burns out.

A second lesson is this: men who personally reject the use of violence but do not engage in confronting other men remain untrustworthy allies in the struggle. A concern for one's own personal purity and for maintaining one's status as a "good guard" in the midst of brutality does little to alter the conditions which perpetuate the violence. Gay men often experience this phenomenon from "liberal" straight men who are tolerant themselves but who fail to speak out against homophobic acts and speech from their male associates. In fact, even the presence of a few "good guards" helps to legitimate the prison system as good, decent, and reasonable.

Each of us is implicated in the violences that permeate our world. Where systemic injustices prevail, no one has clean hands. Just as in a racist society it is a delusion to regard oneself as nonracist, so in a violent society it is impossible to be totally nonviolent, for the institutions we help to maintain by our silence and conformity do the violence for us. Our struggle as men is to become passionately antiracist, antiviolent, antipatriarchal. Fortunately, as Barbara Smith reminds us, "it is neither possible nor necessary to be morally exempt in order to stand in opposition to oppression."[12] What is necessary is to take a stance of resistance, join with others in that struggle, and hold oneself accountable as to how one's own power affects the lives of others for good or ill.

When men become as vocal and organized as women now are in the movement to end violence, among nation states as well as in the family, a major step will be made toward delegitimating and removing the violences from our own lives.

ACCOUNTING FOR THE FAITH
WITHIN US

The struggle to transform ourselves and our world is simultaneously a political and a spiritual process. To believe that a just and nonviolent world is possible requires me to "hope against hope" that my brothers and I may contribute to that transformation, even though violence is deeply entrenched and we face incredible odds. Reclaiming our power to change our lives—and to be changed—is essential to any liberating spirituality. How we name, nurture, and share that power is never a morally neutral or inconsequential matter. The particularities of how we as men experience and articulate our faith will vary, but *what* power we hold as sacred and life-giving needs exploration.

Patriarchal spirituality fosters a quest for transcendence as the highest good, a life beyond vulnerability and dependence on others and an acquisition of absolute control. Allegiance to the male warrior-god sends us scurrying after power-as-domination and in futile search for mastery, for that alienated and alienating power to affect others without being affected ourselves. Small wonder that the "god-*phantasie*" of male supremacy, to use Dorothee Soelle's phrase, is a cold, aloof, and indifferent spectator, who is, literally, "above it all," untouched and untouchable and neither interested in nor affected by human struggles.

To place what is most sacred, valued, and worthy of our loyalty outside the realm of what we see and touch and sense often leads to the abuse and disregard of the integrity of our own bodies, those of others, and of the physical world. By locating what is sacred above and beyond us, we maintain a patriarchal split-consciousness, which allows us to inflict and to suffer pain and violation in pursuit of a transcendent, otherworldly, and unmanifest good beyond ourselves. Violence is often justified in the name of defending such abstractions, including the honor of patriarchy's "Lord God almighty," "Western civilization," and "man's home as his castle." Such abstractions lure us away from the embodied goodness that sustains our lives and only encourage us to distance ourselves from others, as well as from the consequences of our own actions. Those of us who came of age during the Vietnam era experienced the pull of patriarchy toward violence as we struggled against it in order to honor and act upon our deep desire and commitment for peaceful connection with distant people quite different from ourselves. War resistance was as much a spiritual as a political struggle to refuse to become "good soldiers" and to become more powerful lovers of peace and justice.

To honor the flesh-and-blood connections between persons as sacred and inviolate, as well as the web of interrelatedness linking all of life, is to grasp a different experience of transcendence and of the holy. In liberation perspective, transcendence is not a quest for control and mastery but rather the capacity to turn toward the "familiar and evident" and deeply enjoy the pleasure of mutual well-being and at-homeness. That experience, however partial and fragmentary in our lives, affirms that gentleness and power coexist in ways that alone make life worth living. Liberation faith finds its truth in the discovery and enrichment of the "blessed ties" that bind us together with all that is and in the strengthening of genuine solidarity among all peoples. The only spirituality worthy of our devotion is one that cultivates the mutual well-being of bodies and spirits together, ours and all others.

For us men, what faith actually grounds and moves us will be most evident in the actions we are inspired to undertake for our own sake and for the renewal of our world. Not all actions will generate a future for this planet in which life worth living and worth sharing may flourish. Our taking due care to nurture the faith within us and among us will have unavoidable spiritual and, therefore, humanly significant import. With Denise Levertov, may we men be well advised on this score: "Let our different dream, and more than dream, our acts of constructive refusal generate struggle. And love. We must dare to win not wars, but a future in which to live."[13]

NOTES

1. Bell Hooks, *Feminist Theory: From Margin to Center* (Boston: South End Press, 1984), 72.

2. Tony Eardley, "Violence and Sexuality," in *The Sexuality of Men*, ed. Andy Metcalf and Martin Humphries (London: Pluto Press, 1985), 87.

3. Wayne Eisenhart, USMC, quoted by Rick Ritter, "Bringing War Home: Vets Who Have Battered," in *Battered Women's Directory*, ed. Betsy Warrior, 9th ed. (Richmond, Ind.: Earlham College, 1985), 254.

4. J. Glenn Gray, *The Warriors: Reflections on Men in Battle* (New York: Harper & Row, 1970), xviii.

5. Joseph H. Pleck, "Men's Power with Women, Other Men, and Society: A Men's Movement Analysis," in *The American Man,* ed. Elizabeth H. Pleck and Joseph H. Pleck (Englewood Cliffs, N.J.: Prentice-Hall, 1980), 428.

6. Audre Lorde, "Uses of the Erotic: The Erotic as Power," in *Take Back the Night: Women on Pornography,* ed. Laura Lederer (New York: William Morrow & Co., 1980), 299.

7. James B. Nelson, *The Intimate Connection: Male Sexuality, Masculine Spirituality* (Philadelphia: Westminster Press, 1988), 80.

8. Eardley, "Violence and Sexuality," 86.

9. Sally Miller Gearhart, "The Future—If There Is One—Is Female," in *Reweaving the Web of Life: Feminism and Nonviolence,* ed. Pam McAllister (Philadelphia: New Society Publishers, 1982), 281.

10. Gray, *The Warriors,* 175.

11. John Sabini and Maury Silver, *Moralities of Everyday Life* (New York: Oxford University Press, 1982), 83, 51.

12. Barbara Smith, "Between a Rock and a Hard Place: Relationships Between Black and Jewish Women," in *Yours in Struggle: Three Feminist Perspectives on Anti-Semitism and Racism,* ed. Elly Bulkin, Minnie Bruce Pratt, and Barbara Smith (Brooklyn: Long Haul Press, 1984), 71.

13. Denise Levertov, "A Speech: For Antidraft Rally, D.C., March 22, 1980," in her *Candles in Babylon* (New York: New Directions Publishing Corp., 1982), 96.

30

Pornography:
An Agenda for
the Churches

MARY D. PELLAUER

Pornography is a confusing and risky topic, fraught with controversies. Once the issue seemed simple, no matter which side one was on. When *Lady Chatterley's Lover*, *The Well of Loneliness* and *Ulysses* appeared, conservatives rushed to protect the public from these "salacious" texts, while progressives rallied to the cause of artistic freedom and celebrated a new openness about sexuality. Today these simple oppositions concerning porn are gone. Passions run just as deep, but opinions have proliferated. The radical changes in the terms used to evaluate pornography over the past twenty years may leave some of us gasping. The report of the 1970 Presidential Commission on Obscenity and Pornography, which found that there were "no negative effects" of porn, today seems a product of the nineteenth century instead of the late 1960s and 1970s. The 1986 report by Attorney General Edwin Meese's Commission on Pornography paid serious attention to sexually violent and degrading porn, and recorded internal disagreement over whether nonviolent depictions of sexual activities are inherently harmful. Controversy was immediate, with four or five varieties of contending responses being voiced.

But opinions about porn have not spread so wide or so fast as has porn itself. The past twenty years have seen a dramatic explosion of porn products and outlets. Cable television offers sexually explicit movies, and corner drugstores and newsstands feature glossy porn magazines. Dial-a-porn numbers rake in calls and cash from coast to coast. Adult theaters are waning, but only because home video equipment has cut into the market. By one estimate, as many as 40 percent of VCR owners consume porn in their homes (a figure thought to represent 9 percent of all American households). It is estimated that the porn business involves some $8 to $10 billion annually.

In this changed social landscape, discussing porn is both risky and urgent—

perhaps especially so in the churches. Whatever we say about porn may reveal things about us we would rather keep concealed. In some circles, for a woman even to look at pornography, let alone to observe and analyze it, raises suspicions about her morality. Though I see the need to confront pornography as a Christian, I fear touching off a backlash against sexuality and against women in the churches. I often feel tongue-tied in the face of these issues. (Andrea Dworkin, a noted antiporn activist, has suggested that one function of pornography may be precisely to silence women.) Yet we must deal with porn in all its complications.

PORNOGRAPHY AND THE LAWS

Even defining pornography is complicated. The word itself comes from the Greek words for "writing" (*graphein*) and "whores" (*pornē*), and it once meant just that—writing about whores. The difficulty in defining pornography is a problem not only for ordinary discussions but for the courts as well. In a landmark 1957 decision, the U.S. Supreme Court asserted that obscenity is not protected by the First Amendment. In doing so, it defined obscenity, not pornography. The justices said, "A thing is obscene if, considered as a whole, its predominant appeal is to prurient interest, i.e., a shameful or morbid interest in nudity, sex or excretion, and if it goes substantially beyond customary limits of candor in description or representation of such matters."

As any citizen might do, the court appealed to Webster's to define "prurient": "having a tendency to excite lustful thoughts; uneasy with desire or longing; having itching, morbid or lascivious longings," etc. Later the justices referred to "sexual responses over and beyond those that would be characterized as normal," emphasizing that they did not intend to include "material that provoked only normal, healthy sexual desires." At other times the court has affirmed that obscenity applies to material depicting sexual matter "in a patently offensive way." Other qualifications have been made by the court. To be judged obscene, sexual materials must be "utterly without redeeming social value," lack any "serious literary, artistic, political or scientific value," and portray sexual conduct "for its own sake and for the ensuing commercial gains." As is well known, the court leaves many such judgments to the "average individual" and local community standards. On the other hand, judgments of redeeming social value are subject to national standards, not to local ones.

The effect of these broad judgments has been to limit obscenity prosecution to hard-core porn. The best description of hard-core porn may still be Justice Potter Stewart's 1964 comment—that he wouldn't attempt to define it but he knew it when he saw it. Evasive as that may sound, after nine years of investigating porn I have a similar response. What is obscene or pornographic can be dramatically relative. For instance, an acquaintance of mine on the national staff of a Protestant denomination was deeply disturbed when an evangelical conference on porn used a photo of a woman's naked breast among its examples—hardly a case of the material available in porn shops. On the other side of the spectrum, feminists object to the portrayal of violence against or exploitation of women in advertisements that don't feature nudity. A new genre of ads (both print and film), many with an "Old West" theme, features cowboys "roping" women or a group of menacing-looking men approaching a woman who has fallen from a horse (these ads are usually for blue jeans).

For me, pornography is problematic not because it is sexually explicit but because it portrays violence and domination in a sexual context. I have no desire to return to Victorian prudery, to the earlier condemnations of sex as a special source of sin, or even to the lesser silences about sex in our own century. But because I cherish my whole sensual self and believe that good theology calls us to celebrate healthy human sexuality, I find pornography abhorrent.

As a feminist theologian, the greatest concerns I have about porn are not easily addressed by government regulation or prosecution. I am as concerned with the great pool of public sentiment out of which the laws arise and are applied—the "ethos" of the people that is the subject of "ethics"—as I am with the legal issues. Whether or not we favor stepped-up prosecution of obscene materials, those of us in religious communities have a special interest in the formation of character and dispositions—in the moral atmosphere of our society and in a whole range of symbolic concerns. In the nature of the case, these do not bear directly on the legality of acts. The law provides a floor, a minimal standard below which acts of the community are not allowed to fall. Without de-emphasizing the crucial nature of the nation's laws in social-justice matters, we must recall that our theological heritage calls us to far more than the law can pursue.

PORNOGRAPHY AND THE CHURCHES

Churches have shown a new activism and concern about pornography. For example, prior to its merger with other Lutheran bodies, the American Lutheran Church updated its 1974 statement on pornography. The United Church of Canada has also created a new statement, responding largely to concerns about sexual violence. Ecumenical leaders in states such as Pennsylvania have joined to oppose porn. Evangelical groups, such as the National Coalition Against Pornography, claim a burgeoning membership and make use of activist tactics. The new Religious Alliance Against Pornography, composed of both liberals and conservatives, sponsored a White House Conference in the fall of 1986 and organized local groups around the country. A 1985 report on "Violence and Sexual Violence in Film, Television, Cable and Home Video" by the National Council of Churches of Christ suggested that the churches give "priority attention" to the "glut of violence and sexual violence" in the media.

The NCC report led to a 1986 policy statement by the General Board of the National Council which "affirms . . . adherence to the principles of an open marketplace of ideas and the guarantees of the First Amendment to freedom of

speech, of the press and of religion," but which also called on the communication and entertainment media to regulate themselves before censorship returned. In its statement the NCC called for greater involvement by the Federal
Communications Commission in guarding the public airwaves. It also urged
churches to assist their members in becoming more sensitive to the impact of
media violence on families.

If churches are to act responsibly on pornography, they must first of all take
sexual violence seriously. It has by no means been proven that pornography
causes sexual violence. Indeed, since widespread sexual violence predated
widespread pornography, it would be difficult to prove this hypothesis. For
millennia, women have been viewed as property—legal and economic—with the
consequence of sexual ownership and violation. But the fact that there are no
obvious connections between porn and sexual violence does not mean there are
no connections at all.

Certainly the portrayal of rape as something women desire proceeds out of
and reinforces rapist perspectives. Some sex offenders do speak about their use of
porn. Many porn scenarios are strikingly similar to the motives and concerns of
the assailants we know as "power rapists." The chosen woman/victim says,
"No, no, no" but ends up begging to be conquered. The basic plot of many
kinds of porn is the overcoming of a woman's resistance so thoroughly that she is
gratefully orgasmic. Other plots more directly assert that people derive sexual
pleasure from being hurt or hurting others.

Some studies indicate that those exposed to sexually violent depictions are
more likely to accept rape myths, the "need" for violence between men and
women, and "adversarial" views about sex. Under laboratory conditions, the
viewing of scenes of sexual violence correlates with increased aggression toward
women. This effect appears to hold true especially when subjects are previously
incited to be angry at women. (A second large category of rapists is motivated by
anger.) And after viewing depictions of sexual violence, subjects in simulated
court cases are most likely to blame victims and less likely to convict offenders.
These findings have extremely serious implications about the effect of porn on
the health and safety of women.

Many observers of porn believe that its overtly violent content has increased
significantly in recent years. Anyone who looks at porn wares will be struck by
the frequent theme of "bondage" or "discipline." Certainly I will never forget
some images: the black woman chained astraddle a stepladder with an apple in
her mouth; the needle-nosed pliers coming toward a woman's nipple; whips
used and sexual organs wielded like punishing tools, to "teach a lesson." And
violence lurks on the edge of pornographic material that is not explicitly violent.
It is only a short step from systematically degrading people to harming them (as
we have learned from our nation's racist violence at home and abroad).

We in the churches need to concentrate especially upon disentangling sex and
sexual violence from each other. Our theological tradition is less than helpful
here. Classic theologians regularly confused sexuality with sexual violence, often

mistaking rape for adultery. In condemning the sex, they barely noted the violence. (For spectacular examples of the systematic confusion of sex and rape, see chapters 17–30 of Book I of Augustine's *City of God* or Luther's commentary on the rape laws of Deuteronomy 28.) Some of us may be learning for the first time about the devastations of sexual abuse by learning about pornography, and that is necessary. Nonetheless, the ready acceptance of concern about porn in many conservative churches raises serious suspicions that pornography has been singled out for action *because it is sexual,* not because it is violent or actively degrading to women—especially since many conservative Christians have criticized battered women's shelters, sex education and planned parenthood centers. Sexual violence, sexism and sexuality all come together in porn. Disentangling them is a difficult but necessary task.

My conclusion from my work with sexual and domestic violence is that porn is a serious danger to public safety, akin to shouting "Fire" in a crowded theater; but given legal rules of evidence, there may be little hope of convincing courts of this analogy. At the same time, the safety of women and children must be secured by a broad range of prevention and treatment measures. With money for social programs scarce, my own priority is to put cash into more direct action on sexual and domestic violence rather than into prosecuting obscenity. Pornography does contribute to the multiple forces giving rise to sexual and domestic violence, but we cannot afford to be mesmerized by porn as the single issue. Complex judgments are necessary.

If the churches are to deal responsibly with porn, they must also affirm and celebrate healthy human sexuality. While many people may agree that depictions of sexual violence in porn are harmful (half to two-thirds of respondents did so in recent polls), whether all sexually explicit material is harmful is a matter of heated debate. Answers to this question involve the broadest evaluations of sexuality and sexual ethics: What is healthy or unhealthy sexuality? What belongs in public and what in private? What is legitimate education about sexuality? What differences are there between sexuality itself and depictions of it in film or print media? These questions are deeply relevant to porn, and many judgments on them are embedded in the Supreme Court's decisions about obscenity. For instance, what is "healthy" and what is "morbid" sex may be strongly debated. What exactly goes "beyond the limits of customary candor"? Could that mean sexual contact between two unmarried persons, or between two persons of the same gender?

If we look to the Christian tradition for guidance, the answers are disquieting. Any sexuality uninterested in the "procreative ends" of the acts, any sexual conduct focused on sexual joy for its own sake, has historically been condemned. To use contraception in marriage was called criminal, flagitious and debauched; to Augustine it represented "cruel lust or lustful cruelty" (to take but one classic example). In the Middle Ages, masturbation and "unnatural positions" were considered more severe offenses against the ordinances of God than were rape or incest.

These distorted views of sex were not limited to the time before the Reformation (as though Protestants have gotten our theology about sexuality straight). In the mid-19th century, the heyday of Protestant power in the U.S., women were condemned not for being too lusty, as in earlier centuries; rather, Victorians proclaimed women's pure, high and spiritual—i.e., nonsexual— nature. "Purity" was extolled to the extent that women were thought to lack sexual feelings altogether. (Only in the 1970s did we learn that sexual anesthesia is a frequent consequence of sexual abuse.)

Many current pornographic scenarios build on these old mistakes about women's sexuality. Plots often turn on a woman/victim who at first appears to be "good" (nonsexual), but is later revealed, on the flimsiest of pretexts, as a sexually demanding, ultra-lustful creature. These scenarios are often a rebellious comment on Victorian prudishness. Frequently they echo the sexist dualisms that split women into either madonnas or whores. Whatever we think about the legal questions, we have a responsibility to set straight these extremely damaging patriarchal notions about sexuality. The Protestants who propagated these notions helped create the early laws and ethos that gave rise to our present confusing obscenity standards.

Aside from the instances in which it explicitly portrays sexual violence, porn also purveys almost total misinformation about human sexuality. The scenes in porn are endlessly repetitive—boring is a generous judgment. There are no persons, only cardboard caricatures—persons reduced to bits of flesh. There is no intimacy, and no social or personal drama. Further, messages about sexuality that ignore or deprecate *women's* sexuality convey misinformation about *human* sexuality. In our society, let alone in our theologies and churches, we have barely begun to explore women's sexuality from the inside out. Ignorance about the simplest facts of female biology is rampant, and our culture spreads strange ideas about women's sexuality in many more ways than in pornography. We must stop sexist lying about women's sexuality. If we are concerned that "porn is lies about women"—which it surely is—we must be equally concerned that our theologies are not also lies about women.

Finally, unless churches take the economic issues of pornography seriously, we have little hope of being effective in the efforts against it. Christians who may agree that the symbolic dimensions of porn are a serious concern may be wary about tackling its financial side. We often ignore the "material" realities: how much things costs, what the profit is, where the money comes from and goes. We act as though the spiritual and the material were mutually exclusive—itself one of the sexist dualisms of the tradition. But the production and profits of porn are part of its meaning. We have not truly grasped this subject until we see into the shady and exploitative finances of porn.

Some economic dimensions are easier to learn than others. For example, the prices of porn picture magazines and video cassettes are exorbitant. Picture magazines run between $20 to $40. (In areas where video competition is keen, "sales" are common.) These prices are not due to the high costs of producing porn, which is well known for its sleazy pay scales. In March 1986 a *Newsweek* reporter provided some specific figures. A porn movie was made on $120,000 in five days, with a 27-page script, no rehearsals and 18 crew members. If this film attracted an average audience, it would sell about 10,000 video cassettes at $70 each; it would also make larger profits from foreign sales and a simultaneous "softer" version peddled to cable television. It was not the "stars" of this porn flick, however, who raked in cash. The male lead earned $750 per day, the female lead $1,500 per day (top money for the industry)—a pittance in the whole financial deal. But those sums represent big money in comparison to the average woman worker's earnings, and the money often looks good to women with few financial options. This example is among the most benign (see Linda Marchiano's descriptions of the filming of *Deep Throat* for worse). Many porn products are made in "cottage industry" conditions by small-time operators who do not hesitate to use force, violence, blackmail and drugs on the "actors." Porn producers speak of themselves as a legitimate entertainment industry, but their practices are far from legitimate.

Who produces and distributes such work and who pockets the very big bucks are harder questions. Sham corporations, fictitious names and false records are common. In my home state, Minnesota, the finances of the local porn king came to light only after the Internal Revenue Service filed charges of tax evasion against him. Concern over porn's connections with organized crime has been around for many years. The Meese report's conclusions, based on information from law enforcement agencies (who presumably know), tell us that it is too simple to see organized crime (in the sense of the Mafia) at the heart of porn, though there may indeed be payoffs, protection and other such connections involved. But no matter who are its ultimate producers, the processes of making and distributing porn are as saturated with exploitation as are its products. To plumb the multiple meanings of pornography, we must pay as much attention to its economics as to its images.

OBSERVING AND ANALYZING PORN

It is extremely important for us in the churches not to avert our eyes from porn. Before taking a stand, look at it. (This is *not* a recommendation that you become a user or consumer of porn.) Some groups, such as New York City's Women Against Pornography, sponsor tours of porn districts and shops. Many other groups (such as Minneapolis's Organizing Against Pornography, state chapters of Women Against Violence Against Women, and local rape centers) have slide shows available for study groups. Observe the titles, the pictures and the prices. Go into the "adults only" corner of your local home video store. Watch for racism, bondage and titles that appeal to the theme of child abuse. Be respectful in your information-gathering phase. Don't buttonhole customers or workers; if you are female, they may be very defensive about your presence. Look at drugstore racks and newsstands as well. Don't fail to note the true-crime magazines, thought by some to be seriously implicated in sexual offenses. Look at advertising. Think about the differences and similarities in what you see in these different settings and media. Talk to people in churches situated near porn shops about the quality of life in the neighborhood.

The testimony of persons claiming direct harm from porn has been crucial in forging new views about pornography. The women whose bodies are pictured describe coercion. Women sexually abused as children describe the use of pornography in their victimization. Others, often victims of battering or marital rape, tell of partners insisting on trying some practice discovered in porn wares (10 percent of such victims do so in one study). These women report suicide attempts, nightmares, fears, anxieties, shame and guilt—reactions which resemble rape trauma syndrome.

Anyone listening seriously to this testimony will be as changed by it as those who have listened to battered women or rape victims. I will never be able to see another item of pornography without being flooded by questions about the women pictured: Was this one an incest victim? What was it like for her to be filmed chained, smiling, with a knife at her genitals? What was her pay? What percentage of the profit was that? Does she have colitis as a result of the nervous stress? When I go into a porn shop to investigate, the questions multiply. Who are the men in this shop? Why do they look so furtive? Why do they scamper away from me and my companions? (After being in a few porn shops, I find it very difficult to believe the argument put forth by some that porn frees people from hangups.) Who is buying this material and what are they doing with it? Are they showing it to children, saying, "See, it's okay because it's published in magazines"? Are they asking a lover or wife to participate in bondage? Are they using it to "educate" teenage runaways into prostitution?

It may be stressful for many people to look at this material. Frankly, it gives me nightmares, often for weeks. Go with somebody you trust, and process your responses together; this is an appropriate project for a church group. Be as honest as you can. Some people find porn frightening or boring. Some people are turned on by porn; they need the chance to say so and to explore what that means. There is a diverse range of responses. Don't define some as politically incorrect or unchristian. Let yourself have time to experience your feelings, to let them percolate, to let your insights emerge. Take care of yourself.

Christians do not have to agree on everything about pornography. Our experience of life, our priorities, our spiritual depths and our conceptual tools differ greatly. This buzzing diversity in the faith is both the bane and the blessing of our age. We may seriously disagree, for instance, on the Meese report's emphasis on increased prosecution of porn. Everyone who is concerned about porn in even a faintly responsible way is also concerned about freedom of speech. (I am uneasy, for example, with the likelihood that sensitive and honest depictions of women's sexuality or of gay and lesbian life will be found "patently offensive" in a culture that still carries residues of Victorian ideas.) And if we in the churches are concerned that porn provides serious misinformation about sexuality and sexual violence, then we must also take very serious steps to provide accurate and sensitive alternatives—such as supporting rape centers, sex education, and genuine artists who may depict sex in their work.

We all need to pay serious attention to the multiple layers of meaning in pornography, and to the connection it has to the rest of life. We need to guard against reawakening some of the most unsavory chapters in Christian history such as those I have mentioned above. The only way to cope with the many problems porn presents is by going through them, not by evading them or averting our eyes.

Though its primary harms may be to women and children, pornography affects all of us, for it makes serious statements about our world and human life. It asserts that some people are legitimate victims and others legitimate victimizers; it reinforces the worst of our society's hierarchies of inequality and injustice. It asserts that sexual pleasure comes from demeaning, exploiting, objectifying and degrading our partners in the most intimate ways, rather than from an eager and passionate cherishing of the wholeness of that partner. Good theology can be helpful in clarifying what is at stake in porn. It may be due to the limits of my imagination or my theology, but I believe that no one who celebrates healthy sexuality among the many goods of God's creation can affirm pornography.

PART 5

Sexual Orientation: A Test Case for The Church

John Boswell
James B. Nelson
Rosemary Radford Ruether
Dan Spencer

Introduction
to Part 5

Not since the slavery debates of the mid-nineteenth century has the church been engaged by such a troublesome, heated, and divisive ecclesiastical issue as sexual orientation. Homosexuality is *the* scare issue in the churches. It has become a funnel into which is poured a whole range of social fears, many of which have little, if any, relation to issues of sexual orientation. Of course, this is true not only in the churches' internal debates, but in society at large, as the raging controversy about gays and lesbians in the military has demonstrated in recent years.

Yet the church has a particular role in all of this. Even the secular debates seldom remain secular. They frequently return to religious argumentation and claim religious justification. Furthermore, the church has been the primary institutional legitimator of discrimination against lesbian, gay, and bisexual persons in Western culture. Hence, the church has a critical theological-ethical task now. We make no attempt to represent the range of theological viewpoints here. Others have done that.[1] Our purpose in Part 5 is to focus on the issues and assumptions that *underlie* much of the current debate.

John Boswell's essay furnishes a critical historical perspective, reminding us that if gay men and lesbians are the church's most obvious "outsiders" today, they were often "distinguishable insiders" during Christianity's first twelve hundred years. In fact, both priesthood and religious order had a particular appeal for gays and lesbians as the only real alternative to heterosexual marriage. In monasteries and convents same-sex erotic attachments were celebrated in poetry and song, and as early as the fifth century gay clerics took part in homosexual marriage ceremonies and "commemorated special friendships."

From about 1250 onward, however, for a variety of political and social reasons, European society grew increasingly hostile to gay and lesbian people. The church joined these secular patterns of rejection and periodic persecution.

Nevertheless, the supreme irony is that a group currently as marginalized and despised as gays and lesbians could exert—and for the greater part of the Christian era—such a positive influence on the church from within the ranks of its spiritual elite. Boswell challenges the reader to take the whole sweep of Christian history seriously when rethinking sexual orientation.

For this theological task James B. Nelson invokes the use of "the Wesleyan quadrilateral," the formula insisting on the use of all four major sources of Christian insight: scripture, tradition, reason, and experience. (Note that his method is similar to Lisa Sowle Cahill's in Part 1, though he reaches different conclusions on this issue.) Regarding the Bible, Nelson concludes that although the few specific scriptural texts citing homosexual activity simply do not speak directly to our contemporary questions, the scripture's relevance is far more profound than offering specific behavioral norms. With L. William Countryman (see Part 1), he argues that scripture presses us all toward the transformation of our sexual lives in ways that respond to the inbreaking reign of the gracious God.

The second theological source—the church's tradition—gives no more unambiguous guidance on specific sexual expressions than does scripture. Nevertheless, a careful look at tradition challenges a number of unexamined assumptions frequently made in the current debates: that the church has always and consistently condemned homosexual orientation, that the church has always agreed that heterosexual marriage is the normative Christian pattern, and that procreation has always been deemed central to the Christian meaning of genital sex.

Nelson maintains that the third source, reason, is expressed among other places in those contemporary sciences that shed important light on the complex nature of sexual orientation, the question of choice, and the nature of homosexual stereotypes—all important insights underlying the debates. Finally, in combination with the other three, our own sexual experience is a significant theological source. Here the author describes various dynamics of homophobia he has discovered in himself, contending that not only do we need to understand how homophobia works but also we need more adequate incarnational, body-positive, and gracious theologies.

Earlier, Boswell's article raised the question, Why in recent centuries have we drastically altered our prevailing social views of sexual behavior? Why has "homosexual" come to be understood as the primary defining characteristic of a whole group of people, whereas for the majority "heterosexuality" is assumed to be only one part of the individual's personality? Nelson's essay demonstrated how the four theological sources together furnish important correctives to this prevailing assumption. Now Rosemary Radford Ruether's selection extends that discussion.

She maintains that while the traditional arguments against homosexuality—as a sin, a crime, and a disease—do not satisfactorily explain the current fears, it is still important to examine this reasoning. Homosexuality is seen as sinful because, when sex itself is highly suspect, nonreproductive sex becomes the epitome of "a sinful, death-prone instinct." It is viewed as a crime because nonreproductive sex appears to be a deliberate flouting of the natural order that, in turn, undermines society. And it is seen as a disease that can be "caught," an argument augmented by the tragic AIDS epidemic that has been blamed erroneously on gay and bisexual males.

Obviously underlying these arguments is the assumption that sex itself is inherently sinful and legitmated only for reproductive purposes. Further, however, it is assumed that since the two genders are opposite personality types and each needs the other for complementarity, "wholeness" in the sexual relation is possible only when attraction is directed at the other sex. Nevertheless, Ruether contends, the fear and dread of homosexuals by heterosexuals (particularly by males) is inexplicable until we add two additional and interconnected dynamics.

To grasp the first we must recognize that all of us have more bisexual and "polymorphous" sexual capacities than our society's rigid heterosexual indoctrination has led us to believe. If we all have some capacity for same-sex attraction but have been taught disgust over such attraction, homophobia in part is a projection onto lesbian and gay persons of heterosexuals' dreaded fears about themselves. But further, heterosexual conditioning has taken place within a context of patriarchal hierarchy that teaches males a masculinity of dominance and invulnerability. Thus homophobia also betrays men's dread of any (homosexual) relationship in which they might be "penetrated," thus demeaned and dominated by another male. Ruether holds out the hope that as we recognize and deal with these dynamics we can begin to shape a new sexual ethic of loving, committed, and mutual relationships, an ethic applicable to everyone.

While many of us might share that hope, Dan Spencer observes that in the meantime numerous Christian lesbians and gay men have only two choices concerning the church: either to remain closeted or to come out and face hostility and, perhaps, expulsion. Either path leaves one wounded and divided, without community in which to integrate two basic parts of one's identity: being Christian and being gay or lesbian. Hence, in both the United States and the United Kingdom a number of Christian congregations composed largely of lesbian, gay, and bisexual members have emerged, communities in which the identity of the church is located "in the move from the margins *of* community to the margins *as* community."[2]

The gay and lesbian understanding of the church now developing in these communities has a number of distinctive marks. Such an ecclesiology is rooted in the particularities of gay and lesbian experience. It takes the powerlessness born of marginality as a source of strength. It is primarily accountable to its own people's experience in their struggle for liberation. It celebrates human embodiedness as critical to empowerment for justice. It seeks new understandings of leadership, power, and authority. And, such an ecclesiology celebrates its connections with the wider church without sacrificing the need for the supportive community of the oppressed. Such faith communities are true expressions of the church that is called to be one, holy, catholic, and apostolic.

If lesbian, gay, and bisexual people of faith can challenge and invite the rest of the church to experience the gospel without homophobic trappings, as Spencer hopes, that will be a remarkable gift. We would add that by not avoiding this test case for our day, but rather by wrestling deeply with the issue of sexual orientation with all of its implications, the church might gain more theological faithfulness and ethical integrity in other issues as well.

NOTES

1. See, for example, the range of theological arguments included in Edward Batchelor, Jr., ed., *Homosexuality and Ethics* (New York: Pilgrim Press, 1980).
2. Dan Spencer, "Church at the Margins," *Christianity and Crisis* 52, no. 8 (May 25, 1992): 174.

31

Homosexuality and Religious Life: A Historical Approach

JOHN BOSWELL

One of the most difficult aspects of being a lesbian or gay person is the phenomenon of pervasive invisibility: exclusion from any generally recognizable category. This usually happens with persons considered "outsiders" in some way by their contemporaries. Most societies distinguish, consciously or unconsciously, degrees of "acceptability" among persons who are perceived to diverge from the norm, often in three categories: "distinguishable insider," "inferior insider," and "outsider."

"Distinguishable insiders" are, to paraphrase a familiar modern concept, different but equal. They are persons who could be recognized as distinctive if someone had the desire to discriminate, but whose divergence from the norm is viewed in the society at issue as part of the ordinary range of human variation. They are therefore not disadvantaged or segregated, socially or conceptually. Eye color marks such a category in most Western societies; someone might be able to remember which of his or her friends and acquaintances had blue and which brown eyes, but it would hardly make any difference. In the United States the classic example is Protestant church affiliation; though a Presbyterian family may consider the Methodists who live next door to be tragically misinformed theologically, they would not even think of discriminating against them, socially or civilly. The United States was founded, in fact, in no small measure to protect this degree of "separate but equal" status, although it does not extend across the range of Christian theology. Catholics have at many points experienced discrimination, and Jews have never been fully included at a social level.[1]

The second category, "inferior insider," applies to persons whose divergence from some norm is considered tolerable, but who are thereby relegated to inferior social status. The archetype of this category is probably the bottom of the caste system in India. It is not morally or politically wrong to be an

361

Untouchable. Indeed, it is right and necessary that the state and the world include Untouchables, but being an Untouchable relegates one to the bottom of society. Closer to home, I regret to say, women constitute the most familiar illustration. Although few would argue that it is "wrong" to be female, being a woman renders one liable to a lower place in the socioeconomic structure of many Western states. This has been so since the time of Aristotle, who considered women "defective males," because males have taken themselves to be the "norm" and have assumed that female "deviation" from that norm betokens inferiority. This is why the ordination of women is opposed in some Catholic circles. Women "lack" some aspect of the norm of "maleness" presumed to be a prerequisite for sacerdotal functions.

In general, "inferior insiders" occupy positions in which social security is achieved at the expense of access to the upper reaches of social and financial accomplishment. Oppressive as this category is, it is usually preferable to that of "outsiders." "Outsiders" are either not tolerated at all (they are killed, or banished, or incarcerated) or are relegated to nonexistence conceptually. They are political dissidents in totalitarian regimes, Jews in Nazi Germany, the left-handed in much of the world. Even in the United States half a century ago, the left-handed were forced to become "normal"; left-handed people simply could not exist.

Gay people are the most obvious "outsiders" in the modern West. In the ancient world and in the early Christian church they were either not considered a minority at all, or were treated as separate but equal, that is, as "distinguishable insiders." Most people imagine that the modern West has made dramatic strides in the direction of general social tolerance and tend to view pre-modern Europe, especially the Catholic Middle Ages, as the nadir of openness and acceptance. "Medieval" is, in fact, a synonym for "narrow" and "intolerant" in the context of sexuality in particular. But this is anachronistic; in many ways modern systems of determining social consensus about the parameters of the tolerable are much more inimical to the freedom and well-being of minorities.

In the Middle-Ages, gay people were at worst viewed as "inferior insiders." Homosexual activity, no matter how loving or committed, could not be procreative and, according to one view of sexuality, this meant that those who engaged in it necessarily relegated themselves to the inferior category of "sinner." "Sinner" was an inferior position, but also a temporary one, occupied at some times by every living human being since the Virgin Mary. Your neighbor might commit sins you did not, sins you would not even be tempted to commit, but you knew that you yourself were nonetheless a sinner just like your neighbor. Everyone is sinful at times, and no one need be so permanently. Being a sinner did not in any sense remove someone from the map of human types or make one an outsider. In one very real sense, the ability and tendency to sin is the most characteristic moral quality of human beings.

But in modern industrial nations the desirability of persons, actions, and things is assessed against the "norm" of "health." What is physically or mentally "normal" is what would be found in a "healthy" person or society. That this is tautological is not particularly surprising, given the generally low level of philosophical sophistication in political discourse; what is more interesting is that "normality" and "health" are either *characteristics* or conditions, rather than actions or behavior, and one generally has less control over them than over deeds or conduct. The medieval notion of the unholiness of homosexual acts has been transformed by modern discourse into the abnormality of the homosexual "condition." The "condition" is variously conceptualized as a genetic "trait," a psychological "state," an "inclination," or a "preference." Though these terms vary in their implications of permanence and mutability, all suggest an essential, internal characteristic of a person rather than an external, voluntary activity.

The importance of the difference between the modern view and preceding systems of conceptualizing sexuality can scarcely be exaggerated. Contemporary concepts have drastically altered social views of sexual behavior and its significance by focusing on sexual object choice and correlating it with an inherent, defining personal characteristic. The majority supposes itself to have the trait, condition, or preference of heterosexuality, which is "healthy" and "normal," and believes that a minority of persons have the "opposite" trait, condition, or preference, which is "unhealthy" and "not normal." The difference is rendered more profound and alienating by the fact that the "normal" or "healthy" state is generally considered (as were all forms of sexuality in the past) to be primarily behavioral. Because "heterosexual" is conceived to be the norm, it is unmarked and unnoticed. "Heterosexual person" is unnecessary. "Person" implies heterosexual without indication to the contrary. But the normal person is not "heterosexual" in any defining sense; he or she engages in heterosexual activity from time to time, but hardly any information about his or her character, behavior, life-style or interest is inferable from this fact. "Homosexual," on the other hand, is understood as a primary and permanent category, a constant and defining characteristic that implies a great deal beyond occasional sexual behavior about the person to whom the term is applied. Not only, it is imagined, does his or her sexuality define all other aspects of personality and life-style, which are implicitly subordinate to sex in the case of homosexuals but not heterosexuals, but the connotations of the term and its place in the modern construction of sexuality suggest that homosexuals are much more sexual than heterosexuals. That is, in the case of a "normal" person, heterosexuality is assumed to be one part of his or her personality; in the case of a "homosexual" person, sexuality is thought to be the primary constituent of his or her (abnormal) personality.

This partly explains why the very idea of lesbian sisters and gay brothers and priests shocks many people. How could there be gay religious persons? The controlling influence in the lives of religious is presumed to be the absence of sexuality,[2] a sexuality assumed by the majority to be always and everywhere heterosexual; whereas the controlling influence in the lives of gay people is assumed to be overt, abnormal sexuality. Since gay people are not a permitted category, the average person has so little information about them and so little opportunity to consider their lives that the possibility of *sacrificing*, channeling, or dedicating homosexual desire simply is not entertained.

Being outsiders in this way, morally and conceptually invisible to the majority, is one of the greatest problems gay people encounter in modern society. It is especially difficult for gay religious, who are doubly marginalized. They are "outsiders" to other Christians because they are gay, and "outsiders" to most gay people because they are religious. This is a poignant irony on both counts. Not only is homosexual eroticism the oldest and most persistent strand in the Christian theology of romantic love, but Christian religious life was the most prominent gay life-style in Western Europe from the early Middle Ages to the Reformation, about two-thirds of the period since Europe became Christian.

CELIBACY AND THE APPEAL OF
RELIGIOUS LIFE

One of many transformations in the nature of marriage effected during late antiquity and the early Middle Ages was the gradual narrowing of the concept of marriage from an institution filling a variety of needs—such as dynastic, emotional, sexual, or political—to one designed and fit (in the minds of ascetic theologians) for a single purpose, that is, for procreation. Although progeny and the continuation of family lines were prominent in Roman and Jewish ideals of marriage, both of which were influential on early Christians, matrimony also included, in both traditions, aspects of affection, sexual satisfaction, and companionship. For Roman males, moreover, marriage was not expected to constitute the sole outlet for eroticism; sexual interaction with other women, other males, or both was acceptable in Roman society and not considered adultery, although jealous wives were free to object if it displeased them.

Because marriage filled a variety of needs, was conceptualized as a civic duty, and did not limit other possibilities for erotic fulfillment, gay men and women in the ancient world would have had little reason to resist matrimony and much reason to undertake it. But late antique social and philosophical movements, including but not limited to Christianity, increasingly insisted not only that procreation was the sole justification for marriage, but also that it was gravely sinful to engage in any sexual activity outside marriage, or in any acts between spouses not directed at procreation. This made marriage a much less attractive option for most people, both male and female, since it was presented exclusively as a duty to the race, and the role of eroticism and pleasure even within legitimate matrimony was severely disparaged by theologians. "Any love for someone else's spouse or very much for one's own is adultery," warned Jerome,[3] and Augustine urged wives to direct their husbands to prostitutes if they wished to indulge in any sexual activity that was not procreative.[4]

The Christian alternative to marriage, something unheard of and disapproved among Jews and rare among Romans, was celibacy. Although it was not a rule for the secular clergy until the twelfth century, and then only in the West, and although the superiority of the state of celibacy to the married state would not be defined until the Council of Trent in the sixteenth century, from the very beginning of Christian religious life celibacy was a much admired and common ideal.

GAY AND LESBIAN PEOPLE AND RELIGIOUS LIFE

Many men and women entered religious life or undertook celibacy on their own, in response to personal convictions about the superiority of celibacy, reaction against the new and ascetic view of marriage, or both. For obvious reasons, gay people would find the more rigid institution of marriage even less satisfying than heterosexuals, since they would find *no* erotic satisfaction in it, whereas the latter might, incidentally, enjoy procreative activity although such enjoyment was probably sinful in the view of many.[5]

Celibate religious life offered women escape from the consequences of marriage—for example, having to sleep with a husband and bear children—which might not only be unwanted but even life threatening. It afforded both genders a means of avoiding stereotypical gender roles.[6] Women could exercise power in religious communities, among other women, without being subordinated to the male head of a household. Men could become part of a community of equals, all male, without the responsibilities of fatherhood or ruling a household; or they could exercise through the priesthood skills of nurturing and serving otherwise associated with women and considered shameful for men. Men could avoid obligations of warfare and devote themselves to study; women could become literate and learned, an opportunity rare for their sex outside religious communities after the decline of Rome.

It is reasonable, under these circumstances, to believe that the priesthood and religious communities would have exercised a particular appeal for gay people, especially in those societies that treated them as "outsiders" and in which there was no other alternative to heterosexual marriage. Indeed, lesbian and gay people would hardly have needed a spiritual motivation to join a same-sex community of equals. Joining a religious community from about 500 C.E. to about 1300 was probably the surest way of meeting other gay people.

Many non-Christian observers of the Catholic clergy believed that it was disproportionately gay. The Germanic invaders of Roman Europe, Muslims who came into contact with Christians in medieval Spain, and Protestants from the time of the Reformation all charged that Catholic religious tended to be gay. There is doubtless a considerable element of mudslinging in this, but it may also be evidence of ways in which the atypical gender roles of the clergy and religious, and the relation of these to homosexuality, are noticeable even to outsiders. Many clerical observers, with no intention of denigrating their own vocation, also complained about the prevalence of homosexuality in their ranks. Saint Peter Damian in the eleventh century wrote a long treatise, "The Book of

Gomorrha," about homosexuality in the priesthood and claimed that gay clergy confessed to one another to avoid detection. He tried to persuade Pope Leo IX to expel gay people from orders, but in a famous reply, "We More Humanely,"[7] the pontiff refused to do so, arguing that disciplinary action should be taken only against flagrant, very longstanding violations of clerical celibacy.

During the eleventh and twelfth centuries there was, in fact, an enormous struggle over the efforts of the institutional church to enforce the ideal of clerical celibacy. As part of the propaganda warfare that accompanied it, there were frequent charges that homosexuality was playing a large role. An apparently heterosexual priest attacked his bishop for promoting celibacy by claiming that this was a gay-straight conflict. "The man who occupies this [episcopal] seat is gayer[8] than Ganymede.[9] Consider why he excludes the married from the clergy: He does not care for the pleasures of a wife."[10]

RELIGIOUS LIFE AND ROMANTIC ATTACHMENT: THE SECULAR CLERGY

It should not be imagined, however, that gay people were attracted to religious life for subliminal sexual reasons, or that they took ideals of celibacy less seriously than others. For the secular clergy, as noted, celibacy was not binding before the High Middle Ages, and many clerics left records of passionate involvement with persons of their own gender. Some of these may have been purely emotional relationships; others were clearly sexual. The love poetry between Ausonius and Saint Paulinus, bishop of Nola, helped to establish a tradition of explicitly Christian same-sex erotic lyricism that would have a profound impact on Western literature through the time of the Reformation.

> Through all that life may allot
> Or assign to mortals,
> As long as I am held within this prison body,
> In whatever world I am found,
> I shall hold you fast,
> Grafted onto my being,
> Not divided by distant shores or suns.
> Everywhere you shall be with me,
> I will see with my heart
> And embrace you with my loving spirit.
> . . . And when, freed from my body's jail
> I fly from earth,
> Wherever in heaven our Father shall direct me,
> There also shall I bear you in my heart.
> Nor will that end,
> That frees me from my flesh,
> Release me from your love.[11]

Like most residents of the ancient world, Ausonius and Paulinus accepted love between men as a normal variety of human affection, but unlike their pagan contemporaries, they invested it with Christian moral and spiritual significance. The author intends to pursue his love in heaven.

Gay clerics apparently took part in homosexual marriage ceremonies, which were widely known in the Catholic world from the fifth century on. Such ceremonies were performed in Catholic churches by priests and either established what the community regarded as marriages, or commemorated special friendships, in both cases in devoutly Christian terms.[12]

ROMANTIC LOVE IN COMMUNITIES

Monks, too, appear to have taken part in these gay marriages, although most monastic communities required a commitment to celibacy, and this obviously created a conflict. In the Greco-Roman world in which monasticism originated, homosexuality was regarded as a perfectly ordinary aspect of human eroticism, and early religious communities had to come to grips with the possibility of erotic attachment between sisters or monks.

Two basic approaches developed. One, probably influenced by the increasing tendency of Christian thought to reduce human eroticism to the purely functional role of child production, a role it could not properly play in a monastery, condemned human attachments within religious communities and insisted that religious avoid them altogether. This attitude was not specifically antigay. Because homosexuality was not "outside" human eroticism or invisible in the ancient world, it was included along with other forms of sexuality as being improper for those committed to a life of celibacy. It was no worse or better, although perhaps a little more worrisome, because more available in same-sex communities. (Heterosexual religious have, however, in most times and places found it possible to violate rules of celibacy when they wished to.)

Saint Basil's writings are a clear indication of this trend. He expresses both the anxiety of the ascetic that human sexuality not disrupt the sober purity of monastic life, and the assumption that any male might naturally find another male sexually exciting.

> It is frequently the case with young men that, even when rigorous self-restraint is exercised, the glowing complexion of youth still blossoms forth and becomes a source of desire to those around them. If, therefore, anyone in the monastery is youthful and physically beautiful, let him keep his attractiveness hidden, and you sit in a chair far from such a person. Whenever he speaks to you, look down when you respond to him, so that when you gaze at his face you do not take the seed of desire from the enemy sower. Do not be found with him either indoors or where no one can see outdoors, either for studying the prophesies of Scripture or for any other purpose, no matter how necessary.[13]

Basil does not believe that *experiencing* homosexual desire is abnormal or even reprehensible. He simply expects celibate religious to make efforts to maintain their vows, and he thinks that doing so is a worthy struggle. It is not clear from his writings that such eroticism would be wrong for those who have not vowed to give them up, any more than talking is inherently evil because some orders observe silence as a form of monastic discipline.

Another strand of spirituality in religious communities, however, not only accepted but idealized love between persons of the same sex, both in and out of religious life. This approach could find clear precedent in numerous New Testament passages and examples, which it often cited. The ceremony for same-sex union, for example, cited many same-gender couples from Christian history.

> O Lord our God, dwelling in heaven but looking down on that which is below, you who for the salvation of the human race sent your only begotten son, Jesus, and took Peter and Paul and made them brothers by consecration, make also these your servants———and———like those two apostles. Keep them blameless all the days of their lives. Lord of all and maker of humankind in your image and likeness, who gave humans eternal life, consider as worthy of union these two, joined not by nature but by the holy spirit of fidelity and unity of mind, just as you united Serge and Bacchus, Cosmas and Damian, and Cyrus and John.[14]

In the early Middle Ages Walahfrid Strabo, the abbot of the Benedictine monastery of Reichenau, wrote poetry to his friend Liutger evocative of the love sonnets of the Brownings:

> When the splendor of the moon shines from the clear heaven,
> Stand in the open air, and see in the wondrous mirror
> How it grows light in the pure brightness from the moon
> And with its splendor embraces two lovers,
> Divided in body, but linked in spirit by one love.
> If we cannot see each other face to loving face,
> At least let this light be our pledge of love.[15]

This particular monastery, in fact, produced a great deal of love poetry, as did a number of others, including communities of women. The longest and most beautiful examples of premodern lesbian poetry surviving from anywhere in Europe were composed by nuns for each other in southern Germany in the twelfth century.

> To G., her unique rose,
> A. sends the bond of precious love.
> What strength have I that I may bear it,
> That I may endure your absence?
> Is my strength the strength of stones
> That I can wait for your return?
> I never cease from aching, night and day,
> Like someone missing a hand and foot.
> Without you anything happy or delightful
> Seems like mud trod underfoot.
> Instead of rejoicing I weep;
> My spirit never seems joyful.
> When I remember the kisses you gave me,
> The way you refreshed my little breasts with sweet words,
> I would like to die
> Since I cannot see you.

. . . O if my body had been committed to earth
Until your longed-for return,
Or if I could go on a journey like Habakkuk's,
So that just once I could come to where
I saw the face of my lover,
Then I would not care if I died that very hour.
For there is no one who has been born in this world
Who is so lovable and dear,
No one who without feigning
Loves me with so deep a love.
Therefore, I ache without end
Until I am allowed to see you.[16]

Three things are particularly noteworthy about this poem: (1) Although it is uncertain whether the reference to physical interaction describes something real or is a metaphor in the tradition of the Song of Songs, in either event it is clear that carnal love between two women was part of the conceptual framework of the nuns. (2) The love involved, whether physically embodied or not, is clearly a particular erotic passion, and not simply general charity. (3) It is a Christian love, and understood to be incorporated into a Christian, religious life. It is not presented as pagan, or in contrast to virtue, or as an impediment to a holy life. On the contrary, the poem is filled with biblical allusions and references, and is wholly unabashed and unapologetic.

Aelred, the abbot of the Cistercian monastery of Rievaulx, had led quite a wild gay life in his youth, involving multiple partners and passions, but when he entered religious life he took his vow of chastity very seriously. He would bathe in any icy pool to quell his libido—the original cold shower approach. It did not seem to him, however, that he had to give up passionate attachments. On the contrary, he fell in love with several members of his order and wrote candidly about his feelings: "We had but one mind and one soul, to will and not to will alike. . . . For I deemed my heart in a fashion his, and his mine, and he felt in like manner towards me. . . . He was the refuge of my spirit, the sweet solace of my griefs, whose heart of love received me when fatigued from labors, whose counsel refreshed me when plunged in sadness and grief. . . . Was it not a foretaste of blessedness thus to love and thus to be loved?"[17] Such passions did not seem to Aelred a departure from a spiritual life, but a part of it, based on the example of Jesus himself.

We can enjoy this [kind of love] in the present with those whom we love not merely with our minds but with our hearts; for some are joined to us more intimately and passionately than others in the lovely bond of spiritual friendship. And lest this sort of sacred love should seem improper to anyone, Jesus himself, in everything like us, patient and compassionate with us in every matter, transfigured it through the expression of his own love: for he allowed one, not all, to recline on his breast as a sign of his special love, so that the virgin head was supported in the flowers [*sic*] of the virgin breast, and the closer they were, the more copiously did the fragrant secrets of the heavenly marriage impart the sweet smell of spiritual chrism to their virgin love.[18]

Although part of a long tradition, Aelred's views were not universal. His biographer expressed astonishment that Aelred encouraged his monks to hold hands, and noted that many other abbots expelled those who did so from the monastery.

CHANGING TIMES:
THE RISE OF HOSTILITY

Disparagement of personal attachments in religious life eventually triumphed over the tradition of admiration for them, in part because European society grew increasingly hostile to gay people and their feelings from about 1250, and began to treat them as "outsiders" rather than as ordinary sinners. The kind of gay romance that had been so common in religious life since the beginnings of Christianity became not only suspect, but dangerous. Homosexual infractions of rules of celibacy came to seem much worse than heterosexual failings.

The change is evident in the case of Benedetta Carlini, an Italian Theatine nun of the seventeenth century. Given to a convent at age nine, Benedetta hardly had a choice about celibacy. Her parents had decided she was to be a nun; so she was a nun. Quite brilliant and capable, she rose to be the abbess by the age of thirty, at which time she began having ecstatic visions of Jesus. During these she was transformed into a male angel named Splenditello. The other nuns testified that when she was Splenditello she actually spoke and acted in a more masculine manner. As Splenditello, Benedetta had for two years a vibrantly sexual relationship with her companion, Bartolomea, who shared her room.

> At least three times a week, in the evening after disrobing and going to bed, Sister Benedetta would wait for her companion to disrobe and . . . pretending to need her, would call. When Bartolomea would come over, Benedetta would grab her by the arm and throw her by force on the bed. Embracing her, she would put her under herself and kissing her as if she were a man, she would speak words of love to her. And she would stir so much on top of her that both of them corrupted themselves. . . . Splenditello asked her many times to pledge that she would always be his beloved and promised that he would be hers.[19]

Benedetta was deposed and tried when her activities came to light, and ultimately imprisoned in the convent for thirty-five years. She died in confinement. This makes quite a contrast to the tolerance of the High Middle Ages, when prominent bishops published gay love poetry and clerics composed arguments about whether gay or straight sexuality was preferable.[20]

Benedetta's case also suggests, however, that despite increasing hostility and intolerance, homosexuality continued to form a part of religious life. Exactly what the feelings of Benedetta and Bartolomea were remains a mystery. The fact that the former pretended to be, or believed she was, a male while making love to the latter poses difficult questions about "homosexual orientation," but the acts and passions were clearly homosexual, and freedom from or variations on traditional gender roles are in fact an ancient aspect of religious life, as noted above.

It is striking, moreover, that both Benedetta and Bartolomea would accept the idea of a permanent, committed love relationship, regardless of gender, for a nun. Even granting that both believed it was an angel's union with a nun, the idea of a committed erotic relationship for a cloistered nun is an arresting one.

CONCLUSION

The relationship between homosexuality and religious life is a deep and rich one, complicated by shifting patterns of majority attitudes toward gay people and celibacy. Many authors have suggested that gay people have a special gift for religious life not only in the Christian tradition, but in religion generally. Shamans in many cultures seem to be gay, as were the *berdaches* among American Indians, thought to have extraordinary spiritual and religious insights and gifts.[21] Some biologists have argued that gay people tend, for evolutionary reasons, to be particularly altruistic. If such connections are real, they may offer an additional explanation for the traditional attraction of Catholic religious life for gay people.

Gay and lesbian people have contributed much to the human family and to religious life; for example, patterns of selfless devotion not inspired by natural relation, archetypes of love outside the confines of procreative matrimony, compassion for "outsiders," sensitivity to the limits of stereotypical notions of gender. And religious life has given much in return to gay people. Without having entered communities or the priesthood, many would never have discovered their feelings or been able to share them with others. Women especially, who would have been confined to fairly rigid patterns of existence under the control of a husband, have managed to find meaningful relationships with other women, whether sexual or not, and nonsexual relationships, as partners, with religious men. For both women and men, religious life has afforded an opportunity to establish an identity outside the nuclear family, beyond being simply the complement of the opposite gender.

Religious life enabled gay and lesbian people with a vocation to transform their "outsider" status into an advantage. Instead of simply being excluded, they formed part of a group whose "outside" quality was revered and admired by society, because its members devoted themselves to the service of the community and could offer a critique of heterosexual, conjugal society from a disinterested vantage. The superior moral position of the celibate would not have been possible in Judaism or even in pagan Rome, where heterosexual marriage was essential to social standing. It was a Christian innovation to admire those who dedicated their sexuality to something other than pleasure or procreation.

On the other hand, there have been some tragic aspects to the intersection of homosexuality and religious life. Especially in modern times, most gays and lesbians in religious life have been terribly alone. The efforts of early modern and modern Christian societies to make gay people "outsiders" have largely effaced the large and well-developed literary tradition of gay eroticism among the clergy, consigned to oblivion such institutions as the same-sex union, and fostered the illusion that all religious have given up heterosexuality, if, indeed, they ever had any sexuality at all.

Lesbian and gay religious need to reclaim their tradition, publicize it, rejoice in it, and share it with other Christians and gay people. Models of gay Christian religious life embrace nearly every possibility of service to the Lord, from absolute chastity enriched by passionate attachment to another person, to open enjoyment and celebration of eroticism, to permanent unions, with or without physical sexuality. These models should be discussed and utilized as archetypes of Christian love. They are ancient, authentic, and as fundamental to the Christian tradition as heterosexual marriage.

Religious life has probably been the most consistent, widespread, institutionalized, and constructive gay lifestyle in the West during most of the Christian era. It is poignantly ironic that a group as marginalized and despised as gay people should have exerted such an influence on Christian society within the ranks of its spiritual elite, but that the lowly should be glorified and the last become first is, in fact, appropriate to the religion in question. Instead of experiencing their lives as doubly marginalized, as gays among religious and as religious among gays, lesbian and gay people in religious life and the priesthood should recognize and rejoice in the centrality of their position, the importance of religious life to gay culture throughout Christian history, and the prominence of gay people and their feelings and sensitivities within Christian religious life. The intersection is not only an important key to understanding the history of the church and the gay community, but an ongoing, fruitful, and creative one, enriching both traditions today as it has for nearly two thousand years.

NOTES

1. It is worth noting that the ideology of "separate but equal" may be maintained by a society even when the group in question would have a different perception. Most right-handed people are completely unaware of the many difficulties the left-handed encounter in American society, which disadvantages them precisely because *it does not take account* of their variance from the norm and provide for it.

2. This is in itself a misprision in most cases. Most religious sacrifice or channel their sexuality; it is not "absent." But the discomfort most Catholics evince about the subject of sexuality in the lives of religious suggests very strongly that they prefer to believe that priests and brothers and nuns simply do not experience eroticism.

3. "Adulter est in sua uxore ardentior amator. In aliena quippe uxore omnis amor turpis est, et in sua nimis. Sapiens iudicio debet amare coniugem, non affectu." This was widely cited throughout the Middle Ages (for example, by Vincent of Beauvais, *Speculum doctrinale* 10.45), and quoted by the present pontiff, to the consternation of many modern Catholics.

4. *De bono conjugali*, 11.

5. See, e.g., ibid., 13.

6. On this see Elaine Pagels, *Adam, Eve and the Serpent* (New York: Random House, 1988).

7. "Nos humanius agentes"; discussed in J. Boswell, *Christianity, Social Tolerance, and Homosexuality: Gay People in Western Europe from the Beginning of the Christian Era to the Fourteenth Century* (Chicago: University of Chicago Press, 1980), 211–12.

8. Literally, "Ganymedier"; see discussion in Boswell, *Christianity*, 245, 253.

9. A frequent symbol of gay males; see ibid.

10. Ibid., 217.

11. Paulinus of Nola, *Carmen* 11, lines 49ff; text in *Oxford Book of Medieval Latin Verse*, ed. F. J. E. Raby (Oxford: Oxford University Press, 1959), 24; trans. in Boswell, *Christianity*, 133–34.

12. These ceremonies, evident as early as the fifth century and observed by anthropologists in the twentieth, constitute the subject of my forthcoming book, *What God Has Joined Together: Same-sex Unions in the Christian Tradition*.

13. *De renuntiatione saeculi,* 6; *Sermo asceticus,* 323; see commentary in Boswell, *Christianity*, 159–60.

14. From an Italian manuscript of the early Middle Ages, to appear in Boswell, *What God Has Joined Together*.

15. Boswell, *Christianity*.

16. Translated in Thomas Stehling, *Medieval Latin Poems of Male Love and Friendship* (New York: Garland Publishing, 1984), 102–5, no. 113; cf. Boswell, *Christianity*, 220–21.

17. Boswell, *Christianity*, 224.

18. Ibid., 225–26.

19. Judith P. Brown, *Immodest Acts: The Life of a Lesbian Nun in Renaissance Italy* (Oxford: Oxford University Press, 1986), 162.

20. Discussed at length in Boswell, *Christianity*, 8 and 9.

21. This point was probably first argued by Plato (*Symposium* 182, 192); in more recent times it has been made by Edward Carpenter, "On the Connexion between Homosexuality and Divination, and the Importance of the Intermediate Sexes Generally in Early Civilizations," *Revue d'ethnographie et de sociologie* 11–12 (1910): 310–16, and *Intermediate Types among Primitive Folk* (London, 1914). On the *berdache,* see the classic study by Walter Williams, *The Spirit and the Flesh: Sexual Diversity in American Indian Culture* (Boston: Beacon Press, 1986).

32

Sources for Body Theology: Homosexuality as a Test Case

JAMES B. NELSON

It is no news that matters of sexual orientation for some years now have been the most debated, the most heated, the most divisive issues in American church life. While it is typically an issue approached with fears and passions, it is also susceptible to more understanding than many realize. One church's experience in the mid-'80s speaks to the point.

In Riverside Church in New York City, on May 5, 1985, Dr. Channing E. Phillips, one of the associate ministers, preached a sermon, "On Human Sexuality." Dr. Phillips was an African American minister of considerable national stature in both church and public life. Commenting on words in Genesis 1:27, "male and female [God] created them," he said, "It is difficult to avoid the conclusion that heterosexuality . . . is being lifted up as the model of human sexuality. . . . Those are hard words . . . that imply that deviation from the parable of heterosexual relationship ordained by marriage is contrary to God's will—is sin. . . . And no theological or exegetical sleight of hand can erase that 'word of the Lord.' "[1]

Following the sermon, the sacrament of Communion was celebrated, with Dr. Phillips presiding. After Communion, however, a young straight man from the congregation stood up and walked to the Communion table, interrupting the service. Speaking to the congregation, he stated that he could not support the words from the pulpit that morning. He declared that he would stand by the table during the singing of the last hymn, standing there in support of gay and lesbian people. He invited anyone else who shared his concern to join him. Dr. Phillips said, "I don't mind."

About five hundred of the worshipers, including members of the choir and other clergy staff, left their seats to crowd around the chancel to sing the last hymn together. The *New York Times* would report the event in a prominent story.[2]

The senior ordained clergy team of Riverside Church, "the Collegium," quickly did several things. Part of their approach was to address the matter theologically and with pastoral concern. While for some months they had been in a process of discussing sexual orientation, they invited several theologians to help them consider the issues further.[3] They decided that each of the other three clergy would preach on human sexuality—including homosexuality—on the three following Sundays.

On the next Sunday the senior minister, Dr. William Sloane Coffin, said in his sermon:

> I can only begin to imagine the hurt and anger felt by those of you who thought you had found here at Riverside what you had almost despaired of finding anywhere: a church where, despite the misinformation, superstitions and prejudices of our culture, not only black and white could feel at one and at home, celebrating and affirming each other's existence in the name of Jesus Christ, but also gay and straight. I can also understand the pain of others who thought they had heard confirmed their moral apprehensions about homosexuality . . . only to have these apprehensions then questioned by a demonstration—in church yet! . . . Dearly beloved in the Lord, we now have a sharply divided church, one divided by homosexuality, or should we call it homophobia—the fear of, or contempt for homosexuals. . . . However we label it, it is the most divisive issue the churches of America have encountered, or evaded, since slavery.[4]

Later in his sermon, Coffin made his position clear: "I do not see how Christians can define and then exclude people on the basis of sexual orientation."[5] On the following two Sundays, the other two Collegium clergy, the Rev. Eugene Laubach and the Rev. Patricia de Jong, likewise made clear their convictions affirming the inclusiveness of the church regardless of sexual orientation, and also their pastoral concern for all persons of whatever belief on this issue.

Five months earlier, Riverside Church had begun an intentional process of studying the theology and ethics of sexual orientation. A statement affirming the church's inclusiveness was almost ready for congregational action. Then came Dr. Phillips's dissenting sermon and the demonstration. Immediately the Collegium took additional steps to assure a fair and open process of hearing all viewpoints before the congregational vote was taken. A churchwide retreat on the subject was planned to follow the vote.

Congregational action took place in the weeks following the sermons by each of the Collegium clergy. The vote formally declared Riverside Church to be an "Open and Affirming Church"—fully open to and affirming of lesbian, gay, and bisexual persons. It was the first congregation affiliated with the United Church of Christ to make that formal declaration. This action did not mean that Riverside's struggle was finished. Relationships between many African American and white members had been strained, as was true also between gay and lesbian members and some heterosexual members. The healing process would take considerable time. But the church had faced the issue directly and courageously.

Riverside Church was one of the early congregations, and doubtless the most publicized, to enter this process of reconsidering sexual orientation and church practice in light of the faith. There have been many others. Many issues and questions emerge along the way, issues and questions in addition to the theological-ethical ones. But theological-ethical matters are paramount, and they engage our attention here. How shall we approach them?

Protestants typically have asked, first and foremost, "What does the Bible say?" Roman Catholics typically have asked, "What does the church say?" Both questions are crucial. Neither is sufficient by itself.

One of John Wesley's legacies is the "quadrilateral" interpretation of authority, an approach with roots in Wesley's own Anglican tradition, and one still used by many persons in many communions. The quadrilateral formula reminds us that when we do our theological reflection, we must draw on more than one source. Wesley himself gave central weight to the scripture. But, over against the biblical literalizers and simplifiers, he argued that scripture must always be interpreted through the Spirit, with the indispensable aid of the church's tradition (which checks our own interpretation against the richness of past witnesses), reason (which guards against narrow and arbitrary interpretations), and experience (which is personal, inward, and enables us to interpret and appropriate the gospel).[6] Let us apply this approach to the subject of homosexuality, surely a test case for the church in our day.

SCRIPTURE

A friend of mine, a professor of chemistry at a major university but also by avocation a competent and published theologian, was invited to Washington, D.C., several years ago to give the keynote address to a large convocation of government scientists. The convention's theme was the social responsibility of science. My friend decided to open his speech in a way that would get his audience's attention but also make an important point. Here is what he said:

> I have come to Washington today with a heavy heart, for I am convinced that there are sodomites in high places in government. I am convinced that both houses of Congress have many sodomites in them, the President's cabinet is full of them, and I sadly believe that the President himself regularly practices sodomy. Now I want to tell you what sodomy is. The clearest biblical definition of this sin is not found in the Genesis story but rather in the prophet Ezekiel: "This was the guilt of your sister Sodom: she and her daughters had pride, excess of food, and prosperous ease, but did not aid the poor and needy" [Ezek. 16:49]. That, my friends, is sodomy—it is social injustice, inhospitality to the stranger.

My friend remarked that his opening words did get the audience's attention. And he had made an important point: the real issue, whether for those scientists or for all of us, is justice. By implication, he also made another critical point: the importance of careful interpretation of scripture. The Genesis story of Sodom and Gomorrah, one of the major biblical texts used to condemn homosexuality, was centrally concerned not with sex but with the injustice of inhospitality to the stranger. To the extent that homosexual activity was condemned, it was only homosexual *rape*.[7]

When we approach scripture on the question of homosexual expression, or any other issue, we must always ask two questions.[8] First: What did the text mean? What was the writer trying to say? What questions was the writer addressing? What was the historical context? What literary form was being employed? Answering the question, What did it mean? requires our drawing upon the best insights of biblical scholars with their various forms of critical analysis.

Only after having struggled with the first question, can we proceed to the second: What *does* the text mean *for us today*? Whether a particular text has relevance for us now depends on our answer to two additional questions. First, Is the text consonant with our best understandings of the larger theological-ethical message of the Bible as interpreted through the best insights of the church's long tradition and our reason and experience? Second, Is the situation addressed by the biblical writer genuinely comparable to our own? When, but only when, these criteria are met, the text is ethically compelling for us.

Not many texts in scripture—perhaps seven at most—speak directly about homosexual behavior. We have no evidence of Jesus' teachings on or concern with the issue. The subject, obviously, is not a major scriptural preoccupation. Compare, for example, the incidence of texts on economic justice, of which there are many hundreds. In any event, what conclusions can we reach from careful assessment of the few texts in question?

My own conclusions, relying on the work of a number of contemporary biblical scholars, are several:

We receive no guidance whatsoever about the issue of sexual *orientation*. The issue of "homosexuality"—a psychosexual orientation—simply was not a biblical issue. Indeed, the concept of sexual orientation did not arise until the mid-nineteenth century. Certainly, biblical writers knew of homosexual *acts*, but they apparently understood those acts as being done by heterosexual people (they assumed *everyone* was heterosexual). Thus, when persons engaged in same-sex genital behavior, they were departing from their natural and given orientation. Regardless of our beliefs about the morality of same-sex expression, it is clear that our understanding of sexual *orientation* is vastly different from that of the biblical writers.

It is true, we do find condemnation of homosexual acts when they violate ancient Hebrew purity and holiness codes. We do find scriptural condemnation of homosexual prostitution. We do find condemnation of those homosexual acts which appear to be expressions of idolatry. We do find condemnation of pederasty, the sexual use of a boy by an adult male for the latter's gratification.

Note several things at this point. First, scriptural condemnation is also evident for similar *heterosexual* acts—for example, those that violate holiness codes (intercourse during menstruation), commercial sex, idolatrous heterosexual acts (temple prostitution), and the sexual misuse of minors. Further, the major questions that concern us in the present debate simply are not directly addressed in scripture. Those unaddressed issues are the theological and ethical appraisal of homosexual *orientation,* and the question of homosexual relations between adults committed to each other in mutuality and love.

On the other hand, we do find something in scripture that is frequently overlooked in the current discussions. There are clear biblical affirmations of deep love between same-sex adults. I am not implying genital relations in these instances. I simply note that in the instances of David and Jonathan, Ruth and Naomi, Jesus and "the beloved disciple," and others, the scripture seems to hold strong emotional bonding between members of the same sex to be cause for celebration, not fear.

Robin Scroggs's New Testament scholarship provides an example of the help we need on the biblical question. Looking closely at the cultural and religious contexts of the relevant New Testament passages, he discovers that in the Greco-Roman world there was one basic model of male homosexuality: pederasty, the sexual use of boys by adult males, often in situations of prostitution and always lacking in mutuality. He concludes that "what the New Testament was against was the image of homosexuality as pederasty and primarily here its more sordid and dehumanizing dimensions. One would regret it if somebody in the New Testament had not opposed such dehumanization."[9] In short, the specific New Testament judgments against homosexual practice simply are not relevant to today's debate about the validity of caring, mutual relationships between consenting adults. Nor does the Bible directly address today's question about the appropriateness of homosexuality as a psychosexual orientation.

However, the problem concerning direct guidance from scripture about specific sexual behaviors is not unique to homosexual behaviors. The same problem arises with a host of other forms of sexual expression. The scriptures are multiform and inconsistent in the sexual *moralities* endorsed therein. At various points there are endorsements of sexual practices that most of us would now reject: women as the sexual property of men; the "uncleanness" of menstrual blood and semen; proscriptions against intercourse during menstruation and against nudity within the home; the acceptance of polygamy, levirate marriage, concubinage, and prostitution. On these matters some would argue that the cultic laws of the Old Testament are no longer binding, and they must be distinguished from its moral commandments. Such arguments fail to recognize that most of the sexual mores mentioned above are treated as moral, not cultic, issues in scripture.

Those Christians who argue that, since Christ is the end of the law, the Hebraic law is irrelevant, must, if consistent, deal similarly with New Testament pronouncements about sexual issues. Even on such a major issue as sexual intercourse between unmarried consenting adults there is no explicit prohibition in either Hebrew scripture or the New Testament (which John Calvin discovered to his consternation). Indeed, the Song of Solomon celebrates one such relationship. I believe that our best biblical scholarship reaches Walter Wink's conclusion: "There is no biblical sex ethic. The Bible knows only a love ethic, which is constantly being brought to bear on whatever sexual mores are dominant in any given country, or culture, or period."[10]

This is by no means to suggest that these sources have little to say to us. Consider scripture. As L. William Countryman reminds us, the New Testament frames its particular sexual ethic in terms of purity and property systems that no longer prevail among us. Thus, we cannot simply take numerous New Testament injunctions and assume that they apply literally to significantly different contexts. On the other hand, scripture does for us something far more important. It radically relativizes our theological and ethical systems. It presses toward the transformation—the metanoia, the conversion—of the hearer. It presses us to do our ongoing theological-ethical work in ways that attempt faithfully to discern the inbreaking reign and grace of God in our present contexts. Even if many specific scriptural prescriptions and proscriptions regarding sex are not the gospel's word for today, there are still more basic and utterly crucial scriptural foundations for our sexual ethic.[11]

What are some of those foundations? Surely, they include such affirmations as these: the created goodness of our sexuality and bodily life; the inclusiveness of Christian community, unlimited by purity codes; the equality of women and men; and the service of our sexuality to the reign of God. That incorporation of our sexuality into God's reign means expression in acts shaped by love, justice, equality, fidelity, mutual respect, compassion, and grateful joy. These are critiera that apply regardless of one's orientation. Scripture also offers ample testimony that sexual acts that degrade, demean, and harm others and ourselves are contrary to God's intent and reign. But, for more specific application of such scriptural guidance to issues of homosexuality and same-sex expression, we need to read the scriptures in light of the other three sources.

TRADITION

G. K. Chesteron once counseled our taking out "membership in the democracy of the dead." To do so, in Chesterton's thought, is to refuse to submit to that small, arrogant oligarchy of those people whose only virtue is that they happen, at that moment, to be alive and walking about. When we join this democracy of the dead by taking our tradition seriously, we realize that our ancestors in faith and culture have relevant and important insights for us. Truth is not necessarily carried by the book with the latest copyright date.

However, the postbiblical tradition provides no more unambiguous guidance on specific sexual expressions than does scripture. Selective literalism in use of the tradition is almost as common as it is in the use of scripture itself. Most of us would fully endorse the tradition's movement toward monogamy and fidelity. Many of us would endorse the tradition's growth toward the centrality of love as the governing sexual norm. Many of us would celebrate those parts of the tradition that not only tolerate but positively affirm gays and lesbians, including lesbian and gay clergy. But few of us would endorse those elements of tradition which baptize patriarchal oppression, endorse violence against women, oppress lesbians and gays, exalt perpetual virginity as the superior state, or declare that heterosexual rape is a lesser sin than masturbation (since the latter is a sin against nature while the former, while also sinful, is an act in accordance with nature). As with scripture, it is impossible to find one consistent, coherent sexual ethic in the postbiblical tradition.

Of what use, then, is the long sweep of Christian tradition regarding homosexual orientation and expression? On this subject, I believe that tradition most helpfully poses a series of questions—challenges to much of our conventional Christian wisdom.

One question is this: Has the church's condemnation of gay and lesbian people been consistent throughout its history? As Yale historian John Boswell has demonstrated, a careful examination of tradition yields a negative answer. Indeed, for its first two centuries, the early church did not generally oppose homosexual behavior as such. Further, the opposition that did arise during the third to sixth centuries was not principally theological. Rather, it was based largely on the demise of urban culture, the increased government regulation of personal morality, and general churchly pressures toward asceticism. Following this period of opposition, however, ecclesiastical hostility to homosexuality largely disappeared once again. For some centuries there was no particular Christian antagonism toward homosexuality, and legal prohibitions were rare. Indeed, the eleventh-century urban revival saw a resurgence of gay-lesbian literature and leadership in both secular society and the church. Once again, though, hostility appeared late in the twelfth century now as part of the general intolerance of minority groups and their presumed association with religious heresies.

Our conventional wisdom has assumed that Christian history has been all of one piece, uniform in its clear disapproval of homosexuality. In fact, a closer look at the tradition tells us that there were periods of remarkable acceptance. Further, we are reminded to interpret the theological opposition that was, indeed, often present in the context of broader changes occurring in the surrounding society.

Another challenge to us, suggested by the tradition, is this: Has the church always agreed that heterosexual marriage is the appropriate sexual pattern? The answer is no. Singleness, particularly celibacy, was prized above marriage for much of the time from the church's beginnings to the sixteenth-century Reformation. Moreover, a careful look at tradition reveals that heterosexual marriage was not celebrated by Christian wedding services in church worship until perhaps the ninth century. We have no evidence of Christian wedding rites until that time. Obviously, many Christians married during these earlier centuries, but marriage was considered a civil order and not a rite of the church. Curiously, there is some emerging evidence that unions of gay or lesbian Christians were celebrated in some Christian churches earlier than heterosexual marriages. All of this suggests that heterosexual marriage has not always been central as the norm for Christian sexuality.

The tradition suggests a third question: Is it true that procreation has always been deemed primary to the meaning and expression of Christian sexuality? That is, if we do not use our sexuality with the intent to procreate or at least with the possibility of doing so, is there something deficient about it? It is an important question, for the procreative norm has often been used to judge lesbians and gays adversely: "Your sexuality is unfit to bless because your acts are inherently nonprocreative."

Once again, tradition casts large question marks on many current assumptions. In those times wherein celibacy was more highly honored than marriage, it is obvious that procreative sex was not the norm—it was second class on the ladder of virtue. But what of the centuries, particularly since the Reformation, when marriage has been blessed as the normative Christian calling?

Still the answer is no. In the seventeenth century, a number of Christians—especially among the Puritans, Anglicans, and Quakers—began to teach, preach, and write about a new understanding. It appeared to them that God's fundamental purpose in creating us as sexual beings was not that we might make babies, but that we might make love. It was love, intimacy, mutuality, not procreation, that were central to the divine intention for sexuality. Some Puritans, for example, declared that if children were born to a marriage, that was "an added blessing," but not the central purpose of the marriage.

The centrality of love, companionship, and mutual pleasure in the meaning of sexuality has been embraced by most Protestants during the last three hundred years and, in practice, by numerous Catholics, even if not with Vatican approval. The proof in heterosexual relations is the use of contraception as a decision of conscience. Most of us do not believe we must be open to procreation each time we make love—in fact, we believe strongly to the contrary. The curious double standard still exists, however; the procreative norm has been smuggled in the back door and applied negatively to lesbians and gay men.

Thus, while the church's tradition may not give definitive answers to specific questions about homosexual orientation and same-sex expression, it raises questions—these and others—that challenge conventional wisdom and refocus our perspectives.

REASON

In searching for God's truth, theologically and ethically, we need to draw on the best fruits of human reason, a third source from the quadrilateral. Wesley put it this way: "It is a fundamental principle with us that to renounce reason is to renounce religion, that religion and reason go hand in hand, and that all irrational religion is false religion."[12]

One of the ways we honor our God-given reason is in striving for consistency and adequacy in our theological judgments. These two age-old tests of the philosophers are perennially relevant. Consistency eschews the use of double standards. Adequacy prods us to judgments that do justice to the widest range of data.

Reason is also expressed in the various sciences, our disciplined human attempts to understand creation. Biological, psychological, and social sciences can shed significant light on questions of sexual orientation. What, for example, might we learn?

In 1948 Alfred Kinsey and his associates jarred America with the first major study of the sexual behaviors of persons in this society. In his volume on the male, he presented two things that particularly caught the public eye regarding sexual orientation. One was the continuum on which orientations might be represented. Challenging either-or assumption (one is *either* homosexual *or* heterosexual), Kinsey introduced evidence suggesting that we might be "both/ and." The other finding, widely reported in the press, was Kinsey's discovery that at least 50 percent of the male population had experienced homosexual genital relations at some time in their lives, and for 37 percent of them it was orgasmic behavior after puberty. This alone startled many, simply because it appeared to be evidence that same-sex attraction and expression were not just the province of a tiny minority.[13]

Though most of us tend toward one or the other side, it is probable that the vast majority of us are not exclusively either heterosexual or homosexual. Kinsey's conclusions were substantiated by his studies on the American female five years later and by subsequent research by others. Indeed, in recent decades, most sexologists have not only validated Kinsey's continuum but have also added other dimensions to it. While Kinsey was primarily interested in behaviors (genital experiences culminating in orgasm), later sexologists have argued that when other dimensions of orientation—such as fantasy, desire, social attraction, or emotional preference—are added to the picture, it is probable that none of us is exclusively one or the other. Most of us have more bisexual capacities than we have realized or than we have been taught in a bifurcating society. This recognition is of particular importance when we come to try to understand some of the dynamics of homophobia.

Another question on which the sciences shed some light is the origin of sexual orientation. While there is still much debate, at least two things seem clear. One is that our orientations are given, not freely chosen. The likelihood is that they arise from a combination of genetic and hormonal factors, together with environmental and learning factors—both nature and nurture. The other general agreement is that our sexual orientations are established rather early in life, most likely somewhere between the ages of two and five, and thereafter are largely resistant to any dramatic changes. "Therapies" that attempt to change persons from homosexual to heterosexual are now discredited by reputable scientists. Such procedures may change certain behaviors, they may make some people celibate, but they will not change deep feelings and most likely will produce great psychic and emotional confusion. These facts, too, are relevant to the theological-ethical questions.

Further, stereotypes about gay men and lesbians wither under scientific scrutiny. For example, the notion that homosexual males are more likely to abuse children sexually than are heterosexual males has been thoroughly disproved. Linking emotional instability or immaturity with homosexuality, likewise, is no longer scientifically tenable. Granted, lesbians and gay men suffer emotional distress from their social oppression, but this is far different from assuming that the cause of this distress lies in their orientation.

These issues do not exhaust, but simply illustrate, the ways in which the uses of human reason, including the human sciences, provide important insights for our theological reflection and understanding of scripture.

EXPERIENCE

The fourth and last area of insight comes from experience. Wesley was rightly suspicious of trusting all the vagaries of human experience. Experience by itself is not reliable, nor does it give a consistent picture. However, without the validation of scriptural insight by experience as well as reason and tradition, such insight remains abstract and uncompelling. The Spirit, Wesley believed, inwardly validates God's truth through our experience. I believe that is true. And I also believe that we must expand the focus of "experience" to include the careful examination of both individual and common experience to find those things which nurture wholeness and those things which are destructive to our best humanity.

Our experience of *homophobia*, in careful examination, provides one key example. The term refers to deep and irrational fears of same-sex attraction and expression or, in the case of lesbians and gay men, internalized self-rejection. Though the word was coined only within recent decades, the reality has long been with us.[14] Another term, *heterosexism*, more recently has come into use. It too is helpful, for it reminds us that prejudice against gays and lesbians is not simply a private psychological dynamic but, like racism and sexism, is also structured deeply into our institutions and cultural patterns. While I clearly recognize the pervasive realities of heterosexism, in this illustration of the uses of experience in doing body theology I will focus on homophobia.[15]

I lived the first forty years of my life assuming that I was completely heterosexual. That had been my sexual experience, and that was my only awareness. Then, through some volunteer work in urban ministries I came into close interaction, for the first time that I consciously recognized, with a number of articulate gay men and lesbians. They challenged my stereotypes and my homophobia, and they launched me into a process of examining my own experience.

One thing I discovered was that homophobia was a particularly acute problem for males—it certainly was for me. For the first time I realized that my fear of lesbians and gays was connected to issues in my own masculine identity. Gay males seemed to have an ill-defined masculinity, a threat to any man in a society where one's masculinity seems never achieved once and for all and always needs proving. Lesbians threatened my masculinity simply because they were living proof that at least some women did not need a man to validate or complete them as persons.

Gay males were a problem for me also, I realized, because they threatened to "womanize" me (a threat to any male in a sexist society where men have higher status). The gay could treat me simply as a sexual object, a desirable body—not a full person. I had to admit that this was the way that men (myself included?) had treated so many women for so many years. Now the tables were turned.

Examining my experience made me aware, further, that I might be involved in what the psychologists call reaction formation and projection. If it is true that all of us are a mix of heterosexual and homosexual capacities (even though we happen to be considerably more of one than the other), and if it is true that we have been taught by a rigidly bifurcating society to deny the existence of anything homosexual, what do we do with any same-sex feelings that might arise? We vigorously defend against them in ourselves by projecting them onto others and blaming those others for having more obviously what we, to some extent, may also experience. Though I had not been conscious of same-sex desires, I needed also to examine this possibility in my experience, for some capacity was likely there.

Another factor I discovered was simply sexual envy. Looking at gays and lesbians through stereotypical lenses, I had been seeing them as very sexual people. That, in part, is what stereotyping does to the stereotyper—it gives us tunnel vision. I did not see them fundamentally as persons with richly multifaceted lives; I saw them fundamentally and almost exclusively as sexual actors. The result was obvious: they appeared more sexual than I. And this was a cause for envy, particularly to a male who has been taught that virility is a key sign of authentic masculinity.

Still another contribution to my homophobia, I discovered, was intimacy envy. As a typical man, I had difficulty making close, deep, emotionally vulnerable friendships, especially with other men. Yet, deep within, I sensed that I yearned for such friendships. Then I saw gay men closely bonding with each other, apparently having something in friendship that I too wanted—male-to-male emotional intimacy. I was pressed to look at my experience again, this time to see if my intimacy envy and consequent resentment were part of my homophobia.

Further, confronting my own fears meant confronting my fears of sexuality as such—my erotophobia. Though I had long enjoyed the sexual experience, I came to realize that, reared in a dualistic culture, I was more distanced from my sexuality than I cared to admit. Reared as a male and conditioned to repress most bodily feelings, reared as "a good soldier" and taught to armor myself against any emotional or physical vulnerability, I discovered I was more alienated from my body than I had acknowledged. Gay males and lesbians brought into some kind of dim awareness my own erotophobia because they represented sexuality in a fuller way.

The fear of death may sound like a strange contributor to homophobia, but it is likely there. Though in Christian community we are named people of the resurrection, our reassurances in the face of mortality are often grounded much more by children and grandchildren. The thought of childless persons awakens fear of death. And while many gays and lesbians have produced and parented children, they stand as a key symbol of nonprocreating people. In this way also, I realized, they caused me fear, but once again it was fear of myself.

Homophobia thrives on dualisms of disincarnation and abstraction that divide people from their bodily feelings and divide reality into two opposing camps. As never before we need gracious theologies. Homophobia thrives on theologies of works-justification, wherein all persons must prove their worth and all males must prove their manhood. As never before we need erotic theologies. Homophobia thrives on erotophobia, the deep fear of sexuality and pleasure. Homophobia thrives in eros-deprived people because it grows in the resentments, projections, and anger of those whose own hungers are not met. As never before we need theologies of hope and resurrection. Homophobia thrives wherever there is fear of death, for then people try to dominate and control others to assure themselves of their own future. Homophobia thrives on bodily deadness, so deeply linked as it is with sexual fear and repression. Though its varied dynamics are complex, the root cause of homophobia is always fear, and the gospel has resources for dealing with fear.

These are a few of the dynamics of homophobia that I became conscious of in my own experience some years ago. Doubtless, there are others. I have focused particularly on the male experience both because that is my own and because I believe homophobia is a particularly severe problem for dominantly heterosexual males such as I. Nevertheless, it is a disease that affects all of us—female as well as male; lesbian, gay, and bisexual as well as heterosexual. Homophobia is an example of the experience that enters into our theological and ethical reflection on issues of sexual orientation (and many other matters as well). Our awareness of these dynamics in ourselves gives us heightened self-critical consciousness, an important ingredient of theological-ethical reflection.

I have not attempted here to present a fully developed theological-ethical perspective on sexual orientation. My attempt is far more limited. It has been to name and to illustrate some uses of the four major sources of interpretation—scripture, tradition, reason, and experience—so important to the churches' responses to the most troubling and divisive question facing them.

My own bias is evident. Just as homophobic fears are not principally about "them," but about myself and about us all, so also the basic issue is not homosexuality but rather *human* sexuality. Our sexuality, I believe, is a precious gift from God, critically important as part of a divine invitation. It is an invitation that we come together with each other and with God in relationships of intimacy and celebration, of faithfulness and tenderness, of love and justice. Our sexuality is a gift to be integrated fully and joyously into our spirituality. Our orientations, whatever they may be, are part of that gift—to be received with thanksgiving and honored by each other.[16]

NOTES

1. Channing E. Phillips, "On Human Sexuality," May 5, 1985. Quotation taken from a photocopy of the sermon.

2. *New York Times,* May 26, 1985, sec. I, 39.

3. I was one of those called in for consultation, and I subsequently led the church retreat some months later. I mention this because I felt Riverside's events a bit from the inside and not entirely as an outside observer.

4. William Sloane Coffin, "The Fundamental Injunction: Love One Another," Sermons from Riverside, May 12, 1985 (duplicated), 1–2.

5. Ibid., 3.

6. An excellent discussion of Wesley's quadrilateral can be found in Colin W. Williams, *John Wesley's Theology Today* (Nashville: Abingdon Press, 1960), chap. 2.

7. For more detail about the specific biblical texts that make direct references to certain forms of same-sex activity, see James B. Nelson, *Embodiment: An Approach to Sexuality and Christian Theology* (Minneapolis: Augsburg, 1978), chap. 3, n. 7, and chap. 8.

8. Robin Scroggs has formulated these questions succinctly in his important study *The New Testament and Homosexuality* (Philadelphia: Fortress Press, 1983), 123. The entire volume is a persuasive illustration of the application of these questions.

9. Ibid., 126.

10. Walter Wink, "Biblical Perspectives on Homosexuality," *The Christian Century,* Dec. 7, 1979: 1085.

11. L. William Countryman, *Dirt, Greed, and Sex* (Philadelphia: Fortress Press, 1988).

12. John Wesley, in *The Letters of John Wesley,* ed. John Telford, Standard Edition, vol. 5 (London: Epworth Press, 1931), 364. Commenting on 1 Corinthians 14:20, Wesley also said, "Knowing religion was not designed to destroy any of our natural faculties, but to exalt and improve them, our reason in particular." Cf. Williams, *John Wesley's Theology Today,* 30.

13. See Alfred C. Kinsey et al., *Sexual Behavior in the Human Male* (Philadelphia: W. B. Saunders, 1948). See also his *Sexual Behavior in the Human Female* (Philadelphia: W. B. Saunders, 1953).

14. George Weinberg, a psychotherapist, is usually credited with popularizing the term. See his *Society and the Healthy Homosexual* (Garden City, N.Y.: Doubleday & Co., Anchor Press, 1972), chap. 1.

15. For a fuller discussion of the dynamics of homophobia, see Nelson, *The Intimate Connection,* chap. 3, n. 3, and 59ff.

16. For a review of literature on the subject of this chapter, see my article "Homosexuality and the Church: A Bibliographical Essay," *Prism* 6, no. 1 (Spring 1991):74–83.

33

Homophobia,
Heterosexism,
and Pastoral Practice

ROSEMARY RADFORD RUETHER

Homosexuality is the scare issue in the Christian churches today. It is being used as the stalking horse of all the current social fears concerning the disintegration of moral and social structures. We should see antigay fear and hatred as part of a cultural offensive against liberal egalitarian social principles generally. Homophobia is a vehicle for the conservative ideology that links the defense of the patriarchal family with the maintenance of class, race, and gender hierarchy throughout the society. Such a view of society is typically tied with militarism and superpatriotism. The subordination of women and the hierarchy of social classes is seen as part of the "natural order." Since religion is used as the prime support of this social ideology, it is necessary to develop a sustained theological and ethical critique of it and a pastoral practice based on a correct identification of the problem. Although gay people particularly suffer the consequences of it, they are not the cause of the problem. Patriarchal heterosexism is the cause of the problem.

I shall begin with an analysis of the traditional arguments for judging homosexuality as wrong. This lies in three interlocking views of homosexuality as sin, crime, and disease. The Christian tradition that views homosexuality as a sin rests on a view of sexuality as legitimate only within monogamous marriage with reproduction as its primary purpose. As developed by Saint Augustine in the late fourth and early fifth century, this view disregards the relational purpose of sexuality as an expression and means of creating love. Sexuality is seen as inherently debasing to the soul. Even reproductive sexuality within marriage is seen as spiritually debasing. The optimal Christian life-style was that of celibacy.[1] The celibate anticipated the heavenly order of redemption by renouncing sexuality for the "angelic life." Underlying this view of redemption is a quasi-Gnostic anthropology that sees finitude and mortality, and hence the need for reproduction, as characteristics of a fallen order. In the original and future heavenly order, sex, sin, and death were and will be absent.

Saint Augustine sees the blessings on procreation in Genesis as pertaining only to the Old Testament. But this era of the Old Adam has been superseded by Christ, a virgin born of virginal marriage. Although sex and reproduction within marriage are allowable in the Christian era, they are now of inferior value.[2] Married people belong to a moral lower class in the church, the members of which are unable to attain the fullness of the gospel, as do the celibates, who imitate the virginity of Christ and Mary and anticipate the eschatological age.

We see from the above that the traditional view that reproduction is the only legitimate purpose of sex sprang not from a high valuing of children, but from a negative valuing of sex. Sex was the epitome of the sinful, death-prone instinct. Original sin was transmitted from generation to generation through concupiscence, the orgasmic feeling of sexual release. The enjoyment of this experience was regarded with horror as a thing to be restricted as much as possible. It was venially sinful in marriage even when used for procreation, and mortally sinful in every other case. Thus even heterosexual married couples "fornicated," or sinned mortally, when they had sex solely for "pleasure" and avoided reproduction.[3]

In this view, contraceptive, oral, and anal sex, between heterosexuals or homosexuals, were sinful for the same reason. Thus, in much of classical Catholic penitential literature, the sin of sodomy refers not only to homosexual sex, but to any nonprocreative sex. This view is still reflected in the American laws recently upheld by the Supreme Court. These laws make oral or anal sex between heterosexuals or homosexuals illegal. The root of this tradition lies in a view of all sex as sinful, although allowable or venially sinful within procreative marriage. This view sees no autonomous purpose of sex as a means of creating and expressing a love relationship.

These views of nonreproductive sex as sin flow into the condemnation of them as crime. Sexual deviance of all kinds was regarded as a deliberate flouting of the natural order, which, in turn, undermined the social order. Sexual deviants were subversive to the proper order of society and hence a public danger. To flout the natural order was to rebel against God as well, and so sexual deviance was closely linked with heresy. Heretics were typically seen as sexual deviants who practiced "unnatural sex" in the general sense previously defined. Homosexuality was, therefore, seen as an expression of a general spiritual and moral subversion that sought to undermine the established social order. This subversive attitude was typically described as like a disease in Christian literature. It is contagious and spreads through contact.

Although heresy is no longer an official category of crime, contemporary views of homosexuality still preserve much of this classic Christian paranoia. It is seen as contagious, spreading like a disease, and expressing a pernicious subversion of the moral and social fabric of society. The unfortunate development of AIDS, as a disease affecting predominantly, although not solely, male homosexuals, reveals the prevalence of this mentality among North Americans, especially religious conservatives. AIDS is regarded both as a confirmation of the morally diseased condition of homosexuals and as divine retribution against them for their sinfulness. One cannot think of any other medical epidemic in recent times in which the victims have been regarded with such explicitly moralistic hostility. For example, although the link between cancer and smoking has long been established, Americans would hardly dream of regarding cancer as divine retribution for the sinful activity of smoking.

The categorization of homosexuality as disease belongs to an older Christian tradition, but it has been reinforced in recent times by the psychoanalytic profession. Patriarchal psychoanalysis, as developed by Freud, defined homosexuality as a developmental disorder. Freud postulated that infant sexuality is characterized by "polymorphous perversity." That is to say, our original sexuality is nongenital and nongender-specific. As infants we feel sexual all over our bodies and respond sexually to both sexes. But Freud believed that this infantile "perversity" must be overcome by repressing a generalized sexuality in favor of heterosexual genital sexuality, the goal of which is reproduction. Homosexuality is a developmental failure, a "fixation" on an infantile stage of sexuality. Homosexuals are described as "narcissistic." Their attraction to persons of the same gender reflects a self-love that is incapable of loving others.[4] Oddly enough, this view fails to recognize persons of the same gender as distinct other persons from oneself.

Lurking under the charge that homosexuals are narcissistic lies the psychological doctrine of complementarity. Complementarity defines males and females as rigidly opposite personality types. Males must cultivate the "masculine" characteristics of autonomy, force, and rationality; women, the "feminine" characteristics of passivity, nurturance, and auxiliary existence. Only heterosexual sex is directed to the "other half" of this dualism and unites the two sexes in a "whole." Homosexual sex is, therefore, "incomplete," directed toward one's own "half," rather than the other "half."

This condemnation of homosexuality as incomplete and narcissistic is a basic reinforcement of heterosexism. Its doctrine that only heterosexual sex is "whole" is actually based on a truncated human development for both men and women in which both must remain "half" people who need the other "half" in order to be "whole." This truncated personality development reflects patriarchal social roles. The male and female stereotypes are asymmetrical and reflect the dominance-submission, public-private splits of the patriarchal social order.[5]

Against this patriarchal social stereotyping, I would claim that all persons, male and female, possess the capacity for psychological wholeness that transcends the masculine-feminine dichotomy. Once this is recognized, the argument for heterosexuality, based on the genders as complementary opposites, collapses. All sexual relations, all love relations, should be the loving of another person who is complexly both similar and different from oneself. Such relationships should help both to grow into their full wholeness. Complementarity, by contrast, creates a pathological interdependency based on each person remaining in a state of deficiency in relation to the other. The female can't make her own living. The male can't do his own wash or meals. So each "needs" the other to supply these lacks in themselves. The relationship is set up to reinforce this deficiency in each.

To sum up our argument so far: the traditional condemnation of homosexuality has been based on three assumptions: (1) The sexual instinct is lower and bestial, sinful in itself. It is something that can be cut off from higher human spiritual development. (2) The only "natural" and licit purpose of sex is reproduction. Reproductive sex is also seen as a "remedy" of concupiscence—that is, it prevents the male from seducing other women to whom he is not married—but even this is licit only in marriage when the procreative purpose of sex is not impeded. Sex is thus seen as either "functional" or sinfully lustful. The relational purpose of sex is disregarded. (3) Sexual attraction promotes "wholeness" only when directed at the other sex, the two genders being seen as opposite personality types.

All three of these presuppositions must be questioned. We should see sexuality as an integral part of our total psychosomatic being, not something that can be separated out and repressed without damage to our fullness of being. We should recognize that the love-relational purpose of sex has its own integrity and goodness as the creation and expression of bonding, affection, and commitment. It is not dependent on procreation for its justification, and indeed today out of many thousands of sexual acts in the lifetime of any person, only a small percentage can be intentionally reproductive. The defense of marriage between sterile people, sex after menopause, and the acceptance of birth control, including the so-called rhythm method—all tacitly accept the autonomous love-relational purpose of sex.

Once one has accepted any nonprocreative sex to be moral for heterosexuals, one can no longer define homosexuality as immoral because it is nonprocreative. One cannot even say that homosexuals avoid the responsibility to raise children, since celibates also do not raise children, while many homosexuals are raising natural or adopted children. Once one has accepted the understanding of humanity in which men and women are complex psychological wholes, not stereotypic opposites, and that the goodness of relationship lies in mutual support of the wholeness of each, not the mutual deficiency of masculine-feminine interdependence, then the difference between loving and bonding with someone of the same sex as yourself or someone of the other sex can no longer be rigidly distinguished. Both are relationships with another person, with all the complex problems of developing a healthy mutuality, rather than pathological dependency and exploitative misuse of each other.

There has emerged among Catholic moral theologians in the last twenty years a comprehensive effort to revise the traditional Catholic view of sexuality, although these moral theologians are currently very much under fire from the Vatican, which recognizes that its system of social and ecclesiastical control rests on the older definitions of sexual sin. The Catholic Theological Society of America (CTSA) report *Human Sexuality*, published in 1977[6] represents this alternative tradition of Catholic moral theology. The starting point of the moral system developed in this report is that sexual morality or immorality is an expression of moral or immoral human relationality. Relationships are moral when they are mutual, supportive of the full personal growth of each person, committed, and faithful. Relations are immoral when they are abusive, violent, exploitative, keep people in truncated stages of development, and lead to lying, deceit, and betrayal.

This norm of sexual morality, based on moral relationality, eliminates the neat boundaries between moral and immoral sex defined by heterosexual marriage and procreation. Such a norm makes for much stricter judgments about sexual morality in some cases. Much of the sexuality promoted in patriarchal marriage, which, for example, saw the husband as having a right to force his wife to have sex with him, would be regarded as immoral by such a standard. What is moral or immoral sexually becomes more a question of a scale of values than of clear boundaries. No one achieves perfectly mutual love, and perhaps few relationships are totally evil. Rather, such a norm promotes a developmental goal. We are to grow toward healthy, loving, mutual, and faithful relationships, away from abusive and dishonest ones. The morality of homosexual or heterosexual relations is judged by the same standard, rather than by different standards.

In response to the traditional views of homosexuality as a violation of the natural order, or as a developmental disorder, the CTSA report takes seriously the testimony of gay and lesbian people about their own experience of same-gender attraction as "natural" for themselves. Many gay and lesbian people say that they have experienced themselves as sexually attracted to people of the same gender for as long as they remember being sexually aware. Efforts to repress or change this same-gender attraction, in order to conform to dominant heterosexual norms, distorted and violated their spontaneous feelings. Only when they acknowledged their own homosexuality were they able to feel whole and able to express their own authentic being.

This testimony from gay and lesbian experience leads the CTSA authors to declare that homosexual attraction is the natural sexual orientation of a "normal" minority of persons. It is not a deviance from nature, but rather a part of the natural variety of human nature, much as left-handedness is part of a natural variation in humans. We know that left-handedness occurs in about 12 percent of the population, another 85 percent are dominantly right-handed, and some people are ambidextrous. To force left-handed children to conform to right-handedness causes great difficulty when they are learning to read and write. Some societies have indeed regarded left-handedness as "sinister" (the word *sinister* means "left"), and others have devalued left-handed functions. But we recognize today that left- or right-handedness is part of a natural pluroformity in brain "wiring."

The CTSA report argues that homosexual orientation should be seen as a similar sort of natural diversity. This allows the authors to see homosexuality as part of the divinely created "natural" order, rather than as a violation of the natural order. But it also allows the authors to assume that heterosexuality is the dominant orientation of 85 percent of the population, whereas only 10–12 percent are dominantly homosexual. Homosexuals become a natural minority group whose sexuality is an expression of their natures. But they are a small enough group that their existence need not challenge the majority status of heterosexuality. The CTSA report argues against views of homosexuality as either a handicap or something that can be changed by psychological and social coercion. Like heterosexuals, homosexuals are directed to appropriate their natural sexual orientation in a moral development toward healthy, mutual, loving, and faithful relationships.

This revisionist Catholic moral theology is an enormous improvement over the traditional Christian view of sexuality and homosexuality. It has many elements that I wish to affirm, especially the relational norm of sexual morality. Its effort, however, to make homosexuals a fixed natural minority group of 10–12 percent of the population is questionable. It fails to account for the complexity of human sexuality and the shaping of sexuality by society. It does not explain adequately the fear and dread of homosexuals by heterosexuals. Although many gay and lesbian people say they have always experienced same-gender attraction, and are unable to respond to people of the opposite sex, others do not define their experience in this way.

There is some evidence that notions of rigid sex orientation are less prevalent among women than men. Lesbians are more likely to say that their homosexuality is an expression of their general capacity to be sexual, and that this reflects their general capacity to love, to be attracted to and affectionate toward other people, female or male. These women see their lesbianism less as a fixed biological necessity than as a social choice.[7] They would say that they have chosen to love women rather than men because, in a patriarchal society, lesbian relations are less violent and coercive and more conducive to loving mutuality than are relations with males. Since patriarchal society sets up heterosexual marriage as a relationship of domination and subordination, fully moral—that is, loving and mutual—relations are possible only between women. Lesbianism is an expression of this social morality.

Such a definition of lesbianism as a social choice opens up in a different way the question of homosexuality as a preference, rather than as an unchangeable expression of one's "nature." For patriarchal conservatives this would again open the question of changing homosexuals by social coercion. For lesbians this is exactly the sort of society they are avoiding by their choice of lesbianism. This diversity in the experience of gay and lesbian people points, I believe, to the complexity of human sexuality as a social, and not just a biological, reality. We need to ask not just how people "become" homosexuals, but, even more, how people "become" heterosexuals.

I suggest that we return to the Freudian insight that we are "originally" bisexual and polymorphously sexual. Instead of seeing this as an infantile "perversity," we should see it as a clue to the nature and potential of human sexuality. Human sexuality is not narrowly programmed toward genital sexuality, heterosexuality, or reproduction. Indeed what makes human sexuality "human" is its tendency to transcend the limits of biological reproduction and to be oriented toward human relationality. This more generalized capacity for sexual attraction is both exciting and frightening. It is the body's basic experience of vital, pleasurable feelings, awakened in sensual contact with other humans. This is frightening since it also suggests vulnerability, loss of control, giving oneself up to others.

Human cultures have reacted to this ambivalence of sexual experience with various social strategies that channel its use. Sexuality is channeled socially toward heterosexuality and toward committed family relationships in order to assure not only reproduction, but also the stable relationship of the generations in child raising, mutual care, and support of the aged. Western cultures particularly have channeled sexual feeling away from general body experience to a functional, genital sexuality. We develop into adults by deadening most of our bodies, and most of our relationships, sexually. This has been done particularly by males so they could carry on with one another in public relationships without experiencing sexual vulnerability. It was traditionally assumed that any relationships of men with women aroused sexual feelings, so women were to be segregated from public affairs. Civilization, as Freud noted, is based on repression, training people (especially males) to be genitally sexual, heterosexual, and to enter into permanent marriages.

If we are originally bisexual and polymorphous, however, this means that we all have the capacity for sexual attraction and response to people of the same sex. We are not born heterosexual. We are taught to become heterosexual. Most of us accept our heterosexual socialization and develop in ways that channel sexual attraction toward approved marital objects. This includes not only persons of the other gender, but also persons of the "right" race, culture, and social class. Indeed as our society sees it, it is as much a "perversity" to be sexually attracted to persons of another race, religion, or social class as to be attracted to persons of the same gender. Most of us have deeply internalized this conditioning. Although we might feel sexually attracted to a person of the "wrong" race or culture, we might also feel a physical loathing and disgust at our own feelings. This indicates how much our sexuality is a social product.

For some people this heterosexual conditioning fails to "take." They grow up feeling themselves attracted primarily to the same sex, although at the same time sinful and perverse because of these feelings. I suggest that we simply don't know why some people resist this conditioning, any more than we know why most people conform to it. As in all human development, the biological and the social are so deeply intertwined as to be inextricable. If we all have some capacity for bisexuality, and we are all socialized to be heterosexual, the most we can say is that, for some, the attraction to the same gender remains stronger than the weight of this heterosexist social conditioning.

If we recognize a general capacity for same-gender sexual attraction, a capacity that has been repressed, but not killed, by social conditioning in those who define themselves as heterosexuals, we also discover the psychological root of homophobia. Homophobia—the fear, revulsion, and hatred of homosexuals—is a projection onto homosexuals of our fears of our own repressed capacity for same-gender sexual attraction. Having been socialized to hate and fear our own capacity for same-gender sexual feeling, to deny that such feelings exist, we respond with hostility to those who represent this repressed capacity in ourselves. The secret that the homophobe wishes to keep from him- or herself is that he or she, too, might feel sexually attracted to a person of the same gender.

Heterosexuality represents not only a channeling of polymorphous bisexuality toward heterosexual marriage for the purpose of procreation and child raising, but also a socialization that has taken place historically under conditions of patriarchy—that is, under systems of male, ruling-class (and race) domination. We are conditioned to respond sexually to persons not only of the right gender, but also of the right race and class—that is, people who are "marriageable," according to racial and ethnic endogamy and hierarchy. Although dominant males might have sex with such nonmarriageable people, they are not supposed to form any bonds of affection for such sex objects. What is strictly taboo in patriarchy is not so much sex activity itself, but rather *love* for the person of the wrong sex, race, and gender. Mere "sex" is forgiveable for dominant males as long as it does not involve real love and affection for the unmarriageable person.

Sexual conditioning in patriarchy means that this socialization takes place within a system of gender, class, and race hierarchy. Ruling-class males set themselves apart from dominated women and men. They do this by cultivating certain personality and cultural styles associated with dominance and superiority and relegating devalued cultural traits to women and dominated males. Accents, hair and dress styles, the way one moves one's body—all these have been signals that set apart the genders and social classes. In most societies until recently, cross-dressing across not only gender lines but also class lines has been severely tabooed.

One key element in male, ruling-class dominance is sexual control over women and dominated men, while the dominant men themselves remain sexually invulnerable. There are two ways to create this system of sexual control and invulnerability. One is to create a celibate elite that is regarded as above sexuality, morally and spiritually superior to the lower class of sexual people. This celibate elite not only holds itself aloof from sexuality, but also defines everyone else's sexuality by strictly delimiting what they can do, and when and with whom they can do it. In classical Catholicism, the noncelibate are a spiritual and ecclesiastical lower class. They are allowed to be sexual, but only within heterosexual marriage, only for procreation, and never for pleasure "for its own sake."

The second way to be invulnerable and to control other people's sexuality has characterized aristocratic male ruling classes. The ruling-class male allows himself a broad latitude of sexual relations not only with his legal wife, but with mistresses, prostitutes, maids, male paramours, and male servants. But he does so within a framework of strictly defined roles. His legal wife is to be chaste at marriage and strictly faithful after marriage. Since her children must be his legal heirs, any sexual promiscuity on her part is severely proscribed. His other sexual liaisons should be people to whom he has no commitment, usable and discardable at will. Often slaves and servants were not allowed legal marriage to each other at all. They were not allowed to form autonomous bonds with each other that conflicted with the master's use of them.

When we look at this practice of sexuality among ruling-class males, in, say, British upper-class society, it becomes apparent that patriarchy does not rule out either promiscuity or homosexuality for these males. Both are winked at as long as they remain discreet within a public system of heterosexual marriage that will produce legitimate offspring. In patriarchal aristocracy, the homosexual activity of the dominant male does not define him as a "homosexual." This status is reserved for the subordinate male in the relationship. The dominant male typically remains the "penetrator" of both women and subordinate males. To be the "penetrated" one defines sexually one's inferior status. This is the meaning of the Levitical proscription against "lying with another man as you would with a woman. It is an abomination" (Lev. 18:22). What this law presumes is that the male who is "penetrated" is reduced to the inferior status of the female. The law defends the equal masculine status of all males at the expense of all women.

Thus we can say that in heterosexist patriarchal society homophobia reveals two interconnected forms of social and psychological dread. It reveals the dread of recognizing one's own capacity for homosexual attraction in a culture that teaches us to repress and reject this capacity. It also reveals the dread of vulnerability and loss of control by those who define their masculinity as dominance and invulnerability and fear that, in the homosexual relation, they may be flung into the "penetrated" and hence the demeaned and dominated position. For this reason homophobia also tends to be more virulent in males than in females. Once women have gotten over the denial of their capacity for same-sex attraction, they do not have the same fears of being demeaned and dominated by other women that men have toward other men.

This analysis of homophobia as rooted in a patriarchal social system of dominance and repression makes questionable any pastoral strategy that regards homosexuals as the primary problem, who are to be helped by counseling or therapy. First, it is essential to correctly name the problem as lodged in the system of heterosexist domination, rather than in its victims. We need, then, to ask how all of us, men and women, homosexual or heterosexual, celibate or noncelibate, have been damaged in our fullness of spiritual, moral, and psychosomatic development by this system. The correct naming of the issue is itself enormously therapeutic, taking the burden of fear and self-hatred from individuals and allowing them to claim the complexity of their own experience.[8]

There is a need not only for ways of thinking and communicating that correctly name the problem, but also for ways of ritualizing and celebrating this claiming of our experience. We need rites of "coming out" by which lesbians and gay men can heal themselves of their internalized self-hatred and affirm and be affirmed in their authentic personhood in community. There is also a need for covenanting celebrations by which lesbian and gay male couples can affirm and be supported in committed relationships. In my book *Women-church: Theory and Practice of Feminist Liturgical Communities,*[9] two lesbian couples have developed such coming-out and covenanting rites out of their own experience and religious traditions.

Perhaps as more of us acknowledge the complexity of our sexual potential, it will become less necessary for some to identify themselves as homosexual over against a heterosexual majority. As we recognize the pluriformity of our sexual potential and experience, and the way we have been shaped in our identities by conformity to or reaction against the dominant social conditioning, we can begin to explore a new sexual and social ethic of moral development toward mutual, loving, and committed relationships. Such moral development does not entail a denial of our capacity for many-sided sexual feeling, but it does entail choosing, out of a multiplicity of possibilities, certain particular people with whom we open ourselves to deeper relationship and vulnerability, with whom we choose to journey into the bonding of committed love and friendship. In the context of such a committed relationship we can then appropriate our sexuality not as something biologically necessitated, or as socially coerced, but as a freely chosen way of expressing our authentic humanness in relation to the special others with whom we wish to share our lives.

NOTES

1. Augustine, *De sancta virg.* 45, in "Misogynism and Virginal Feminism in the Fathers of the Church," *Religion and Sexism: Images of Women in the Jewish and Christian Tradition,* ed, R. Ruether (New York: Simon & Schuster, 1974).

2. Augustine, *De nup. et concup.* 1, 14–15, in *Nicene and Post-Nicene Fathers,* ed. P. Schaff (Buffalo: Christian Literature Company, 1887), 5:269.

3. Augustine, *De bono conj.* 3, in *Nicene and Post-Nicene Fathers,* 13:400; and Ruether, "Misogynism and Virginal Feminism in the Fathers of the Church," 164.

4. Sigmund Freud, *Civilization and Its Discontents* (New York: W.W. Norton & Co., 1961).

5. Karl Barth, *Church Dogmatics,* vol. 3, no. 4 (Edinburgh: T. & T. Clark, 1961), 116–240.

6. A. Kosnik, W. Carroll, A. Cunningham, R. Modras, and J. Schulte, *Human Sexuality: New Directions in American Catholic Thought* (New York: Paulist Press, 1977).

7. See Carter Heyward, *Our Passion for Justice: Images of Power, Sexuality and Liberation* (New York: Pilgrim Press, 1984); and Mary E. Hunt, *Fierce Tenderness: A Feminist Theology of Friendship* (New York: Crossroad, 1991).

8. Task Force on Gay/Lesbian Issues, *Homosexuality and Social Justice* (San Francisco: Archdiocesan Commission on Social Justice, 1982).

9. Rosemary Radford Ruether, *Women-church: Theory and Practice of Feminist Liturgical Communities* (San Francisco: Harper & Row, 1986).

34

Church at the Margins

DAN SPENCER

Many of us grew up in the church and experienced it as a place of nurture, healing, and redemption—until we realized our gay identities. At that point we faced two primary choices: remain closeted and increasingly experience the world through a split existence, or come out and face hostility and expulsion from the church. Either path left us wounded and divided, with no community in which to integrate two fundamental parts of our identity, being gay and being Christian.

This basic contradiction—between our faith that God is a God of love and compassion and our experience of hatred and contempt from the church and society—has caused us to cry out "How long, God?" Why do we experience so much pain, suffering, confusion, and hatred, and how long until we are simply accepted and loved for who we are? Why is the very community that names you central to its faith the one that drives us away? Where do we go and what do we do to experience your love?

At least initially many of us go to nongay people to find validation, and our approach to the church is usually apologetic: "Please let us in, we're just like you." But we are not just like others. Our experiences have shaped us differently. Eventually we start to realize that we need each other to begin to name our difference, and reflect together on how it affects our faith.

This need for communities of wholeness, where we can affirm and are affirmed in our identity as gay and Christian, has led to a gay and lesbian experience of church that differs from the dominant church. Our ecclesiology is rooted in our liberating efforts to *resist* heterosexism and homophobia, and to *celebrate* our identity and uniqueness. As a result, it locates the identity of the church in the move from the margins *of* community to the margins *as* community. . . . The task now is to articulate the distinctive marks of the emerging gay and lesbian ecclesiology.

Self-identification is critical to the liberation of subjugated groups and peoples. This process includes claiming personal and communal history, as well as reclaiming the group's history from the distortions and mystifications of the dominant perspective. It is key not only to a sense of identity and validation, but also to the energy required for empowerment. A gay and lesbian ecclesiology must be rooted in the *particularities of gay and lesbian experience.*

At the same time, we must not universalize any particular experience. Like gender, sexuality cuts across every other particularity. All of us, moreover, are shaped by multiple experiences and identities. A liberating gay and lesbian ecclesiology will recognize its partial and fragmented nature, and will be sensitive to the power dynamics, to the contradictions and particularities within the community.

The *ecclesia* of lesbians and gay men will be *a community at the margins:* of the society, the broader church, our communities and families of origin. Gay men and lesbians typically find ourselves at the margins of whatever other community we belong to, whether these communities are shaped by racial or ethnic identity, by class location, or by religious affiliation. Claiming the particularity of our identity as lesbian or gay usually cuts us off from our communities of origin, which might otherwise serve as liberating sources in our struggles. We cannot simply return to our roots for sources of liberation, but must forge new sources from the communities we create.

Because of this, many lesbians and gay men of faith resonate with Fortunato when he likens our faith journeys in the church to that of exile, being placed on the very margins of communities from which we expect nurture and life.[1] Others have used the analogy of a community of urban refugees, since many of us have felt forced to leave our places of origin to seek community and shelter in large cities. A gay and lesbian ecclesiology recognizes the need to provide faith communities that allow the space both to grieve our losses and to "embrace our exile" to discover the resources that come from life at the margins. It embraces the prophetic strand of Christianity that recognizes the power that comes through weakness, from life at the margins, without romanticizing the costs of powerlessness.

A gay and lesbian ecclesiology is *accountable first and foremost to its own people:* the community of lesbians and gay men who seek to integrate our Christian faith with the ongoing struggle for liberation: it takes seriously the nature of difference between and among gay people. It welcomes all lesbian- and gay-supportive persons, while also affirming the need at times for gay- or lesbian-only space.

In addition to traditional Christian sources, a gay and lesbian ecclesiology makes use of *three primary sources* to shape its understanding of mission as the praxis of liberation: the historical experience of resistance and struggle by lesbians and gay men; spiritual and cultural resources located in contemporary lesbian and gay experience; and analysis of power relations to identify and root out heterosexist structures.

The thoroughly androcentric and often patriarchal and heterosexist nature of scripture make its use as a liberating resource problematic. Hence the gay and lesbian experience of church encourages appropriation of those parts of the Bible and tradition that empower gay people while encouraging the community to construct its own sacred texts and scripture. In this sense a gay and lesbian ecclesiology joins feminist theologians in moving beyond Latin American liberation ecclesiologies to apply a critical analysis not just to traditional interpretation of biblical texts, but to the texts themselves. Lesbian feminist theologian Carter Heyward is helpful in reminding us that scripture is holy and authoritative "only insofar as we who read, study, preach, or teach it do so in a spirit of collaborative, critical inquiry steeped in collective struggle for radical mutuality between and among us all on the earth."

The *ecclesia* of gay men and lesbians is an *embodied community* that works to repair the damage of theologies that are anti-body and anti-sexuality. Our ecclesiology emerges from a liberating as opposed to liberal understanding of community, one centered on the practice of justice. Gathering for support as a gay and lesbian people by itself is not sufficient for justice. Lesbian and gay faith communities must use this critical support to empower their resistance to gay oppression and to struggle to transform society and the wider church.

The response of lesbian and gay faith communities to a church that is pervasively abusive towards them will have *moments of separation and integration*. Our ecclesiology must understand and be able to read the advantages and shortcomings of each. Moments of separation into autonomous gay or lesbian space are critical for affirming and deepening our identities, and often free us for worship and thanksgiving that may not be possible in integrated environments. The danger of separation is that it can lead to isolation and sectarianism. It can also in time lead to conservative tendencies as separated communities eventually build up and acquire their own set of institutional privileges.

Moments of integration with nongay Christians lead to possibilities of ecumenism, connecting particularly with other communities of struggle. They also keep clear and present the contradictions the community experiences, as those who benefit from and perpetrate heterosexist oppression may be sitting in the pew next to you. The danger of integration without separation is in having to divert time and energy constantly to justify one's presence and in eventually internalizing the hatred and abuse of the oppressor.

Because it emerges from an embodied community that seeks mutuality in relationships, a gay and lesbian ecclesiology is marked by *attention to issues of power and authority*. Our practice seeks new understandings of power and authority, and new models of leadership.

Our experience of church is not ideologically separatist, and we are therefore *committed to and celebrate relationship with the wider church*. Such relations, however, must be shaped by a nonapologetic stance. We can no longer devote the bulk of our energy and resources to trying to convince homophobic sectors of the church that we should be allowed in. We *are* in. We *are* the church *now*. The stance of our ecclesiology toward the broader church is therefore *confessional* (this is how we experience God in our lives) and *invitational* (how do you experience God's presence?).

Faith communities of lesbians and gay men seek to be a place of reconciliation with nongay sectors of the church. Combining the Pauline understanding of justification that reconciles alienated groups in the church with an evangelical commitment to liberation, a gay and lesbian ecclesiology affirms that reconciliation and unity happen through joint efforts to bring about justice through combating homophobia and other forms of injustice. For this to happen, however, conversations with the wider church must be sensitive to power. We must recognize how our relations have been formed and structured along lines of oppression and privilege, and make our conversations accountable to this recognition.

Following this overview, it is fair to ask: In what sense is the ecclesia of lesbians and gay men an expression of the true church of Jesus as one, holy, catholic, and apostolic? Here are some initial thoughts:

Gay and lesbian church is marked by *unity* to the extent we participate in and invite other churches into the practice of justice. Grounded in the particularity of lesbian and gay experience, the faith communities of lesbians and gay men call attention to and invite others to join in the struggle against the concrete sins of homophobia and heterosexism, while joining others in struggles to transform whatever threatens life.

A gay and lesbian expression of church is marked by *holiness* to the extent we identify unconditionally with the mission of God in saying *Yes* to all that brings life and *No* to all that threatens life. It experiences holiness from within the perspective of faith in its efforts to transform homophobic attitudes and practices and heterosexist structures in church and society, understanding that the persecution and suffering its resistance generates is never justified, but may serve as an indicator of fidelity to practicing the reign of God.

Gay and lesbian church is *catholic* to the extent that we understand God's preferential love for us not as something we merit over others or keep within our community, but as an invitation to the whole church to abandon its search for God through alliances with oppressive forms of power, and to join us at the periphery in the experience of power in unalienated relationship.

Finally, gay and lesbian church is *apostolic* to the extent that we remain evangelical in our identity, proclaiming and practicing with joy the reign of God in the particularity and concreteness of lesbian and gay struggles for liberation in all its fullness.

Marks of our apostolicity include the denunciation of homophobia and heterosexism as incompatible with the apostolic witness to the Gospel of Jesus, inviting conversion to the Gospel through renunciation of anti-gay attitudes and practices, and commitment to the liberation struggles of lesbians and gay men. Gay and lesbian church is apostolic as well to the extent we reach out in solidarity to other churches in their struggles for justice, practicing mutuality in the sharing of our burdens. In each case the traditional marks are given meaning and content through the practice of justice of lesbians and gay men, understood from the perspective of faith as practice of the reign of God.

Why do we stay in the church? We stay because our communities are forging an ecclesiology that shatters the image of a heterosexist church as the locus of God's liberating love by grounding our identity as church in the praxis of gay and lesbian people of faith. These emerging faith communities offer both challenge and invitation to the broader church to experience the Gospel of Jesus free of homophobic trappings, to join us in celebrating, with the early church, "once you were no people, now you are God's people." That's the Good News. It's worth staying for and offering to others.

NOTE

1. See John E. Fortunato, *Embracing the Exile: Healing Journeys of Gay Christians* (New York: Seabury, 1983)—ED.

Acknowledgments

The essays reprinted in *Sexuality and the Sacred: Sources for Theological Reflection* first appeared in the following publications and are reprinted with permission:

CHAPTER 1. "Notes on Historical Grounding: Beyond Sexual Essentialism," in *Touching Our Strength*, by Carter Heyward. Copyright © 1989 by Carter Heyward. Reprinted by permission of HarperCollins Publishers Inc.

CHAPTER 2. Reprinted from *Between the Sexes*, by Lisa Sowle Cahill, copyright © 1985 Fortress Press. Used by permission of Augsburg Fortress.

CHAPTER 3. Reprinted from *Dirt, Greed, and Sex*, by L. William Countryman, copyright © 1988 Fortress Press. Used by permission of Augsburg Fortress.

CHAPTER 4. From "Sexual Ethics," by Margaret Farley. Reprinted with permission of The Free Press, a Division of Macmillan, Inc., from *Encyclopedia of Bioethics*, Warren T. Reich, Editor in Chief, vol. 4, 1575–1587. Copyright © 1978 by Georgetown University.

CHAPTER 5. © 1984 by Audre Lorde; excerpted from *Sister Outsider*, published by the Crossing Press, Freedom, Calif., by permission of the Charlotte Sheedy Literary Agency, Inc.

CHAPTER 6. "Wonder, Eroticism, and Enigma," by Paul Ricoeur, from *Sexuality and the Modern World, Cross Currents*, Spring 1964, © by Cross Currents Corporation.

CHAPTER 7. "Sleeping like Spoons: A Question of Embodiment," by John Giles Milhaven, from *Commonweal*, vol. 116, no. 7 (April 1989): 205–07.

CHAPTER 19. "Appropriate Vulnerability: A Sexual Ethics for Singles," by Karen Lebacqz. Copyright 1987 Christian Century Foundation. Reprinted by permission from the May 6, 1987, issue of *The Christian Century.*

CHAPTER 20. "Sex before Marriage," by Monica Furlong, in *Christian Uncertainties,* by Monica Furlong (Cambridge, Mass.: Cowley Publications, 1982), 114–16. Reprinted with permission of Cowley Press.

CHAPTER 21. "Sex within Marriage" from *Sexual Integrity,* by Jack Dominian (London: Darton, Longman & Todd, 1987), 88–105. Reprinted with permission of Darton Longman & Todd Ltd. Australian reprint rights granted by Collins Dove.

CHAPTER 22. Selected excerpts from *Celibate Passion,* by Janie Gustafson. Copyright © 1978 by Janie Gustafson. Reprinted by permission of Harper-Collins Publishers Inc.

CHAPTER 23. *Presbyterians and Human Sexuality 1991:* The 203rd General Assembly (1991) Response to the Report of the Special Committee on Human Sexuality, Including a "Minority Report" (Louisville, Ky.: Office of the General Assembly, Presbyterian Church (U.S.A.), 1991), 56–62.

CHAPTER 24. "The Change of Life" from *Becoming Woman: The Quest for Wholeness in Female Experience,* by Penelope Washbourn. Copyright © 1977 by Penelope Washbourn. Reprinted by permission of HarperCollins Publishers Inc.

CHAPTER 25. *Presbyterians and Human Sexuality 1991:* The 203rd General Assembly (1991) Response to the Report of the Special Committee on Human Sexuality Including a "Minority Report" (Louisville, Ky.: Office of the General Assembly, Presbyterian Church (U.S.A.), 1991), 56–62.

CHAPTER 26. "AIDS, Shame, and Suffering," by Grace Jantzen, in James Woodward *Embracing the Chaos* (London: S.P.C.K.), 22–31. Reprinted with permission of The Society for Promoting Christian Knowledge.

CHAPTER 27. "AIDS, High-Risk Behaviors, and Moral Judgments," by Earl E. Shelp, *The Journal of Pastoral Care,* vol. 43, no. 4 (Winter 1989): 325–35. Reprinted with permission of *The Journal of Pastoral Care.*

CHAPTER 28. Excerpts from "Violence against Women: The Way Things Are Is Not the Way They Have to Be," by Marie M. Fortune, *The Drew Gateway,* vol. 58 (Fall 1988): 38–50. Reprinted with permission of Drew Theological School.

CHAPTER 29. "Refusing to be 'Good Soldiers': An Agenda for Men," by Marvin M. Ellison, from Susan E. Davies and Eleanor H. Haney *Redefining Sexual Ethics* (Cleveland: Pilgrim Press, 1991), 189–98. Reprinted with the permission of The Pilgrim Press.

CHAPTER 30. "Pornography: An Agenda for the Churches," by Mary Pellauer.

Copyright 1987 Christian Century Foundation. Reprinted by permission from the July 29–August 5, 1987, issue of *The Christian Century*.

CHAPTER 31. "Homosexuality and Religious Life: A Historical Approach," by John Boswell, in *Homosexuality in the Priesthood and the Religious Life*, ed. Jeannine Gramick (New York: Crossroad, 1989), 3–20. Reprinted with permission of Jeannine Gramick.

CHAPTER 32. "Sources for Body Theology: Homosexuality as a Test Case," in *Body Theology*, by James B. Nelson (Louisville, Ky.: Westminster/John Knox Press, 1992), 55–71. Reprinted with permission of Westminster/John Knox Press.

CHAPTER 33. "Homophobia, Heterosexism, and Pastoral Practice," by Rosemary Radford Ruether, in *Homosexuality in the Priesthood and the Religious Life*, ed. Jeannine Gramick (New York: Crossroad, 1989), 21–35. Reprinted with permission of Jeannine Gramick.

CHAPTER 34. "Church at the Margins," by Dan Spencer, *Christianity and Crisis*, vol. 52, no. 8 (May 25, 1992): 174–76. Reprinted with permission. Copyright © 1992 Christianity & Crisis, 537 West 121st Street, New York, N.Y. 10027.